Encyclopedia of Furniture Materials, Trades and Techniques

The cabinet-maker's shop, all belts and wheels
And whining saws, would thrill me with the scream
Of tortured wood, starting a blackened plank
Under the cruel plane, and coming out
Sweet-scented, pink and smooth and richly grained;
While in a far off shed, caressingly,
French polishers, all whistling different tunes,
With reeking swabs would rub the coloured woods,
Bringing the figured surfaces to light;

(John Betjeman, *Summoned by Bells*, 1960)

Clive Edwards

Encyclopedia of Furniture Materials, Trades and Techniques

ASHGATE

Published by
Ashgate Publishing Limited
Gower House
Croft Road
Aldershot
Hants GU11 3HR
England

Ashgate Publishing Company
Old Post Road
Brookfield
Vermont 05036–9704
USA

British Library Cataloguing-in-Publication data
A catalogue record for this book is available from the British Library

Library of Congress Cataloging-in-Publication data
Edwards, Clive, 1947-
Encyclopedia of furniture materials, trades and techniques/Clive Edwards.
    p. cm.
Includes bibliographical references.
ISBN 1-84014-639-7
1. Furniture—Encyclopedias. 2. Furniture making—History—Encyclopedias. I. Title.
NK2205.E34 2000
749'03—dc21   00-025076

ISBN 1 84014 639 7

Printed on acid-free paper
Typeset in Palatino by Tom Knott
Printed in the United Kingdom at the University Press, Cambridge

Contents

List of figures

Colour plates   BETWEEN PAGES 134 AND 135

Preface and acknowledgements

As in any such work, the research of previous authors and scholars has been of paramount importance in developing the entries. The bibliographies indicate the number of sources that have been drawn upon. These include the works of important earlier furniture historians, including Ralph Edwards, John Gloag, Margaret Jourdain and Robert Symonds. More recently Geoffrey Beard, Adam Bowett, Edward Cooke, Benno Forman, Christopher Gilbert, David Hanks, Peter Thornton and Lucy Wood have been among the many scholars whose writings have influenced my research on furniture. The development of furniture studies has been progressed enormously by the publication of journals which are of great value to any researcher. These include in particular *American Furniture*, *Furniture History* and *Regional Furniture*. In many of the entries in this Encyclopedia, specialist bibliographies are given, which often refer to the vast storehouse of magazine and journal articles.

The research has been supported by a number of institutions. I should first like to thank the Idlewild Trust for generously making a grant that has ensured the publication of this work. My thanks also go to the Arts and Humanities Research Board for funding a travel grant which enabled me to visit the United States, in particular the Winterthur Museum Library and High Point, North Carolina. In addition, I have been given much helpful support by the Regional Furniture Society. Special thanks go to Chairman Christopher Claxton Stevens for his kind and generous assistance, and to the Regional Furniture Society Committee for supporting the successful funding application to the Idlewild Trust. I should also like to thank colleagues at Loughborough University who have helped in many ways.

The staff at a number of museums and libraries have been staunch helpers, in particular the following: the librarians at the Bernice Beinenstock Furniture Library, High Point; High Wycombe Public Library; D. H. Hill Library, University of North Carolina; Grand Rapids Public Library; the Winterthur Museum Library. James Yorke of the Furniture and Woodwork Collection archives in the Victoria and Albert Museum was, as always, very obliging. Many other individuals have been generous with their help including Margaret Ballardie, Geoffrey Beard, Tony Berry, Adam Bowett, Roderick Butler, Simon Feingold, Paul Greenhalgh, Noel Riley, Michael Rowlands, Eleanor Thompson, Philip Walker and Gillian Walkling.

I should also like to thank Pamela Edwardes for having faith in the project and for seeing it through to publication. Finally, I am grateful to Lynne Edwards for her considerable support and help over what has been a long and sometimes difficult time.

Introduction

The original concept behind this work is derived from a programme, instigated by the late Clive Wainwright at the Victoria and Albert Museum and supported by the Commissioners of the 1851 Exhibition, which involved the locating and recording of information relating to the techniques and materials used in furniture-making in the 19th century. I then realized that a development of this exercise to cover the major historic periods could be a useful contribution to the literature on furniture history. The scope has had to be limited principally to British and American furniture and furnishings of the period 1500–2000, with diversions to other periods and countries as required. These diversions are necessary firstly to indicate origins of material and processes and secondly to locate the growing international nature of the furniture industry as it developed over that particular period.

The methods or techniques of construction and production and the materials used create an interaction assisted by tools and machines. The description of materials and techniques based on the criteria of when, how, who, where and why, with appropriate examples, is the basis of this Encyclopedia. It is not intended to be a stylistic or technical manual, but a reference aid for furniture scholars and others interested in what furniture and furniture-making are about.

It is important in a work of this kind to indicate what is not included. Generally there is no discussion about the design elements of furniture, and therefore consideration of pattern books, trade labels and design terms are generally omitted. The Encyclopedia is historically grounded and in no way intended as a guide to making furniture. In a work such as this, despite relying heavily on the research of other scholars, the responsibility for its content lies with the author, and therefore I would quote the words of Thomas Chippendale: 'The correction of the judicious and impartial I shall always receive with diffidence in my own abilities and respect to theirs.' (*Gentleman and Cabinet-maker's Director*, Preface, 1762).

Guide to use

The entries themselves are cross-referenced in two ways: the textual reference, which is fully capitalized, refers the reader to an expanded article; at the end of a text, the reader may be referred to more general background reading and reference material, as appropriate. There are two bibliographical reference systems: works cited in the entries and used more than once are listed in the Bibliography at the end. Works relating to a specialist topic can be found at the end of the particular entry. Where possible, examples of documented usage have been given to illustrate the use of a material or process.

In the entries that refer to different types of wood, the meaning of descriptive terms is as follows:

Figure: The decorative effects or markings on longitudinal or side surfaces of converted timber. These are produced by a combination of early and late wood, growth-ring structure, colour, damage and method of conversion. There are many types, including crotch, curly, fiddleback, ribbon or stripe, roe, mottle, birdseye, blister or quilt and feather.

Grain: Wood cell structure which relates to the growth pattern of the tree. Straight follows the axis; cross deviates; spiral relates to twisting of wood elements; interlocked relates to the changing spiral direction in each growth season; wavy and curly refer to undulating structure caused by compression in growth.

Texture: The relative cell diameters in softwoods or the relative pore sizes in hardwoods. The terms fine, medium and coarse classify the range of sizes from small to large. Timber weights (seasoned) are given approximately in kilograms per cubic metre with Imperial equivalents. The botanical names of current commercial timbers have been derived from BS7359:1991.

A – Z entries

Abrasives

The object of abrasives in furniture-making is to level the wood fibres and thus create a smooth and unblemished surface ready for finishing. Various methods have been used (see below). The Ancient Egyptians used sand as an abrasive for wood surface preparation, thus starting a method that has continued unabated. Since then, various attempts have been made to improve the process, including the use of fish skins, brick dust, grasses and various minerals. The introduction in the later 18th century of prepared sheets of abrasive 'paper' made from discarded scraps of glass glued onto a backing marked the beginning of a more reliable abrasive technique. These coated-paper abrasives also used calcined or ground pumice mixed with varnish that adhered to the paper ground. An improvement on paper-backed abrasives was the introduction of abrasive-coated cloths, which were introduced in the 1870s in the United States. These, in combination with the use of sanding machines which were fitted with rotary drums or continuous belt equipment, marked the gradual decline of hand-sanding for most commercial work.

In the late 19th century, two much harder and longer-lasting abrasives were introduced initially in the United States: aluminium oxide and silicon carbide (see below). In the 20th century advances in abrasives have followed scientific developments to a degree. A whole range of specialist abrasives have been developed to work faster, to remain firm under strain, and to be more reliable in regular use.

Aluminium oxide

An abrasive material produced and developed in the 1890s. Aluminium oxide (created using bauxite crushed, calcined, mixed with additives and electrically heated in a furnace) produced an extremely hard-wearing abrasive material. It has been widely used in the 20th century for sanding work on hardwoods and light metals.

Brick dust

A 17th-century term meaning powdered brick. During the 18th century the use of brick dust in combination with some oils constituted both an abrasive and a finishing process: the combination makes a putty-like substance, which gently rubbed and polished a surface. The method involved sifting brick dust through a cotton stocking onto the oiled surface and then polishing the surface with a lead weight wrapped in a carpet until it was glossy. John and William Myers of Wheldrake, Yorks (1778) recorded the method:

To polish mahogany doors oyle it over with linseed oyle over night then in the morning take sum brick dust put it into a silk stocking or anything that is fine then dash it over the door and take a piece of new carpitt or any woolon cloth and rub it. Oyle coats after another with brick dust and oyle until you make a glow till you can see youre self in it.
(Cited in Gilbert, 1991, p.18)

Brick dust was widely used for polishing timber in conjunction with oils prior to the introduction of FRENCH POLISH in the early 1820s: indeed Sheraton noted that 'the general mode of polishing plain cabinet work is … with oil and brick dust' (1803, p.289).

Emery paper

A natural abrasive of corundum and magnetite, which is formed into sheets by sieving the emery onto glued paper. It was mainly used for finishing metals. English emery was especially recommended by Plumier (1749) for polishing iron and steel. In 1793, toolmaker Christopher Gabriel had in stock 11 reams and 6 quires of 'paper-emery' (Goodman, 1981, p.31). Emery cloth was patented in December 1830 (Pat.no.6044).

Fish skins

A number of types of fish skin have been used by furniture-makers for polishing surfaces. Skate skins were used in Roman workshops (Pliny, ix, 40, xxxii, 108), and their use continued right into the 19th century. For example, London maker Samuel Norman's inventory of 1760 included 41 fish skins and 5 dozen fins and some scouring paper, as well as 6 rubstones (Kirkham, 1969, p.508). The variety of skins used depended on region, but shark skin was often used in Europe, whilst in America, cabinet-makers in the 18th century used nurse fish or dog-fish skins. All these skins were successful abrading agents, as they possessed large numbers of small sharp 'teeth' (dermal dentils) which gently rubbed the wood fibres. Roubo (1772) remarked upon *'la peau de chien de mer'* and singled out the fins (*'oreilles de peau de chien'*) as the very best, as their grain was the finest and did not scratch so much. Sheraton mentioned 'The skin of dogfish or sharks, used for cleaning up chair work or in some parts of cabinet work' (1803, p.210). In the mid 19th century dogfish skin was still considered to be more durable than GLASS PAPER but less convenient: 'the scales which are hard and pointed stand up obliquely so cut effectively in one direction only'. Despite its inconvenience, its flexibility and advantage of not leaving any deposit meant that it was still recommended for fine work and especially used when wrapped around the finger as a file effect (Holtzapffel, 1846, p.1060).

Flint or quartz paper

A natural abrasive that was made into a cheap substitute for sandpaper which was widely used in the 19th century for wood finishing before garnet paper was developed. Chalk flint paper was similar but much tougher, and was used for very hard woods.

Flour paper

Similar to glass paper but using very fine glass particles as a coating.

Garnet paper

A high-quality abrasive paper using a natural vitreous silicate mineral to provide a sharp cutting surface for all wood types. Developed in the 1870s, by 1880 it was widely available to woodworkers. In the 1930s it was recognized as the most extensively used abrasive in US wood finishing.

Glass paper
Aka Cabinet paper. An abrasive preparation that was probably made to replace fish skins. Originally made from broken wine-bottle fragments which were sieved onto a pre-glued paper or cloth surface. Glass paper was known in Paris in the 18th century, especially for abrading metal, but it appears that it was not until the early 19th century that glass paper was widely used in furniture-making, although a 1760 reference is made to 'scouring paper' (Kirkham, 1969, p.508). An 1830 recipe for glass paper describes how cabinet-makers should take broken window glass, pound it up, then take cartridge paper, cover that all over with glue, and then sieve the glass powder over it until covered, and allow to dry. It was claimed that this was 'much better than any you can buy, sand being regularly mixed with the glass and coloured to deceive the purchaser' (Siddons, 5th edn, 1830, pp.2–3).

Rushes
See Grasses (Dutch rushes)

Sandpaper
An abrasive sheet used to abrade the surface of wood and metal before finishing. Sand has been used as an abrasive since early times but its use as sandpaper appears to have begun in 1828 in the USA. In the mid 19th century it was described as being made 'with common house sand … but in other respects exactly like glass paper to which it is greatly inferior' (Holtzapffel, 1846, p.1091).

Silicon carbide paper
In 1891 Edward Acheson developed silicon carbide papers, trademarked as Carborundum, which were made from coke and clays heated to extreme temperatures in electric furnaces. Sometimes called 'wet and dry', the abrasive is very tough in either state. It is used as a dry paper for sanding hardwoods and has been used in conjunction with zinc-oxide powder to rub down French polish.

Steel wool
An abrasive pad, made in a range of degrees of abrasiveness which is widely used for surface preparation, especially in finishing systems. Introduced in the last quarter of the 19th century, it is made from specially processed thin matted metal fibres and is often known as wirewool.

Carborundum Co (1991), *The First 100 Years 1891–1991*, Niagara Falls.
Norton Co (n.d.), *Abrasives: Their History and Development*, Worcester Massachusetts: The Company.

ABS plastic
See Plastics

Abura (*Hallea ciliata*)
A West African hardwood timber introduced into Europe in the 1920s which was particularly popular during and after World War II. It has an average density of 570 (36 lb/cu ft), is light brown to pale red-brown in colour, with a fine even texture, a variable grain and a weak striped figure. Commonly used for interior work and for simulating traditional timbers and veneers in reproduction work. Aka Bahia.

Acacia
See Robinia, Myrtle

Acana
Imported into England *c*.1915, it was a heavy timber with a density of 960 (65 lb/cu ft). It had a deep purple plum colour and was likened to BEEFWOOD. Probably the same as Almique (Howard 1920). Aka Donsella.

Acapu
See Partridge wood

Acid catalysed lacquers
See Lacquer

Acid stain
See Stains

Ackerwood
A little-known timber of unknown origin which was described in 1830 as a 'cinnamon coloured timber' (Knight, 1830, p.179).

Acle (*Albizzia acle*)
A timber sourced in the Philippines. A dark brown walnut-like wood, it is hard, durable and heavy, with a fine texture and crossed and curly grain which is easily worked and seasons well. Recommended as a cabinet wood in the mid 20th century.

Acrylic
See Plastics

Adhesives
The need to fix surfaces together meant that some forms of adhesives would be required from very early on in furniture-making. They have mainly been used for structural assembly or to apply decoration, but have also played an important part as a binding agent in gesso, sizing and in the manufacture of timber products. They are divided here into three categories: animal, synthetic and vegetable.

ANIMAL GLUES
The original and most universal adhesive. This glue is made from the boiled bones, hides, blood and carcases of many animals, and, when purified, sets into a gelatinous mass. When heated, this becomes liquid and it is its instant 'grab' when applied hot that makes it ideal for cabinet-making purposes, especially rubbed joints, the fitting of corner blocks and hand veneering processes, although its final setting time can be up to twenty-four hours. Another benefit is that by warming the glue the effect can be reversed. Animal glues are forms of broken-down collagen (connective protein) which vary in purity from the rough remains of the tannery or slaughterhouse to fine fish bladders and small animal skins. There is also a distinction between bone glue and hide glue: the former is made from boiled, crushed animal bones, which are heated and steamed, and then run off; the hydrolysis process finishes the preparation. For the latter, hide parings are prepared, washed at high temperature and the collagen run off in the same way as bone glue.

Egyptian wall paintings in the tomb of Rekhmire (1575–1300 BC) show glue pots similar to 20th-century models. However, it appears that glues were not much used in Egyptian furniture construction, although it was used for preparing GESSO as well as an adhesive for inlays and veneers. The Romans and Greeks also used animal glue for carcase construction and decorative applications.

The development of a range of glues is shown in recipes from 12th-century texts. Theophilus offers one made from stag horn and hides, another made from cheeses and quicklime, as well as one derived from fish (c.1120, pp.26–7). By the 17th century John Evelyn was disparaging about 'cheap glue', which was made by 'boiling the sinews etc. of sheep's trotters, parings of rawhides etc. to a jelly and straining it' (1662, p.240). In his time the best glues were supposed to be pure hide or fish glues. This understanding continued into the 19th century. The various types of animal glues included those from Russia and Italy, which were based on the skins and parings of hides while London glue was made from animal tissue as well as bones.

Fish-based glues were not particularly strong, but were often used for fine and delicate work. Cennini noted that in 15th-century Florence fish glue was used because 'it is excellent for mending lutes and other fine paper, wooden or bone objects' (1437, p.66). Cennini also claimed that glue made from the remains of goats was useful for wooden work, especially for 'making lutes, tarsio, fastening pieces of wood and foliage ornament together, tempering gesso and doing raised gesso'. Two hundred years later John Evelyn confirmed the ichtyocolla (fish) glues as being most suitable for fine and delicate work (1662, p.240). In the 19th century isinglass (fish gelatine) dissolved in 'common gin or spirits of wine' was a component of refined glue made from fish bladders. It was especially used for ivory work and was known as diamond cement (Holtzapffel, 1846, p.154).

Other types of animal-derived glues include casein from soured milk (or sometimes cheese), where the casein is precipitated in the form of curds which, when mixed with slaked lime (calcium hydroxide) makes a true cement. Casein adhesives were also known to the Ancient Egyptians, and were used in North Africa well into the 20th century. They were revived in central Europe c.1800 but were not widely used until the 1914–18 period when they were employed in aircraft construction. These glues were not popular as they introduced too much water into the wood and had a tendency to stain tannin-rich timbers. Rabbit-skin glue was a particular adhesive employed in GILDING as a primary sealant for surfaces, although it is not now a defining term. Egg white, also known as glair, has been used as a size preparation as well as being mixed to make BOLE more workable and tacky. Blood-albumen glue was patented by A. M. Luther in 1896 as a result of a search for a waterproof glue to use in plywood. The recipe included water, ammonium hydroxide and hydrated lime, but was restricted to the manufacture of hot-press plywood (see PLYWOOD and BOIS DURCI).

One of the main problems prior to the 19th century was the storage of glues. Craftsmen usually had to make up their glues each time they were required, as the prepared animal glue had no keeping qualities. In the early 19th century commercially produced glue 'cakes' were successful, enabling glue to be stored until required. These were known as English, Cologne, Fish, French, Medal, Russian or Scotch, according to quality and manufacturing process. Later developments included glues in a powdered or granular form, liquid glues that had lower gel points, as well as glues with added preservatives. Animal glue remained popular well into the 20th century, when it was widely used for secondary or assembly gluing without the application of heat and for a relatively speedy turn round. It was also used for corner block gluing by the RUBBED JOINT method and to build up table legs ready for lathe turning to shape, as well as for many veneering applications. In mainstream work animal glues have now been mainly replaced by synthetic glues for many operations in the furniture industry (see below).

SYNTHETIC (AKA WHITE) GLUES

A whole range of improved and special-purpose glues have been developed in the latter half of the 20th century, which bond at the molecular level, making it possible to join any two surfaces. They are based on (a) solvents which swell, dissolve and then bond upon evaporation; (b) polymers which are applied as a film in solvents, such as contact adhesives; (c) dispersants which use mechanical adhesion using water based glues; (d) heat setting, using thermoplastic solids melted between the parts to be joined; (e) reactive glues based on epoxy resins and polyesters. Many of these glues often respond to heat and therefore can have vastly accelerated setting times. These were originally used in conjunction with radio-frequency heating, introduced in the 1940s, which used electrodes fitted to jigs so that a current passed through the glue line.

Contact adhesives

These are later 20th-century products based on rubber solutions. They are applied, allowed to dry and then joined under pressure. They are particularly associated with plastic laminates, upholstery foams and fabrics.

Hot melt glues

These are applied by gun or in sheet form. Hot melts are used for edge veneering and other non-structural work by being applied at a high temperature, which is followed by a quick cooling to set the join. They can be useful in bonding dissimilar materials.

Formaldehyde group

Melamine formaldehyde (MF)

Used as a coating layer for decorative laminates, and from the mid 20th century (c.1939 on) for general assembly of wood products as they only leave a light-coloured glue line.

Phenol formaldehyde (PF)

A moisture-resistant adhesive based on the same synthetic resin as used in Bakelite. It required heat and pressure to melt and harden and was not good at gap-filling, so was wisely used as a plywood glue, especially after 1930. It was used in film form so plys could be 'laid up' in a press to make plywood or decorative panels.
See also Plastics

Resorcinol formaldehyde (RF)

An all-purpose glue that bonds a range of materials. A post World War II development, it was used for laminating and assembly only, as it leaves a dark glue line. It cured without heat but with a catalyst, resulting in a very strong bond.

Urea formaldehyde (UF)

A synthetic resin which cures in acidic conditions with an added hardener. It was developed from around 1931 and used as a secret component of aircraft manufacture in England during World War II. It was used for laminated sections formed by vacuum presses as well as by high-frequency welding techniques. Sometimes these adhesives were supplied as films: a thin paper coated on either side with the resin was applied to the flat surfaces, and pressure was applied to bond the components. These glues are widely used in the late 20th century for laminating, veneering, and assembly operations. Being water resistant and gap filling, they are a major resin component of PARTICLE BOARD.

PVA

Originating in about 1930, PVA glues (polyvinyl acetate) or 'white glues' are thermoplastic water-based glues that set as the water diffuses into the material being glued.

VEGETABLE GLUES

These glues are made from a range of starch granules (polysaccharides) found in substances such as tapioca, dextrine, rye-flour, rubber and soya-bean dissolved or digested in a solution of caustic alkali. The starch glues have been used for plywood and veneer work as well as for light work such as table linings. They were first introduced as 'apparatine' in Germany c.1870. They then became important in the United States around 1910, especially as plywood adhesives. A range of specialist rubber-latex based glues have also been designed for many applications including contact adhesives for plastic laminates and for certain upholstery and foam work.

Buller, J. (1993), 'Adhesives in the Furniture Industry', in *Furniture Journal*, June, pp.24–8.
Cummins, J. (1986), 'Visit to a glue factory', in *Fine Woodworking*, March/April, pp.66–9.
Darrow, F. L. (1930), *The Story of an Ancient Art: From the Earliest Adhesives to Vegetable Glue*, Perkins Glue Co, Lansdale, Penn.
Masschelein-Kleiner, L. (1985), *Ancient Binding Media, Varnishes and Adhesives*, Rome: ICCROM.
Pinto, E. H. (1948), *Wood Adhesives*, London: Spon.
Skeist, I. (1990), *Handbook of Adhesives*, New York: Van Nostrand.

Adze

A wood-cutting tool with the blade set transversely to the handle and used for the same purpose as a modern jack or smoothing PLANE, that is preliminary preparation or rough work. As opposed to an axe, horizontal strokes are thus used with an action similar to that of a pick-axe. Originally made from stone, the blade passed through a bronze and then a copper phase (Egyptian) and an iron phase (Roman), to be most recently made from steel. Egyptian models were initially thin-bladed with straight edges; later they were cast in copper with a flared blade, 12–27 cm (5–11 in) long, which was lashed to a shaft.

Adzes continued as an essential part of the CARPENTER's tool kit, and were clearly useful for particular as well as general situations. Moxon wrote of the adze: 'Its general use is to take thin chips off timber or boards and to take off those irregularities that the ax by reason of its form cannot well come at; and that a plane (though rank set) will not make riddance enough with' (1677, p.119).

In more recent times many models were made for specific uses, including the chair-maker's adze which often had a gouge-shaped blade. This was used to chop out the seats of Windsor chairs – a process known as bottoming (see CHAIR-MAKERS). The bottomer or seat-shaper would hold the board between his feet and strike the timber across the grain to remove wood and shape the seat. The dangers of this activity can be judged by the references to 'Billy no-toes', the seat-bottomer.

Small, short-handled versions known as carvers' or sculptors' adzes are used for the quick removal of waste wood in carving work.
See Bosting

Afara (*Terminalia superba*)

A hardwood sourced in West Africa during the early 20th century with an average density of 560 (35 lb/cu ft). One variety has a light yellowish-brown colour resembling light oak, whilst the other has an olive or grey-black streaked figure. They have a moderately fine and uniform texture with straight or wavy grain. They have a tendency to split when nailed, but are suitable for rotary veneer-cutting as well as turning. The black heartwood is used for highly decorative veneers. In the solid they have been used for framing, lipping and drawer work. Aka Limba or Korina.

African black walnut

See Mansonia

African blackwood

See Blackwood

African cherry

See Makoré

African mahogany

See Mahogany

African padouk

See Padouk

African pencil cedar

See Cedar

African rosewood

See Bubinga

African satinwood

See Avodiré

African walnut

See Walnut

Afrormosia (*Pericopsis elata*)

A West African hardwood, introduced in the later 20th century. It has an average density of 700 (44 lb/cu ft). The heartwood is a yellowish brown which, when cut, darkens to a medium orange-brown. The wood resembles TEAK, but is stronger and finer textured and lacks teak's oily nature, making it easier to glue. It has a straight grain and a plainish figure. This has meant that in the second half of the 20th century it has been used for framing of teak-veneered furniture as well as being used in the solid and in veneer together. Its popularity was at a height during the period 1960–75.

Afzelia (*Afzelia spp.*)

An African (West and Central) hardwood, with an average density of 750 (47 lb/cu ft). It is orange-red in colour with a medium texture and an interlocked grain with a weak striped figure. Although probably known as a timber in the 18th century, in the 20th century it has been used as an alternative to teak where strength is not a factor.

Agalloch

See Calambac, Eaglewood

Agate

A semi-precious stone, agate is a semi-transparent and translucent variegated chalcedony, with the pigments arranged in stripes or bands or blended in cloud-like colourings. They are classed according to source, with the Indian stones from Goa being especially prized. Sardonyx agate, black or brown with milk-white bands was prized in Antiquity and revived in the 15th and 16th centuries. The Florentine PIETRE DURE masters favoured the blue-green German or ochre-brown Sienna agates. The stones can be stained to increase their colour intensity, which is due to variations in porosity. The stone was also used as a GILDER's burnisher. Stalker and Parker noted that: 'of late Aggate and pebbles are more highly esteemed [than dog teeth]' for such purposes (1688, p.60).
See also Pietre dure

Agba (*Goßweilerodendron balsamiferum*)
A West African hardwood which was introduced commercially to England at the British Empire Exhibition of 1924. With an average density of 560 (35 lb/cu ft) it is yellowish pink to reddish brown with a fine texture and is similar in colour to GABOON MAHOGANY. With a natural finish it suggests light-coloured mahogany and was employed for 'modern' furnishing schemes in the 1950s. In the 1950s some manufacturers stained it and sold it as mahogany. Veneers have been used for middle-range furniture in the post World War II period, sometimes sold under the name of TOLA. In the 1960s it was also recommended for contract, school and church furniture. It has been known as pink mahogany or NIGERIAN CEDAR.

Ageing
The deliberate attempt to make a piece of furniture look older than it is, through the process of 'antiquing' furniture by mechanical, chemical and other methods. These have included sand blasting, hammering, staining, hitting with chains and so on. In the 19th century, when demand for 'antiques' was developing, it was common to use a caustic solution of potash to prematurely age woodwork; this effect could also be achieved by the application of soap leys. In 1897 H. Buyten invented an ageing process for woodwork using a sand-blasting method (Pat.no.24381). Artificial ageing methods are still used today in reproduction furniture. Aka Distressing.

Ailanthus (*Ailanto*) (*Simaru aliente*)
A timber from the East Indies, Japan and China. With an average density of 600 (38 lb/cu ft), it is a durable timber, greyish yellow-orange with a satin lustre which resembles ASH. Not much used in the 20th century, but 'although not common, [it] is appreciated by cabinet-makers' (Boulger, 1908).

Air cushions
Cushions constructed with impervious materials and inflated with air appear to have been made in the early 17th century. Cushions and mattresses were made for outdoor use from oiled skins filled with air via a valve according to Du Fouilloux (1611). (Du Fouilloux, 1611, *The Noble Art of Venerie or Hunting*.) In mid-18th-century Paris, pigs' bladders were inflated and used as cushions (Thornton, 1984, p.155). In the 19th century the concept of air cushions and air beds was further explored, often as a palliative for invalids. The development of waterproof, rubber-coated textiles that could be seamed and fitted with a valve, meant that a wide variety of applications could be adopted, and a number of processes were patented in the first half of the 19th century.

In 1813 a patent was taken out for air-filled beds 'rendered impervious by treating with a rubber solution' by John Clark of Bridgwater, Somerset, England. It was recommended for use with water, steam or other fluids (Pat.no.3718). In 1816 Samuel Pauly patented a seamless substance (the peritoneal covering of the blind gut of animals) that could be filled with air (Pat.no.4000). In 1835 Thomas Hancock made air-bed cushions from cloth lined with caoutchouc (Pat.no. 6849). Coincidentally (maybe) the Philadelphia firm of Hancock and Co had '9 velvet air cushions' in stock in the same year. In 1851 an inflatable bed-chair was exhibited at the Great Exhibition. None of these ideas seems to have been completely successful.

In the 20th century, with advances in rubber and plastic technology, the concept of air-filled cushions for seating were revived. In 1942 Elliot Equipment in England patented the Elliot chair made from inflated Numax, a PVC-coated fabric that covered a cushion on a metal or timber frame. In 1948 American designer Davis Pratt utilized the inflated inner tube of a tyre to make a cushion seat mounted on a welded steel frame. This idea has been followed by a variety of inflatable 'air chairs' usually with some form of plastic casing, the most famous perhaps being the 1967 'Blow' chair by Zanotta, which used the newly developed heat seaming of clear PVC to make an air-filled, see-through, 'throwaway' chair.
See also Plastics, Coated fabrics (Water beds)

Air drying
See Seasoning

Air(e) wood
This term usually refers to SYCAMORE or MAPLE veneers stained with an oxide of iron to make them a greenish-grey colour. In 1830 Siddons gave instructions for dyeing wood a silver-grey shade. This required a mixture of rusting iron, vinegar and water, which when boiled was ready to receive the veneers. LOGWOOD and NUT-GALLS (see Stains) were then added and the whole recipe was boiled regularly for two hours a day until the required colour veneers were achieved (Siddons, op.cit., pp.26–7). This coloured timber has been known as HAREWOOD since the 19th century. Aka Silverwood.

Akle
See Acle

Akund (*Calotropis procera*)
See Kapok

Alabaster
A very soft gypsum that is mostly pure white and translucent, although yellowish and red varieties are known. This see-through facility occasionally allowed images to be painted on the reverse of the stone.

Oriental alabaster
A limestone substance differing from ordinary alabaster. It may be translucent white or reddish-yellow marked with undulating bands or streaks of yellow amber to dark red-brown. In the 16th and 17th centuries the harder, more variegated alabaster from North Africa was favoured. These varieties were classified as the *cotognino* or onyx, *fiorito* with yellow-brown or red colourings, and *marino* with a red-blue veining on a pale green background. Alabaster was used in PIETRE DURE and for the central slab of table tops. Roman stone-work tables of the 16th and 17th centuries incorporated several kinds of alabaster, as well as occasionally using the translucent varieties. In 1768 Richard Hayward supplied Croome Court with 'a 10′ 2″ Alabaster for a table including labour and mouldings' (Beard, 1993, p.101). Alabaster was also mined in Derbyshire in the 19th century.

Alder (*Alnus glutinosa*)
A hardwood timber found in many temperate areas of Europe and West Asia. It has an average density of 520 (33 lb/cu ft). When cut, it is greenish-white but soon oxidizes to an orange red-brown colour which can be confused with mahogany. Alder is straight-grained with a fine, even texture and its solid surfaces show a watered effect when flat sawn, or mild flecking when cut on the quarter. It can have a knotted figure like MAPLE, which has made it attractive to cabinet-makers for centuries. Evelyn records that 'the swelling bunches which are now and then found in the old trees afford the inlayer [with] pieces curiously chambletted and very hard' (1662, p.37). According to Rolt,

alder was in 'great use among turners for household furniture' (1761). Alder has been a popular furniture timber in mainland Europe for marquetry and veneered surfaces. Scandinavian, and in particular Swedish, cabinet-makers employed it, whilst in France, especially during the Napoleonic wars when mahogany was difficult to obtain, alder veneers were popular, particularly those cut from the roots. The taste for decorative root veneers was still prevalent in 1846 (Holtzapffel, p.72). In Britain, the timber was mainly used for country furniture, especially in the North and Scotland: 'suitable specimens are, however, comparatively rare, and they are usually sought after by those who have a partiality for articles made of native grown timber' (Blackie, 1853, p.46). In Scotland the finer timbers were immersed in a peat-water and lime mix as a preservative, which also gives the wood a good mahogany colour. This was then used as the so-called 'Scots mahogany' (Loudon, 1844, p.1681).

Red alder (*Alnus rubra*)
The red alder from western North America is an important timber in the USA. With an average density of 530 (33 lb/cu ft) this variety is pale yellow to reddish-brown, even textured, and straight grained. It has been used for furniture, utility plywood and for veneers. The natural defects such as knots, burrs and streaks also make decorative veneers. In America during the early 20th century it was particularly used for core panels and exposed parts of cheaper furniture, as it stains easily in imitation of mahogany or walnut. Later it was used for upholstery frames. It has been imported in the solid into Europe during the mid 20th century as 'western red alder'.

Alerce wood (*Fitzroya cupressoides*)
A South American (Chile) timber allied to Larch. It has a density of *c*.440 (28 lb/cu ft) with variable reddish hues. It is straight grained, brownish-red with a fine even texture. It is used locally for furniture.

Alexandria wood
Referred to in the *Cabinet-Makers' London Book of Prices and Designs of Cabinet-work …* of 1793. No further references have yet been traced.

Algerian fibre
A natural fibre, produced by a shredding and curling process of the split leaves of the dwarf Algerian palm that grows extensively in North Africa. Although naturally green, it is often dyed black (to imitate hair?). It was widely used as a first stuffing in upholstery work as it retained its body reasonably well. It has been said that top-quality Algerian fibre is equivalent to poor-quality hair. Aka *Crin d'Afrique*.

Algerine
A woollen fabric originally from Algiers, but in the later 19th century the name referred to a striped cotton (or cotton and silk) cloth used for covering sofas, for hangings and curtains (Eastlake, 1878, p.99).

Alginates
Fibres produced from seaweed which have been utilized as upholstery stuffing.
See Alva Marina

Alisia wood
See Whitebeam

Alkanet
See Stains

Allegozant or Alligazant
According to Sheraton, a 'kind of Black rosewood' (1803, p.335). In 1762 an 'allagazante table' was listed in a Powderham inventory (Gilbert and Murdoch, 1993, p.51). In 1774 Thomas Chippendale supplied Burton Constable with '2 very neat bookcases made of fustic, cross banded with Allegozant …' (Gilbert, 1978, p.280).

Alligator wood (*Guarea trichilioides*)
A pinky-brown West Indian timber, similar to mahogany, but not abundant. Its particular characteristics were noted by Sloane: 'The smell of the trunk is sweet like musk or that of an alleygator [sic] whence the name' (Sloane, 1725, vol.2, p.24). In 1774 Long included 'Musk or alligator wood' amongst a list of woods exported from Jamaica for cabinet work.
See also Muskwood

Almique (*Manikara albescus*)
A red-brown wood from Cuba and Guianas. It is hard, compact and heavy and takes a fine polish.
See Acana

Almond (*Amygdalus communis*)
(a) A dull red-tan timber with an average density of 690 (43 lb/cu ft). It has deeper-coloured veinings like TULIPWOOD, and is found in southern Europe and the Mediterranean region. The timber nearer to the roots has been known as false LIGNUM VITAE. Almond was used in 18th-century French marquetry and for OYSTERING. In the early 20th century it was used occasionally for turnery and marquetry.

(b) Almond (*Chuckrasia tabularis*) also refers to an Indian timber (aka Chittagong wood) with a density of 780 (49 lb/cu ft). It has a pink-red stripe, a straight grain, and selected logs can show a range of figures. It resembles SAPELE MAHOGANY and has been used for both solid work and marquetry.

Aloes wood
See Calambac, Eaglewood

Alone (*Rhodognaphalon breviscuspe*)
A West African and South American timber with an average density of 560 (34 lb/cu ft). It is pale reddish-brown with a tendency to discoloration by fungal attack. It is straight grained and coarse textured. Widely used in the 20th century for core stock, plywood and furniture-making.

Aluminium
A lightweight, silvery-coloured metal which can be manipulated in all the standard metal-working processes including casting, rolling, extruding, forging and drawing, as well as spinning and stamping. In contact with air, aluminium rapidly becomes covered with a tough, transparent layer of aluminium oxide that resists further corrosive action, thus making it especially suitable for exterior furniture.

The commercial source of aluminium is bauxite, an impure hydrated aluminium oxide. Experimentally developed and successfully produced by the 1850s, the decorative possibilities of aluminium were soon noticed and it was used in jewellery and for inlays in papier mâché furniture. In the latter case it was in 1863 (Pat.no.145) that James Betteridge patented a method of inlaying aluminium into PAPIER MACHE as a decorative medium. Aluminium was not introduced commercially until 1886 when American Charles Hall and Frenchman Paul Héroult independently and almost simultaneously discovered that alumina, or aluminium oxide, would dissolve in fused cryolite and could then be decomposed electrolytically to a crude molten metal. A low-cost technique, the Hall-Héroult process, is still the major method used for the commercial production of aluminium.

By the end of the 19th century Austria developed some of the earliest applications of aluminium as furniture decoration. One of the earliest innovative uses of the new material was by architect and designer Otto Wagner. His project for the Austrian Postal Savings Bank in Vienna c.1906 included bentwood furnishings, which used an expensive and contrasting material, aluminium, for detailed effects on the legs, arms and 'bolts'.

However, aluminium as a structural material was only seriously introduced into furniture in the 1920s. Aluminium's benefits were seen as its corrosion resistance, light weight, malleability, flexibility and resilience, and not least its silver-like finish. When compared with tubular STEEL however, its relative weakness was a disadvantage and any designs had to build in a degree of support that was not necessary in steel. The development of the alloy Duralumin in Duren [Germany], which was made of 95 per cent aluminium, 4 per cent copper and 1 per cent manganese, created an alloy which age-hardened so that its tensile strength increased rapidly in a few days.

Examples of light metal furniture were shown in Paris exhibitions in 1921 and 1924 (*Metal Industry*, May 1931, p.457), whilst in the 1920s the United States Aluminium Co of Buffalo produced aluminium chairs for sale in European as well as home markets. Weighing less than 3 kg (8 lb), they were decorated in a range of coloured enamels (*Cabinet Maker*, 20 October 1928). The business of making furniture was initially an off-shoot of the main production of this company:

part of the Buffalo works where aluminium bodies were being made, was turned over to the furniture division. Production and sales organisations were assembled, jigs and tools were manufactured for a representative number of designs and a small stock was accumulated. As soon as regular production could be established the prices of pieces dropped sharply.

(*Iron Age*, 1935, 136:30–3)

In the 1930s the aluminium used for furniture was of a high strength corrosion-resistant alloy containing small percentages of silicon and magnesium. These alloys were known as 51S in the USA, Silmalec in England, Almasilium in France and Anticordal in Germany. In 1935 it was said that 'almost every hotel that was built … had to have at least one public room in which aluminium furniture was the outstanding piece of decoration' (loc.cit.).

In Europe it was Marcel Breuer whose name is first associated with the design of aluminium furniture. His work stems from mid 1932 (German Pat.no.170985), but it was in 1933 when the Alliance Aluminium Company of France sponsored an international competition, the '*Concours international du meilleur siège en aluminium*', to find the best aluminium chair, that the value of aluminium as a furniture material was fully demonstrated. It appears to have generated wide interest in the international design community as the competition attracted entries from 14 countries, comprising 209 chair designs, of which 54 were in prototype.

Developments continued in Europe for specialized applications such as furnishings for the airship company, Zeppelin. The German firm of L. and C. Arnold supplied aluminium tubular-framed chairs for the airship Hindenburg in 1935. The combination of light weight and a modern image was clearly attractive to the airship-builders, although the cost of aluminium was to prohibit any mass-production ideas, despite aluminium frames also being used for seating by other aircraft companies.

1   *Aluminium-framed table and aluminium-framed BA chairs by Ernest Race, 1947.*

A little later, in 1938, Swiss designer Hans Coray won a competition for a chair to be used in the Swiss National Exhibition. He designed a lightweight aluminium chair which was primarily for outdoor use (it weighed only 3 kg/6 lb). In this case the use of aluminium was not just a practical one. Aluminium had long been known as the 'Swiss metal', as it was in Neuhausen that Héroult built his first facility for manufacturing aluminium in commercial quantities (see Plate XXI).

After the end of World War II a revival of interest in aluminium as a commercial material was clearly a response to both the timber shortage and the over-supply of aluminium created by the war effort. The British Utility furniture scheme included aluminium divan bedframes, and plans were made for a range of coloured aluminium-framed dining chairs c.1946–7. There were serious moves to use surplus aluminium from aircraft manufacture by the furniture industry, but Gordon Russell, who was charged with investigating the feasibility of the idea, suggested it would only work if there was a complete timber shortage. Nevertheless, one of the most famous British chairs of the 20th century was undoubtedly the aluminium BA chair. Designed and manufactured by Ernest Race, its success can be seen in the fact that, between 1945 and 1969, 250,000 chairs were produced.

In the United States, the aluminium industry had grown by 600 per cent during wartime, and by 1945 it was clear that industrial promotion of aluminium was necessary to utilize the increased capacity. The aircraft industry had been a major user of aluminium, so it is not surprising to find that the Cessna Aircraft company produced a storage unit with drawers lined in aluminium. In contrast, the 'Airlume' upholstery range by the San Hygene Upholstery Co was made with aluminium frames, but when upholstered, the furniture was indistinguishable from the traditional wooden versions.

Aluminium suppliers continued to promote the use of their material and they positively encouraged product development. The future for aluminium in furniture seemed to lie in components as well as single-use design. Aluminium had been successfully used by Saarinen in the bases of his 1956 Tulip chair-and-table group, interestingly in combination with glass-reinforced plastic. In 1958 Charles and Ray Eames developed an important range of chairs called the 'Aluminium Group' which were intended for indoor or outdoor use. The chairs' lightness was achieved by using the hammock seating principle in combination with a cast aluminium frame. Costs were high due to the sand casting and hand-finishing processes, so they were most usually purchased for interior use.

Aluminium continued to be considered suitable for furniture use and was thus promoted. In 1961 the British Aluminium Company sponsored a furniture design competition. The winning design was for a contract bed-frame and the second prize went to a design for an outdoor chair. The third prize was awarded for an aluminium swivel base for a chair. The idea of component parts was further developed, since extruded tube, cast or spun aluminium was an ideal material for a range of fittings and swivel-chair bases. In addition it was widely used for aluminium extrusions that were applied to all sorts of furniture including 'pole' storage systems, as well as accessories.

In recent years aluminium has again been a favoured material for avant-garde designers. Phillipe Starck has used it extensively for chair frames (Louis 20, Stool) and the Spaniard Jorge Pensi has taken the Swiss Landi chair idea and produced the Toledo chair in the same idiom, but for the Spanish outdoor market. The sculptural effects achieved by Australian designer Marc Newsom and his Lockheed Lounge chaise longue, which uses riveted plates of aluminium upon a fibreglass shell, show that the material can still be innovative and contemporary.

See also Anodizing, Magnesium

Anon. (1931), 'Aluminium in the construction of furniture', in *The Metal Industry*, 1 May, pp.457–60.
Cologne (1991), *Aluminium, das Metal der Moderne*, Cologne: Stadtsmuseum Exhibition Catalogue.
Long, R. G. (1990), 'A perfect metal for design: aluminium furniture and tableware from 1850–1945', MA Thesis, Parsons School of Design and Cooper Hewitt Museum.
Nishikawa, Tomota (1935), *Siège en aluminium*, Tokyo: Unpublished dissertation.
Smith, G. (1995), 'Alcoa's aluminum furniture', in *Pittsburgh History*, 78, Summer, pp.52–64.
White, J. Noel (1973), *The management of design services*, London: Allen and Unwin. [Case study on Race]

Aluminium oxide
See Abrasives

Alva marina (*Zostera marina*)
A dried seaweed imported from the Baltic, used as an inexpensive upholstery filling in the 19th century, especially for the edges of first stuffing. Webster noted it was 'well spoken of as a stuffing for mattresses as it does not harbour vermin' (1845, p.297), however, it was later pointed out that 'alva marina has been objected to for stuffing mattresses as likely to absorb damp; the saline properties would, nevertheless, prevent its giving cold. Other weeds and mosses, the products of Italy and America, are used for the same purpose, and are cheaper than horse-hair and wool' (Bitmead, 1912, p.17). It was generally out of use by the early 20th century. Aka SEA GRASS, Eel grass.
See also Mattresses, Moss

Amaranth (*Peltogyne paniculata*)
See Purpleheart

Amarillo
A group of timbers found in tropical America, especially Venezuela (*Aspidospermum vargassii*) and Brazil (*Terminalia odorata*), which are generally golden to reddish-yellow in colouring and used as dye woods.
See also Arariba, Fustic, Canarywood, Vinhatico

Amber
A fossilized resin that has been used in jewellery and precious objects for centuries. It is mined in Poland and found on the Baltic sea shore. It was particularly used in furniture by cabinet-makers in Augsburg and Nuremburg as a decorative veneer or inlay in the period of exotic cabinet production during the 17th century. The valuable nature of the material meant that it was used as a symbol of status or prestige. For example, King Charles I owned 'a cabinet of yellow amber garnished with silver guilt [sic], with an ebony boxe' (Jervis, 1989, p.283). The famous amber throne of Hapsburg Emperor Leopold I from 1677 still exists in fragments in Vienna Kunsthistorisches Museum. In 1684, amber-decorated cabinets were given as gifts to the Siamese ambassador by the French court.

Amber has also been used to make a VARNISH resin as it is one of the hardest natural resins. By melting amber at high temperatures into thin sheets and then crushing this into powder and again mixing with a drying oil such as LINSEED, then heating again for a period, a fine varnish can result. However, the cost, the resultant yellowy colour, and the many weeks' drying time mitigated upon its success. As it is also the least soluble, 'amber varnish' often contains little true amber.

Baer, Winfred (1982), 'Ein Bernsteinstuhl für Kaiser Leopold I', in *Jahrbuch der Kunsthistorische*, XCII, pp.91–108.
Dahlstrom, A. and Brost, L. (1996), *The Amber Book*, Tuscon: Geoscience Press.
Reineking von Bock, G. (1981), *Bernstein, das Gold der Ostsee*, Cologne: Callwey.
Williamson, G. C. (1932), *The Book of Amber*, London: Benn.

Amboyna (*Pterocarpus indicus*)
A mildly fragrant wood related to the PADOUK with an average density of 560–640 (35–40 lb/cu ft). It is exported from the Philippines and the Molucass group of islands. The burr wood, which is usually light yellow to blood red with a wavy interlocked or crossed grain is comprised of small knots and curls which are highly decorative and can be used in the solid or as a veneer.

A timber called 'amboina' was used in the 18th century, exported from the Dutch East Indian port of Amboina, but it is not clear whether this was the same timber. In the 19th century the name amboyna referred particularly to the burrs. In 1830 Knight noted that it 'is now very much used in cabinet work. It is of various colours, and the shades are generally small. It arrives in logs of two feet wide' (1830, p.179). Twenty years later, cabinet-makers were advised that amboyna

is an exceedingly beautiful and highly-ornamental wood. Its available size, figure, and colour recommend its use in the manufacture of small cabinets. It is besides, frequently used in veneering more extensive surfaces, such as loo table and tea table tops. In such cases, from the irregularity of form in the wood, and from the abrupt and transitory character of the fibre, the joinings require to be waved and indented.
(Blackie, 1853, p.42)

The commentary ended by noting that it was difficult to finish, and often required the action of oil and PUMICE stone to level the surface, which could darken and deteriorate the appearance somewhat. Finally it was noted that amboyna 'is now of less frequent use than formerly'. Its use was again revived in Europe, especially in Paris, in the early 20th century.

In the mid-19th century, amboyna wood, imported from Singapore, was also known as Kiabooca wood (Malay Kaya Boka). As Kiabooca it was shipped '2 to 4 foot long, 4 to 24 inches wide and 2 to 8 inches thick. It resembles the burr of the yew-tree' (Holtzapffel, 1846, p.89). Aka Lingoa wood, Narra.

American beech
See Beech

American birch
See Birch

American black ash
See Ash

American black walnut (*Juglans nigra*)
See Walnut

American cherry
See Cherry

American chestnut
See Chestnut

American cloth
See Coated fabrics

American elm
See Elm

American holly
See Holly wood

American horse chestnut
See Buckeye

American lime
See Basswood

American locust
See Robinia

American maple
See Maple

American plane
See Buttonwood, Sycamore, Plane

American red gum (*Liquidambar styraciflua*)
A timber native to the eastern section of the United States from Connecticut to southern New York, which has an average density of 560 (35 lb/cu ft). The red-brown heartwood, which may be handsomely figured with darker streaks, contrasts with the whitish colour of the sapwood. Although they are the same timber, the sapwood is sometimes known as hazel pine and the heartwood as satin walnut, the 'hazel' not having developed the darker wood on account of its natural habitat. Red gumwood was used as a furniture timber in the American Colonial and Federal periods, especially in the New York region. It was recognized as relatively easy to work with and finish.

It was 'very light and takes a brilliant polish, it is sometimes sawn into excessively thin laminae and employed by the cabinet-makers in New York for veneering' (Loudon, 1844, p.2051).

During the early 20th century, in the United States, red gum was widely used for imitating walnut or mahogany, especially for the structural parts of cabinet work. During the 20th century, in Europe, it has been known as 'satin walnut' and was used in the production of inexpensive bedroom suites. According to Boulger, the gum remaining in the timber caused it to twist and warp, therefore 'it is only used for cheap bedroom furniture, not being fit for rooms in which fires are lit' (1908, p.182). By about 1925, improved seasoning and veneering techniques had removed the difficulties, and its ease of working and finishing made it a more important timber. By the 1950s red gum was the most widely used wood in the American furniture industry. This wood has also been used to make plywood as well as being used in the solid and as a core-wood for veneering. Old inventories sometimes use the name Bilsted for this timber. Aka Sweet gum.

American red oak
See Oak

American walnut
See Walnut

American white ash
See Ash

American white elm
See Elm

American white oak
See Oak

American whitewood
See Basswood

Amyris (*Amyris balsamifera*)
A West Indian, Central American and Florida timber with an average density of 1000 (64 lb/cu ft). It has a whitish sapwood and a yellow to medium-brown heartwood with a fine uniform texture, a variable grain, and is often streaked. Discovered in Martinique *c*.1695 and known in France as *bois de Rhodes*, it was used for inlays and turnery in the 18th century. It was also known as Candlewood on account of its high resin content, and was mainly used for the extract of oils. The oil made it more valuable as an apothecary's wood than it was as timber. Aka *Lignum rodium*.

Anan (*Fagraea fragrans*)
A hard and heavy Burmese timber with an average density of 800 (50 lb/cu ft). It is yellow or light brown with streaks of white, darkening to deep gold-brown. It has a variable texture and grain with a mottled effect figure. In 1920 it was noted that 'if it became known in England … it would be particularly prized for the makers of chairs and other work of like character' (Howard, 1920, p.84). It has been used for cabinet work and as a veneer.

Andaman padouk
See Padouk

Andiroba (*Carapa guianensis*)
A Central American timber closely related to the MAHOGANY family with an average density of 640 (40 lb/cu ft). It is lustrous reddish-brown, often with streaks, with a moderately fine and even texture, and variable grain. It is prone to splitting, but as it resembles mahogany, it has sometimes been used as a substitute. It has also been used for corestock for plywood as well as supplying decorative veneers. In about 1900 it was specifically recommended for picture frames and small ornamental cabinet work. By 1920 it was denigrated as having little to commend it (Howard, 1920, p.67) but it was still recommended as a cabinet wood in Britain and America during the 1950s. Aka Brazilian mahogany, Crabwood.

Angelim (*Andira inermis*)
A Central and South American timber with an average density of 800 (50 lb/cu ft). Red-brown to very dark brown or black, it is often highly figured. It has a straight grain and a coarse and uneven texture. The 'feathered' figure when tangentially cut gives rise to alternative names such as PARTRIDGE or PHEASANT wood.
See also Cabbage bark, Partridge wood

Angica wood
See Cangica wood

Animal glues
See Adhesives (Animal)

Anime
See Resins

Aningeria (*Aningeria spp.*)
An African timber with an average density of 530 (33 lb/cu ft). Cream to tan with a pinky tinge, it has a straight grain, occasionally producing a mottled effect. With a medium to coarse texture, it is fairly easily worked and takes a fine polish. Used in the 20th century for furniture, plywood and selected decorative veneers.

Annotto (Anatta)
A red dyestuff obtained from the seed capsules of *Bixa orellana*, a West Indian tree. Often used to give a gold tone to lacquer.

Anodizing
A process of artificially thickening the natural protective oxide film which often forms on ALUMINIUM. Colour can be introduced into the porous film before the final sealing process. The process is based on a version of electrolysis, using an acid solution of chromic or sulphuric acid. The process has been used in the latter part of the 20th century for colouring and decorating small furnishing items such as chair frames, trolleys and trays.

Antiaris (*Antiaris toxicaria*)
A West African timber with an average density of 410 (26 lb/cu ft). It is a white to yellowish-grey timber with a rather coarse and uneven texture and an interlocked grain with a striped figure. Although a rather poor-quality timber, it is easy to work, so it was used in England in the 1960s for interior work in cabinets. The wood somewhat resembles OBECHE. Selected logs offer decorative veneers.

Antique dusting
A technique used in reproduction furniture-making, suggesting dust deposited in open wood pores over time. It is made from 'antiquing slush' produced by mixing wax, rottenstone, and dry colour, which was wiped over a surface and allowed to settle. Used as a finishing process in the USA, especially during the 1930s.

Antlers
See Horn

Applewood (*Malus sylvestris*)
A European fruit wood with an average density of 770 (48 lb/cu ft). It is pale reddish-brown or yellow-to-biscuit colour. It has a close, fine texture often with tiny knots and it is very hard. As with most fruit woods the timber is restricted in size due to the relatively small size of tree, so its use in furniture is limited. In the Middle Ages it was employed in Southern Europe, whilst in the 17th century it was used for inlay and applied carving in Northern Europe. It has been worked into TUNBRIDGE WARE, for turned work and for the legs, as well as for stretchers and spindles of regional chairs. It was occasionally used as a decorative veneer in continental Europe during the early 19th century, and is still used for turnery, carving and inlay work. Known in France as *bois de pommier*, it was one of the BOIS INDIGENES.

Appliqué
(a) A method of decoration that is applied rather than being worked into the material directly. Although it may refer to other materials, it usually refers to a textile cut-out in a decorative shape, which is then applied onto the surface of another fabric with an embroidery stitch or by COUCHING. By using contrasting colours and fabric types, often upon a plain ground, a three-dimensional effect can be created (a 16th-century example made for Henry VIII in black velvet on white satin with arabesque motifs is in the Burrell Collection, Glasgow). The Spangled Bedroom chair covered in red satin with applied cloth of gold and silver, at Knole, is a superb example of the process; other fine examples are in Hardwick Hall, Derbyshire. During Elizabethan and early Stuart times plant and animal motifs, worked on canvas, were cut out and fixed to plain-ground fabrics, often velvet, for use as cushions and hangings.

(b) In North America, the term appliqué has also been used to refer to raised wooden panels up to 3 mm (⅛ in) thick, which offer a display surface for rare and exotic timber veneers (including burr poplar, ash and walnut) which are then incorporated into cabinet work.

Apricot wood (*Armeniaca vulgaris*) or **Abricotta** (*Prunus armeniaca*)
The wood of the apricot tree, native to Armenia. Compact and yellow, it is used in turning but only to a limited extent due to the rarity of sound timber.

Apron piece
An applied section of timber that is fitted to the front rail of a chair or kneehole cabinet to give a decorative feature, having no particular constructional value. For example, chairs with deep apron pieces might conceal a pot.

Aqua fortis
See Stains and staining (Nitric acid)

Aquilaria
See Eaglewood

Arabesque marquetry
See Marquetry

Araracanga (*Aspidosperma*)
See Peroba rosa

Arariba (*Centrolobium paraense*)
A tropical South American timber with an average density of 840 (53 lb/cu ft). The colour varies from yellow (such as Amarillo) to orange-red, all variegated with dark-red to black stripes. It has a variable grain and a medium texture. Used in the 20th century for cabinet-making both as solid and as veneers. Aka Balaustre.

Arbutus wood (*Arbutus unedo*)
A small tree originating from the Mediterranean region but grown extensively in Southwestern Ireland. It is reddish-brown, with a hard close grain that is prone to splitting. Used in the 19th century for souvenir wares and small furniture such as chiffoniers, davenports, and so on. It was fully exploited by using roots and branches, as well as the trunk. Aka Strawberry tree.

'Killarney Inlaid Woodwares', in B. Austen (1989), *Tunbridge Ware*, London: Foulsham.

Archil (*Roccella tinctoria*) also **Orchil**
A species of lichen known since the 15th century as a dyestuff, giving a rich red-purple tincture. It was sourced in the Canary Islands and fermented with alkali (such as ammonia) to draw the dye, but it had a tendency to speedily fade. In 1830 Siddons noted its use as a stain for the 'common red [colour] for bedsteads and common chairs' (1830, p.2).

Arkwright
A maker of meal or corn bins which were known as 'arks' in northern England. They used a CLAMPED front with pegged and WEDGED construction combined with cleft boards and a simple overlapping technique for the top. See Construction, Pegs

Armchair-maker's saw
See Saws

Armorply
A man-made board comprising PLYWOOD and a thin sheet of metal developed along with a number of other special-use plywoods in the 1930s.

Armozeen or **Amarzine**
A silk taffeta-like fabric used for hangings and curtains. In the 18th century it was imported from France, Italy and the East Indies. According to Postlethwayt (1751), the East Indian versions were inferior. In the Chiswick House inventory of 1770 there were 'three blue Armozeen festoon window curtains' (Rosoman, 1986, p.98). In the 19th century, a heavier ribbed version was used for curtains and covers.

Armure
A broad class of fabrics with 'pebbled' surfaces. Originally a heavy silk fabric with this effect, later made from a range of fibres, but especially cotton. In America during the early 20th century, armure was recommended for couch covers and *portières*.

Arris
A bevelled edge that is often found on fluting. The term is first recorded in 1677 for a decorative feature or detail deriving from the French *areste* meaning a sharp ridge created when two plane surfaces meet. The sharp edge of the flutes on an Ionic column are an example. Although considered an example of fine carving, the result can be prone to damage if too 'sharp'. Nicholson suggested that flutes should be less than a semi-circle to maintain the arris and went on to say that though 'a sharp arris is the perfection of the workmanship it is often taken away to avoid injury' (1826, p.7).

Arsedine
A word of unknown origin referring to a gold coloured alloy of copper and zinc (such as brass).
See also Dutch gold

Art Deco
A style label applied to architecture and design produced in a *moderne* style between c.1918 and 1939. Its name is derived from the *Exposition internationale des arts décoratifs et industriels modernes* held in Paris during 1925. The style embraced mechanization and machine motifs, as well as a wide range of popular imagery, including sources as varied as jazz, Ancient Egypt, African culture, China and Japan, engineering and machinery as well as contemporary avant-garde art. The best furniture, often from French houses, is finely crafted with exotic materials, and may be associated with names such as Ruhlmann, Dunand and Lalique. The styles were frequently adapted to commercial designs and produced in volume, in a parody of the fine work of the artist-decorators. The style was popular throughout Europe and North America.
See Bronze, Gaboon, Glass, Iron, Ivory, Leather, Palm, Rosewood, Shagreen, Tortoiseshell

Art fibre
(a) An early-20th-century (c.1904) American term that refers to a twisted paper 'string fibre' used for manufacturing chairs, especially as FIBRE-RUSH.
See also Fibre-rush, Lloyd Loom

(b) Also used as an abbreviation for 'artificial fibre' which usually refers to early-20th-century cellulosic products like rayon.

Art Nouveau
A deliberate attempt to create a new style which grew in the 1880s and died during World War I, reaching a zenith in the Paris Exposition of 1900. It was characterized by particular stylistic elements including the whiplash, human figures and curving and tendril-like lines applied to decorative arts. The style also embraced fine craftsmanship and the ethos of individuality which encouraged commissioned work. Although attempting to be radically different, many of the designs were rooted in developments of previous styles including Japonisme, ARTS AND CRAFTS and early Celtic work. In particular, furniture design either developed as the sinuous curvilinear style exemplified by Hector Guimard, Emile Gallé and Henry van de Velde or followed a more geometrically based model such as the work of Charles Rennie Mackintosh. Both these styles were to influence MODERNISM.
See also Bronze, Copper, Marquetry

Arts and Crafts
Although named after the Arts and Crafts Exhibition Society founded

in 1882, its origins are to be found some thirty years earlier. In the 1850s critics of design were keen to return to 'handicrafts' as opposed to faceless factory production. The romantic socialism of John Ruskin and William Morris led to the establishment of Guilds which developed furniture (amongst other decorative arts) which was intended to be true to the materials used, honestly designed and made, and which would express the craftsmanship within the product. The hallmark of the movement is simple furniture designed in a vernacular tradition, often made of OAK but using a range of finishes including PAINTING, EBONIZING, INLAY, CARVING and CERAMIC TILES. The movement reached the USA in the 1870s and was espoused by Frank Lloyd Wright, Gustav Stickley and others. Its influence has remained in the crafts, and it has had a revival in the latter part of the twentieth century. It has also been seen as a precursor to MODERNISM in terms of its theories.

Ash wood (*Fraxinus excelsior*)

A European hardwood (also found in Western Asia and in North Africa), with an average density of 720 (46 lb/cu ft). It has a cream to pale-tan colour, with occasional black heart, a hard texture and an open straight grain with a fine figure, and pores, rings and rays that are easily definable. It is tough and elastic but fairly easy to work. Ash is ideal for chair-making as it bends well.

Its bending qualities were first exploited by the Ancient Egyptians for making compound bentwood ash bows. In Roman usage ash was recognized as a 'moist' wood, particularly suitable for resilient bed frames. Ash continued to be a valuable timber for both rural and urban furniture-makers. From the 1650s onwards it was used for drawer linings in chests. In addition, ash has been widely used for country furniture, especially for legs and struts, as it cleaves or is riven into boards easily and can be bent to shape. It was also a favourite timber for turned chairs over a very long period from the Middle Ages to the 19th century. It has been an important part of the chair-makers' trade, being widely used for Windsor chairs, especially for the bows, cresting rails, legs, sticks, stretchers and splats. Evelyn recorded that

some ash is curiously camleted and vein'd, I say, so differently from other timber, that our skilled cabinet-makers prize equal with ebony, and give it the name of green ebony … but to bring it to that curious lustre so as tis hardly distinguished from the most curiously diapered olive, they varnish their work with the China varnish … which infinitely exceeds linseed oil.
(1662, p.53)

Ash burrs were highly prized in 18th-century furniture both in America and England, whilst in France the decorative value of *loupe de frêne* was popular with Empire and Restauration designers. Like other indigenous timbers, ash found favour in many European countries during the Napoleonic wars when imported exotic timbers were less accessible (see BOIS INDIGENES). In the later 19th century ash was considered especially suitable for the insides of cabinets as well as in the solid for bedroom suites. Ash was also valued for kitchen tables, as it was less likely to splinter.

Ash takes stain well. When permanganate of potash solution is applied, it can imitate oak (see STAIN). This effect was used during the mid 1950s in Britain, where ash table tops were stained and sold as an 'oak finish' with the legs of chairs and tables made in solid ash. In the latter part of the 20th century, ash stained black, known as 'black ash' has been a popular finish.

American black ash (*F. nigra*)

A light, medium-tan to dark-brown timber, it is akin to white ash and has been used for similar purposes, especially chair-making. It was widely used for components, especially seat rails and stretchers. It is particularly noticed for a process of de-lamination of the annual rings, which can create ash splints. These were used to BOTTOM the seats of chairs in New England probably from the late 17th century and were called 'checked seats'. The black ash was sometimes used for veneer bandings in early Federal furniture. In the early 20th century it was widely used for furniture and interior finishing, with burrs being highly valued.

American white ash (*F. americana*)

A greyish-white to light-tan coloured timber, with a straight grain, older timbers having a cross-figuring effect known as curly ash. It has an average density of 680 (42 lb/cu ft). In America the timber was widely used for turned chairs during the 17th century. It was also used for chair frames during the Federal period.

This timber is not as hard or as tough as the British variety, thus its more amenable working properties encouraged extensive exports to Britain in the 19th century. American or Canadian white ash was therefore widely used for British cabinet work in this period. It was especially used for the interiors of robes, chests and the like, as well as for drawer work including sides and bottoms. It was noted that ash 'gradually and to a considerable extent superseded the other woods used for the interior fittings of chests of drawers, wardrobes and similar articles of furniture' (Blackie, 1853, p.12). The attraction was the 'entire absence of smell … and the ease it is wrought as compared with cedars etc., formerly in use for the purpose to which ash is now applied' (idem). In the early 20th century white timber was also much sought after for bedroom furniture in the USA. Although by the 1920s it was classed as a low-use medium-grade furniture timber, it was still widely used for kitchen furniture in America during the 1950s. As with black ash, the 'splints' from the laminae of the tree were prepared by crushing the fibrous early growth wood to make strips for chair bottoming, called checked seats.

Hungarian ash

An ash variety sourced from Hungary. It was popular as a furniture wood in Austria in the later 18th century and in western parts of Europe at a similar time, and remained so into the mid 19th century. This was due to the finely figured, burred and wavy curls, or zigzag grain found in that species, ideal for the flat surfaces of bedroom and dining furniture. The effects were sometimes called 'watery ash' or 'ram's horn'.

Japanese ash (*F. mandschurica*)

This variety is found in South East Asia and has an average density of 570 (36 lb/cu ft). It is a straw or biscuit to light-brown colour, with a fine even texture and a usually straight grain. It is used for cabinet work, both as a solid and as a veneer. Selected logs produce veneers with a range of figure including the 'peanut shell'. This highly figured veneer has been occasionally used in furniture-making. Imported into the United Kingdom from around 1908, it was especially favoured in Scotland. It was introduced into America around 1920. Aka Tamo.

Mountain ash
See Rowan

Olive ash

Ash logs with dark brown to black heartwood markings are sometimes known as olive ash and have been converted into decorative veneers.
See also Green ebony

Aspen (*Populus tremuloides*)
A North American timber with an average density of 440 (28 lb/cu ft), which is greyish-white to light brown in colour, with a fine and even texture and a straight grain. It is recognized as being tough and shock resistant. In the 20th century it has been used for wardrobe backs and drawer bottoms. It has also been converted into EXCELSIOR.

Assembly
See Construction

Astragal
See Moulding

Astragal plane
See Planes

Atlas
A silk satin fabric manufactured in the East Indies which was plain, striped, or flowered. It was noted by Celia Fiennes on her visit to Fetcham Park in 1712, where she saw: 'one ground bed chamber which was an Indian attlass [sic] white very fine' (Fiennes, 1982, p.240). It was still recognized as a rich Indian satin in the early twentieth century.

Atomic wood
A semi-synthetic wood produced in America during the 1960s. Timber was impregnated with a plastic resin and irradiated by being placed in a vacuum chamber, where air and gases were removed and replaced with a monomer. The timber was then bombarded with gamma rays causing polymerization and resulting in a solid wood-plastic composite. Certain firms experimented with it as it was much stronger and more durable than plain timber, and in addition had a ready-made finish. The Lockheed Aircraft Company experimented with this material and branded it Lockwood.
See also Densified wood

Auger
A basic boring tool, with a long shank and a cutting edge with either a single or double (Jenning's) helical twist, a screw point and a handle fixed at right angles to allow turning by hand. Early literary references to augers are found in Pliny and the *Odyssey*, and the tool appears to have been well known in Roman times. The enormous variety of cutting edges, shapes and styles for specialist work testify to the value of this tool for many generations of wood-workers. The nose or shell auger with a simple semi-circular cutting edge fixed to the end was introduced in the Middle Ages, whilst the twist augers, with their improved capabilities, were developed in the later 18th century. The double twist auger of Jenning's pattern ensures clean, accurate holes in cabinet work by using the small screw thread to start the hole, by removing the debris as it cuts, and by cutting with the doubled sharp edge. 'Chest augers', made in a tapered half-conical shape, were used in Windsor CHAIR-MAKING.
See also Bit and Brace

Australian beefwood
See Beefwood

Australian blackwood
See Blackwood

Australian red cedar (*Cedrela toona*)
A hardwood found in India, Java and Australia that is not a true cedar. The timber is similar to mahogany but with a density of 440 (28 lb/cu ft), and a reddish-brown colour with darker streaks. It is straight grained, with a moderately close but uneven texture, and was widely used by early settlers. In the early 20th century it was recorded that 'it is largely employed in furniture and joinery-work, and beautiful veneers are obtained from the junction of the branches and the stem … it takes a fine polish, and is suitable for dining-room furniture &c.' (Spon, 1901, p.149). In the later 20th century, decorative veneers cut to display a silver ray figure, were used for furniture panels. Aka Toon wood or Indian mahogany.

Australian satinwood
See Satinwood

Australian silky oak (*Cardwellia sublimis*)
See Oak

Australian walnut
See Walnut (Queensland)

Aventurine or **Venturine**
A variously coloured quartz mineral which contains particles of mica, commonly brown or reddish-brown. Factitious aventurine has been made from a brownish-coloured glass, flecked with copper crystals, especially in Murano since the 16th century. The effect was also re-created by sprinkling powdered bronze, gold or copper onto wet lacquer surfaces. In Japan and Europe it was used in conjunction with lacquering and japanning to create a spangled surface effect. The process was explained by John Evelyn:

By venturine is meant the most delicate, and slender golden wire such as embroiderers use, reduced to a kind of powder, as small as you can file or clip it; this strew'd upon the first layer of pure varnish, when dry, super-induce what colour you please; and this is prettily imitated in several lackes. (1662, p.239)

Aventurine lacquer was popularized by the Martin brothers in Paris during the 18th century. It was also known as speckles: a form of decorative painting that appeared to imitate aventurine effects.

[speckles] are of divers sorts as golden, silver, copper and many other colours, some finer, some coarser, which are to be used according to the fancy of the artist and as the nature of the matter may require; they are used on mouldings, outsides and insides of bowls, cups, and boxes, drawers etc. (Salmon, 1672, p.862)

To lay speckles after a piece is painted or varnished, 'before it is dry, put some of your speckle into your sieve … and gently shake the sieve over the place you design, till they are all speckled according to your intention' (Salmon, op.cit., p.903).
See also Lacquer

Avodiré (*Turraeanthus africanus*)
A West African hardwood with an average density of 600 (38 lb/cu ft). It has a light yellow to golden-yellow or amber colouring with a generally straight, but sometimes wavy, irregular grain which produces a mottled figure when quarter sliced. There is not normally much distinction between sap and heartwood. Plain timber resembles a light-coloured, fine-textured mahogany, but the figured timber is more like Ceylon satinwood. The irregular grain effect of quarter-cut decorative veneer has been used for English cabinet work since the late 18th cen-

2 *Back board of English commode, c.1773. The framed-up construction shows the unusual feature of the stiles tenoned into the rails.*

tury and avodiré remains a valuable marquetry wood in the 20th century. Plain avodiré has sometimes been used as an alternative to mahogany in cheap furniture manufacture, whilst the figured variety has been used as an alternative to sycamore as well as a decorative veneer. Aka African satinwood.

Awl
A hand tool with a sharp spike designed to pierce holes in soft materials, for example leather and some woods. The awl with a square cross section and a tapering pointed blade was used for boring hardwoods and veneers close to edges, as it avoided splitting as the square section breaks the fibres rather than splitting them. Although often used for piercing pilot holes in timber, the awl also functioned as a scribing tool to provide marks to assist in cutting out woodwork.

The upholstery craft also used awls, especially the 'garnish' or 'straining' awl, whose function was particularly for enlarging holes in leather and cloth. The 'pritch' awl was used to mark out cloth, especially leather, for button plans: the 'stabbing' awl was used to make holes in tough material prior to sewing.
See also Bradawl, Prickall

Ayan (*Distemonanthus benthamianus*)
A West African timber with an average density of 690 (42 lb/cu ft). It is a yellow-gold to orange-brown colour with a fine to medium texture, a variable grain, and a mottled figure effect. It is hard, brittle and difficult to work, but has been used in the 20th century for joinery and carcase work. Occasionally logs supply very finely figured veneers. Aka Nigerian satinwood.

Back boards
A CONSTRUCTION term that refers particularly to the framing panels of mirrors, dressing glasses and the backs of cabinets. These may be simple boards nailed to the carcase, or more sophisticated panels or framed sections designed for better protection against movement. The range of finishes is very wide and includes painted, stained, veneered or unfinished.

The use of separate back boards was introduced with framed up construction methods in the 17th century. The range of fixing methods used since then include horizontal planks nailed to rebates, frame and stile panelled sections, and boards dovetailed to stiles. They are often finished with a wash or stain of varying dark colours. Sheraton was quite specific about the nature of back boards for particular objects. In cheval mirrors he suggested 13 mm (½ in) mahogany framed in four panels, rebated to receive 6.4 mm (¼ in) panels to make a frame of light weight, that would need a lead weight to balance it. He suggested that back boards of large mirrors were to be of 38 mm (1½ in) deal in 4 or 6 panels with thin back boards ploughed into the framing (1803, p.25). By the mid 19th century 13 mm (½ in) 'deal' was considered to be appropriate for common cabinet back boards, whilst 'good work' was made from 25 mm (1 in) thick deal and sometimes framed in 2 or 4 panels. In batch-produced early-20th-century English cabinet work it was common to paint the back boards of chests and cabinets with a yellow-green ochre paint. Late-20th-century production furniture often utilizes PLYWOOD and HARDBOARD panels for backing cabinets.

Back flap hinges
See Hinges

Back painting
See Verre églomisé

Back plates
The part of a handle ensemble that rests against the timber and supports the handle itself. The handle's pins or screws pass through the plate and are fixed in the door or drawer by a pin or nut. The back plates were initially cast in BRASS but after about 1780 they were also manufactured by stamping methods. Other materials have been used for back plates including SILVER, GLASS, ENAMEL, SHEFFIELD PLATE and ceramic material.
See also Brass

Back saw
See Saws (Back)

Back spring lock
See Locks

Back tacking
An UPHOLSTERY technique that allows fabric to be secured by hidden fixings. It involves cutting the materials to be used (that is, there may be more than one top cover) to the size required. The top edge of the outside top fabric is placed face down on the top of the frame. A strip of starched muslin or card is placed so as to form an edge and is tacked or stapled through the fabric to the frame. The cloth is then pulled over the muslin or card to show the face side. The bottom of the fabric panel is then tacked in the usual way on the lower underside of the frame. The method also works for batch work, and in the latter part of the 20th century ready-made tacking strip has been used in factory upholstery work.

Backing grade veneer
A veneer category that identifies inexpensive and usually plain veneers that are applied to the backs of decorative veneered components to give equilibrium to the whole panel. In some cases they are used as a base for transfer PRINTING of more exotic patterns.

Bagasse board
A man-made PARTICLE BOARD made from the pulpy residue of sugar cane after extraction. The ligno-cellulosic composition of bagasse is similar to wood and therefore has been used to manufacture boards for furniture parts such as table tops since the 1950s.

Hesch, R. (1968), 'Manufacture of particle board from bagasse', in L. Mitlin (ed.), *Particle Board Manufacture and Application*, Sevenoaks: Pressmedia Ltd.

Bahia
A timber named after Bahia state in Brazil.
See Brazilwood

Baize
An open, loosely woven woollen fabric with a long nap, usually dyed green, blue or red, widely used for billiard and card table tops. Known since at least the 16th century, it was sometimes combined with DAMASK LEATHER to make PROTECTIVE covers for pier tables and so on. During the 18th century it was used for protecting a range of furniture types, including covers for sideboards, linings for mirror glasses and cases. Rolt noted that 'The looking glass-maker likewise uses [baize] behind their glasses to preserve the tin or quick-silver, and the case-makers to line their cases' (1761). It was also used as protection for clothes in cupboards. In 1767 Chippendale invoiced Nostell Priory: 'To a very large mahogany clothes press ... sliding shelves, covered with marble paper and Bays aprons' (12 November 1767, cited in Gilbert, 1978). The practice continued into the early 19th century as Sheraton recorded that baize 'is used by cabinet-makers to tack behind clothes press shelves to throw over the clothes' (1803, p.40).
See also Bay(e)s

Bakelite
See Plastics

Balata (*Mimusops spp.*)
A timber from the northern coast of South America, especially Guiana. Although known since 1696 in France, it is difficult to find examples of use in the 18th and 19th centuries. By the 20th century it was considered a normal furniture timber, especially in France.
See also Beefwood, Bulletwood

Balaustre (*Centrolobium paraense*)
The American name for Arariba.

Ball fringe
See Passementerie (Fringes)

Balsa wood (*Ochroma lagopus*)
A very light South American timber with an average density of 140 (9 lb/cu ft). White to oatmeal in colour, with an even texture, it is moderately firm in relation to its weight. Its light weight is one of its most important characteristics. Hardly used in furniture-making for this reason, it has been employed for cores in PLYWOOD sandwich construction (stressed skin) as well as in aeroplane manufacture (especially 1939–45).

Balsam
See Resins

Balsamo (*Myroxylon balsamum*)
A timber with an average density of 990 (62 lb/cu ft), it is a pink to purplish-red timber with wavy markings that can be nearly black. Similar in appearance to East Indian ROSEWOOD but lighter in colour. Aka *Oleo vermelho*.

Bamboo (*Bambusa*)
In the Far East, the indigenous bamboo (*bambusa arudinacea*) has been an important material for many centuries in house building, roofing, and in the making of simple furniture. Its use in furniture-making can be traced to India in AD 200, although it is more commonly recognized as a product of China or Japan. Bamboo may be worked 'green', but is preferably seasoned before use for furniture. Woodworking tools and joints are used to prepare and assemble bamboo into furniture, but there has to be allowances for the particular hollow nature of bamboo. For example, joints are often reinforced by split bamboo wrappings. Bamboo may also be shaped by heating and bending over a former.

A particular European taste for bamboo furniture occurred in 1757, when Sir William Chambers first published designs for bamboo furniture. Chairs were the main item to be given the bamboo treatment, although in many cases the bamboo furniture of the period was in imitation bamboo. During the late 18th century imports of bamboo were also made into America, and some manufacturers soon introduced imitation bamboo furniture into their ranges. For example, Samuel Gragg advertised bamboo fancy chairs in 1809. In England, the exotic tastes of the Prince Regent gave a spur to the introduction of bamboo into the 'Chinese' furnishings of the Royal Pavilion at Brighton, with many of the projects being produced in imitation of real bamboo. Some furniture examples supplied by Elward, Marsh and Tatham were made from a mix of real and imitation bamboo, combined with authentic lacquered panels. The taste continued into the 19th century and was especially employed in making bedroom or fancy chairs. Nicholson noted that 'bedroom chairs are frequently constructed' of bamboo (1826, p.1).

The imitation of bamboo was evidence of its success. Sheraton describes how beech was turned into chair parts, which were then painted and flecked to imitate bamboo, whilst turned legs fashioned to imitate bamboo were used in a wide variety of furniture types (1803, p.29). Although it fluctuated in fashion, by the mid 19th century, bamboo was being imitated in materials other than wood. Cast iron chairs painted to imitate bamboo caused particular consternation to the *Journal of Design*: 'We really had imagined that society was getting tired of the conventional upholsterer's bamboo with its three black strokes and splashes to indicate foliations: but here it is breaking out in the most inveterate form, upon a material least of all calculated to support the attack' (2, 1850, p.202). Later in the 19th century firms such as the Vantine Emporium in New York were importing quantities of ready-made furniture from the East. On the other hand, much allegedly oriental furniture was made from imported raw materials in city factories. These makers produced ranges of occasional furniture such as side tables, what-nots, flower stands, and the like. For example, the Boston firm of James E. Wall seems to have specialized as a bamboo furniture-maker between 1881 and *c*.1895.

France also developed a business in bamboo furniture. In 1859 Joseph Cavoret applied for patents to protect his particular methods of imitating bamboo, whilst the business of Perret & Fils & Vibert made a speciality of bamboo furniture for export. They were particularly associated with a range of bamboo produced in three different colours – red, white and black – which appears to have been successfully sold in America.

Imports of bamboo raw materials were also made in England, and the first bamboo furniture-makers, Hubert Bill, operated from *c*.1869.

By 1910 there were over 130 manufacturers working in the business of bamboo furniture. The bulk of the trade was situated in the East End of London, but the biggest establishment was founded in Birmingham. This city became a centre for the trade, and large quantities of the fashionable products were made by the firm of W. F. Needham. His business started in 1886 and used his patent process to make a range called Ferrum Jungo. This method used a system of metal sockets and shoes which avoided the problems of splintered ends of poles and the usual nailed joints becoming loose. The business was so successful that by the mid 1890s he employed over 300 workers who produced over 4000 pieces of furniture per week. Despite, or perhaps because of, the considerable success of real bamboo furniture, it was still found that some manufacturers of more conventional furniture continued to use the imagery of bamboo in their products. George Hunzinger of New York produced chairs with turned legs in imitation of bamboo, whilst the European firm of Thonet included bamboo styles in their range of BENTWOOD furniture. Throughout the 20th century bamboo has continued to play a minor part in the repertoire of furnishings. In the 'contemporary' furnishing style of the 1950s it played a role, being lightweight and flexible. In the 1980s it was seen as ideal for the conservatory living style.

Bamboo has also had other roles to play in furnishings, since it was also suitable for interior decoration. Split and varnished sections could be used for beading around panels, ceiling decoration, dados, cornices and mantles, and even stair rods. It has been pressed into service for cornice poles, fire-screens and shelving, as well as for the more common jardinières, chairs and chair companions. The use of bamboo in cane-edge UPHOLSTERY and bedding is also worthy of mention. It was used to provide upholstery with a flexible but shape-retaining front or side edge, prior to the development of ready-made spring units which were complete with a flexible metal edge built in (see Plate XIX).
See also Faux bamboo

Brown, T. W. (1893), *Bamboo Work for Amateurs*, Leeds: T. W. Brown.
Farrelly, D. (1984), *The Book of Bamboo*, San Francisco: Sierra Club Books.
Hasluck, P. N. (1901), *Bamboo Work Comprising the Construction of Furniture, Household Fitments and Other Articles in Bamboo*, London: Cassell.
Walkling, G. (1979), *Antique Bamboo Furniture*, London: Bell and Hyman.

Band saw
See Saws

Banding
A technique that employs small ribbon-like sections of VENEER to provide a decorative edge to a surface. These may be the same as the main surface or a contrast to it. Depending on the methods used, the effects will be either straight (cut with the grain), cross (cut across the grain), or feather (cut at an angle to the grain). A wide range of designs can thus be made from these basic cuts. The designs include dentil, check, rope, domino, herring-bone, diamond or chevron. The timbers most often used for bandings include BOXWOOD, BLACKWOOD, MAHOGANY, ROSEWOOD, TULIPWOOD and SATINWOOD, sometimes bordered with STRINGING. Bandings are often made up into blocks using the chosen veneers which were then cut through. This saves time and allows a degree of expertise to be acquired in their making as well as providing a wide range of designs. At the end of the 18th century and onwards there was a trade in the supply of ready-made bandings and decorative inlays. This trade was usually carried on by veneer merchants who met this need along with their main business.

Banding as a decorative technique required some skill in aesthetic judgement. Sheraton warned against using bandings that detracted from the main veneered timber panels, and discussed the harmony of contrast:

Some degree of excessive contrast is admissible with safety when the ground veneer is less delicate, or poor faulty wood; ... Poor wood, doubtless is least deserving of much banding, but stands most in need of it. On the other hand, the contrast produced by banding may [be], and is as frequently, too weak for the ground veneer, in which case considerable expense proves of no use. This is always the case when poor tulip wood, or even the best of it, is joined to mahogany, for it turns by the air nearly to a mahogany colour.
(1803, pp.175–6)

Banding plane
See Planes, Banding

Bantam work
See Japanning, Lacquer

Barberry or **Berberry wood** (*Berberis vulgaris*)
A timber native to Britain and North America, barberry usually grows as a shrub with usable stems up to 10 cm (4 in) in diameter. It is a fine yellow colour, close grained with a streaky light-to-dark heartwood. Barberry was used for inlays in 17th-century European furniture, for turnery and marquetry, and it also found favour with the manufacturers of TUNBRIDGE WARE.

Bargello work
See Stitches (flame)

Baroque
A style of art, architecture and design that originated in early-17th-century Rome and then spread throughout Europe, reaching England in the latter part of the century. It is characterized by a unity of the arts expressed in exuberant decoration, a grand scale of display but still using many Renaissance motifs. The taste for luxury goods encouraged the design of furniture to reflect status and power by the use of exotic materials and overly theatrical styles which often relied on contrasting textures, materials and shapes. Auricular designs and exuberant carving combined with luxurious textiles, LACQUER work and gilded finishes were among the hallmarks of Baroque art. This style ensured a role for carvers and gilders in the production of furniture, which is evident in the products of the Restoration, William and Mary and Queen Anne furniture and decoration.
See Boulle, Cabinet-maker, Ebony, Ivory, Marquetry, Pietre dure, Tortoiseshell, Walnut

Barrs
(a) An 18th-century name for the stretchers on chairs. In 1736 Mrs Purefoy ordered 'chairs of wallnut tree frames with 4 legs without any Barrs' (*Purefoy Letters 1735–53*, 1931, pp.102–3). By the end of the century the term had changed its meaning and the upright sections of chair backs were referred to as bars (see (b)).

(b) Sheraton refers to bars as the 'upright square pieces of mahogany, about a quarter inch thick one way, and three quarters the other, which form sometimes the whole, and at other times only a part of the baluster or back' (1803, p.33).

Basil or Bazil
See Leather

Basketwork
See Wicker

Basswood (*Tilia americana*)
A timber native to the eastern coasts of Canada and the USA, it is sometimes called AMERICAN LIME in the UK. It has an average density of 410 (26 lb/cu ft). It is pale brown to an almost white colour, with a fine texture and a straight grain, but being soft, it is not very strong in terms of wear. Despite this it has been widely used in furniture-making. In the 19th century it was sometimes used for general furniture, but it has most frequently been used in the 20th century for light cabinet-making and carving, and for interior cabinet work, chair-seats and cheap furniture. It was a favoured veneer for trunk-making in the early-20th-century United States, and in the solid it was used for kitchen table tops. Basswood was also converted by spiral cutting to give plys of timber which produced thin boards for core-stock work such as plywood (Boulger, 1908, p.137). The inner bark has been used for woven chair seating, which may account for the name as a corruption of bastwood. Aka American LIME.

Baste tacks
See Stitches

Battenboard
A 20th-century pre-fabricated board (introduced in the 1920s) in which strips or battens of timber (up to 7.5 cm/3 in wide) are sandwiched together under a veneer on either side. Originally made in sheets up to 1.52 × 4.60 m (5 × 15 ft), they enabled cabinet carcase work to be completed quickly and securely. The boards were especially valued for their strength-to-thickness ratio, which enabled cabinets to be designed and made with slimmer panels. They were used in high-quality furniture during much of the 20th century.
See also Blockboard, Laminated board

Baudekin
Originally an embroidered material with a gold thread warp and a silk weft, introduced into Europe in the 11th century and used for regal garments or church hangings. Later adapted for canopies of state as 'Baldachins'. The term later still was applied to rich shot silks and even plain silks. In 1509 the inventory of Edmund Dudley records 'a testar of bawdiken embrodrid' (Beard, 1997, p.282).

Bay(e)s
A coarse woollen cloth with a worsted warp and woollen weft and a long nap. Introduced into England from France and Netherlands during the 16th century. It was used for stiffening and lining. Not as heavy as BAIZE.

Baywood
See Mahogany

Bead
See Mouldings

Bead mosaic
A decorative method of setting strung glass beads into composition laid onto a wooden core to decorate furniture. During the mid 18th century the Van Selow family of Brunswick developed the process. In England in the later 19th century the idea was revived. The beads were mounted directly into a cement or glued onto board panels which were then fitted into furniture items. The objects decorated in this way ranged from pole screens to sideboards.

Anon. (1874), 'Bead mosaic for furniture and decoration', in *Furniture Gazette*, 14, March.
Bilza, B. (1969), *Fürhre durch die Schausammlung Perlmosaiken von J. M. van Selow*, Brunswick: Stadtischen Museum.

Bead saw
See Saws

Bead work
(a) A term used by cane-seat makers that indicates a common seat made with only single strands of CANE.
See also Cane and Caning

(b) An English embroidery technique favoured in the period 1660–1700 as an alternative or addition to STUMPWORK for mirrors, picture frames, boxes and cushions. It was revived in the 19th century and used in conjunction with BERLIN WOOL-WORK. Beads could be needled onto a canvas pattern or directly to the ground work material already mounted. It was particularly used for *prie-dieu* chairs and stools.

Bearer
A general term that indicates a load-bearing component in cabinet-making. The term is most commonly used in drawer-bearers.

Beaumontage
A STOPPING made from beeswax, RESIN and a few flakes of SHELLAC. The mixture is melted and colouring is added. When required, it is warmed and applied where the filling may be needed. Aka stopping out wax.

Bed
See Bed springs, Bedstead, Mattress

Bed cord or **Bed lines**
Rope that was used to make a suspensory framework fitted to holes drilled in a bed frame to support mattresses. 'Bedlines and cord &c.' were in the stock inventory of an Essex grocer in 1692 (Steer, 1969, p.213). The use of bed cords lasted well into the 19th century, but by this time they were only part of the supporting system. In 1840 instructions in the *Workwoman's Guide* included the following information about assembling beds: 'The sacking is next tightly laced up with strong cord, and ought to be pulled together and knotted by a man as a woman is scarce strong enough to do it effectually' (p.191).

Bed-joiners or **Bedstead-makers**
By the beginning of the 18th century the production of bed frames was often in the hands of specialist makers who called themselves bed-joiners, or later, bedstead-makers. For the most part they were joiners or assemblers of cut parts, so they were not considered amongst the most skilful of workmen. The specialism seems to have lasted until well into the 19th century, since they are recorded as having established a trade union in the 1820s and their identity remained separate when Mayhew wrote on the woodworking trades in 1850:

the bedstead-maker has not to cut out his material in the same way as the cabinet-maker, as the posts are fashioned by the turner or the wood-carver ready for his purpose, and the other portions of his work are prepared by the sawyer in the sizes he requires. He is the putter together of the article, in every

3 *Tucker's patent bed frame with sprung slats, c.1860, marketed by Smee and Co, London.*

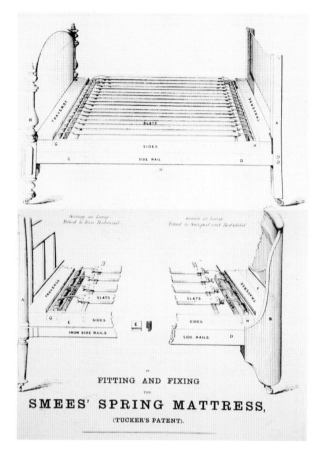

FITTING AND FIXING
THE
SMEES' SPRING MATTRESS,
(TUCKER'S PATENT).

part, except the insertion of the sacking bottom, which is the work of the porter.
(*Morning Chronicle*, Letter, LXIII, 1 August)

Apart from making bedsteads, part of their work involved house visits to clean beds and frames.

Bed-key
An instrument for tightening BED SCREWS, used in assembling wooden head- and footboards. The tool had two or more arms with various sockets or turnscrews.
See also Bit

Bed mechanisms
Contrivances that enable beds to be moved, hidden, adapted or otherwise changed have been in existence for many centuries. Tutankhamun owned a folding hinged bed and since then there have been scattered references to a variety of mechanical devices adapted to beds. Patents were often obtained for these devices, one of the earliest English ones dating from 1620 (Pat.no.16).

The bed mechanisms fall into three categories: those for invalids, those for comfort and those for concealment. The first category includes bed-chairs, sitting up beds, and beds that can be changed without involving the removal of the occupant. The second category, related to the first, includes alarm beds, special upholstery or springing systems, as well as beds designed for comfort when travelling (for example, camp beds). The third category includes press beds, and

a wide range of folding, wall, cupboard and piano beds. Although arousing interest in the 18th century, it was during the 19th century that a highly developed fascination in the possibilities of mechanized beds occurred. In the 20th century the addition of electric motors to beds has taken the comfort concept even further.

Bed-post machine
A specialist early-20th-century wood-working machine that was used to bore the holes and make the slots at each end of bed rails or in bed posts, for the purpose of fitting the rails to the posts.

Bed-screw
A large wooden screw used for holding together the posts and beams of a wooden bedstead. Beds usually had four long screws for attaching the sides and four short ones for fixing into the head and foot ends. A double-screwed bedstead referred to rails that were fixed by two bolts into each post. These screws were tightened with the BED-KEY.

Bed slats or Laths
A simple method of supporting a mattress and bedding by laths or boards of wood fitted across the width of the bedstead. They were illustrated by Roubo in 1771 (Plate 242), although they did not usurp the cord and sacking arrangement until the late 19th century. In the mid 19th century the London wholesalers William Smee developed a flexible spring bed frame which was made up from tension spring-loaded wooden slats running the length of the bed. In the later 20th century flexible laminated wood lathes which have an integral springiness, fitted in conjunction with rubber grommets, have improved the slat system greatly, although simple wooden slats are still widely used in inexpensive bed frames.
See also Springs (Wood)

Bed springs
The commercially successful integration of springs into the bed frame occurred in the mid 19th century when, in 1846, Edward Cottam patented a 'Rheiocline' or spring bedstead which could be fitted to any bed frame (Pat.no.11,241). The bed spring mounted on side irons fitted to head- and foot-boards remained an integral part of the 'bed' until the development of the divan base which was then used to support the mattress.

In the second half of the 19th century the woven wire 'mattress' spring, mounted on a pine frame was introduced to provide a support for the mattress overlays (first patent January 1865, no.99). These were usually fitted with a woven wire mesh which could be tightened by bolts working on a moving cross-member. The frames could also be fitted with hourglass springs with an overlaid wire mesh. The 'combination bottom' made from an angle-iron frame with tension springs at one or each end, fitted to wire links, was a cheaper version. This new sort of 'elastic' mattress was recommended by Lady Barker (1878) as 'it resembles a coat of mail and possesses the triple merit in these travelling days, of being cool, clean and portable' (Giedion, p.385). These ready-made supports were intended to fit onto side irons which were themselves located onto the bed frame itself. The free-standing versions were often made from wire mesh or linked wire held by small tension springs. A wide range of inventive models of bed-spring systems were developed in the later 19th century and early 20th century.
See also Mattress, Springs

H. Myer and Co Ltd (Bedding manufacturers) (1976), *Myer's First Centenary 1876–1976*, The Company.

Bedded mouldings
See Mouldings

Bedstead

Bedsteads, being the support or framework for springs, beds and bedding, have been made from wood, brass, iron or steel. The standard form of bedstead consisted of a head and foot end of various designs. These were linked by wooden rails and posts or angle irons which were side rails with dovetails cast at each end so they could be mounted onto the sockets fitted onto the head and foot ends. In some cases, the top flanges of the side irons were fitted with eccentric oval studs which had light gauge steel laths with punched oval holes fitted over them. The studs were then turned with a key, thus tightening the laths across the width. To avoid buckling the frame, a stretcher bar was fitted below and between the sides. The bedstead supported a BED SPRING or upholstered bed base. This arrangement began to be abandoned in the 1920s–30s in favour of divans, although bedsteads have returned as part of the furnishers' repertoire.
See also Bed springs, Chills, Mattress, Side irons

Beech wood (*Fagus sylvatica*)

A European hardwood extensively used for furniture-making. With an average density of 640 (40 lb/cu ft), a pale to pinkish-brown colour, and an even texture, this straight-grained timber has distinctive flecks of darker brown. One of the strongest furniture timbers (but prone to decay), it may be used in the solid and as veneer, often for producing PLYWOOD. Beech is a widely used and multi-purpose furniture timber as it is easy to work, strong, tough, difficult to split, and takes a range of finishes well. Easily shaped by bending, it is also ideal for TURNING and chair-making.

Known to the Romans, it was used by them for many items of furniture including beds, chairs and tables (Pliny, xiv, 229). Its value has been recognized ever since. Evelyn observed of beech that 'with it the turner makes dishes, trays, rims for buckets and other utensils, trenchers, dresser boards etc. likewise for the wheeler, joyner, for large screws, and [the] Upholster for Sellyes, Chairs, Stools, Bedsteads etc.' (1662, p.47). The ubiquitousness of beech was commented upon by Abraham Cowley (1618–67) who wrote:

Hence in the Worlds best years the humble shed,
Was happily and fully furnished;
Beech made their chests, their beds, and joyn'd stolls,
Beech made the board, the platters and the bowles.
(Cited in Pinto, 1962, p.40)

Beech has been widely used not only for the items mentioned above but also for chair frames, drawer sides, table framings and so on. After 1660 it was recognized that, due to its blandness, it was especially suitable as a surface for decoration. Therefore it was often used as a base for imitating other woods. Evelyn discovered that cabinet and chair-makers polished beech to look like EBONY, and to imitate WALNUT. He wanted it banned as it was so easy to use as a fake:

[Beech is] so obnoxious that I wish the use of it were by a law prohibited [to] all joyners, cabinet-makers and such as furnish tables, chairs, bedsteads coffers etc. They have a way to black and polish it so as to render it like ebony, and with a mixture of soot and urine imitate the wall-nut …
(Evelyn, 1662, p.47)

The use of beech is perhaps most well-known in chair-making. After the Restoration, side chairs were made from beech, often caned with an ebonized finish. This section of furniture-making was highly lucrative, and a branch of chair-makers who specialized in this trade were

established (see Cane chair-maker). However, in the 18th century, the proneness to decay was recognized as a problem when beech was also used as a chair-making timber, 'it is also wrong for any person to buy Beechen Cane-chairs, because the cane will last a great deal longer than this wood' (Ellis, 1742). Nevertheless, beech was ideal for turning parts, and therefore a great many turned chairs have been made from this timber. Later, the production of English Windsor chairs would rely on the beech tree, amongst others, to supply the material for legs, spindles and backs. It was also widely used as a framing timber for upholstered furniture as well as for many structural purposes in cabinet work. In France, *bois d'hêtre* was extensively employed by the specialist *menuisiers* in making seat-furniture frames.

In the 18th century beech was again used as a base for imitations. It was stained to resemble the more expensive MAHOGANY, as well as being used as a foundation for carved, gilded, japanned or painted furniture. In the early 19th century beech was still used as a base surface for popular imitation-bamboo decoration, and also for STAINING to simulate ROSEWOOD. Its value to cabinet-makers was again recognized by contemporary authors: 'The cabinet-makers chief woods are mahogany and beech; … In London, beech is almost the only English wood made use of at present by the cabinet and chair-makers' (Marshall, *Planting and Rural Ornament*, 1796, cited in Symonds, 1955). Sheraton noted that:

[Beech is] much used in mill work, amongst plane-makers, and chair-makers. It requires to be kept dry, and will then prove long lasting, but being exposed to wet and much dampness it will rot very soon … Boiling it in red stain is

5   *German patent automatic wood-bending machine capable of multiple bends, c.1876.*

hurtful to it, and before japan colour be laid on to it, it should have a thin coat of white lead and oil. [Regardless of these problems] it is brought to London in great quantities from 1 inch boards to 5 inch planks and is now the cheapest in use.
(1803, p.45)

During the 19th century beech took on another role as the raw material for large-scale manufacturing of BENTWOOD chairs. The great Central European beech woods supplied the bentwood furniture industry with much of their requirements. Firms, especially Thonet, deliberately established their factories close to the timber supplies, well away from the cities. This enabled them to exploit the forests and to use inexpensive local unskilled labour to manipulate and manufacture the products in factories.

In the mid 19th century beech was widely used for common bedsteads, furniture and for carved moulds, where it was used for the composition ornaments of picture-frames. It was also still stained to imitate rosewood and ebony (Holtzapffel, 1846, p.74). By 1853 a change in taste meant a lesser role, so that 'the uses to which it is applied are, to furnish rails for common and easy chairs, stocks and scrolls for couches and sofas, stocks and posts for bedstead etc.' (Blackie, 1853, p.11).

In the first half of the 20th century British makers used stained beech in simulation of Jacobean oak, Georgian walnut and mahogany. In the second half of the century, when there was a taste for light-coloured timber in furniture, beech was often left in its natural colour and simply finished with a clear varnish. Scandinavian makers, especially the Danes, favoured this particular treatment. Beech has remained a valuable timber for upholstery frames as much for its tack-holding properties as anything else.

American Beech (*Fagus grandifolia*)
A timber with a density of 740 (46 lb/cu ft). With a slight reddish-brown tinge, it is similar in most respects to European beech, though rather coarser.

Beefwood (*Causarinaceae*)
There is some confusion over nomenclature regarding the term Beefwood. It appears to derive its name from the pigment of the timber which resembles the colour of beef meat. Beefwood is a catch-all term for those timbers unidentifiable (during the 20th century) except by their colour. Contenders have included BULLETWOOD OR BALATA.

The main source is probably BOTANY BAY oak (*Causarina*). Knight suggested that beefwood was a native of New Holland, of a pale red colour and not as cloudy as mahogany. It was mainly used for banding since although it was up to 275 cm (9 ft) in length, it was only available up to 33 cm (13 in) wide (1830, p.178). Holtzapffel considered that Botany Bay oak was the best contender for the name beefwood, although he described it as being more red than mahogany, with occasional dark veins (1846, p.74). In the 19th century it was used for turnery, veneers and borders of small cabinets and in Tunbridge ware (Blackie, 1853, p.48).
See also Botany Bay wood, Bulletwood

Belladine fringe
See Passementerie (Fringes)

Belt sander
See Machines (Sander)

Bench
A woodworker's workplace, equipped with a range of accessories as

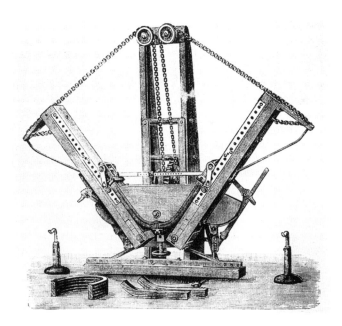

required. Simple planks on legs had been used from Roman times up to the medieval period. By the 17th century a framework of constructed squares or legs and rails was made up. By the 18th century vices were a common addition to the bench, with the L-shaped vice especially being used in Europe.

Bench planes
A general name for a range of hand-operated planes used in the workshop.
See Planes

Bench screw
A 'tool' for holding work fast on the carver's bench. The screw, up to 30 cm (12 in) long, was passed through a hole in the bench and fitted into a pilot hole in the base of the piece of timber to be worked upon. This method allowed the wood to be held firm with nothing in the way of the carver's workspace.

Bending
The techniques associated with wood bending appear to have been known to the Ancients and have been used ever since. Examples of furniture pieces found in tombs in Phrygia from the 8th to the early 7th centuries BC point to the early use of this process. Timbers can be bent in a variety of ways. Primitive methods include shaping a growing tree, heating cut timber over fire, or weighting down pieces and using gravity to create a curve. Later more controlled techniques of bending timber include (a) kerfing, (b) steam bending of laminated and solid wood, (c) built-up laminations.

Built-up laminations
By using thin veneer strips cut to size and laid into a pre-cut former or jig and then glued together, a vast range of shapes can be built up to suit a shape or design, particularly curved and bent shapes.
See Laminations

Kerfing
A method of slitting or cutting grooves across the width of timber to

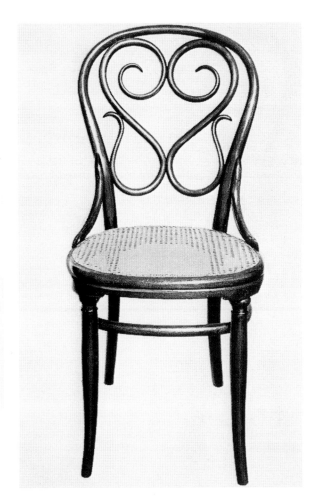

FAR LEFT
6 American bentwood 'fancy' side chair by Samuel Gragg, patented in 1808.

LEFT
7 Thonet No.4 chair, dated post 1865. Manufactured from solid bentwood and fixed with screws.

lessen the internal stress and achieve a curvature or shaping. The process reduces the strength of the timber but is useful in small areas such as curved doors or drawer fronts. Kerfs can be cut into solid timber or blockboards. Once cut, a glued-on piece of cloth was sometimes used to cover the kerf.
See also Keys

Steam bending of solid wood

When certain timber pieces are heated and moistened, they become pliable; then, when fixed into a shape, they will dry and cool into that shape. The result of the bending process is likely to have been used by Ancient Egyptians (for example, for chariot wheels), while reference to the Greek *klismos* chair seems to show that the Greeks were familiar with wood-bending techniques. Theophrastos mentions woods that, although tough, are easy to bend (Pliny, V, vi, 2; V, vii, 3, 4): the MUL-BERRY and the wild fig were seen as especially useful for bending work. Although bending techniques were widely used by other wood-workers, their use in furniture was to be particularly associated with the manufacture of Windsor chairs (see Chair-making, Windsor).

Until well into the 19th century the process was not easy to control. Sheraton was concerned that cabinet-makers who attempted bending processes risked shrinking the wood, therefore he recommended the application of measured amounts of moisture and fire heat only. In conjunction with this he suggested sizing or oiling the surface to be bent before the heat application and then, once it was ready, to immediately fasten it into place (1803, p.46).

The success of bending was clearly based on improvements to a range of jigs or formers which could help to control and stabilize the wood during the bending process. In simple situations wooden members can be bent by being held in position and fixed against pegs placed in a drilled board, so as to follow the required contour. This involved a degree of risk as the stretching pressure on the outer part is in contrast to the crushing of the inner part of the curve. This could result in splits and crush marks. To avoid such problems, the use of iron formers shaped to the required contour of the part were often employed. This allowed makers to introduce a range of shapes rather than just simple curves. The example of the Thonet company's iron jigs demonstrates this well. Initially this forming was operated by hand, but mechanical methods have been introduced which allow a number of wooden parts to be bent at once to the required shape (see Bentwood, below).

Bentwood

Although solid wood bending was an ancient practice, it was not until the 18th century that attempts were made to rationalize the process. The earliest English patent for bending wood was taken out by John

Cumberland in 1720 (Pat.no.427). Another patent for a wood-bending process taken out by John Vidler in 1794 (Pat.no.2020) referred to 'Bending timber for circular work without injury to the grain'. This applied particularly to cabinet-makers as well as shipwrights as it used a series of 'concaves and convexes' (or cauls) with weights and balances to help bend the wood to shape.

The most spectacular bending of solid wood in the early years of the 19th century (c.1808) was achieved in the United States by Samuel Gragg. The details of his patented method of bending side rails, seat and back stiles and even complete sides have been lost. However, it can be assumed that some form of steam bending was used, as the curves are too precise for heating alone. Although Thonet is associated with bending solid wood, his early experiments were concerned with making furniture from LAMINATIONS. The laminations suffered from problems with poor glues and subsequent de-lamination, so were abandoned. His success came from the gradual change from the use of laminations of wood to bent solid wood (see Plate XV).

The Thonet process was as simple as it was successful. Metal 'formers' of a pre-determined shape were devised that would accept the ready-cut wooden rods once they had been steamed to make them flexible. Once the wood components cooled and dried in the formers they were 'set' in the required shape. This process was used for all the components except seats. The principle of clamping hot steamed timbers remains the same in today's bentwood chair-making industry.

Exner, W. (1876), *Das Beigen des Holzes, ein für Möbel, Wagen und Schiffbaume wichtiges Verfarben, mit besonderer Rücksichtnahme auf die Thonet'sche Industrie*, Vienna: Bernhard Friedrich Voigt.
Harwood, B. (1994), 'Two early Thonet imitators in the United States: The Henry I. Seymour chair manufactory and the American Chair-Seat Company', in *Studies in the Decorative Arts*, II, I.
Kane, P. (1971), 'Samuel Gragg, His bentwood fancy chairs', in *Yale University Art Gallery Bulletin*, XXXIII, Autumn, pp.26–37.
Ostergard, D. (ed.) (1987), *Bentwood and Metal Furniture 1850–1946*, New York: American Federation of Arts.
Portoghesi, P. and Massobrio, G. (1975), *La seggliola di Vienna. Thonet and the History of Bentwood Technique*, Turin: Martano.
Vegesack, A. (1987), *Das Thonet Buch*, Munich: Bangert Verlag.
Wilk, C. (1980), *Thonet: 150 Years of Furniture*, New York: Barrons.

Benzoin
See Resins (Benzoin)

Bergame, Tapisseries de
See Tapestry

Berlin wool-work
A form of NEEDLEWORK which is particularly associated with mid-19th-century upholstered chair or seat covers. It was mainly produced by amateurs working with German woollen yarns which were worked into square meshed canvas using cross or tent stitches. The introduction of machine-made double thread canvas helped to ensure perfect correspondence between the exactly counted cross stitches and the published paper patterns supplied on squared paper. Berlin was the centre of production and sale of the yarns and patterns, with the earliest patterns being published in 1804. However, it was not until 1831 that the first serious importation of patterns and yarns into England began, by a Mr Wilks of Regent Street. By the early 1840s the method became highly fashionable so that by the mid 1840s designs were sometimes printed directly onto the canvas with instructions issued in letters and numbers. In 1846 Henry Wood published fifty designs suitable for furniture in his *A Useful and Modern Work on Cheval and Pole Screens, Ottomans, Chairs and Settees for Mounting Berlin Needle work*.

The designs were often in the *style troubadour* with elements of images from the works of Walter Scott or other fashionable Victorian artists, however the most popular appear to have been floral designs of great variety. By the 1850s restrained designs, often on a white background, were giving way to black backgrounds with harshly coloured woollen yarns (resulting from the development of coal-tar dyes in Germany), offering stained-glass brilliance. The resultant work was widely used for mounting into pole screens and firescreens.

In the 1870s and 1880s, especially in the USA, a variety of Berlin work was introduced. It used the same method of stitching, but the loops were trimmed to tufts and the whole design was made through a heavy ground fabric and a canvas. When finished, the canvas was removed, thread by thread, leaving the wool-work on the base cloth. The ubiquitousness of Berlin wool-work meant that it was regarded as synonymous with embroidery, but by 1912 it was apparently 'rarely employed except as a covering for footstools or chairs' (Bitmead, 1912, p.33).

Hughes, Therle (n.d.), *English Domestic Needlework, 1660–1860*, London: Abbey Fine Arts.
Morris, Barbara (1962), *Victorian Embroidery*, London: Jenkins.
Proctor, Molly G. (1972), *Victorian Canvas Work*, London: Batsford.
Vincent, Margaret (1988), *The Ladies Work Table: Domestic Needlework in Nineteenth Century America*, Allentown PA: Allentown Art Museum.

Berlinia (*Berlina spp.*)
A Nigerian and West African timber with an average density of 720 (45 lb/cu ft). Reddish pale brown to dark brown with irregular purplish markings, it has a variable interlocked grain and a coarse texture. Used for cabinet-making and for decorative veneers for marquetry work in the 20th century. Aka Rose zebrano.

Bermuda cedar (*Juniperus bermudiana*)
See Cedar

Betty(e) saw
See Saws

Bevel
(a) A chamfered or sloped edge which is usually applied to glass or mirror plate. The angle of bevel is variable, ranging from a sharp crystal cut to the so-called 'Vauxhall mirror bevel', which is designed to be less than a 7.5 degree angle in order to make it flat and elongated.

(b) A tool made up of a straight stock with an adjustable blade that can be fixed open at any angle to assist in SETTING OUT work. A range of types have been made to suit particular crafts.

Bible front
An upholstery method that has been used to give sharp definition to the edges of upholstered work. It is made in conjunction with the first stuffing. A row of stitching is placed crosswise around the edge of the seat in a herringbone shape. The feather stitch is applied to the top to compress the edge into a sharp line of stuffing.

Biedermeier
A term used to describe art and design developed in Germany and Austria (and Scandinavia) between 1815 and 1848. It reflects a simple, unpretentious style of furnishing which was based on the tastes of the bourgeoisie. The name is derived from *bieder* meaning plain or unpretentious and *meier* a common German surname. The style was developed from Empire and later-18th-century English models. It is

characterized by elegant and simple shapes using stripped-down classical motifs. The use of BOIS CLAIRS and BOIS INDIGENES as well as large expanses of exotic timber veneers was also characteristic. The development of the spring seat in Germany was part of the desire for comfort expressed by the middle-class patrons of the style.

See also Cherry, Laminations, Poplar, Springs

Bilsted
See American red gum

Bindings
A term used by upholsterers to describe 'the various kinds of narrow laces used to strengthen and ornament the edges of any sort of curtain, drapery, or bed furniture' (Sheraton, 1803, p.51). They included silk or silk and worsted ribbons, and silk-covered LACES, and were usually 2–2.5 cm (¾–1 in) wide.

See also Passementerie

Birch wood (*Betula spp.*)
A straight-grained, fine-textured European timber with an average density of 650 (41 lb/per cu ft), being nearly white to light brown in colour. It bends successfully under steaming and stains and polishes well, and is popular for PLYWOOD as well as for high-quality CHAIR FRAMES. Its oils were used in the preparation of Russia LEATHER.

Although Evelyn considered birch to 'be of all others the worst of timber' (1662, xvi) it was employed throughout the 18th century in Europe for vernacular furniture. Rolt noted that the birch tree 'though very indifferent, is used by turners for chairs, and other domestic things' (1761). In the late 18th century fashion allowed birch to be used as a decorative veneer, as certain cuts resembled SATINWOOD. The burrs were also favoured at this time. Sheraton considered 'this wood [to be] very useful, being both light and tough and a sort of cream colour' (1803, p.51). According to Loudon, birch was particularly popular with Scottish Highlanders for all their furniture and wooden equipment. He noted that 'for cabinet-making birch is of little use till it has attained the age of sixty or eighty years at which age [it] is little liable to warp or to be attacked by worms' (1844, p.1697). But its appeal was clear: 'it is considerably used in furniture; some of the wood is almost as handsomely figured as Honduras mahogany, and when coloured and varnished, is not easily distinguished from it' (Holtzapffel, 1846, p.74).

At the very beginning of the 20th century it was reported that 'a new industry has been recently started in Russia in the manufacture of birch three-ply planks [that is, plywood] for export to India for tea chests. The logs are cut rotarily … and three thicknesses are then glued back to back with their grains crossing so as to correct warping' (Boulger, 1908, p.166). Its use in the solid also changed: 'For many years it was extensively used for furniture of all kinds, but of late, except for inexpensive chairs, it has largely gone out of fashion' (Howard, 1920, p.29). However birch remained a popular timber in Sweden and Finland, used either naturally light or stained darker, as veneer or intarsia or as a surface for plywood.

American birch (*Betula*)
A popular timber in Boston, Salem, and other areas of New England from the later 18th century. In the mid 19th century it was reported of imports into England that: 'for a long period, it has furnished the staple commodity in use, for almost all the purposes for which hardwood is required: and more recently, the finer specimens of it have been employed in the manufacture of bed-room, hall and even draw-ing room furniture' (Blackie, 1853, p.7). The virtues of birch were that it was 'well suited for the manufacture of hall furniture, when the design of it is rather plain than enriched with carving: also for bed-room furniture, when the apartments in which it is to be placed are not large' (ibid.). Birch was also highly regarded for its grain structure and the reflective qualities this gave: 'for when finished in French polish they [furniture specimens] possess a transparent appearance, suggestive of coloured crystals or precious stones, having the light reflected from a surface polished at different angles, rather than a plane surface of wood' (ibid.). In the early 20th century it was widely used in the northern states of America for furniture, sometimes stained to imitate mahogany and cherry. It continued to be exported to England and used for bedroom furniture and was sometimes called sweet or mahogany birch. Aka Colonial mahogany.

Black birch (*Betula nigra*)
An American timber with a density of 590 (37 lb/cu ft). It has a light to medium tan colour with a coarse texture and a variable grain. It was the earliest of the American birches to be imported into Europe and the most common in the 19th century and into the 20th century. By the early 20th century it was noted that 'the black or cherry kind is most esteemed and is largely used for plain furniture' (Spon, 1901, p.128). The figured varieties have been used for veneer.

Canadian or yellow birch (*Betula alleghaniensis*)
A Canadian and North American timber of average density 645–780 (40–48 lb/cu ft). It has a fine and even texture with a variable grain and occasionally curly markings much like the American birch but lighter in colour. It has a whitish sapwood and yellow or reddish-brown heart, with rays seen as dark flecks in quarter-cut stock. A common wood in the furniture of French Canada, it was also used after 1780 as a substitute for SATINWOOD, in both the solid and veneer. Birch was also used as a base for painting as it showed no grain through the finished surface. In the second half of the 19th century it was widely imported into Europe. Large quantities were brought into the United Kingdom for making up into bedroom suites and chests, taking advantage of the decorative 'roey' figure. It is also often used for high-grade plywood, and the curly or flame effects are still valued. Widely used in 20th-century veneer and construction, and sometimes stained red to imitate mahogany, or brown to imitate walnut.

Karelian (Masur) birch
This Finnish and Russian timber has been prone to attack by larvae (*Agromyzia carbonaria*), which have produced a particular marked effect called pith flecks. This creates a decorative veneer which has a pale background overlaid with variable colourings of gold to brown. The effect is best revealed by rotary cutting of the affected logs, hence it was mainly used in veneer or plywood form. First used as a base for MARQUETRY work and later as a full surface finish, it remained popular until the end of the 19th century. In the 20th century, the Masur birch was revived in PLYWOOD and LAMINATES, and successfully used in some of the furniture work of Alvar Aalto.

Paper birch (*Betula papyrifera*)
A birch with a heavy white sapwood and a pale brown heart. It has a density of 620 (39 lb/cu ft), a straight grain and an even texture. In the 1850s reference was made to the paper birch as a valuable tree which supplied 'the feathered and variegated portions taken from the regions of the trunk whence the branches spring'. American cabinet-makers, especially from Boston and surrounding New England areas used these veneers for cabinet work (see Tomlinson, 1854, pp.1019–20). In the early 20th century Boston cabinet-makers still used this

veneer especially where a curl in the grain was formed when branches separated (Boulger, 1908, p.142). This timber has been widely used as veneer as well as for plywood in the 20th century.

Bird-cage
A name given to the tilting arrangement developed in the 18th century to operate a tilt-top table. It is so arranged that the pillar of the table fits through its base, whilst the table top is hinged to the top edge of the cage. It allows the simple tipping up of the top when the table is not in use, but remains stable when let down. Roubo describes tables fitted with these devices as *tables à l'Angloise* (Roubo, 1774, p.973 and Plate 329).

Bird's beak lock
See Locks

Bird's-eye maple (*Acer*)
See Maple

Biscuit joint
A particular form of dowel joint using a 'biscuit' of compressed beech that fits into pre-cut slots for a range of jointing applications including mitring, butt, and edge-to-edge joints. When (water-based) PVA adhesive is introduced, the wooden biscuit expands for an extremely tight fit. It was used in the latter part of the 20th century in conjunction with an electric biscuit jointer.

Bit
A boring tool fixed by a spring or chuck into a stock. The variety of models is extensive and in 1803 Sheraton (p.53) noted that four dozen types were regularly used by cabinet-makers. Bits were also developed by sections of the furniture trade for specific jobs. The fluted bedstead bit was devised to bore holes through bed posts into the side rails, so that a BED SCREW could be fixed through. The chairmakers' bit, also called a 'spoon bit' (a name derived from its shape), produced a fine smooth hole for chair parts such as legs, stretchers and dowelling, as well as for cane seat holing.

Black ash
See Ash (black)

Blackbean (*Castanospermum australe*)
An Australian hardwood with an average density of 720 (45 lb/cu ft), a straight grain (sometimes interlocked) and close texture, it was introduced into England at the British Empire Exhibition in 1924. Blackbean has an attractive figure, and a rich brown colour with grey-brown streaks, with the look of European walnut, though coarser in texture. The timber has been widely used in veneer for fine cabinet-making and decorative joinery. Aka Moreton Bay chestnut.

Blackbutt (*Eucalyptus pilularis*)
An Australian timber with a density of 880 (55 lb/cu ft). Pinky brown, it is usually straight grained with a moderately fine texture. It is easily split, but it takes a good polish and has been used for decorative veneers.

Black cherry (*Prunus serotina*)
See Cherry

Black gum
See Tupelo

Black locust
See Locustwood, Robinia

Black oak
See Bog oak

Black Sea walnut
See Walnut (Circassian)

Blacksmith
An ironworker whose association with furniture-making has existed for centuries. They supplied furniture-makers and upholsterers with particular requisites, particularly ironwork for attaching to furniture. This would on occasion include LOCKS, handles, HINGES, opening and closing mechanisms, ties, and so on. For upholstery they made iron FRAMES to fit wooden seats as well as ratchets, STAYS and other fittings. On occasions blacksmiths have also made furniture in wrought-iron. This taste found particular expression in the work of the *ferronier* in France in the 1920s and later, and much more widely in the 1950s.
See also Brazier, Iron

Black walnut
See Walnut (American)

Blackwood, African (*Dalbergia melanoxylon*)
An East African timber with an average density of 1200 (76 lb/cu ft). It is dark purple-brown with black streaks, and takes a finish well. It is extremely hard and heavy and is usually only available in short lengths, so is mainly used by the inlay and turnery trades. Aka Mozambique ebony, Black Botany Bay wood.

Blackwood, Australian (*Acacia melanoxylon*)
An Australian hardwood used in fine furniture with an average density of 640–710 (41–5 lb/cu ft). Golden brown to dark reddish-brown, but becoming black when washed with lime water, it is generally straight grained but occasionally supplies a fiddle-back effect in veneers, which is considered very desirable.

It was exported in large quantities in the second half of the 19th century for piano manufacture and bagpipe making. It is an excellent turning timber and for a time, around 1890–1910, replaced mahogany in the manufacture of billiard tables. By the beginning of the 20th century it was noted that 'within the last few years it has been introduced extensively into the manufacture of the finer description of furniture, such as drawing room suites, and is found far superior to walnut, owing to its strength and toughness' (Spon, 1901, p.128). In 1920 it was recorded as 'second only to Cedrela Toona [red cedar] as an Australian cabinet wood' (Howard, 1920, p.33). Still considered a furniture wood in the 1950s, although less well known.

Blackwood, Chinese
See Rosewood, Indian

Blackwork
An EMBROIDERY style worked in black silk on white linen, especially in Spain and England in the 16th century. Although used for apparel, it was also intended for decorating cushions and pillow covers. The 1601 Hardwick Hall inventory listed '3 curtains wrought with black silk needlework upon fine holland cloth with button and loops of black silk' (Boynton, 1971, p.23). Aka Spanish work.

Blanket stitch
See Stitches

Bleaching
A surface preparation for furniture woods, made either from oxalic acid crystals or hydrogen peroxide, intended to lighten them. The effects on pine or oak are well known, but, when fashion dictates, curiosities can be created such as 'blonde walnut' or 'blonde mahogany', popular in the 1960s.

Blind fret
The result of applying cut FRETWORK to a solid substrate. The fretwork appears as a feature on the base and loses its lightweight quality. This form of decoration is often associated with mid-18th-century 'Chinese Chippendale' designs.

Blind stitch
See Stitches

Blind tacking
See Tacking

Blind tracery
See Fretwork

Block
See Corner blocks

Block clamping machine
See Machines

Block fringe
See Passementerie (Fringes)

Block front
(a) An American treatment of the front of cabinets in which there are three curved divisions. The centre section is concave whilst the two outer sections are convex. The panels are most usually cut from the solid, thus requiring considerable skill and use of material. The form is particularly associated with Boston and Newport makers dating from 1760–80. Shell motifs commonly feature on this work.

(b) The term is also applied generally to a cabinet made in three sections, whereby the centre section is either recessed or protruding in relation to the two side sections.

Block plane
See Planes (Block)

Blockboard
A prefabricated timber product developed in the early 20th century, in which wooden core strips, not exceeding 2.5 cm (1 in) in width, are laid randomly together, glued and then veneered to make panels. Its advantage lies in the larger sizes and stable form that makes this material ideal for carcases, table tops and so on. Aka Lumbercore in America.
See also Battenboard, Laminated board

Bloodwood (*Eucalyptus corymbosa*)
A heavy timber from Australia with an average density of 960–1000 (60–5 lb/cu ft). It is found in a range of red shades, with a medium-coarse texture, and an interlocked grain and little figure.
See also Eucalyptus, Ironbark, Muninga

Blue John
Decorative fluorspar that was mined extensively in Derbyshire (Treak Cliff at Castleton, Derby) in the 1770s, and was used occasionally for decorative inlays on cabinet work, and, in rare cases, for furniture (for example, the table top in Castleton Museum). Bands of blue-purple are interspersed with other coloured bands, but the colour of the stone may be lightened by the application of heat. Blue John was also turned and polished to show the crystals to their best effect, but it often needed to be bound in some form as it was frequently flawed.

Ford, T. D. (1955), 'Blue John Fluorspar', in *Proceedings of the Yorkshire Geological Society*, vol.30/1.

Boarded construction
See Construction

Board jointer
See Machines

Boasting
See Bosting

Bobble fringe
See Passementerie (Fringes)

Bodger
The term originally referring to a travelling dealer, but from the 19th century it indicated forest wood-workers who worked in the beech woods of the Chiltern Hills in southern England. Their trade consisted of setting up a camp, complete with a home-made pole LATHE, cutting down the required timber, and then TURNING chair parts in the forest. The heyday of this craft was during the 19th and early 20th centuries (see p.26).
See also Chair-making

Mayes, L. J. (1960), *The History of Chairmaking in High Wycombe*, London: Routledge.
Sparkes, Ivan (1989), *Wycombe Chairmakers in Camera*, Buckingham: Quotes Ltd.

Bodying in
The process of filling the grain of a surface before the finishing stages of POLISHING.
See Fillers

Bog oak
OAK timber that has been preserved in a peat bog. The very dark colour, caused by iron impregnation, meant that this timber was ideal for INLAY and applied decoration. However, bog oak was considered to be the wood that presented the most inconvenience and trouble to cabinet-makers: 'Proprietors on whose land it is found, are naturally fond of having it made into articles of furniture, but are little aware of the difficulty of the task' (Blackie, 1853, p.19). It was suggested that the best use for bog oak was in veneer whenever possible, as this limited the warping and drying that was inherent in solid bog timber, although the art of carving solid bogwood was revived in Dublin in the early 19th century. Aka Black oak.
See also Bogwood

8 *A Chilterns bodger working on chair parts: (a) using a drawing knife (b) turning spindles on a pole lathe.*

Bogwood

Any variety of timber that has been found submerged in a bog or marshy area. The best-known species include APPLE, OAK, POPLAR, MAPLE, LARCH and YEW. The submergence of the timbers causes a blackening of the wood which superficially often resembles EBONY. Bogwoods were used in the 16th and 17th centuries for ornamental in-lays. In Ireland, during the 18th century, these woods were made into rustic-style furniture and sent to the English market, especially for garden and conservatory furniture. In the 19th century bog-yew was used for fine furniture and carved panels. The London Exhibition of 1851 displayed a number of pieces by William Jones of Dublin. The exhibition also showed specimens of veneers taken from the roots of the 'bog Scotch fir', which were considered 'well worthy of notice and suggestive of a more extensive use of this pre-Adamite timber for cabinet-making' (Tomlinson, 1854, p.1018).

Hughes, G. B. (1971), 'Irish bog-wood furniture', in *Country Life*, 7 May.

Bois clairs

A general term used to describe the lighter-toned timbers such as bird's-eye MAPLE and BIRCH with their bright blonde colouring, which were popular in France, Russia and Eastern Europe in the early 19th century.

Bois durci

An imitation plastic-like material, made to resemble EBONY, designed to reproduce carved work at a lower price and more quickly than by any hand method. It was patented in France in 1855 by Charles

Le Page, and introduced into England in the same year (Pat.no.2232, 5 October 1855). Bois durci was composed of rosewood sawdust, ani-mal blood and water, which were mixed, heated and then allowed to dry. The albumen of the blood amalgamated with the dust and made a firm agglomeration. The dry material was then pressed into moulds, and pressure from a hydraulic press was applied with heated platens. The compression and heating resulted in a fusion of the material into the desired mould shape. Another method involved making impres-sions into the material with a steel die stamp. It was used for ebony-like carvings, medallions, heads, rosettes and paterae. The result was a highly finished imitation ebony carving that was apparently about one third of the cost of true carvings. Mostly used for added decor-ation to ebony cabinets that were popular in the second half of the 19th century, although references can still be found in 20th-century trade literature.

See also Wood substitutes

Grant, M. H. (1939), 'Medallions in Bois-durci', in *Connoisseur*, 104, October, pp.190–2.
Pinto, E. (1953), 'A forgotten plastic', in *Country Life*, CXIII, 16 April, pp.1152–3.
— (1970), *Tunbridge and Scottish Souvenir Woodware*, London: Bell. See chapter on Bois durci.

Bois indigènes

A term referring to the indigenous timbers of France especially those that were employed in cabinet-making during the late 18th and early 19th centuries. There was official encouragement for their use from *c*.1800 as a result of the English 'Continental System' that blockaded French imports. In 1810, the *Société d'Encouragement à L'industrie* founded a prize for the use of native timber furniture, and in 1811 all official furniture was ordered to be made from indigenous woods. This meant that highly notable cabinet-makers, such as Lignereux and the Jacob Brothers were involved in making furniture from native French woods. The timbers used included ELM with knotted roots and twists (*l'orme galleux*), PLANE tree, YEW root and ASH.

Ledoux-Lebard, Denis (1976), 'Empire furniture in bois indigènes', in *Connoisseur*, 778, December.

Bois repoussé

A French method of imitation CARVING, invented *c.*1876 by M. Ley. The process used cut steel dies that were applied to the wooden surface with immense pressure, to produce relief carvings of up to 2 cm (¾ in) in depth. The resulting 'carvings' were then used for panels, friezes, medallions, borders and the like. Commentators declared that this process was:

not a sham, and therefore has a claim for durability and solidity which has never been possessed by any previous discovery; and moreover, the grain of the wood being horizontal, in contra-distinction to an American device [STEEL CARVING] which could only give the pattern on the end grain of the wood – an obviously false principle – gives the work exactly the same appearance as if produced by the wood carver.
(*Practical Magazine*, 6, 1876, p.108)

Bole

A fine earth of velvety smoothness being composed of a clay and iron oxide. Bole is used in water GILDING as a preparatory surfacing material. It is applied to GESSO surfaces to further smooth and level them before the final finishing processes are applied. Available in a range of colours, including red, blue and yellow. Red is often used for large flat areas, and blue for parts of the work that are to be in high relief. Bole also refers to a mix of dry colour and glue, used in some other preparatory processes of gilding.
See also Gilding

Bolection moulding

See Mouldings

Bolt

(a) A timber trade term for a section of a short log – either sawn or split.

(b) Metal fastenings with a cylindrical shank, a shaped head and a thread, to be used in conjunction with nuts. Special models are used in particular applications.

(c) Cabinet fittings that engage into recesses to hold doors tight against the frame of a cupboard or similar. Sheraton lists brass bolts for bookcases ranging from 5 to 75 cm (2 to 30 in) in length, as well as iron or brass bolts for dining tables (1803, pp.64–5).

(d) Bedstead bolt (see Bed screw).

Bolted construction

See Construction

Bombanga (*Macrolobium coeruleoides*)

A West African timber with a density of 600 (38 lb/cu ft), it is yellow to light brown with a straight grain and a fine even texture. An excellent furniture wood in the 20th century.

Bombazine

A twill weave cloth made from silk warp and worsted weft. Developed in Bruges, it was a form of DIMITY. Introduced into England in the late 1560s–70s, it was woven in Norwich and later in London. It was piece-dyed in a variety of colours but by the mid 19th century was mainly black. Bombazine was especially used for curtains. The well-known 1677 inventory reference to 'white bumbasine' curtains in the wardrobe room of Ham House refers to bombazine (Thornton and Tomlin, 1980, p.164).

Bombé

A feature of cabinets in which the carcase was designed to swell out at the front and sides. The construction of such cabinets meant that a certain amount of BUILT-UP WORK had to occur to ensure a moulded or shaped base, prior to VENEERING.

Bone

Bone, antler and ivory are similar hard skeletal materials, while HORN is a keratin-based material, not to be confused with the others. The whiteness of bone is superior to IVORY but its fibrous structure is weaker, making it easier to break. A process of treatment involving soaking in a solution of water, sodium carbonate and lime for twelve days, and subsequently boiling, helped to whiten the bone. Hydrogen peroxide, a bleaching agent which is easy to apply, is a quicker method of whitening. After treatment, bones can be dyed or tinted as wood.

Bone has often been used as a form of decorative inlay in many furniture-making traditions, the earliest being Egyptian. In the eighth century AD it was used as a decoration for caskets and chests. The Frank casket in the British Museum, made from whalebone, is a fine example which has a very interesting assembly method (see Mac-Gregor, 1985, p.109). From the 15th century, the use of bone as a form of CERTOSINA inlay was practised in North Italy. This resulted in geometric patterns based on Islamic models which were recognized by the contrast between white bone and dark wood. The 1556 Gage inventory lists items 'garnished with collorred boone [coloured bone]' ('The Gage Inventory of 1556', *Sussex Archaeological Collections*, XLV, 1892). During the mid 16th century writing desks were made in Germany which were inlaid with biblical scenes made from bone.

During the 18th century, recipes for the manipulation and dyeing of bone were given, especially for red and green colourings and in imitation of tortoiseshell for Boulle work (Dossie, 1758, pp.441–4). In the 20th century bone has been occasionally employed as a decorative inlay.
See also Adhesives, Horn, Ivory

Jervis, Simon (1972), 'Antler and horn furniture', in *Victoria and Albert Museum Yearbook*, London: Victoria and Albert Museum.
MacGregor, A. (1985), *Bone, Antler, Ivory and Horn*, London: Croome Helm.

Bone finish

An American wood finish popular in the 1930s for bedroom suites, dinettes and occasional items. This gave a flat white enamel lacquered effect to wooden furniture. Also known as Egyptian or Antique white.

Bonegrace

Narrow curtains used in the 17th and 18th centuries, which were hung at the corners of beds. In conjunction with the larger side curtains they completely enclosed the occupant and avoided draughts.

Bonnet top

An American treatment for the tops of pedimented case furniture. The broken pediment is fitted to the whole top, either in one piece, or by fixing side coverings to the front and back parts of the pediments.

Book matching

A method of matching VENEERS, in which the first leaf of a bundle of veneers is opened as the page of a book and matched at the edges with its fellow.
See also Veneering

Bordering

(a) A term that identifies best CANE work using three skeins of cane, sometimes as thin as 1.5 mm (⅟₁₆ in) wide. Sheraton likened the work of this quality to some canvases (1803, p.126).
See Cane

(b) The decorative gold 'tooling' stamped as a border into leather table tops and bureaux flaps.

Boring machine

See Machines

Bosting or Boasting

A preparatory process in CARVING. The shaping of the outline of a carving by gouging and sawing to a predetermined plan before the final detailed finishing. The basic block shape may be built up by gluing blocks together. By the early 19th century bosting could be part of the division of labour: 'In small factories it is common for one carver to begin and finish the whole of the carving. But where there are a number of hands employed, and in pieces that require much skill, the other [bosting by one and carving by another] is the most preferable way' (Sheraton, 1803, pp.62–3).

Botany Bay wood

(a) A name applied by Sheraton to a range of woods imported from Australia especially from the Botany Bay area in New South Wales. He lists four types of timber which are labelled Botany Bay, but none are accurately described: 'the olive, the orange, the flesh and the brown' (1803, p.88–9). In 1811 the *London Cabinet-maker's Union Book of Prices* listed work to be done in Botany Bay wood, which was to be charged at the same rate as rosewood.
See also Beefwood, Blackwood

(b) African black Botany Bay wood.
See Blackwood (African)

Bottom linen

A coarsely woven linen sackcloth or canvas which is used to cover the webbing in upholstered work. It is a support for the filling and may be cut so that the edges can be turned in over a roll of filling material to create a 'French edge'.

Bottoming

The process of cutting out the wooden seat shape of chairs (especially Windsor types) with an ADZE. The work was originally done by a bottomer. Bottoming also refers to the process of weaving RUSHES, ash splints, bark strip and the like over the seat rails to form a chair-seat bottom. Aka Saddling.
See also Adze, Chair-makers

Boulle or buhl work

A form of MARQUETRY which has been particularly associated with the cabinet-maker André Charles Boulle (1642–1732). The work was based on the use of a variety of materials as veneer in conjunction with each other, to create a spectacular effect. These could include fine timber veneers or metals such as brass and pewter, as well as mother-of-pearl or tortoiseshell.

Originating in 16th-century Italy, the technique was brought to France by Italian craftsmen and was perfected by the Boulle workshop. Boulle work is best known for its designs worked with shell background inlaid with brass, known as *première partie* and brass inlaid with shell known as *contre partie*. The early process of cutting the shell, timber or metal was either as a sandwich of parts or individually cut and mounted using patterns. However, by the early 19th century, Peter and Michelangelo Nicholson were clear about the method:

In joining this ornament with that to which it is to unite, the part for the ornament and that for the ground must be glued together, drawn upon the one, and laid upon another such piece joined in the same manner, but placed in reverse order; then the design being drawn upon the one, and the whole substance making one thickness, is cut by means of a fine bow saw, thus producing four parts joined in twos reversed to each other. (1826, p.3)

The finished work was often further embellished by ENGRAVINGS, with back painting in colours or the application of coloured foils.

In the 18th century the aesthetic of Boulle work was both imitated and copied, as well as being interpreted in other ways. The brass inlay work into mahogany was very fashionable in England (see entry on BRASS INLAY), whilst in France a taste for the original style of Boulle ensured work for makers such as Etienne Levasseur (1721–98). With the revival of interest in French designs in the early 19th century, a new demand for Boulle work arose. A number of well-known makers established themselves about this time. In 1816 Louis Le Gaingneur set up a 'buhl manufactory' in Edgware Road, London, and by 1817 Thomas Parker of Air Street, London, was advertising himself as a Cabinet and Buhl Manufacturer. In Paris the Wassmus family, specialized in satisfying the French demand.

Features of this revived taste were techniques devised to make the supply of Boulle work easier. Initially these simplified the process of cutting-out the metal by stamping it, or in some cases by pressing the metal into the wood veneer. As with most techniques there were attempts to mechanize the process to meet a growing demand. In 1830 a machine for 'buhl-cutting' was made by a Mr McDuff, a member of the London Mechanics Institution, who won a prize of £10 for the best machine invented in the year. McDuff was a working turner who devised an arrangement that allowed a frame with a reciprocating saw to be mounted onto an existing wheel-operated lathe. The machine had the benefit of freeing both hands and allowing the work surface to be flat. This method still used a saw process similar to the original 'donkey' method, but apparently reduced the time and improved the efficiency.

The cutting-out process was also speeded up by the use of stamping techniques for the metal (usually BRASS) sections of the work. In 1839 Andrew Ure's *Dictionary of Arts, Manufactures and Mines* described Boulle decoration in which he mentioned the use of punches to cut out the shapes required, and in 1856 Digby Wyatt noted that 'stamps or punches are sometimes used in buhl work of brass or wood, but only to a limited extent'. Initially the techniques were used to revive old designs rather than create new ones. Digby Wyatt commented on the practice of makers using the techniques to doctor old furniture rather than design new models. He said: 'It is a great pity that much of the ingenuity and dexterity which are now brought to bear in doing-up old foreign work, should not be devoted to the improvement of our contemporary productions' (1856, p.294).

In 1863 *The London Cabinet-makers' Union Book of Prices (supplementary)*, gave a note that 'Buhl borders stamped into veneer tops are charged at half the price of banding'. Other methods of obtaining Boulle effects without great cost included substitution of materials. The process of using a mixture of tin and quicksilver mixed with size was suggested as an alternative to the more costly silver inlay. Another process, devised by a Mr Cremer, involved a method of applying a mix of japan and copper to a base frame to create an effect that resembled Boulle, but was made for between a tenth and a twentieth of the cost. The method involved engraving a copper plate, then taking an impression of this in gutta percha, onto which was deposited a film of copper. The whole surface was then painted with strong japan colour and this was built up and stoved between each layer. When it was as thick as the excised parts it was rubbed down to the copper surface leaving the japan colour in the excised parts of the pattern. Naturally this process required a substantial demand in order for it to be an economic proposition. The attraction of combinations of materials meant that many other makers produced marquetry furniture throughout the 19th century in various mixes, including wood veneers, brass and mother-of-pearl. The so-called 'works in three woods' refers to a mid-19th-century Boulle process which uses for example, mahogany, rosewood and satinwood cut in the manner of Boulle work in order to produce three different grounds, motifs and centres respectively.

Although tastes changed, the commercial production of Boulle continued, although one commentator was concerned about standards of workmanship. In 1890 the magazine *Furniture and Decoration* noted that 'The modern manufacturers saw out simultaneously ten or twenty sheets and the whole result is so rough and paltry that to call it Boulle is a calumny on the name' (October, p.280).

Bemrose, W. (1872), *Manual of Buhl and Marquetry*, London: Bemrose and Son.
Fuhring, P. (1992), 'Designs for and after Boulle furniture', in *Burlington Magazine*, CXXXIV, pp.350–62.
Gilbert, C. and Murdoch, T. (1993), *John Channon and Brass Inlaid Furniture 1730–1760*, New Haven and London: Yale University Press.
Kirkham, P. (1980), 'Inlay, marquetry and buhl workers in England c.1660–1850', in *Burlington Magazine*, 122, pp.41–9.
Ledoux-Lebard, Denis (1984), *Les ébénistes du siècle 1795–1889*, Paris: Les Editions de l'amateur.
Levy, Martin (1989), 'Sincerest form of flattery (Boulle revival)', in *Country Life*, 15 June, pp.178–81.
Massie, F. (1990), *La marqueterie Boulle*, Paris: Biro.
Nicholson, P. and M. (1826), *The Practical Cabinet-maker, Upholsterer*, London: H. Fisher & Son and P. Jackson.
Randle, R. H. (1969), 'Templates for Boulle singerie', in *Burlington Magazine*, 111, pp.549–53.
Salivate, de, F. (1962), *Les Ebénistes du XVIII Siècle*, Paris.
Samoyault, Jean-Pierre (1979), *André Charles Boulle et sa famille: Nouvelles recherches, nouveaux documents*, Geneva: Droz.
Wilson, G. (1972), 'Boulle', in *Furniture History*, VIII, pp.47–69.

Boulle cutter

A specialist branch of the marquetry working trade. Originally Boulle work had been produced by cabinet-makers, in many cases by those who concentrated on this particular form. The revival of Boulle work in the early 19th century again encouraged specialists to concentrate on this form of decoration. Between c.1820 and 1870 they plied their trade and were distinguishable from the less skilful craft of the brass inlayers. Mayhew recorded a conversation with a buhl-worker in c.1850 that noted:

there are two kinds of buhl-cutting, 'plain' and 'French ornament'. The plain is mother of pearl laid on to the veneer, the 'French ornament' is brass and green shell (foreign snail shell) greatly variegated. The brass is cut first and fitted into the wood, and then the brass is cut to admit the green shell … The buhl worker then introduces a wire scroll into the pattern and a few little brass pips [tacks]. When finished I clean it off with a 'toothing iron' and a file. When its [sic] so cleaned off its sent to the cabinet-maker … then its sent back to me to engrave.
(*Morning Chronicle*, Letter LXIV, August)

In England the 1851 census listed '50 buhl cutters and workers', but after 1870 it was no longer a business proposition to remain in the craft. In a guide to finding work in various trades, Boulle-cutters were recommended to 'apply to the old furniture and curio dealers who want repairers, inlayers and workers' (Williams, 1881). In France, however, the specialism remained a distinct part of furniture-making and the marquetry tradition.
See also Marquetry workers

Bow front

The convex front curve, shaped like the outline of a bow, usually found in chests of drawers and cabinets. It is achieved by BUILT-UP work or by COOPERED joints.

Bow lathe

See Lathe

Bow saw

See Saws

Box lock

See Locks

Box maker

A specialist woodworker who made wooden boxes as containers. By the mid 18th century the craft had declined to such an extent that they were described as 'no more than bungling joiners employed chiefly in making boxes and cases for packing' (Campbell, 1747, p.255).

Boxwood (*Buxus sempervirens*)

A widely dispersed timber found in Europe, Western Asia and North Africa with an average density of 940 (59 lb/cu ft). It is light yellow or brown with a straight grain, a fine uniform texture and little figure. It is hard and dense, but relatively easily worked. It cuts very cleanly with sharp tools and is used for fine turning. It is difficult to season and convert, sometimes being allowed to rest in damp sawdust for a period.

Box has been used widely for INLAY and MARQUETRY since ancient times especially as a contrasting timber to ebony and metals. Egyptian evidence shows that the finest supplies came from Syria and Phoenicia, where it was considered an excellent wood for cabinet work (varieties were still known as Persian, Turkish or Abyssinian in the mid 20th century). Its popularity continued with the Assyrian domination of the Middle East, whilst in Greece and Phrygia it was used in combination with yew. In the 16th and 17th centuries and especially in the 18th century, it was employed as inlay and border (STRINGING) in European furniture. In the 17th century the figured wood from the root of the tree was particularly valued as they 'furnish the inlayer and cabinet-maker with pieces rarely undulated and full of variety' (Evelyn, 1662, p.156). In the 19th century two varieties were particularly identified: the European (mainly Spain) and the Turkish.

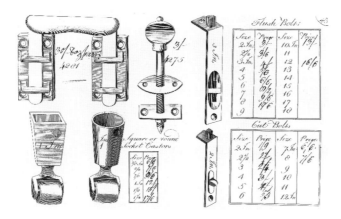

The former was small in diameter – 2.5–12.5 cm (1–5 in) – and the latter was larger – 6.5–35 cm (2.5–14 in).

Cape or East London boxwood
See Kamassi

Maracaibo or West Indian boxwood (*Gossypiospermum praecox*)
A Venezuelan timber with an average density of 840 (53 lb/cu ft), a fine even texture and a straight grain, used as a substitute for true boxwood, being available in larger sizes.

Larson, P. D. (1996), *Boxwood, its History, Cultivation, Propagation and Description*, Boyce, Va: Foliar Press.

Brace
(a) A simple, elegant tool which uses a crank motion especially for holding BITS. For chair-making a special brace was used. This comprised a wooden brace with wide arms, a small head and a socket chuck. The revolving head fitted into a BREAST BIB. Aka Stock.

(b) Another name for CORNER BLOCKS. Sheraton noted that they are 'lipped in at the angles of the seat of a chair, to prevent the girth webbing from warping or straining the rails' (1803, p.91).

Bracket foot
A cabinet foot shaped like a bracket. The exact contour would vary with the prevailing fashion. In some cases the brackets were built up with small blocks at 90 degrees to each other (strong) with a surface finish applied over. Other kinds were solid throughout with a vertical grain (less strong). Sheraton displayed a preference for bracket feet over turned stump feet, on the grounds of elegance and strength (1803, p.91).

Brads
See Nails

Bradawl
A chisel-pointed AWL used to bore pilot holes in timber. Used initially with the chisel point against the grain, it can be worked to move the fibres sideways to produce a clean hole.

Braid
See Passementerie

Bramah lock
See Locks

Branch or Branched cloth
A cloth with a figured pattern in the pile or weave, probably resembling branches or limbs.

Brass and brasswork
Brass is an alloy of copper and zinc, which makes a soft yellow metal. By varying the percentage of copper to zinc, a variety of colours of brass may be achieved. The common brass averages two thirds copper and one third zinc and gives a warm yellow-red colour. Over two thirds of copper, with 10–15 per cent of zinc, makes the alloy golden and is known as gilding metal. Pinchbeck has about five parts copper to one part zinc. Brass with less than 60 per cent copper is called Muntz metal or yellow metal and is often used for castings.

The pre-18th-century method of brass smelting used zinc ore with copper surrounded by a charcoal flux. When heated to melting point, the zinc becomes gaseous; at that temperature (850°C) the copper absorbs the zinc in chemical combination. As it cools, the gases escape leaving pit holes and impurities in the metal. This is known as the cementation process. The metal is then ready to fabricate as required. Although brass was first manufactured in England c.1568, it was not until 1693 that full-scale brass casting commenced in England after a licence was given to John Lofting. By the second half of the 17th century brass had begun to displace iron in the manufacture of cabinet mounts, and it has remained a standard ever since. In the 18th century a method of brass production called speltering was developed, which was able to mix the two metals together without the problems of working directly with ores. In 1738 William Champion patented a method of distilling pure zinc (Pat.no.564) by downward distillation, which enabled it to be added to molten copper creating a more manageable product, but its commercial success was not until later in the century. In 1784 James Emerson, once an employee of William Champion, produced brass in this new manner which Richard Watson described as being 'more malleable, more beautiful, and of a colour more resembling gold than ordinary brass is' (*Chemical Essays*, London: printed for T. Evans, 1784, pp.47–8). Later developments in zinc production further improved the process, and nowadays it is generally made by electrolysis.

There are numerous methods of producing brasswork for hardware which follow a sequence. The first stage is the making of a model. The moulder then prepares a mould from the model and then 'runs' the casting. When cold, the chaser cleans it up and finishes the work, and finally polish or lacquer is applied. The following methods are used to create brasswork: casting, drawing, pressing and stamping.

CASTING
Patterns of the object to be cast were made from boxwood or lead and had casting sand packed around them. The number of patterns would vary depending upon the complexity of the piece. Molten brass was then poured into the shapes made in the sand and allowed to rest until set. Once set, the chaser or finisher cleaned up the item with emery, pumice or tripoli, usually leaving the casting marks on the rear. The lost-wax (*cire perdue*) method used a wax model made round a clay (fired) core and wrapped within an outer casing of clay and plaster. The whole was heated in an oven until the wax melted; liquid metal was then poured in to replace the wax. When cooled, the clay was broken out and the work was ready for finishing. Gravity die casting

is a technique where the molten brass is poured into a steel or copper die. It flows into the spaces by gravity, is allowed to cool, and is then removed. Pressure die casting is similar to gravity die casting, but the molten metal is forced into the mould under pressure thus enabling multiple copies to be made at one time.

DRAWING

The working of brass by drawing through different-sized holes in a template creates rods which can be processed. Furniture handles, for example, had their bails and plate cast, whilst the post or pommel pins were made from drawn brass.

PRESSING

The drop press: A method known as 'book piercing' which produced cut-out shapes for borders, inlay and buhl work. The lower part of the die was a bed with the design cut into it. The brass sheet was laid over this and an identical, but pierced, copy of the bed was laid over. Punches were located into the perforations on the top sheet so that, when pressure was applied, they cut through the metal to make a copy of the required design.

STAMPING

In 1769 John Pickering patented a method of stamping designs into brass in a drop press, which immediately enabled the brass workers to produce ten times as many items in a day than was possible by the old methods (Pat.no.920, 7 March). The design was cut into a steel block, and an impression was taken of this in brass (called the force). Brass sheet was placed on the block and the force was dropped and stamped. The new stamping method also allowed a reduction in the thickness of the metal used. In the older system, plates of $c.1–1\frac{1}{2}$ mm ($\frac{1}{32}–\frac{1}{16}$ in) thick were common, whilst with press stamping, a sheet of $c.\frac{1}{2}$ mm ($\frac{1}{50}$ in) metal could be safely used. In 1777 Marston and Bellamy patented a method of stamping ornament which was described as 'the stamping upon plated metal, gilt, and other metals … all sorts of figures, decorations, ornaments and other devices for cabinet furniture and lock furniture' (Pat.no.1165). Birmingham was the centre of the stamping trade and here the brass workers worked closely with the die-sinkers, who were responsible for cutting the master blocks; a pair of dies being required for each design. Patent methods were applied to brass work in the 19th century. In 1811 William Jenkins improved a method of making flat-backed handles and rings to save labour and material (Pat.no.3450).

TUBES

From $c.1825$ brass tube became available for furnishings. In 1827 Robert Winfield patented a process of manufacturing tubes or rods into bedstead components (Pat.no.5573). However, the *Art Union* still referred to brass tube as a novelty when reporting on the 1844 Paris Exhibition. In 1847 Peyton and Harlow obtained a patent for taper tubing (Pat.no.11765), but one of the most important brass inventions was in 1848 when Ward devised a method of tube drawing called the yielding die method. By the second half of the 19th century the simplicity and relative ease of brass bed manufacture was commented upon by Timmins: 'it cannot be said that there is any special machinery used, the only machines used in addition to the ordinary lathes, drills etc. for assisting hand work are those producing the various tubes for the post and pillars' (1866, p.282).

The artistic decorating movement and the Aesthetic movement of the later 19th century encouraged the use of brass, for discreet embellishment as well as the main component of furnishing items. In furniture these were usually occasional pieces such as magazine racks, plant stands, small tables and the like. In the latter half of the 20th century a revival in brass furnishings occurred. The taste for Victorian styles encouraged brass beds to be reproduced, and military style furniture with brass corners and embellishment were revived. Brass was also used in tube and square sections for making table frames, used in conjunction with glass or stone tops.

Brass foil

A Dutch process which consisted of beating brass metal to a foil consistency from a thin sheet, which was then used as a substitute for gilding metal. It was made from an alloy consisting of 11 parts copper to 2 parts zinc.
See also Dutch gold

Brass inlay

Famous as a component of BOULLE work, brass inlay as a technique of decoration has also been used in other furniture. In the mid 18th century a particular form of British furniture centred around the work of John Channon, who used brass as inlay both discreetly and dramatically. In the early 19th century brass inlay became a hallmark of the productions of the period. Brass was used for decorative silhouettes and ornamental borders, using a cutting technique called 'book piercing' (see above, Pressings). This was particularly effective as a contrast to fashionable dark woods. Brass was also used for decorative beads that were fixed onto sharp points and used in early-19th-century furniture (see Plate VIII).
See also Dutch gold

Aitken, W. (1866), 'The early history of brass and brass manufacture in Birmingham', in S. Timmins (ed.), *Resources, Products and Industrial History of Birmingham*, London: R. Hardwicke.

Eccleston, B. (1989), 'R. W. Winfield and the Birmingham brass trade', in B. Tilson (ed.), *Made in Birmingham*, Studeley: Brewin.

Fennimore, E. (1991), 'Brass hardware on American furniture, Parts 1 and 2', in *Antiques*, May, pp.948–55, July, pp.80–91.

Gentle, R. (1975), *English Domestic Brass 1680–1810, and the History of its Origins*, New York: Dutton.

Gilbert, C. and Murdoch, T. (1993), *John Channon and Brass-inlaid Furniture 1730–60*, New Haven and London: Yale.

Hayward, C. (1965), 'English brass inlaid furniture', in *Victoria and Albert Museum Bulletin*, January and April.

Hiley, E. N. (1957), *Brass Saga*, London: Benn.

Peyton, E. (1866), 'Manufacture of brass and iron bedsteads', in S. Timmins (ed.), *Resources and Products of Birmingham and Midlands*. Reprint 1967 Frank Cass: London.

Schiffer, P. N. and H. (1978), *The Brassbook*, Exton, Penn: Schiffer.

Brass nail

See Nails

Brazier

A worker in brass. In the 18th century this was a trade that supplied furniture-makers with 'locks of all sorts, hinges of various kinds and different materials; chases and handles for cabinet work, nails, woodscrews, and generally all sorts of brass and ironwork that are useful for furniture or any part of furniture' (Campbell, 1747, p.177). For most of the 18th and 19th centuries Birmingham (England) was the centre of this trade both for domestic and export needs. In 1767 Birmingham brass founders were considered 'ingenious artists [who] make an infinite variety of articles as sconces, cabinet handles, escutcheons, hinges, cloak pins etc.' (Sketchley's *Directory*, 1767, cited in Fennimore, 1991, p.953).

Braziletto (*Caesalpina brasiliense*)

See Brazilwood

Brazilian mahogany
See Andiroba

Brazilian rosewood
See Rosewood

Brazilian walnut
See Imbuia

Brazilwood (*Caesalpinia sp.*)
A heavy hardwood of Brazilian origin with an average density 1200–1300 (75–80 lb/cu ft), which has a bright orange colour with stripes of red, toning to dark red or reddish brown. It sometimes resembles certain cuts of Cuban mahogany. It was originally imported from the Far East from the Sappan tree (*C. sappa*). In *c.*1500 the Portuguese discovered a new region (later to be named Brazil) which had a supply of timber very like Sappan. The name was transferred to *C. echinata* and supply became a Portuguese monopoly from 1623. Brazilwood was occasionally used in the 17th century for inlays, no doubt since it was only available in short lengths of no more than 20 cm (8 in) in diameter. Its greatest value lay in its role as a dyewood. Sheraton noted that Brazilwood (or Brasiletto) was 'an American wood, of red colour and very heavy', adding that 'the wood is imported for dyers, who use it much' (1803, p.95). Aka Bahia, Brasilette, Brasiletto, Limawood, Pernambuco or Sappanwood.

Breast bib
A specially designed support for the chair-maker's BRACE favoured by Windsor chair-makers. It was fitted over the shoulders with a light harness and sat on the breast with a cut-out for the handle of the drill to fit into. This ensured that the chair seats could be drilled with maximum force from the maker's body, and the correct angle was maintained when drilling with brace and bit.

Brick construction
A method of building up parts of carcases, drawer fronts and the like by using an overlapping brick-laying technique with timber blocks. This enables curved shapes (for example, table rims) to be created simply and firmly. Martin described the making of circular rims for tables and drawer fronts. They are 'cut out of deal from 1.5 to 3 inches thick, laid one over the other by breaking or intersecting the joints as in brickwork. Care however must be taken that the grain runs as long as possible at the ends for the tenons or dovetails' (1819, p.116).

Brick dust
See Abrasives

Bridle joint
See Joints

Broadcloth
A fine quality plain cloth of double width (exceeding 72.5 cm/29 in) usually between 135 cm (54 in) and 157 cm (63 in), used not only for garments but also for bed-hangings and table-cloths. Usually dyed black or indigo, it was considered the best of all woollen materials. In 1609 the Lumley inventories listed '3 bedds of Broadcloth vidz one purple, one carnation, one green' (Walpole Society, 1918, p.40). The 1693 inventory of Margaret Thatcher of Boston, Mass., included '1 red broad cloth suit of curtains and valaines' (cited in Montgomery, 1984, p.179).

Brocade
Usually a richly figured textile, often with a gold or silver thread 'brocaded' or inserted into parts of the design by supplementary wefts which are not part of the weave structure. Probably of ancient Chinese and Indian origin, they were woven in Italy (Lucca) in the 13th century. By the 16th century it was noticed that 'clothe of silke, brocado and divers sorts of merchandise came out of Persia' (Hakluyt, 1589, II, 215). In the 17th century upholstery covers were sometimes brocaded with gold or silver threads and this practice continued into the 18th century. By the mid 18th century brocade was defined as 'a stuff of gold, silver or silk, raised and enriched with flowers, foliages, or other ornament according to the fancy of the merchant, or manufacturer, who invents new fashions' (Postlethwayt, 1751). Brocade now refers to multi-coloured fabrics that create a brocaded effect but have various coloured yarns woven right across the weft of the fabric.

Brocatelle
A material with linen or cotton wefts and silk warps with a raised design featured in the warp caused by stuffer yarns. It first appeared in England in Norwich *c.*1590. It has been used for hangings as well as upholstery. Evelyn recorded seeing 'a chair and desk covered with brocatelle … and cloth of gold' (*Diary*, 9 July 1669). Postlethwayt described brocatelle as 'a kind of stuff proper to make hangings and other furniture. A slight stuff made with cotton, or coarse silk in imitation of brocadoes [sic]. There are some all silk, & others all of wool' (1751). In the later 19th century a linen warp and woollen weft or mixes of cotton were used. Nowadays any woven fabric with a plain ground and a raised woven design is called a brocatelle.

Bronze
An alloy of copper and tin usually in the ratio of nine parts copper to one of tin. Bronze has been used for many centuries as a furniture-making or decorating material. Its first use appears to have been in Assyria and Egypt, and it was later used by the Etruscans, *c.*500 BC. Surviving examples of bronze furniture include thrones, chests, tables, couches and the well-known Etruscan circular barrel chairs which used bronze sheet as cladding. Its use was continued by the Romans for benches, couches, chairs, tripods and tables, as well as for decorative furniture parts such as legs, locks, hinges, corner ornaments, and fulcra (decorative attachments) for sofa scroll arms.

Bronze returned to furniture-making in the 17th and 18th centuries, one example being the cast supports for a Vatican library table by Valadier (1789). However, it was for furniture mounts that bronze was most well known. These were often gilded, and in France were known as BRONZE DORÉ. They could also be left natural and in 1807 Thomas Hope in his *Household Furniture* suggested allowing bronze metal mounts to develop their own green patina for decorative effect (1807, Plate 11). This effect was also produced artificially (see Vert antique). In the London 1851 Exhibition bronze bedsteads were exhibited by Gandillot of France, but the taste remained esoteric. During the 20th century bronze was sometimes used by French *décorateurs* for fabricating furniture in an Art Nouveau or Art Deco style.
See also Gilt-bronze mounts, Ormolu, Speculum, Vert antique

Hunter-Steibel, P. (1984), Exhibition catalogue: *Elements of Style: the Art of the Bronze Mount in Eighteenth and Nineteenth Century France*, New York: Rosenberg and Steibel.
— (1985), 'Exalted hardware: the bronze mounts of French furniture', in *Antiques*, 127, January, pp.236–45.
Richter, G. (1926), *Greek, Etruscan and Roman Furniture*, Oxford: Clarendon Press.
Steingraber, S. (1979), *Etruskische Möbel*, Rome: Breitschnieder.

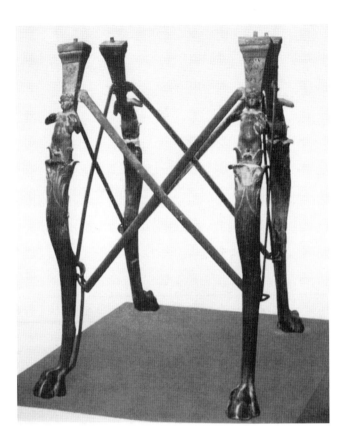

sliced veneer, although in the 1950s it was used in France for solid cabinet work and marquetry. When rotary cut, it produces a decorative veneer called kevazingo. Aka African rosewood.

10   *Roman bronze table-frame with sliding cross-braces to allow for folding.*

Buckeye (*Aesculus octandra*)
A timber from eastern USA with an average density of 480 (30 lb/cu ft), a creamy-white colour and an even texture, which is used for plywood. It is similar to English horse CHESTNUT and has been known as American horse chestnut.

Buckram
In the early 14th century buckram was a loosely woven cloth made from hemp, cotton or linen. It was used unstiffened as a case-cover material or for beds. In 1586 Sir Edward Littleton owned '2 bedsteads with a branch buckram canopye and gilt belles with curtains' (West, 1962, p.111). The 1604 Tart Hall inventory lists a 'long shovel board table with cover of old yellow buckram' (Cust, 1911, p.99). Its use as a lining material is specifically noted in the Byelaws of the Upholsterer's Company (1679), which refer to 'any tester or valance of silk, camlet, cloth, kersey, serge, say or of any other stuff but such as they shall lyne with buckram, callico or canvas …' (Houston, 1993, p.58). Since the 15th century buckram has also been stiffened with gums, flour paste or china clay (*c*.45 per cent of weight) and used for reinforcement work in valances and the like.

Buckram-maker
A specialist craft supplying the upholsterer with BUCKRAM. Campbell noted that 'it requires but little ingenuity to learn the art, nor is there much made of it when acquired' (1747, p.176).

Buhl-cutting machine
See Boulle work

Built-up work
A name for a range of cabinet-making techniques that use a number of parts to make a shaped section or component. These might be BLOCK, BRICK, LAMINATES, PLYWOOD or VENEERS or various other solid sections cut to shape. They were usually intended to be further finished. For example, cabinet-makers were responsible for building up block shapes for the turner: 'A vase (glued up for the turner) twelve joints in ditto' was part of the price of a pedestal (*Cabinet-makers' London Book of Prices*, 1793, p.147). The methods were also used for bombé shapes, rims, doors, mouldings and so on.

Bull-nose plane
See Planes

Bullen nail
See Nails

Bulletwood (*Manilkara spp.*)
A Central American timber with an average density of 1000 (65 lb/cu ft), whitish to light brown sapwood with a light red to dark red-brown heartwood. Known in the 19th century and confused with BALATA and BEEFWOOD.

Bullion fringe
See Passementerie (Fringes)

Bulrush
See Grasses

Bronze doré
A French term for gilded bronze, normally having the mercury GILDING process as the method of application.
See Bronze, Gilt-bronze mounts, Ormolu

Bronzing
The imitation of bronze carried out by PAINTING techniques.
See also Vert antique

Broom (*Cytisus scoparius*)
A European and Mediterranean shrub producing timber of limited use in furniture-making as the source is so small (*c*.5 cm/2 in diameter). It has been used occasionally, a bureau made for Blair Castle in 1756 being a rare documented example. Loudon noted that in Spain and France 'it is much used for veneering from being finely veined' (1844, p.596).

Brown ebony
See Cocuswood, Partridge wood

Brown oak
See Oak

Bubinga (*Guibourtia demeusei*)
A West African furniture wood introduced in the 20th century. It has an average density of 880 (55 lb/cu ft), is red-brown with red-purple veinings, with a coarse texture and an interlocked grain, while the pores often hold pockets of reddish gum. Chiefly used as a sawn or

11 *A cabinet on stand decorated and 'carved' by the burned-wood process. Shown at the 1851 London Great Exhibition by the Wood-Carving Co of Pimlico, London.*

Bunya pine (*Arucaria bidwillii*)
See Pine

Bureau action
A variety of methods have been used to operate the fall flaps of bureaux. These include manual or automatic wooden sliders, or LOPERS, that support the lowered flap from below; brass QUADRANTS that are fitted to the inside edges of the flap to allow fall, and fall flap stays that may be simple or friction versions.
See also Cylinder fall

Burgauté work
Burgau is a thick reddish-mauve MOTHER-OF-PEARL from a Neareastern shell which has sometimes been used in Europe for the decoration of small boxes. *Lac burgauté* is a form of raised gilt decoration on lacquer, based on a black ground with inlaid burgau shell although the term may refer to any lacquer-work with mother-of-pearl inlay.
See also Lacquer

Burlap
A coarse CANVAS made of jute and hemp, often used for wrapping-bags for transport or (especially in USA) for upholstery spring cover-

ing and other tasks. A finer variety was also used for curtains in the late 19th and early 20th centuries.
See also Hessian

Burma padouk
See Padouk

Burmese sandalwood
See Kalamet

Burned wood-carving process
The idea of mechanically using heat to char and burn a surface so that a decorative effect was produced was a successful mid-Victorian process. It took the idea of PYROGRAPHY and made it into a commercial process that produced carved-effect furniture and other wooden objects. In the 1840s devices which used heated-iron moulds were exploited by the Patent Decorative and Carving Works in London. Another process by the Wood-Carving Company produced successful results that were claimed to be some quarter of the price of hand carving. The third company in this period was The Burntwood Carving Company who used mechanized hot brands to produce a 'patent xylopyrography', which produced some fine quality carving effects.

The main imitation carving method was not carving in the true sense of the word, but was rather a sophisticated embossing technique, based on the idea of burning out a pattern into the wood with an iron mould, pressed onto a dampened surface. The process involved using pressure of between 10 and 30 thousand kilos (10 and 30 tons), and it was apparently possible to obtain up to 250 impressions before the mould needed to be re-chased. After approximately 500 impressions the mould had to be renewed. (See also Embossing.)

An iron mould is first cast from a plaster or wood model. The iron mould is heated to a red heat, and applied to a piece of wood, previously damped, with great force, and repeated until the wood is burned to the required form. The char is then cleaned off, and any undercutting that may be required done by hand; when the operation is finished it has the appearance of old oak.
(*Civil Engineer and Architects Journal*, July 1841)

Some results of other pyroligneous processes were displayed at the Manchester Exposition of British Industrial Art held in 1846. The *Art Union* illustrated a chair produced by the Patent Wood-Carving Company which was 'highly carved' in the late-17th-century manner, and they recorded that it was sold for the sum of thirty shillings (January 1846).

The Guattari process used heated moulds to burn or char away parts that were not required, using variably controlled heat and pressure. It was noted at the time that hardwoods were best suited to this process, but softer woods could be hardened by the removal of gums and sap and replaced with a glue to harden the wood (*Furniture Gazette*, 26 October 1878, p.28). In 1897 the Cameo Woodworking Company used patent pressing machinery and exhibited the results at the Furniture Trades Exhibition in London that year.
See also Poker work, Xulopyrography

Allwood, R. (1996), 'Machine carving of the 1840s and the catalogue of the Patent Wood Carving Company', in *Furniture History*, XXXIII, pp.90–126.
Edwards, C. (1993), *Victorian Furniture, Technology and Design*, Manchester: Manchester University Press.

Burr
A term that applies to an abnormal growth on a tree. Burrs are caused by fungal attack, severe pollarding, natural growth irregularities, or by numbers of small buds that fail to grow out. Burr veneers are

sought after as they can reveal highly decorative and distinctive patterns. Although many trees can develop burrs, ASH, ELM and OAK are particularly valued in this form, but the most well known are WALNUT, THUYA and MAPLE.

Burying timber
See Seasoning

Butt hinge
See Hinges

Butt joint
See Joints

Butterfly hinge
See Hinges

Butterfly wedge
See Joints

Butternut (*Juglans cinera*)
A native American timber, with an average density of 440 (27 lb/cu ft). It is light yellowish-grey with tinges and dark streaks, with an almost white sapwood. It has a moderately coarse texture and a straight grain. It is without strength, so is only used for decoration, often being stained to match black walnut. Known since the mid 18th century as a furniture timber in America, it is sometimes called white walnut and, during the 19th century especially, was used stained as a substitute for BLACK WALNUT. Also used plain in the USA in Eastlake-inspired furniture.

Button polish
See Resins: Lac

Buttoning
A method of fixing upholstery fillings, which followed TUFTING and was used from the late 18th century. The silk or wool tufts used in the 17th and 18th centuries were to some extent replaced in the late 18th century by buttons or rings. Loudon noticed that 'small rings are used covered with the same leather as the chair; these rings being found to look as well as, and wear better than, tufts of silk; at the same time they do not harbour dust' (1839, p.1049). By the middle of the 19th century, as designs demanded more stuffing and more cover, deep buttoning, as opposed to float buttoning, was developed, which ties the buttons through the stuffing to the foundation canvas. The buttoning was a technical imperative to hold the stuffing into place, but it soon became a distinct aspect of upholstered furniture. The *crapaud*, sofa, confidante and chesterfield are all 19th-century examples of upholstery buttoning, usually in conjunction with spring suspensions.

As buttoned or tufted upholstery was a major feature of the later 19th century, it is not surprising that attempts were made to try and simplify the process by mechanized means. But it was not until the end of the century that a satisfactory method was marketed, mainly in the USA. The tufting machine produced a 'quilt' of backing, stuffing and material top-cover buttoned together, which could then be applied to a sprung frame with much more speed and ease than the traditional built-up process. These machines were known as 'hay-balers' by the workers. Naturally this encouraged the division of labour and a consequent reduction in the skill required for upholstering chairs and sofas.
See also Tufting

12 *Elm burr veneer showing the typical pattern found in burr woods which has been sought after by cabinet-makers for centuries.*

13 *A 'Pompadour' chair. The metal-framed chair is deep-buttoned to keep the stuffing in place, but also to create a sumptuous look. English, c.1860−80.*

Buttoning (Cabinet work)
A method of fixing wide panels by rebating a wooden or metal block, the button, to fit a groove on the inside frame rail, thus allowing the board a degree of movement but maintaining it in place. Used in the 18th century for fixing carcase tops and in the 19th century for high-class joinery especially.

Buttons and loops
A 17th-century method of joining valances and covers 'sides to edges' with a braid loop fixed over a button. In 1601 Hardwick Hall had '3 curtains … with button and loops of black silk' (Boynton, 1971,

14 *A French caricature of a menuisier-ébéniste (cabinet-maker), c.1670–90, by Nicolas de l'Armessin. The tools, templates and measuring equipment represent those available at the time.*

Habit de Meniusier Ebeniste.

p.23). By the 18th century these had become decorative, in order to disguise HOOKS AND EYES.

Buttonwood (*Platanus occidentalis*)
A reddish-brown American timber which is hard and cross-grained. In the later 17th century it was mill-sawn in Massachusetts and used for cabinet-making and sometimes for chair-making. It was introduced into England from Virginia around 1640, but due to its liability to warp it was often only used for simple furniture such as bedsteads. In 1800 timber merchant Nathan Coombes of New Jersey was advertising 'handsome button-wood bedstead sets' (cited in Kebabian and Lipke, 1979, p.44). In the USA during the early 20th century improvements in seasoning meant it could be used for drawer sides, and was popular for plywood drawer bottoms when used as quarter-sawn ply veneer. Aka American plane or Sycamore (USA).
See also Plane, Sycamore

Cabbagewood (*Andira inermis*) **and Cabbage bark**
'The black-cabbage tree, the wood of which … is in high estimation among carpenters and joiners' (Stedman, 1796, II, xxiii, p.164). Holtzapffel noted that PARTRIDGE wood was called Cabbage wood in H.M. Dockyards in the mid 19th century.
See also Angelim, Partridge wood

Cabinet-maker
The term now refers to those whose business it is to make items of furniture of many different types. Perhaps the definition should relate simply to those items that are veneered, as this is the origin of the distinctive nomenclature. Cabinet-making methods were first used in the 16th century in northern Europe, possibly even earlier in Italy. The equivalent term in France for a cabinet-maker is *ébéniste* referring to the use of ebony veneers that were the province of this craftsman. By *c.*1660 the full effects of the continental skills of cabinet-making were being introduced into England. Pepys reveals a lot about the trade when he described how he went 'over the water to the cabinet-makers and there bought a dressing box for [Betty Michel] but would require an hours time to make fit'. He returned later and 'staid in the shop above seeing the workmen work, which was pretty, and some exceeding good work, and very pleasant to see them do it, till it was late quite dark' (*Diary*, 11 February 1667). In 1685 the cabinet-maker was described as a specialist worker who 'Smootheth hewn boards with a Plain upon a workboard, he maketh them very smooth with a little plain, he boarth them throw with an Auger, carveth them with a knife, fasteneth them together with Glew and Cramp irons and maketh Tables, Boards, Chests &c …' (Comenius, cited in Welsh, 1966, p.183). This description does not mention veneering and probably reflects the confusion of nomenclature in this period.

The mid 18th century saw the full development of the cabinet-maker as the supreme furniture craftsman, but Samuel Johnson simply defined him as 'one who makes small nice drawers or boxes' (*Dictionary of English Language*, 1778, London: W. Strahan). However, by 1747 some cabinet-makers were described as very wealthy: 'many of their shops are so richly set out they look more like Palaces, and their stocks are of exceeding great value' (*General Description of all Trades*, anon.). The best description is found in *The London Tradesman*:

The Cabinet-Maker is [the Upholsterer's] right hand man; he furnishes him with Mahogany and Wall-nut tree Posts for his Beds, Settees of the Same Materials, Chairs of all Sorts and Prices, carved plain and inlaid. Chests of Drawers, Book-Cases, Cabinets, Desks, Scrutores, Dining, Dressing and Card Tables, Tea-Boards, and an innumerable Variety of Articles of this Sort. The Cabinet-Maker is by much the most curious Workman in the Wood Way, except the Carver; and requires a nice mechanic Genius, and a tolerable Degree of Strength, though not so much as the Carpenter; he must have a lighter Hand and a quicker Eye than the Joiner, as he is employed in Work much more minute and elegant. A Youth who designs to make a Figure in this Branch must learn to Draw; for upon this depends the Invention of new Fashions, and on that the Success of his Business. He who first hits upon any new Whim is sure to make by the Invention before it becomes common in the Trade; but he that must always wait for a new Fashion to come from Paris, or is hit upon by his neighbour is never likely to grow rich or eminent in his Way. A Master Cabinet-Maker is a very profitable Trade; especially if he works for and Serves the Quality himself; but if he must serve them through the Channel of the Upholder, his Profits are not very considerable.
(Campbell, 1747, p.171)

The prestige of cabinet-makers was not altogether universal. In 1740 Batty Langley claimed that

cabinet-makers were originally no more than spurious indocible chips, expelled by joiners, for the superfluity of their sap … Tis a very great difficulty to find one in fifty of them that can make a bookcase etc., indispensably true, after any one of the five orders, without being obliged to a joiner for to set out the work and make his templates to work by.
(1740, Introduction)

Later the cabinet-making trade was seen as being 'one of the leading mechanical professions in every polite nation in Europe' (Sheraton,

1803, p.115). There was a trend in the later 18th and early 19th centuries for craftsmen to begin to specialize in particular types of cabinet work. By the mid 19th century the lower end of the trade was full of divided labour and specialisms often involved in scamping, whilst the better quality cabinet-makers remained able to work a range of skills especially in the quality, comprehensive manufacturing firms.

During the 20th century a revival of small craft-based workshops has been a feature of British and American furniture, although these are generally of a small scale and are not in competition with the mainstream manufacturers. In addition, cabinet-making craft skills are still used for specialist repair and conservation work.

Forman, B. (1971), 'Continental craftsmen in London 1511–1625', in *Furniture History*, pp.94–1120.
Gate, W. C. (1962), 'Journal of a cabinet-maker's apprentice', in *Chronicle of the Early American Industries Association*, XV, 3, September.
Kirkham, P. (1988), *The London Furniture Trade 1700–1870*, The Furniture History Society.
Pradere, A. (1989), *French Furniture-makers*, London: Sotheby.
Vaughan, A. (1984), *The Vaughans, East-end Furniture-makers*, London: ILEA.
Wills, G. (1974), *Craftsmen and Cabinetmakers of Classic English Furniture*, Edinburgh: Bartholomew.

Cabinet-making
See Construction

Caffa
See Caffoy

Caffar/Caffart/Caffard damask
The name 'caffard' appears to originate from the French word for 'counterfeit'. In this sense it is an inferior DAMASK of silk warp and linen, or wool and linen, or other combinations for the weft. During the 18th and 19th centuries they had a satin ground and the patterns were often in Oriental designs. Sheraton (taking a definition given by Postlethwayt in 1751) noted that caffart damask was 'made in imitation of the real thing, having woof of hair, coarse silk wool or cotton. Some have the warp of silk and woof of thread' (1803, p.191).

Caffoy
A satin ground fabric with a woollen pile woven in imitation of silk velvets and damasks, probably first imported from Abbeville, France. Woven from *c.*1577 by immigrant Flemings, largely in the Norwich

area of East Anglia, it was popular in the 17th and early 18th centuries for upholstery, bed hangings and wall coverings. An early reference (1590) to caffoy occurs in the bed furniture of Lady Morison at Cassiobury (Beard, 1997, p.31). In the 1726 Erthig inventory there are also references to caffoy upholstery covers.

Calamanco
A worsted material related to SATIN with a high gloss, hot-pressed effect, glazed with a coating of beeswax, often twilled and chequered in the warp so that the checks show on one side only. Originally from Flanders, the term was first recorded in England in 1592 and refers to Norwich manufacture. Norwich was still the centre of the trade in the early 19th century. These glazed worsted fabrics were used for hangings and upholstery as well as for dress materials (Postlethwayt, 1751, i, 428). Sheraton recorded that calamanco was 'a sort of woollen stuff manufactured in England and Brabant. It has a fine gloss, and is chequered in the warp, whence the checks only appear on the right side. Some calamancos are quite plain, others have broad stripes adorned with flowers, some with broad stripes quite plain, and others watered' (1803, p.121).
See also Everlasting, Russell

Cummin, H. (1941), 'Calamanco', in *Antiques*, 39, April, pp.182–4.

Calamander wood (*Diospyros quaesita*)
An ebony which is also called coromandel wood, Indian or Macassar ebony. A product of several species of the ebony family of trees from the Indian sub-continent. It grows in rock clefts, making it difficult to extract roots, which are often the most attractive part of the tree wood. With an average density of 1100–1200 (70–5 lb/cu ft), and a light-brown colour with black stripes, it is a hard, fine-grained wood, ideal for cabinet work. The dark-brown to black heartwood is streaked with lighter bands and it has a fine even texture with a mostly straight grain. The timbers were variously known as calamander, calemberri and omander.

Introduced in the early 1800s, it was first used as a veneer and for banding. Sheraton described coromandel as resembling black rose-wood but intermingled with light stripes being 'a foreign wood lately introduced into England, and is much in use by cabinet-makers for banding' (1803, p.180). Sheraton recognized its value and fashion by giving a recipe for imitating it. By 1830 calamander was 'wrought into chairs and particularly into tables', but was 'not regularly imported into the country, all that is here has been brought over by private gentlemen returning from that colony for their own use' (Knight, 1830, p.179). Knight described it as being 'used in large works, like zebra and rosewood' (ibid., p.178).

By 1853 these hard timbers were 'easily cut by the veneer saw, and as easily wrought upon the turning lathe, for which they are peculiarly well adapted; and all of them for very elegant furniture woods', although 'it was frequently scarce in the market' (Blackie, 1853, p.41). The description continues and confirms Sheraton:

Generally expressed, its appearance is something between rosewood and zebrawood, with a red hazel or chocolate brown ground figured with black stripes and marks. The darkest kind of wood is that most seen in this country, and is known as calamander; a lighter coloured variety somewhat striped is called calemberri; and a third kind, almost as light in shade as English yew, but possessing a ruddier hue, and partially veined and marked with darker tints, is called omander.
(op.cit., p.41).

15 The cabinet-makers' shop in the Harris Lebus factory, c.1910. Although the firm was an important and large-scale enterprise, the labour-intensive aspect of assembly work is aptly shown.

In the 1870s it was used for dressing-cases and fancy work. By 1908 it was becoming scarce and hence was one of the most valuable timbers of India and Ceylon.

Calambac

A timber particularly sourced from Timor. According to Rolt, as Calambourg wood, this was a timber 'brought from the East Indies in large long logs; its use being for the making of beads, turnery and cabinet work' (1761), whilst Roubo (1772) said it resembled olivewood and was light, porous and of a greenish colour tinged with red.
See also Eaglewood

Calambourg

See Calambac

Calembeg

See Calambac

Calemberri

See Calamander wood

Calico

A plain-weave cotton cloth originally from Calicut, which could be plain or printed. The range of textiles listed under the generic name of calico is wide, and include plain, printed, stained and dyed versions as well as CHINTZ and muslins. Imported from India in the late 16th century onward, it was later manufactured in Europe. In 1675 Edward Sackville was supplied with 'watered callicoe' and 'stained callicoe' for hangings (Beard, 1997, p.294). *Chambers Encyclopedia* described calicoes as being of 'divers kinds, plain, printed, painted, stained, dyed, chints, muslins and the like' (1753). Twenty years later, Dr Johnson described it as 'an Indian stuff made of cotton; sometimes stained with gay and beautiful colours' (1773). The material was used for upholstery covers as well as for hangings and lining. By the early 19th century calico was also a white or unprinted cotton cloth in England and a printed cotton cloth with no more than two colours in America. George Smith noted that calico should 'be glazed mellow; the small chintz patterns holding a preference in point of effect, especially for draperies' (1808, p.xii).

Down-proof calico is a tightly woven cloth finished by waxing which is used as a feather cushion case. In an unbleached version it is used as a final covering before a top cover (often hide) is fitted. Calico is also used to encase pocket SPRINGS.

Irwin, J. and Hall, M. (1971), *Indian Painted and Printed Fabrics*, Ahmedabad: Calico Museum of Textile.

Calimango

A plain-weave worsted fabric, often with narrow colour stripes, made in Yorkshire in the second half of the 19th century. The striped cloth was sometimes used for chair seats during that time.

Callipers

A simple but valuable tool based on a pair of legs, either straight or shaped, which are connected by a joint. They are used for transferring, dividing or repeating a measurement, or for checking the regularity of turned parts. They are also used in the scribing process when fitting boards, for example, against an uneven surface. Sheraton gave 'Calliber-Compasses' (sic) as an alternative name saying these were 'used to take the diameter of round or swelling bodies' (1803, p.122).
See also Measuring

Cam fittings

A special fitting used in knock-down CONSTRUCTION often of nylon or mild steel, which comprises a circular peg in one component and a circular boss in the other, so that, when brought together and the screw in the boss is tightened, a close joint is made.

Cambric

A fine plain-weave linen (and later cotton) cloth mainly used for clothing. It was sometimes used for drapery in the early 19th century.

Camlet or Chamlet

An important upholstery material which was originally a ribbed cloth made from worsted or goat hair. It could be treated in a number of ways to make differing effects, all with varying names (see Harrateen, Moreen, Grosgrain and Cheney). English camlets were made from Norwich worsted, whilst the Low Countries made camlets from goats' hair or a hair and silk mix, with Brussels camlets being the benchmark. Originating in the 13th century, it was noted by Camden that the wealth of Coventry 'arose in the last age from its woollen and camblet manufacture' (*Britannia*, 1610, cited in Ralph Edwards, 1964, p.110). Katharine of Aragon had silk 'chamlette' bed covers at Baynard Castle in 1535 (Clabburn, 1988, p.242). The applied decorative effects were clearly a feature through the 17th century. In 1620 Sharpe and Wilton took out a patent (Pat.no.17) for a new method of making camlets 'in the Turkish manner', achieved by cold rather than hot pressing. John Evelyn also recorded that he 'went to see … the pressing and watering … [of] grosgrans and chamblettes with weights of an extraordinary poyse put into a rolling machine' in Tours (*Diary*, 8 May 1644). In 1698 Celia Fiennes saw 'camlet and mohair beds' in the Cupola house at Bury St Edmunds (1982, p.139). In 1736 it was described as a 'sort of stuff made of camel's hair, silk etc., mixd' (Bailey, *Dictionarium Britannicum*). Postlethwayt (1751) has the best definitions:

figured camlets are those of a single colour, on which have been stamped, or imprinted, various figures, flowers, foliages, &c. This is performed with hot irons, which are a kind of moulds, that are passed under a press at the same time with the stuff. The figured camlets only come from Amiens and Flanders. The trade of them was formerly pretty considerable; at present there are but few of them sold, which serve commonly for church ornaments, or for making some household furniture … Wave camlets are those on which a kind of waves have been impressed, as on tabbies, by making them pass several times under the calender … Water camlets are such, which being taken from the loom, undergo a certain preparation with water, after which they are put into the hot press, that renders them smooth and glossy.

Later still, Sheraton described camlet as 'a stuff sometimes of wool, silk and sometimes of hair especially that of goats, with wool and silk' (1803, p.122). His description is clearly taken from the 'Bailey' source and was still used, well into the 19th century.
See also Paragon

Cummin, H. (1942), 'Camlet', in *Antiques*, 42, December, pp.309–12.

Campaign fringe

See Passementerie (Fringes)

Campeche or Campeachy

See Stains (Logwood)

Camphor

See Resins

Camphorwood (*Cinnamomum camphora*)
A timber native to China and Japan. It has an average density of 680 (41 lb/cu ft), with a grey-yellow and brown colouring and a strong scent. It has been traditionally used for travelling chests and boxes. Camphorwood was recommended in restrained terms to 19th-century British cabinet-makers: 'Its dimensions, but chiefly its fragrance, are its sole recommendations for cabinet work and that only for internal finishings' (Blackie, 1853, p.44). During this period it appears to have been imported in quantity, both in log and large plank form, and was particularly used for entomological and ornamental cabinets. By the turn of the century it was no longer considered a commercial timber.

Borneo Camphorwood (*Dryobanalops aromatica*)
See Kapur

East African Camphorwood (*Ocotea usambraensis*)
An East African timber with an average density of 570 (37 lb/cu ft). It is yellowish-brown darkening to deep brown, with a moderately fine texture and an interlocked grain resembling African walnut, and therefore used both in solid and veneers, especially in the mid 20th century.

Canadian birch
See Birch wood (Canadian)

Canadian silkywood
See Birch wood

Canadian white ash
See Ash (American)

Canalete (*Cordia spp.*)
See Princewood

Canarywood
A name applied to a variety of timbers:
(a) A light orange to yellow wood from *Persea indica* and *P. canariensis*, native to Madeira and the Canary Islands. It was an inferior form of mahogany, known in the 18th century as Maderah and later as Madeira MAHOGANY.

(b) In 1853 canarywood was recorded as a Brazilian timber which was golden yellow to light orange, sometimes streaked with yellow-brown and often defective toward the heart, therefore it was not used much except for marquetry and turning (Blackie, 1853, p.44), although Holtzapffel considered it 'very proper for cabinet work, marquetry and turnery' (1846, p.79).

(c) American WHITEWOOD (*Liriodendron*).
See Poplar, Tulipwood, Vinhatico

Candlewood
See Amyris

Cane and caning
Cane is a generic name for the stems of various reeds, grasses and palms which may be used whole or split. The types include solid canes such as Malacca cane which is nut brown in colour and has a very durable surface. It is one of the strongest canes and is ideal for contract furniture. The Palembang (Brown cane) is also used whole – that is, with its outer bark on – although it is slightly thicker, so is tougher and more wear-resistant. The Tohiti cane is also thick (12–

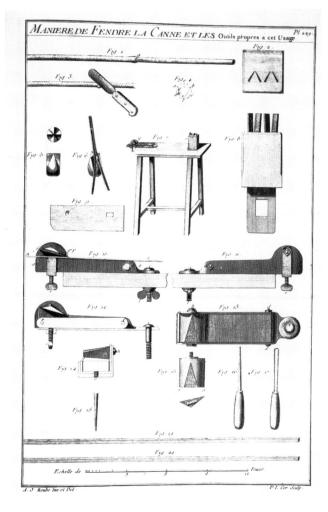

16   *The preparation and cutting of cane, and the tools required of the caner, c.1761–88.*

30 mm/½–1¼ in) and used for frames. The Sarawak cane (8–18 mm/ 5⁄16–11⁄16 in thick) is a yellow colour with a glossy finish bark which when split is widely used for seats. The Segah cane (4–10 mm/⅛–⅜ in thick) with a glossy finish, is also used for seats. (See also BAMBOO canes.) Cane also refers to the pared and split outer skin of the RATTAN palm (*Calamus rotang*), whereas REED is the core of the rattan palm. These plants grow to exceptional lengths between 30–75 m (100–220 ft) with a diameter, when fully grown, of up to 6 cm (2.5 in). Caning is the process of using the split canes that can offer both a structural and decorative element to furniture. They are usually interlaced to form a mesh seat or back support within a chair frame.

Cane had been imported into England and Europe in the first half of the 17th century, but was not used to any extent for furniture until caned seats became popular after the Restoration. The English makers exported caned furniture into parts of the world where textiles were impractical. This caned-furniture trade was so successful that in 1689 a petition for the suppression of cane chair-making was made by the woollen-cloth trade in an effort to halt the alleged damaging effects on their business. They complained that 'since cane chairs have been in use, the trade [in woollen cloth] has decayed and is lost, now the said poor that used to be employed beg their bread; and the Town and others near it, without some redress will come to ruin' (cited in

Symonds, 1951, 'English Cane Chairs 1', in *Connoisseur*, March). The cane chair-makers responded by saying that

about the year 1664, Cane chairs &c.came into use in England which gave much satisfaction to all the Nobility, Gentry, and Commonalty of this Kingdom for their Durableness, Lightness, and Cleanness from Dust, Worms and Moths, which inseparably attend Turkey-work, Serge, and other Stuff-Chairs and Couches, to the spoiling of them and all furniture near them that they came to be much used in England, and sent to all parts of the world. (loc.cit.)

The French taste for cane began around 1720, with Savary des Bruslons noting that 'Rotin was a form of cane which was split into pieces and was made up into furniture providing a large trade in England and Holland and recently in France' (1723). Caning had a variable fortune during the 18th century. However, it was revived for Chinese-style chairs, and Chippendale noted that 'such chairs are very proper for a ladies dressing room, they commonly have cane bottoms with loose cushions, but if required thay have stuffed seats and brass nails' (1762, p.3). By the 1770s caning was out of fashion again until the very late 18th century when a renewed demand for light fancy chairs came into vogue. Sheraton recorded this change in taste and noted that 'caning cabinet work is now more in use than it ever was known to be at any former period' (1803, p.126). Cane was employed for ends of bed frames, borders, round chairs, bed steps and 'anything where lightness, elasticity, cleanness and durability, ought to be combined' (op.cit.). The fineness of the work in Sheraton's time was divided into single, double or triple strands of cane worked, the last and best quality being called BORDERING.

In the 19th century caned seats remained popular whether for steamer chairs or bentwood side chairs. For much of the century caning was carried out by hand labour (usually female), but in 1870 William Houston, engineer of the American Wakefield Rattan Company, invented a power loom to weave sheets of cane for seating use. In 1875 Wakefield's rivals, the Heywood Company, and their engineer Gardner Watkins developed their own cane-weaving machines, but more importantly they patented a machine process that cut a groove in the surface of the seat-frame rim, and avoided the need for drilled holes. Other patents covered the processes of fitting seat fabric (of woven cane or other type) in the groove and securing it tightly with glue and a triangular wooden-wedge strip. Later 20th-century techniques continued to avoid the necessity for drilling multiple holes and employing special labour to cane seats, especially when woven sheets of 'synthetic' cane became available.

See also Lloyd Loom, Rattan, Reed, Wicker, Willow

Adamson, J. (1993), *American Wicker*, New York: Rizzoli.
Brown, N. (1984), *Cane and Rush Seating*, London: Batsford.
Harwood, B. (1994), 'Two early Thonet Imitators: The Henry I Seymour Chair Manufactory', in *Studies in the Decorative Arts*, Bard Graduate Center, New York.
Kirkham, P. (1985), 'Willow and cane Furniture in Austria, Germany and England, c.1900–1914', in *Furniture History*, XXI, pp.128–31.
— (1986), *Harry Peach: Dryad and the DIA*, London: Design Council.
Ottilinger, E. (1990), *Korbmöbel*, Salzburg: Residenz.
Roubo, J. A. (1771), *L'Art du menuisier-carrosier*, pp.624–34, Paris: Académie des Sciences.
Saunders, R. (1983), *Collectors' Guide to American Wicker Furniture*, New York: Hearst Books.
Symonds R. W. (1951), 'English cane chairs', Part 1, in *Connoisseur*, 1127, March.

Cane chair-maker

A relatively short-lived specialism, but cane chair-making was a very successful trade during the period 1670–1720. The specialist trade that was established in England to satisfy the demand for cane-bottomed chairs in the latter part of the 17th century was supported by a Cane Chair-makers' Company. Their contribution to the economy may be judged from the following petition statement:

[Cane chairs] came to be much used in England, and sent to all parts of the World; which occasioned the Chair-Frame Makers and Turners to take many Apprentices; and Cane Chairs &c. coming in time to be Carved, many Carvers took Apprentices, and brought them up to Carving of Cane-Chairs, Stools, Couches, and Squobs only: And there were many Apprentices bound only to learn to Split the Canes, and Cane those chairs, &c. (Cited in Symonds, 'English Cane Chairs', 1937, p.125)

The petition continued to (over- ?) state that by 1688 'Six Thousand Dozens of Cane Chairs, Stools, Couches and Squobs' were made every year and over two thousand dozens were exported annually. The popularity of these exported English chairs can be seen in the adoption of the term 'Englische Stuhlmacher' for a German cane chair-maker. By the 1720s changes in fashion meant the decline and demise of this specialist branch of chair-making although it was revived in the late 18th century in conjunction with FANCY CHAIR-MAKING.

Symonds, R. W. (1937), 'English cane chairs, the rise and decline of an industry between 1664–1747', in *Antique Collector*, 8, pp.102–6.

Cane edge

A method of giving shape to the leading edges of upholstered seats (and divans) by tying strips of flexible BAMBOO or other cane to the springs to maintain the finished shape. When a seat has been first sprung, the cane (or metal imitation) band is bent to the shape of the front rail, then tied to the top rims of the front springs. It is held in place by being fitted into holes in the sides of the frame, providing a lever-like arrangement so as to allow it to move when the springs are compressed.

Canella

A general name for timbers from the *Lauraceae* family: Aniba, Nectandra, Imbuia and Ocotea. Louro Preto is a late-20th-century trade name for this timber. Aka Sweetwood.

Cangica wood

A timber from Brazil, also called Angica. It is similar to rosewood but lighter and more yellow-brown, often straight-grained and plain. In the 19th century, logs were imported of only 15–26 cm (6–10 in) in diameter, but it was used still for cabinetwork and turning (Holtzapffel, 1846, p.78).

See also Snakewood

Cantilever furniture

Chairs that are designed and made with leg support only at the front or back, allowing the cantilever tension principle to support the load, are said to be cantilevered. The principle has been used in conjunction with STEEL bar and tube, wood LAMINATIONS and PLASTICS. An early cantilever development was published in the *Wiener Möbel Journal* of 1851. Ferdinand List showed a design for a suite of furniture which was intended to have a cantilevered underframe of either cast iron or laminated wood, with a conventional upholstered seat and back. The cantilever was more successfully used in the 1880s for tractor and farm machinery seating and various attempts were made subsequently to adapt the idea for furniture. An American patent of 1889 devised cantilevered chairs fixed to a circular table for steam-ship use (US Pat.no.96,089), based on steel rods similar to the more successful tubing of the 1920s. Although a spring-loaded cantilever 'lawn' chair

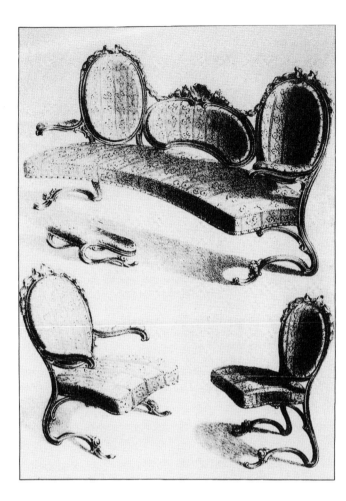

was patented in America between 1922 and 1924 (US Pat.no. 1,491,918), it was shown to be impractical, so the first accepted domestic model was introduced by Mart Stam in 1926 and was quickly followed by other designs by Mies van der Rohe and Marcel Breuer.

The cantilever principle was also applied to laminated wood and plywood chairs in the work of Alvar Aalto during the 1930s. He used Finnish birch plywood, which was inherently springy, to produce a curved seat and back section which was then fitted in-between two laminated arm and skid frame supports. Once the principle had been established, the idea became accepted widely and manufacturers have since produced cantilever chairs in ALUMINIUM and PLASTIC as well as STEEL and wood.

Macel, O. (1990), 'Avant-garde design and the law; litigation over the cantilever chair', in *Journal of Design History*, vol.3, nos 2/3.

Macel, O. and Kuper, M. (1993), 'The chairs of Heinz Rasch', in *Journal of Design History*, vol.6, no.1.

Stuhlmuseum Burg Beverungen (1986), *Der Kragstuhl*, Berlin: Alexander Verlag.

Canvas

A material woven from fibres such as hemp, linen or cotton which could be made in a variety of textures and weights. Used unbleached as the base for various NEEDLEWORKS, for the undersides of chairs, and dyed for seating such as stools, deck chairs and tubular steel stacking chairs. In medieval times it was occasionally used as a base

for painted work mounted on chests. Henry Shaw (1856) recorded a medieval chest with wrought-iron works 'the spaces between covered with canvas, on which are painted imitations of fruit and flowers' (cited in Kirk, 1981, p.186). Canvas was also exceptionally used at Tart Hall in 1641 'for two beds to keep the gnats away' (Cust, 1911).

Canvas work

A term used to define the work applied to decorate cushions in the 17th century, and upholstery in the 18th century. Tent, cross or Irish STITCH, worked on canvas, formed the basis of this work.
See Needlework

Caoutchouc

A rubber-like solution used for producing an impervious and air-tight seamless material that could be made into cushions and air-beds. After Mackintosh's invention of rubberized fabric in 1823, some furniture-makers began to experiment with its possibilities. The most obvious use was for air or water beds.
See also Air cushions, Coated fabrics (Water beds)

Cape boxwood
See Kamassi

Carbon fibre
See Plastics

Carbonizing
See Seasoning (Carbonizing and smoking)

Carcase or carcass

The made-up frame of a cabinet before it is fitted out with drawers, doors or hardware. Special terms such as 'wing' carcase and 'bottom' carcase refer to the parts of cabinets that are fitted to the side or below other parts respectively.
See also Construction

Carcase back
See Back boards

Carcase divisions

The main interior fittings of a cabinet carcase. These might include centre divisions, DUST BOARDS and shelves.

Carcase saw
See Saws

Cardboard

Cardboard has been used as a furniture material to take advantage of the high strength of paper materials when bent and laminated. The earliest use of paper as a constructional material (as opposed to papier mâché) appears to be Hans Gunther Reinstein's German patent process from 1908. This process used cardboard as 'an autonomous self-supporting material'. Although the furniture produced from this patent process continued to be made up to 1929, it never became a mainstream development. In the 1970s Canadian architect Frank Gehry used laminations of corrugated paper laid at right angles to each other, to create a firm yet bendable material for furniture-making. His range of Easy-Edge furniture was well received both in terms of design and as an ecologically responsible use of materials. In the 1990s cardboard was revived as an environmentally-friendly furniture

17 A design for a suite using the cantilever principle by Austrian upholsterer Ferdinand List, c.1851. Although probably never put into serious production, it is a precursor of 20th-century cantilever chairs.

material with desks, chairs and tables made from packing-case quality cardboard.

See also Papier mâché, Paper

Dry, G. (1982), 'Hans Gunther Reinstein und seiner Möbel aus Pappe', in *Kunst in Hessen und am Mittelrhein*, XXII.
Martens, B. and Tschuppik W.–M. (1995), *Das Kartonmöbel: Industrielle Herausforderung oder Experiment?*, Vienna: Technical University.
Robinson, J. (1950), 'Can furniture be made of cardboard?', in *Canadian Art*, 8/2, pp.70–7.

Cardcut

A form of lattice ornament cut with a FRETSAW. The term usually refers to the low relief carved decoration found on 18th-century 'Chinese Chippendale'-style furniture. It is often laid over a solid ground.

Carpenter

The earliest craftsmen to be involved with furniture-making were carpenters who were responsible not only for house-building, but also for the loose and fixed furnishings within an interior.

In medieval Europe, the carpenters organized themselves into guilds as did most tradesmen. In England the Carpenters' Company had its first charter granted in 1477. There were continual disputes as to their role in relation to joiners, which were never really resolved. The carpenter generally made furniture that was boarded and nailed together, whilst the JOINER used woodworking joints and produced a more refined result. The distinctions between carpenter and joiner came to a head in the 17th century when the two were apparently clearly demarcated. In 1632 the Committee of the Court of Aldermen decided that joiners were allowed to make furniture of a more complex nature (see JOINER), and conversely carpenters were limited to the following:

All drapers tables, all tables for taverners, victuallers, chandlers, compting house tables and all other tables made of deale, elme, oake, beeche or other wood nayled together without glue, except all sorts of Tables either nayled framed or glued being moveable.
All Sesterne stooles, washing stooles, Ducking stooles and all other stooles whatsoever that are to be headed with oake, elme, beeche or deale and footed with square or round feete except all framed stools glued or pinned.
(Cited in Wolsey and Luff, 1968, p.17)

The distinctions were not upheld by the carpenters, and in 1672 the joiners had to petition again for enforcement of the 1632 rules. The carpenters ingeniously argued that they were all of the same craft and it was the joiners who had set themselves apart, so it was unfair to penalize the basic craft in favour of an offshoot. By the mid 18th century the distinction was becoming blurred again. *A General Description of all Trades* noted:

Carpentry and Joinery, that part especially belonging to house-work (and even Undertaking or furnishing of funerals) are often performed by the same persons, though the work of [the Joiner] is much lighter and reckoned more curious than that of carpenters; for a good joiner can often do both well, but every carpenter cannot work at joinery.
(Anon., 1747)

This acknowledgement of the position of carpenters is probably because cabinet-makers were by then the supreme furniture-makers and had supplanted both the carpenters' and the joiners' once-held roles. However, the City judgements and ordinances had no power beyond the confines of the City of London, and many craftsmen continued to combine roles.

By 1803, in London, carpenters were recognized as those workmen who framed roofs and floors, whilst the joiner was responsible for the doors, windows and so on. In provincial situations the carpenter's work remained limited only to the wood material he worked with. Adam Smith described a country carpenter as one who 'deals in every sort of work that is made of wood … He is not only a carpenter, but a joiner, a cabinet-maker and even a carver in wood, as well as a wheelwright, ploughwright and a cart and waggon maker' (Book I, 3, p.20, 1776). Therefore in rural situations, beyond guild control, the role of the carpenter was much more varied than might be assumed.

Alford, B. and Barker, T. (1968), *A History of the Carpenters' Company*, London: Allen and Unwin.
Higenbotham, S. (1939), *Amalgamated Society of Woodworkers, Our Society's History*, Sussex University.
Jupp, E. B. (1887), *An Historical Account of the Worshipful Company of Carpenters of the City of London*, London: Pickering and Chatto.
Pinto, E. H. (1964), *The Origins and History of the Worshipful Company of Furniture-makers*, The Company: Robertsbridge.
Rose, Walter (1937), *The Village Carpenter*, reprint 1987, Cambridge: Cambridge University Press.

Carpet (Saddle bags)

In the 19th century carpets were used as upholstery cloth. They included authentic hand-woven Oriental rugs as well as machine-made carpets. The latter category included velvet, Brussels, tapestry-Brussels, Wilton and Axminster weaves. The velvet, tapestry and Brussels have a printed pile warp, invented in the 1830s, whereby the pattern was printed on elongated yarns and when made up created the design, with velvet being cut and tapestry-Brussels uncut. Brussels and Wilton weaves had pile warps of dyed yarns that were carried along the length of the cloth underneath the carpet, when not required for the design. This made for a material stiffer than the velvet types. Axminster carpeting used pre-dyed yarns that were prepared on spools or reels. They could be made wider than the standard 69 cm (27 in) and were used more for flooring than upholstery, although upholstery examples have been recorded. Used from the 1850s, carpet remained a popular choice for inexpensive suites and folding chairs until the end of the century. Carpet upholstery was revived in the later 20th century as 'Kelim' (rug) upholstery.

Carton pierre

See Papier mâché

Cartridge paper

See Paper

Carver

A craftsperson who embellished furniture and furnishings (amongst other woodwork) using a wide range of tools and techniques. Since at least the Middle Ages the wood carver was a co-worker alongside the joiner and then the cabinet-maker. As in many examples of craft divisions, the distinctions between job descriptions were a continual cause for concern. In a judgement of 1632 regarding a dispute between joiners and carpenters, the question of carving was also dealt with. The London Court of Aldermen defined carving as joiners' work (item 19, Jupp, 1887, pp.295–9, l.10, ref.: Symonds 1937) 'all carved workes either raised or cutt through or sunck in with the Grounde taken out being wrought and cutt with carving tooles without the use of plaines, (this should be under the province of joiners)'. By the end of the 17th century, a specialized division of labour had occurred within the carving craft. When designs for cane chairs called for carved work 'many carvers took apprentices, and brought them up for carving of cane

Beard, G. (1985), 'Some English woodcarvers', in *Burlington Magazine*, CXXVII, October, pp.686–94.
Davidson, E. (1978), *The Simpsons of Kendal, Craftsmen in Wood 1885–1952*, Lancaster: University of Lancaster.
Heckscher, M. (1969), 'Gideon Saint: An 18th century carver and his scrap-book', in *The Metropolitan Museum of Art Bulletin*, 27, pp.299–311.
Mayhew, H. (1850), Letter LXIV in *Morning Chronicle*, 8 August.
Symonds, R. W. (1950), 'Craft of the carver and gilder', in *Antiques Review*, December, pp.13–20.

18 Late-16th-century plank-construction English oak chest. The chip carving is comparatively crude, but effective.

chair, stools, couches, and squabs only' (cited in Symonds, 1937, *English Cane Chairs*).

By the 18th century the craftsman often combined the joint roles of carver and gilder not only because of the connections between the two crafts, but also to enjoy some continuity in employment due to the vagaries of taste. According to Collyer, the carver in the mid 18th century

requires much ingenuity, a lively and elegant fancy, skills in drawing, with great neatness foliages, fruit, flowers, birds, heads, &c. a good eye, and a steady hand. The Frame being prepared is sent to the carver who finishes it in two different manners as the work requires: either carving in the wood entirely, and afterwards causing the work to be gilt, or cutting the figures first roughly in the wood; after which the whole is covered with several coats of whiting to a considerable thickness; which when dry, the carver wets with a brush and finishes the figures by making such strokes and embellishments on the whiting as is agreeable to his pattern.
(1761, p.150)

The specialization in parts of the carving craft continued, so that in mid-18th-century London a trade existed for carved mirror and picture frames (see Looking-glass maker) as well as for carved furniture parts such as posts, testers and chair frames. In 1803 Sheraton could still talk of four classes of carver which included architectural work, internal decoration in furnishings (including pier glasses, cornices for windows and beds), chair work and ship work. However, the carving trade collapsed due to changes in taste in the early 19th century. T. Martin noted that

There are only eleven master carvers in London, and about sixty journeymen (though at one time there were six hundred). Many of the latter are now very old. They make no show of their work and live only in private houses. Carving in wood has long been in the background as a branch of the arts.
(1819, p.159)

Hardwood carving for furniture was revived in the 1830s, as fashion dictated, but softwood work was never to be important again in furniture due to COMPOSITION materials taking over. The large volume of ecclesiastical work as well as changes in styles generally created a demand for skilled wood carvers. The divisions between cabinet and chair carving were revived, with cabinet work being the province of the more accomplished carvers, so by 1851 the English census recorded 1241 carvers and 4930 carver/gilders. Even with the development of CARVING MACHINES, there was still a need for carving masters and finishers into the early 20th century.
See also Chair carver

Carver's bench screw
See Bench screw

Carver's clip
A removable screw-threaded turn-button with serrated and clawed edges. They were screwed to the bench to hold down work in progress.

Carver's tools
See Bench screw, Carver's clip, Chisel, Cramp, Mallet, Planes, Punches, Riffler

Carving
As one of the most important decorative elements of furniture throughout many periods and locations, furniture carving has ranged from the most elementary scratch marks through to full-scale sculptural work. Carving methods varied widely (see below), so that only simple tools were required for basic jobs (for example, gouges and chisels), whilst more complicated work required a range of other chisel types, rasps and punches. Specialist tools included the carver's BENCH SCREW, designed to hold wood blocks secure with free access; the CARVER'S CLIP which, when used in pairs, secured work on a bench; a wider range of carving CHISELS (over 1000 variations); a carver's CRAMP; a selection of chip-carving knives; a carver's MALLET, a router PLANE for the flat recessed parts of work; a range of carvers' PUNCHES (with a variety of designs on their ends), and the riffler (a double-ended file used for smoothing curved parts). The various types of carving are as follows:

Chip (knife chip)
An unsophisticated method of decorating flat surfaces. The wooden panels were marked out with a compass point and a scribe. The de-

19 English carved and gilded mahogany and pine console table, with gesso top, c.1746. The rococo style demanded highly skilled carving.

to stand out in relief. Alternatively, the level surface could be left with the compressed material standing out as a different shade.

Imitation

The desire and need to imitate hand carving resulted in a range of processes and materials developed since the 18th century. These include moulding materials, mechanical processes, turning or 'machine' carving (see Carving machines below). The demand for carved furniture and interior woodwork increased in the 19th century, so that these processes became a necessity. In addressing this matter the *Practical Magazine* discussed substitutes for wood-carving and concluded that imitation and real carving could exist side by side. Discussing the BOIS REPOUSSE carving, they said: 'In truth hand work, from its costliness, never can obtain a general demand and from that very circumstance it is evident that this discovery opens a new chapter in the history of taste as applied to the ornament of dwellings without interfering with the venerable art of the artificer in wood' (vol.6, 1876, p.108). But they also warned of poor quality reproductions: 'the popularisation of art, which has been characteristic of society during the last thirty years has induced many attempts to imitate the sculptured handwork of the artificer … but public taste and the voice of authority has condemned them on the grounds of their unreal nature' (loc.cit.).

See also Bois repoussé, Bois durci, Burned-wood carving, Compositions, Wood substitutes, Steel carving, below

In the round

A carving process that produces free-standing items that can be applied to furniture. These range from simple finials and table legs to full sculptural works. The process involves rough shaping or bosting before gradually finer profiling. Originally the carver had to tackle a block of wood as a stone carver might, but by the early 16th century carvers were working in cooperation with the joiner or cabinet-maker. The joiner made up blocks of timber with the grain running up and down to ease the carving process.

Low relief

A carving used for detail work (possibly with a stippled or pricked background) with only a slight projection from the surface. It was a low-relief carving process using geometrical patterns on horizontal surfaces which was popular in the late 16th and early 17th centuries.

Pierced

A method of carving in which the work is cut through in some parts (pierced) and left closed in other parts. This method has been used on a wide range of furniture including highboy pediments, dining-chair backs, and easy chairs and sofas. In order to ensure some dimensional stability, there was often a need to provide extra support by preparing the timber to be worked into LAMINATIONS. This enabled the carver to pierce the work without fear of breakout. Some of the most extraordinary examples are found on the work of 19th-century furniture-maker Henry Belter.

Reeding and fluting

Carving with a half-round tool that produces a gouged effect either raised or incised.

See also Machines, Mouldings

Scratch (incised)

Carving made by incised shallow cuts into the timber, producing linear grooves on the plain surface to create a drawn look. It has no depth or illusion of depth. Mainly used on carpenters' boarded work and country-made cabinet-work up to the 18th century.

sign was then chipped with a sharp knife from two differing angles to the same point, to produce triangular cavities or inverted pyramids. Chip carving was particularly used between the 13th and 15th centuries, but persisted in some areas beyond this period. More recently, special sets of knifes with skewed or straight blades for cutting the patterns associated with chip carving have been made.

Gouge

A form of carved ornament in a regular pattern, produced by gouging out shallow depressions so that a pattern then stands in relief. Particularly used on cupboards, chests, beds and the like in the late 16th and 17th centuries. The background is often punched to produce a matt surface in contrast with the polished raised design.

High relief

This form of carving, based on the undercutting of timber, is usually considered to be of the best quality as it combines a degree of artistic as well as manual skill. The motifs are carved so that they stand proud, either completely separately or as part of a panel.

Hydrographic

Hydrographic carving was invented by Cowan and Stuart of Liverpool in the 1880s. It involved pressing cut dies into wood to a predetermined depth. The surface was then planed level. After that, the material was 'relaxed' by water or steam and this enabled the pattern

Steel carving

A process of imitation carving produced by steel dies that were impressed into the wood, which had been roughly shaped already, under pressure into the end grain. In 1870 the Ornamental Wood Company of Bridgeport, Conn., USA, had nearly 300 designs in rosewood, mahogany, black walnut, oak or ash. It appears to have been a successful product since it was recorded that a large manufacturer in the USA was using as many as 10 to 12,000 pieces per month (Bitmead, 1873, p.66).

See also Embossing

Strap

See Low relief, above

Sunk

See Gouge, above

Beecroft, E. (1976), *Carving Techniques*, London: Batsford.
Bemrose, W. (1862), *Manual of Woodcarving*, London and Oxford: J. H. Parker and Sons.
Hasluck, Paul (1910), *Wood carving, Comprising Practical Instructions, Examples and Designs Including 1146 Working Drawings and Photographic Illustrations*, London: Cassell.
Jack, G. (1903), *Wood Carving Design and Workmanship*, London: Hogg.
Miller, F. (ed.) (1884), *Wood Carving Practically, Theoretically and Historically Considered with Notes on Design as Applied to Carved Wood*, London: Wyman.
Oughton, F. (1976), *History and Practice of Woodcarving*, London: Stobart.

Carving machines

These mechanical devices were something of a cross between a lathe, a drill and a pantograph, devised to replicate carved work. Most machines were designed to bost out the work and the result often needed hand finishing. Although developed in the late 18th century, it was not until the mid 19th century that they really became important in the business of wood-carving. By which time the machine's products were being used by architects, builders, decorators, upholsterers, shipbuilders, pianoforte manufacturers, cabinet and frame makers and others. A distinction must be drawn between machine-carving proper and other machines that produce mouldings or relief-type 'carving'. This distinction is important because full machine-carving is a different process from moulding or routing designs into wood. Essentially, full machine-carving is a process of copying an original in which the workpiece or the cutters moved, whereas moulding is basically a mechanized use of the planing principle using a variety of shaped cutters, either on their own or combined with fret-cutting and routing. The results and applications of these two processes are quite different: one being a substitute for the hand-carving process of bosting, and the other being a decorative shaping process.

The major development of the carving machine had to wait for the machine-tool industry to expand so that it was possible to produce quantities of machines at reasonable prices. It was the application of the steam engine that enabled the first efficient combination of machines of varying descriptions to be applied to a production process associated with turning woodwork. The most important example of this was the block-making machinery devised by Brunel and employed by the Royal Navy in the Portsmouth Dockyards from the early part of the 19th century. Although this particular arrangement was exclusive due to the size and cost of the project, it does have a place in this history. The block-making did not include in its processes carving in a decorative sense, but the cutting and shaping of intricate designs to a standard pattern was indicative of a trend towards using machines to manipulate wood in traditional woodworking situations.

One of the first machines to achieve true carving as its object was invented by James Watt. In fact he developed two machines: the Eidograph in 1809 and the Diminishing machine in 1811. Further attempts to produce successful carving machines continued, and in 1822 John Buckle of Mark Lane, a merchant in the City of London, obtained the patent rights to a carving machine invented by J. P. Boyd of Boston (Pat.no.4652). Buckle's machine operated on the idea that a model was inserted into the machine and copies would be cut from blocks set in parallel with the original model. However, he gives no details of its application to making furniture parts and it would appear that this machine carried out a multiple turning operation rather than being a proper carving machine.

Another attempt was made in the patent taken out by Joseph Gibbs in November 1829 (Pat.no.5871). Gibbs's patent machine was based on the idea of having the model to be copied set on a platform with the tracer; below it, on another platform, the drill acted onto the copy block. Interest in mechanical carving, especially in relation to sculpture, was continued by Cheverton, who developed a machine that could be used to produce copies of sculpted works. This machine was based on the pantograph principle and had the ability to enlarge or reduce the original. Although the machine was essentially like Watt's version, Cheverton was able to patent his machine in 1844.

The first patent taken out, that directly relates to machine carving in its specification title, is William Irving's patent of 1843 (Pat.no.9962). This patent, with the title of 'Machinery and apparatus for cutting or carving substances to be applied for inlaying and for other purposes', was important in the early history of machine carving as it was the first to replicate a proper carving operation. It was also important because it was the basis of the well-known Jordan machine improvements. Jordan's invention which was patented in 1845 as a 'machine

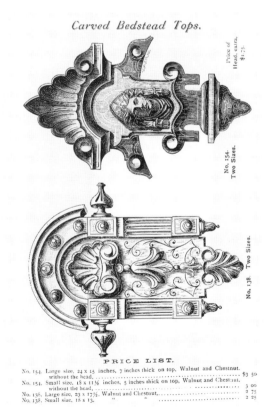

Carved Bedstead Tops.

Price of Head, extra, $1.75

No. 154. Two Sizes.

No. 138. Two Sizes.

PRICE LIST.

No. 154. Large size, 24 x 15 inches, 7 inches thick on top, Walnut and Chestnut, without the head, ... $3 50
No. 154. Small size, 18 x 11½ inches, 5 inches thick on top, Walnut and Chestnut, without the head, ... 3 00
No. 138. Large size, 23 x 17½, Walnut and Chestnut, ... 2 75
No. 138. Small size, 18 x 13. " " 2 25

21 *Solid-wood bedstead carvings by A. Roda of Rochester, New York, c.1876. In the USA the market for ready-made components developed rapidly due to the lack of skilled labour in relation to the demand.*

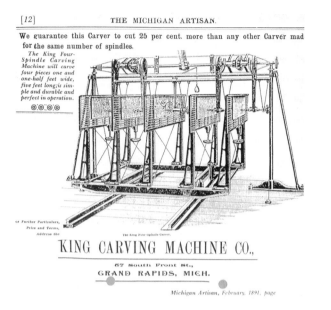

[12]   THE MICHIGAN ARTISAN.

We guarantee this Carver to cut 25 per cent. more than any other Carver mad for the same number of spindles.

The King Four-Spindle Carving Machine will carve four pieces one and one-half feet wide, five feet long; is simple and durable and perfect in operation.

ⓞⓞⓞⓞⓞ

or Further Particulars, Price and Terms, Address the
The King Four-Spindle Carver.

KING CARVING MACHINE CO.,
57 South Front St.,
GRAND RAPIDS, MICH.

Michigan Artisan, February, 1891, page

and apparatus for cutting, carving and engraving' (Pat.no.10,523) was a new departure in machine construction, but (as he admitted) it was not a new invention in its own right. With the arrival of Jordan's machine there were then three distinct methods of producing carving or carved effects competing with each other. The essential difference between Jordan's machine and those of his predecessors was that his machine worked on the principle that the solid material to be carved had movement given to it, whilst the tools remain virtually stationary. This enabled the operator to trace the model to be copied and also to produce two or three copies simultaneously. The main rival machine was Irving's. In this machine the material to be carved was fixed on a table which turned on a centre. The cutting tool was guided by a cast-iron pattern, so that the cutter drilled out the pattern according to its depth and shape. The third competing method was the pyrographical or imitative carving which relied on heated iron moulds to burn away the excess wood and char the surface to the required pattern (see Burned wood-carving process).

Despite some new initiatives, such as Cunningham's patent carving machine, many commentators considered the carving machine unnecessary. Richards wrote of it in the following terms:

As to the history of carving machines thus far, leaving out special cases and taking the results generally, it has been an even race against hand labour, to say the best, and gives no great promise of gain in the future. In this assumption we are guided by the only fact that is reliable in the matter, which is that carving in both England and America, as well as on the continent is mainly done by hand.
(1872, p.44)

As late as 1880 the *Scientific American*, in reporting on the manufacture of parlour furniture, said 'it is found more economical in practice to do a large proportion of the carving by hand, rather than fit up the knives and patterns for the machine for all the new and elaborate designs in carving which are always being introduced' (6 October).

Although it appears that Jordan's patent was known in the United States, it was not until the last twenty-five years of the century that there was a meaningful development of carving machines there. The major development came when bosting or multiple carving machines were developed in the 1870s. In 1889 the *Cabinet Maker* was suggest-

ing that the American-made Moore carving machine was so simple that it could be operated by a boy, and therefore 'no manufacturer who employs carvers and has any quantity of duplicate carvings to make can afford to be without a machine, as it will save its cost in three months' (*Cabinet Maker*, 1889, July, p.25). This machine operated its counterbalanced cutters from the side, thus saving on space and easing operation. The ability to 'carve' by machine was compared with hand labour more than once. An observer of the American industry in 1906 remarked that 'the automatic carving machines supplanted the laborious process of removing by hand superfluous wood preparatory to the final artistic touch of the hand tool, which infuses life into each upturned leaf as guided by the skilled carver' (Goss, 1906, pp.1037–8, cited in Ettema, 1981).

By early 20th century Jordan's principle was re-used for automatic carving machines which could complete eight 61 × 13 cm (24 × 5 in) carved figures in an hour and three quarters, without supervision. His principle still remains for multiple-cutting machines now. In the 1990s ANC routing machines that perform the job of 'carving' as well as machines based on the pantograph principle of bosting out carvings from a template, are also being used in the modern furniture industry. These machines rough out copies of the original, ready for the master carver to finish by hand. These are mostly used for high-quality reproduction furniture for the contract trade.

Allwood, R. (1996), 'Patent Wood Carving Co', in *Furniture History*, XXXII, pp.90–126.
Edwards, C. D. (1998), 'The mechanization of carving, the development of the carving machine especially in relation to the manufacture of furniture and the working of wood', *History of Technology*, vol.20, pp.74–102.
Hughes, G. (1954), 'Mechanical carving machines', *Country Life*, CXVI, 23 September.
Jordan, T. (1847), 'On carving by machinery', in *Transactions of the [Royal] Society of Arts*, supplementary volume, part 3.

Case rods

A metal rod fitted round the top of a bed tester to support protective curtains. They have been used since at least the 17th century.

Casein glues

See Adhesives

Cassimere

A twilled soft woollen cloth of medium weight, patented in England in 1766 by Francis Yerbury (Pat.no.858). Described as a thin superfine cloth, it was woven in plain and fancy types which were widely used for clothing, but it was also employed as a furnishing fabric. In 1808 George Smith suggested that drawing-room draperies should have 'under curtains of muslin or superfine cassimere' (Smith, 1808, p.1). For eating rooms, he went on to say, 'a material of more substance is requisite than for rooms of a lighter cast' and 'for such purposes superfine cloth or cassimeres will ever be the best' (ibid., p.xii).

Cast iron

See Iron

Castors

The idea of a wheeled arrangement to facilitate the movement of furniture was devised prior to 1600. Baby cages were equipped with wheels and early records include castors in Catena's painting of the Holy Family *c.*1520 (cited in Edwards, 1964, p.112), and in a 1582 Perugian inventory there is 'a seat with four wheels' (Thornton, 1991, p.188). It is likely that these early wheels were applied to invalid chairs either to assist self-propulsion or to allow others to move the person easily. Castors were clearly in use in England at the end of the 17th century, as by 1690 there was a distinct castor-making trade in London.

Originally castors were no more than hardwood globular shaped 'wheels' rotating on an axis but they could not swivel. By 1700 vertical spindle pins connected to jaws fitted with axles, meant that the wheel could rotate in every direction. Soon after this, the ball-shaped wooden castors were fitted with metal axles and this was quickly improved upon by using rollers rather than balls. By the 1730s the wooden rollers were superseded by leather wheels, and other wooden parts were gradually replaced by brass. These new models consisted of a quantity of leather discs fitted together between brass horns, the horns themselves being fixed to a hidden plate. Choice was wider by the mid century. For example, Samuel Norman listed 'two-wheeled castors, field-bed castors and unspecified castors' in his inventory of 1760 (Kirkham, 1969, p.508). By the 1770s complete brass castors were available in three styles: (a) a simple plain jaw with a tapered or square socket above and a fixed axle revolving roller below; (b) a plate and peg castor fixed by screws passing through the plate. The wide roller was partly hidden by a canopy to the jaws and the swivel peg was accommodated by a small hole in the wooden frame of the furniture item; (c) friction castors, available with both screw and socket fixing. The distinctive idea of the friction roller was that small wheels fitted between the surfaces of the jaw and the plate helped to reduce friction, thus assisting movement. Sheraton (1803, pp.138–9) lists these varieties and others which included plate castors, square and round socket, claw castors and bed pillar castors. Socket castors provided fertile ground for decoration with a wide range of motifs from lion's paws to tulips. The variety can be seen in early-19th-century pattern books. Many of these were made in iron or brass, but smaller ones were still supplied with boxwood wheels.

The first half of the 19th century was an innovative period for castor design. Between 1811 and 1851 there were twenty-four English patents granted for improvements to castors, and in the nine years between 1867 and 1876 an astonishing sixty-five separate English patents were granted in relation to castors. Design improvements continued with changes to the castor such as extending the arms of the jaw in order to spread the weight more evenly, and supplying screw-in castors with a built-in screw on the plate.

The desideratum of castor designers was to have the movement support directly over the greatest point of weight. This was developed over the 19th century. The ball and socket castor was developed by Thomas Sturgeon in 1811 (Pat.no.3406). This design took the form of a solid ball mounted in an inverted cup, with a screw-on lower section which was partly open to allow the ball inside to swivel in all directions. The top portion of the ball cup was fixed against rollers to avoid friction between the outer and inner socket. Patents for castors include John Loach's 1812 models with cast-iron frames covered in brass sheet (Pat.no.3548). By 1815, the use of a steel-lined socket base for the brass spindle avoided brass-on-brass friction. The Barron castor (Pat.no. 3976/1816) had a steel base which pressed onto the brass horns (jaws) and again avoided friction to a degree.

From about 1840, and into the second half of the 19th century, brass-mounted, baked-clay wheels or rollers in either brown or white vitrified china, were common. In 1851, Frederick Geithner invented and patented a particular glazed earthenware wheel which was sometimes decorated with hand-coloured designs (Pat.no.13,828). One idiosyncratic idea was to use glass balls for castors. A patent for these was taken out by a Mr Adgate and the castors were manufactured by

23   A triple-wheeled castor with laminated-leather main wheel. Mounted on a commode, c.1770.

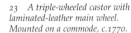

24   A triple-wheeled brass-friction castor, c.1771, fitted to a commode supplied to Harewood House by Thomas Chippendale.

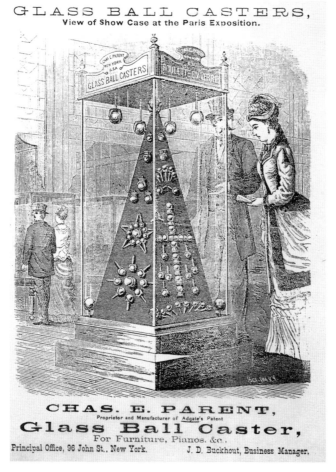

GLASS BALL CASTERS,
View of Show Case at the Paris Exposition.

CHAS. E. PARENT,
Proprietor and Manufacturer of Adgate's Patent
Glass Ball Caster,
For Furniture, Pianos, &c.
Principal Office, 96 John St., New York.   J. D. Buckhout, Business Manager.

Charles Parent of New York. Strangely, these were first designed to protect the occupier of a chair from lightning strikes. Later these glass castors were used on exotic horn chairs, and the Tiffany Studios incorporated glass-ball castors in some of their chair designs.

In the 20th century castors became sophisticated items, often incorporating ball-bearings with a circular casing (Orbit or Shepherd types), rollers with plastic wheels, 'slipper' designs incorporating a glide and swivel, versions with wheels that act independently of each other and even self-braking castors.

Catalpa (*Catalpa speciosa*)
An American timber with an average density of 400 (24 lb/cu ft) which resembles BUTTERNUT. Greyish-brown, sometimes with a pale blue-lavender tinge, it is a light and moderately weak wood but works easily and has been occasionally used in cabinet work during the 20th century.

Cativo (*Prioria copaifera*)
A Central American timber, medium to light brown streaked, with a fine texture and a straight grain.

Cat's-tail
Although the word has referred to a fur for the neck, it also refers to reedy marsh plants with brown furry spikes that resemble a cat's tail.

Cat's-tail grass has at various times been used as an upholstery filling. These fillings were referred to in England as early as 1474 (in conjunction with thistle down) as an inferior and unsatisfactory material: 'feather beds and bolster stuffed with thistle down and cats tails … [have] been deceivably made to the hurt of the Kings liege people' (cited in Houston, 1993, p.5). Over three hundred years later, in 1803, Richard Wevill's inventory of his Philadelphia upholstery business still included 'a small cattial mattrass' valued at $2.50 and 'a lot of cat-tail' valued at $1.0 (P. C. O'Donnell, 'Richard Wevill, Upholsterer', in E. S. Cooke (ed.), *Upholstery in America and Europe from 17th century to WWI*, 1987, p.117).
See also Grasses (Reed-mace)

Caul
A term derived from the idea of a membrane. In furniture-making it is a mould that is heated, greased and applied to glued-up veneer and ground work, in order to weight it down and assist the adhering process, sometimes on both sides at once. Cauls are held by screw pressure and can be curved or flat, or even specially shaped for a particular part of a job. In the early 19th century they were made from wainscot or deal. Sheraton explains that 'sometimes thin wainscot is used for cauls, and by heat made to bend to a crooked surface' (1803, p.140). In the case of card-table cauls, they were of 2.5 cm (1 in) deal banded with wainscot to ensure stability and flatness, but Sheraton expressed doubts about the efficacy of this method. Cauls were also made from ZINC sheet and cast iron. In the cabinet-making workshop of George Bullock there was 'a large cast iron plate with iron screws and two stoves for drying and laying veneers, faced with lead' (Levy, 1989, p.182). There were also fifteen caul screws and mahogany beds in the same workshop (ibid., p.201). Zinc cauls were still used in commercial workshops well into the 1950s.
See also Veneering

Cavity foam
See Latex

Caviuna (*Machaerium spp.*)
A South American (Bolivian and Brazilian) timber, brown to dark purple-brown, often streaked, being hard and heavy with a variable texture and grain. It has been used in the 20th century as ROSEWOOD and is considered a rosewood variety. Aka Jacaranda.

Cedar (*Cedrus spp.*)
True cedar is botanically a softwood of which there are a number of varieties including Lebanon cedar (*Cedrus libani*) sourced in the Middle East, *Cedrus atlantica* found in North Africa, and deodar (*Cedrus deodara*) from the Indian sub-continent (especially Afghanistan). Cedar has an average density of 570 (35 lb/cu ft) and is an aromatic yellowish-brown wood which grows to a large size, thus providing extensive planks. It has a medium to fine texture, a clearly marked grain and gives a fine finish. The name Cedar also refers to varieties of Cupressus (Port Orford cedar, yellow cedar); Juniperus (Pencil cedar, African cedar); Cedrela (Central American cedar); Australian Cedar and Thuja (Western red cedar).

Known and used by the Ancient Egyptians as a furniture-making wood, it had problems with a rough grain and a tendency to shrink in seasoning, but was considered preferable to indigenous woods. The Lebanon cedar was widely imported into Egypt for building and furniture-making; for example, Tutankhamun's tomb held a cedar chair. In 16th-century England cedar was imported from Italy, especially for making up into chests as it was widely believed that the scent from the timber would repel worm and moth. In the second half of the 17th century chests of drawers made of cedar were widely popular for similar reasons. In 1793 the *Cabinet-maker's London Book of Prices* specifically charged extra for clothes-shelves and drawers made from cedar (p.264). Although previously much used for heavy construction and outdoor furniture, in the later 20th century cedar has been used for furniture-backs in the cabinet trade.

African pencil cedar (*Juniperus procera*)
This was used in East African furniture-making and has been used in England for the linings of furniture, especially wardrobes.

Bermuda cedar (*Cedrela odorata*)
A Central American timber of a reddish-brown colour, with a uniform texture and usually a straight grain. Used locally for construction work and furniture-making, it was also exported to England and America. In 17th-century England it was used for ceiling construction and wall panelling. John Evelyn mentions cedars as an ideal wood: 'I cannot but suggest that our more wealthy citizens of London, every-day building and embellishing their dwellings, might be encouraged to make use of it [cedar] in their shops at least for shelves, counters, chests, tables and wainscot, &c' (1662, p.148).

Eastern red cedar (*Juniperus virginiana*)
An American variety, also called pencil cedar. It has a strong aroma and a reddish-tan colour with a fine texture and a straight grain. Thomas Harriot (1587) wrote about the benefits of exporting cedar:

A very sweet wood, and fine timber, whereof if nests of chests be there made, or timber thereof fitted for sweet and fine bedsteads, tables, desks, lutes, virginals, and many things else (of which there has been proof made already) to make up freight with the principal commodities, will yield profit.
(Hakluyt, 1589, p.51)

In 1682 Carolina was apparently 'cloathed with odoriferous and fragrant … Cedar and Cyprus Trees, of … which are composed goodly boxes, chests, Tables, Scritores, and Cabinets … Carolina [cedar] is esteemed equal … for grain, smell and colour … [to] Bermudan Cedar, which of all the West Indian is … the most excellent' (Ashe, 1682, cited in Beckerdite, 1997). In the mid 19th century it was imported into England in 15–25 cm (6–10 in) squares and was used for the inside work of small cabinets. It has been used widely in the USA for bedroom furniture.

Spanish cedar (Havana cedar) (*Cedrela odorata*)
Another variety from the West Indies and parts of Central America (especially Cuba and others). A timber with an average density of 480 (30 lb/cu ft). A member of the mahogany family, so not a true cedar; it has a red to red-brown heartwood with a variable texture and a straight grain. It has been widely used for cigar-boxes, drawer linings, trays and casings. Aka Havana cedar or Cuba wood.

Sheraton described two varieties: One he called the West Indian variety which had an agreeable smell but was only available in small-diameter logs, and the other he called Spanish, with an offensive smell but which was cheap and often 'broad enough to do without jointing', therefore useful for drawer linings, robe trays, boxes and chests (1803, p.141). The Spanish cedar or bastard mahogany was used in the mid 19th century for 'inferior furniture, for the ground framing and panelling of veneered doors, and in carcase work for the gables and insides of sideboards, wardrobes, commodes and chests of drawers' (Blackie, 1853, p.38). This was still the case in the 1920s in the USA, when it was used for drawer bottoms and mirror backs, although much went to making cigar boxes. Modern uses for these 'cedars' are in plywood and furniture-making.

Celluloid
See Plastics (Cellulose nitrate)

Cellulose
(a) A chemical compound that occurs in the cell walls of plants. Cellulose acetate was dissolved in acetone and used as dope in World War I for coating plane wings and so on. The material was transferred to polishing technology and became the basis for cellulose LACQUER.

(b) Viscose, made by treating cellulose with strong alkali and carbon disulphide was widely used to make 'rayon' for furnishing fabrics in the 20th century.

Worden, E. C. (1911), *The Nitrocellulose Industry*, New York: Van Nostrand.

Cement
See Stopping

Centripetal springs
See Springs

Ceramic plaques, inlays and tiles
The taste for porcelain inserts as decoration on cabinets was developed in France in the second and third quarters of the 18th century. The use of Sèvres porcelain tops fitted to small tables as well as plaques painted in floral designs in Louis XVI furniture met a demand for colour, practicality and status. Dealers such as Poirier and Daguerre made a speciality of supplying this form of decorated furniture which was often made by superb craftsmen such as Adam Weisweiler, Martin Carlin and Bernard van Risenburgh II. The designs and quantity of ceramic work that was applied varied enormously, and in some cases whole table tops would be mounted with porcelain panels. The famous ceramic-topped Table of the Grand Commanders (1806–12), made for Napoleon, was ingeniously mounted on a ceramic pillar with the weight being held by metal plinth and rod support.

In England Josiah Wedgwood also promoted plaques for insertion into small cabinets. Sheraton noted their use: 'In the freeze [sic] part of the commode is a tablet in the center [sic], made of exquisite composition in imitation of statuary marble. These are to be had, of any figure or on any subject at Mr Wedgewood's [sic] near Soho square.

26 Wedgwood ceramic inlays on a neo-classical revival commode, c.1880. These sorts of inlays were especially popular in the later 19th century.

27 Detail of ceramic inlay.

by makers such as Alexander Roux, who used porcelain plaques to decorate his cabinets. Designed to be fitted to ebonized carcases, they were also intended to harmonize with THUYA, AMBOYNA or SATIN-WOOD, often combined with ORMOLU mouldings. However, it was the incorporation of ceramic tiles, rather than porcelain plaques that found a popular fashion in the latter half of the 19th century.

In 1867 Bruce Talbert designed a sideboard with polychrome enamel plaques and in the 1870s a taste for tiles was urged, both by Eastlake and Talbert. In the United States, the Herter Bros made bedroom suites in the 'Art furniture' tradition which used tiles with Japanese-influenced designs on them, whilst the firm of Kimbel and Cabus used tiles in a similar way to Talbert. The *London Cabinet-makers' Guide* referred to plaques as being a comparatively recent introduction, 'and their use might be very usefully extended' (Bitmead, 1873, p.66). Bitmead commented favourably on both porcelain plaques and art tiles, and said 'there is no reason why they may not be made instructive as well as artistic' (loc.cit.). Art furniture incorporating tiles by such designers as Burges and Bevan soon became the basis for a popular taste, so that the middle-market manufacturers incorporated tiles into hall chairs, stands and jardinières as well as bedroom wash stands, sideboards, flower boxes and the like. According to Bitmead these were often of 'a richness and artistic expression rivalling that of oil-painting, and quite as effective and much more durable' (1873, p.66). From the 1880s onward, tiles were also used in combination with BAMBOO for the developing mass market. The art furniture taste continued, and was met by such firms as Liberty and Co, who incorporated tiles by De Morgan in the 1890s.

A renewal of demand for tiles in furniture occurred in the 1960s and 1970s, when they were incorporated into coffee tables, dining tables and worktops. Recent demand for reproduction Victorian designs have revived the use of tiles in this style of furniture as well.

Kelly, A. (1965), *Decorative Wedgwood in Architecture and Furniture*, London: Country Life.
Lemmen, H. van (1989), *Tiled Furniture*, Aylesbury: Shire Album.

Certosina

A decorative INLAY process that has Arabic origins, that since the 9th century seems to have been transferred to Spain and Sicily. It was fashionable in 15th-century Italy, especially in Lombardy and Venice. The inlay used polygonally-shaped tesserae of wood, bone, metal and mother-of-pearl in geometric patterns.

Ceylon mahogany
See Jackwood

Chaff
See Straw

Chair carver

A specialist sub-contracting craftsman who produced any carved furniture (other than picture frames) for other craftsmen. They developed as a specialism from the later 17th century and remained important through the first half of the 18th century. *The London Tradesmen* described how

the cabinet-makers and upholsterers employ a species of carvers, peculiar to themselves; who are employed in carving chairs, posts and testers of beds, or any other furniture whereon carving is used. Their work is slight and requires no great ingenuity to perform it; I mean he needs no elegant taste in the general art of carving who performs that used at present upon furniture. (Campbell, 1747, p.172)

They are let into the wood, and project a little forward' (1793, pp.444–5). The initial black basalt bas-relief cameos soon gave way to the famous Jasper-ware. These were then used to decorate chairs, cabinets, secretaires and the like by such firms as Gillows, Ince and Mayhew and Seddon. Robert Adam's integrated interiors seemed to naturally require matching items of furniture with appropriate porcelain inserts, and Sheraton promoted them as well. It was not only English makers who used Wedgwood's wares. The French maker Weisweiler used their plaques and, in some high-quality Spanish commodes, Wedgwood or Buen Retiro porcelain inlays were used.

The taste for porcelain plaques in furniture continued into the 19th century, especially for exhibition pieces. For example, Worcester porcelain inserts in chairs were displayed at the Great Exhibition in 1851, whilst in 1855 Jackson and Graham displayed a cabinet with Minton plaques, and in 1867 Wright and Mansfield showed a cabinet with green jasper-ware Wedgwood plaques. In the mid 19th century the French taste returned to a revival of porcelain inserts, particularly in *meubles d'appui* which were made with lavish bronze mounts and exotic timbers to combine with the porcelain, creating a very rich effect. In the 1870s bas-reliefs in stoneware, in imitation of the *gris de Flandres* by Doulton, were used in panels set in frames, rather than inlaid. Bitmead noted that porcelain plaques also 'form at the present time a favourite decoration for ebonised (or ebonised and gilt) furniture and are made of Wedgwood and Sèvres china. The designs are generally emblematical. Panels display similar treatment, with highly coloured figures on gold grounds' (Bitmead, 1873, p.66).

This fashion was also adopted in the United States in the 1860s

The carvers once specialized in the carving of cane-seated chairs and stools during the periods of popularity in the late 17th and early 18th centuries. Chairs remained the staple work for the hardwood carver during the first half of the 18th century, with the combination of fine mahogany and a vibrant rococo style, but this taste died with the onslaught of neo-Classicism. During the mid 19th century, the revival of a range of styles, especially the Gothic, meant that hardwood carving once again became prominent. Until the 19th century, the chair carver had been responsible for all hardwood carving, both on chairs and cabinets, but from the 1830s distinctions between cabinet and chair work became evident. The chair carver remained less skilled than the 'revived' cabinet carver.

See also Cane chair-maker, Carver

Chair frames

A term that generally refers to the wood or metal frames, or the skeleton of an upholstered item including 'show-wood', or the exposed parts on a plain or side chair. The frames may be variously described, including open, upholstered, iron back, show-wood, KD, sprung edge, stuffover, drop-in seat, folding, rocking and reclining.

METAL FRAMES

Amongst the earliest metal chair frames were Etruscan types made from BRONZE. The Romans also used bronze and iron for frames. Various IRON frames were also used for special chairs in the Middle Ages, but iron frames for upholstered chairs were only developed in France in the early 19th century. In the 1830s the construction of a *bergère en gondole* used an iron frame to give a shaped contour to the back. It was then completely upholstered, and the only evidence of the iron frame was the slight give when the chair was used. The use of iron frames continued throughout the century and were still illustrated in text books into the 20th century. The base frame was wood, but 3.75 cm (1.5 in) iron rods were forged to the required arm and back shape, fixed to the frame and then built upon as normal upholstery work. A little later STEEL spring wires were attached, one by one, and bent into a form and bound together to secure into a shape. All these effects need deep-buttoned upholstery skills to complete them, and were called Turkish wire backs.

Exposed iron frames were yet another matter in the design and manufacture of upholstery. The Birmingham firm of Peyton and Peyton, leaders in the manufacture of brass and iron beds, exploited the patent of Angelo Sedley (Pat.no.2742, 1860). This patent used a metal rack and pin mechanism to allow the user of their chairs to adjust the rake of the back of the chair from upright to fully reclining. The more sophisticated Equilibrium couch, with an iron frame, japanned bronzed or made in brass, was partially demountable as well as having a reclining backrest. These and other versions of folding metal chairs were popular for many years. Their light weight, their portability when folded, and their relative cheapness led to a long life. The most popular image of these was in the use by invalids, and in many cases they became known as invalids' chairs.

With the development of metal tubing in the 20th century, ALUMINIUM, STEEL tube and rod were included in the repertoire of the upholsterer. In conjunction with metal frames in the late 1940s, the hammock principle used in upholstery based on aircraft seating, was further developed. This design was again taken up in the 1960s and early 1970s, when there was a fashion for chairs made from chromed tubular steel fitted with hammock supports and cushions.

Another example from post World War II was the manufacture of upholstery frames made from cut or rolled sheet steel. Although

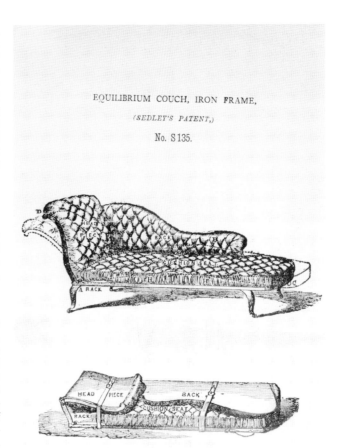

28 An iron-framed 'Equilibrium' folding couch based on Sedley's patent, c.1860.

29 A welded-steel chair frame based on the strap versions of the later 19th century, c.1955, English. Note the rubberized hair which was particularly suitable for upholstering these shaped chairs.

30 *Chair frame of rolled steel, c.1955, English. Used in place of wood, but the design is based on traditional shapes and takes no account of the material's special capabilities.*

introduced to save timber, they used the same shaped designs as pre-war wooden models. Metal frames using steel, rods, aluminium extrusions and so on were also utilized for lightweight organic shapes as well as to re-interpret traditional models.

PLASTIC FRAMES

Although there were sporadic developments in the use of PLASTICS as chair frames, it was only with advances in technology and design strategies during the 1960s, that chairs were produced which incorporated frame, structure and seating in one item. The plastics revolution that allowed this was responsible for an incredible range of very varied objects, including the Sacco chair of high-resistance foamed polystyrene balls, the Blow chair in inflatable PVC, the Pratone of integral foamed polyurethane foam, or even the Up chair, made from polyurethane foam, vacuum-packed in a box which 'came to life' in your living room as it was unpacked. However, it is important to remember that these fashion chairs did not generally make inroads into the essentially conservative world of domestic upholstery. The developments that affected mainstream manufacture were plastic SHELLS and components. Chair shells were made from plastics that were moulded from GRP (see GLASS), expanded POLYSTYRENE or moulded urethane foams. These could be produced on a large scale by specialist manufacturers, but upholsterers still put on the fillings and top fabrics. Important innovations in plastic components during the later 20th century include pre-formed plastic arms, wings and leg sections and even complete plastic frames for 'traditional style' chairs. See also Plastics

WOODEN FRAMES

The traditional method of upholstery-frame making often relied on a separate craft of frame-makers. These craftsmen built wooden frames to a specification and then delivered them to upholstery workshops. These were usually a framework for the fixing of suspensions and coverings, and in many cases were completely hidden after up-

holstering. At various times fashion created 'show-wood' upholstery, which called for exposure of the frame. This varied from a hint, such as an arm knuckle, to a fully polished show-wood frame with loose seat and back cushions, which demanded considerable woodworking skills.
See also Chair-makers, Chair-making

OTHER FRAMES

Chair frames have been made from PARTICLE BOARD, HARDBOARD and many combinations of these and other materials. Cheap furniture frames of the later 20th century are likely to include these sheet materials, as well as plastic and KD components.

Chair-makers and **Chair frame-makers**

Chairs have been made by a variety of makers including JOINERS, TURNERS, COFFERERS and basket-makers, as well as specialist chair-makers. The techniques of woodworking are completely different from upholstery, so this necessitated the division of labour in chair-making from an early stage. The demarcation disputes that established the independence of the turners, carvers and joiners must have meant that, at some time around the end of the 17th century, a designation of chair-maker was coined. It does not appear to be a co-incidence that the title of chair-maker gained currency around the time of the popularity of caned, turned and carved chairs in the 1670s onward. Demarcation of trades was a problem in this period. The combination of joinery and turning skills required to make these chairs is demonstrated in the example of Thomas Stapleford of Boston, Mass. In 1684 he is referred to as a chair-maker. By 1695 he is regarded as a chair frame-maker and in 1717 he is supplying joined cabinet work.

In England, Francis Croxford is described in the *Daily Post, c.*1730, as a chair- and cabinet-maker whose stock included about one hundred dozens of varying chairs. By 1747 CANE CHAIR-MAKERS had moved into making other chair types as well, no doubt as an economic necessity. The specialization of the trade is further recorded: 'though this Sort of Household Goods [chairs] is generally sold at the Shops of the Cabinetmakers for all the better kinds, and at the Turners for the more common, yet there are particular makers for each' (Anon., *A General Description of All Trades*, 1748). This trend continued. Sheraton recorded that

chair-making is a branch generally confined to itself; as those who professedly work at it, seldom engage in making cabinet furniture. In the country manufactories it is otherwise; yet even these pay some regard to keeping their workmen constantly at the chair, or to the cabinet work. The two branches seem evidently to require different talents in workmen, in order to become proficient. In the chair branch it requires a particular turn in the handling of shapes to make them agreeable and easy.
(1803, p.145)

By the mid 19th century Mayhew recorded how 'the chairmaker constructs every description of chairs and sofa but only the framework. They had their own society but suffered as trade changed to supply direct to the seller' (*Morning Chronicle*, 1 August 1850). In 20th-century factory-scale production the chair frame shop is usually distinct, and it is common for furniture-makers to buy in frames from specialist suppliers.

Pallot, B. (1989), *The Art of the Chair in Eighteenth Century France*, Paris: ACR-Gismondi.
Symonds, R. W. (1938), 'The chairmaker', in *Connoisseur*, November, pp.234–40.

FAR LEFT
*31 An Egyptian wooden-frame
chair from the 18th dynasty. This
type of chair has established the
type-form that is almost
universally recognized.*

LEFT
*32 An American Windsor chair
showing many of the features
common to the type, including
the hoop back, spindles, dished
seat and pegged or wedged
construction, c.1765–95.*

Chair-making

Although there is any number of designs and patterns for wooden chairs, there are particular procedures and processes that are often the basis of their making. When joiners made chairs, they were working with panelled construction and mortise and tenon joints. This was followed by chairs made particularly by the turner, using turned components to make a variety of sections, which then complete the frame. These usually include back uprights, front legs, seat rails and aprons, stretchers (if used), back and top rails, ladders or splats and the seat. Pinned or pegged mortise and tenon joints or dowelled joints were most common, and the tenoning of the long rails and dowelling of the short rails has been common practice in English chair-making.

Chair-makers also developed particular methods to simplify making or to solve problems. For example, chairs with drop-in seats had frames made with rebates in thin side rails which were combined with a simple wooden corner block or brace. Seats that were designed to be over-upholstered had thicker rails and larger braces to accept the tension of the webbing. Stiles and centre splats were tenoned into top rails but often left loose in the shoe to allow for movement. Armchairs, which required stability, had the arms screwed to seat rails and into back stiles, while stretchers were tenoned into legs.

Although there have been many changes in materials and design, the chair-maker working in wood is still restrained by the limitations of material, ergonomics and appropriate construction.

See also Corner blocks, Chair frames, Shoe piece, Turning

Windsor Chair-making

The development of common stickback chairs was derived from the stool, via the back stool to the comb-back chair to the Windsor chair, all having the same simple jointing techniques based on wedging. The manufacture of these chair types was based on either a factory or craft system.

In England the work of the BODGER was the first stage in the traditional method of making Windsor chairs. The bodger located a stand of timber and established a temporary woodland camp. Once the selected timber had been cut down, it was sawn and the logs were split into billets which were chopped to a rough leg shape with an axe and 'cleaned-up' with a drawing knife. The billets were then put to the pole lathe where the shape was finalized and patterns cut. They were then passed to the chair factory.

The benchman was responsible for preparing the sawn parts of a chair, including the banisters (vertical bars in the chair back), the bow, the splat and the seat. The favoured tool was the frame saw which was more versatile than the open handsaw, as it allowed the blade to be adjusted to any angle. The process of cutting out the decorative main back splat was laborious as it required a hole to be drilled for the particular part of the design, the bow-saw blade being run through, the cut made, and the blade removed. The process had to be done for each cut of the design.

The bottomer provided the sawn seats for the chair-maker. His main tool was the hollowing adze. The seats of elm plank some 5 cm (2 in)

33   The workshop of Jack Goodchild, a chair-maker from Naphill, Bucks., c.1950.

The finisher/stainer cleaned down the made-up chair with nitric acid and then immersed it in a dipping tank with the selected solution for staining the particular chair. Chairs were polished or finished by oiling with linseed oil, some were waxed and others were shellac-polished, and yet others had a full French-polish treatment to produce either a glossy or matt finish.

Caners undertook the seating of the same chairs. This was often done by women or children, sometimes working from home. With a minimum of equipment, the range of caning patterns could be easily learnt and applied as required (see CANING). In many cases individual craft-based chair-makers undertook all the above tasks themselves.

Cotton, B. (1990), *The English Regional Chair*, Woodbridge: Antique Collectors Club.
Crispin, T. (1992), *The English Windsor Chair*, Stroud: Alan Sutton.
Evans, Nancy G. (1979), 'A history and background of English Windsor chairs', in *Furniture History*, XV, pp.24–53.
— (1996), *American Windsor Chairs*, New York: Hudson Hills Press.
Fitzrandolph, H. E. and Hay, M. D. (1977), *Rural Industries of England and Wales*, vol.1, reprint.
Forman, B. (1988), *American Seating Furniture 1630–1730*, New York: Norton.
Jenkins, J. (1972), *The Craft Industries*, London: Longman.
Massingham, H. & J. (1943), *Men of Earth*, London: Chapman and Hall.
Mayes, J. L. (1960), *The History of Chair-making in High Wycombe*, London: Routledge.

Chair mechanisms

For various reasons since early times, chairs have been made to be demountable, collapsible, reclining, convertible into beds, rocking, suspensory, or even trapping. The need for chairs for travel, for space-saving, for multiple functions or even for amusement has meant that a number of mechanical methods have been devised to deal with the demands. These include X frames, scissors shapes, interlaced comb-like joints, patented mechanisms, tip-up and other connecting devices.

Hinges are probably the earliest and simplest form of mechanism. The Ancient Egyptians had folding stools which used a pin pivot, and the later medieval *faldstuhl* was designed with hinges for folding and portability. Mechanisms to make chairs portable have been developed ever since. These are usually self-evident and can be very sophisticated, but often work on a simple principle – for example, the 'colonial chair' with its loose-jointed frame members, strips of canvas or leather with a pivoted backrest.

Multiple function furniture, especially chairs, have been popular for centuries. Evelyn noted a 'conceited chair which folded into so many varieties as to turn into a bed, a bolster, a table, a couch' (*Diary*, 28 November 1644). These sorts of chairs were not necessarily space-saving or even dual-purpose. The ingenuity and amusement value was often important.

The taste for comfort encouraged ideas in adjustable chairs, so that in the 17th century iron STAYS and staples (often silvered or gilded) were used to adjust and recline chair backs on a ratchet. The reclining principle with an enormous number of variations has remained ever since, probably reaching its hey-day in the mid to late 19th century. See also Springs

Edwards, C. (1998), 'Reclining chairs surveyed, health, fashion and comfort in evolving markets', in *Studies in the Decorative Arts*, VI, no.1, pp.32–67.
Harwood, B. (1997), *The Furniture of George Hunzinger*, Brooklyn Museum of Art.

Chalcedony

A hard stone being a fibrous variety of quartz, which comprises stones such as cornelian (bright red to pale yellow) and heliotrope (dark

thick and 45 cm (18 in) square were sawn to outline shape by the bottomer. The adze cuts away unwanted timber to create the distinctive seat shape with a variety of thicknesses ranging from the full 5 cm (2 in) to barely 1 cm (½ in) in parts. The seat as left by the bottomer still needed careful finishing as it was still ridged and furrowed with cutting marks.

The bender supplied the chair-maker with bent bows made from sawn ash for common work and cleft yew for better-quality products. The selected parts were roughly squared with a drawing knife and then steamed or boiled until they were pliable. The use of a bending mould to shape the steamed timbers was required for every pattern of bow. Some makers used pre-drilled steel plates or wooden blocks so that a variety of shapes could be pegged out rather than creating a new mould for each model.

The framer, the actual chair-maker, prepared the rough parts sent in by the above workmen: he bored seats for legs and bored legs for stretchers; cut mortise and tenons for other joints and wedges; glued the chair up if necessary. He also finished it with a shave and scraper. The framer used a specially devised block, which was a low bench with three dowels let in to the bench-top. With the help of a wedge, chair legs could be held tight in this arrangement for boring. Variations on the arrangement of the block would include tool holders, notches for trimming round timbers, and a hollowed grease box for greasing the bits and saws. He traditionally used an extensive tool kit including the breast bib and its associated brace, spoon shaped bits, spokeshaves, scrapers, as well as other standard woodworking tools.

34 An advertisement for Minter's Archimedean screw reclining chair, c.1845. One of many patented reclining mechanisms popular throughout the 19th century.

green with red flecks). Oriental chalcedony with its milky transparency was very rare but was used in Antiquity and the Renaissance for hard-stone inlays, in particular for Florentine work. Chalcedony sometimes was given a silver backing to create a particular luminescence.

Chalons

An upholstery textile related to DORNIX. It is a medieval and Renaissance term (celone) for a tapestry and a bed cover. Double chalons were woven full width, doubled over and then quilted through and used for beds. Chaucer in 'The Reves Tale' writes:

and in his own chamber hem made a bed
With shetes and with chalons fair y-spread.
(*Canterbury Tales*, c.1387, lines 4139–40)

Chamfer

The method of shaving an exposed edge of a frame so that it will not be so liable to splitting and scratching in use. It was often made into a decorative feature, and is something of a hall-mark for 19th-century Gothic revival woodwork as it clearly revealed constructed decoration. A cornering tool took off the sharp edge or ARRIS to leave a level flat edge to a timber section. Chamfers are produced with DRAWING KNIVES, ROUTERS or SHAVES. Chamfers may be plain, concave, convex or moulded.

Changeable

An early term for tabby-weave textiles with warps and wefts in differing colours or shots, intended to allow light reflection to reveal the changeable colouring in differing aspects. In 1601 Hardwick Hall inventory recorded 'curtains of Chaungeable taffety', and in another room 'a quilt of chaungeable taffetie sarcenet' as well as 'five curtains of chaungeable damask' (Boynton, 1971, pp.24, 25, 26).

Channel moulding

See Mouldings

Charcoal polishing

A method of polishing used at the end of the 19th and during the early 20th centuries, which was invented by French cabinet-makers to attempt to recreate the dense colour of ebony in other woods. The wood was coated with a solution of camphor and followed by a coating of sulphate of iron, water and nut-galls. Once dry, the surface was brushed down and charcoal was rubbed into the grain, followed by a rubbing with linseed-oil and turpentine mix. The result was a fine dead-black colour.

Charring

See Poker work, Xulopyrography

Chassis (*à chassis*)
A removable upholstered seat or back panel, e.g. a DROP-IN seat.

Check
A plain weave fabric with differing warp and weft colours that create a checkered effect in the cloth. The effect can also be printed. Although initially used for a number of purposes, they were especially popular from the mid 18th century for bed hangings and slipcovers. In a description of Manchester and its surroundings in 1795, John Aikin noted that 'an application of the lighter open striped checks to bed-hangings and window curtains forty years since introduced the making of furniture checks, which have almost set aside the use of stuffs in upholstery' (cited in Montgomery, 1984, p.197).
See also Crankey, Decker work

Cheney
A worsted furnishing material based on a plush pile on a ground of warp yarns. Broad or narrow, they were woven using bright colours which were sometimes watered or striped. Commonly known as China or other corruption, it derives from the name 'Philip and China', itself based on the French words *felpe* meaning plush and *chaîne* meaning warp. It was introduced into England by the Walloons and was made in Norwich at least by 1608. By the mid 17th century it was known in America. A 1656 account of household furnishings from Cambridge, Mass., recorded 'Philip and Cheny curtaines in graine with a deep silke fringe on the vallance and a smaller on the curtaines' (cited in Cummings, 1961, p.2). In 1710 the library of Dyrham Park was furnished with 'five pieces of scarlet and green cheny hangings, and six window curtains and valances of the same' (Walton, 1986, p.61). It was still used as a furnishing fabric in the mid 18th century.

Chenille
An ornamental corded fabric made from very short lengths of thick twisted wool or soft thick silk which are attached to an inner cord to completely surround it. This resembles a caterpillar (French *chenille* = hairy caterpillar). Carpet or cloth may also be made from these lengths. It was popular in the mid 19th century, especially for portière curtains.

Cherry (*Prunus avium*)
A timber of average density of 600–640 (38–40 lb/cu ft). It is pinkish-yellow to dark brown with an even texture, a flecked grain and a pale ray figure. It is often available in large planks and is easily polished. Although admirably suited for fine furniture and cabinet work it is often found in country-made items as well. Evelyn commented that it was 'sometimes … fit to make stools with, cabinets, tables especially the redder sort, which will polish well …' (1662, 1, XI, p.181). Cherry is very well suited to turning work, and has been used for table legs and chair stiles, including Windsor chairs and was particularly associated with provincial chair-making. Holtzapffel noted that cherry 'when stained with lime [quicklime dissolved in water] and oiled and varnished, closely resembles mahogany'; he added that 'it is much used for common and best furniture and chairs, and is one of the best brown woods of the Tunbridge turners' (1846, p.80).

Always popular on the European continent in the 19th century, especially in Austria, South Germany and France, it was used as veneer during the Biedermeier period, along with other fruit woods. In France, cherry was extensively used for *meubles usuels*. This was confirmed in 1853, when it was reported that cherry was 'little used by cabinet-makers and specimens of it are rare [in England], but in France and other parts of the Continent where this tree abounds, it is extensively used by the cabinet-maker, turner and musical-instrument maker' (Blackie, 1853, p.46). During the 20th century cherry was employed for decorative inlays in furniture by designer-craftsmen such as Ernest Gimson and others. During the latter part of the century (especially the 1970s onward) cherry veneers have been used for bedroom and dining suites.

Black or American cherry (*P. serotina*)
A timber from the eastern half of the USA and southern Canada with an average density of 580 (36 lb/cu ft). The sapwood is whitish to light red-brown, while the heartwood is similar in colouring to mahogany. With a uniform texture, and a generally straight grain, it works and finishes well. It was widely used in New England and New York in the colonial and early Federal periods for general cabinet work, seat components such as medial braces and seat rails, as well as for fine quality work. Small amounts of this timber were imported into England from 1733, but it was never as important as the indigenous variety. Although apparently scarce in the 1920s, it was revived in the USA for French provincial-style furniture in the 1950s. Aka American mahogany.

Wild cherry (*P. virginiana*)
An American timber which, like other cherrywood, resembles mahogany. In the mid 19th century Bigelow noted that 'in the manufacture of cabinet work it is much used as a cheaper substitute for mahogany' (1840, p.103).

Cherry birch
See Birch wood (American birch)

Cherry mahogany
See Makoré

Chestnut
American or Wormy chestnut (*Castanea dentata*)
A timber that is similar to oak in appearance with prominent growth rings but without the silver-ray effect. A fungal disease sometimes affects the tree and causes the so-called 'wormy chestnut effect'. Rarely used in America until the later 18th century, when it was employed for interior work and drawers. Chestnut has been used in the 20th century in America for the cores of cabinets that are to be veneered. It has also been used for making reproduction period furniture and supplying decorative veneers.

European, Sweet or Spanish chestnut (*C. sativa*)
A native of North Africa, Asia Minor and parts of Europe, with an average density of 570 (35 lb/cu ft), it is a pale brown to whitey-biscuit shade. It resembles oak in colour and texture, but is more easily worked and is devoid of the silver grain when cleft or quarter cut. It has a coarse texture with a straight to spiral grain. It was used on occasion for Renaissance furniture, but was always in competition with fine oak. Evelyn says that 'Chestnut is (next the Oak) one of the most sought after by the Carpenter and Joyner. This timber also does well (if kept dry) for columns, tables, chests, chairs, stools and bedsteads, tables, chests, chairs, stools' (1662, p.57). It has been used for the wooden parts of PASSEMENTERIE, as well as a substitute for SATINWOOD in certain cuttings during the later 18th century. Sweet chestnut was used as a substitute for oak in 'oak style' furniture of the 1950s as its properties are similar.

Horse-chestnut (*Aesculus hippocastanum*)
A native of Northern Greece and Albania, it was introduced into Europe in the 17th century. It has an average density of 520 (32 lb/cu ft), and is a creamy white to pale yellow, sometimes tinged with pink. The whiteness is dependant upon the time and nature of the felling. It has a close texture and is often spiral or cross grained. It is used for turned work and occasional carving or inlay, although it is not very durable, whilst the whiter timbers are often used as a base for dyed timbers and HAREWOOD. In the early 20th century it was occasionally used for cabinet-making and for window-blind wood.

Japanese horse chestnut (*A. turbinata*)
Very similar to European horse chestnut, some proportion of it having a wavy or curly figure, creating a mottled effect.
See also Buckeye

Chills
Usually an iron mould designed to make 'chilled' castings. The name has been adopted to refer to the cast-iron brackets that hold bed side-irons to head and foot boards.
See also Bedsteads

Chinese blackwood
See Rosewood, Indian

Chinoiserie
The European imitation of Chinese or similar motifs in design. Developed fully by the later 17th century, it was a taste that lasted well into the 19th century. Although chinoiserie is particularly associated with ceramics, the technique of JAPANNING was developed for furniture to imitate oriental lacquer work. During the 18th century the use of FRETWORK, pierced CARVING and oriental and pseudo-oriental detail was often combined with rococo motifs, in a range of furniture including beds, screens and cabinets. A number of designers, including Darly, Chippendale, Chambers, Ince and Mayhew, and Linnell produced patterns for furniture in the chinoiserie style. In the 19th century orientalism manifested itself in bamboo furniture and in various commercial revivals of 18th-century styles.
See also Rococo

Chintz
A furnishing cloth made from calico, with a painted or printed design, often given a glazed finish. The Hindi term *chint* (*chitta*) means spotted cloth, so the anglicized corruption is evident. The original chintz was not glazed, and the word referred to any Indian printed cloth (see Palampore, Pintado). The later, fully-glazed version is made by applying pressure and starch; pressure only is applied to the semi-glazed version. First introduced to Europe from India via France in the 1570s, it was soon brought into England. As early as 1626 specific bed hangings were occasionally imported, but by the 1680s a large business was established in imported ready-made bed draperies. Chintzes were soon widely used in furnishing schemes. Pepys recorded that he 'bought my wife a chint, that is a painted East Indian Calico for her to line her new study' (*Diary*, 5 September 1663). In 1676 a patent (Pat. no.190) was granted to William Sherwin for 'a new way of printing and staying' calico. The madder-mordant technique was adapted for the use of wood blocks, so that cloth could be printed in the Indian manner.

At the beginning of the 18th century, Daniel Defoe noted that chintzes had 'crept into our houses; our closets and bedchambers,

curtains, cushions, chairs, and at last beds themselves' (*Weekly Review*, 31 January 1708). The taste for these sorts of imported material created unrest within weaving communities, and in 1701 all printed, stained or dyed calicoes were banned from use or wear. This Act was amended in 1736, but it was not until 1774 that the restrictions were fully lifted. By 1788 Hepplewhite was able to recommend the use of printed cotton fabrics for bed hangings (1788, p.18).

In the early 19th century chintzes designed specifically for chairs had their patterns printed so that they were centred on the seats and were supplied with a matching border. Sheraton noted that chintz 'may now be had of various patterns on purpose for chair seats, together with borders to suit them' (1793, p.374). These borders were often intended to match the curtains and other hangings of a room, with the designs based on the furniture print for curtains, a filler with a small overall print, and the chair seat with the design (usually flowers) centred.

By the 1820s chintz was no longer highly fashionable; George Smith deprecatingly recorded how 'printed calicos may answer extremely well for secondary apartments, or for those in houses of persons of small fortune; but they are not at all suitable for persons of rank and splendid income' (1808, xii–xiii). However, the ever-practical Loudon noted that, for the modern villa, 'chintz is generally preferred for bed curtains as it admits of being washed' (1839, p.1079). At the end of the century, a glazed finish distinguished chintz from CRETONNE. By the beginning of the 20th century, chintzes were recognized to be 'so advantageous in price, durability, and appearance, that they are often employed instead of silk fabrics' (Bitmead, 1912, p.35). Chintz has been a staple of the English cottage and 'country house' style, fashionable in the later 20th century. Aka Furniture prints.
See also Calico, Printed cotton

Bredif, J. (1989), *Classic Printed Textiles from France 1760–1845, Toiles de Jouy*, London: Thames and Hudson.
Irwin, J. and Brett, K. B. (1970), *Origins of Chintz*, London: Victoria and Albert Museum.

Chip carving
See Carving (Chip)

Chipboard
See Particle board

Chipfoam
An upholstery material made from plastic FOAM that has been shredded. It may be bonded into a variety of shapes or packed loose as a filling. It has been used in the late 20th century for cushions, preformed upholstery components and the like.

Chipolin
An 18th-century French VARNISH and paint technique intended to create a china-like surface effect, which reflected light. It was used as a primer for carved work as well as for interior woodworks. By applying up to twelve coats of white paint, followed by coats of clear varnish, the brilliant effect could be achieved. Havard noted that the twelve layers required for the technique made the carvings appear coarse (1887, p.814), and consequently the technique was abandoned.

Chisel
A bladed cutting tool with a multitude of uses and variations. The chisel types are numerous, but can be divided between general-purpose 'firmer' types, paring chisels for fine woodworking, mortise

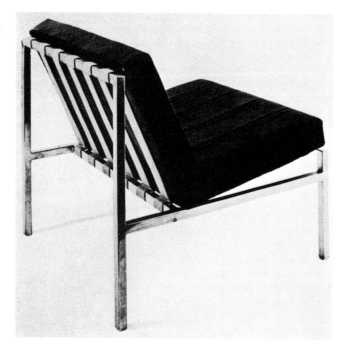

35   A chair designed by Robin Day for Hille of London, showing chromium-plated steel section with latex-rubber webbing supporting leather-covered cushions, c.1960.

chisels for cutting joints and heavy work, and special-purpose designs for carvers, turners and other tradesmen. Chisels have been used since Neolithic times, made in various materials including bronze. Pre-Dynastic Egypt used small copper chisels, which remained popular for engraving and small work. Chisels with handles, capable of having pressure applied to cut grooves and gouges in depth were used during the First Dynasty (c.3000 BC). The distinctions between the firmer and mortise chisels were known in Roman times, and in some cases the chisel design has not altered since these early models.

Some of the more particular designs are the bevelled-edge chisels, which give good clearance when trimming dovetails; butt chisels used for housing hinges; cabinet chisels used for paring and fine work; carving chisels (of which there are over a thousand patterns); CHAIR-MAKERS' chisels for cutting mortises; drawer lock chisels; and a range of TURNERS' chisels specifically for that craft. The CARVING chisels are identified by the profile of the cutting edge. The straight chisel has a flat cutting edge, whilst the gouge has a curved shape. The Fluter and Veiner have deeper profiles and the parting chisel has a V-shaped groove. The quaintly named Macaroni, Flutaroni and Backaroni are rectangular-shaped for finishing sides and recesses and for finishing detail.

Chittagong wood
See Almond

Chromium plating
A metal finish derived from lead chromates that imparts a shiny resistant surface to metals. Although discovered in 1798, and developed in France during the mid 19th century, chromium-plating techniques were little used for furniture until they were taken up in conjunction with tubular steel in the early 1920s. The process resists corrosion and maintains a bright shiny finish, but it was its image of modernity and its machine-like qualities that made it so appealing to both high

and popular styling. It has continued in use as a treatment for metal framing for upholstery, tables and chairs ever since.
See also Nickel plating

Sully, A. H. and Brandes, E. A. (1967), *Chromium*, London: Butterworth.

Chuglam
See Indian silver greywood

Circassian walnut
See Walnut

Circular saw
See Saws

Ciseleurs doreurs
The French name for a craftsman who worked in ORMOLU, specifically performing the operations of chasing and GILDING.

Citronnier (*Citrus medica*)
French name for a Mediterranean timber related to the satinwoods. It has an average density of 720 (45 lb/cu ft), a pale yellow to tan colour with a uniform texture and a hard, close grain. It was periodically used by ébénistes in France and Germany in the 18th century as a contrast to darker wood surrounds, although according to Roubo 'it was not much in use at present' (1774, III, p.773).

Citronnier is also a name applied to other yellow woods including AMYRIS, FUSTIC, SANDALWOOD and SATINWOOD.

Citronwood
See Thuya

Clamp
(a) According to Sheraton (1803, p.151) and Loudon (1839, p.306), a clamp was a small fillet of wood that was let into the edges of table tops, leaves or doors to stabilize the frame. The technique was still being used in the mid 20th century.
See also Lipping

(b) In tool terminology a clamp is another name for a CRAMP, of which there are many varieties for particular applications.
See Cramp

Clamped front
See Construction

Close nailing
See Nailing

Cloth of gold, silver
A textile using metal threads that were either woven into cloth or used in narrow weaves such as ORRICE work. Originating in the 13th century, it was introduced into England in the early 17th century from Spain and Italy. The best varieties were made only from the metal 'yarn', whilst others were worked in a silk foundation. It has been used for both upholstery and bed hangings. In 1582 Edward Baker supplied '30 cushions of similar cloth of gold tissue, cloth of gold and velvet and satin of diverse colours, part embroidered with cloth of gold cloth of silver and satin of diverse colours, Venice gold and silver …' (Beard, 1997, p.284). The gold threads were made in a variety of ways: The Venetians gilded vellum, cut it into strips and wrapped it

around threads; in Germany, especially at Augsburg and Nuremberg, gold-plated silver bars were drawn out into wires which were flattened and wound round thread. Straight metal thread was called *filé*, whilst the spiralling version was *frisé*.

See also Tissue

Coachwood (*Ceratopetalum apetalum*)

An Australian hardwood with an average density of 640 (40 lb/cu ft), a pinkish-brown colouring and a pleasant odour. It has a fine and even texture, a straight grain and a flecked figure on a quartered surface. Introduced in the 20th century, it can be a very satisfactory furniture wood, both in the solid and in veneer. Aka scented satinwood.

Coade stone

An artificial material similar in looks to fine limestone, with a pale cream-colour finish. Eleanor Coade established her factory in 1769 in Lambeth, London. The products were widely used for statues, torchères, plaques and pedestals through the second half of the 18th century and into the early years of the 19th century. Although generally associated with building materials, this artificial stone composition has been used for furniture parts. The Coade Stone Company also produced SCAGLIOLA for the furniture trade.

Kelly, Alison (1974), 'Furnishing from Coade factory in Lambeth', in *Furniture History*, X, pp.68–70.
— (1978), 'Mrs Coade's stone', in *Connoisseur*, vol.197, no.791, January.

Coal

The use of cannel (or parrot) coal in the mid 19th century to make decorative items, including furniture, was both a manifestation of the Victorian love of the eccentric and exotic, as well as a means for mine owners to present memorable gifts. The key figure in this craft was the Scotsman Thomas Williamson who exhibited various examples of coal furniture in the mid 19th century. The coal was easily carved and polished, but had to be fitted up with iron connections to ensure stability. In 1855 a table and a bench were made as furnishings for Osborne House, Isle of Wight, but it remained an esoteric taste.

Coal was also used as part of a composition. In 1852 William Pidding patented a method of making furniture from an amalgam of coal, peat, shrubs, shells, bark and the like, which was mixed with glue, and 'carbonized' (Pat.no.13911/1852). The process was to pulverize the coal, mix it with the other ingredients, and then create shapes by moulding.

See also Compositions

Jones, D. (1987), 'Coal furniture in Scotland', in *Furniture History*, XXIII, pp.35–8.

Coated fabrics

Coated fabrics, which were all based on a pliant top layer applied to a fabric base, have a long history. Waxes, rubber, gums, oils and plastic materials have all been used. For furniture use, coated fabrics were usually intended to be an imitation of LEATHER. These originated in the 14th century, were developed in the 19th century, and were improved in the early 20th century, resulting in a wide range of coated fabrics.

AMERICAN CLOTH
See Leather or Oil cloth, below

LEATHER OR OIL CLOTH
From the 14th century oiled cloth was made to look like leather. Linseed oil and clay fillers were applied and calendered to a base

cloth, and allowed to dry. The surface was levelled, dried in a heated oven, and then rolled. The process was repeated several times. Three or four coats of enamel paint were applied by roller, and grain effects could also be applied by the same means. In 1627 a patent was obtained for the production of oil cloth by I. Wolfer (Pat.no.40). The royal use of oil cloth is later recorded in 1677, when John Casbert supplied '45 yards of green oyled cloth to make 4 curtains and a tester for the Queen's volary' (Beard, 1997, p.291). In the early 19th century Sheraton particularly noted, with reference to protective covers for tables and the like, that 'lately they have introduced a new kind of painted canvas, varnished, and very elastic in its nature, and will probably answer better than leather' (Sheraton, 1803, p.336). This is probably a reference to a contemporary leather cloth.

In 1850 the British firm Storeys of Lancaster were still making leather cloth for upholstery, with linseed oil as the main ingredient, and the trade name Rexine was introduced by the British Leathercloth Manufacturing Company. A cloth with a nitro-cellulose base was introduced in the 1850s as an imitation leather. This was made from castor oil, cellulose nitrate and colouring matter. In 1856 four further patents were granted for improvements in leather cloth, including Rowley's, which was based on a mix of albumen, china clay, and a coating of naphtha solution of gutta percha (Pat.no.1652). By 1884 Storeys of Lancaster manufactured leather cloth using a cellulose nitrate amylacetate mixture which, when combined with castor oil, gave a degree of flexibility to the material.

George Cole described leather cloth as 'a name given in England to a cotton cloth prepared with a glazed and varnished surface to imitate Morocco leather, used for carriage trimming, known in the United States as enamelled or oil-cloth' (1892). In the 19th century it was part of the upholsterer's stock in trade and was widely used for covering dining room and library furniture, especially chairs, tables and desk tops. For chair coverings, 'American cloth is treated in a manner similar to leather, and the same allowances for fullness will answer very well' (A Working Upholsterer, *Practical Upholstery*, 1883, p.5).

36 *The fashion for imitation leather reached new heights with the development of polyurethane coatings (PVC). This English 'Valencia' upholstery group is typical of the period, c.1974.*

During the early 20th century English manufacturers produced versions of American cloth in particular, the trade names being Keratol and Rexine. Similar developments occurred elsewhere with Fabrikoid, by du Pont, becoming a famous American trade name. Aka American cloth, wax cloth, *toile cirée*, Lancaster cloth.

MOROCCO CLOTH

A version of leather cloth introduced in the mid 19th century and designed to replicate Morocco LEATHER. It was clearly considered a suitable material in the mid 19th century.

A most perfect imitation of morocco [leather] by the application of a preparation of caoutchouc, or gutta percha, to the surface of a plain woven or twill cotton cloth. The surface is corrugated in imitation of morocco, and is coloured and varnished so as to present all the external appearance of that kind of leather. The elasticity is perfect, showing no tendency to crack, and so far as time has at present tested its durability, this appears to be satisfactory. Its cost is less than one-third that of morocco, and from the width of the cloth, it cuts to much greater advantage in the covering of articles of furniture, for which, as well as carriage linings, particularly railway carriages, it is coming largely into use.
(G. Wallis, 1854)

PVC

Leather cloth was eventually replaced by a flexible PVC. Although the idea of a flexible surface applied to a backing cloth was not new (see above), it was only with the introduction of PVC (polyvinylchloride), used since the 1930s, that improved flexibility and a lesser chance of cracking, made it truly popular as an upholstery cloth. By the 1940s, imitation leather, based on PVC, was a commercial proposition. These flexible-textured vinyl fabrics were very popular post-war for many kinds of upholstery work as they could be used 'traditionally' or through vacuum-forming processes.
See also Plastics (Polyvinyl chloride)

RUBBER CLOTH

The use of rubber to produce coated textiles provided a waterproof or inflationary capability. Coal-tar oil, which was a good solvent for rubber, produced a solution which, when pressed between two cloths, made a waterproof substance (see patents *c.*1813: no.11832 and others). The use of rubber cloth in furniture included Hydrostatic or water beds (see below) and inflatable chairs. At the 1851 Great Exhibition Thomas Hancock, who worked with Charles Mackintosh, exhibited an inflatable bed-chair in India rubber.

WATER BEDS

The idea of an impermeable sheet was more useful for water beds than for air beds. In 1823 Charles Mackintosh had patented his waterproof cloth, so it is not surprising to find that it was soon applied to furniture items. By the 1830s the air-filled bed had given way to water cushions and beds as they were more comfortable to use, particularly

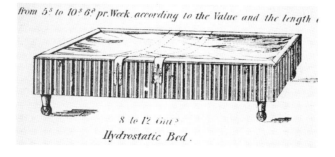

37   An advertisement for Minter's Hydrostatic water bed, c.1840s.

with regard to reduced heat retention. The Hydrostatic (water) bed devised by Dr Arnott is one example. It was simply a wooden box-shaped bed which was lined with lead or zinc to make it watertight. A sheet of India-rubber cloth was loosely fitted to the edges and frames, shutting in the water which flowed through a cock at one end. The bed was then made up normally (Loudon, 1839, p.337).
See also Cellulose

Brunn, M. (1990), 'Treatment of cellulose nitrate coated upholstery', in *Upholstery Conservation Pre-prints*, pp.449–55, America Conservation Consortium, East Kingston, N.H.
Christie, G. (1964), *Storeys of Lancaster, 1848–1964*, London: Collins.
Gooderson, Philip (1996), *Lord Linoleum, Lord Ashton of Lancaster*, Keele: Keele University Press.
Meikle, J. L. (1995), 'Presenting a new material: From imitation to innovation with Fabrikoid', in *Decorative Arts Society Journal*, 19, pp.8–15.
Neuberger, R. (1934), 'History and development of the leathercloth industry', in *Upholstery*, 1, no.4, July.
Seymour, R. B. and Mark, H. F. (eds) (1989), *Organic Coatings: Their Origin and Development* (Proceedings of the International Symposium on the History of Organic Coatings held 11–15 September, 1989 at Miami Beach, Florida, USA), New York: Elsevier.
Thorp, V. (1990), 'Imitation leather; structure composition and conservation', in *Leather Conservation News*, Spring, pp.7–15.

Coatings
See Finish

Coccus lacca
See Lacquer

Cock bead
See Mouldings

Coco fibre (USA)
See Coir fibre

Cocobolo (*Dalbergia retusa*)
A timber from the Pacific region of Central America with an average density of 1100 (68 lb/cu ft). It is orange-red with black stripe or mottle effect, with a fine texture and irregular grain. It was used as a fancy cabinet wood for turning, inlay and TUNBRIDGE WARE in the 20th century. Howard noted that it 'deserves much wider use, but is insufficiently known' (1920, p.64). In the later 20th century it has been used as a rosewood substitute. Aka Granadillo (Mexico).

Coconut wood (*Cocos nucifera*)
The timber of the coco palm can be classified as wood, although it is markedly different from conventional wood, being a monocotyledon. It is grown on the Indian sub-continent and in the East Indies and provides a hard timber of a medium brown shade, offset with deep red-orange deposits in the pores which are revealed as 'quill marks' in longitudinal surfaces (hence Porcupine wood). The outer part of the stem is the only usable portion of the tree and was used during the 19th century especially as a veneer for work-boxes. In the mid 19th century it was noted that 'the palm woods are sparingly employed in England for cabinet and marquetry work, and sometimes for billiard cues which are considered to stand remarkably well; they are also turned into snuff boxes etc.' (Holtzapffel, 1846, p.98). Aka Palmyra.
See also Palm, Porcupine wood

Cocuswood (*Brya ebenus*)
A West Indian wood, mainly from Cuba, with an average density of 1200 (75 lb/cu ft). The heartwood is dark brown to nearly black with

38   *An X-frame seat showing the art of upholstery as practised by cofferers, c.1554. The hessian-covered horse-hair stuffing, the gilt nails and the luxurious textiles were soon to become trademarks associated with the upholsterer.*

cursors of that craft. The carcase work was usually of poor timber, as the bulk of the effort went on the external appearance of the tooled leather, nailing and fabrics used. An account from 1581–2 of the work of the royal coffer-maker, Thomas Grene, indicates the fine effects that could be achieved:

To Thomas Grene for timber work of 19 chairs, 6 high stools, 24 square stools and 11 footstools of walnut and other timber of which some are covered with tissue, cloth of gold, and velvet and various colours, and some embroidered and lozengered with Venice gold, silver and silk, fringed with similar gold, silver and silk, the aforesaid chairs having backs lined with satin and pillows of fustian filled with down, gilt scutchions, some with pommells of gilt wood and some with pommells of copper gilt, great gilt bullion nails, small gilt nails girth web, sackcloth for the iron work, canvas cloth, cases of cotton and leather and all other necessaries to the same pertaining …
(Royal household accounts, cited by Symonds, March 1941, p.103)

By the 18th century the cofferer's business had changed to become that of trunk-maker, with little reference to furniture.

Symonds, R. W. (1941), 'The craft of the coffer maker', in *Connoisseur*, March, pp.100–5, 133.
— (1942), 'The craft of the cofferer and trunk maker', in *Connoisseur*, CIX, January–June, p.40.

Coil spring
See Springs

Coir fibre
A fibrous material derived from the husks of the coconut palm. Long known as a rope or matting material, it seems to have been introduced *c.*1845 (Webster, p.297) as an intermediate filling in upholstery, and has been widely used as such since then. In that year John Barsham patented a method of manufacturing matting for cushions and mattresses from coir fibres and the like (Pat.no.10884). The best is made from long fibres and is artificially curled, like hair. It works best when needled onto hessian to form pads which are fitted over spring upholstery. In the 1950s it was recorded as the most widely used upholstery fibre filling in England. Aka Coco or Ginger fibre.

Colonial
A general term referring to architecture, furniture and interior decoration produced in America before the Revolution. Early Colonial, produced in the 17th century, reflected the styles brought by immigrants which were continually updated as tastes changed in Europe. The later Colonial period, between about 1710 and 1776, was an interpretation of Georgian styles which were firmly based on Classical ideas but which developed a character of their own. The coastal cabinet-makers of Boston, Philadelphia, New York, Charleston and so on developed their own particular interpretations of the style. From the 1870s the Colonial revival renewed an interest in the traditional furniture of the 18th century as well as restoring a taste for simple, but elegant farmhouse furniture styles.

Other Colonial styles, for example Dutch, Spanish and French, were developed in countries influenced by the immigrants who in many cases fused the vernacular and their own traditions to create a style.
See also American red gum, Mahogany

Colophony
See Resins (Rosin)

Colouring
See Stains and staining

veinings, a fine texture and a variable grain. In the late 17th and the 18th centuries it was an important cabinet wood, imported in quantity from Jamaica and used for oyster veneers for cabinet work. During the 18th century it also provided vividly striped veneers which are now confused with LABURNUM. By the 19th century it was used for high-class turnery and wood-wind instrument making, but was not recommended for furniture due to its small size and changeable colour. *The Cabinet-maker's Assistant* explained: 'This [timber] does not possess the necessary qualities of a good cabinet wood: its small size, (2–8 inches in diameter) frequency of heart faults, general inferiority in figure, and above all, its liability to change in colour, unfit it for extensive use' (Blackie, 1853, p.43). Confusingly the wood has been described as LIGNUM VITAE or West Indian or Jamaica EBONY.
See also Green ebony, Granadillo

Cofferer or Coffer-maker
During the 15th and 16th centuries the cofferer was responsible for producing wooden chests or coffers (banded with iron), as well as trunks, cradles and even chairs (X-framed), often covered with leather. A cofferers' guild was established in London as early as 1328. Like other guilds they tried to restrain any competing trade. In 1483 they were 'like[ly] to be undone' by the importation of Flemish furniture and were able to obtain an import prohibition order. By 1517, the Cofferers were absorbed into The Company of Leather Sellers who obtained powers to 'maintain standards in work covered and made of leather and trussing coffers …' (Symonds, 1941, p.101). The cofferers developed skills in upholstery work and can be considered as pre-

Comb joint
See Joints

Combing
A range of decorative finishes applied to a painted or coloured surface in which various shaped combs are dragged through the wet surface to create patterns either of particular wood grains (see GRAINING) or to create effects in coloured paint. Although not strictly a graining process, it used the grainer's tools to make patterns in flat colour panels on cabinets. During the 1920s and 1930s zigzags and scrolls were particularly chosen for colour-combing effects.
See also Graining, Painting

Commesso
See Pietre dure

Compass plane
See Planes

Compass saw
See Saws

Composite board
Any form of built-up boards used for specific applications, which has thick core sections and thinner plys of wood or other material applied to each side of the core. This may then be veneered with face veneers or left with the alternative finish. Composite boards sometimes had other materials in their core. These ranged from asbestos for insulation to vermiculite or balsa for lightness.
See also Blockboard, Plywood

Composite veneers
A man-made veneer which is produced by gluing a quantity of stacked veneers together and applying pressure to them. When dry, they are cut at 90 degrees to the original plane to produce a striped or mottled effect, in fact a veneer of veneers. It was first used in the early to mid 19th century, using distorted veneers able to create a mottled effect. It was particularly associated with TUNBRIDGE WARE in this period. In the later 20th century the technique was utilized so that plain wood veneers could be used to create a decorative finish (trade name: Fineline), which had a vogue in the latter part of the 20th century.

Compositions
The use of compositions in furniture-making has been part of the repertoire for centuries. Most composition material was based on a particular recipe mix that could be moulded or shaped to the required patterns, particularly to imitate carved work. Examples abound for substitute carving, for example, in 1592 the Fontainebleau accounts list components (bas-reliefs, cornices) which were moulded from 'paper, wax and other materials' (Benhamou, 1991, p.7). In 1693 an English patent was granted to Marshal Smith and Thomas Puckle for 'making a composition with wood capable of being run onto moulds in a liquid state, for beautifying rooms, embellishing cabinets, &c.' (Pat.no.317). An early-18th-century recipe tells how to take moulds from a carved section and make duplicates for application to objects:

Make a Glew-water stronger than any Size, yet weaker than Joyners melted Glew: mix Whiting in fine powder therewith, till it is as thick as Paste or Dough; knead it very well, wrapping it up in a double cloth; in which it may lye and get heat from the fire for you are not to let it get cold, for then it will harden, and so be unfit for use. Once ready put into moulds or around carvings then when set glue the sections into place on the frames and when dry, paint gild or japan.
(Salmon, 1701, p.911)

In the third quarter of the 18th century compositions made from a range of materials were developed. Fibrous slab produced from plaster and a range of vegetable matter was devised to produce moulded ornaments for mirrors and chimney pieces by William Walton. In 1786, Obadiah Westwood patented (Pat.no.1576) an 'improved composition' of ground rags, glue, flour and water intended to make trays, caddies, and frames for pictures and looking-glasses.

Variations on this theme continued in the 19th century. Nicholson (1826, pp.3–4) describes a simple composition method in which fine glue is mixed with shavings and sawdust, put through a sieve and poured into a mould. It is then weighted down and, when dry, can be glued, needle-pointed or braded to a surface. The simplest method was to press whiting and thin glue into an oiled mould (E. Cunnington, Pat.no.882/1853). In 1862 Thomas Ghislin patented a process of converting seaweed mixed with glue, gutta percha and India rubber to form a 'plastic' material which was alleged to be a good substitute for ebony (Pat.no.2035). He also proposed boiling the mixture in a solution of sulphuric acid to harden the material to produce an imitation of stag horn. This material would then be used as a substitute for horn, ivory and such like.

Inevitably, the show-case of the 1851 Great Exhibition was the place to display a board material made from a mixture of moss-peat and sawdust devised by J. A. Bampton. In the same year Moses Poole patented 'Improvements in the manufacture of tables, sofas, bedsteads etc. …' His improvement was based on producing a hard substance from India rubber and sulphur with or without other materials. It was proposed that the resulting product was then either made into veneers for use on wooden frames or wrapped round iron-framed furniture (Pat.no.14299). Later developments in composition were either based on versions of the plaster processes or were PLASTIC based.
See also Coal, Plastics, Veneers, Wood substitutes

Thornton, Jonathan (1985), 'Compo, The history and technology of plastic composition', in AIC Preprints, AIC: Washington, pp.113–26.
Witt-Dorring, C. (1993), 'A group of early seat furniture with composition decoration from the Danhauser factory', in Furniture History, XXIX, pp.147–60.

Compression moulding
A method of PLASTIC fabrication that feeds plastic powder or pellets into steel moulds, which are then heated under pressure via a male former to take the shape of the female mould.

Compression wood
Timber that has been stressed under compression, for example, the underside of a heavy branch or a distorted standing tree. The distorted wood is often revealed by spiral markings and the wood is usually darker.

Concertina side
See Table opening and extending mechanisms

Concrete
The use of concrete as a furniture material seems unlikely, but is only an extension of using stone which has had a very long existence. In 1940 it was suggested that cast plaster or concrete panels could substitute wood for shelving and the like. It was also suggested that

these panels might be veneered with wood to hide the raw concrete (Tomrely, 1940, p.94). In 1954 Willy Guhl, a Swiss designer, devised a simple garden chair from fibrated concrete, which performed well. The concrete was set into organic shapes whilst still wet, and used for weatherproof chairs. Its specific use as an outdoor material has been widely exploited for public seating and benches. In the 1980s, concrete was used for furniture, including stereo cases and chests of drawers.

Conifer

The word refers to evergreen trees that usually bear cones. PINE, SPRUCE, LARCH and FIR are amongst the common timbers that are now often lumped under the general term of DEAL.

Construction (Cabinet)

The technique of making a piece of furniture ranges from the very simple shaping of a naturally suitable object (Dug out) to the application of the full range of cabinet-making skills, including timber selection and SEASONING, preparation, JOINTING, DRAWER construction, VENEERING, MARQUETRY, metal or ceramic decoration, FINISHING, and so on. The diversity of types and traditions in furniture construction through many centuries, let alone the differences across and within country boundaries, has meant that although the major techniques have been widely adopted, there have been numerous variations on themes. The simple chronological divisions between carpentry-based, joinery-based cabinet-making and factory construction are useful to a degree, but do not allow for the many overlaps and divisions within the history of furniture construction. Like much in furniture history, whilst there is change there is also much continuity of practice.

Indeed, many of the techniques that have been applied to furniture in the last 2000 years have been developed from ancient furniture-makers. The scarcity of timber meant that their construction techniques had to adapt to these specific circumstances. For example, Egyptian carpenters used a technique of alternating concave and convex boards in carcase construction. They cut out and filled knots and blemishes in the scarce timber rather than discard a whole section. In the same spirit, scarf joints were used to utilize smaller pieces of timber. Boards were joined by tongues of hardwood inserted at regular intervals in mortises cut into each board thickness. Parallel wedges were required and often had butterfly joints added. Tongue and groove joints were used for ivory covering plates; whilst corner jointing methods included mitres and halving joints. Cabinet construction itself was based on mortise and tenon, dovetail and mitred joints. The shortage of timber also resulted in the application of veneers and built-up panel work.

From this brief list it can be seen that many of these techniques have been transferred to the repertoire of furniture-making which has developed since the Middle Ages. Although the changes were slow, piecemeal and overlapping, the major developments are outlined below.

BOARDED

A simple method of making furniture with solid wooden boards. The boards were flush BUTT-JOINTED, or rebated and held with pegs or nails. As boards were often not wide enough to make a full side, they were often nailed to the stiles and rails, or in some cases slip-tenoned along the edges to be fastened together (see Biscuit joint). They may also have been joined with primitive DOVETAIL JOINTS. This method enabled RIVEN or sawn timber to be used without further working, and it remained a constructional form until the 18th century in certain

districts. The propensity for timber to shrink, even if seasoned, meant that the boarded construction would often split and warp, thus the application of iron banding and elaborately worked HINGES was a necessity that turned into a decorative feature as well. This limitation also meant that objects were usually limited to box-like forms such as chests, stools, benches and boxes. Carpenters' furniture was recognized as being made from boards simply nailed together.

BOLTED CONSTRUCTION

A system that bolts the carcase sides between the plinth and cornice using screw bolts. Bolt holes were drilled into side panels and the nuts were fitted into the top and bottom panels. When tightened they created a good fit. Established in the European industry in the 19th century, the technique was imported into America and England with migrant workers. It was a forerunner of knock-down methods.

BUILT-UP WORK

The problems arising from the use of solid wood as a basis for veneering (especially before controlled seasoning) was addressed by built-up work. Built-up framing, either in plies or blocks, is evident in much of the superior work of the 18th century. In terms of cost and function, it was a most satisfactory way of producing *bombé* or curved shapes. Built-up curved work was made in a variety of ways: Firstly, solid sections could be cut into small curves, and then jointed together edge to edge; secondly, small blocks were shaped and then built up like brickwork; thirdly, laminates of wood were vertically aligned; and, lastly, kerfs were cut into a rail or skirt allowing them to be bent into a curve. These various techniques all demonstrate a variety of solutions to a design problem, aimed at achieving a particular stylistic interpretation within certain parameters. Drawer fronts were often made from built-up timbers, especially useful in the case of shaped fronts, for commodes for instance. Some card tables produced in the 1760–70s have their tops formed from cross members, framed by shaped muntins, the flush under-surfaces supported by a central strut, and the shaped friezes built up in three layers. Not only were friezes and drawer fronts built up. The use of LAMINATES was another example of a practical design decision. Sheraton explained how card table tops, which need to be as flat as possible, were to be made. His jointing method was remarkably similar to some modern boards: 'I take it to be the best to rip up dry deal or faulty mahogany, into 4 inch widths, and joint them up. It matters not whether the pieces are whole lengths, provided the jump joints be crossed' (1793, Appendix p.17). Mahogany LIPPINGS were then tongued into the ends of the tops, and slips were glued to the sides, so once veneered they created the appearance of solid mahogany.

The built-up system was not limited to fancy shapes or card tables. Sheraton suggested this method as a general expedient to counteracting movement. In his design for a Universal table he advised that 'The bed panels [for the top] are sometimes glued up in three thicknesses, the middle being laid with the grain across, and the other two lengthways of the panel to prevent warping.' The underframe of the Universal table was to be made 'of faulty mahogany or of wainscot veneered' (op.cit., p.358). Round surfaces were also treated in a similar manner. Arch tops were glued up in thicknesses round a CAUL, whilst curved doors were either framed and panelled or 'glued up in narrow slips of inch mahogany and clamped' (loc.cit.). These techniques, based on trial and error, were realistic solutions to particular problems.

Some of the results however, could be very ingenious. An 18th-century method of turning pilasters demonstrates this. Because pilasters were attached after the carcase was made, it was necessary for

39   *Dug-out armchair, ash with elm seat, c.1760–1800. The continuity of well-established practices long after the need has passed is a feature of furniture-making.*

veneered, other procedures clearly had to be developed. The simple method was the technique of holding tops on with blocks, which were glued and fitted under the top board and side rails. Further changes, perhaps related to poor adhesion problems, meant that by the 1740s gouged recesses were being made to accommodate screws which held tops to frames (see Buttoning). These were not universal methods by any means, but the examples simply demonstrate the continuing pragmatic approach to construction that furniture-makers used, according to their particular circumstances.

As has been indicated, cabinet-making was based on the application of veneers onto a pre-formed carcase which was hidden beneath the surface. The basic principle of this kind of work is the construction of a rigid carcase, often using dovetail joints, to which a number of other items including doors, drawers and fall-flaps might be fitted. The revival of veneering in association with this method of working meant that less important timbers could be used for the carcase and the expensive exotic timbers could be used sparingly for surface decoration. Once the basic cabinet-making methods were established, various developments and changes were made as taste and demand required.
See also Cabinet-maker

CLAMPED

Some chests from the medieval period onward were based on a stage in-between primitive nailed board construction and panelled construction. Boards were cut with tongues or tenons on their ends, which then located into grooves in the vertical stiles or posts that 'clamped' the boards together. The ark is a favoured form of clamp work made by the CARPENTER, or ARKWRIGHT.

DUG OUT

The extremely elementary process of cutting a log, squaring it up, hollowing out the inside and using one part of the off-cut sides as a lid, is a basic technique that required only simple carpentry tools. The interior timber of the log was excavated with axes and/or burnt out and finally cleaned up. The lid was secured with iron hinges and a set of straps and locks. The dug-out process was also used for making chairs, using hollow trunks as chairs or by the more laborious process of actually hollowing out a trunk into a rough chair shape. This method was used from the medieval period until the 18th century in rural areas.
See also Rustic furniture

EXPOSED JOINTS AND CONSTRUCTION

In the 19th century, the revival of a taste for medieval-inspired work resulted in cabinet-makers again working in solid wood, their obvious construction details exposed as part of the style. The pinned mortise and tenon is one such example. Apart from stylistic matters, the exposed construction was a 'revealed' truth which indicated honest workmanship to some critics. Changes in construction were again made during the 19th century, in response to economic demands which had increased the market, and continued to do so into the 20th century. Many of these changes also had to take into account the increased quantities required, the poor training of furniture-makers and the need to control costs.

FRAMED CARCASE

A technique devised to take advantage of multi-ply and laminboards towards the middle of the 20th century. It took veneered boards (1.27 cm/½ in thick) and tongued them into fillets, posts or pilasters, which were then assembled to make cupboards, cabinets or wardrobes, with appropriate plinths and bases.

them to be turned. They were initially planed square, then rebated to the angle of fixing. This angle was then fitted with a fillet of deal that was glued in lightly for easy removal after turning, thus keeping the rebate intact. The piece was then turned to shape and could easily be fitted when finished.
See also Brick construction

CABINET-MAKING

Fundamental changes in construction occurred during the 17th century with the use of veneers, dovetail jointing and improved drawer construction. However, distinctions between joinery and cabinet-making can be rather arbitrary as cabinet-makers used mortise and tenon joints for example, and joiners used dovetails, but the refinement was really in the change from working with solid wood, using joinery techniques, to cabinet-making using the skills of fine jointing, veneering and flush-carcase making. For example, prior to the introduction of veneering, table frames and tops were usually pegged together through the surface. When the top surfaces were to be

JOINED OR FRAMED

This construction type, also called panelled construction, was known in Ancient Egypt where mortise and tenon joints for frames were used. It was a useful method of construction, so continued in the Mediterranean region. For example, the 7th-century *Codex Amiatinus* shows a book cupboard with panelled doors. By the 14th century, in northern climes the panelling technique was particularly used for lining walls (wainscoting). The benefit of the process was that thin panels of wood could rest in grooved frames or stiles, joined up by mortise and tenon joints, so that the panels were free to move in relation to fluctuations in moisture content, thus avoiding the problem of splitting that occurred when they were nailed. The transfer of technique from building to furniture was conducted by the same craftsman: the joiner. Initially, during the 15th century, the panels were long and narrow and often cut from a single plank. By the later 16th century squarer panels were introduced, made up from wider planks or joined widths. Early panels were stepped to fit the grooved frame, but by the 17th century they were chamfered at the edges. During the 18th century panel construction was used to imitate cabinet-making work by using flush panel work. Panelled construction remained a feature of furniture-making, usually as the method of preparing the backs of even the best-quality work.

See also Joiner

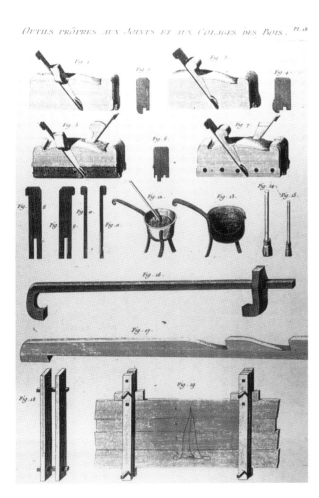

BOTTOM LEFT
40 The tools and technique used for the preparatory jointing and gluing of planks to make up flat boards, France, c.1770.

LEFT
41 An impression of an American furniture factory in 1885. It shows the extensive use of machinery including sawing, planing, carving, shaping and sanding.

KNOCK-DOWN OR PANEL CONSTRUCTION

A form of furniture-making which allows objects to be dismantled and reassembled. It has its origins in the dry jointing techniques of Ancient Egypt, and has been used on occasion ever since. The knock-down (KD) method was revived seriously in the 18th century as a response to the pressures of space in exporting furniture, as well as meeting the requirements of travellers. The design of metamorphic and patent furniture sometimes relied on this construction method. During the 19th century designs were further developed as export markets grew. The example of the bentwood industry demonstrates this practice well.

During the 20th century, due to advances in precision machining, particle board panels, improved packaging and a willingness for consumers to assemble furniture in their own homes, the KD manufacturing methods have grown extensively. Swedish and Danish expertise in the 1930s onward was fuelled by their export market, and the development of specialist KD fittings that allowed for simple dry jointing ensured the success of the method. In conjunction with this form of construction was the prepared 'panel' processing in factories, which has become the standard for bulk production. Although this is a long way from cabinet-making in the true sense, it is a highly developed and efficient operation that meets the demands made upon it.

MACHINE WORK

The advent of machine tools began to change the nature of the craft of furniture-making in the later 19th century. Bitmead singled out the CIRCULAR SAW as the prime aid to the cheap furniture-makers (known as slop-makers). He suggested, not unnaturally, that this assisted them in mitring, parallel and tapered work, so its value to the slop-makers was enormous. Bitmead thought that 'The cheap furniture-makers could not work at the price they do if they did not use this saw'. It is important to remember that these saws were very often worked by foot treadle and did not necessarily imply factory conditions. Bitmead then identified the FRETSAW as the next most useful tool for cabinet-makers. This again was operated by a treadle and was essential for curved work and fancy work. The third tool he mentioned is the Toupie, or 'Improved rotary moulding cutter' (Bitmead, 1873, p.74). This simple machine, operated like a SPINDLE MOULDER, was a quick and simple tool to incise designs into panels or 'carve' shapes in sections of timber. He identified the particular benefit of this tool in the following way: 'For Gothic or medieval work it is invaluable, as more chamfering can be done by it in one hour than could be done by hand-work in a day' (Bitmead, loc.cit.).

These machines could be employed by small-scale workshops but by the end of the 19th century another major change began to affect the furniture industry. The growth of larger manufacturing concerns, in conjunction with powered machinery, meant that further division of labour often reduced even more the need for constructional skills. Indeed, by the early 20th century, methods of construction began to be adapted to new materials such as PLYWOOD and LAMINATED BOARDS, as well as metals and later PLASTICS.
See also Machines

PLY FRAME WORK
The combination of lightly constructed framing with a sheathing or covering of plywood. The technique was developed after World War I for covering mortised and tenoned frames. It fell into disuse when laminboards were employed to make framed carcase work. However, it was revived for the British wartime Utility Scheme.

SCAMPING
A 19th-century term referring to a particular method of construction in which makers produced carcases in several parts, which were 'put together with thumbscrews'. In 1873, Richard Bitmead described the continental systems of carcase construction which 'offer some very good examples of quickness and quantity, but not quality'. Bitmead went on to describe the process of making 'French cabinets' that were known to the trade as 'steamers'. The process he described did not allow any joints in the framework of the carcase; it was made of machined pieces that were then nailed and dowelled together. He remarked that: 'Carcases are seldom dovetailed together; the ends are merely rabbeted with the saw, and French nailed together. In the French cabinets there are neither mortises, tenons, nor dovetails used; the circular saw does the whole' (1873, p.67).

42 *The painted foot of a commode, c.1775–80, showing the demountable screw fitting. Although not a true knock-down construction, it is an expedient way of ensuring safe conduct for a fragile component of a piece of furniture.*

During the 19th century the growing number of small masters who set up in business to make furniture on their own account soon found out that they were unable to make a living by using traditional methods, so they had to skimp. This was often done by using poor-quality materials, but the construction suffered as well. An early example was the making of curved pieces. To make curves correctly, according to T. Martin, pieces of shaped wood cut out of deal 3.75–7.5 cm (1.5–3 in) thick were laid one over the other by breaking or intersecting the joints, as in BRICKWORK, to the required thickness. He continued: 'some cut a piece of inch deal, and after bending it, glue a piece of canvas on the inside; but this is a bad and weak practice …' (Martin, 1819, p.116). The re-use of second-hand timber was another cost-cutting process. Table-makers would purchase old teak taken from ship-breakers, to use as the bulk of the pillars for loo-tables and the like. Turned, artificially stained and veneered, these apparently passed as walnut (see Bitmead, 1873, p.78).

WEDGED
Whilst the demand was for basic storage or support furniture, the wedged construction was the simplest method. It was based on a timber board or slab (that is, a table or bench top) that had legs or supports fitted through holes in the surface. The legs had slots cut into them and were then wedged with pegs.

Bonnett, D. (1956), *Contemporary Cabinet Construction and Design*, London: Batsford.
Booth, D. (1935), 'Notes on the construction of cheap furniture', in *Journal of the R.I.B.A.*, 42, July.
Denning, D. (1931), *The Art and Craft of Cabinet-Making; a practical handbook to the construction of cabinet furniture, the use of tools, formation of joints, hints on designing and setting out work, veneering, etc.*, London: Pitman.
Goodman, W. (1979), 'Classical Greek joinery', in *Working Wood*, 1, (vol.1, no.3), pp.20–3.
Hasluck, P. (1907), *Examples of Cabinet Work and Joinery*, London, Cassell.
Hewett, Cecil (1988), 'English Medieval cope chests', in *Journal of British Archaeological Association*, 141, pp.105–23.
Keeble, A. L. (1930), *Cabinet-Making Theory and Practice*, London: Longmans, Green and Co.
Moore, N. (1987), 'A Chester cabinet-maker's specification book', in *Regional Furniture Journal*, vol.1.
Nosban, M. (1843), *Nouveau Manuel complet du menuisier, de l'ébéniste et du layetier*, Paris: Roret.
Sturmer, M. (1982), *Handwerk und Hofische Kultur: Europaische Möbelkunst in 18. Jahrhunderts*, Munich: Beck.
Symonds, R. W. (1940), 'Craft of the cabinet-maker', in *Connoisseur*, May, pp.200–7.
— (1946), 'Craft of furniture-making in the XVIIIth century', in *Antique Collector*, March/April, pp.54–9.
— (1950), 'Provincial furniture-making in eighteenth century England', in *Country Life*, 27 January, pp.220–3.
Trent, R. F. (1985), 'The chest of drawers in America 1635–1730, A postscript', in *Winterthur Portfolio*, vol.XX, pp.31, 48.
Walton, Karin-M. (1976), 'Eighteenth century cabinet-making in Bristol', in *Furniture History*, XII, pp.59–63.
Watson, F. J. B. (1969), 'The craftsmanship of the Ancien Regime', in *Apollo*, XC, 91, September, pp.180–9.
Wells, P. and Hooper, C. (1909), *Modern Cabinet Work, Furniture & Fitments*, London: Batsford.

Continuous hinge
See Hinges

Contre-partie
The results of cutting various materials together to form interlocking patterns (i.e. tortoiseshell and brass); it can also refer to the panel with less valuable material predominating.
See also Première-partie, Boulle work

Conversion

A general term that describes the sawing of timber baulks into smaller parts to maximize their best-use value as planks, deals, boards, billets or VENEERS. The original method of timber conversion from log to boards was to split the timber along the grain (RIVING). This remained popular for centuries. The most important development was the use of a saw to cut timbers into pre-determined planks. The Ancient Egyptian method of tying a baulk to a post and cutting with a pull-saw was followed by trestle or pit-sawing (see below). Indeed the pit-saw method was the most common method in England until the early to mid 19th century by which time steam-powered SAWMILLS were fully developed. In mainland Europe it was usual to use large trestles to support the timber to be cut above ground, whereas in England the digging of a pit was more usual.

The employment of water-powered sawmills, especially in North America, was common practice by the 18th century. Preliminary sawing or 'breaking down' was done by large circular or vertical saws. The choices after this depended upon the particular log and the end-use requirements. By the early 19th century steam-powered mills were becoming commonplace in the USA.
See also Sawmills

Bastard sawing
A cutting that shows the growth rings at angles of between 30 and 60 degrees with the board faces.

Flat sawing
This method saws straight through the log tangentially to the annual rings, giving attractive grain patterns in walnut and pitch pine, for example. This method is also called slash sawing, through and through or tangential sawing.

Pit sawing
From Roman times onward in mainland Europe the trestle support was a usual method of supporting logs to be cut. It was not, it seems, until the early 16th century that the pit-sawing process was introduced, and even then only in particular areas. England, Denmark, North-west Germany and Belgium appear to have taken to the idea, but in other cases the trestle remained the popular method. The pits were large holes in the ground about 1.80 m (6 ft) deep, 3.60–4.30 m (12–14 ft) long and 0.90–1.20 m (3–4 ft) wide. The log to be cut was laid over the pit on bars and held with timber dogs. The top sawyer

(top dog) was then able to snap a chalk line as a cutting guide and he then remained responsible for following this mark. The bottom sawyer, standing in the pit, supplied the power on the down stroke. The KERFS produced by this method reveal a straight but slightly angled set of parallel marks which are distinct from the kerfs made by vertical or rotary sawing machines.

Quarter rotary conversion
Logs are sliced and peeled circumferentially and therefore produce unusual grains; for example, bird's-eye maple. See VENEERS.

Quarter sawing
To reduce warping and to expose the medullary rays, the cutting of timber boards should allow the annual rings to be at right angles to the surface. By cutting the log down to the centre and then cutting the log into quarters so that the cuts follow its radius, the desired effect can be achieved easily. Woods cut in this manner often produce silver and ribbon grain.

Slicing
A guillotine knife-cutting process that cuts previously prepared logs intended for producing VENEER, either vertically or horizontally.
See also Riving, Sawmills, Saws, Veneering

Berg, G. (1957–8), 'The Sawing by hand of boards and planks', in *Folk-Liv*, XXI–XXII, pp.1–11.
Forman, B. (1970), 'Mill sawing in seventeenth century Massachusetts', in *Old-Time New England*, 60, Spring, pp.110–30.

Coopering and coopered joints

A method of making curved or shaped surfaces, derived from the craft of coopering (barrel making). Long, narrow, bevelled strips of timber are joined together to the shape of a former, then glued and held by clamping boards at top and bottom. Once the pieces have set, the COMPASS plane smoothes the surface which can then be veneered in a CAUL. The system is used for both vertical and horizontal applications. The vertical former consists of shapes for bombé door fronts and sides, and the horizontal former can be found in bureaux cylinder falls, for example. Coopering methods were also sometimes employed to make chairs, tubs and buckets.

Copaiba (*Copaifera langsdorfii*)

A Brazilian timber with an average density of 800 (50 lb/cu ft). The heartwood is reddish brown with darker streaks, with a variable grain and a medium-to-fine texture. Widely used for furniture-making in

43 *The extensive timber yard of the furniture manufacturer Harris Lebus of London, c.1910, gives an indication of the large scale that manufacturing had reached by the beginning of the 20th century.*

44 *A saw-pit and sawyers, photographed in High Wycombe, England, c.1905. The longevity of methods and processes which were satisfactory remains a feature of furniture-making.*

the 20th century. A resinous juice – copal oil and copaiba RESIN are obtained from this tree, which may be used in the preparation of VARNISH.

Copal resin
See above and Resins

Coping saw
See Saws

Copper
Although copper was used for edge tools in Ancient Egyptian times, it is as a furniture decorating material that it is now known. During the Middle Ages, copper was used as an adornment for chairs, beds and stools. For example, in the 12th century copper sheets were decorated with molten tin, and then applied to furniture (Theophilus, 1120, p.149). Copper has been used in conjunction with other materials, especially in Boulle work, but also as inlay in 17th-century cabinets. There are also examples of painted copper panels (frequently round or oval) being affixed to later-18th-century commodes. Around 1762, Frenchman Msr Destorges was recorded as a specialist maker of lacquered copper panels which were to be used in furniture decoration. Furniture-makers in the Arts and Crafts tradition in the late 19th century (as well as in the later Art Nouveau style) employed decorative copper panels in their work in addition to using copper hinges and mounts.
See also Enamelling

Copper pin nail
See Nails

Copperplate
See Printed cotton

Copy lathe
See Lathe

Coralwood (*Adenanthera pavonina*)
A timber found in India, Burma and the West Indies with an average density of 890 (56 lb/cu ft). When first cut, it is a yellowish shade, but as it matures it reveals a bright golden-red to coral shade. It takes a fine polish and may be mistaken for MAHOGANY. Known since at least the mid 17th century, as King Charles I owned 'a table of coral in waves' at Windsor (Jervis, 1989, p.287). A little later it was noted that 'the Aquitztil of New Spain … [is] an elegant tree called coral wood' (*Philosophical Transactions*, XVII, 620, 1693). In 1920 it was said that 'it would be useful in this country as it already is in India for cabinet work. It has not been imported commercially, but supplies are likely to be available in the near future' (Howard, 1920, p.4).

Cord, decorative
See Passementerie

Cord seats
A form of interwoven cord made from twisted, treated, brown kraft paper. It was widely used for bottoming chairs in the second part of the 20th century, and is especially associated with Danish dining chairs. Other varieties of cord seating have included GRASSES, reeds and extruded cellophane and plastic tube which is often associated with exterior or patio furniture, originally in the 'contemporary' style of the 1950s.

Cordia
See Freijo, Kalamet

Cork
Cork is a light, springy, buoyant substance that is derived from the bark of the cork-oak tree (*quercus suber*) which grows in the Mediterranean region. It has many uses in commercial applications but its use in furniture is limited to decorative finishes, often in the form of veneers for table tops, chair frames and accessories.

Corn husk
See Straw

Cornel
See Dogwood

Corner blocks
A shaped and angled piece of timber that is fixed between the rails at the joints of chairs and settees, to give strength and to combat timber movement. In the case of chairs the block types vary considerably. They may be open struts that are fixed into grooves in the side rails, or solid triangular or oblong blocks that are glued or screwed into position. The corner block was also called a 'brace', a term used amongst chair-makers for a piece of timber which was intended to 'prevent the girth webbing from warping or straining the rails' (Sheraton, 1803, p.91). They may also be used by cabinet-makers for strengthening feet. Bracket feet often have an interior corner block which is fixed with the grain running in the opposite way to the face material.

Corner plates
A late-20th-century method of fixing table legs to rails at the corners. The leg is fitted with a threaded screw which is placed into a shaped plate which fits into grooves cut into the rails. A wing nut tightens the assembly, so they are ideal for KD (knock-down) CONSTRUCTION.

Coromandel wood (*Diospyros*)
See Calamander

Coromandel work
See Lacquer

Cotton flock
A natural fibre derived from the cotton plant. Extensively used as yarn in textile manufacture as well as an upholstery filling. Short cotton fibres or linters are made into a loose cotton felt for application as wadding in upholstery processes. Used in this form since the mid 19th century and sometimes known as linter felt or cotton felt. As a WADDING it has been used in the 20th century to give a smooth feel over hair and eliminate the noise factor from springs.

Cotton velvet
See Velvet

Cottonwood (*Populus Sp.*)
A North American timber with an average density of 470 (29 lb/cu ft). Grey-white with a smooth even texture, named after the 'hairy' seeds resembling cotton puff. Used in the 20th century for veneers, cross banding and plywood work.
See also Aspen

Couching
An embroidery technique that produces a pattern by sewing lengths of cord to the support fabric by small over-and-over couching stitches. Couching is used for gold, silver, wool or silk cords that are too large for needlework directly. It is often employed in conjunction with other techniques such as APPLIQUE, border or scroll work.

Countersink
The process of cutting a tapered edge to a drilled hole to accommodate the screw-head without protrusion. The process requires a small tool with a cone-shaped cutter which is often a BIT or small hand-tool.

Courbaril (*Hymenea courbaril*)
A Central to South American or West Indian timber which is sometimes designated as LOCUSTWOOD. It has an average density of 830 (52 lb/cu ft). It is a rich reddish brown with streaks of varying hues, having an even but medium-coarse texture and an interlocked grain. Although used in the 18th century, it was very difficult to work, and its colour was fugitive, so it only occasionally replaced mahogany. As locustwood it was revived and praised in the mid 19th century.

This wood possesses all the important qualities of a valuable cabinet-wood. In dimension of timber, in colour, figure, and texture it is well suited to the manufacture of the larger and more expensive articles of furniture. It has hitherto been comparatively little known to British cabinet-makers, but from the elegant and ornamental character of the articles of furniture, manufactured in this wood and shown by the Austrians in the Great Exhibition, it is probable that it will soon be introduced into general use in this country.
(Blackie, 1853, p.47)

In the mid 20th century Courbaril was recommended for bentwood work and turning. It is also a source of copal RESIN.

Crabwood (*Carapa guianensis*)
See Andiroba

Crackle and Crackling finish
A network of fine cracks on an otherwise smooth surface. It is the result of applying rapid drying materials over slower drying ones. As a decorative finish, a failure has been turned into an 'effect', this being especially popular in the 1930s.

Cramp
A holding and tightening tool that has a number of variants in cabinet work and chair-making. G cramps, in a wide variety of sizes, are portable and used for many holding needs, while sash cramps are used for cramping-up and holding frames during gluing. A range of special clamps are produced for curved or corner work. Mitre cramps are used for accurate mitring, whilst fretwork or buhl cramps hold timber or veneers together while they are being cut. Sheraton defined a cramp as 'a four foot long iron tool with a screw end and a movable shoulder or arm which can force the closure of mortise and tenon joints' (1803, p.183). The process was mechanized in the 20th century.

Cranked hinges
See Hinges

Crankey
A checked linen ticking for a mattress. George Wyndham was supplied with 'a thick border'd crankey hair mattrass' by Chippendale in 1777 (Gilbert, p.286). In 1786 T. T. Byrd of Virginia was supplied with a 'wool cranky matrass' (Montgomery, 1984, p.207). The term was still current in the 1830s.

Crape
See Crêpe cloth

Crash
(a) Unbleached linen used as a basis for embroidery, especially in the mid 19th century.

(b) A rather coarse heavy fabric made from irregular tow yarns in a plain weave. Printed effects were often applied.

Crêpe cloth
A fabric made of various types of fibres (especially worsteds, silk) with an irregular and crinkly surface, obtained by using hard twisted thread or yarns, by embossing processes, by printing with caustic soda, or by weaving with varied tensions. Although best known as a dress fabric, it was occasionally used in America during the late 19th century as an upholstery fabric (Adrosko, 1990, p.108).
See also Cretonne

Cretonne
Originally a French term for unglazed printed cotton or linen cloth. Known in the 18th century as a heavy cloth with a hemp warp and a linen weft used for curtains and linen, it has been popular since the later 19th century for loose covers and upholstery work. 'New' cretonnes, a mix of hemp, linen and cotton, were produced in the 1860s. They were printed with delicate patterns and to some extent superseded CHINTZ. Eastlake noted that 'The new cretonne now used for bed furniture, &c., is a good substitute for chintz, in so far as it will wash and does not depend for effect upon a high glaze' (1878, p.101). In 1882 it was recorded that cretonne was 'a French name for a cotton fabric which has latterly superseded, to a considerable extent, the use of chintz for upholstery work' (Caulfield and Seward, 1882, p.95). Cretonne was particularly recommended for bedroom furnishings including dressing tables and bed drapery. Particular printed effects could be achieved, which included a different print on either side to make them reversible, or imitation tapestry designs with pigments that soaked into the soft, but twisted yarns to give a slightly worn effect. In 1927 it was said that: 'Crêpe fabrics are also sometimes printed with decorative designs, and sold as a light and cheap material known as "cretonne", which is employed extensively as loose coverings for furniture' (Nisbet, 1927, p.103). It is now a cotton fabric with a thicker warp and a thinner weft, having a lightly ribbed effect.

Crewel work
Crewels were originally the two-ply fine worsted yarns derived from warp ends and used for embroidery. The 18th-century use of the word crewel meant 'worsted': loosely twisted wool yarns for embroidery. In this case the term refers to the yarn and not to the stitches or design. Crewel now refers to embroidery of fine two-ply worsted woollen yarns on plain linen, used in the late 16th and 17th centuries to decorate hangings, especially beds. The designs, often floral, may have been derived from imported Indian cotton patterns.

English work was made on FUSTIAN or occasionally DIMITY. Up to the 1750s satin, long and short stem, knot and other stitches were used, and in later pieces so much yarn was used that the design appears in low relief. The designs were often drawn (stamped) on base cloth ready for embroidering. For example, Lady Forbes (1683) left 'a web of green stamped cloth for bed hangings' (cited in Rowe, 1973, p.106).

In the latter half of the 19th century the fashion for crewel work was revived as an antidote to BERLIN work. Anon, (1881), *The Young Ladies' Treasure Book* writes about crewel work:

The stitch used in crewel work is very old and very simple; but it is the least mechanical of all stitches used in fancywork, and much discretion in its practice is left to the worker; it is like hatching in chalk and water colour drawing: so that the effect be good, it signifies but little what means the artist takes to produce it. This freedom gives a peculiar charm and fascination to working in long-stitch, which indeed has not inaptly been called painting with the needle.
(1881–2, p.752)

Cummings, A. L. (1961), *Bed Hangings*, Boston, Mass.: SPNEA.
Montgomery, F. (1979), 'A set of English crewel work hangings', in *Antiques*, CXV/2 February, pp.330–41.
Rowe, A. P. (1973), 'Crewel embroidered bed hangings in Old and New England', in *Bulletin, Museum of Fine Arts*, Boston, 71, pp.102–66.

Crocus
A coarse linen SACKCLOTH used by upholsterers in the 18th century, especially in America.

Cross banding
See Banding

Cross-cut saw
See Saws

Cross grain
A particular feature of early- to mid-18th-century walnut furniture but also applicable to many other designs, cross-grain work is usually found in MOULDINGS which have the grain running across the moulding rather than along it. The contrasting lay of the grain makes a decorative variation to the main body.

Cross stitch
See Gros Point

Crystal
See Rock crystal

Cuban mahogany
See Mahogany

Cucumber wood
See Magnolia

Cuir bouilli
See Leather

Curled hair
See Hair

Curved forms
See Bending, Built-up work, Coopering

Cushions
A bag or case made from various materials in which is enclosed a filling, designed to soften seats or to be directly sat upon. This simple definition belies the enormous range of cushion shapes, styles, fabrics and various fillings that have been employed in their making. Cushions have at various times been used in conjunction with upholstered chairs and sofas, used on the floor, on beds or on chairs as bolsters, with stools or side chairs; they have been crucial, either as support or simply as a decorative addition.

Ancient Egyptian examples of cushions survive which are linen covers filled with water-fowl feathers. During the medieval period cushions were important and portable decorative accessories. By the 16th century, cushions were sheepskin (leather) lined, stuffed with FEATHERS and finally covered with cloth TAPESTRY or embroidered. These were based on two pieces of cloth laced round the inner bag. In 1509 the Dudley inventory included 'A cussion of purpull velvett, ij cussions, the one side of crymson damask and the oder side black satin' (Beard, 1997, p.282). By 1600 the envelope case had developed. Cloth of gold, satin damask and velvet silk were used as covering for cushions at this time, while applied EMBROIDERY became a common decorative method for cushions well into the 17th century. The techniques included fine tent stitch, or cross or Irish stitch, and STUMPWORK.

In the 17th century *carreaux*, or squab cushions, were based on leather-lined floor cushions, a Moorish tradition introduced via Spain. A *porte-carreau* was a cane frame designed to support the squab cushion, sometimes tufted, often en suite with a bed and its hangings, and used in the late 17th century. Bordered squab cushions were made for use with cane-seated chairs and were usually fixed with tasselled cords to the chair back. Squabs were firmer and made like a mattress with boxed sides, whilst the underside of the cushion was often lined or bottomed with an inferior material. In the 17th century references to 'baggs filled with down' are found, although the fillings would be down and lamb's wool or a white horsehair and wool mix for the best quality.

During the 18th century, Chippendale suggested that a sofa 'when made large … have a bolster and pillow at each end, and cushions at the back, which may be laid down occasionally and form a mattress' (1762, Plate XXIX). During this period some squab cushions were supplied with valances and loose covers. Sheraton recorded that 'cushions are stuffed with hair in a canvas case and are then quilted or tied down and have loose cases into which they slip' (1803, p.186). Their popularity grew through the century. In 1821 Maria Edgeworth wrote: 'I am now writing in a delightful armchair – high backed antiquity – modern cushion with movable side cushions with cushion elbows lying on the lowest of low arms, so that there is just comfortable room to sit down in a place between cushions' (Letters from England 1813–44, cited in Clabburn, 1988, p.161).

In the 20th century cushions comprise a wide variety of loose upholstery. They refer both to the interiors such as LATEX cushion or spring-filled cushion as well as to the use or style. The standard cushion has been supplemented by floor cushions, bean bags, scatter cushions, pillow cushions as well as the traditional models.
See also Air cushions, Latex, Needlework, Passementerie, Springs

Cut cupboard locks
See Locks

Cut velvet
See Velvet

Cutting-out board
An essential part of the basic equipment of a 'traditional' upholsterer. The board was made from timber of 3 cm (1.25 in) thickness and not less than 3.60 m (12 ft) long and 0.90 m (3 ft), or 1.50 m (5 ft) if making mattresses, in width; this stood upon TRESTLES. It was important for the front edge to be planed quite straight so as to act as a guide when fabrics were cut out.

Cylinder fall
Originally an 18th-century device for the front closure of a desk or bureau, the cylinder fall is usually a curved quadrant-shaped front cover fitted on pivots, so that when lifted it will disappear into the back of the cabinet. Early examples are often made up from thin slats that are coopered and then have canvas glued on the back, the front being veneered. The actual weighted balance may be a quadrant iron (unequally weighted iron bar fixed to the edges of the flap), a fan-shaped iron fitted to the quadrant, or a counterbalance arrangement. Sheraton describes the method of making in his *Cabinet Dictionary* (1803, p.186–9). A number of variations are possible, including a shelf that moves forward upon operating the cylinder fall. The cylinder fall is still used for certain bureau fronts.
See also Stay, Tambour

Cylinder hinges
See Hinges

Cypress wood (*Cupressus spp.*)
Botanically a softwood, it is a native of Persia, Asia Minor and southern Europe, and has a density of 440 (28 lb/cu ft). A yellowish tan to reddish colour with streaked veins, it is hard, durable and close grained. Used in Ancient Egypt for furniture and coffins, and by the Greeks and Romans for receptacles, it was a useful timber for chests as it had a pleasant scent. During the Gothic period cypress was widely used in Italy, Spain and southern France for cabinetry. Evelyn recommended it for 'chests and other utensils' as 'resisting the worm and moth and all putrefaction to eternity' (1662, p.145). At the beginning of the 19th century, Sheraton still suggested it for chests and musical instruments as it was even then considered resistant to worm (1803, p.139). By the end of the 19th century it was not considered commercially valuable. In the 1920s cypress veneers cut from stumps and crotches were sold in the USA as FAUX SATINÉ. More recently it has been used for frames and linings.

Damask
A reversible figured material woven in a compound weave, often of silk or wool (or any suitable yarns), deriving its name from Damascus. The particular pattern is the effect created by the contrasting warp-float and weft-float faces of a satin weave. Damasks are usually divided between multi-coloured patterned fabrics and 'table' damasks which are self-coloured, relying on the reflection of light upon the woven pattern for effect.

Damask was initially manufactured in Damascus and then Italy, especially Venice and Genoa. These centres remained the chief European suppliers until the 17th century. However, in the 16th century other centres of supply did develop, especially at Norwich and later in Spitalfields (*c.*1570) in London. Although particularly used for bed hangings, it was common practice to use damask for upholstery. The Lumley inventory of 1609 listed 'two damask chaires, three low stools of damask and two long quishions of damask' (*Walpole Society*, 1918, VI, p.41). By the mid 17th century, silk weaving was a flourishing industry in England. Damask was constantly in demand for furnishing and there are numerous references to its use. Nevertheless damasks of 'foreign' origin were the most esteemed.

In the 18th century, damask was so highly regarded as a furnishing textile that made-up work was often supplied with PROTECTIVE covers. Bimont recognized the reasons for this popularity: 'The material which is most used for all sorts of furniture is damask. It has a brilliance that other sorts of materials do not have … When it is strong it has two advantages: the first is that it is better suited for use on seats, the second is that the flowers show up better' (Bimont, 1770, p.209).

It still held an important position in the 19th century. George Smith noted that in 'elegant Drawing rooms plain coloured satin or figured damask assumes the first rank, as well for use as richness' (1808, xii–xiii). During the 19th century substitute yarns were used to lower the price of silk damasks. Worsted yarns, silk warps and cotton wefts, as well as wool and cotton mixes produced the damask effect at a cheaper price. Mixed damasks (linen warps and jersey or silk wefts) and worsteds were being used especially in upholstery.

In the mid 20th century damasks were also woven with a cotton warp and rayon weft, and have also been widely used as a TICKING on mattresses and divans.

See also Caffar, Caffoy, Harratine, Lampas

Thornton, P. (1965), *Baroque and Rococo Silks*, London: Faber and Faber.

Damask leather
See Leather

Dammar
See Resins

Danta (*Nesogordonia papaverifera*)
A West African timber with an average density of 720 (46 lb/cu ft). It has a reddish-brown colour with an interlocked grain and a fine texture. It has been used in the later 20th century as a plywood timber, for veneers and for cabinet-making.

Dark yellow wood (*Rhus rhodamthema*)
A Queensland timber described as 'soft, fine grained, and beautifully marked'. It was available up to 61 cm (24 in) wide and was once 'highly esteemed for cabinetwork' (Spon, 1901, p.131).

Darnix
See Dornix

Deal
Many coniferous softwoods have now been aggregated under this general title. Originally, a deal was a unit of measurement that referred to sawn boards, usually more than 23 cm (9 in) wide and not more than 7.60 cm (3 in) thick and at least 1.80 m (6 ft) long. Sheraton noted that deals (which word he considered derived from the Dutch *deel*, meaning a part load) were 'fir or pine timber that was cut into thin portions' (1803, p.191). It is now generally used to refer to sawn pine or fir timber. However, its use as a furniture wood description is found in the 1588 Howard House inventory, which listed a 'table of fine deale' (cited in Edwards, 1964, p.301).
See also Pine (Scots) and Spruce

Decalomania
See Découpage work

Decker work
Calico cloth, printed with a check design, often used for loose covers. Chippendale supplied 11 m (12 yds) 'fine decker work printed calico for chair covers' to Ninian Home at Paxton House in 1774 (Gilbert, 1978, p.274).
See also Check

Découpage work
Another name for LACCA POVERA. In the 18th century a form of amateur japanning was known as *découpage* work. Ladies were taught how to paste prints onto selected objects and then cover them with several layers of lacquer to imitate lacquering. The cities of Boston and New York were centres for such techniques in America during the mid

18th century. In the latter part of the 19th century and the first half of the 20th century the application of transfers to furniture was carried out both by amateurs and factory production lines. The process was simply to wet the surface with a dampening agent (for example, alcohol), place the transfer onto the surface, allow to dry and remove the paper, finally protecting the image with a varnish finish.

Sayer, Robert (1762), *The Ladies Amusement or the Whole Art of Japanning Made Easy*, London: printed for Robert Sayer.
Wing, F. (1965), *The Complete Book of Découpage*, London: Pitman.

Degame (*Calycophyllum candidissimum*)
A Central and tropical South American and West Indian timber with an average density of 810 (51 lb/cu ft). It has a wide sapwood, which is white to light brown with an olive brown heartwood, a variable grain and a very fine and uniform texture. Used for turnery, carving, and fine cabinet-making, often as an alternative to LANCEWOOD. Aka Lemonwood (USA).

Denim
Originally *serge de Nîmes* (denim). A strong twill-weave cotton fabric usually plain coloured. Fashionable in the late 19th century, it was recommended by Codman and Wharton for 'willow armchairs with denim cushions' (*Decoration of Houses*, 1897, p.29). It was later used for upholstering under-seat cushions (platforms) in mid-20th-century American upholstery work. Figured denim has also been used for upholstery work.

Densified wood
In this *c.*1950 technique, which created a man-made timber product, a large number of veneers were taken and then impregnated with resin and bonded under extremely high pressure. Its resultant strength and weight precluded it from general furniture-making, but it was used for shaped feet and similar items. It was more widely used in the factory for making moulds and jigs for regular production parts. Another version was to impregnate wood veneers with urea resin. This material, called Parkwood-Textolite was made by the General Electric Co, and was used to make table-tops which were resistant to heat and spillage.
See also Atomic wood

Deodar (*Cedrus deodara*)
A sub-species of CEDAR found in the western Himalayas and North Africa. It has an average density of 570 (35 lb/cu ft) and is light brown, with a straight grain and a medium to fine texture. It was introduced in the mid 19th century and mainly used for garden furniture.
See Cedar

Diachromatizing
A decorative process invented in the latter quarter of the 19th century by H. C. Webb of Worcester, England. It was a method of dyeing or staining wooden surfaces with a pattern that penetrated the surface, so was longer lasting than a simple surface treatment. This method had the benefit of not being prone to wear and abrasive removal. Examples of diachromatized furniture were exhibited at the International Health Exhibition of 1884 in London.

Diamond matching
A method of using decorative VENEERS so that four consecutive leaves from the bundle are cut in such a way that they are 'matched'

to make a diamond shape. They can be reversed to make a crossed effect.

Diamond tufting
See Tufting

Diaper work
(a) A repeating pattern, often found in MARQUETRY, INLAY, and woven material designs, in which the pattern is a system of criss-crosses resulting in triangles and diamond shapes. It is particularly represented in veneered parquetry designs on 18th-century French furniture. Aka *Jeux de fond*.

(b) A name for cloth with diagonal shapes woven in lozenge shapes usually referring to household linen.

Die cutting
A later-20th-century version of STEEL CARVING, which usually works in conjunction with plywoods. It is a factory process in which decoratively shaped plates of sharp steel cut plywood panels to create an effect rather like fretwork.

Dimity
A variety of fabrics have been called dimity. Originally made in Italy as a kind of coarse cotton or flannel, it was first produced in England during the 17th century from wool; it was later woven as a cotton and linen fabric, usually in opaque white or light shades, with a corded and slightly striped effect achieved by alternating warp and weft-faced stripes. The *Mercury Dictionary* noted that 'the term was given by Indian traders to a cotton cloth of the fustian character, and usually figured with raised stripes, giving the appearance of embossing due to thick weft floats' (c.1950, p.177).

In 1696 'Dimetty … which is called Pillis Fustian is of great use

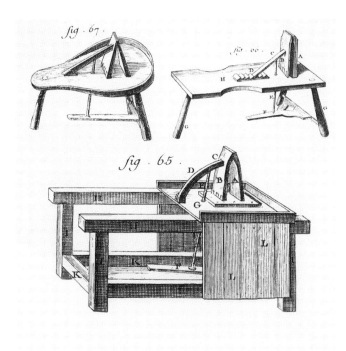

to put feathers in for pillows' (*Merchants Warehouse*, cited in *Oxford English Dictionary*). During the 18th century it was used for covering bolsters and mattresses, and Parson Woodforde 'had the two best chambers to sleep in and very handsome they were both very fine white dimity furniture very full and fringed' (*Diary*, 2 May 1792). Hepplewhite found that 'white dimity, plain or corded, is peculiarly applicable for the [bed] furniture, which with a fringe of gymp head, produces an effect of elegance and neatness truly agreeable' (1794, p.18), whilst Ackermann showed stamped dimity as 'an entirely new article for white beds and other furniture' (Ackermann, 8, 47, November 1812, p.304). It remained popular, as Loudon noted, for modern villas: 'dimity curtains, for both beds and windows, are considered in good taste, especially in the country where they keep long clean' (1839, p.1080). Dimity was also used throughout the 19th century for slip covers, especially in the USA. In the 1880s it was still used for bedroom hangings and furniture.
See also Bombazine

Cummin, H. (1940), 'What was Dimity in 1790', in *Antiques*, 38, July, pp.23–5.

Distressing
See Ageing

Dogwood (Cornus)
Aka cornel
(a) The *Cornus florida* is an American timber from the eastern USA, with an average density of 800 (51 lb/cu ft). It is a hard and heavy timber with a straight grain and a fine texture, coming from a small tree. The sapwood is the only usable part and is light yellow to pale pinky-brown. Aka American boxwood.

(b) The *Cornus sanguinea* is a native to Britain and, like the American variety, straight grained with a fine and uniform texture, smooth grained and varying from tan yellow to bright yellow-red colouring. It turns well and has been used for shuttles and bobbins and was occasionally used for inlays in the 16th and 17th centuries.

Dolphin hinge
See Hinges

Domes of silence
A range of circular, metal furniture accessories developed in the 1950s, that are fitted to the wooden legs of (usually) chairs or small furniture, to assist in the silent movement of the chair on wooden floors or to glide over carpeting.

Donkey
The donkey is a name given to a variety of devices intended for holding fast timbers or veneers while they are being worked on. The Windsor CHAIR-MAKERS used a particular donkey for shaping chair top-rails and splats which were held in a vice. MARQUETRY and BOULLE workers used a donkey which was nicknamed a 'neddy' in the mid 19th century.
See also Horse

Dornix (Darnex or Dornick or Domeck)
A linen-warp and wool-weft fabric used for upholstery, curtains and table covers, but especially associated with bed covers. The name probably derives from Doornick, the Dutch name for Tournai (Flanders), where it was originally made. It was introduced into England (Norwich) in the 15th century by Flemish weavers and it re-

47   Three examples of French marquetry 'donkeys', c.1760–70. The lower example, which is bench-mounted, would require the artisan to stand rather than sit as in the other two examples.

mained popular into the 17th century. Dornix was woven on large looms, often with repeat patterns in widely varying scales, but when used for upholstery the chosen patterns were comparatively large. Dornix is distinguished by its relatively coarse texture and it is likely that it was akin to the 'tapisseries de BERGAME', the so-called 'poor man's tapestry'. In 1601, Hardwick Hall had an embroidered bed with 'a curtain of darnix and a piece of buckerom about the bed to cover it' (Boynton, 1971, p.23). In a less fashionable Essex inventory of 1672 there was '… 1 Livory board and Darnix Cloth, 1 standinge joined bed with Darnix curtains and vallents' (Steer, 1969, p.125). It was rarely used after the beginning of the 18th century.

Dotter
A measuring stick devised by chair-makers. It is about 41 cm (16 in) long with a shoulder at one end as a stop and a metal point at the other end (that is, nail or screw). By tapping the pointed end where required on the timber, it 'dots' a mark where the piece is to be bored or drilled. This ensures a degree of alignment between components.
See also Measuring

Double-end tenoner
See Machines (Tenoner)

Double nailing
See Nailing

Double-stuff stitching
See Stitches and Stitching

Douglas fir (*Pseudotsuga menziesii*)
An important softwood (but not a true fir) native to Western North America that produced much of the plywood in use during the latter part of the 20th century. It has an average density of 530 (33 lb/cu ft), is pink to reddish-brownish biscuit colour with a straight grain. A marked contrast between early and late wood gives a prominent growth ring structure which shows itself as a contrasting light and dark stripe. During the 1950s it was widely used for wardrobe ends, table tops and whitewood and kitchen furniture as it wears well. Aka Oregon or Columbian pine.

Dovetail
See Joints

Dovetailer
See Machines and machinery use

Dovetail maker or template
A simple device made from either thin hardwood or sheet brass, for marking out dovetail shapes ready for hand cutting of joints.

Dovetail saw
See Saws

Dowel and dowel joint
See Joints

Down
The soft, feathered undercoating of water fowl consisting of the light down clusters without any quill shaft. Known since ancient times as a luxurious CUSHION or MATTRESS filling. The use of down for

mattress fillings was recorded by Chaucer in the mid 14th century in his *Book of the Duchesse*: 'Of downe of pure doves white, I will give him a feather bed' (1369/70). In the early 18th century, Queen Anne was supplied by Hamden Reeve with 'a large fine dimity bed tick and bolster covered with white satin and filled with seasoned swans down containing ninety pounds of down in them' (Heal, 1953, p.149). Mixed with feathers, it has been a favoured cushion filling for loose cushions on upholstery to the present time.
See also Feathers

Dragon's blood
See Stains

Drawboring
A joinery method which incorporates pegging a mortise and tenon joint with dowels. The holes in the tenon are closer to the shoulder than the holes in the mortise (i.e. offset), so that when the dowel is driven through, the joint is tightly drawn together. Moxon suggested the degree of offset should be only 'about the thickness of a shilling' (Moxon, 1703, p.88.).

Draw knife
See Drawing knife

Drawer plane
See Planes

Drawer or Till lock
See Locks

Drawers
Originally called tills or [with]drawing boxes. In the 17th century drawers were made with rebated sides that fitted into front panels, which were often nailed home. The drawer bottom was rebated into the front and nailed to the base of the sides. To allow this drawer to work simply, a groove was cut into the exterior side of the drawer up to 13 mm (½ in) deep, so it was necessary that the drawer sides were made from relatively thick timber. The grooves accommodated wooden runners which were fixed inside the carcase to support the operation of the hung drawer. There was no progress on reducing the chunky drawer frames until a new support system was devised.

In the late 17th century, side-drawer runners became obsolete as soon as the drawer was so arranged as to run on a wooden-base platform. This meant that the underside of the drawer had to be fully rebated and glued to avoid nail damage, but it was also possible to construct drawers with daintier narrow sides. By the 18th century this developed into drawer bottoms that were rebated about 3.2 mm (⅛ in), with the result that the bottom of the side edge projected. This was strengthened by a fillet, 13–19 mm (½–¾ in) thick. These runners underneath the drawer cause wear and tear which make a channel on the carcase. Although improvements in the late 17th century incorporated the dovetail joint, the early through-dovetails meant that a moulding had to be applied to hide the open joint on the drawer front. Once the lapped dovetail was used, the surface could be decorated as required and finished with a simple cock beading.

Eighteenth-century dovetails continued this development but became narrower and often more numerous. By the end of the 18th century MUNTINS for partitioning drawer bottoms were being applied to large drawers to enable them to be made economically and safely. At the turn of the century and into the 19th century, quarter-round mouldings were fixed into the inside edges of drawers. These both strengthened and tidied the drawer interior.

Cheaper cabinets allowed for the drawer divisions to be dovetailed into the carcase side while the drawer supports were often nailed to the side panel, in the manner of the previous century. This method created a problem as the rails acted as battens and hindered the movement of the carcase panels, thus causing splitting. Conversely, on expensive work, it has been known for the drawer bottoms to be made by the 'frame and panel' method to completely avoid splitting. Whilst quality drawers often have linings made from oak, pine is more common on vernacular items.

By the 20th century the virtues of the hand-made joint were only exploited by followers of the Arts and Crafts movement: for most other work the use of machine-cut dovetails, mortise and tenons, and so on was to be standard until new materials changed the technology of drawer making. However, even in large factories drawers had to be 'fitted' by hand, using sand paper, planes and scrapers to ensure a good fit at the final assembly stage. This changed with the development of PLASTIC extrusions which snap together to make a drawer shape. These were ideal for the new KD designs which require to be flat packed. The potential of flat-pack drawers which required no assembly was a boon to this form of manufacture. This method was also extensively adopted for factory making where semi-skilled labour could be employed.
See also Joints (Dovetail)

Drawing knife

A tool with a flat or curved blade from 4 cm (1.6 in) to 20 cm (8 in) long and up to 6.4 cm (2.5 in) wide. The blade is normally chisel shaped, and the tapering tangs (one on each end) are turned upwards to receive wooden handles. The tool has been used in a wide range of woodworking trades, where they are generally used to remove surplus wood and for chamfering and rounding. They are often used in conjunction with a shave HORSE.

Already known in Ancient Egypt and used by Viking carpenters, the modern version was common by the mid 17th century. Moxon noted that it was 'seldom used about house-building but [was] for the making of some sorts of Household-stuff as the legs of Crickets [low wooden stools], the rounds of ladders' (Moxon, 1677, p.122). In chair-making in particular, the drawing knife was a very versatile tool. The TURNER used it to shape chair legs and stretchers prior to final turning, whilst in general chair-making it was used for almost all the preliminary shaping work. The drawing knife was also used to 'tune' the pole of a pole LATHE by shaving away the underside, to tension the springiness as accurately as possible. The chair-makers often made their own versions called 'lined and steeled draw knifes'. These were home-made adaptations which split the metal edge and allowed a tool steel blade to be fitted in, giving superior quality cutting with the original flexibility.

Dressing marks

The ridges and furrows that sometimes remain upon secondary timber surfaces. They may either indicate a product of the pre-machine age, or a lack of finishing.

Driers

Any material that is added to a liquid that assists the polymerization and drying process. Red lead, litharge, turpentine and zinc sulphate are all ingredients of traditional driers that have been used by gilders, paint and varnish-makers for many centuries.

Drills

Generally a tool, or the cutting piece inserted into a tool, that makes holes in materials. The earliest drill appears to be the bow-drill used in Ancient Egypt, where the bow string was fitted round a rod with a cutting end. Pressure was applied to a cup held on the top of the stock, while the bow was pulled to and fro. This drill form was supplemented in the Middle Ages by the BRACE which allows continuous rotation and also accepts the torque needed to make larger holes. It is now loosely used to refer to machine and hand drills as well as the BITS they use. The breast drill and hand drill, although still having a place in the furniture-maker's tool kit, have been generally superseded by the electric power drill and its wide range of attachments.

Driver

A description for a person from at least the 16th century who was employed to separate the DOWN from FEATHERS and who removed lumps from feather mattresses, probably with the assistance of bellows. In some cases, the driver also made new bedding, bolsters and pillows.

Driving bolt

A specialized 18th-century tool designed with a hollow shank intended to drive decorative bolts into work. It fitted over the bolt or nail and pushed them home. In this way the nail's gilding was not damaged as it surely would have been had a hammer been used.
See also Prickall

Drop-in seat

A ready-made upholstered seat pad and frame designed to 'drop in' to a chair seat frame without fixings. Introduced in the early 18th century, they have been in use ever since. These seats are usually upholstered with webbing and stuffing and may sometimes be sprung with zigzag SPRINGS in later examples.

Drugget

A 'sort of stuff, very thin and narrow, usually all wool, and sometimes half wool and half silk, having sometimes the whale [rib] but more usually without' (Chambers, 1752). It was occasionally used for curtains and linings. In 1710 the old nursery in Dyrham Park was recorded as having 'three pieces of grey druggett hangings' (Walton, 1986, p.63).

By the mid 19th century drugget was a more coarsely woven fabric used as a protective cloth for tables, carpets and floors. 'They are chiefly employed to lay over another carpet, to preserve it when the room is in daily use, and openly removed for company...' (*Workwoman's guide*, p.202).

Drum sander

See Machines (Sander)

Ducape

A plain-woven, stout silk poplin (that is, slightly corded) fabric known since the 17th century, but mainly as a dress textile. It is a form of GROSGRAIN but is softer in texture. According to Beck, it was introduced into England by the Huguenots, *c*.1685.

Dug out

See Construction

Duralumin

Heat-treated aluminium alloys (including copper) with the strength of mild steel but much lighter. Named after Duren in Germany.
See Aluminium

Durance or Durant

A material that was imported into England by 1660 and was made from 'thred or silk'. In the 18th century it was a plain weave, glazed worsted variety of TAMMY or EVERLASTING, but finer than either. Chippendale supplied Durant as a curtain lining for the Dumfries House commission (Gilbert, 1978, p.138). In the later 19th century it was used for window blinds. In the 20th century it was recorded as a heavy felt, woven to imitate leather, in a buff colour with a smooth finish similar to a billiard cloth. Durance was also a name given to buff leather, hence the crossover of names (*Mercury Dictionary*, c.1950, p.194).

Dust board

A term for the fully-fitted boards set between individual drawers within a chest to maintain cleanliness and security. May be variable in size, that is, either the full thickness of rails or thinner than side rails.

Dustproof joints

See Joints

Dutch elm

See Elm

Dutch gold

A mixture of 80 per cent copper and 20 per cent zinc (for example, brass) which produced a distinct gold-coloured alloy used for Boulle work. When beaten into thin leaves, it was also employed as a substitute for gold leaf in the 18th century. An 18th-century notice described it as

copper gilt … and beaten into leaves like the genuine. It is much cheaper; and when good greatly [imitates] the effect of the true at the time of its being laid on the ground; but with any access of moisture, it loses colour, and turns green in spots and indeed in all cases its beauty is soon impaired, unless well secured by lacquer or varnish.
(Dossie, 1758, p.369)

The 1731 inventory of the firm of Bastard of Blandford (Dorset) lists 'a large quantity of Dutch gold' valued a £1.16.0d, along with various items of gilding equipment (Legg, 1994, p.29).

Dutch rushes

See Grasses

Dyes and Dyeing of wood

The staining and colouring of furniture woods occur most often in the finishing processes. The dyeing process gives colour right through; STAINING, on the other hand, only gives a surface colour. Dyeing appears to have been most satisfactory in the case of veneers. They were soaked in water, dried and then placed in dye baths, ensuring an even take-up of colour. Until the introduction of synthetic dyes in the 19th century, the origin of most dyes was from vegetable matter (berries and barks and pulverized tree woods, treated with solutions). Sheraton noted that 'the art of staining wood was more in use at the time when inlaying was in fashion, which required most of the primitive colours; at present red and black stains are those in general use' (1803, p.308). In the 19th century, experiments with dyes included in-troducing colour into a tree whilst it was still living, by letting roots ingest coloured liquid supplied to the tree in the years before cutting (*Scientific American*, 3 (37), 3 June 1848, p.296). These ideas were not always welcome. For example, the process invented by a Dr Boucherie for injecting dyes into woods that were to become part of marquetry panels was denounced because it was thought that these processes 'have presented a dangerous facility to the designers and workmen' (Wyatt, 1856, p.294). Some timbers and veneers were pre-stained by the converters or the cabinet-makers, ready for use. During the 19th century this was a Parisian veneer speciality, and dyed veneers have been subject to the vagaries of fashion ever since.
See also Annotto, Archil, Brazilwood, Diachromatizing, Fustic, Stains and staining (Alkanet) (Log-wood)

Eaglewood (*Aquilaria agallocha*)

Sourced from the Far East and India, this wood is the ALOES timber of biblical times, and is also known as PARADISE WOOD or AGALLOCH. It is a resinous wood, with an aromatic odour, a straight grain and a medium coarse texture. The usable centre part of the trunk is coloured in a variety of red and green hues which combine with growth ring markings for a very decorative effect. Eaglewood was apparently first known in Europe in 1539 when Jean III of Portugal visited Malacca. More widely known in France: for example, in 1686 Siamese ambassadors presented some of the timber to the court, and it was used in the 18th century for marquetry (Roubo, III, 1769–75, p.770).
See also Calambac

East African olivewood

See Olivewood

East Indian rosewood

See Rosewood (Indian)

East Indian walnut

See Kokko

Eastern red cedar

See Cedar

Ebéniste

The French term for a cabinet-maker who works mainly with veneers, as opposed to a *menuisier* who usually works in solid wood. When ebony was introduced into French furniture-making in the early 17th century, it was particularly used for veneering. The workers in this wood were soon called ébénistes, and were clearly distinct from *menuisiers* who specialized in solid and carved wood work. The dynamism of French (especially Parisian) furniture-making in the 18th century was based on the trade organization which segregated the making from the retailing on the one hand, and the employment of foreign trained labour on the other. It has been estimated that a third of the Parisian workforce was made up from first or second generation immigrants during the 17th and 18th centuries. This created a network of employers bound by family ties, who were particularly located in the Faubourg St Antoine, thus benefiting from locational as well as familial factors.

The divisions of labour were noted by Roubo: 'The menuisier-ébénistes, for the most part, do not make the carcases themselves but have them made at rock bottom prices by other menuisiers who do nothing else' (1771, p.453). Nevertheless, Roubo considered the ébéniste to be an artist who needed not only practical skills but also a wide knowledge of other matters. Roubo included in this a knowledge of the gluing, dyeing, shading and polishing of all wood species used in cabinet-making; a knowledge of a diverse range of materials, including ivory, shell, mother-of-pearl, tin, copper, pewter, silver and precious stones; and in addition, a knowledge of chemistry was thought necessary for the preparation of stains and tints, as well as skills in drawing and designing with taste (Roubo, 1772, p.763). The skills of the French cabinet-makers not only ensured a market for their work at home and abroad, but also set a standard that others were measured against. Sheraton considered that 'cabinet work is more strikingly improved [in France] than any other branch of mechanical trade whatever' (1803, p.115).

Auslander, L. (1996), *Taste and Power, Furnishing Modern France*, Berkeley: University of California Press.
Janneau, G. (1975), *Les Ateliers parisiens d'ébénistes et de menuisiers aux XVIIe et XVIIIe siècles*, Paris: Editions Serg.

Ebonizing

The process of producing a finish that resembles EBONY by staining and polishing with dyes and stains. The methods were well known in the 18th century. Sheraton gave a recipe (taken from Barrow's *Dictionarium Polygraphicum*, 1758) using pear-tree wood and other similar grained woods, which were given a 'wash with a hot decoction of galls, and when dry, adding writing ink, polishing it with a stiff brush and a little hot wax' (1803, p.205). The so-called 'German ebony' was made by steeping woods such as sycamore, fruit wood, and beech into a mix of blue or black aniline dyes, dissolved in alcohol. In the 19th century ebonized BAYWOOD or blackwood was particularly used by designers working in the Aesthetic style. In the 20th century ebonizing continued to be a simple way to give inexpensive woods an exotic look. In the 1950s and 1960s black lacquered or painted legs and frames were supplied to cabinets and tables, often in combination with brass ferrules. These acted as a contrast to the glossy finishes of wood or plastic laminates that the cabinet or table was mainly constructed from.
See also Charcoal polishing, Lampblack

Ebonite
See Plastics (Vulcanite)

Ebony (*Diospyros spp.*)
A hard and heavy timber with an average density of 1150 (72 lb/cu ft). In colour it ranges from black, to purple-brown and grey intermingled, with a fine texture, and a straight or only slightly irregular grain. The timber is hard and brittle and is very difficult to work, but takes a fine finish. There are different varieties and countries of origin for ebony. The Ceylon ebony (*D. ebenum*) and West African (Cameroon and Nigeria) ebony (*D. crassiflora*) are generally uniformly black, whilst Macassar ebony (*D. celibica*) and Ceylon COROMANDEL (*D. quaesita*) often have striped or veined heartwood. The Indian subcontinent supplied *D. tomentosa* and *D. roylei*, whilst *D. ebenaster* came from the East Indies. Whatever the source, the tree is rather small, thus limiting the amount of usable timber, therefore it was mainly used for mosaic work, inlay, turnery and small cabinet work.

Ebony was employed by the fashionable court circles of Ancient Egypt, both in the solid and as veneer. For example Tutankhamun's tomb housed a solid ebony bedstead. Ebony timber was considered valuable enough to have been collected as booty, paid in tribute or given as a diplomatic gift. Amenhotep III gave the King of Babylon beds in ebony overlaid with gold and ivory as well as head-rests

and chairs made in ebony and decorated with similar treatments. The Romans used ebony as a veneer and examples of medieval use are also recorded. In 1357, Edward III had 'an ebony chaire with a leather case' (Eames, 1977, p.189).

However, in the 16th century it was widely imported into Europe, mainly from the East Indies, and was then particularly used for veneering cabinets in Germany or for making small decorations in the Dutch taste. By *c.*1600 the Augsburg cabinet-makers were concerned that imitations of ebony would devalue their work, so they stamped cabinets with *eben* to distinguish them (Kreisel, 1970, p.105). During the 17th century, the South German Kunstschrank was developed with ebony as the prime cabinet wood, while in Italy ebony was widely used for table cabinets. In many of these cases the choice of ebony was as a foil to the bright-coloured decoration supplied by precious stones, tortoiseshell, ivory and the like. The problem of imitating ebony grew. By the beginning of the 18th century, ebony was widely imitated by paintings, or staining. (See EBONIZING.) Sheraton (borrowing from Barrow's *Dictionarium Polygraphicum*, 1758) said that 'the black ebony is not at present so much in use as it formerly was, since there have been discovered so many ways of giving other hardwoods a black colour' (1803, p.204).

By the 19th century ebony regained favour, although it was not easy to use. *The Cabinet-maker's Assistant* (Blackie, 1853) listed Mauritius ebony (*D. ebenum*) as the best, but it was only available in diameters from 15 to 20 cm (6 to 8 in). It was prone to splitting upon drying, so was often immersed in water for many months and, when removed, was bound with iron rings to hold it in place during seasoning. The second half of the 19th century was the great age of international exhibitions and, amongst the furniture showpieces, none were more spectacular than the ebony cabinet work exhibited by various countries.

African ebony (*Dios. crassiflora*)
A jet-black ebony with an average density of 1000 (64 lb/cu ft). Imported from the end of the 19th century, but mainly used for instrument making as it was more inert and less attractive in colour and grain.

Andaman ebony (*Dios. marmorata*)
A decoratively marked ebony species from Ceylon and the Andaman Islands with an average density of 1000 (64 lb/cu ft). It is a grey-brown timber with darker brown or black bands which alternate on quartered surfaces to produce 'zebra stripes'. On end grain, a pattern of brownish-black spots give a marble-like appearance. It has a smooth, fine, even texture with a straight grain. It was used for cabinets and decorative veneers, and as a substitute for CALAMANDER wood in the early 20th century. Aka ZEBRAWOOD, East Indian ebony or Marblewood.

Ceylon ebony (*Dios. ebenum*)
A very heavy, fine textured black wood with some brown striping, but less than Marblewood or Macassar ebony. Logs are converted to small sizes, to avoid splitting.

Green ebony
See Green ebony

Indian ebony (*Dios. melanoxylon*)
An ebony variety widely located in India and South East Asia. It has been used locally and exported since the 18th century.

Macassar ebony (*Dios. celebica*)
Aka Indian ebony, COROMANDEL, CALAMANDER (*D. quaestia*) wood. A hardwood with a deep brown colour, with varying black or brown

stripes. Texture is fine and even, but it is a difficult timber to dry and to work. Highly valued for veneers, inlay and small works. Imported by the Dutch in the 17th century via Macassar, which was the principle port of exit on the SW of Celebes islands. Used for cabinets especially during the 1920s.

Madagascar ebony (*Dios. perrieri*)
An ebony variety from Madagascar, imported into Europe in the mid 17th century first by the Portuguese, then the Dutch.

Mauritius (*Dios. ebenum*)
According to the *Cabinet-maker's Assistant* (Blackie, 1853), ebony from Mauritius was the finest, hardest, blackest and most costly form of ebony, but was only available in 15–20 cm (6–8 in) diameter. In the early 20th century, it was still considered the source of the best quality ebony.

Eder
The OSIERS obtained from WILLOW wood used to make frames.

Edge treatment (Cabinetry)
Cabinet work has often required edge finishing by decorative means, for example CHAMFER, CARVING, MOULDINGS, FITTINGS. In veneered work the edge treatments, amongst others, include BANDINGS, LIPPINGS, FILLETS, metal trims.

Edge treatment (Upholstery)
The completion of edges in upholstery work, both internally and externally, is an important part of the process. Edges give definition to the required shape or outline of an upholstered seat. The earliest method seems to have been a simple BRAID or PIPING that defined the shape. By the early 18th century squared edges were being fabricated, echoing the square frames of easy chairs. These built-up edges were formed by fixing WEBBING along the side and front edges so that it stood proud of the frame. The HAIR stuffing was pulled to the side by stitches sewn through the side web so as to build up a firm edge. By the later 18th century the so-called French edge was introduced. This was made from a rolled pad of hair or GRASS that was inserted into an overlapping flap of linen extending from the first covering. This sewn-in edge former gave a crisp shape to the neo-classical styles that were fashionable at the time.
See also Bible front, Cane edge, Passementerie, Rolled edge, Tacking

Eel grass
See Grasses (Sea wrack)

Elder wood (*Sambucus nigra*)
A European timber with an average density of 700 (44 lb/cu ft). White to lightish yellow wood with no visible grain, it is similar to HOLLY. It has been used as inlay and also for cheaper turned chairs. In France it was known as *bois de sureau*.

Elemi
See Resins

Elm wood (*Ulmus spp.*)
A hard, tough timber with an average density of 550–640 (35–40 lb/cu ft). With a pale dull brown colour, a coarse texture and a bold figure, it takes a fine finish and bends well. Sometimes it is tough to work, due to its crossed fibrous grain. It has had a tendency to buckle in

seasoning, but this can be overcome. The horse dung immersion process (see SEASONING) was recommended for elm in the same way as other timbers, to enhance colour and figuring. The European use extended to Scandinavia and northern Europe and it was particularly popular in the early 19th century in France as *bois d'orme*.

American or White elm (*U. americana*)
A Canadian and eastern American timber with an average density of 610 (39 lb/cu ft), it has a pale brown sapwood and a deeper brown heartwood, often with a reddish tinge. It is coarse textured with a mostly straight grain. Despite being indigenous to the eastern seaboard it was not widely used, although large quantities of elm were exported from Canada to the British Isles in the mid 19th century. In the early 20th century this wood was cheap and widely used as a cabinet wood and in some cases for exposed parts. Aka ORHAM WOOD (Canada).

Dutch elm (*U. hollandica*)
Similar to the common elm, but recognized as being stronger and firmer in texture than its common relation.

English elm (*U. procera*)
An important timber, it is commonly used for Windsor chair seats, table legs as well as single-plank table tops. The Penshurst Place table at 8 m (26 ft) is a fine example. In 1485 'a dressing bord of elmen' was recorded (Eames, 1977, p.64). John Evelyn recalls the use of elm for the making of 'trunks, and boxes to be covered with leather; coffins, for dressers and shovelboard tables of great length' (1662, p.44). He also recommends it for the carver: 'by reason of the tenor of the grain, and toughness which fits it for all those curious works of Frutages, Foleage, Shields, Statues and most of the Ornaments to the Orders of Architecture, and for not being much subject to warping' (Evelyn, loc.cit.). In 1726 it was still recommended for dressers because 'it will not break away in chips like other timbers' (Neve, 1726, p.258). In the mid 18th century there were attempts to treat elm with acids and stains to simulate mahogany.

Elm burrs and twisted growths that revealed highly decorative veneers have been widely used on cabinet work. This taste continued into the 19th century, when Ackermann recorded that 'The manufacture of British woods such as the pollard oak and elm, cut transversely near the roots, is now so well understood, and so beautiful when thus applied, that they need no recommendation to the admirers of superior furniture' (Ackermann, R., January 1824, Plate 135). Twenty years later the taste was still popular. Loudon recorded how 'The knobs which grow upon old trees are divided into thin plates by cabinet-makers particularly in France and Germany; and when polished they exhibit very curious and beautiful arrangements of the fibres which render this wood extremely ornamental for furniture' (1844, p.1380). The reason it went out of use was that it required a high degree of skill to lay and finish the veneers, which were notoriously difficult to fit.

Its utilization in the solid for chairs was recognized by Sheraton who noted that elm was used instead of beech for country chair-making (1803, p.205). By the mid 19th century it was remarked that 'although at present it is rarely used except for the commoner sort of Windsor chairs and similar articles, not more than twenty years have elapsed since it formed a principal material for drawing room furniture of the best description' (Blackie, 1853, p.14). During the 20th century it was still used for Windsor chairs and was also employed for other cabinet work.

Smooth leaved elm (*U. carpinifolia*)
A European hardwood with an average density of 580 (36 lb/cu ft). It is a dull reddish-brown with a straight grain and a medium density. Used for furniture and upholstery frames. Selected logs produce decorative veneer. Aka French elm.

Spreading elm (*U. effusa*)
Valued in continental Europe for its markings for turnery, cabinet-making and gun stocks.

White (Rock) elm
See Orham wood

Wych elm (*U. glabra*)
An elm species which grows in northern Europe, northern and western Asia and north Africa. A tough timber with an average density of 680 (42 lb/cu ft). It shows a clear differentiation between sapwood and heartwood. The heartwood is light brown with a greenish tinge, sometimes even streaks of green. It has a straight grain and its distinctive rings give a handsome figure on quarter-sawn timber. Pollarded wych elm also provided a very rich veneer (Loudon, 1844, p.1405).

Embossing
The process of moulding surfaces so they are in relief.

(a) In plywood work, chair seats were sometimes embossed with hot plates carrying a design which caused parts of the surface to stand in relief. The panels were then rolled flat and cooled, creating an embossed effect. The technique was called 'Flachbrand' or 'Thermoplastic' and was developed and widely used in the bentwood furniture of Thonet and others in the later 19th century.

(b) A late-20th-century process that produces a raised or three-dimensional pattern on a substrate. The method starts with a carver who prepares a model of the required design. Over this a silicone rubber mould is poured, and when set, removed and filled with ceramic slurry. When this is set hard, a beryllium-copper alloy is poured over the ceramic mould. Once this is cold, the copper mould is ready for the embossing chamber where a mix of heat, pressure and time allow the mould to 'emboss' the prepared wood or MDF substrate with the original pattern.

Embroiderer
A person who embroiders or puts on decoration to cloth. A long history of ecclesiastical sponsoring of embroideries was brought to an end with the Reformation, so that embroiderers had to turn to other clients to ply their trade. In many cases they were employed by households to prepare and finish upholstery work, much of which was 'worked' by the women of the house. However, professional embroiderers were employed for both costume and furnishing embroidery by the monarch and aristocracy, certainly by the late 16th century. In 1591, the Bacon accounts record payments 'to the embroiders sonne for 24 weeks 3 days at 3s the weeke' for embroidering bed hangings (Clabburn, 1988, p.102). In 1649 Randle Holme showed an image of a 'chair made by an Imbrautherer' (Book 3, XIV, p.14). But if Celia Fiennes is correct, women still took an active role in this work. She recorded in 1712 that in the Queen's Closet at Hampton Court 'the hangings, chaires, stooles, and screen the same, all of satten stitch done in worsteads, beast, birds, images, and fruites [were] all wrought very finely by Queen Mary and her maids of honour' (1982, p.241). By the 18th century embroidery was a commercial proposition for both upholsterers and specialists. For example, Elizabeth Watson ran an embroidery business from her shop at the Sign of the Wrought Bed. In 1706 she was selling ready-made embroidered bed hangings as 'wrought beds from £7 to £40 packed, with all sorts of fine chain stitch work' (Heal, 1953). In 1747 Robert Campbell defined their work:

Embroiderers may be reckoned among the dependants of the Lace-man; as in his shop the greatest part of their rich work is vended, and he furnishes them with all materials for their business. It is chiefly performed by women; is an ingenious art, requires a nice taste in drawing, a bold fancy to invent new patterns and a clean hand to save their work from tarnishing – few of the workers at present can draw, they have their patterns from the pattern drawer, who must likewise draw the work itself, which they only fill up with gold and silver, silk or worsted, according to its use and nature.
(1747, p.153)

Embroidery
See Fustian, Needlework

Emery paper
See Abrasives

Enamelling
(a) A smooth, hard and glass-like coating fused by heat onto a (usually) metal surface. The technique of enamelling, long known to jewellers, was adopted during the second half of the 17th century as a decorative process for furniture and mirrors. A vitreous paste was used to decorate brass castings. The fashionable colours included light turquoise, white, green, black, purple and red. Decorative enamelled copper was also used for drawer handles and hardware in late 18th and early 19th centuries.

(b) An early-20th-century furniture finish prepared by coating a surface with a mix of whiting and size. When set, this was rubbed down smooth and finished with a transparent French polish.

Enbowing plane
See Planes (Moulding)

Endive marquetry
See Marquetry

Engraving
The inscribing of lines and or designs onto bone or metal components

48 *A page from an English illustrated catalogue showing 'stamped commode handles with enamel centres', c.1770. The enamelling technique was part of a trend in the later 18th century for lightly applied decoration to cabinets.*

of furniture, especially BRASS, has been a feature since the 17th century. It was usually the work of a specialist engraver employed by the cabinet-maker. The technique is particularly associated with Boulle work and early- to mid-18th-century brass inlaid furniture.

Escutcheon
(a) Armorial shields that occupy a central place on the pediments of cabinets or other items.

(b) More commonly the term refers to keyplates and covers that fit around a keyhole as a decorative feature. Cartouches with modelled ornament have been common for escutcheons, but they may also simply be pivoted cover plates.

Espagnolette lock
See Locks

Etchwood
A form of decorative plywood, usually Douglas Fir, in which a pattern was created by scraping the grain with a series of rotary action wire brushes. This was used in the mid 20th century as a decorative finish, as it made an etched effect on the surface ply, revealing something of the substrate as a contrast.
See also Plywood

Eucalyptus wood (*Eucalyptus sp.*)
A family of Australian timbers, having over 250 species. A number of these are gum trees. Australian white ash, BLACKBUTT, Karri, JARRAH, red river gum, TASMANIAN OAK, and white-topped box are all members of the family. They have been used by Dutch cabinet-makers in their East Indian colonies as well as by Australasian furniture-makers.
See also Bloodwood, Gumwood, Ironbark

Euonymus
See Spindle wood

Everlasting
A satin weave textile mainly used for coat linings and shoe tops, that is occasionally found in upholstery work. As 'lasting' it was used in the USA in the later 19th century as a substitute for HAIRCLOTH.
See also Durant

Excelsior
A trade name for a cheap 19th-century upholstery stuffing made from thin spiral shavings of woods, such as HICKORY, CEDAR and POPLAR. In the USA it was also known as 'pine state hair'. In 1868 a US Patent (Pat.no.75728) was taken out for a machine to manufacture excelsior, and it was still being used as an inexpensive stuffing material in the 1920s. Wood wool is a similar material, but is often produced with very thin timber shavings. Aka Shruff

Extrusion process
A method of fabricating plastics, in which the dry pelleted material is extruded through heated dies or nozzles and cooled upon exit to create a continuous profiled object of uniform section.

Facing
A piece of superior wood that is fitted over a lesser quality base wood. It is not necessarily a veneer, although the effect is similar.

Fancy cabinet-making and makers
A term applied in the early part of the 19th century, which referred to cabinet-makers who made small items such as work-tables, writing tables, boxes, dressing-cases and so on, often devising new or novel designs and using 'fancy' or exotic woods. Although specialist makers of small fashionable items had been established in the latter part of the 18th century, the introduction of machine-cut fancy wood veneers in the 1820s encouraged the development of a specialist group of makers. The fancy cabinet-making trade was highly divided with specialists in particular styles as well as those working in specific areas such as the fitting up of the interiors of boxes and cases, or the fixing of the fabric linings. In England, by the middle of the 19th century, the work had degenerated into the so-called 'dishonourable trade', witnessed by growing evidence of poor and scamped workmanship.
See also Lining

Mayhew, H. (1850), *Morning Chronicle*, Letter LXIV, 8 August.

Fancy chair-making and makers
The term 'fancy chair' is recorded as being used in the 1780s in both England and America. In 1786, a consignment of '14 fancy back chairs open cutt, shap[ed] feet with cane seats, very neatly japanned green and white and drawn into sprigs of flowers' were sent by John Russell, royal chair-maker (cited in Kirkham, 1988, p.21). The description perfectly shows the typical features of fancy chairs: the light frame, cane seat, japanned finish and painted or stencilled decoration, noted by Hepplewhite in 1788.

Several of these designs [for chairs] are particularly adapted to this style, which allows a framework less massy than is requisite for mahogany; and by assorting the prevailing colour to the furniture and light of the room, affords an opportunity, by the variety of grounds which may be introduced, to make the whole accord in harmony, with a pleasing and striking effect to the eye. Japanned chairs should have cane bottoms, with linen or cotton cases over cushions to accord with the general hue of the chair.
(1788, p.1)

By the early 19th century the term fancy chair-maker was in common currency and indicates the speedy growth of the specialism. They were generally made from beech or birch, were painted in light colours or japanned, and were considered to be very elegant and attractive. Indeed they often cost more than mahogany chairs. To meet the demand which grew rapidly from the turn of the 18th century, a trade of specialist fancy chair-makers developed. In 1803, in London, there were at least six businesses, specializing in fancy chair-making only, as well as general chair-makers who no doubt also made fancy chairs to order. However, by the 1830s the taste had declined and the specialist trade proved no longer profitable.

Fancy chairs also had a great popularity in the first half of the 19th century in America. They were made in cities and rural communities alike, but in terms of style they were often derived from Sheraton's patterns. The woods used included MAPLE, BEECH and other softwoods suitable for JAPANNING. In American examples, CANE was particularly used for seats, but they were also often made from RUSHES or FLAGS. An 1812 advertisement from New York records:

Asa Holden, 32 Broad Street, has a superb assortment of highly finished fancy chairs, such as double and single cross, fret, chain, gold, ball and spindle back, with cane and rush seats etc., of the latest and most fashionable patterns. The cane seats are warranted to be American made, which are known to be superior to any imported from India.
(Rider Lea, 1960, p.38)

They were widely used to furnish steamboats and were known as 'steamboat fancies'. Fine examples of fancy chair-making were found in Baltimore, while Pittsburgh became well known for bulk production of fancy chairs. The trade was important enough for a fancy chairmaker's trade society to exist in America. The famous firm of Lambert Hitchcock was established in 1825 at Hitchcockville (Rivington) Connecticut and made chairs from machine-turned parts that were then decorated and STENCILLED. The finish imitated the effect of japanning by using a dark background and decorating the surface with stencilled designs using metallic powders.
See also Painting

Boram, John (1999), 'Eighteenth Century fancy chairs from High Wycombe', *Regional Furniture*, XIII, pp.7–16.
Evans, Nancy Goyne (1996), 'Nomenclature of Vernacular Seating', *American Furniture*, pp.38–51.
Rider Lea, Z. (1960), *The Ornamented Chair, its Development in America, 1700–1890*, Rutland Vermont: Tuttle.

Fat Bag
A dolly (bag) 7 cm (3 in) in diameter, containing a suitable fat (for example, suet), wrapped in hessian. Used by mattress makers to grease needles and thread before buttoning.

Faux bamboo
A particular paint effect for wooden or metal frames to imitate BAMBOO, which had a particular vogue in the early 19th century. Discussing bamboo furniture, Sheraton wrote that 'these are, in some degree, imitated in England, by turning beech into the same form, and making chairs of this fashion, painting them to match the colour of the reeds or cane' (1803, p.29). However, there were limits to this taste. In the mid 19th century the *Journal of Design* commented upon a Coalbrookdale cast-iron hall chair that was painted to imitate bamboo:

no bamboo chair could ever exhibit the ridiculous bits of ornament which disfigure this, nor could it have been made without ties and points of connection, all of which are here omitted. We really had imagined that society was getting tired of the conventional upholsterers bamboo with its three black strokes and splashes to indicate foliations; but here it is breaking out in the most inveterate form, upon a material least of all calculated to support the attack.
(1850, vol.II, p.202)

As a paint technique it has been revived periodically ever since.
See also Bamboo

Faux satiné
A cut of CYPRESS crotch veneer, often from stumps, which produces timbers similar in colour and texture to SATINWOOD. Used for furniture in the USA in the 1920s.

Feather banding
A form of CROSS BANDING which has two thin widths of veneer laid diagonally to each other to produce a feathering effect. Often found on drawer fronts of late-17th- and early-18th-century cabinets.

Feather bed
See Mattress

Feather stitch
See Stitches and stitching

Feather work
The use of feathers for decorative work has been part of furnishing for

49 An English side-chair, painted to simulate bamboo, c.1770. This example does not pretend to replicate bamboo exactly, rather it creates an impression as part of a whole decorative scheme.

well over three hundred years. The first significant use was for crestings of beds. Randle Holme recorded their use: 'The tester adorned with plumbes according to the colours of the bed' (1649, Book III, xiv, 16). The decorations were often made from egret (from the French, *aigrette*) feathers but more usually they were made from white, occasionally coloured, ostrich feathers. Plumage of all sorts was supplied and fitted by a feather-dresser who worked in cooperation with the upholsterer. In rare cases feathers were used to make complete ensembles of tester, bed cover, and matching wall and upholstery decoration.

By the 19th century feather work was used to describe a decorative technique often employed by amateurs, which consisted of covering buckram or other foundation with a design made from birds' feathers and sewn over the base. Used for valances, picture frames, chairs, brackets, fire screens and clothing, the range of feathers used was only limited by the imagination.

Cassidy-Geiger, M. (1999), 'The *Federzimmer* from the *Japanisches Palais* in Dresden', in *Furniture History*, XXXV, pp.87–111.

Feathers
The plumage from a wide variety of birds used for practical and decorative purposes alike. The range includes chicken, swan, goose, eider (Hudson's Bay feathers), heron and ostrich feathers. Used in Ancient

Egypt for cushion fillings, feathers are still best known as MATTRESS or CUSHION fillings. The feathers are distinguished between live, that is plucked from a living bird, and those removed from dead birds. The former, being considerably more elastic, are the most sought after. A difference is also made between scalded feathers and dry pulled feathers. Scalded feathers refers to soiled feathers that had to be washed and cleaned; dry pulled feathers being simply plucked and dried in an oven.

The supply of feathers was apparently subject to unscrupulous interference, and the need to scrutinize the trade was soon recognized. In 1495 an Act against Upholsterers was passed that remarked upon 'corrupte stuffes, that is to say of scalded feders and drie pulled feather togedre and of flokks and feders togedre, which is contagious for mannys body to lye on …' (cited in Houston, 1993, p.9). However, when used properly they made luxurious beds. In 1539 Giles Corrozet honoured the

Delicate soft and luxurious bed,
bed of tenderest down,
Bed of good and fine feathers …
(*Blazon of the Bed*)

Apparently most of the 16th- and 17th-centuries' imported feathers came from Antwerp, although other centres did supply them, for example Bordeaux, Burgos and Denmark. In 1637, Ralph Grynder supplied Queen Henrietta Maria with '46 pounds of fine Burgis feathers to fill the seat and winges …' (Beard, 1997, p.289). The use of feathers and down for upholstery fillings (as well as bedding) was common practice by the latter part of the 17th century. In a further attempt at quality control in 1679, the London Upholders' company maintained that no upholsterer should

mingle … any flocks and feathers together to put on sale or shall put to sale … any corrupt or stinking feathers in any bedd bolster pillow cushion or in any cowches squabbs chairs or stooles and that every person using the said art or mystery shall cause his or her feathers to be cleansed of dust and quill before the same be put on sale.
(Cited in Houston, 1993, p.57)

Feathers remained important to the 18th-century upholsterer. For example, Chippendale maintained two feather rooms at his London premises, and another upholsterer, Paul Sanders, listed in his inventory 21 kg (46 lb) of seasoned down, 218 kg (480 lb) of feathers, feather bags, as well as beating frames and poles for feathers (Beard, 1997, p.13). The beating frames and poles indicate that proper handling, that is drying and cleaning, was an important part of good practice then as now. Feathers were 'dressed' by airing, or driven by being beaten in a bag to loosen the dirt (see DRIVER).

Sheraton had to warn against a clearly continuing problem of quality control: 'Several very imposing arts are practised by brokers and dealers in feathers which the strangers and fair trader ought to be aware of' (1803, p.208). The international nature of the feather trade continued into the 19th century with eider down imported from Denmark, using Hudson's Bay suppliers, while swans' down was imported from Danzig. By the end of the century, feather imports concentrated on German and Russian sources, along with a continuing home supply. During the 19th century (1830s onward) the method of cleaning and purifying was by steaming, although in their 1835 inventory the Philadelphia business of Hancock and Co refer to a 'kiln' for drying feathers. In the 20th century feathers have remained as an upholstery filling as well as continuing in use for quilts, eiderdowns and duvets.
See also Down

Federal

The Classical revival that developed towards the end of the 18th century in America coincided with the newly acquired status of the United States. The term covers furniture and decoration made between 1785 and 1810 and is particularly associated with regional work specific to areas and craftsmen, created in an often discreet classically based style. In Boston the Seymours were well known, whilst in Salem it was the Sandersons and Samuel McIntyre who led the field. Duncan Phyfe is typical of the Grecian taste associated with New York furniture, whilst in the same city, C.-H. Lannuier developed his version of the French Empire style. Although mahogany remained popular, the Federal style also espoused CHERRY, MAPLE and WALNUT especially in the rural areas. Exotic woods such as bird's-eye maple and SATINWOOD were used.
See also American red gum, Ash wood, Cherry, Holly wood, Lead, Satinwood, Verre églomisé

Fern work

See Leaf decoration

Ferret

A stout cotton or silk tape. The name probably derives from the Italian *fioretti* for floss silk. In 1764 William France supplied Sir Lawrence Dundas with 'green lutstring curtains ferreted with silk ferret and every other peculiar' (Beard, 1997, p.307). Ferret was sometimes specified for Venetian blind drawstrings in the 19th century.

Fibreboard

A homogeneous sheet material made from bonded wood fibres. It is less expensive and less strong than plywood but may be used in non-structural situations. In England in 1898, early experiments based on the breaking down of fibres of cellulose material, especially hot-pressed waste paper, led to the development of hardboard or Masonite. In around 1908, Canadian manufacturers used ground wood to make pulp boards, but it was soft and of a low average density. The main innovations came in the early 1920s when wet pulpwood was compressed in hot presses to produce rigid sheet boards, suitable for furniture applications. (Developed by Masonite Company USA from 1926.) Used mainly for space filling in drawer-bottoms and cabinet backs, its image has perhaps suffered in quality furniture use because it has also been a favoured 'do-it-yourself' material. It has been produced in a wide range of sizes and finishes. From 2 to 12 mm (c.⅛ to ¾ in) thick with the standard smooth face, it can be patterned on the surface with moulded or embossed effects. A 'tempered board' is standard hardboard with resin impregnations, which makes it stronger and more water resistant.

Hardboard has been used for building furniture in a variety of methods. The use of hardboard for panels in CHAIR FRAMES, introduced post World War II, had advantages over plain dowelled frames in that the pressure was absorbed over a wide area and not solely on the joints. The assembly can be stapled and the regularity of production as well as skill level is constant. The use of hardboard as a structural skin in chair frames, using single curvature shapes, was developed in the 1970s in England but did not appear to be successful. In cabinet construction, the single and double 'skin and frame process', although losing popularity by the 1970s, was a potential method of cabinet framing to reduce weight whilst retaining dimensional stability. A timber frame with a hardboard surface fitted to it on one or both sides was considerably lighter than the equivalent particleboard solid product, but the assembly was more time-consuming, so it fell from favour.

FIRA (1975), *Hardboard in Furniture*, Stevenage: FIRA.

Fibrefill
A later-20th-century upholstery filling made from crimped polyester fibres matted together to make a thick wrap usually in conjunction with polyurethane foam interiors.

Fibre glass
See Glass fibre reinforced plastic

Fibre-rush
A material made from twisted PAPER that resembled cord. The fibre used was derived from wood pulp reduced in a solution of sulphuric acid, which produced a paper of greater strength than did the alternative soda process. First used in 1904, when an American firm, the Western Cane Seating Co, produced a chair made from woven fibre-rush over a wooden and RATTAN frame. The machinery for fully developing the idea was designed by H. Morris, an employee of the Ford Johnson Furniture Company of Chicago. They gave the name of 'Fibre-rush' to this new WICKER-like material. By 1912, over 15 per cent of the 'wicker' market was being met by just four manufacturers who used fibre-rush. By 1930 fibre-rush furniture accounted for an astonishing 85 per cent of all 'wicker' furniture made in the USA.
See also Lloyd Loom, Wicker

Gandre, E. (1930), *Fibre Furniture Weaving*, Milwaukee: Bruce Publishing.

Fielded panel
A form of panelling technique that followed architectural styles in the 17th and 18th centuries and was often used on cabinet doors. It was formed by a raised panel, framed by mouldings. Alternatively it could be made from the solid. Moxon describes how 'You may (if you will) bevel away the outer edge of the pannels and have a table in the middle of the pannel' (1677).

Figure
The figure of a timber is the result of the angle of cutting and refers to the decorative pattern of the internal structure of the board or log. Radial cutting is most common in revealing figure; for example, quartered oak and chestnut reveal 'flash' or 'silver' figure. Similar effects can be found in beech, while sycamore offers a flame figure and plane tree gives lacewood. Quartered exotic timbers such as ebony and rosewood reveal vertical stripes, whilst straight cut versions will give irregular blazes of colour. Other methods reveal differing figure. For example, crotch, formed at the point that the tree forks into two large branches, is found by cutting timbers tangentially. The contrast between sap and heartwood is also figure, for example, laburnum oysters, royal walnut and the feathering of walnut crotches. Irregular grain structures offer a range of figure styles including feather, ray, fiddleback, blister, ribbon, curl or butt.

BURRS reveal some of the most extreme examples of figure and are highly prized, while the timber's growth rings offer an obvious figure caused by plain sawing through the rings, revealing the variations that are caused by different growth patterns in various years.

Filigree
In metal work, filigree is decorative open-work producing lace-like patterns usually in solid gold and silver. It has also been copied in less expensive materials such as paper, parchment and so on. Originating in the 15th century and using metal mainly for devotional works, it was revived post-1650 when strips of paper duly crimped, stiffened, rolled and twisted were mounted onto panels with threads. Seeds and shells, papyrus rinds, tree bark and gilt-edged and painted paper were also used to create patterns. This form of decoration was later a pastime for 18th-century ladies, and patterns and models were published for their use. In addition, some furniture was especially designed with inset panels ready to take the paper scroll work. In 1786 ladies were supplied with 'a profusion of neat elegant patterns and models of ingenuity and delicacy suitable for tea-caddies, toilets, chimney-pieces, screens, cabinets, frames picture ornaments etc.'. It was added that 'the art [of filigree] affords an amusement to the female mind capable of the most pleasing and extensive variety; it may be readily acquired and pursued at a very trifling expense' (*New Ladies Magazine*, cited in Edwards, 1964, p.318). Skilled workers could use up to 135 rolls of paper per 6.5 sq cm (1 sq in), each fitted individually. The technique was called quilling in America.

Christy, Betty, and Tracy, Doris (1974), *Quilling, Paper Art for Everyone*, Chicago: Regney.
Robertson, Hannah (1777), *The Young Ladies School of Arts Containing a Great Variety of Practical Receipts, in Gum-flowers, Filigree, Japanning, Shell-work, Gilding, … &c.*, Edinburgh: Printed for Robert Jameson, Parliament Square.

Fillers
The preparatory process of filling, intended to fill pores and level the surface, is one of the first operations in wood finishing. A variety of methods have been employed. GESSO was the earliest method used by Ancient Egyptians. Others included rubbing the surface with linseed oil and using a flat pumice stone to make a mash, so the grain would fill as required. In other cases, waxes and resins mixed with colouring matter could be used to stop up blemishes. In the early 19th century plaster of Paris, dyed or stained and mixed with a liquid binder, was suggested for filling open grain before the final finishing. By 1900, filling methods included the following: the use of plaster of Paris rubbed in with a damp cloth; wet plaster of Paris rubbed over the whole surface and then cleaned off; Russian fat, plaster and suitable pigment laid in hot and then wiped off; and even mutton suet rubbed into the surface and then cleaned off.
See also Beaumontage, Compositions, Imitation wood, Stopping

Fillet
A term used for a number of differing applications:
(a) A strip of wood used to support a shelf.
(b) A plain timber band used to distinguish varieties of mouldings.
(c) A slip of wood used to edge a panel or table top.

Fillings
See Upholstery fillings

Fillister
See Planes

Fineline
See Composite veneers

Finger joint
See Joints

Finish
The finishing of wooden furniture in a variety of systems to enhance, protect or decorate has been an essential part of the furniture-maker's

50 *A line of women workers spray-polishing cabinets in the Harris Lebus factory during the 1950s.*

repertoire since early days. Resinous coatings have been found on furniture dating from the 8th century BC. Traditional methods of furniture finishing (see below) have stood the test of time and remain in use. However, the possibilities offered by the discoveries and inventions of science and their application to the furniture trade were noticed in the early 19th century. In 1829 a furniture-maker's guide astutely commented that:

The researches of the chemist are daily adding to a stock of information valuable to every department of the arts and sciences; among these the cabinet-maker and upholsterer will find many peculiarly serviceable – witness the modern improvements in cements, varnishes, gilding, polishing and every other part of ornamental decoration.
(Stokes, 1829, pp.vii–viii)

This explosion of information was demonstrated by the wealth of practical volumes on the subject of furniture finishing, along with many articles in magazines and dictionaries that were published throughout the 19th century. By the 20th century the beginnings of scientific involvement in the preparation and application of standard factory-made finishes marked the end of the personal recipes and concoctions that were manifest up until then. By the late 20th century, finishing had become a complex and highly developed part of the manufacturing process. Up to eleven different coating operations may be required for a finish. These include sap equalizer, prestain, overall stain, washcoat, combination stain, sealer, glaze stain, lacquer, pad accent/splatter or antique glaze, two coats of lacquer and rub finish. All these now belong to the province of the science of finishing.

Finishing systems can be roughly divided into four broad groups; these encompass the decorative and illusory treatments as well as purely functional ones.

The first group comprises those systems used with the intention of either enhancing or protecting the natural grain of the timber by providing a defensive coat. As a protective measure, finishing was intended to keep the surface usable and practical.
See POLISH (FRENCH POLISHING), WAX POLISH, VARNISH

The second group relates to ideas of disguising the quality of the timber, altering its appearance or colour, or imitating another type of timber or material. It is not surprising to find that methods were devised to give an inexpensive timber the look or colour of a more fashionable or higher quality one.

See CHARCOAL POLISHING, COMBING, DIACHROMATIZING, DYES, EBONIZING, GRAINING, JAPANNING, MARBLING, PLASTIC LAMINATES, PRINTING, STAINS, VERT ANTIQUE, XYLOGRAPHY

The third group is made up of the decorative finishes that are applied to furniture, to ornament them without necessarily attempting to imitate.
See AGEING, ANTIQUE DUSTING, BLEACHING, CRACKLE, DECOUPAGE, EMBOSSING, FROSTING, GILDING, HIGHLIGHTING AND SHADING, INLAY, LACQUER, LEAF DECORATION, MARBLING, MARQUETRY, PAINTING, PICKLED FINISH, POKER WORK, XULOPYROGRAPHY, SILVERING, STENCILS, VENEERS

The fourth group is related to colouring the surfaces, where the colouring or dyeing of different woods was legitimately used to produce a colourful marquetry or inlay pattern. In either circumstance, the process often took place on pale-coloured timbers, such as holly, pear, and beech that were relatively easy to acquire and able to take the colour and polish well. (See DYES, LACQUERS, JAPANNING, PAINTING, STAINING.) Colour changes can also be made by many of the finishes mentioned. In addition to these wood-based finishes, attention has been given to decoration and finishing of metal. (See ANODIZING, CHROMIUM PLATING, ENAMELLING, LACQUER, OXIDIZING, PAINTING, POLISH, SANDBLASTING, TOLE)

Collier, J. W. (1967), *Wood Finishing*, Oxford: Pergamon.
Dresdner, M. (1999), *The New Wood Finishing Book*, Newtown, Conn.: Taunton Press.
Frank, George (1999), *Classic Wood Finishing*, New York: Sterling Publishing.
Oughton, Frederick (1982), *The Complete Manual of Wood Finishing*, London: Stobart & Son.
Pattou, A. B. and Vaughn, C. L. (1944), *Furniture Finishing, Decoration and Patching*, Wilmette. Illustration: F. Drake and Co.
Penn, T. Z. (1984), 'Decorative and protective finishes 1750–1850', in *Bulletin of Association for Preservation Technology*, xiv, pp.3–40.
Siddons, G. A. (1825), *Cabinet-makers' Guide*, London: Knight and Lacey.
Thomas, M. (1985), *Furniture Finishes and Related Materials*, Stevenage: FIRA.

Finishing equipment

Once machine processes were established for finishing in the late 19th century, a number of developments either related to the process itself or later, to the needs of the flow-line, were made. These include spraying, coating and the final processes of drying and curing.

Coating

A method of passing flat panels along a conveyor that runs under a suspended tank of lacquer, so that it flows a film of lacquer evenly over each panel ensuring an economic and accurate finish. It is ideal for flat pack designs.

Dryers and curers

Rather than allow finishes to dry by evaporation or solidification, modern late-20th-century finishes are best set or cured by methods such as hot air, infra-red or UV curing processes. These speed up setting times and ensure a regular result, and can be built into a flow-line production system.

Spray finishing

A method of applying finish which was in full use by the 1920s in larger enterprises. The conventional spray is a jet of lacquer combined with a jet of air designed to break the lacquer into droplets as it is expelled and to re-establish itself as it settles on the object. A refinement of this process is the airless spray, in which the pressure in the pot forces small lacquer droplets through a fine nozzle at high velocity. Further development resulted in the electrostatic spray, in which each droplet of lacquer is given an electrostatic charge. The object being sprayed is then earthed so that the droplets are attracted directly to it and produce a wrap-around effect, avoiding any overspray. This was ideal for chair-frames and intricately shaped objects. More recently the robotic spray has been developed. There is a variety of automated spraying techniques for large-scale production methods which can include control and memory devices.

Fir (*Abies spp.*)
See Douglas fir, Pine

Fish-mouth spring
See Springs

Fish skins
See Abrasives, Shagreen

Fittings
A general name for the metal or plastic accessories that are part of the operational additions to furniture.
See Back plates, Bed-screw, Bolt, Bureau action, Cam, Castors, Chair mechanisms, Corner plates, Domes of silence, Glides, Hinges, Hooks and eyes, KD, Locks, Plates, Platform rocker, Stays, Table opening and extending mechanisms, Weights, Wheel mechanisms

Adolphe, J. (1890), *Present-day Furniture Fitments and Decorative Detail*, London.

Flags
The term flag was early English for reed. It now refers to endogenous plants such as Iris, but in early use indicated any REED OR RUSH used for BOTTOMING chairs.
See Grasses

Flake board
See Particle board

Flame stitch
See Stitches

Flannel
A woollen cloth of loose texture usually without nap, sometimes used for hangings as well as for PROTECTIVE COVERS. Hangings made from flannel are listed in the 1603 inventory of Hengrave (Clabburn, 1988, p.245), whilst in the 1710 Dyrham Park inventory there was recorded a 'great cedar chest' in which were 'several large parcels of flannel for covering the furniture' (Walton, 1986, p.67). During the 18th century, thick flannel material was recommended for the inside backs of large mirrors, to provide a soft bed for the silvered glass. It was also used to line leather chair covers. George Smith noted in 1808 that 'Salisbury flannel has been much used [for drapery]' (p.xii). According to Beck, by the end of the 19th century, 'flannel was usually sold white' (1882).

Flies
Extension pieces sewn to the sides of top outer coverings of upholstery work that are not seen, but are needed to complete the tight covering of chairs and the like. They are usually of HESSIAN or CALICO, thus saving on the cost of the main cover.

Flint paper
See Abrasives

Flitch
See Veneers

Float buttoning
See Buttoning, Buttons

Float glass
See Glass

Flock
See Woollen flock

Florentine mosaics
See Pietre dure

Flour paper
See Abrasives

Fluting
A decorative treatment for furniture in which hollow channels are cut into columns or side-by-side along friezes or table tops. Although special machinery for 'fluting wood for columns' was patented in England by Leonard Hatton in 1776 (Pat.no.125), machines to prepare flutes and wave mouldings were already published in 1774 by Roubo (*L'art de menuisier en meubles*, Plates 312–15). By the 1870s the process was very simply done with a lathe.
See also Mouldings

Foam, synthetic
A cushioning and suspension product used widely in the later-20th-century upholstery industry. Its manufacture is based on the interaction of a polyol and an isocyanate with water, in which a reaction is created so that polymers form and gas generation causes expansion. The introduction of plastic (polyether) foam as an upholstery material broadened the range of possibilities for upholsterers especially in the finished profiles of their products. Initially introduced as a substitute for LATEX, it could also soon offer its own possibilities.

First discovered in 1848, its significance as a material was not recognized until 1937 when Dr Otto Bayer discovered the polymerization process from a family of organic chemicals known as polyurethanes. Wartime developments encouraged experimentation, so that by 1952 Farben-Fabriken Bayer had developed flexible polyurethane foams and in 1953 the Du Pont Corporation also announced their process. The products were mainly used in the textile industry until the 1960s when polyether upholstery foams developed, which encouraged use in seating applications. Many avant-garde designers in the 1960s used plastic foams to create eye-catching and flamboyant designs deliberately planned for short runs and limited editions. In the popular market, foam-engineered products included mattresses, complete bed-settees and easy chairs.

The more recent developments in plastic foam technology have resulted in a range which has a wide choice of densities and hardness factors, special features like fire retardancy, and ancillary developments that have included polyester wraps (FIBREFILL) which give a softer feel and look to cushions, as well as variable average density made-up cushions that give support and comfort.
See also Latex

Foils
Plastic and impregnated paper foils which can be printed to imitate

a wide range of designs are treated like VENEER. Introduced in the 1970s, they have provided manufacturers of inexpensive furniture with an ideal surface treatment for chipboard panels and the like. The foils are usually printed with a wood grain effect to simulate real timber veneers. The added advantage of PVC and ABS foils with their inherent strength and flexibility made them ideal for vee jointing (one piece MITRING) and folding operations in the factory. Decorative paper foils are strengthened with fillers and laminated to the substrate direct from rolls, thus ensuring a reliable surface. Resin-impregnated papers are often applied to HARDBOARD where strength is not required, and used for decorative wardrobe backs and drawer linings.

Folding wedges
A pair of wedge-shaped pegs used to tighten boards that are to be jointed to make a panel. Used in place of CRAMPS, they are especially suited to curved work (in conjunction with shaped bearers).

Fondeurs-ciseleurs
French metal-casters and chasers who worked bronze mounts before the final gilding by the *doreur*.

Four cutter
See Machines

Four point platform
A mid-20th-century upholstery suspension method that used rectangular rubber sheets fitted with fixing points in each corner, which were anchored to hooks in the corner of seat frames. Often used for show-wood upholstery, the diaphragm effect spread loads evenly and allowed for thinner cushions. Originally developed for the motor industry, it was a simple and effective upholstery support for both show-wood and metal-framed upholstery.

Fox wedging
A method of jointing, in which wooden wedges are inserted into the end of a tenon so that they spread the tenon when it is inserted into a stopped mortise, ensuring a very tight fit.

Frame saw
See Saws

Frame-maker and Frames
This trade specialized in the manufacture of picture and MIRROR frames. It was noted in 1636 that 'the art of making cases or frames for looking-glasses had until late time been only known or exercised in Holland' (cited in Howarth, 1984, p.11). Ralph Freeman refers to a maker who has 'discovered how to make a frame the same himself and for that purpose has devised and fitted with engines and tools (never known in this Kingdom before) and is now able to furnish the whole Kingdom with these commodities' (Howarth, loc.cit.). Frame-makers were certainly soon established in London. Pepys records how he went 'to the frame-makers, one Norris in Long Acre, who showed me several forms of frames to choose by: which was pretty, in little bits of moulding …' (*Diary*, 30 April 1669). By the mid 18th century, mirror and picture frame-makers were described by Campbell:

There are a set of joiners who make nothing but frames for looking-glasses and pictures, and prepare them for the carvers. This required but little ingenuity or neatness, as they only join the deals roughly plained in the shape and dimensions in which they are required; if the pattern chosen for the frame is to have any large holes in it, these they cut in their proper places, or, if it is

to have mouldings raised in the wood, they plain them on, but they leave the carver to plant on the rest of the figures.
(1747, p.174)

The development of machine-cut mouldings and COMPOSITION ornament, and the mitre cutter, along with the collapse of the frame-carving trade in the early 19th century, meant that the frame-maker simply became an assembler or a joiner.
See also Looking-glass maker

Freijo (*Cordia goeldiana*)
A Central American (especially Brazilian) timber with an average density of 590 (37 lb/cu ft). It has a yellow to brown heartwood with streaks, it is straight grained and works well for fine cabinetry and decorative veneer. Introduced into Britain *c*.1946, it has been used as a substitute for teak.

French edge
See Edge treatment (Upholstery)

French hair
A mocking name for hay as an upholstery filling. Crofton particularly referred to hay intended for making a rolled edge in upholstery as 'French hair' (1834, p.2).

French lacquer
See Vernis des Gobelins and Vernis Martin

French polish(ing)
See Polish

French walnut
See Walnut

'French work'
See Construction (Scamping)

Fret-cutter
During the 19th century the demand for fretted designs and FRETWORK grew to a point where there developed a separate trade of fret-cutter who produced fretted parts for supply to furniture and piano makers. They also made small items which they sold themselves. Fretted trusses are illustrated in the *Journal of Design* (1851, 2, p.193) as supplied by Samuel Sandy, a London fret-cutter. Although fret-cutters tried to maintain a mystery around their trade, the development of cheap and simple fret machines in America in the 1880s encouraged manufacturers, large and small, to use the new machines and brought about the demise of the specialist.
See also Fretwork

Fretsaw
See Saws

Fretwork and Fretwork machines
The term 'fretwork' simply describes a wide range of decorative woodwork (or metal) based on cutting thin timber or metal (with a FRETSAW) to form patterns that are either left open or backed in some way. Fretted work can be used as a decorative component of table tops or chair frames. It is also applied to a solid ground, when it is purely decoration, and it is sometimes known as BLIND FRETWORK. It should not be confused with pierced CARVING.

The fashionable Chinese and Gothic tastes of the 18th century encouraged the use of both blind and open frets, often in the form of trellises. Fretwork was particularly used for trim to trays, tables, and *torchères*. These were vulnerable to breakage and therefore, although some frets were cut from single boards, it was common to find that a LAMINATION had been prepared to encourage strength and stability in an otherwise fragile design. Sheraton noted the return to fashion of frets cut from metal:

Frets were much introduced into cabinet work anciently, but have been laid aside many years since. At present however, we seem to incline to them again, but with a material difference, the ancient frets being cut out of thin mahogany and the modern cast in brass, which is doubtless much to the advantage of the work. (1803, p.214)

The lamination methods remained into the 19th century: 'Fret-panels are ordinarily wrought of three thicknesses, the middle one being made to cross the grain of the others. In frets of rosewood, stout veneers are considered sufficiently thick, in those of mahogany, the centre thickness is most frequently ¼ inch beadwood [sic]' (Blackie, 1853, p.34). A report on a pianoforte manufactory in Grays Inn (London) noted that the decorative fretwork panels for piano fronts were 'formed of three separate veneers joined into one thickness in such a manner that the crossing of the grain in each veneer imparts an extraordinary degree of strength' (Strauss, G. L. M. et al., 1864, pp.306–7).

By 1855 a treadle-operated BAND SAW was introduced which gradually replaced the hand fretsaw in businesses, so avoiding the 'double' job of holding the saw as well as cutting out the design. The development of the mechanical fretsaw to a state of reliability and the fact that the power source could be human, steam or later electrical, stimulated its speedy adoption. The fret machine's success in relation to other machines was considered by one commentator in 1878:

The application of machinery in the ordinary sense to cabinet works is not at present very extensive. The harder and more difficult materials which are used, and the greater variety of work, have hitherto prevented any wide use of the machines which are used in joiners' work. Still there are some excellent fret-cutting machines which have in great measure superseded hand-cutting in this branch and provide a very cheap and effective means of decoration. (Paris, 1878, p.96)

It was noted in 1882 that 'among the somewhat numerous attempts which have been made of late to hit the popular taste in the matter of furniture, nothing probably has hit with more conspicuous success than fret-cut work' (*Cabinet Maker*, 1 May). This encouraged further developments. In 1885, W. Robertson, a cabinet-maker from Alnwick, patented (Pat.no.15518) a method of decoration involving a process of joining thick and thin bars of wood together temporarily and then fret-cutting designs through them. The thinner piece was then inserted into the thicker one and attached to a carcase. It was alleged that this would ensure that the piece appeared integral rather than applied.
See also Saws (Fret) (Jigsaw)

Bemrose, W. (1868), *Fret-cutting and Perforated Carving*, London: Bemrose and Son.
Denning, D. (1895), *Fretwork and Marquetry*, London: Upton Gill.
Luff, R. W. (1974), 'Fretwork decoration', in *Antique Collector*, 43, pp.141–6.
Sawyer, G. A. (1875), *Fretsawing and Woodcarving for Amateurs*, Boston, Mass.: Lee and Shepard.
Spielman, P. R. (1992), *Victorian Gingerbread, Patterns and Techniques*, New York: Sterling.

51 An advertisement for the English Fleetwood scroll saw used for fretwork, c.1880. The simple blower device to remove sawdust is a useful attachment.

Frieze

A woollen fabric with a napped finish (frise) designed for warmth and comfort. Used for wall hangings and bed curtains from the 17th century. The inventory of Tart Hall (1641) records amongst many entries for frieze, 'for this room [Great Chamber] there is a suit of freeze hangings in the Wardrobe' (Cust, 1911). In some cases it appears that 'freeze' was intended as a winter hanging cloth which was replaced yearly by summer hangings. By the end of the 18th century it was mainly used for clothing. Sheraton defined it as 'woollen cloth or stuff for winter wear, being friezed or knapt on one side; where probably it derived its name' (1803, p.215).

Fringes
See Passementerie

Frisage
See Parquetry

Frisé

A later-19th-century pile (often mohair) fabric with uncut loops, used for upholstery, especially in the early 20th century. Various effects may be made by varying the pile, by cut and uncut loops, by yarn types or printed effects.

Froe

A cleaving or splitting tool with a blade 15–30 cm (6–12 in) long, which is fitted to a handle set at right angles. The froe, used in conjunction with a MALLET, is a speedy and efficient way to split logs along the grain and to rough out components, especially for chairs.

Frosting

A colour contrast applied over WICKER furniture. The colour ground was first applied, then other shades were applied over and partially wiped off leaving a two-tone effect. The technique was widely used in the 1930s.

Fruitwoods

See Apple wood, Cherry, Mulberry, Pearwood, Plum, Service wood

Bowett, A. (1993), 'Fruitwoods in British furniture-making', in *Furniture Journal*, December, pp.41–5.

Fumed oak

A chemical process of colour change for oak furniture, which is produced by exposing oak to the fumes of ammonia within an airtight container. Woods with high tannin content will darken on exposure to ammonia gases. The tannic acid reacts, producing a particular shade, depending on the oak variety. Popular in the late 19th and early 20th centuries, the greyish-brown colour obtained, which faded to a yellowish-brown, was used in the so-called 'quaint style' of furniture. Fuming was also used extensively by Gustav Stickley (1857–1942) to give American white oak furniture a 'rich nut brown' shade. It was also used in factory-made furniture of the early 20th century. In many cases the fumed results were often uneven and had to be adjusted by hand colouring and finishing. In the later 20th century it has been mostly used for ecclesiastical work.

Functionalism

More a concept than a style, although it has been used as a label for both, it originally referred to the idea that objects that function well and are made economically with no intentional aesthetic are the best designed objects. The result is often austere and puritanical, but can be elegant and rational. In the nineteenth century some of Pugin's furniture designs come close to this ideal. Functionalism encouraged the innovative use of new materials (PLYWOOD and ALUMINIUM) as well as adaptations of older methods (BENTWOOD). In the 20th century, functionalism and the slogan 'form follows function' were soon applied as a label to modernist-inspired products which were made in this way and which were often based on the ideals of the Bauhaus. Functionalism soon became a style that was adopted by mainstream manufacturers and architects alike.
See also Modernism

Furnishing tweed

Used in the 1950s and 1960s for 'contemporary' furniture upholstery. Harris and other Island tweeds were popular accompaniments to open-sided teak framed sofas and chairs.

Furniture cord

See Passementerie

Furnitures

A general term to include all textile fabrics used in bed and upholstery work, including brocades, cretonnes, reps, tapestries and many others.

Fustet (*Rhus cotinus*)

A timber from the Venetian SUMACH tree, with a green-yellow and brown veined colouring. Probably used in European furniture as an inlay as well as for a yellow dye. Also known as young FUSTIC.

Fustian

A category of mixed-fibre twilled fabrics, usually of linen warp and cotton weft with a smooth and short nap pile. They probably originated from Spain and were used since the Middle Ages for clothes and bed hangings. Fustian of Naples was used as an upholstery material in the Tudor court and was brought by Walloons to Norwich, *c.*1554. Other imported varieties included Holmes (Ulm), Myllion (Milan) and Jeans (Genoa) fustian. Fustian was also used as a base for EMBROIDERY: In 1687 an American, Samuel Sewall, asked Daniel Allen in England to buy for his wife 'white fustian drawn, enough for curtins, wallen, counterpaine for a bed, and half a duz. chairs with four threeded green worsted to work it' (cited in Cummings, 1960, p.25). Fustian remained a base for embroidery. In *c.*1727, John Wood described how 'such [furnishings] as was of linnen, consisted either of corded Dimaty or coarse Fustian; the matrons of the city, their daughters and their maids flowering the latter with worsted, during the intervals between seasons to give the beds a gaudy look' (*A Description of Bath*, cited in Ayres, 1981, p.24).

Fustian remained popular throughout the 18th century. In 1710 the Terras Bed Chamber of Dyrham Park was furnished with 'a white fustian covering quilt' (Walton, 1986, p.59). Sheraton, citing Chambers (1751), says that 'right fustians should be made of cotton yarn both woof and warp but a great many are made, the warp of which is flax, or even hemp' (1803, p.219).

Renamed in late 18th century as Manchester velvet, then velour. Hepplewhite commented that 'The Manchester stuffs have been wrought into bed-furniture with good success' (1789, p.18). It continued to be used through to the early 19th century. Now a thick velvety twill cotton with a short pile or nap usually dyed olive, leaden or other dark colour.

Fustic (*Chlorophora maclura tinctoria*)

A yellow wood imported from tropical America and the West Indies in the 17th and 18th centuries. It has an average density of 910 (57 lb/cu ft), with a golden yellow heartwood darkening to browny-red, and is usually coarse-textured with a straight grain. Well known as a dye wood, it is also used as veneer and as inlay. Evelyn recorded how 'our inlayers use fustic, locust, or acacia; brasile, prince and rose-wood for yellows and reds, with several others brought from the Indies' (1662, p.240). In 1772 it was used by Chippendale for an inlaid press of fustic and black rosewood made for Garrick (Gilbert, 1978, 1, p.246), but by the early 19th century its use had been discontinued. Sheraton noted that it 'was introduced in cabinet-work above twenty years since; but as it was found to turn by the air and heat of the sun to a dead brownish hue, it was laid aside as unfit for such purposes' (1803, p.219). In the mid 19th century it was known primarily as a dyewood, but was also used in mosaic cabinet-work and for turning. Aka YELLOW WOOD. Known as 'old fustic' to avoid confusion with ZANTE or FUSTET.

Gaboon (*Aucoumea klaineana*)

A central and western African timber with an average density of 420 (27 lb/cu ft), it is light pinkish brown in the heart with an even medium texture and a variable grain. It was introduced in the late 19th century from French Africa. Although used for Art Deco furniture in the 20th century, it has been primarily a blockboard and plywood species. It has also been used in the solid as a MAHOGANY substitute. Aka Oukoumé.

Galloon
See Passementerie

Galuchat
See Shagreen

Garnet paper
See Abrasives

Garnet polish
See Resins (Lac)

Gauffrage or **Gaufré**
A French term for blind embossed effects often used on VELVETS.

Gauge, marking
A versatile tool used to mark out work, usually by scratching a mark at a pre-determined spacing. A range of models have been produced, including the mortise, side, mullet and the circular cutting gauge.
See also Dotter

Gedu Nohur (*Entandrophragma angolense*)
An African hardwood with an average density of 560 (34 lb/cu ft). Its characteristics are similar to SAPELE. It is a dull reddish-brown, medium hard with some interlocked grain. An early-20th-century import that was used widely in the second half of the 20th century for cabinet work in both veneer and solid, often as a substitute for African mahogany.

Genoese velvet
See Velvet

Gesso
A mixture of gypsum (plaster of Paris or whiting) or precipitated chalk and glue size (usually made of parchment, rabbit-skin or gelatine), occasionally with other materials added such as linseed oil, cotton fibres or sugar for particular recipes. Originally known to the Ancient Egyptians and used as a surface FILLER and smoother and as an adhesive for inlays. It was applied on poor quality timber to cover it or as a surface for painting upon. It was also employed as an adhesive to hold gold or silver foil to timber.

Since the Middle Ages, when it was referred to as 'white' (modern whiting), it has been mainly regarded as a base for painting or gilding upon. This led to its use later in the 15th and 16th centuries for the preparation of Italian cassone work. Gesso was revived in the latter part of the 17th century, where it was used for relief work and for picture frames. In this work, the contrast between raised, gilded and burnished surfaces, and matt backgrounds was very effective and gesso should not be considered a poor substitute for wood carving. In the very early 18th century some designers specialized in gesso work. William Kent became well known for his side tables, stands and frames which all employed gilded gesso, whilst the firm of Gumley and Moore specialized in gesso furniture with low relief detail. Gesso eventually fell out of favour for furniture until it was revived by Arts and Crafts makers, although it has remained a ground for gilding.

A particular feature of gesso work since Egyptian times has been the

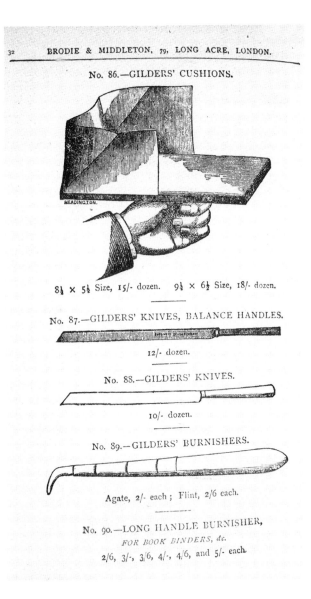

52 *An English advertisement for gilders' equipment, c.1880. It includes the cushion, a variety of knives and burnishing tools.*

use of strips of linen cloth laid between the base timber and the gesso to even out any movement through shrinkage. This practice has continued in Florence.

Gilder
A specialist craftsman who was employed in the finishing process of GILDING. During the 18th century gilders started to call themselves picture frame gilders and this continued as a nomenclature into the 19th century. It indicated a lessening of the contact with furniture-making. Although gilding and carving were separate crafts, the consolidation of the two into one business became common as fluctuations in taste meant that either specialism would be fashionable at various times. The cachet of the name 'carver and gilder' remained long after most frames were made from composition materials, in which the worker simply put together the frames and gilded them.
See also Gilding

Gilding

The application of a thin layer of GOLD leaf to a prepared surface to create a gilded effect, which is often burnished to a bright finish. Gilding may be applied to a variety of surfaces, including gesso, wood, glass, ceramic and metals.

The application of gold leaf was well known in Antiquity, and the technique has continued in painting and the decorative arts ever since. Two forms of gilding have been used since the Middle Ages, one based on oil application and the other on water. In the case of gilding on wood, the process starts with a firm but malleable GESSO paste base which is applied to the underframe. In oil gilding the base may be a painted layer of white lead or red ochre in oil. This was built up in six to seven coats, earlier coats having more glue in them, to a final thickness of 1.6 mm ($\frac{1}{16}$ in). Once dry, the gesso was rubbed down to extreme smoothness. If applied over carving, the sharpness would need to be restored by re-cutting with gouges. The next step was to seal the gesso with BOLE. The gilding (either oil or water) can then commence. Gilders used a range of specialist equipment including a brush or 'tip' made from camel hair fixed between two thin pieces of card; a cushion made from cloth layered on wood covered with chamois to cut the gold leaves; a parchment 'wall' to stop draughts; paint brushes of various sizes; sharp knifes to cut the leaf; and a 'bob' of chamois-covered cotton wool to press leaves on to the work.

FIRE OR MERCURY GILDING

For metal work, fire gilding was once widely used. It was a gilding process for metal (usually bronze or silver) which used either gold leaf or an amalgam of gold and mercury (six parts mercury to one part gold). For either method mercury had to be applied to the cleaned metal surface, either by brushing the mercury all over or, later, by dipping in a mercuric nitrate solution. The next step was to apply the gold leaf to the surface, burnish it and then heat it to remove the mercury. The second process used an amalgam of mercury and gold which was applied to the surface. The mixture was forced through chamois to remove superfluous mercury so that the amalgam was reduced to about two parts mercury and one gold. The item was then warmed so that the mercury mix could be applied with a brush or knife. The object was then heated to vaporize the mercury, leaving a gold deposit on the surface. The gold layers were then burnished with beeswax, red ochre, verdigris, copper, alum, vitriol or borax to give colour and lustre to the gold. The process was highly detrimental to health and has been abandoned, although the particular effect is difficult to replicate with safer methods. The importance of the colouring processes associated with gilding were based on chemical colouring methods. One process dipped the gilded object into yellow colouring matter (including turmeric, sulphur and yellow arsenic), whilst another method was to apply tinted gilding wax and reheat the object to re-deposit it upon the surface.

Although some commentators were dismissive, it was successfully employed by Matthew Boulton in the later 18th century. Later on, Nicholson, discussing mercury gilding said that 'it is from this species of gilding that French furniture derives its brilliancy'. He went on to say: 'As far as our experience goes, it will not stand the humid-atmosphere of this country; nevertheless the nature of this gilding which enables the French to add such spotty brilliancy to exceedingly plain wood work was worth enquiry' (Nicholson, P. and M., 1826, p.10). It was the favoured metal gilding method from the Middle Ages to the mid 19th century, when it was usurped by electrogilding, patented in 1839 by Elkington.

GERMAN GILDING

The application of silver leaf or other substitute, which is then finished with a gold-coloured lacquer.
See also Gold leaf, Gold size

OIL GILDING

The simpler and less costly of the processes, it is more durable and less affected by atmosphere. Oil gilding could go over gesso or be applied directly on unprepared surfaces. The first stage of oil gilding is the application of a mordant, which was often cooked linseed oil mixed with colouring matter (for example, ochre, raw sienna). It was painted on and left until tacky, after which time the gold leaf could be applied. It was not burnished.

WATER GILDING

Sheraton noted that water gilding 'has doubtless the advantage of oil gilding, but is attended with much trouble and expense' (1803, p.227). This method, which produces a fine lustre due to burnishing (which is unavailable on oil work), can only be applied to a gesso surface. It uses wetted BOLE mixed with 'glair' or, more commonly, parchment size as a mordant. The surface must be made wet in order for the gold to adhere. The leaf is laid down one square foot at a time onto the sticky size, and adheres by capillary action. When dry, the gold is burnished. (Sections of the object to be gilded may then be glazed with another colour bole, usually purplish red-brown, but perhaps blue if the gold finish is to be 'white or pale lemon' in colour.) In the best work a second coat of leaf is applied, known as double gilding. The burnishing was originally carried out with dogs' teeth, but by the mid 17th century pieces of AGATE or hard stone set in long handles were used.

Bigelow, D. (1991), *Gilded Wood Conservation and History*, Madison, Conn.: Sound View Press.
Cennini, C. (1933), *The Craftsman's Handbook*, trans. D. V. Thompson, New Haven, reprint 1960, New York.
Goodison, N. (1974), *Ormolu: The Work of Matthew Boulton*, London: Phaidon.
Mitchell, F. S. (1908), *Practical Gilding, Bronzing and Lacquer*, London: Trade Papers Publishing.
Practical Carver and Gilder's Guide and Picture Frame-maker's Companion, The (1850), London: pub. Brodie and Middleton.
Society of Gilders (1876), *The Gilder's Manual: A complete practical guide to gilding in all its branches: designed for all trades in which gilding is used, including silvering: together with picture framing, picture repairing, and much other useful information, valuable receipts, &c.*, reprint 1990, Washington, DC: Society of Gilders.
Stalker, J. and Parker, G. (1688), *A Treatise on Japanning, Varnishing and Guilding*, London: Tiranti reprint 1960.
Symonds, R. W. (1950), 'Craft of the carver and gilder', in *Antiques Review*, December, pp.13−20.
Watin, J.-F. (1773), *L'Art du peintre doreur*, Paris: Grangé et Durand.

Gilt-bronze mounts

Gilt-bronze metal was used for the manufacture of a number of items for the interior. In the case of furniture the material was especially used to make mounts.

The process of making mounts started with the *fondeur* who set a model or cast of the object into a sand bed. Molten BRONZE was poured into the cavity and a rough casting was acquired. After being cleaned up, the mount was passed to a *ciseleur* who, with a variety of tools, decorated the surface with chasing, cutting and burnishing techniques. The mount was then ready for GILDING. The result effectively alloyed the metals. After the initial gilding, other processes were involved to improve colour. The scratch brush cleaned the object so that it might be re-heated to redden the colour by further amalgamating the gold and brass. Chemical colouring could occur by dipping the gilt object in a boiling yellow colouring matter. This was followed by a final burnishing with an AGATE or dog tooth (Goodison, 1974, p.70).

The matt gilding process, as devised by Pierre Gouthière (master in 1758), coated the required areas to be left matt with a chemical mix, heated the item then plunged it into cold water. A fine and even ground surface was achieved without chasing, which was combined with highly burnished parts. Fixing the mounts was usually by screw and later by less obtrusive lugs.

Methods of simulating gilt-bronze were explored. In the mid 18th century a process was applied to acid-cleaned bronze by coating it with a varnish, often tinted to look like gilding. In the Biedermeier period, mounts were stamped from sheet metal, whilst other imitations were moulded in plaster and gilded to resemble gilt-bronze. See also Bronze, Bronze doré, Gilding, Ormolu

Gilt leather
See Leather

Gimp
See Passementerie

Gingham
A plain-weave cotton fabric made with dyed yarns, often in stripes and checks with multiple-stranded warps and wefts. Originating in Malaya, it was widely used in the 18th century for case covers and upholstery. A 19th-century version was made from linen.

Girdling
See Seasoning

Girth web
See Webbing

Glass
A versatile material basically made from a mix of 75 per cent silica, 10 per cent lime and 15 per cent sodium or potassium oxide, glass has been associated with furniture since Ancient Egyptian times. Its early use was for decoration as inlaid mosaic glass pieces, but due to financial and practical constraints, it was not until the 16th century that it became an increasingly important part of the furnishing repertoire. The history of the development of glass was driven by changes in technology that gradually improved its quality, size and availability. These changes were first initiated from the *cristallo* which was a clear glass developed around 1450 by glass-workers in Murano (Venice).

Glass has been used for a range of components of furnishing work, but particularly for MIRRORS, glazed doors and painted glass panels. Glass was also used as part of the structure of some furniture. Early examples of high-style use include Louis XIV's novelty table and similar products in Medici Florence. A glass piano was extant in Hampton Court in 1598, and a virginal (c.1600) at the Victoria & Albert Museum is decorated with polychrome glass rods, whorls and florets. Further examples include 17th-century Neapolitan cabinets, and work from the St Petersburg Imperial Glass Factory. The Italian influence continued into the 18th century and is evidenced by Lady Mary Montagu who visited Venice in 1756 and saw 'a set of furniture, in a taste entirely new. It consists of eight large armed-chairs, the same number of sconces, a table and a prodigious look glass, all of glass' (*Letters and Works of Lady Mary Montagu*, vol.2, 1861, reprint 1970, p.302).

In the early 19th century various publications attest to the rising attraction of glass as a furniture material, including *The Manufacture of Ornamental Glass* (1823, London) and the *Manuel complet de fabricants de verre et de cristal* (1829, Paris). The famous firm of F. and C. Osler of Birmingham, England, were manufacturers of a variety of glass items for interiors. Established in 1807, their heyday in glass furniture was post 1851. Although chandeliers and table pieces were the main part of the output, some spectacular glass furniture was also made. The range included stools, settees, bedheads, cradles, thrones, tables, mirrors, *étagères* and sideboards. Although Osler's supplied a home and continental market, their most successful outlets were located in North India. In 1878 in the Paris Exhibition, they displayed an amazing sideboard with a breadth of 259 cm (8 ft 6 in) and a total height of 441 cm (14 ft 6 in). In the late 19th century the French Baccarat company made glass furniture that was well known, and in the USA the Libbey glass company also made furniture pieces for exhibition.

During the 20th century glass became a popular medium in a variety of styles. Pierre Legrain's glass piano, and Art Deco glass furniture by Lalique contrasted with modernist uses such as Denham Maclaren's glass chair and table. By the 1960s, the popular market employed smoked or clear glass table tops for dining and occasional tables, whilst later in the century glass became almost sculptural in its use with the creations of Danny Lane (see Plate XVII).

BLOWN GLASS
An early process (aka broad or Lorraine) involved blowing a 'bubble' of glass until it reached the appropriate size when it was then cut into a tube, sliced and flattened before it was annealed. Alternatively it was blown into a mould which was then opened, the glass was reheated and flattened, annealed and then it was ready for use. It was used for mirrors in Venice from c.1500 in plates up to 208 × 121 cm (82 × 48 in).

CROWN GLASS
A piece of glass blown into a bubble which is then placed on an iron surface and spun rapidly so that it spreads out from the centre into a rough circular form. After heating and annealing, it is finished by cutting the flat 'edges' away leaving a 'bulls-eye' at the centre. By the early 18th century it was deemed more important than the broad glass. In 1710, Zacharias Conrad von Uffenbach described the Vauxhall glass works and the glass-making process:

First they take out a great mass, which they repeatedly blow up in a circle and then they again make red-hot, when it is large enough, they take it to the so-called pulpit which is really a chair raised on several steps, below which a man stands with a pair of scissors and cuts the great bubble in pieces, then it is laid on a large sheet of iron, on which the glass is stretched. On this it is placed in the cooling oven and smoothed out with an iron resembling a scraper; then it is stood in an upright position and left for three days to cool. The panes are then sold to other people who cut and mount them, making mirrors of them, this is a special trade followed by many people in London.
(Cited in Wills, 1971, p.56)

Ordinary drawn window glass is not entirely uniform in thickness, because of the nature of the process by which it is made. The variations in thickness distort the appearance of objects viewed through panes of the glass. The traditional method of overcoming such defects has been the use of polishing and grinding.

FLOAT GLASS
The grinding and polishing necessary in the case of plate glass has been widely supplanted by the cheaper float-glass process. It is made by pouring molten glass onto a molten tin metal surface so that when it cools it forms a natural surface, completely smooth and absolutely uniform. The temperature is high enough to allow the surface im-

perfections to be removed by the fluid flow of the glass. The temperature is gradually lowered as the glass moves along the tin bath, and the glass passes through a long annealing oven at the end. Invented in 1959 by Pilkington Bros, float glass provides undistorted vision and reflection.

PLATE (CAST) GLASS

There continued to be limitations on the size of glass sheets until the development of cast glass. Put simply, this was a process of pouring molten glass onto an iron plate (table) covered with sand, which was then made smooth with a roller before the annealing process. After annealing, the plate was ground and polished on both sides. This practice was devised by Bernard Perrot in the 1680s and developed at St Gobain in Picardy. Large-scale manufacture was established in France at that time. In 1691 Robert Hooke and Christopher Dodsworth were licensed to 'exercise and put into practice the new invention of casting plate glass, particularly looking glass plates'. In fact by 1735, as noted in the *Dictionarium Polygraphicum*, 'the method of running and casting large looking-glass plates has been considerably improved by our workmen in England' (Barrow, 1758). The certain profitability of glass-making encouraged the establishment of the British Cast Plate Glass Co in St Helens and London in the mid 1770s. The ability to produce large plates reflects a desire to lessen the importation of French glass and keep the trade national. Sheraton confirms the change when he mentions that pier glasses could be made in London in sizes from 91 × 152 cm (36 × 60 in) up to 190 × 297 cm (75 × 117 in). In 1839, Loudon referred to glass for bookcases as being of plate glass or still of

flatted crown glass produced by heating the glass quite hot in an oven, on a flat iron plate laid perfectly level, to which the heated glass adapts its surface; the operation is performed for cabinet manufacturers, and others who require perfectly flat glass by a distinct group of artisans called glass annealers. (p.1053–4)

Manufacturing improvements in the 1840s reduced prices, and the repeal of duty in 1845 brought down prices further. By 1869 plates as large as 360 × 182 cm (142 × 72 in) were being made. Plate glass is now made by rolling the glass continuously between double rollers located at the end of a forehearth. After the rough sheet has been annealed, both sides of it are finished continuously and simultaneously.

PRESSED GLASS

The pressing of molten glass into cast-iron moulds using a plunger. A process patented in the USA in 1826, which introduced a major change to small glass item manufacture.
See Glass knobs

Glass decoration

A number of methods of using glass as MOSAIC, BEAD or other form of decoration have been introduced into furniture. Very early examples are found in Ancient Egyptian work. Although occasionally employed since, it was in 1786 that a glass cutter, Thomas Rogers, patented a process which used coloured, stained and clear glass to particularly produce decorations for furniture, looking-glasses and the like (Pat.no.1568). In the same year John Skidmore devised a method of ornamenting furniture with 'foil stones, Bristol stones, paste and all sorts of pinched glass, and every other stone glass and composition use or applicable to the jewellery trade' (Pat.no.1552). The success of these processes is not recorded, but they do indicate an interest in trying to develop exotic decoration for furniture. Some time later, in 1848, Elisabeth Wallace patented a process of using coloured

glass to replicate marble (Pat.no.12075), but again the success and use of this idea is not known.
See also Bead mosaic

Glass fibre
See Glass fibre reinforced plastic

Glass fibre reinforced plastic (GRP)

One of the most important sub-divisions of PLASTICS is the combination of glass fibres and plastic (Polyester) resin, commonly known as 'fibreglass'. The fibre web was laid onto a moulded shape and the resin was applied over it. Pressure was applied and the material was allowed to set. Although GRP had been experimented with, it was in the Organic Design in Home Furnishing Exhibition held in 1940 in MoMA, New York, that it was really exploited for its 'organic' possibilities.

In 1948 the Eames's DAX chair, the first self-supporting one-piece glass reinforced plastic chair shell, won second prize in the 'Low Cost Furniture Competition' in New York. This was the first chair to have a moulded fibreglass seat in which the natural surface of its materials was exposed. Further developments in GRP shells for chairs came with Eero Saarinen's Womb chair of 1948. The methods of GRP production were based on either a hand lay-up method or a moulding system. The idea of a complete one-piece chair made from a material like GRP was considered by Saarinen. His 1956 Tulip chair had an integral GRP seat and back but was supported by an aluminium base. In 1966 the true benefit of GRP was developed when Helmut Batzner produced his famous Bofinger stacking chair. This was one of the first 'one piece plastic chairs'. The commercial development of GRP was particularly evident in the manufacture of chair shells as well as one-piece chairs based on the original ideas mentioned. GRP continues to be a versatile and sculptural material for innovative designers.

Glass knobs

Decorative handles made from glass and used on drawers and cupboards. Introduced into American furniture c.1810, they warranted comment from a visitor to New York: 'I would remark that the cabinet work executed in this city is light and elegant, superior indeed I am inclined to believe to English workmanship. I have seen some with cut glass instead of brass ornaments which have a beautiful effect' (Fearon, 1818).

Glass (painted or stained)

Although stained or painted glass is rare in furniture-making, it has been used on occasion. There are several examples of settees and chairs which have painted glass panels glued to the wood and held in by mouldings. Console tables were also treated to this decoration, with the aprons and legs decorated in painted glass. Marie Antoinette's famous *serre bijoux* (1787) and some fancy cabinets made in Baltimore 1795–1801 attest to this. They are often referred to as VERRE EGLOMISE. A further example of true stained glass use may be found in early-19th-century fire screens (Loudon, 1839, p.1072), as well as fire and room screens made in the late 19th century.
See also Bead mosaic, Mirror glass, Verre églomisé

Barker, T. G. (1960), *Pilkington Bros. and the Glass Industry*, London: Allen and Unwin.
Caldwell, I. (1989), 'John Gumley, The glass makers', in *Antique Collector*, 60, January, pp.40–6.
Clarke, T. and Bourne, J. (1988), 'Louis XIV's glass table', in *Apollo*, CXXVIII, November, pp.334–9.
Doley, A. (n.d.), 'Le Meuble en verre', in *Œil*, 309, April, 46–53.

Goncalez-Palacios, A. (1971), 'The Prince of Palagonia, Goethe and glass furniture', in *Burlington Magazine*, CXIII, pp.456ff.

— (1985), 'A Neapolitan cabinet decorated with painted glass panels', in *Furniture History*, XXI, pp.11–15.

Hollister, P. (1992), 'Louis XIV's glass table', in *The Magazine Antiques*, 142, September, 324–33.

Podos, L. (1991), 'Glass furniture', in *Glass Club Bulletin of the National Early American Glass Club*, 165, Fall, pp.8–16 and 166, Winter, pp.3–16.

Smith, J. P. (1991), *Osler's Crystal for Royalty and Rajah*, London: Mallett.

Symonds, R. W. (1936), 'English looking-glass plates and their manufacture', in *Connoisseur*, 97, pp.243–9.

Wills, G. (1965), *English Looking-glasses, a Study of Glasses Frames and Makers, 1672–1820*, New York: Barnes.

Wilson, K. and Nelson, K. (1996), 'The role of glass knobs in glass making and furniture', in *Antiques*, May, pp.750–9.

Glass paper
See Abrasives

Glazing bars
Rebated bars set in frames to support window glass. The application of false glazing bars on a pane of glass to create an effect has been practised more recently. It is obviously cheaper to glue bars onto glass rather than to glaze a made-up and often intricately panelled door frame. Not all glazing bars were made from timber. Discussing bookcases, Hepplewhite noted 'The ornamental sash bars are intended to be of metal, which painted a light colour or gilt will provide a pleasing effect' (1794, p.9).

Glides
An attachment for the feet of tables and chairs, based on a ball and socket joint. Originally devised by the Shaker community so that chairs could be safely tilted, they were an integral part of some of their chair designs as they were built into the back legs. A variant was introduced commercially in the 1950s which was made from brass or plastic, with a pin fixing, which allowed easy movement and avoided rucking carpets or scratching floors.

Glues
See Adhesives

Go bars
Go bars are flexible wooden rods which are fitted between the ceiling of the workshop and the piece of work. They were a simple but effective method of applying pressure upon veneered components especially. In 1728 Chambers noted their use for larger veneered works which were too big for the hand PRESS. Roubo describes something similar as a *goberge*, which was pressed against a sand cushion to hold the veneer tight against a curved surface (1772, p.855, Plate 295) – it is a possible derivation of Go bars. This method of fixing veneers was also common practice in the 19th century and has continued into the 20th century as a specialized system.
See also Lancewood

Gold
A precious metal associated with furniture since Antiquity. Used in solid, sheet or leaf forms, it imparts a particular grandeur to any furniture item. Egyptian royal furniture used gold foil to cover frames which had previously been prepared with a layer of gesso. Beaten gold sheet was applied to a timber frame, the fixings being made with small gold or silver nails. Solid gold was occasionally used for Roman furniture. However, gold is mostly associated with GILDING.

53   *The application of go-bars in a 20th-century piano factory, c.1960, demonstrates the longevity of techniques that do not require further development to be successful.*

Gold leaf
Gold leaf, the basic material for gilding work, is gold that has been hammered to *c*.1 micron thick. The gold leaf used has ranged from 24 carat to 15 carat for ordinary work, with 22 carat being generally used. The leaf is also available in a range of gold colours and qualities based on alloys that influence colours, so that shades of red, yellow, green-white can be made by adding various proportions of copper and silver to the gold during refining. Modern leaf foils are attached to carriers and so can be easily transferred to surfaces. Because of its inertness it will not tarnish and therefore maintains its richness throughout its life.
See Gilding

Gold size
A preparatory foundation for surfaces prior to gilding with gold leaf. It is usually made from fine oils, and colouring such as ochre or vermilion mixed to the colour gold to be applied. Stalker and Parker gave a full recipe:

Gum animae one ounce, gum efpaltum one ounce, lethergi of gold half an ounce; red lead, brown umber, of each the like portion. To these shut altogether in a new earthen pipkin, large enough to hold one third more than you put in, pour of linseed oil a quarter of a pint, of drying oil half a pint, with which you may be furnished at the colour shops.
(1688, VII, p.28)

In the 19th century ready-made japanners' or house painters' sizes were available, the former being a quick-drying version.

THE MICHIGAN ARTISAN.

Grand Rapids Panel Company,
Manufacturers of
ELASTIC GRAINING PLATES
For producing the finest
Imitation French Burl Veneer, and
Imitation Mahogany Crotch Veneer,
ALSO ON
Improved Graining Machines for Furniture Panels.

Goncalo alves (*Astronium fraxinifolium*)

A central South American, especially Brazilian, timber with an average density of 940 (59 lb/cu ft) which is varied in colour from a reddish-brown to dark brown with black streaks similar to ROSEWOOD. It has a medium texture and an irregular interlocked grain, and has been used in the 20th century for high-class furniture and veneers.

See also Zebrawood (UK), Tigerwood (USA)

Gothic and Gothic revival

The change from the monumental Romanesque style to the lighter, more intricate and decorative style that was later called Gothic occurred from the mid 12th century and was developed and elaborated until the full flowering of the Renaissance in the mid 15th century. Gothic furniture is characterized by the use of architectural motifs and decoration, solid timbers, iron attachments and applied decoration especially PAINTING or GILDING. The construction of furniture based on working in the solid was reserved for carpenters and joiners, although turners were also employed for furniture-making. Although UPHOLSTERY was rare, it first developed during this period with the work of the cofferers.

The Gothic revival began in the 18th century with William Kent and Batty Langley producing designs in the revised taste. It was further developed as a romantic or picturesque style in the later 18th century. By the early 19th century the Gothic revival had been codified by Pugin who was able to design complete interiors and furniture with a confident medievalism. During the mid nineteenth century the Reformed Gothic returned to the origins of the style and removed the superfluous and 'wedding cake decoration' to create a more honest interpretation. The Gothic was closely linked to the ARTS and CRAFTS movement, although the styles are not interdependent.

Gouge
See Chisel

Gouge carving
See Carving

Grain

A relative term that has a range of definitions which are dependent on context. It may refer to decorative effects, growth-ring placement, early and late wood contrast, relative cell size, the surface appearance or the direction of cells. Generally it refers to the pattern of longitudinal cells in relation to the direction of growth. When the fibres of the tree are parallel to the length of the trunk, they are said to be straight. Any deviation from this is referred to by comparison or style: Cross, diagonal, spiral, and wavy are self-explanatory, while interlocked describes the way in which the fibres in each growth layer change direction and can cause interesting FIGURE. As grains are natural and varied, the angles of cutting will also affect the resultant grain pattern on the exposed surface.

Graining

A method of imitating natural wood-grain by various paint techniques by either using various tools or machines. Graining required tools including common brushes, sash tools of different sizes, camel hair pencils, graining rollers, and horn combs made for the purpose. It was used in Roman times and was attacked as a travesty even then. Pliny bemoaned the 'monstrous invention devised of destroying the natural appearance of tortoiseshell by paint, and making it sell at a still higher price by a successful imitation of wood' (xvi, 232, cited in Richter, 1966, p.126). Centuries later, painting surfaces to imitate more costly woods was common practice. In 16th-century Augsburg 'many of the craftsmen paint all sorts of wood that they have worked with colours, and sell it as naturally grown coloured wood' (Ritz, 1971, p.7). A 1598 inventory from the Villa Medici in Rome listed items *legno tinto di noce* (worked to look like walnut) and with *tinto di nero* (ebony look) (see Thornton, 1991, p.92).

Although an interest in graining continued during the following centuries, it was the 19th century that encouraged a massive revival of graining as a method of imitating costly woods (and other materials) to satisfy the expanding market. In 1823 graining processes were described as 'the imitating, by means of painting, various kinds of rare woods; as satin wood, rose wood, kingwood, mahogany etc., and likewise various species of marble' (Nicholson, M., 1824, p.417). The growing demand caused a number of patent methods to be devised. For example, a correspondent of the *Mechanics Magazine* (19 July 1842, p.21) described a process which he had devised to achieve the appearance and texture of bird's-eye maple. The process simply involved placing veneers of common woods such as plane, birch, and others between warmed wave-grooved rollers, which distorted the fibres of the wood sheets. When they had set and been cleaned off, they apparently had the appearance of bird's-eye maple. In 1850 Samuel Jacobs took out a patent (Pat.no.13,300) for a wood-graining machine, and in 1857 Clayton patented (Pat.no.488) a machine for embossing and ornamenting woods. In this instance 'inferior woods' were passed between heated rollers, which were engraved with the design, either in relief or intaglio. Pressure then transferred the design to the wood surface. In 1856 there were two further patented processes: F. Whitehead patented (Pat.no.2352) a method of decoration using heaters and tracers, and T. Williams also devised a process (Pat.no.2112) to imitate costly woods. Attempts to transfer the facsimile of fine grains to otherwise plain wood were patented (Pat.no.3184) by William Dean in 1869. His process enabled copies of fine-grained wood to be transferred to any flat or irregular surface. The process was brought to a fine art by the Grand Rapids Panel company in the USA who, during the later 19th century, manufactured so-called Elastic Graining Plates designed to produce fine imitation French burl [walnut] veneer and imitation mahogany crotch veneer, amongst others.

These patented machine techniques never usurped the hand-graining work of the skilled painter-grainer in either the 19th or the 20th century. The well-known Kershaw panels, representing imitation wood grain and marbling, were the epitome of the hand craft. However, it was objects like cheap bedroom suites and chairs grained to fashionable effect in the mid to late 19th century that became the main work of grainers.

In the 20th century the 'graining' of metal furniture developed, especially for use in contract situations. Like other paint techniques, graining enjoyed a revival in the last quarter of the 20th century.

See also Combing, Marbling, Printing

Mussey, R. (1827/1987), *The First American Furniture Finisher's Manual: a reprint of 'The cabinet-maker's guide' of 1827*, New York: Dover.

Reynolds, H. (1812), *Directions for House and Ship Painting*, New Haven: Eli Hudson.

Scaffner, C. V. and Klein, S. (1998), 'American grain painted furniture 1790−1880', in *Folk Art*, 23, 36−43.

Siddons, G. A. (1830), *The Cabinet-maker's Guide*, London: Sherwood, Gilbert and Piper.

Smith, J. (1676), *The Art of Painting*, London: Crouch.

Sutherland, W. G. (1892), *The Art of Graining and Imitating Woods*, Manchester: Decorative Arts Journals Ltd.

Whittock, N. (1827), *The Decorative Painters' and Glaziers' Guide*, London: Isaac Taylor Hinton.

Granadillo

A name for a number of West Indian woods which are hard, red, aromatic and supply figured timbers. It is also the name given to the red ebony used by French cabinet-makers in the mid 19th century. Aka ROSEWOOD, Bois de Grenadille.

See also Partridge wood

Granite

A granular crystalline rock which is usually light grey, white or light red in colour. Occasionally it has been used for furniture. In 1762 Benjamin and Thomas Carter supplied Croome Court with 'two Granate tables at a cost of £73.00' (Beard, 1993, p.98). It has continued to be used on occasions for table tops, ever since.

Grasses

Any plant of the *Gramineae* family which includes cereals, reeds and bamboos. Many varieties have been used since Ancient Egyptian times in furniture-making, especially for BOTTOMING chairs and stuffing upholstery work. They were also used for polishing.

Bulrush (*Scirpus lacustris*)

Growing up to 3 m (10 ft) high in wet marshy areas, it has a smooth stem completely free of leaves and nodules, making it an ideal bottoming material. It is a member of the Sedge family and, although called rush, is not botanically of that family.

Cotton grass

See Sedge, below

Dutch rushes (*Equisietum*)

The horsetail rush that was widely used for POLISHING in the 17th to 19th centuries due to its high silica content. Mentioned by Stalker and Parker who said that 'You should furnish yourself with rushes, which are called Dutch rushes, with which you must smooth your work before you varnish it … You may buy them at the Ironmongers' (1688, p.2). Over 150 years later Holtzapffel noted that

it is gathered in pieces two or three feet long; which are interspersed by knots at distances of four to six inches. The rush is usually the size of a writing quill, of a greenish-grey colour, with a groovy surface that feels rough like fine glass paper, from the quantity of silex disseminated throughout its exterior surface. (1850, p.1053)

Directions given require

a dozen or more short pieces or joints of the rush just divested of the knots and tied up at the ends as a faggot [which] are used with water … After a sufficient period, and when the rush feels inactive, it is laid by and allowed to dry, when it is again used in the dry state and serves to bring up a polish nearly or quite equal to that produced by tripoli. (op.cit., p.1124)

In the 1870s reference books were still suggesting Dutch rushes to give a final polish to surfaces. Aka Shave grass.

Flags

The common name for the wild iris, sweet sedge or sweet flag, although the term can refer to a range of grass or water plant species. Flags were used for bottoming chairs in New England during the 17th century.

Marsh (*Juncus effusus*)

Any grass that grows in marshy ground, especially *g. spartina*. It was used as a stuffing material in 17th-century upholstery in America and England. Initially bunches of grass were arranged to cover the seat and back with the protruding ends packed over the frame to protect the leather covers from chaffing. In more sophisticated work, grass was prepared in rolls which delineated an outline which would then be filled with hair.

Prairie

A wire grass from the prairies of North West America, which in the later 19th century was converted into a pliable twine and used in the manufacture of woven 'wicker' style furniture.

Reed-mace (*Typha*)

Reed-mace has long sharp leaves growing round the base and has the easily recognized brown furry sausage-shaped flower. Called CAT's-TAIL in the USA and, mistakenly, bulrush in England. Aka Fen down.

Seagrass

In its natural state seagrass is a coarse grass or sedge. It belongs to the *Cyperus* family which is a native of Bengal, though may be found in China and Malaya where it is used for basket making. The natural colour of seagrass is somewhat like rush and is used for seating stools and chairs. It is, however, much easier to use than rush as it is available in long lengths, does not require damping, and it allows for a greater variety of patterns.

Sea wrack grass (*Zostera marina*)

A dried seaweed upholstery filling material described as

found on the coast of Norfolk; abundantly in the Orkneys and Hebrides; and on the northern shores of the German ocean. When gathered it is repeatedly washed in fresh water, to deprive it of all its saline particles; and being dried in the sun it is twisted into thick ropes and in that state sent to the manufacturer who has it untwisted and cut into short lengths for use. (Loudon, 1839, p.325)

Aka Eel grass, ALVA MARINA.

Sedge (*Carex claudium*)

A grass-like flowering plant that grows in marshy areas. Sedges are generally distinguished from grasses by their triangular stems and by leaves with closed sheaths. The stems and leaves of many genera, including the bulrush, are used for components of furniture, especially chair bottoms. William Nicholls of Bedwardine in Worcestershire had 'one segg chair and one segg stool' (West, 1962, p.117). Cotton grass is used in pillow stuffing.

In a different context entirely, a variety of sedge (*Carex stricta*) was used to weave into furniture. This wire grass was used in the manufacture of Prairie Grass furniture from 1900 by a subsidiary of the

American Grass Twine Company. The range was available in 'natural Green' or 'Baronial brown' and was sold under the trade name of Crex. The taste for this range lasted until World War I when woven-paper substitutes took over much of the trade.

Wire grass (*Carex stricta*)
See Prairie grass, above

See also Bamboo, Rush seats

Carey Howlett, F. (1990), 'The identification of grasses and other plant material used in historic upholstery', in M. A. Williams (ed.), *Upholstery Conservation*, pp.66–91, East Kingston, VT: American Conservation Consortium.

Green construction
The process of making furniture from unseasoned wood. This form of construction requires different skills to those for seasoned woodworking; for example, the process of ovaling of members such as round mortises and dowel ends so that as the wood dried, a close fit was obtained. Evelyn noted that 'the greenest timber is sometimes desirable for such as carve and turn' (1662, p.217).

Abbott, M. (1989), *Green Woodwork*, Lewes: GMC Publications.
Alexander, J. A. Jnr (1978), *Making a Chair From a Tree. An Introduction to Working Green Wood*, Newton, Conn.: Taunton Press.

Green ebony
Green ebony is most commonly a variety of EBONY which has greenish colourings. The Indian ebony *Diospyros melanoxylon* is a source of green ebony as well as the true black. The mutation results in a green, grey or brown colouring in the heartwood. Other timbers which are not true ebonies have also been called green ebony. The ASH is one such timber.

In 1853 green ebony was described as a

product of the West Indies generally and is imported chiefly from the island of Jamaica, in pieces from 3 to 6 feet in length … The heart wood is of a brownish green and is highly resinous, like rosewood; and like black ebony it is straight grained, and cleaves easily. It is used in turnery and marquetry.
(Blackie, 1853, p.41)

This may be the same timber as COCUSWOOD which also supplied a 'green ebony'.

Green oak
See Oak

Grenadillo
See Granadillo

Grenoble wood
A 17th-century term for a French variety of WALNUT.

Grevillea (*Grevillea robusta*)
An Australian species which is similar to 'silky oak' with a density of 560 (35 lb/cu ft) and with a pink colour, toning down to pale brown upon exposure. A prominent feature is the 'silver flash' effect figure that resembles true oak. In the 20th century it has been used in Britain as an oak substitute.

Grey oak
See Oak

Greywood
See Harewood

Grisaille
A method of painting, often using grey, olive or buff tints, to represent objects in relief. These designs were sometimes painted in friezes and medallions on later-18th-century satinwood or japanned furniture.

Grosgrain or **Grosgram**
Any plain weave textile which has a corded effect caused by heavier weft yarns. In particular, silk or silk mixture cloths made from grosgrain yarns (large rounded twists) that produced a thick corded-effect fabric, suitable for upholstery. The name derives from the French *gros* meaning 'thick'. One of the new draperies, its use was recorded in 1643 as an upholstery cover in Worcester House: '1 elbow chair and 8 stools of silver figured grograine' (*Archaeologia*, vol. XCI, cited in Clabburn, 1988, p.246). John Evelyn noted a visit 'to see the manner of chambletting silk and grosgrains at Monsieur La Dorees in Morefields' (*Diary*, 30 May 1652).
See also Camlet, Ducape, Tabby

Gros point
An EMBROIDERY technique which uses cross-stitches in woollen yarns worked across double threads of canvas to make an even tapestry-like effect. It is heavier and coarser than petit point. This stitch and petit point were characteristic of embroidery work from the 16th century at least. It has been used for table covers, cushion covers and bed furniture and even wall-hangings. During the 17th and 18th centuries the stitch was particularly employed on chairs, settees and fire screens.
See Needlework

Guadeloupe wood
See Mahogany

Guanacaste (*Enterolobium cyclocarpum*)
A central South American timber, with an average density of 490–600 (30–37 lb/cu ft). It has a light yellow sapwood, a brown, occasionally reddish colour heartwood, a coarse texture and an interlocked grain. Used for cabinet work and veneering in the 20th century.

Guarea (*Guarea cedrata*)
A West African timber that has similar qualities to mahogany. It has an average density of 610 (39 lb/cu ft) and is pinkish-brown in colour with a fine texture, a straight or wavy grain and sometimes a mottled or curly figure. Imported from the early 20th century, it has been used both as a plywood species and for veneers, often as a substitute for mahogany. Aka Nigerian pearwood or cedar.

Gums
Gums and resins are referred to frequently and the distinctions need to be noted. Gums are usually soluble in water and hydrophilic, and are generally insoluble in organic solvents such as alcohol. RESINS on the other hand are insoluble in water or hydrophobic and are more or less soluble in solvents. Examples are gum arabic and gum tragacanth which were used as binders for water-colours.
See also Resins, Varnish

Gumwood
A timber from a range of resinous trees.
See American red gum, Eucalyptus, Tupelo

Gutta percha (*Sapodilla*)

A gummy substance derived from the juice of the *Palaquium gutta*, a tree found in the Malay archipelago. When heat softened it could be reset in moulds. Although it was known from the 17th century, it was not until 1844 that the possibilities of gutta percha as a furniture material were developed. In 1846 Charles Hancock set up the Gutta Percha company and patented the processing and applications of it as an inlay or veneer (Pat.no.11,208). It was thought that gutta percha would be an ideal substitute for wood where carving and ornament were required. Its malleable and elastic qualities meant that it could be moulded into almost any shape required, thus making it a strong contender for imitation carving, for instance. The *Art Union* said that 'Copies of old oak panelling taken in gutta-percha have preserved in the most remarkable manner every trace of the original. The grain of the wood, its abrasion by age, its colour and of course its pattern being preserved with the utmost fidelity' (1848, p.39).

Gutta percha showed promise in the manufacture of many articles, however it never really became part of the furniture-maker's repertoire as it was vulnerable to direct heat and was easily marked by fingernails and other abrasions. Nevertheless the 1851 Great Exhibition showed a large sideboard decorated with gutta percha ornament in its natural colour. The material's qualities were described as combining the three-fold advantage of 'lowness of price, elegance of form, and absence of fragility' (Exhibition Jury Reports, Class XXVIII, 1851, p.598). 'All those different articles of furniture, the price of which is so enhanced by carving, are capable of being reproduced by means of pressure and thus multiplied at a low price' (op.cit., p.598).

Its elastic properties were also applied to a form of springing which anticipated the rubber PLATFORMS that were common one hundred years later. At the 1851 Exhibition, H. Pratt displayed a brass chaise-longue fitted with 'elastic' gutta percha sacking (Class 26, Item 403). Despite its apparent promise, it was never a mainstream furniture material.

Anon. (1858), 'The application of gutta percha to the arts', in *Universal Decorator*, p.35.
Clouth, F. (1903), *Gutta percha and Balata*, London: Maclaren and Sons.
Collins, J. (1876), 'Gutta percha and India-rubber', in G. P. Bevan (ed.), *British Manufacturing Industries*, London: Edward Stanford.
Gutta Percha Company Catalogue, Science Museum Library, London, nos 1984–1101.

Hackberry (*Celtis occidentalis*)

A southern Canadian and eastern American yellow-green to brown timber with an average density of 640 (40 lb/cu ft). It has a fine texture and an irregular grain, which works well but is not strong. Occasionally used for furniture, especially chair bottoms, as a substitute for white ELM. Aka Nettletree (USA).

Hair

Animal hair has been used extensively in the furnishing trades both as an upholstery stuffing and for weaving into cloth (see HAIRCLOTH). Curled horsehair is considered one of the best traditional upholstery fillings as its resilience remains for long periods. A spring is set permanently by boiling or steaming tightly twisted ropes of prepared carded hair which give the effect of many resilient individual fibres.

The early use of animal hair in upholstery is evident in the plea made by the Upholder's Company in 1495. They complained of persons who used very poor quality hair and brought the craft into disrepute. Therefore in 1495 an 'Act against Upholsters' was passed which forbade the use of 'horse hair, fen downe [reed mace], neetis [oxen] hair, deers hair, and goats hair which is wrought in lyme fattes

55   *A sideboard exhibited at the 1851 London Great Exhibition. It is ornamented with gutta percha 'carvings'. The idea was never very successful for furniture and it soon fell out of use for this purpose. Other materials and compositions had established themselves, and the properties of gutta percha were not enough to replace the existing materials.*

[grease], and by the heat of a man's body, the savour and taste is so abominable and contagious that many of the Kings subjects [have] thereby been destroyed' (cited in Houston, 1993, p.9). Horsehair began to be more valued as upholstery methods developed. In 1660–1 Charles II had John Caspert supply him with chairs which specified 'curled hair to fill the chair back' (Thornton, 1978, p.225). By 1679 its value was so widely recognized that attempts began to imitate and substitute it in upholstery work. By this time it was also used as a mattress filling.

In the 18th century it appears that it was common practice to re-use old hair by teasing it out and adding new when needed. However, problems with quality control remained. In 1819 it was commented that

The best picked hair is made of horse or bullock tails, and should not be mixed with short hair. This is the case however with common hair, and the quality of the article is known by the greater or lesser quantity of the short kind that is introduced.
(Martin, 1819, p.115)

In the 20th century hair has been rubberized and formed into pads,

but loose curled hair still remains part of the traditional upholsterer's repertoire.
See also Haircloth, Rubberized hair

Hair substitutes

Although a number of cheaper alternatives were introduced into upholstery work from the 17th century (see Upholstery fillings), it was during the 19th century that a number of attempts were made to develop reliable replacements for horsehair. In 1806 Dr Charles Berenger took out a patent (Pat.no.2949) for a hair-substitute, which simply supplanted cheaper hogs' hair for horsehair, and in 1840 John Bachelard devised a process of using curled waste-cork shavings mixed with wool and hair as an upholstery filling (Pat.no.8581). In 1843 Richard Brooman patented the use of fibres obtained from con-vulvuli plants (Pat.no.9863) and in 1862, Thomas Ghislin patented 'improvements in the treatment of certain foreign plants and the application of fibres derived therefrom' (Pat.no.2035). These plants were broken down and their fibres used as stuffing or might be woven into cloth or as a substitute for horsehair.

The more successful substitutes were coir fibre, Algerian fibre and excelsior.
See also Upholstery fillings

Haircloth or Horsehair material

An upholstery textile woven mainly from horsehair, but has also been made from camel, goat or even dog hair. It is woven at an average 69 cm (27 in) width (varying between 36 cm/14 in and 102 cm/40 in, depending on the hair length) in sateen, twill and repp weaves, as well as plain, striped, chequered or damask effects. The fabric had a linen or cotton warp and a hair weft, giving a glossy appearance.

Its first use appears as a backing for the 'holes' in aumbrys in the 15th and 16th centuries and is referred to by Randle Holme as a covering material for arks (1649). The cloth made from 'mane' fabric was used for covering chairs, especially dining chairs, from the 1760s. By the end of the 18th century, Hepplewhite still recommended that 'mahogany chairs should have the seats of horsehair, plain, striped, chequered, &c. at pleasure' (1794, p.2).

Haircloth was also popular in the 19th century due to its strength, imperviousness and cleanability. In the mid 19th century its silk effect gave it the name of 'satin hair' in America. However, Christopher Dresser pronounced it 'inartistic in its effect' (1873, p.72), so it is not surprising to find that during the 1876 Centennial Exhibition 'modern fashion has driven this material from fashionable drawing rooms; but its durability still causes it to be retained in unambitious apartments' (cited in Adrosko, 1990, p.108). It still remains an upholstery fabric.

Haldu (*Adina cordifolia*)

A timber from India and Burma with a density of 650 (41 lb/cu ft). It is pale yellow, darkening to deeper yellow on exposure, with a fine texture and a moderate density. Used occasionally for furniture.

Halved joint

See Joints (Bridle)

Hammer

A wide range of striking tools are called hammers, many devised specially for particular jobs. The double-faced CHAIR-MAKER's hammer with a smooth, sometimes convex head is used instead of a mallet for 'legging-up' chair frames, as it does not split end grain or mark surfaces so badly. The UPHOLSTERERS used a cabriole hammer with a

6.4 mm (¼ in) diameter head, a tack hammer with a magnetized 16 mm (⅝ in) diameter head and a claw hammer. In the 19th century, French makes of upholstery hammers were preferred by British upholsterers. It was also a standard tool for CABINET-MAKERS, who used a variety of hammers including claw, cross-peen, pin (for driving small nails, veneer pins and so on), tack, veneering (see VENEERING), and War-rington hammers (general-purpose).

Hammock

The original hammock was a net or canvas strip that was slung be-tween supporting uprights and was probably brought to Europe from the Caribbean in the late 16th century. The form has been adapted by many designers as a support in seating. An early example would be the deck chair (in the 19th century, called a hammock chair) which has a canvas support slung from the top rail and fixed on the front seat rail. The idea of a fabric sling support was also used for metal rocking chairs in the mid 19th century as well as for J. B. Fenby's (1877) fold-ing camp chair. Forms of hammock upholstery suspension in the 20th century include plastic sheet, leather and cotton cloth. Variations are numerous and include the well-known Hardoy chair, designed in 1938 with its hammock support fitted to a demountable metal frame, as well as more conventional chairs made from tube metal frames with polypropylene sheet, supporting cushions.

Giedion, S. (1948), *Mechanisation Takes Command*, New York: Oxford University Press, pp.471–9.

Hand saw

See Saws

Handscrew

A clamping device made from two parallel hardwood blocks 254–457 mm (10–18 in) long, about 25–50 mm (1–2 in) square. They are fitted with large wooden screws which bring the jaws together to clamp the work.

Hard maple

See Maple

Hardboard

See Fibreboard

Hardstones

See Pietre dure

Hardware

See Hinges, Locks

Hardwoods

A botanical definition which has no relation to the strength of the tim-ber. It refers to the timber derived from broad-leaved deciduous trees classified as angiosperms (as opposed to conifers). They are more complex in structure than softwoods. Hardwoods are also defined as porous woods (as opposed to non-porous conifers) and are known as ring porous (concentrated in early wood) or diffuse porous (even distribution throughout), referring to the structure of the pores in a ring.

Harewood

(a) Figured sycamore (or curly maple wood), which is stained with ferrous sulphate (oxide of iron). This reacts with the wood and produces a silver grey colour, but is prone to fading to a browny-grey. Used as veneer for marquetry work. Aka Mousewood, Greywood. See also Air(e) wood, Dyeing

(b) Also a name for a SATINWOOD species imported into England, known as concha satinwood (Howard, 1920, p.95).

Harratine or **Harrateen**
A watered (moiré) worsted fabric used in the 18th century for bed furnishings. It was an important woollen furnishing fabric which had a hot-pressed design applied, imitating damask. Popular prior to the 1750s after which it tended to be replaced by more washable textiles. In 1726, the Boston upholsterer Thomas Fitch wrote to a client of this material: 'I concluded it would be difficult to get such a Calliminco as you propos'd to cover the ease chair, and having a very strong thick Harratine which is vastly more fashionable and handsome than a Calliminco. I have sent you an ease chair cover'd with sd Harrateen which I hope will sute you' (cited in Montgomery, 1984, p.256). In 1731 'one new harrateen bed, bedstead and Cornish all compleat never used' was listed in the inventory of the Bastards of Blandford (Legg, 1994, p.29). By 1882 it was described as 'an imitation of Moire in commoner material for purposes of upholstery' (Beck).

It has also been used to refer to a linen fabric. Esther Hewlett (1825) suggested that 'If you have curtains … the best are linen check harrateen' (cited in Cummings, 1961, p.26).
See also Moreen

Hartshorn or **Ammonia**
See Stains

Hasp lock
See Locks

Haunch tenon
See Joints

Havana cedar
See Cedar

Hawthorn (*Crataegus oxyacantha*)
A European timber which is yellowish-white, hard, fairly heavy and with a tough, fine, close grain. It has limited use, due to its small size, but it has been used as a substitute for boxwood in inlay work.

Hazel (*Corylus spp.*)
Also known as nutwood, or *bois de cordier*, it is a pinkish-white to reddish-tan timber with a close uniform texture and a straight grain. Although its small dimensions restrict its use, the butts are valued for veneers. Used for European vernacular furniture as well as Germanic city furniture and marquetry, especially in the 19th century. In the later 19th century it was employed as timber for bedroom suites in England.

Hazel pine
See American red gum

Heartwood
The inner part of a tree, the chief function of which is to support that tree. It does not have any living cells as compared to the sapwood. It is usually heavier, harder and more durable than the outer sapwood, although in some species it is difficult to distinguish.

Hemlock (*Tsuga heterophylla*)
A North American softwood with an average density of 500 (31 lb/cu ft). It is straight grained and has a fine even texture. It has a light yellowish-brown background with a clear growth ring figure which is often reddish brown. Hemlock is a useful timber for concealed parts of cabinets and painted work, although selected logs are used for decorative veneering.

Japanese hemlock (*Tsuga diversifolia*)
Sourced in Formosa, it has an average density of 450 (29 lb/cu ft), a pale brown colour with late wood bands giving a red-purple cast, and a variable grain and coarse texture. Particularly used for decorative veneers in the 20th century.

Hemp (*Cannabis sativa*)
A fibrous stem of the Indian hemp plant which has been used for HESSIAN, scrim, canvas and sacking, though it has been replaced in recent times by jute. Discarded flax or hemp fibres make TOW. Hemp fibres as tow have also been used as an upholstery filling.

Herring-bone or **Feather banding**
See Banding

Hessian
A woven cloth made from linen or jute fibres, sometimes called CANVAS, it is often woven 183 cm (72 in) wide specifically for upholstery purposes. Varieties include the tightly woven tarpaulin version or spring canvas for covering springs, woven with flat threads, and the SCRIM version with rounded threads used as a covering of the first stuffing which is stitched into place (scrim stuffing refers to this process). Hessian is also used for lining interiors of frames. It is available in various weights from 210 to 448 g (7.5 to 16 oz). Also known as BURLAP or Forfar.

Hickory (*Carya sp.*)
A hardwood, native to eastern North America with an average density of 790 (49 lb/cu ft). It has a reddish-brown heartwood (red hickory) with a pale sapwood (white hickory), which are sold separately. It is extremely tough with high tensile strength, but its open-pored grain makes for poor nailing. Typically straight grained and with a coarse texture, it is difficult to work as it splinters easily. Rather like ASH but stronger, it turns well and is good for bentwood. Hickory is widely used for chair work, particularly for components such as crest rails, spindles and stretchers. Famous as the raw material for late-19th- and early-20th-century 'rustic' Adirondack chairs. The Old Hickory Chair Co used poles (saplings) bent into shape and fitted together using a patent metal frame. Seats and backs were then fitted with woven material made from strips of the inner bark. It is also used for plywood and veneer as well as construction work in the 20th century.

Kyloe, Ralph (1995), *A History of the Old Hickory Chair Company, and the History of the Indiana Hickory Furniture Movement*, Lake George, NY: Ralph Kyloe Antiques.

High relief carving
See Carving

Highlighting and shading
A skilful process of finishing cabinet work by blending out a coloured stain and varnish to create a rubbed effect. It was popular in the 1930s.

Hinau wood (*Elaecarpus dentalus*)
A yellowish-brown close grained coniferous wood common throughout New Zealand. At the end of the 19th century it was said that Hinau 'makes a very handsome cabinet wood' (Spon, 1901, p.134).

Hinges

A method of joining parts of furniture together so that they will open, close, fold or otherwise move as required. Hinges may be made from many materials including woods, metals and plastics. Developments in technology have continually improved hinges in material, type and operation.

Early Egyptian hinges of metal (copper) may be found on the furniture of Tutankhamun: simple butt hinges of gold as well as copper hinges. Wood pin hinges were used from *c*.1400 BC in substitute for wooden pivots used previously, although wood pin hinges were still common in the 12th and 13th centuries. Iron hinges followed in the form of strap or butterfly shapes up to the 15th century, and strap hinges were still in use in the 16th century. However the butt type was common by then, initially made from iron until brass started to be used also, later in the 17th century. Although steel or brass remain the standard for hinges, nylon and other plastics have been used in the latter part of the 20th century. The wide variety of types is indicated below.

Back flap
A simple hinge that allows flaps to rise and fall easily. Used on bureaux falls as the screws are further from the edge than butt hinges and the flanges are bigger. Frequently used in association with rule joints.

Balance
Designed for the fall-fronts of secretaires. They are fitted to the side of the fall so that the weighted end can rise and fall in the side panels, enabling the fall flap to close itself when it reaches 45 degrees (see Sheraton, 1793, Plate 52).

Butt
A metal hinge which is let into two panels in such a way that they will close together without strain. Found on furniture from the 17th century, they were commonly used on doors and lids. Originally butt hinges were made from thin strips of wrought-iron which were bent over double, so leaving a rounded fold for the insertion of a pin. Later versions, which were made by machine, had plates cut from the solid with the end curled over to make the pin slot. In the early 19th century the range of butt hinges included: the 'stop' butt which limited the degree of opening; 'rising' butt hinges designed to clear carpets; 'slip off' butt hinges to allow simple removal of doors; 'lap over' butt hinges which raise work above the edge; and the 'desk' butt hinge which is a standard butt with a wider strap. Flush hinges do the same job but are more suitable for lighter work.

Butterfly
A medieval iron hinge mounted on the surface of items such as cupboard doors. Its open design resembles the wings of a butterfly, hence the name. They were not common after the later 18th century.

Continuous
See below, Piano hinge

Cranked
Used for lay-on doors in high-quality work enabling a full return opening.

Cylinder
A hinge that allows a door to open 180 degrees. Cylinder parts are inserted into pre-drilled holes so that they are nearly invisible.

Cylinder soss
A patented hinge that is mortised into the edges of the boards to be fitted so that it is completely hidden when doors are closed. It works on an enclosing comb principle.

Dolphin
A name referring to the outline of a hinge designed to be used on fall-fronts of secretaires or writing drawers.

H shaped
A decorative hinge with the flanges longer than the bolt, giving an H shape outline. More elaborate examples were called 'cocks heads' in the 17th century.

L shaped
A special hinge described by Sheraton as being for 'shaving and dressing tables: [they] are adopted for strength, for the ell part returns on the front and back edge of the swinging part and greatly secured the top' (1803, p.252).

Lift-off
A hinge with a pin on one plate and a socket on the other, enabling the hinged component to be removed at will.

Necked or Offset
A hinge with the flap offset from the pin so that, when opened, it will allow the door to clear projections.

Piano
A continuous hinge (up to 2 m/6½ ft) which is used to give a very strong fitting. It is cut to size as required.

Pin
Basic part of a simple hinge whereby the pin acts as a pivot for straps. They may be of wood or metal. Early wooden examples may be found in 12th- or 13th-century items. Sheraton recommends their use 'to avoid the disagreeable appearance of the knockle of common but-hinges' (1803, p.252).

Quadrant
A combined STAY and hinge designed to support flap, but only used where space for a stay is available.

Rule joint
A simple hinge designed to allow flaps to drop on gate-leg tables, for example, with an ovolo edge.

Staple
A type of simple hinge in which two metal cotter-pins are inserted through timber edges and splayed open to fix in place in such a way that the two rings on each end can be first linked to form a pivot.

Stop
A hinge opening only to a certain point. This is achieved by two adjoining knuckles having opposing offsets which interlock.

Strap
A hinge with an elongated plate used to screw to the face of doors on cupboards and cabinets. It may be plain, shaped or decorated. Found on a wide range of cabinet work from the Middle Ages. This hinge form was revived in the latter part of the 19th century under the influence of the Arts and Crafts movement. They are also used for desks and furniture with a narrow fixing space.

Swan neck
Described by Sheraton as particularly associated with folding camp tables (1803, p.252). The hinge allows the table top to turn over onto itself and be held by a hinge. The name derives from the graceful curved shape of the two arms of the hinge.

Holdfast
A traditional tool for the workshop known since Roman times. It consists of a figure seven-shaped piece of iron bar let into a hole on the bench. By knocking it on the top it would grip a work-piece, by another blow it would be released. Modern versions have quick-acting screws. Moxon described 'The hold-fast, let loose into round holes ... in the bench: its office is to keep the work fast upon the bench, whilst you either saw, tennant, mortess or sometime plain upon it' (1677, p.65).

Holland
A plain linen cloth imported from Holland since the 15th century, that was used for case covers and blinds among other uses. When finished with a glaze, it has been used for roller and spring blinds since the 18th century. It was particularly recommended for removable covers and for chair-back cushion 'caps' in the mid 19th century. The *Workwoman's Guide* explained that 'Holland covers are the most durable but look cold' (1840, p.206).
See also Protective furnishing

Holly wood (*Ilex aquifolium*)
A hard creamy-white hardwood being a native of Europe and Western Asia. With an average density of 800 (50 lb/cu ft), it has a slightly flecked but irregular grain, with little or no figure. To preserve the white colour, the wood needs to be converted immediately upon felling and stored in shade. In Britain, boiling and careful drying also worked to preserve colour. In the case of veneers, they were hung up after cutting to avoid stain contact. In the case of billets for turning, they were boiled, then covered with sacking to exclude air, and allowed to develop a mildew surface which was brushed off at intervals until they were dry.

Holly wood has been widely used in inlay, intarsia, banding and marquetry. It is often used as a substitute for BOXWOOD or, when stained black, as a substitute for EBONY. In the 17th century Evelyn recommended placing holly veneers under thin ivory to raise the profile of the ivory material (1662, p.161). Sheraton confirmed that it was 'much in use amongst cabinet-makers for corner lines and other purposes. It is capable of being dyed a good black and is used as such for ornamenting cabinet work' (1803, p.253). In the 19th century it was used by TUNBRIDGE WARE makers for the best work, especially that which was to be painted in water colour or used as a contrast. Mayhew particularly noted that 'of holly the Tonbridge ware is made ... and is employed for stringing' (Letter LIX, 4 July 1850).

American holly (*Ilex opaca*)
Similar to the European holly and used for veneers and cabinet work detail, in the Federal period especially. It was particularly used for stringing, either in its natural colour or stained.

Honduras mahogany (*Swietiana macrophylla*)
See Mahogany

Honduras rosewood (*D. stevensonii*)
See Rosewood

56   An American horn armchair, c.1880–90. The use of animal horns was part of a taste related to a later-19th-century interest in the wild and the exotic.

Honey locust
See Locustwood

Hooks and eyes
(a) Used to describe the stirrup-shaped clips that slot into fittings to join dining-table leaves to make a full table top.

(b) A method of fitting loose covers around chair frames using small metal hooks and small ring-shaped 'eyes' sewn to each side of the opening. In 1686 Jean Poictevin invoiced work for the Queen's Bedchamber for 'false covers for the chairs and stools silk, tape, rings, hoocks and eyes. £20' (cited in Beard, 1997, p.292). They remained in favour until the introduction of ZIPS in the early 20th century. In some cases wall hangings and bed furnishings were also fixed by this method.
See also Buttons and loops

Hoop pine
See Pine

Horn and Antlers
A natural white, yellow-white or black substance derived from the horns of certain animals. Preliminary preparation of horn included soaking, marrow removal and then cutting into three sections: the tips, biscage (main section) and throat. The biscage or tube part and the

throat were heated and then opened by cutting so as to lay flat. The horn was then pressed, rasped, reheated and squeezed until the required thickness was achieved to create a transparent and level sheet. Marquetry workers use sheets 1 mm (c.¹⁄₁₆ in) thick (horn may be up to 6 mm/¼ in for cattle and 25 mm/1 in for buffalo). Horn has been used for itself and as a substitute for TORTOISESHELL. Its use has not only been in inlay and marquetry work. In 1829 James and Thomas Deakin patented a method of making handles and knobs and other parts of cabinet and household articles from animal horn (Pat.no.5753), and in 1838–40 the Houghton Patent Buffalo Horn Furniture Company of 44 Farringdon Street, London was in business.

The use of steer horns in American furniture was particularly popular, especially in the last quarter of the 19th century. Some firms in Texas specialized in the manufacture (for example, Wenzel Friedrich), and made chairs, sofas, tables and hall stands, all using full horn material. Friedrich boiled the selected longhorns to soften them for shaping and paring. Each horn was then filled with plaster of Paris and fitted with a wooden block to seal the horn and provide a fixing point. The naturally laminated form of horn material also meant that it could be used when flattened as table-top finishes and aprons to chairs. Another 19th-century centre for horn furniture was Chicago. The massive stockyards ensured an enormous supply of by-products from animals, and these naturally included horns. The Tobey Furniture Company began to specialize in this unique style, and by 1881 had developed quite a reputation for 'chairs with polished horn for backs, and they are as modern as the Texas cowboy and as inimitable' (*Inland Architect and Builder*, cited in Darling, 1984, p.78). By the last decade of the century, horn furniture was widely available, no doubt as much for its representation of the Wild West, as its intrinsic novelty.

Antlers
The branched horns of a stag or male deer. Although antlers had been used in interior decoration on and off since the Middle Ages, it was not until the mid 19th century that their use for furniture was seriously considered. In the first quarter of the 19th century the Austrian firm of Josef Danhauser designed a number of furniture pieces using antlers and animal heads. The German firm of Rampendahl were exhibitors at the 1851 Exhibition, where they showed a range of specimens of stag horn furniture, while other firms based in Frankfurt had already established an antler furniture tradition especially for the furnishing of hunting lodges. The exhibiting of such furniture continued in other later exhibitions, but the items always remained novelties. Other firms included Kraftverkehr of Bitterefield, R. Friedrich Bohler who won a silver medal for stag horn furniture, and Jetley and Co of London who made items from samba deer horn or Indian antelope, which were shown at the Philadelphia Exhibition of 1876.

Imitation horn
A method of imitating horn was devised in the 18th century, which involved dipping wire mesh into a bath of fish glue and allowing a film to build up by repeated dippings. When varnished, it was apparently quite adequate as a horn substitute (*Almanac sous Verre*, 1799, cited in Benhamou, 1991).
See also Compositions, Tortoiseshell

Jervis, Simon (1972), 'Antler and horn furniture', *Victoria and Albert Museum Yearbook*, London.
MacGregor, A. (1985), *Bone, Antler, Ivory and Horn*, London: Croome Helm.
Rogers, Alan (1993), 'The horn furniture of Henry Metz', in *Maine Antique Digest*, 21, 8, August, 8B–9B.

Hornbeam (*Carpinus betulus*)
A timber native to Europe with an average density of 750 (47 lb/cu ft). It is yellowish-white in colour with little figure, although flecked on quarter-cut surfaces. It is occasionally used as a substitute for ebony, when dyed black. It is rare in cabinetry as it is difficult to work, except as veneers and inlay; however, it is common in turnery. Sheraton said 'This wood being of a close and hard texture in the grain, is much used by turners' (1803, p.255). It is also widely used for piano actions. During the 18th century it was occasionally used for decoration, and in French marquetry it was known as the *bois de charme*.

Horopito (*Drimus/pseudowintera axillaris*)
An evergreen tree from New Zealand, which was recorded as a 'very ornamental in cabinet work, making handsome veneers' (Spon, 1901, p.134). Aka Pepper Tree or Winter's Bark wood.

Horse
(a) A device specially made for working veneers with a MARQUETRY saw. The operator sat astride the seat and clamped the parcel of veneers between the jaws of a foot-operated vertical vice. This left the hands free to manipulate the saw and adjust the parcel. In 18th-century France the curved jaws were fixed to a work bench with the pedal fixed below so that the marquetry-worker stood up to cut the shapes.
See also Donkey, Saw horse

(b) A support for rising desk tops or inclining mirrors which may have lead weights for adjustment. *Cabinet-makers' London Book of Prices* noted prices for making 'a glass made to slide under the drawer, with a horse hinged to the back' (1793).

Horse-chestnut wood
See Chestnut

Horseflesh mahogany
See Sabicu

Horsehair
See Hair

Housed joint
See Joints

Housed mouldings
See Mouldings

Hungarian ash
See Ash

Huon pine
See Pine

Hydrographic carving
See Carving

Idigbo (*Terminalia ivorensis*)
A West African hardwood species with an average density of 580 (36 lb/cu ft). It is a light yellow to pale brown colour with an uneven texture, a variable grain and a well marked growth ring figure with occasional brown striping. Flat sawn stock has a distinct superficial re-

semblance to OAK. It has been widely used in 20th-century furniture, joinery, decorative veneers and plywood.

Imbuia (*Ocotea porosa*)
A Brazilian hardwood, sometimes known as BRAZILIAN WALNUT, with an average density of 720 (45 lb/cu ft), a yellowish-brown colour, a fine to medium texture, a straight grain and a variable figure. It is used in Brazil for furniture, while quality veneers are exported to Europe for decorative finishing.

Imitation carving
See Carving

Imitation inlay
See Inlay, Marquetry (Imitation inlay and marquetry)

Imitation leather
See Coated fabrics

Imitation marquetry
See Marquetry

Imitation tortoiseshell
See Tortoiseshell

Imitation wood
See Bois durci, Bois repoussé, Compositions, Graining, Wood substitutes

Impregnation seasoning
See Seasoning

Improved tacks
See Tacks

In the round carving
See Carving

Incised lacquer
A decorative process to build up layers of differing colour lacquers which can then be cut through (incised) in a pattern to reveal the various colours under the top coat.
See Lacquer.

Indian cedar or **mahogany**
See Australian red cedar

Indian laburnum (*Cassia fistula*)
A timber sourced in India, Sri Lanka and Burma. It is hard and heavy at 970 (61 lb/cu ft), with a brick-red colour, darkening upon exposure. One authority considered that its close grain 'would [make it] useful for turning, inlay and fine cabinet work' (Howard, 1920, p.47).

Indian laurel (*Terminalia alata*)
A South-East Asian hardwood timber with an average density of 870 (53 lb/cu ft), which is similar in colour, figure and character to Italian WALNUT: dark brown with wavy streaks which supply highly figured veneers. It is straight grained, with a coarse but firm texture. The timber works well and takes a fine polish. Introduced in the early 20th century, it has been used in chair-making and for cabinet veneering. It is not a true laurel.

Indian mulberry (*Morus indica*)
See Mulberry

Indian rosewood (*Dalbergia latifolia*)
See Rosewood

Indian silver greywood (*Terminalia bialata*)
A handsomely figured wood sourced from the Andaman Islands with an average density of 660 (42 lb/cu ft). It has a greyish-white to smoky lightish-brown background, with darker streaks. Fairly straight grained with a medium texture. It has similar properties to oak, but is mainly used as a veneer. When plain timber, it is called CHUGLAM.

Indian white mahogany (*Canarium emphyllum*)
Aka Dhup

Injection moulding
A process used in furniture manufacture in conjunction with PLASTICS. The granulated plastic material is placed into a hopper which feeds a prepared mould. The mould is then heated, the granules melt and the liquefied material takes the form of the mould. When set, the mould is opened and the item removed. Very high speeds of processing can be achieved.

Inlay
An ancient decorative technique that has many variations of material but is simply the filling of cut-out shapes in solid parts by another, usually contrasting material. The let-in materials include assorted woods such as ASH, BEECH, BOG OAK, EBONY, FRUITWOOD, HOLLY, PEAR, POPLAR, SYCAMORE and YEW, as well as BONE, HORN, IVORY, MOTHER-OF-PEARL, PLASTICS, STONE, TORTOISESHELL and such like.

Early inlay techniques, which often used ebony, were employed in Ancient Egypt. The sections were quite thick (*c*.2 mm/⅛ in and 4 mm/¼ in) and would have initially been fixed with resin. The use of glue as a fixative followed later in the new Kingdom period. Other materials used by Egyptian craftsmen for inlay work included GLASS, precious stones and metals. For example, the back of Tutankhamun's throne is decorated with inlaid faience, carnelians and gold. In Greek literature there are many references to the inlay technique, for example, Penelope's chair which was inlaid with ivory and silver (*Odyssey*, XIX, 56). This taste continued into Roman times where inlay could demonstrate wealth by using precious jewels, metals, and so on. However, horn, ivory and coloured glass were also used for their decorative effect.

During the 15th century, inlay was employed by central European makers, especially for cupboard decoration. In the 16th century, inlay techniques became popular in conjunction with oak furniture. During the late 16th and early 17th centuries, inlays comprised of holly or poplar woods for light tones and BOGWOODS for dark tones with some red coloured woods, for example CHERRY, for ornament. A particular inlay of compressed wood shavings has been found in eastern counties of England. In the case of geometric inlays, bone was used as well as timber. In 1662 Evelyn noted the wide range of timbers used for inlay work at that time. He noted that the indigenous woods included 'berbery for yellow, holly for white', whilst of the foreign timbers 'our inlayers use fustic, locust or acacia, brazil, prince and

57   *An English oak chest showing panelled construction and decorative inlay work, c.1655. The simple trompe l'œil feature in the top centre is probably derived from intarsia originals.*

rosewood for yellows and reds with several others brought from both Indies' (1662, p.240).

Although replaced by MARQUETRY as a fashionable finish from the mid 17th century, inlays have continued to be used in combination with solid work in a variety of cabinet works. The technique was particularly revived as an honest and simple decoration by makers working in an Arts and Crafts tradition.

Metal inlays
The particular use of metals, including BRASS, COPPER, PEWTER, SILVER, as inlaying was a very ancient practice which has been revived on occasions.
See Boulle, Brass inlay

Forgione, J. (1973), *Wood Inlay: Art and Craft*, New York: Van Nostrand.

Inlayers
See Marquetry workers

Intarsia
The term intarsia causes some confusion as it is derived from the Italian word which refers to all kinds of inlay (including marquetry). The verb is *intarsiare* and workers were known as *intarsiatori*. It is accepted that intarsia is a particular form of inlaid decoration for furniture and architectural panels that is distinct from other types of wood decoration including inlay, certosina and marquetry. It is a process which builds up a pictorial design by setting timber pieces 3–6 mm (⅛–¼ in) thick into recesses cut into a solid ground. The process was intended to provide colour by using stained or shaded timbers set

against a dark background. Originally, intarsia incorporated trompe l'œil perspective designs, often using humanistic motifs, such as books, globes and other trappings of Renaissance learning. Motifs also included architectural perspectives of imaginary buildings, both complete and in ruins, and it was these that could be found both in furniture and architectural woodwork.

Intarsia appears to have originated in Tuscany (Italy) in the early 14th century and was initially used for the decoration of religious buildings. An early use was in the choir stalls of Orvieto Cathedral by Giovanni Ammannati who died c.1340. Later examples can be found in the chapel of the Palazzo Publico, Siena, executed by Domenico di Niccolo de Cori (1415–28). The process matured in Florence and was at one time considered equal to painting. Vasari gave details of artists who worked in the medium, and credited Francesco di Giovanni as the originator of the process. He also noted that Brunelleschi taught perspective to artists by using intarsia examples (1550, p.305).

Apart from the religious applications of intarsia, it was also sought after for use in secular situations. These could be for cabinets and *cassone*, but also for decorating interior wall panelling. Perhaps the most famous use in a domestic room was the decoration of the *studiolo* of Federigo de Montrefelto, in the Ducal Palace at Urbino. Constructed c.1470 and still in situ, the small room is enlivened by amazingly skilled intarsia decoration. The trompe l'œil effect is achieved by creating the illusion of half-open cupboards with their contents tantalizingly on display, shelves with life-like objects and architectural detail which is featured all round the room. (A similar example by Francesco di Giorgio for the Palazzo Gubbio is now located in the Metropolitan Museum of Art in New York.)

In Italy, by the mid 16th century intarsia was moving out of high fashion and gradually becoming a craft rather than the high art it had once been. Work in hard-stones replaced the supremacy of wood. However, the strong influence of Italy meant that intarsia became attractive to South German cabinet-makers. The high-quality intarsia work from Augsburg and Nuremberg was evidence of their expertise in the field. The famous *Wrangelschrank* made in Augsburg during 1566 is a fine example of the cabinet-maker's skill. Intarsia can often be found on the back and top as well as the front and sides of a cabinet, clearly an indication of prestige.

From Germany the influence of intarsia decoration spread further north. By the mid 16th century it had reached Bohemia. Towards the end of the 16th century parts of the Low Countries had developed the skills to use intarsia work, particularly Zeeland and Antwerp, both using the imaginary architectural scene to decorate the fronts of cupboards and chests. With the development of veneering and the MARQUETRY process, which was much more adaptable, intarsia became less important.

RELIEF INTARSIA
This technique prepares panels in order to combine flat intarsia with other work in relief. The craft that produced this heightened perspectival effect was centred on the city of Eger in Bohemia, and was at its height during the mid 17th century. In the 19th century, the work of Henri Fourdinois (1830 until post 1894) has connections with this technique, although his own method was patented. His work introduced delicate relief carvings that were let into the body of the cabinet, sometimes from the rear of the panels. The reliefs were usually in contrasting timbers, such as box, which were set off particularly well against an ebony ground.

Ames, Kenneth (1976), 'The furniture of Fourdinois', in *Antiques*, 110, August, pp.336–43.

Beblo, Hans (1958), *Die Intarsia und Ihre Techniken*, Augsburg: Wolfgang Zimmer.

Bruggemann, Erich (1988), *Kunst und Technik des Intarsien*, Werkzeug und Material, Munich.

Flade, Helmut (1986), *Intarsia: Europaische Einlegekunst aus Sechs Jahrhunderten*, Munich: Beck.

Hamilton Jackson, F. (1903), *Intarsia and Marquetry*, London: Sands and Co.

Irish stitch

See Stitches (Flame)

Iroko (*Milicia excelsa*)

A timber of West and East African origin with an average density of 670 (41 lb/cu ft). Introduced in the late 19th century, it is strong and durable, with a light yellow to deep gold and dark brown colour with lighter markings. It has a coarse texture, an interlocked grain and has been used as a substitute for teak. Sometimes called African teak.

Iron

The distinctions between iron and STEEL are that cast iron has up to 5 per cent carbon, and steel is an alloy of no more than 2 per cent carbon with other proportions of metals as required. Iron working was known and practised from *c*.1500 BC but its use was limited to small items and utility objects such as pots, kettles, guns and firebacks. The first furniture application was wrought iron.

WROUGHT IRON

The simplest form of iron was originally produced by heating charcoal and iron ore together to produce 'bloom' or pig iron. This could then be hammered to remove impurities and made into iron bars which could be shaped to requirements or passed to slitting mills to cut into smaller rods. Modern wrought iron is made by refining cast iron through a re-heating process that reduces the carbon content by the presence of iron oxide. The low carbon content means that it is relatively free from impurities and has a fibrous structure giving a good tensile strength.

Wrought iron was used by the Romans for folding chair frames in the *Sella curulis* model and the tradition survived into the early Middle Ages for various aspects of furniture construction. For example wrought-iron bars and straps were often used for making chests stronger and more structurally sound. (One of the earliest known items using wrought-iron bands is in the Abbey Church of Saint-Etienne, Obazine, Corrèze, France.) The material was also recognized for its potential decorative value which was often exploited along with its structural necessity.

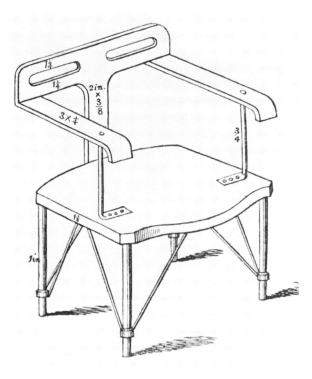

59 An early idea for a chair made with iron tube, iron bar and a wooden seat, showing an unusually clear understanding of the materials and their design capabilities, c.1839.

The connection between iron and bedsteads and their ability to avoid bugs and fleas was an early consideration that was often revived. As early as 1393 in the *Ménagier de Paris*, iron beds were used as a deliberate precaution against this problem, and the famous Parisian hospital, the Hôtel Dieu, was supplied with iron bedsteads upon its establishment in 1623. In the 17th century iron bedsteads were noted by Evelyn, 'the bedsteads in Italy are all of forged iron gilded, since it is impossible to keep the wooden ones from the Chimices [bugs]' (*Diary*, 8 August 1645). Iron beds continued to be made for illustrious clients, although by the end of the 18th century they were also in demand for other applications. Armies were becoming important customers whose volume orders encouraged large-scale production. The usefulness of wrought iron for beds was revived in the early 19th century. Loudon illustrates a range of beds from a simple stump bed to a fine French bed, which used iron slats and frames as a deterrent against the vermin found in wooden beds, although the development of iron tubes eventually took over part of this function (1839, p.329).

In addition to beds, the use of iron for special seats continued. This is demonstrated by the chair made for the Duchess of Suffolk. In 1466: 'a chaire of state of yren [iron], covered with purpell satyn fur'd, and a case of leather thereto' was supplied to her (Parker, 1859, p.115). In other cases, spectacular iron furniture was the result of a liaison between the blacksmiths, locksmiths and iron founders and even armourers. One of the most spectacular is the iron chair made in 1574 by Thomas Rucker of Augsburg for the Emperor Rudolph II (*Burlington Magazine*, June 1980, pp.428–32). Other furniture types were occasionally made from iron, including braziers, torchères, pole screens and the *pie de puente* tables from Spain. These wooden tables used wrought-iron stretchers to join the legs and tops together giving the advantage of strength to a demountable construction.

As a decorative medium, wrought iron was revived in the 1880s

58 Iron bedsteads were among the first institutional furniture. This example was intended for use in workhouses, c.1836, English.

RIGHT
60 *Cast iron was often used to imitate other materials or was worked in historic styles rather than using its intrinsic qualities. A cast-iron console table, c.1860.*

FAR RIGHT
61 *Cast iron was also used in extraordinary designs. This bedstead by Dupont of Paris was shown at the 1851 London Great Exhibition.*

especially by French designer Emile Robert. In the early 20th century, wrought iron was an ideal material for the fashionable Art Deco furniture with a whole range of decorative items being designed and made by French designers in particular. They included Brandt, Subes, Piquet, and Poillerat. Edgar Brandt remains the most notable. During the 1920s his wrought-iron work included mirror frames, lamp bases, screens, console tables and a wide range of other accessories.

After World War II, wrought iron was again used as a lightweight and decorative material for furniture. The 1950s 'contemporary' designers used it, often enamelled in colours, for garden or patio furniture as well as for small occasional tables, shelving and other accessories. Its combination with glass was particularly popular, and in these cases the metal was often painted white.

CAST IRON

Cast iron is made by melting iron ore in a furnace at a high temperature. The iron absorbs some of the carbon from the fuel. Once melted, the liquid metal is drawn off into ingots or made directly into castings. Although known and used for a wide range of products since the 15th century, the benefits of cast iron for decorative furnishings were particularly acknowledged in the 18th century, especially for architectural applications that required multiple castings of the same object, for example railings, balconies and panels. To accommodate the demand for finer quality work, changes had to occur in the manufacturing technology. The first major development was the blast furnace designed to be fired by coke, developed by Abraham Darby from 1709. This increased temperatures and produced a more fluid iron. Alongside this, the development of sand moulds was also crucial for making finer castings. By the 1780s two-thirds of furnaces making iron had switched from charcoal to coke-burning. In conjunction with this improvement in quality, was the use of steam engines for air blasting, and the introduction of the puddling process which helped to reduce costs. The introduction of the cupola blast furnace by Wilkinson in 1794 meant that foundries could be separate from the blast furnace. These changes made the cast iron material suitable for bulk production of household items, including various ranges of furniture.

The possibilities of iron for chests of drawers, bookcases and bureaux were seriously considered in England in 1809 by Benjamin Cook. According to him these could be japanned to imitate costly woods, or the panels could be painted; the mouldings might be Gothic or any other form, and the drawers 'might be made with light iron framing: filled up with wire work, which would make them very light'

(*Furniture Gazette*, 10 June 1882, p.361). However, one of the earliest designers to actually use cast iron as a furniture material was Prussian architect K. F. Schinkel, who between 1820 and 1825 devised a range of cast-iron outdoor furniture. These were simply made with two identical cast sides held together by wrought-iron rods. It was this simple formulation that has remained a basis for much outdoor furniture produced since then.

The British and North American manufacturers of cast iron were initially interested in products such as stoves and grates, but by the 1840s they recognized a growing market for both interior and exterior furnishings. One of the first British commentators to be enthusiastic about the possibilities of cast-iron furnishings was John Claudius Loudon. His illustrated designs included early applications of iron to chair-making, and these have sometimes been seen as precursors of early-20th-century products. Loudon explained that cast iron made 'an exceedingly light yet stable chair, weighing less than most oak ones' (1839, p.32). Although he published some very unusual chair designs, he was also attuned to the contemporary demand for inexpensive ornament. Loudon pointed out that, 'where carved work or much ornament is to be executed in furniture, cast iron will always be found cheaper than wood, even though small numbers only of the article were wanting' (loc.cit., p.318). For utilitarian purposes cast iron was ideal. For example, the 'stump bedsteads made entirely of wrought-iron, the place of the canvas or seating bottom being supplied by interwoven iron hooping which is manufactured by Messrs Cottam and Hallam' were common for workhouse furniture in the 1830s (loc.cit., pp.331–2). Others were also active in this climate of development in cast iron. In France, the Pihet brothers were making cast-iron furniture, and in America around 1849, Thomas Warren unashamedly used cast-iron frames for his famous CENTRIPETAL SPRING chairs, which were widely accepted.

Amongst many, perhaps the most important name that is associated with cast-iron objects is the Coalbrookdale Iron Company. The company, which was founded early in the 18th century and was responsible for the first iron bridge built in the 1770s, began to make ornamental castings in the 1830s. The 1851 Great Exhibition entry by the Coalbrookdale Company showed the range of items that were being produced by that time: cast-iron chess-tables; hall or console tables in cast iron, unusually painted in white and gold with marble top; a large table with cast-iron legs painted oak; an intricate iron casting, bronzed and marbled of a hall-table, arranged with pedestals for hats, coats and umbrellas; armchairs, and 3-tier plant stands.

Cast-iron products were often decorated so that the ironwork would imitate other materials in attempts to make them acceptable to domestic consumers. For example, Loudon had suggested that iron chairs should be painted in imitation of oak, and that table pedestals might be BRONZED. In addition to wood grains and metallic finishes, the great variety of coatings might include FAUX BAMBOO, silvering, or simply painting in red, brown or black. One firm even produced iron-framed bedsteads that were in imitation of PAPIER MACHE (*House Furnisher*, 1 June 1871, p.65). These supposedly unsuitable treatments were not confined to England. In the United States, Gervase Wheeler was admonishing against the practice of GRAINING iron furniture to look like wood, but came out in favour of BRONZING and GILDING. This was because he thought such processes did not suggest another material, but a higher or different quality of iron (Wheeler, 1851, p.208). Whatever the merits of the various finishes were, there was no doubt that iron had to be treated, as the foundry finish was unacceptable; it was therefore a prime candidate for an illusory image, both from a practical and a marketing point of view (see Plate XIII).

IRON TUBE

Around 1828 Gandillot et Cie in Paris began to develop chairs with iron tube frames. They were soon able to produce chairs from reinforced hollow iron tubes, which were, however, painted in imitation of wood, ebonized or even painted with flowers or other designs (Halphen, 1845, pp.55–6). In 1839 Loudon illustrated an iron chair fabricated from cast iron with gas tubing for the supports (1839, p.320). In *c.*1851, the Austrian firm of Kitschelt used metal tubing to create the internal frames of sofas and chairs as well as tables and dining chairs, but the design of the whole suite remained in a traditional form.

The development and use of metal tube was particularly applied to rocking chairs. The use of iron was referred to in an article on invalid furniture published in the USA in 1845. A very simple representation of the metal rocker had the concise caption: 'a rocking chair for exercise … It is made wholly of iron, with a stuffed covering but not very heavy' (Webster, 1845, p.306). In France, Charles Léonard offered *fauteuils américains* from his iron furniture factory in the 1860s, and this iron chair form continued in popularity for much of the century.

IRON BAR AND ROD

The use of iron bars and rods as part of the internal construction of some 19th-century furniture became a feature. For example, a device which prevented warping in made-up wooden panels was considered, in which holes were bored through the panels and strong iron wires inserted at intervals across the piece. These acted as clamps to prevent warping but were not affected by shrinkage in the width. A main use of iron as a hidden constructional material was in seat furniture. The origins of this method of framing are difficult to trace, however; it seems that the earliest mention of iron-framed upholstered chairs originates in France. In the 1830s the construction of a *bergère en gondole* used an iron frame to give a shaped contour to the back. It was then completely upholstered and the only evidence of the iron support was the slight give in the back when the chair was used. In 1834 Le Bouteiller illustrated such a *fauteuil en fer garni* in his furniture pattern book. The use of iron frames, later often referred to as 'Turkish chairs' continued throughout the century and they were still being illustrated in text books well into the 20th century. (See also CHAIR FRAMES.)

In the late 1980s the taste for found objects, bricolage and a will to experiment encouraged some artist-designers to use metals of all sorts in their work. From discarded cast-iron components as a raw material for sculptural furniture by Tom Dixon, to designs ranging from the

62 *Although using an innovative material, iron tubing, Kitschelt's suite is based on traditional designs, c.1851.*

elegant to the extravagant by André Dubreuil, art metal work and furniture have come together again.
See also Steel

Himmelheber, Georg (1996), *Cast-Iron Furniture*, London: Philip Wilson.
Ottilinger, Eva (1989), 'August Kitschelt's metal furniture factory and Viennese metal furniture in the nineteenth century', in *Furniture History*, XXV, pp.235–49.
Snyder, Ellen M. (1985), 'Victory over nature, Victorian cast-iron seating', in *Winterthur Portfolio*, 20, Winter.

Ironbark (*Eucalyptus spp.*)

A heavy Australian timber with an average density of 950–1120 (60–70+ lb/cu ft). It has a greyish-brown to reddish-chocolate brown colour with a moderately fine even texture, an interlocked grain and occasional streaks. It is difficult to season, cut or machine and it has a dulling effect on blades.

Iron tacks

See Tacks

Ironwood

A term first recorded in 1657 in the *Oxford English Dictionary* (OED) that is a catch-all for a large number of heavy, usually tropical timbers. As an accurate description it is useless, since many countries in various parts of the world have a timber designated as ironwood, for example, in the USA, LIGNUM VITAE is designated ironwood.

Ivory

This material is the exceptionally hard dentine from the tusks of the elephant, hippopotamus, walrus and narwhal. The curved layers of dentine intersect one another, so that the internal structure is elastic and finely grained. The elephant tusks can weigh between 70–80 kg (154–76 lb) and these are sawn into sheets 1–1.3 mm (*c.*¹⁄₃₂ in) thick with a band saw or a veneer saw.

Ivory has been used as a decorative medium in furniture-making since early times. Panels of ivory for decorating bedheads and chair backs have been found in Assyrian tombs dating to the second millennium BC. Egyptians made small legs from ivory as well as using it for inlay. It was also sometimes used in the solid (e.g. Roman couches). The practice of ivory embellishment of furniture continued in the early medieval period with the chair in St Peters, Rome, as well as the famous throne of Maximian (Ravenna), fitted with ivory panels in Byzantine fashion (see Plate I).

During the Renaissance, designers incorporated ivory inlays into cabinets and tables, whilst in Spain the Mudejar marquetry of coloured woods and ivory in geometric patterns continued the contribution of ivory as a white foil for other materials. The CERTOSINA process also occasionally used ivory. During the 16th century French- and Antwerp-made cabinets were veneered with ivory in combination with other exotic materials. Whilst in Germany, court artisans used ivory extensively as decoration for cabinets, and Augsburg was a particular centre for this work which was sent all over Europe. In England, King Charles I owned 'ivory cabinets', and the 1677 inventory of Ham House listed an 'ivorie cabinet'. These were veneered in ivory, but could also be engraved and stained green as part of MARQUETRY practice.

The impact of colonial decorative ideas can be seen in Spanish *varguenos* with inlaid ivory plaques, as well as Spanish and Portuguese colonial furniture from Goa and the East. These Goan cabinets were often inlaid in an ebony ground. In India the Mughal style from the 18th century used ivory veneer to entire surfaces as well as for inlays and mounts. The centre of such work was Vizagapatam near Madras. Cabinets, work-boxes, mirrors, and revolving 'Burgomaster chairs' in the Dutch taste, and later in a Hepplewhite style, were all made in this area.

In the 19th century ivory working techniques appealed to Victorian tastes. For example, the Dieppe ivory technique was a regional practice from Northern France, which applied thin carved slices of ivory to the frames of chairs, tables and mirrors. Rather more subtle was the later-19th-century ivory inlay tracery work used to contrast with dark timber cabinets by well-known cabinet-makers such as Jackson and Graham, and Collinson and Lock. Edwardian suites were often decorated with small motifs of ivory in the backs of wood-framed chairs and settees.

The association with luxury continued with the use of ivory decoration by French ébénistes in the early 20th century, especially with work in the Art Deco style.

Imitation ivory
Derived from vegetable ivory (*Phytelephas macrocarpa*) which has been obtained from the palm tree nut.

Burack, B. (1984), *Ivory and its Uses*, Rutland, Vermont: Charles E. Tuttle.
MacGregor, A. (1985), *Bone, Antler, and Horn, the Technology of Skeletal Materials Since the Roman Period*, London: Croom Helm.
Simpson, E. and Payton, R. (1986), 'Royal wooden furniture from Gordion', in *Archaeology*, New York, vol.XXXIX, 6, pp.40–7.

Jacaranda
See Rosewood

Jack plane
See Planes (Jack)

Jackwood (*Artocarpus integrifolia*)
A native of India and a variety of bread fruit tree, it has an average density of 680 (42 lb/cu ft). The wood is yellow when first felled, but turns to a dull red mahogany colour upon exposure. The timber resembles a poor-grade mahogany hence its alternative name of CEYLON MAHOGANY. It was used widely in India in the 19th century for furniture and was imported into England in logs 0.9–1.5 m (3–5 ft) in diameter for furniture use. In the mid 19th century it was described as follows:

in colour [it] resembles a rather coarse and inferior variety of mahogany. In cross section, the concentric rings are seen to be variously and alternately

coloured in different shades of brown, the wood in plank presents a minutely streaked appearance, which at near view, imparts to it considerable richness and elegance. The general colour of the wood, when first cut is yellowish brown, which deepens on exposure to a reddish brown … In India jack wood is extensively employed for all purposes in house carpentry and furniture; and in England for cabinet work, marquetry and turnery.
(Blackie, 1853, p.48)

It was still used in the early 20th century for furniture.

Jamaica mahogany
See Mahogany

Jamaica rosewood
See Amyris

Japanese ash
See Ash

Japanese beech (*Fagus crenata*)
Used as European beech

Japanese horse chestnut
See Chestnut

Japanese maple
See Maple

Japanese oak
See Oak

Japanning
European imitations of oriental LACQUER, using lacquer made from shellac are called japanned work. The best recipes were based on mixes of SANDARAC or seed lac mixed with MASTIC, Venice TURPENTINE, COPAL resin, gum ELEMI, BENZOIN, or COLOPHONY, dissolved in ethanol or turpentine (see LAC). Many coats were applied for backgrounds (black, dark green, red and yellow) whilst raised designs were built up by a composition of gum arabic, sawdust and colouring matter which was then gilded (see Plate IV).

The process began with priming. Initially the practice was to use a whiting and size binder, but this was rejected in the latter part of the 18th century as liable to peel and crack off and was replaced by two or three coats of coarse shellac varnish. A base of nine coats of prepared whiting and glue (GESSO) was applied in three stages, each rubbed down with RUSHES. When dry, the surface was sealed with seed-lac VARNISH. The design was then drawn in outline and then built up with a mix of whiting, bole and gum. When this built-up surface was dry, the design was painted in with water-colour, carved out in detail and smoothed down. Details were accentuated by GILDING or silvering or by a contrasting colour. A burnishing by dog's tooth was followed by two final coats of varnish.

Coloured backgrounds were made with additives to the ground varnish. In the case of black, japanning varnish was mixed with LAMPBLACK for the base coats. Then seed lac mixed with lampblack and turpentine was applied, followed by up to twelve coats of pure seed lac, tinted with lampblack. After drying, it was polished with TRIPOLI and then cleaned down. A final polish using lampblack and oil finished the surface.

Introduced into England in the second half of the 17th century, it was soon highly fashionable. Samuel Pepys recorded a visit to

'Greatorex's, and there he showed me his varnish which he hath invented which appears every bit as good as the Indian' (*Diary*, 23 May 1663). In 1688 Stalker and Parker published *A Treatise of Japanning and Varnishing*, with 'designs or patterns for japan work in imitation of the Indians for Tables, Stands, Frames, Cabinets etc.'. They had very particular opinions about quality. In the introduction to their work they note how 'some [japanners] have more confidence than skill and ingenuity, and without modesty or blush impose upon the gentry such stuff and trash, for Japan work, that whether tis a greater scandal to the name or artificer I cannot determine' (loc.cit., p.xvi). This was not the only problem. In 'The case of the japanners of England' the following complaint was made:

But the Merchants sending over our English patterns and models to India, and bringing in such vast quantities of Indian lacquered wares (especially within the last two years), great number of families are by that means reduced to miserable poverty. And the large quantities of japan'd goods expected shortly to be brought from the Indies, will not only tend to the ruin of the Japan-trade here in England, but also obstruct the transportation of our English lacquer to all Europe, which is a considerable advancement to His Majesties Customs whereas the Indian lacquer being exported from hence draws back the custom.
(Cited in Symonds, 1955, p.27)

A class of japanners was therefore established who were to pioneer imitative techniques. Activity in England was hectic: Edward Hurd and James Narcock petitioned for a patent for lacquering in 1692. In 1695 a 'company of patentees for lacquering after the manner of japan' was established, who successfully lobbied Parliament for an increase in import duties on foreign lacquer work. By 1697 the patentees were offering cabinets, secretaires, tables, stands, looking-glasses, and tea tables in a Japanese style. In 1701 William Salmon published instructions for 'japanning wood with colours [including] black, white, blew, common red, deep or dark red, pale red, olive coloured, chestnut coloured, lapis lazuli' (pp.890–7). He also noted recipes for 'marble japan' and 'tortoiseshell japan' (loc.cit., pp.897–902). Salmon also distinguished differing work: 'as japanwork is both plain and embossed, and is wrought most in gold and other metals; so the bantam work is also plain and carved, and is wrought, lots of it in colours, with a very small scattering of gold here and there' (loc.cit., vol.II, pp.916–18). Other developments were also recorded:

[Japanning] is performed by applying 3–4 layers with colour first, then two of pure varnish uncoloured … Before it is dry they sift some venturine or gold wire reduced to powder over it, and then cover with as many layers of pure varnish as render it like polished glass: and lastly rub it over with tripoli, oil of olive or a hatters felt.
(Chambers, 1728)

By the mid 18th century, japanned work was still referred to as 'a kind of Indian painting and carving in wood resembling Japan-work, only more gay' (Chambers, 1752). A little later, Robert Dossie noted that japanning was 'not at present practised so frequently on chairs, tables and other furniture of houses except tea waiters, as formerly' (1758, p.407). Dossie further remarked that 'one principle variation on the manner of japanning is the using or omitting any priming or undercoat on their work to be japanned. In the older practice [of] such work [it] was always used … but in the Birmingham manufacture it has always been rejected' (loc.cit.).

The development of decorative lacquers in France was particularly successful and these were widely sought after. Interest in lacquerwork was enshrined in the establishment of a section of the Manufactures royale des meubles de la couronne in 1672, entitled 'Ouvrage de la Chine'. The famous Martin family obtained a Privilège for lacquer manufacture in 1730, renewed it in 1744, and again in 1753. Such was their success that VERNIS MARTIN has become a generic name for French lacquer work of this period. The French superiority in lacquerwork, urged the Society for the Encouragement of Arts, Manufactures and Commerce to offer a prize for a result equivalent to the French product. The prize was eventually awarded to a Stephen Bedford in 1763.

Although the craft of japanning was separate from furniture-making, the supply of finished lacquer items was often a part of the furnishers' normal trade. For example, while Daniel and Joseph Mills traded specifically as 'Japanners and Cabinet-Makers' at the Japan Cabinet and Cistern in Vine Street, London between 1768 and 1777, other leading firms were quietly meeting the demand as and when required. In 1772 Chippendale made Edwin Lascelles 'a large commode with folding doors vaneer'd with your own japann with additions japann'd to match' (Gilbert, 1978, p.206). This seems to confirm the re-use of existing or imported lacquer work.

Full-scale japanning gradually declined in popularity and it began to be replaced in the latter part of the century by varnishing processes laid over painted work. A different fashion was noted by Hepplewhite when he said that japanning was 'the new and very elegant fashion … arisen within these few years'. The idea was to finish chairs 'with painted or japanned work, giving a rich and splendid appearance to the minuter parts of the ornaments, which are generally thrown in by the painter' (1794, p.2).

In America lacquerwork had been imported by the 1690s. By the beginning of the 18th century, japanning was already carried out in Boston and this became a centre for such work. Their process used maple or pine as the base wood, which being denser, did not require a gesso foundation for the surface. The pattern could be built up directly onto the wood by being modelled in gesso, which was then rubbed down and varnished. A final clear varnish was then applied.

Nineteenth-century japanning techniques were often based on a bleached shellac and camphor mixture. The base was sealed with this varnish and the built-up sections were made from diluted whiting and gesso. The varnish with powdered pigment was then brushed on, with up to ten coats being applied. Decoration was applied at this stage with powder pigments in varnish and black ink. Three or more coats of clear varnish were then applied, each being rubbed with fine PUMICE powder. The top coat was finished with whiting and oil, which was fully removed by cloths for the final polish. The importance of japanning in this period was closely associated with PAPIER MACHE work, but by the later 19th century the trade in japanned furniture had nearly died away.

The uses of japan and varnish were not always designed to imitate oriental products. In many cases the finish was an imitation of another more valuable material such as tortoiseshell. In 1742, John Baskerville took out a patent for a 'new method of making and flat-grinding thin metal plates', which, once fabricated, were japanned and varnished to produce 'fine glowing mahogany colour … or an imitation tortoise-shell'. They were designed to be 'applied to the frames of paintings and pictures of all sizes, looking-glass frames, the front of cabinets, buroes, … and every other sort of household furniture' (Pat.no.582). Other methods using metallic bases included figure paintings that were made on copper panels and TOLE or tin-painted panels which were often let into the surface of cabinets.

See also Fancy chair-making, Lacca povera, Lacquer, Papier mâché, Tole, Vernis Martin

Bourne, Jonathan (1984), *Lacquer: An International History and Collector's Guide*, London: Bracken Books, in association with Phoebe Phillips Editions.

Hill, J. H. (1976), 'History and technology of japanning', in *American Art Journal*, VIII, 2, November.

Huth, Hans (1971), *Lacquer of the West. The History of a Craft and Industry 1550–1950*, Chicago: University of Chicago Press.

Siddons, G. (1830), *The Cabinet-maker's Guide*, 5th edn, London: Printed for Sherwood, Gilbert and Piper.

Stalker, J. and Parker, G. (1688), *A Treatise of Japanning and Varnishing*, Oxford.

Werner, A. (1985), 'An eighteenth century japanner's garret', in *Tools and Trades Journal*, pp.84–96.

Jarrah (*Eucalyptus marginata*)

An Australian hardwood with an average density of 800 (50 lb/cu ft). It is pinkish to dark red in hue, turning to a deep brownish-red upon exposure. The texture is even, moderately coarse and usually straight grained. It is a heavy, hard timber and as SWAN RIVER MAHOGANY was used by colonial cabinet-makers in the 19th century. In the 20th century it was recommended as a cabinet wood and an ornamental veneer.

Jasper

A variety of quartz which is completely opaque. It shines brilliantly when polished and gives a range of effects from plain to chromatic. The source in the name describes the type: for example, Corsican Sea is a green colour, Sicilian Golden is a yellow colour. The Florentine and Bohemian manufacturers of PIETRE DURE used it especially in ideal landscape designs for table tops. In England it was occasionally used: prior to 1649, King Charles I owned a cabinet 'of greene jaspers garnished with silver guilt' (Jervis, 1989, p.282), and in 1767 Richard Hayward supplied Croome Court with '9′ 4″ of jasper for two tables and working the same' (Beard, 1993, p.100).

Javawood

A very loose description of a timber probably based on its point of origin. Java wood was listed in George Bullock's stock-in-trade sale of 1819 (Levy, 1989, p.183) and was recommended as a 'table wood' in Ackermann's *Repository* (February 1825, Plate 145).

Jelutong (*Dyera costulata*)

A timber from Malaya and Indonesia with an average density of 470 (29 lb/cu ft). It is a creamy pale-brown colour, with a fine even texture and a straight grain. May be stained after tapping for latex, but has been used in the 20th century for plywood stock.

Jetquitiba (*Cariniana spp.*)

A Brazilian timber with an average density of 570 (36 lb/cu ft). It is a creamy-white to light-red to pinkish-brown colour, with a fine and even texture, and a straight grain. Very durable, but often hard to saw. It has been an important timber in the South American furniture industry in the 20th century.

Jeux de fond

See Diaper work, Marquetry

Jiffy tuft

See Tufting

Jig

Jigs or saddles are pre-formed holders for component parts that are designed to allow tools or machinery to follow a pre-determined path so that each piece is prepared speedily and uniformly. Jigs in conjunction with BAND SAWS, SPINDLE MOULDERS and high speed ROUTERS are especially efficient. Machine attachments are forms of jigs, for example a DOVETAIL attachment to a router.

Jigsaw

See Saws

Joined or Framed work

See Construction

Joiner

Joseph Moxon neatly defined joinery as 'an art manual, whereby several pieces of wood are so fitted and join'd together by straight lines, squares, mitres or any bezel that they shall seem one intire piece' (1677, p.63). The separation of the carpenter (as a general wood-worker) and the joiner (as a specialist joiner of panelling, fittings and furniture frames) occurred during the 14th century. Early references to the craft of joining frames rather than nailing them together occur in 1386 and again in 1412 in the Oxford English Dictionary (OED). In 1413 in the city of York, a joiners' organization was established, and in London, in 1440, the Mystery of the Joyners of the City of London was allowed to elect two Wardens with the power of search. The London company's charter was granted in 1570.

The position of the joiners vis-à-vis the carpenters had long been unsatisfactory, so in 1632 a dispute with carpenters over demarcation led to a victorious decree that joiners be allowed exclusive rights over the making of most furniture. The London Court of Aldermen decreed that joiners were entitled to make:

All sorts of bedsteads whatsoever (onlie except Boarded bedsteads and nayled together)
All sorts of chayres and stooles which are made with mortesses and tennants
All tables of wainscotte walnutte or other stuff glewed with fframes mortesses or tennants
All sorts of formes framed made of boards with the sides pinned or glewed
All sorts of chests being framed duftalled pynned or glued
All sorts of cabinets or boxes duftalled pynned or glued or joyned
All sorts of cupboards framed duftalled pynned or glewed
[Then follows a number of joinery work items related to fitting up]
All frames for pictures …
All carved workes either raised or cutt through or sunck in with the grounde taken out being wrought and cutt with carving tooles without the use of plaines.
(Jupp, 1887, pp.295–9)

The Joyners also had a demarcation dispute with the Turners, so court also decreed that

whatsoever is done with the foot as have treedle or wheele for turning of any wood we are of opinion and do find that it properly belongs to the Turner's and we find that the turners ought not to use the gage or gages, groove plaine or plough plane and mortising chisells or any of them for that the same do belong to the Joyners trade.
(loc.cit.)

However, when it suited them, they would join forces with other guilds, for example with the old adversaries, the carpenters, to resist the incorporation of sawyers. Joiners remained important in the furniture-making trade until the end of the 17th century when the CABINET-MAKER, FRAME-MAKER, and CHAIR-MAKER gradually usurped them from their position. Although the joiners continued to make furniture in rural districts, in urban centres they worked in a building and architectural capacity having little to do with free-standing furniture.

See also Bed-joiners, Cabinet-maker, Carpenter

Forman, Benno (1974), 'The Joyners' company in 1694', *Furniture History*, X, p.12–14.
— (1988), *American Seating Furniture 1630–1730*, New York: Norton.
Jupp, E. B. (1887), *An Historical Account of the Worshipful Company of Carpenters of the City of London*, London: Pickering & Chatto.
Lane, S. E. (1968), *The Worshipful Company of Joiners and Ceilers or Carvers: a Chronological History*, published by the Company.
Symonds, R. W. (1946), 'Craft of the joiner in medieval England', in *Connoisseur*, December, pp.17–23, 98–104.

Joints and jointing

Jointing in furniture CONSTRUCTION is clearly fundamental, but joints can be divided into four basic divisions: The first of these are joints meant for widening boards to make a suitable panel. These include the butt and coopered joints. Secondly are the joints for fixing narrow pieces of wood at right angles, to make a variety of frames. These include the various mortise and tenon joints and mitred joints. Thirdly, joints for fixing wide panels together at right angles. Here are found dovetails, housed joints and large mitres. Finally, the mechanical joints which include the rule, finger and knuckle joints. In addition are lippings, rebated (or rabbetted) joints and dowels, which are also jointing methods for special purposes (see below).

Although quite sophisticated jointing methods were used in furniture-making by the ancient craftsmen of Egypt and Rome, it was not until the Middle Ages that these aspects of the craft took on a revival. Even so, the carpenter who made furniture still often used quite primitive methods. For stools and benches, a simple notch might be cut into the top of a leg, then pushed into a pre-cut hole in the top board; finally a wedge was inserted into the notch for strength. In the case of box-like structures, the simplest method was to nail or peg boards at right angles. When it was found that the wood split, iron bandings were introduced to hold the chest together. Although primitive, they appear to have been effective.

As the carpenter's work gave way to the joiner and the re-introduction of the mortise and tenon joint, the nature of furniture-making took its first fundamental change. Joined construction meant that thinner panels of wood could be mounted into a prepared frame, thus giving the solid panel sufficient room for expansion and contraction. This innovation, no doubt borrowed from interior panelling work, meant that the warping and splitting tendencies of solid wood were reduced.

In practice, the process meant that the muntins of a chest were tenoned and the rails mortised into them to produce a rigid frame. Improvements in this process included the pegging of the tenon through the mortise at points of high stress. The development of the mitred joint was also associated with the frame construction process. However, as developments in cabinet-making evolved in the 17th century, especially with the introduction of VENEERING, jointing methods had to change again. The fundamental change was in carcase construction and this was most evident in the development of the chest of drawers and other cabinets with drawers. Panel frames using the mortise and tenon joint gave way to flush-framed carcases, which required a particular jointing method to provide continuous connection along edges of end grain. The dovetail joint was found to be the most suitable.

In conjunction with the rise of cabinet-making and the development of a range of furniture types, there was a need for other types of joints in furniture. For many of the basic purposes, the various construction joints were used. The butt joint, sometimes in conjunction with a tongue and groove, was used to join timber in its length, whilst the coopered joint would assist in the making of bow-front or serpentine-shaped work. Housing joints were used for fixing shelves and non-structural parts of a cabinet, whilst the dowel was used widely in chair-making and sometimes in circular frameworks. As furniture design became more sophisticated, the range of mechanical joints, such as the rule, finger and knuckle, were introduced for special purposes, such as flaps, gateleg tables and screens.

Bridle
A version of the mortise and tenon principle which has the 'tenon' cut in the body of a rail and the mortise cut out of the end of a rail. It is used to fix two differing widths of rails such as a table leg and table top rail, or for acute angle work. Also for faced-up grounds for doors and skeleton grounds for fixing. Aka halved joints.

Butt
A wood joint known in Ancient Egypt, that has the end of one piece butted to the side face of another. It usually has to be further strengthened, either by dowels or metal KD bolts. It may be glued or nailed.

Butterfly wedge
A decorative joint in the shape of two triangles joined, used to link two boards together with a decorative feature.

Comb
A method of joining two pieces of wood end to end. Also used as a name for a 90 degree angle joint used for drawers and boxes, where tongues fit into kerfs.

Coopered
See Coopering

Dovetail
A joint devised for woodworking, which uses a fan-shaped or 'dovetail' shaped projection at one end, which is designed to fit an equal-sized cut in another end. Originating in fourth dynasty Egyptian furniture for boxes and coffins as well as in ivory work. It appears in medieval work pre 1104. In that year a chest containing the body of St Cuthbert was recorded as being 'joined and united by the toothed tenons of the boards which come from this side and from that to meet one another' (Eames, 1977, p.228). Further developed in the 14th century for caskets and small box work, it was common by the 15th century in Italy. In 1565–73 Cooper's *Thesaurus Securicla* defined 'a swallow tayle or doovetayle in carpenters work which is a fastening of two pieces of timber or bourdes together that they can not come away'.

Initially they were crude, often very wide and coarse and sometimes held with a nail for extra grip. However, the use of the dovetail joint meant that sections of timber for drawer sides and carcases did not need to be so thick, so the proportions were gradually slimmed down and over time became more elegant. The original dovetail joint was known as the through-dovetail, as both the pin and the slot had exposed end grain. This was soon found to be unsatisfactory for the adhesion of veneer, so the stopped or lapped dovetail was developed, which had the advantage of providing a side grain surface.

All dovetails were originally hand cut, either by chisel or saw. Evidence of saw use, in which small horizontal cuts may be seen on the inside front corner of a drawer, will show where the maker has overshot the cutting line. Very often a scribing mark can also be found to guide the craftsman in his measuring, and often there is slight irregularity in the size and spacing of the cuts.

Types of dovetail:
(a) Through-dovetail is the simplest form in which the joint is completely seen. Used for decorative work, but end grain is shown.
(b) Single or half lapped usually has a lap or cover so that the pins are

hidden. Particularly useful for drawers where the fronts are likely to be veneered.

(c) The double lapped is the same as the single but the lap is cut on both parts of the joint, making a 'secret' dovetail. This joint has been used for tops of bureaux and cabinets.

(d) Slot or housing dovetails are cut in the width of the timber rather than the thickness and are used in plinths, cornices, shelves, legs into pedestals, and so on.

(e) Stopped-slot dovetail is used for joining T stretchers where a pull is exerted.

(f) Secret mitre dovetail is a combination of mitre and dovetail made so that the finished joint looks like a butted mitre.

See also Machines (Dovetailer)

Dowel

A small wooden peg made to join timbers together, usually at right angles. Used since the Ancient Egyptian period (3000–2500 BC), it must be ranked as one of the oldest joints. In Egyptian furniture-making it appears to have also doubled as a cramping method. The dowel was widely employed in the work of the joiners who used it to peg boards together. Dowels could be round, rectangular or dove-tailed (axe shaped). The dowel has also been widely used for chair-making. In the late 17th century they were used for fixing chair seats to legs and back rails, the results not always being satisfactory. How-ever the dowel has remained a crucial jointing method ever since. In upholstered chair-frame making, the dowelled joint has little to sur-pass it and the term 'dowelled, screwed and glued' has been widely used as a benchmark of quality in chair-frame making. In later-20th-century construction, the dowelled joint has taken the place of the mortise and tenon, particularly in KD and self-assembly furniture.

Dustproof

Halved simple woodworking joint that joins two pieces of timber in an L or T section. It is not especially strong, so is mainly used for non-structural work or is enhanced by dowels or screws. Sometimes used in conjunction with dust beads (felt or rubber).

Finger

A movable, interlocking joint hinged to a rail, with a centre pin, used for brackets and fly rails.

Haunch tenon

A woodworking joint that is based on the mortise and tenon, but in this case leaves a portion of the tenon uncut (called the haunch) so as to avoid any tendency to warp.

Housed

A simple range of joints known to Ancient Egyptians, for shelves and non-structural work. These include simple housing, stopped housing (conceals groove at front), dovetail housing, barefaced housing (sim-pler to cut and with a tapered shape to make fitting easier).

Knuckle

A mechanical joint which is related to the rule joint, allowing a pivot-ing action. Often used on the brackets for the flaps of Pembroke tables.

Lashed

A jointing system used by the Ancient Egyptians which used thongs of leather or hide, linen string or copper bands. Recesses or holes were made into the wooden frames to take the thongs which were then tied off.

Mitre

A joint in which two pieces of material meet at right angles, creating a mitre which is used for corners in many wooden constructions es-pecially picture frames, boxes, architraves and plinths. Mitre boxes and blocks are used to assist accurate cutting. Mitres were known to the Ancient Egyptians and most were held by diagonally fixed pins, often with additional lashing or round dowels. Mitre joints may be fixed by glue, loose tongues, dowelling, veneer keys set in saw kerfs on the outside of joints, or mechanical bolts.

The Mason's mitre was cut into solid material containing a mortise, the tenon rail then coming up to meet it and the angle being cut on the joint to give the impression of a mitre.

The Tongued mitre is a mitre joint with a separate tongue that is in-serted for extra grip and strength into the joint.

Mortise and tenon

A mortise is a deep groove cut into a rail to receive an appropriately shaped piece in a muntin called the tenon, cut so that the two will fit together. The mortise was described as 'a square hole cut in a piece of stuff to entertain a tennant to fit it' (Moxon, 1677, p.113). The joint is used for all kinds of framing, in chair construction and in table work. The use of pegs or dowels in the DRAW-BORE process pulls the tenon tightly into the mortise as the hole is slightly off line. Common in Ancient Egyptian work, it has remained a fundamental joint ever since.

Types of mortise and tenon:

(a) The concealed mortise and tenon joint is the basic joint in which the tenon completely fits the mortise.

(b) Bare-faced mortise and tenon allows a thin member to be tenoned into a thicker part to finish flush to one side. This ensures that the mortise is cut away from the edge.

(c) Haunched mortise and tenon in which the width of the tenon is re-duced to prevent upward movement. A small shoulder or haunch is left on the tenon as it is cut.

(d) Stub or blind mortise and tenon is a joint in which the tenon is cut short so that the end grain is not visible through the mortise.

(e) Through-mortise and tenon is the simplest form of the joint. The end grain of the tenon is visible through the mortise.

(f) Wedged mortise and tenon is a through-joint which has been pegged with small wedges for added strength as well as decor-ative appeal.

(g) Long and short shoulder mortise and tenon is used when connect-ing rebated parts so that the rebate remains true.

(h) Mitre mortise and tenon is used when working mouldings on their inside edge.

Rubbed

The simplest form of jointing two boards together by rubbing and then clamping the two glued surfaces to obtain adhesion.

Rule

A hinged joint introduced in the early 1700s, cut in such a way as to prevent a gap showing. Particularly used for table flaps and screens where the ovolo edge of the top is seen, rather than a gap.

Scarf

For joining timbers in the length without increasing the cross-section area. First used in Ancient Egypt to join short-cut end grain timbers, and fitted in conjunction with a butterfly wedge.

Tongue and groove

A simple but effective joint for widening boards. The tongue and the groove are cut in the length of the board, giving a good gluing surface. Loose tongues may be fitted between two grooves.

See also Biscuit joint, Construction, Drawers, Machinery

Bairstow, J. (1984), *Practical and Decorative Woodworking Joints*, London.
Goodman, W. L. (1979), 'Classical Greek joinery', in *Working Wood*, 1/3, Autumn, pp.20–3.

Juniper (*Juniperus sp.*)
An evergreen softwood with an average density of 500 (*c*.30 lb/cu ft). It is a yellow to tan-brown colour with a mild scent, a fine uniform texture and a straight grain. Juniper was used in Egypt and was also enjoyed by the Romans on account of its variegations. It was occasionally used for furniture-making in the late 17th and early 18th centuries. Evelyn mentions that 'we might perhaps see some [of the bushes] rise to competent trees fit for many curious works; for tables, chests, small carvings and images' (1662, p.138). In 1672 an Essex inventory included '1 juniper chest' (Steer, 1969, p.126). It was particularly used by Scandinavian cabinet-makers, especially in the early 19th century.
See also Cedar

Jute webbing
See Webbing

Kalamet (*Cordia fragrantissima*)
A Burmese timber with an average density of 800 (50 lb/cu ft). It is red-brown with darker streaks. Also known as Burmese sandalwood and Cordia. It is difficult to work, but has been used for cabinet-making and joinery work in the later 20th century.

Kamassi (*Gonioma kamassi*)
A South African timber with an average density of 990 (62 lb/cu ft). It is a pale yellow colour, with a fine even texture. It is hard and close, with the properties of BOXWOOD and is sold commercially as such. In 1793 it was recorded that 'Camassi wood is merely a shrub, and consequently produces small pieces only which serve for veneering' (Thunberg, 1793, II, 110). Kamassi has been used for inlay and small cabinet work as a substitute for true boxwood. Aka Cape boxwood.

Kapok (*Bombax ceiba*)
The seed fibre or vegetable down of the Ceiba tree and plant, which is grown widely in Java and India, especially Calcutta. Processed like cotton, it has been used as an upholstery filling since the 18th century. In 1761 Rolt noted that 'capoc' [kapok] was used for beds, cushions and pillows'. It remains in common use as a loose filling for cushions and quilts and, a paper-backed version is made for upholstery wadding. A fibre known as *akund* with similar properties has been imported from Africa, but is considered inferior.

Zand, Stephen (1941), *Kapok, a Survey of its History, Cultivation and Uses*, New York: Lincoln.

Kapur (*Dryabolanops spp.*)
A hardwood sourced in Malaysia and south eastern Asia with an average density of 700–780 (44–48 lb/cu ft). It is light to deep-red brown in colour, with a coarse but even texture and a camphor-like odour when first cut. Kapur has been used for furniture in the 20th century but has been found to be hard to work. Aka Borneo camphor-wood.

Karelian birch
See Birch

Kauri pine (*Agathis spp.*)
See Pine

Kauri resin
See Resins

Kauvula (*Endospermum diadenum*)
A timber from the Papua New Guinea area with an average density of 400–480 (25–30 lb/cu ft), a pale-yellow to straw-brown colour, a straight grain and a coarse, even texture. Selected grades have been used for cabinet work and veneers in the 20th century.

KD (knockdown) fittings
A range of specially designed accessories intended to be fitted into pre-finished panels or boards for later assembly. Particularly used for later-20th-century flat-pack furniture. There are three basic types: threaded fittings in which a bush is inset on one component while the other is locked with a metal screw or barbed plug; interlocking fittings in which both components screw together; and cam-action fittings with a hook-operated linkage. The range is enormous in type and material but includes dowels, bolts, connectors, nuts and bolts, bushes and screws, nylon butt joint blocks and cam fittings.
See also Construction (Knock-down)

Langston, C. (1978), *Knock-down Furniture and Fittings*, FIRA Bulletin, 63.

Kerf
See Bending

Kersey
A thick woollen or worsted twill weave material developed in the 13th century but occasionally used as a covering for upholstery in the 17th century. In 1603 an inventory of Hengrave Hall included a 'great foulding skreen of seven foulds with a skreen cloth upon it of green kersey' (cited in Gloag, 1990, p.589). Although recognized as a clothing material, it was also used in America for upholstery. In 1666 a Boston inventory recorded 'pieces of Kersie wrought for chairs and stools' (cited in Montgomery, 1984, p.273).

Kevazingo
See Bubinga

Keys
Thin slips of wood let into saw KERFS and fixed with glue at the joints of two parts of a piece of work to strengthen the joint.

Kiabooca wood
See Amboyna

Kiln drying
See Seasoning

Kingwood (*Dalbergia cearensis*)
A Brazilian timber botanically related to ROSEWOOD, it has an average density of 1200 (75 lb/cu ft) and is produced in short billets, not usually exceeding *c*.2.5 m (8 ft) in length and 5–17.5 cm (2–7 in) in diameter. The timber has distinctive variegated colours from violet-brown with dark streaks, to a golden yellow through to black, and is straight grained with a fine texture.
The French cabinet-makers of the Louis XIV and XV periods

particularly favoured it. Kingwood is also found in the Gillow records during the 1760s, and from *c*.1770 it was employed for cross banding. In 1839 it was noted as useful for small cabinet work and borders, and by 1879 it was 'chiefly used for drawing room furniture' (Bitmead, 1873, p.78). It is still used today for veneering, oysters, inlay bandings and marquetry. The name Kingwood seems to be a 19th-century invention. Aka Violetwood (USA), Guiana-wood.

Kit furniture
See Construction (Knock-down)

Knife chip carving
See Carving

Knitted fabrics
With the development of variously shaped plastic shells and tubular metal frames for chairs in the 1970s, the demand for a stretch fabric was self-evident. Weft-knitted textiles including jersey, double jersey and interlocked, all of which have good stretching properties, were employed as upholstery cloths for shaped frames.

Knockdown (KD) (Packaged Furniture)
See Construction

Knots and knotting
An important part of the traditional upholstery process and a necessary skill that was required to build up a seat platform that would give satisfactory service.

(a) Lashing: An upholstery technique for tying coiled seat and back springs into a firm but flexible whole. There are double and centre versions with the twine running twice diagonally across the spring sets.
(b) Loopknot: A special upholstery knot used for tying in springs.
(c) Return tying: A method in which a length of twine was put through the middle of a run of springs and returned over the top of the same springs.

Knotted pine
See Pine (Ponderosa)

Knotted work
In the later 17th century knotted threads were applied as decoration to chairs and covers in a similar fashion to GALLOON. In the early 18th century the work was applied to monochrome bed hangings and covers. The knotted threads were sewn to a linen ground in a range of patterns.

Knuckle joint
See Joints

Koa (*Acacia koa*)
A wood sourced from the Philippines and Hawaii with a density of 680 (41 lb/cu ft). It is reddish to dark brown in colour with a pronounced stripy figure, an interlocked grain, and a medium texture. Used for high-class furniture and decorative veneers in Hawaii but also imported into Europe.

Kokko (*Albizzia lebbek*)
An Indian and Burmese timber with an average density of 610 (39 lb/cu ft). It is a grey-brown colour with darker streaks and has a superficial resemblance to walnut, hence an alternative name, EAST INDIAN WALNUT. A hard and difficult timber to work, which can be highly polished. First recorded in 1862, even in 1920, Howard could write that 'a small quantity has been used for decorative furniture work in England but it is not yet generally known or appreciated' (1920, p.306). Used in the early 20th century in the USA for decorative furniture, especially for Pullman cars. By the 1950s this wood was listed as a common commercial furniture wood.
Aka Koko(h).

Kyabuka
See Amboyna

L shaped hinge
See Hinges

Laburnum (*Laburnum anagyroides*)
A timber indigenous to northern Europe which was introduced to the British Isles in the 16th century. It has an average density of 880 (55 lb/cu ft), a medium-fine texture and a straight grain. It is a decorative timber with a yellowish tint with brown streaks, shading to an almost pinky-brown. When cut, it has a distinctive light and dark patterned effect caused by sap and heartwood which makes it ideal for inlay, parquetry and oyster veneering. This usage was especially popular in the later 17th century. It was fashionable again in the 19th century because 'when of larger dimensions, no timber is fitter for cabinet work of all kinds. It takes a fine polish, it looks well and it is durable. Chairs made from it are far stronger than mahogany' (Knight, 1830, p.164). In the early 20th century it was used for drawer and door handles by designer craftsmen, but by the mid 20th century it was sometimes used for veneered carcase tops; it was said, however, that it was 'seldom used because its possibilities are seldom known' (Sheridan, 1953, p.12).

Jones, D. (1992), 'The laburnum tradition in Scotland', in *Regional Furniture*, vol.VI, pp.1–10.

Lac
See Lacquer, Resins

Lacca povera
Poor man's or counterfeit (*contraffata*) lacquer is an apt description for this 18th-century imitation work. An Italian, especially Venetian, imitation of oriental lacquering, it relied upon decoration formed by cut-out prints stuck to a surface and then varnished many times over. The firm of Remondini produced printed designs in sheets specially for the purpose. These included chinoiserie figures, huntsmen and shepherdesses. The technique was particularly appropriate for secretaires, chests and screens, although it may be found on most types of furniture. It was one of a number of forms of decoration that was carried out by cabinet-makers and amateurs alike.
See also Découpage work

Kisluk-Grosheide, D. (1996), 'Cutting up Berchems, Watteaus, and Audrans, a lacca povera secretary at the Metropolitan Museum of Art', in *Metropolitan Museum Journal*, 31, pp.81–97.
Simpson, J. (1989), 'Lacca povera furniture', in *Architectural Digest*, 46, February, pp.168–73.

Lace
See Passementerie

Lacewood
See Plane wood

Lacquer
Lacquer is a liquid coating applied to surfaces, which then dries to a hard finish. There are four major forms of 'lacquer':

(a) The Far Eastern *Urushi* lacquer which dries by oxidative polymerization through exposure to high humidity,
(b) Lacquer based on resins dissolved in oils or solvents,
(c) Lacquer made from insect secretion, principally shellac,
(d) Synthetic or cellulose-based factory-made lacquers.

In addition, imitations of the Eastern lacquers are known as JAPANNING and VERNIS MARTIN.

RESIN-BASED LACQUERS
See Varnish (Shellac)

URUSHI
These 'true' lacquers were produced from the sap of the sumach tree (*Rhus verniciflua*). Once the sap had been tapped from the tree, any impurities were removed by sieving, then the water content was reduced by heating. Colourants could be added to the viscous liquid or it was left clear. The preparation of lacquer was very time-consuming and there was a wide range of techniques, but generally the final effects were either plain, carved, incised, inlaid, sprinkled or gilded. In most cases the base wood had to be prepared very precisely. This initial stage was followed by the application of layers of cloth, filler and lacquer which, when set, were covered (depending on the design and recipe) with up to fifty or more lacquer coatings. These coatings required a drying period of one to five days between each one. The finished result was a very hard, durable surface which is resistant to acids, alkalis and hot water. Urushi lacquer originated in China in a decorative form by the 4th century BC, and was introduced into Japan in the 3rd century BC. Urushi lacquer remained an exclusive and desirable product for centuries in the Far East. With the opening of trade routes in the 16th century it became very desirable in the West.

The Portuguese reached Japan in 1542 and they began to share the trade with China, but the monopoly enjoyed by the Portuguese lasted only until it was broken by the British and the Dutch. Eventually the Dutch took over the trade and in conjunction with China, remained in control until the 19th century. Chinese incised lacquer was taken by boat to ports on the Indian Coromandel coast, which were used from the late 17th century by the English East India Company as staging posts for shipments of all traded items from the area. The coast gave its name to the work when it first arrived in Europe. Folding screens were amongst the most important items, not only because they were spectacular, but also because they were easy to transport. From the 16th century, Japanese lacquer, called Namban ware, was imported by the Dutch directly from Japan. Incised lacquer was also sent from the Dutch trading station called Bantam in western Java, which again gave its name to the work. The excitement this work instilled in Europe was evident. In 1598 Jan Huyghen van Linschoten wrote

They cover all kinds of householde stuffe in India as bedsteddes, chairs, stools, etc., and all their turned woodworke, which is wonderful common and much used throughout India: the fayrest workemanshippe thereof cometh from China, as may be seene by all things that come from thence, as desks targets, tables, Cubbordes, boxes, and a thousand such like things, that are all covered and wrought with Lac of all colours and fashions.
(Cited in Huth, 1971, p.21)

Nearly one hundred years later John Evelyn commented upon 'that incomparable secret of Japan and China varnishes which hitherto have been reserved so choicely among the virtuosi' (30 July 1682). However, it is evident that lacquer was made in Japan specifically for export.

As demand grew, European cabinet-makers had to turn their skills towards making imitation Oriental lacquer. As the lac tree was not available in Europe, and the craze for oriental lacquer work did not abate, the search for a substitute was made and found in SHELLAC. The result is called JAPANNING.

The 20th-century European introduction of the skills of Urushi lacquering began in France when difficulties with varnishing aircraft propellers in World War I aircraft encouraged the French to import Southeast Asian lacquer workers to deal with the problem. From 1918 onwards the skills of these workers were applied to fashionable objects. The following description also refers to Urushi work: The wood was smoothed with pumice covered with pasted fine silk and then smoothed with powdered stone. Both sides of the object were treated the same, that is, twenty coats of lacquer each side with a rubbing down and drying period of four days between each coat. Drying was carried out in a humid atmosphere in a dark room with constant running water. The most important designers associated with this work were Eileen Gray and Jean Dunand along with the technical encouragement of a Japanese craftsman, Sougawara. Dunand developed particular techniques including the crushed-eggshell inlay process for screens and table tops. Dunand describes lacquering as a labour of love:

Twenty coats of lacquer are needed, no forty, since each layer must be repeated on the other side lest the wood warp ... In fact it is not forty operations that are needed but one hundred, because after each coat, the surface must be rubbed and before each of the twenty coats there is involved a drying process lasting four days. What may surprise you is that the drying is done in a humid-atmosphere in a dark room with constantly running water, and the finest results are achieved during a full moon. So now you understand how very oriental in character is this work!
(Garner, 1973, p.4)

SHELLAC
Shellac sourced in Asia was used to prepare a varnish. Shellac, introduced into Europe during the 16th century, was also used as an ingredient in coloured varnishes that imitated Far Eastern lacquer.
See Japanning, Lacca povera, Resins, Varnish, Vernis Martin

SYNTHETIC LACQUERS
Modern plastic lacquers polymerize by catalyst into resistant surface finishes. The first stirrings of change in the development of finishes was as a result of experience during World War I. The benefits of CELLULOSE ACETATE, used as 'dope' for aircraft during 1914–18, was that it could be converted to cellulose nitrate which was an element of nitro-cellulose. This product was the basis of the cellulose lacquer, which became standard in the industry. Its main advantage was that it could be sprayed directly onto furniture, thus reducing costs of time and materials as it lost solvent and therefore dried quickly.

By the 1920s nitro-cellulose spraying was commonplace in large factories. Initially it was applied with hand guns, in individual booths, with rise and fall turn-tables. Experiments with automatic spraying were based on the simple idea of mounting a gun, which was controlled by an electric eye on a beam over a moving runway. After many trials it was discontinued as it needed a throughput of many articles of the same type to make it efficient. However, the use of cellulose, with its quick-drying facility enabled the polishing shop to be conveyorized. This allowed interior spraying, overhauling, spray matching and hand finishing to be done as a continuous operation. The conveyors were extended to the warehouse so that finished goods would go straight to storage without being man-handled.

The economic reasons for introducing mechanical polishing were clear: the machines could be operated by semi-skilled labour. It was not only the machines that saved money. For many years polishing had been women's work and as female labour rates were one third less than the male rates, the economies were clear.

The technique of application of finishes using synthetic lacquers like cellulose was usually to spray on and then 'pull over' the finish with thinners; it was then cut down and the lacquer re-applied. The 'pull over' method used in Britain temporarily softened the lacquer and required some hardening time. In the United States a quick hardening lacquer which allowed immediate packing was used, to avoid the drying time experienced in British factories.

During the 1960s the development of phenolic resins and synthetic resins with special properties such as heat resistance were becoming popular with the trade as well as with the public. The most important development was of synthetic lacquers that provided greatly enhanced resistance to heat, water and spirit damage. Acid-catalysed finishes used a process whereby the solids were converted into a film by a catalyst. The formulae may include urea and phenol formaldehyde, melamine and other resins. The matt finishes that were a result of the use of these spray-applied lacquers were ideal for the fashionable teak-finished furniture. More recent developments include the use of pre-catalysed lacquers which make the application much easier.

For furniture that required a gloss finish, the use of polyester lacquers was ideal. Its mirror-like finish was extremely hard and was perfectly suited to flat panel construction. Other lacquers such as polyurethane are very strong and resistant to household damage and have become one of a range of alternative finishes.

Along with the new finishes, revised methods of application had to be devised. It was in this area of the industry that the change from a craft to a science was most noticeable. The development of curtain-coating and roller-coating methods, which offered economic precision application of paints and lacquers, enabled panels to be finished on line, thus superseding spraying.
See Finishing equipment

Acid catalysed lacquer
A two-part furniture-finishing system introduced in the 1960s, using resins and solvents which interact when subjected to the acidic catalyst. The resultant cross-linking produces a film that is increased in its resistance to heat and solvents, but is non-reversible. The finished surface has a high resistance to heat and solvents. These finishes are therefore often specified in contract situations. Pre-catalysed lacquers react to exposure and evaporation and were widely used in later-20th-century domestic furniture finishing.

Polyester lacquer
A two-part lacquer of polyester resin and a catalyst. When reacting, they build up a thick film with high resistance to damage and capable of a high gloss finish.

Polyurethane lacquer
A finishing process that has been outstanding for adhesion, flexibility and resistance to damage. The lacquers are toxic unless the proper safety precautions are followed and this has led to a decline in their use in the latter part of the 20th century.

See also Aventurine, Chipolin, Japanning, Lacca povera, Resins, Varnish, Vernis Martin

Baarsen, R. (1992), 'Japanese lacquer and Dutch furniture in the seventeenth and eighteenth centuries', in *Antiques*, 141, April, pp.632–41.
Bourne, J. et al. (1984), *Lacquer; an International History and Collector's Guide*, Crowood Press.
Garner, P. (1973), 'The lacquer work of Eileen Gray and Jean Dunand', in *Connoisseur*, May, pp.2–11.,
Gibson, A. J. (1942), 'Story of lac', in *Journal of the RSA*, 17 April, pp.319–35.
Huth, H. (1967), 'Lacquer in Rome', in *Apollo*, 85, May, p.336.
— (1971), *Lacquer of the West*, Chicago: University of Chicago Press.
Jones, A. (1937), *Cellulose Lacquers, Finishes and Cements. Their History, Chemistry and Manufacture*, London: C. Griffin and Co.
Kesel, W. G. de (1989), 'Lacques flammande du XVIIè. siècle', in *L'Estampille*, 223, March, pp.28–39.
Koizumi, G. (1923), *Lacquer work: a practical exposition*, London: Pitman.
Mannelli, G. (1967), 'Lacquer in Venice', in *Connoisseur*, 166, September, pp.5–9.
Stalker, J. and Parker, G. (1688), *A Treatise on Japanning and Varnishing*, Oxford.

Laid cord
An UPHOLSTERER's twine made by layers of cord twisted together so as to avoid stretching. It is employed to lash SPRINGS into position when creating a fully hand-built sprung seat. The best quality is made from flax, lesser quality from HEMP.

Laminations
Variable-sized strips of wood that are joined together with the grain running in the same direction, as opposed to PLYWOOD which has grains running at 90 degrees to each other. The strength thus achieved in this man-made process is found in the direction of the grain of the material. This idea has been widely utilized in the manufacture of arms and legs for chairs. It works particularly well when a single laminated board or tube can be cut into strips, each of which is a ready-made arm or leg section.

This process was known to 18th-century cabinet-makers, who used the technique to make rims for tables and other items. The patent lists record that Samuel Bentham in 1793 devised a method of 'giving curvature to wood' by dividing it into thicknesses (Pat.no.1951). A few years later, around 1802, the French ébéniste Jean-Joseph Chapius built chairs using 6.4 mm (¼ in) thick wood slats which, when glued together, bent and then shaped, made semi-circular legs for chairs. It was common practice in 1819: 'upper rails for circular bason stands: glued in three thicknesses, all running lengthways of the grain. The two inner thicknesses are of deal and the outside one of mahogany' (Martin, 1819, p.115).

The two most famous exponents of laminated wood in the 19th century were John Henry Belter and Michael Thonet. Belter, originally from Wurttemberg in Germany, emigrated to America in *c*.1840 and

63 Detail of the rear back of a Belter sofa showing the laminations as parallel lines, c.1856.

began experiments with laminations to create shaped forms for the frames of sofas, chairs and beds. Whilst the bedsteads followed the simple smooth surfaces of the Biedermeier style, Belter's work on chair frames used the lamination process to incorporate the Rococo Revival style. One version of Belter's process used a cylindrical assemblage of built-up 'staves' (usually made from two veneers at right angles to each other). These staves were placed against a heated shaped core, and further slightly wider staves were placed against the first layer with overlapped seams. Any number of layers may be added with an attractive wood on the first and last faces. The whole assembly was then glued and pressed between the inner core and the outer shaped mould and left to dry for twenty-four hours. The outer mould was removed, leaving a barrel-like built-up piece which was cut into sections ready for application to a seat frame.

In Europe, Thonet pursued his work on laminations. He constructed chairs out of laminates of thin wood soaked in glue baths, so as to achieve hitherto unknown degrees of bending. In July 1842 an Austrian patent was granted. However, Thonet soon discovered that the laminating process was time consuming, expensive and did not survive the extremes of temperature that his furniture might be subjected to. For these reasons he moved towards the BENDING of solid wood. Nevertheless, for traditional cabinet-making the laminating process remained an important method.

By the mid 19th century, making curved or 'sweep-work' by gluing up timbers in thin thicknesses in a caul or mould was still common practice. The Thonet company returned to experimenting with laminates for chair-making in the 1880s. This time they tried to produce a chair which was cut out from sheets of laminations rather than building up thin sections, but again it was not successful. However, laminations soon became widely used in avant-garde furniture as components of pieces, and the process was used industrially from the end of the 19th century.

The commercially successful development of laminated furniture was further developed in the 1930s when Alvar Aalto perfected the sculptural possibilities offered by the process of bending laminated BIRCH wood. The laminating technique was also suitable for cabinets and, in 1946 in the USA, the Plymold Corporation produced a desk from bent laminations. The desk was particularly innovative in its drawer construction as it only used three elements, the back and sides being moulded in one-piece laminate. This was to become a commonplace method in the 1970s. In the 1950s a similar idea used hoops of wood made by a continuous strip of veneer wound on a core to build up a piece to the required thickness for rims of tables. However in England, even by 1955, one critic was disappointed to find that the successful war-time laminating technique used in the Mosquito aircraft had not been exploited by the furniture trade:.

Laminated bends presuppose new, and for this country, strange forms and these the trade has generally rejected in preference to forms derived from the more conventional methods of construction. The attitude of the trade towards the bending of laminated wood is disappointing, especially as it is merely one facet of the furniture manufacturers' deeply rooted antagonism to any change. (Farr, 1955, p.4)

Developments have continued and in the early 1990s architect Frank Gehry designed and developed a range using the concept of basket work to 'weave' thin laminations into a rigid chair. Seven layers of MAPLE wood (50 mm × 2 mm/c.2 in × ⅟₁₆ in) were formed into chair shapes which had the seat and support integral with each other. The use of thermosetting glues eliminated the need for any other structural support.
See also Plywood

64 The manufacture of prefabricated laminated chair components in quantity appealed to designers in the 1930s. Laminated chair arms destined to become the frame of chairs, designed by Alvar Aalto and manufactured by Artek, 1937–47.

Hewitt, B., Kane, P. and Ward, G. (1982), *The Work of Many Hands: Card Tables in Federal America 1790–1820*, New Haven: Yale University Art Gallery.
Vincent, C. (1967), 'John Henry Belter. Patent parlour furniture', in *Furniture History*, III.
— (1973), 'John Henry Belter. Manufacturer of all kinds of fine furniture', in *19th Annual Winterthur Conference Report*.

Laminated board

Not to be confused with laminated wood. This material is made from strips of solid wood (lumber) which are glued together and veneered both sides to make up a flat board material. There are three main types which are differentiated by the thickness of the core strips. BATTEN BOARD in which the core strips are up to 75 mm (3 in) wide, BLOCK-BOARD with strips about 25 mm (1 in) and laminboard with strips only 7 mm (¼ in).

These forms of board were introduced in Germany around 1860 under the name of *Tischlerplatten* (cabinet-maker's board) (Wood and Linn, 1942, p.117). In 1883 the American Indianapolis Cabinet Co began to manufacture desk tops with a five-ply construction with a lumber core and in 1890 the Louisville Veneer Mills made desk tops for the Globe-Wernicke Co with a lumber core and a cherry veneer face and reverse. In Germany, versions were developed by Richard Kummell, which had core blocks of about 25–30 mm (1–1+ in) width, produced by the Deutsche Holzplattenfabrikk at Rehfelde by 1910. By 1921 experiments had led to a reduction in the size of the core strips to about 3.3 mm (⅛ in).

In 1927 Shirley Wainwright introduced the idea of laminboard (laminated board) to English furniture-making to try and avoid the problems of jointing sections of solid wood to make up panels. This apparently coincided with 'a vogue for a simpler type of furniture depending for decorative interest on choice veneers rather than on mouldings, carving or fanciful contours' (Wainwright, 1927, p.58). Wainwright praised Austrian furniture in which 'lamination has been accepted as a structural necessity of cabinet work for a long time' (loc.cit.). Another commentator declared: 'laminated board has become not only a desirable but an essential and inescapable element in furniture construction' (Weaver, 1930, p.63). Weaver seems to have hoped for nothing less than a minor revolution in design from the use of laminboard:

Laminated board gives to furniture the same character that the use of steel and concrete tends to produce in architecture. Thus at length we may confidently look forward to a genuine revitalisation of design and decoration proceeding

not from successive waves of imitative fashion but from the truthful application of a material of which the practical and decorative possibilities seem to be limitless.
(op.cit., 1930, p.74)

In the latter part of the 20th century laminated boards are often combined with a number of ply veneers to make composite boards.

Wainwright, S. (1927), *Modern Plywood*, London: Benn.
Weaver, L. (1930), *Laminated Board and its Uses. A Study of Modern Furniture*, London: Fanfare.
Wood, A. D. and Linn, T. G. (1942), *Plywoods, Their Development, Manufacture and Application*, Edinburgh: W. & A. K. Johnston.

Lampas

Originally a painted or dyed textile from the Coromandel coast of India. Subsequently it referred to a weaving system using a two-warp and two-weft system to introduce one weave technique into another, as with twill on satin. It is now a furnishing textile made from silk (and sometimes metallic threads) in a compound satin weave which creates a two-colour damask by using two sets of warp yarns which bind the figure wefts and ground wefts respectively. A brocaded effect is achieved, but lampas does not have the floating wefts typical of brocade, indeed the pattern wefts of lampas are woven into the cloth giving a banded effect which is non-reversible.

Lampblack

A pigment of almost pure carbon. It was collected from the results of burning resins, oil or wood in a confined space. The dense black smoke given off by the partial burning causes soot to collect on the walls and ceiling of the space. It was widely used in 19th-century furniture decoration, especially in EBONIZING processes and PAPIER MACHE work. Sheraton gave detailed instructions on the preparation of black for japanning chairs and considered lampblack preferable to 'ivory black' (prepared from burnt ivory or bones) as it was more opaque (1803, p.54).

Lancewood (*Oxandra lanceolata*)

A West Indian and Central American wood with an average density of 990 (62 lb/cu ft). It is a paler yellow colour than BOXWOOD, which it is sometimes substituted for. It has been imported in poles 7.60–15.20 cm (3–6 in) in diameter. In the 19th century it was used for billiard cues and rules and, when steamed and bent, for springs and bows. Its elasticity and springiness made it ideal for GO BARS.
See also Degame

65 An easy-chair, c.1955, English, showing the use of tension springs and pre-formed latex cushions. These new materials introduced better quality upholstery, made less expensively.

Lapis lazuli

A deep ultramarine-blue semi-precious stone, sometimes with pyrite crystals giving a sparkling effect, used for decorating cabinets and other furniture, particularly in the 17th century. It was also popular for use in PIETRE DURE where less pure varieties with white flecks were used to give the image of sea foam or clouds. During the Renaissance it was sourced from Afghanistan, later some varieties came from France, but from the late 18th century onward, Russia was the main source.

Lapped dovetail joint
See Joints (Dovetail)

Larch (*Larix spp.*)

A European softwood, introduced into England *c.*1629, with an average density of 560–600 (36–8 lb/cu ft). It is reddish-brown to pale yellow with a fine uniform texture and a straight grain. Evelyn noted that it 'bears polishing excellently well, and the turners abroad much desire it' (1679, p.116–17). It was sometimes used for carcases in the late 18th century, whilst in France *bois de melèze* was used both in solid and veneer. Larch was introduced to Scotland *c.*1727 by the Duke of Athol, and timber from the estate was later made into furniture for the Duke by George Bullock, a cabinet-maker well known for his interest in using indigenous timbers. In the later 20th century larch has been sliced for decorative veneers taking advantage of the light and dark streaks that resemble pitch pine. It was widely used in the UK, post World War I for the framing of BED SPRINGS.

Laser cutting

Lasers, introduced in the late-20th-century furniture industry are particularly used for the cutting out of precision shapes in panels. Lasers are devices that amplify light and produce very hot and powerful directed light beams, that can effectively vaporize material. In conjunction with computer-designed 'blueprints' which can turn the laser on and off at will, complex parts can be cut smoothly, accurately and quickly to a very high degree of precision. The process works equally well for wood or metal or for large or small projects including marquetry.

Lashed joint
See Joints

Lashing
See Knots

Lasting
See Everlasting

Latex

Natural latex is a plant exudation obtained from the rubber tree *Hevea brasiliensis*. As a suspension in an aqueous solution, it sets by evaporation. It was first brought to Europe in 1735 but was not developed commercially until the 1820s as rubber. Its main use in furniture has been in its conversion to upholstery foams which were developed in the late 1920s. Experiments began at the Dunlop company, where a food mixer was used to whisk liquid latex with additives and then 'cured' in an oven. The result was a flexible and resilient sponge material that returned to shape after being pressed. A typical process of making latex foam mixes the latex with chemicals such as sulphur, soaping agents and anti-oxidants. After maturing, the mix is foamed with air. It is then poured into moulds and steam heated to vulcanize (cure) it. The later process uses a foam mixture to partly fill moulds; these are then closed, and a vacuum applied so that the material expands. After being frozen solid, CO_2 is blown through to gel it. It is then cured at a higher temperature and finished. Initially, the moulding method in which the cured latex shape was removed from a mould meant that it was not reversible. Later developments include: Pincore latex, a process in which the liquid mixture is baked in a mould with numerous thin pins penetrating it. This makes a reversible material with no mould limitations. Synthetic rubber-styrene butadiene latex is often blended with natural latex to provide a variety of densities and other features.

Dunlop's first commercial use of Dunlopillo was in 1929 when their latex cushioning was used in cockpit linings; by 1930 cavity moulded cushions were being supplied to the automobile industry. The contract markets (auditoria, office, hall and vehicle seating) accepted the new material well. However, most domestic furniture manufacturers were reluctant to change. In 1946 it was still referred to as a 'new' filling material.

As late as 1951 a British industry commentator thought that 'the potentialities of latex foam for upholstery and the influence it can exert on the design of chairs and seating units have not yet been fully realised' (Desbrow, 1951, p.2). Like many new materials, latex foam was clearly versatile enough to be used not only as a substitute but also to become the basis for completely new designs. The benefits of latex cushioning were such that it gave the designer much more flexibility than the traditional methods. The costing of the cushion-making was much easier due to the regular shape of the cushion, and it was the logical choice for contemporary furniture due to its shape-retaining capabilities. It was also promoted for hygienic mattresses and pillows. The development of PLASTIC FOAMS has had an impact on the role of latex in the late 20th century.
See also Foams, synthetic, Webbing

Desbrow, R. (1951), 'Latex foam in furniture design and manufacture', in *Rubber Developments*, vol.3, pp.2–11.
Murphy, E. (1966), 'Some early adventures with latex', in *Rubber Technology*, vol.39, June, pp.ixxiii–xxxiv.
Young, D. (1954), 'Freedom of design with latex foam', in *Latex foam in furniture, Report of a conference organised by the British Rubber Development Board*, May, London.

Lathe

A tool or machine that allows materials to be shaped whilst being rotated (turned). Although the Ancient Egyptians were familiar with the technique of turning by bow or strap, there is no firm evidence that they used lathes. Rather the lathe was probably developed around 1000 BC in central Europe, and by 200 BC was widespread throughout Europe. Prior to these developments, circular work appears to have been made on the principle of a potter's wheel with the vertical lathe operated by two persons, one cutting and one pulling alternately on a rope around the workpiece. Hence the term 'thrown or turned' (chairs), which links turners and throwers in the same technique.

The next stage, the turning-lathe frame of table height, based on the POLE lathe principle was common by the early Middle Ages. This operated with a drive wheel which had an extended axle called a mandrel. The importance of the table lathe was that with adjustable stocks or ends, differing sizes of material could be worked on with simple changes. Another advantage was that by standing up, the turner could apply pressure with both hands and use his body weight to ease the cutting process. However, the disadvantage of non-continuous motion still needed to be addressed. (See Pole lathe, below.)

Theophilus describes the use of lathes with a crank device for metalwork (1100–40, p.180). The development of the treadle lathe with a cranked flywheel and sometimes additional power sources meant that the making of parts for chairs and stools slowly improved. The treadle lathe, which combined a great flywheel for heavy work and a treadle wheel for lighter work, generally superseded the pole lathe by the mid 18th century. However, the pole lathe did survive until the early 20th century.

Although cabinet-makers had lathes in their workshops, for example, George Bullock had a 'turning lathe with large hand wheel, ditto with foot wheel', the separate trade of TURNER inevitably meant a different path of development. By the early 19th century the centre lathe had become a very powerful machine worked by a large wheel, turned by one or more men. The growth of steam 'turning mills' in the 19th century increased the specialization, and for much of the trade the complete separation of turning components occurred at this time (but see Pole, below).

Bow
A simple form of lathe that employs a bow used as the drive, fitted round the piece to be worked which is held between centres. The bow string is looped round the workpiece and pulled back and forth whilst the working tool is applied to the piece. This lathe remained in use by the Byzantines, and still continues in some regions today.

Copy
A machine so designed that the lathe is able to hold a master model and reproduce it many times from inserted blanks.
See further, Carving machine

Pole
A particular form of lathe that has been known and used for many centuries by joiners and other woodworkers. It is most well known in relation to BODGERS, as it could be set up in woodland without any power source, other than human. It could also be fitted into a workshop. The pole lathe consists of two beams of wood which are parallel but a few inches apart, so that there is a groove between them. This groove has two wooden stocks fitted into it, which can be moved by adjusting the holding wedges, according to the size of billet to be worked. The driving power is a 3.6 m (12 ft) ash or larch pole firmly fixed to the ground or by an overhead connection. One end of a chair leg is tapped onto the fixed end, and the other end is fixed to the adjustable stock. As there is no driven chuck, a piece of string joins the top end of the pole to the floor-mounted foot treadle, and is wrapped once round the material to be turned. By pressing the foot treadle which is hinged, the pole bends and the material turns, and once released, it springs back again. The work is then adjusted for true running. The nature of the forward turn means that the chisels can only work on the down stroke. The pole lathe was ideally suited to turning legs and stretchers since, in most cases, the work could be done in one setting as the driving cord remained in the middle of the workpiece.

In 1850 Mayhew noted that 'About fifty years ago, the pole lathe, which is worked without a wheel was in general use ... The pole lathe is still used in the country especially in Buckinghamshire where "rapparee" [painted bedroom] chairs are principally turned out of beech' (Mayhew, Letter XVII, 29 August 1850). The pole lathe remained in isolated use until the 1950s.

Treadle or wheel
An alternative power source for a lathe was foot power or by a rotating wheel, which could be hand powered. These were well known in Moxon's day and feature in 18th-century woodworking tracts. By

RIGHT
66   Pole lathe, c.1770, French.

FAR RIGHT
67   Pole lathe, c.1763, English.

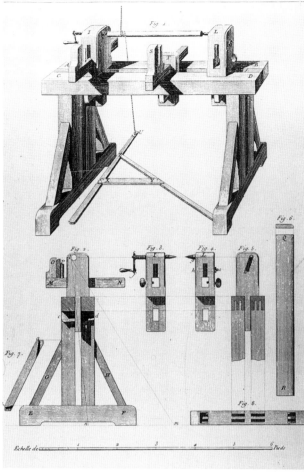

the early 20th century treadle-operated lathes were still common in woodworking establishments.

See also Turning, Turners

Abell, S. G., Leggatt, J. A. and Ogden, W. G. (1956/1987), *A Bibliography of the Art of Turning and Lathe and Machine Tool History*, North Andover, Mass.: The Museum of Ornamental Turning Ltd.
Holtzapffel, C. (1846), *Turning and Mechanical Manipulation*, London: Holtzapffel & Co.
Maurice, K. (1985), *Sovereigns as Turners*, Zurich: Verlag Ineichen.
Woodbury, R. S. (1961), *A History of the Lathe to 1850*, monograph 1, Cleveland: Society for History of Technology.

Lauan

White lauan (*Shorea spp.*)
A timber sourced in the Philippines with an average density of 590 (37 lb/cu ft). It is a pale grey timber turning pale pinky-brown upon seasoning, with a medium-fine texture and a 'roey' grain. It was introduced in Europe in the early 20th century for general furniture and cabinet work. Aka Philippine mahogany.

Red lauan (*Shorea spp.*)
See Meranti

Laurel (*Laurus nobilis*)

A decorative timber introduced into England in the 16th century. Its pinky-white colour ensured that it was used for inlay work. A hard and tough timber, it generally has a fine texture and usually a straight grain. It is not an important cabinet-making wood due to the small sizes available.
See also Indian laurel

Lead

A heavy bluish-grey metal that is soft and easy to work. Sheet lead has been used in furniture-making to line tea canisters, pedestals, cupboards and for coolers as a refrigerant in the later 18th century. Lead WEIGHTS were also used in metamorphic furniture to facilitate movements and counter-balances. Lead was also used as moulded ornament in the 18th century in conjunction with carved work such as mirror frames and ornaments.

Lead inlay

The use of lead inlay has been recorded both in wood and in conjunction with brass. Lead was occasionally used as a decoration in chests as early as 1230 (Eames, 1977, p.150) and much later as a filling for worked-brass ornamental borders used in the early 19th century.

Lead moulding

American upholsterers occasionally used a strip form of lead or pewter in late-Federal and Empire furniture. It was used in place of piping, as the soft metal followed the contours of the chair frame well.

Leaf decoration

An 18th- and 19th-century technique for creating a leaf pattern. By pasting leaves onto a wooden surface and then exposing the same to sulphur fumes, the wood will turn a darker shade, dependent upon the length of time of exposure. When the leaves are removed, the shapes will be seen in the original (lighter) wood colour. The method was used for surface decoration. In 1853 Eliza Cunnington patented an invention which was a process of decorating table tops with ferns pressed under glass, sometimes with feathers added to create an image of pictorial inlay (Pat.no.882). The process entailed selecting suitable natural leaves, pressing them and then gluing them to a previously stained carcase. A final coat of copal varnish sealed the surface.
Aka Oppuntia

Leather

Leather is a generic name given to hides prepared by a currier. Large animal hides and small animal skins from reptiles and birds provide leather. In the case of hides, the outer hair layer and the inner fleshy layer are removed, leaving the corium (with hair follicle grain marks) to be turned into leather by tanning. The basic techniques are: (a) Chamoising or treating with oils and fats; (b) Tawing (soaking) with minerals such as alum and salt; (c) Tanning with vegetable matter such as bark, sumach, and such like. Traditionally, tanning was done with tree barks and roots. By the 18th century the processes included tawing with alum with added fats, egg yolk and flour. Modern methods now include the addition of chrome and alum tanning agents to speed up the process. The mineral tanning, which uses mineral salts such as chrome sulphate, completely tans the hides in twenty-four hours. Once tanning is complete, the hides may then be split layerwise and treated to give a finer and more correctly balanced grain. Pickling in weak acid or salt solution follows. The skins which result are then processed as upholstery leather by dressing, shaving and dyeing. They are finally oiled and stretched, coated, polished and finished.

Leather has been used by furniture-makers for many tasks, both functional and decorative. These include jointing thongs, seat and upholstery covers, cushions and protective covers for cabinet work, wall-hangings and writing surfaces. One of the early uses was as strap thonging for lashed joints in Ancient Egyptian furniture. The structural use occurred from an early age with sling seats fitted to X-framed chairs. Details of other uses are commonly found in inventories. In 1423 Henry VI had Spanish leather covers for tables, and in 1534 Katherine of Aragon enjoyed cushions of 'lether, lyned withe yalowe cotton to the same'. The range of leathers available by the 16th century indicates an already sophisticated market. The 1582 *Book of Rates* noted 'Skinnes for leather … Basill, buffe for cushions, portingale [Portugal] red hides, roan, salt, Spanish, spruce and swan skinnes' (Willan, 1962). In the 18th century the range of upholsterers' leathers is indicated by the inventory of Samuel Norman. His stock included brown damask skins, white sheep skins, rone skins, bazil skins and gilt skins (Kirkham, 1969, p.509).

By the 19th century, leather was chiefly used for upholstery work and table tops. In 1839, a patent was taken out by Henry Brown for making VENEER from the skins of animals for plating furniture (Pat. no.8193). Its success is unknown but it anticipated later schemes where leather was used to cover hard furniture. Leather has been and remains an important upholstery and decorative finish for all sorts of furniture.

BASIL OR BAZIL

Sheep skin tanned in bark. Sheep leather was specifically used only for linings and not for top covers according to the 17th-century byelaws of the Upholder's Company. It was also used for covering inexpensive trunks in the later 18th century. As this material was comparatively thin, the use of brass corners and studs helped to reduce premature wear. In 1801 it was regarded by one writer as 'an inferior leather … [which] tears almost like paper' (W. Felton, *Carriages*, cited in Legg, 1994, #56). In the 20th century it has been used for upholstery.

CALVES' LEATHER

A specific description of a particular hide derived from young bovine animals. A 1691 Essex inventory specifies '5 calves leather chairs' (Steer, 1969, p.207).
See also Gilt leather, below

CUIR BOUILLI

When leather is wet it can be manipulated into shapes, and when dry will retain its new shape. The process can be speeded up by immersing the leather in boiling water, hence *cuir bouilli*. Once moulded, the leather was often treated with an oil or wax finish ensuring flexibility and waterproofing for covering furniture chests, trunks and boxes. An early example is recorded in 1337 when the Lord of Naste had '1 coffre de cuir boulit' (Eames, 1977, p.135). Widely used during the 16th century, it had a renaissance in the 1840s and 1850s, when leather was reduced to a pap by shredding and boiling and was then pressed into moulds to make embossed work which was used on mirrored frames and chairs. In the 1851 Great Exhibition, Leake of London exhibited a chair upholstered with embossed *cuir bouilli*.

DAMASK LEATHER

A 17th- and 18th-century method of processing leather to imitate the patterns of damask material, by embossing with heat. The treated leather was most often used for PROTECTIVE COVERS or cases for furniture, for example, library tables and sideboard tops, although John Cobb provided 'candle spots of brown damask leather' to Croome Court in 1769 (Beard, 1993, p.103). It was also popular in Italy during the early mid-18th century for chair covers. Siddons, writing in 1830, gave full instructions to show cabinet-makers how to prepare damask leather: 'Produce a block of wood 2′6″ × 2′ wide, draw patterns and carve out so it matches sides to sides and end to end. Strain the leather dry on the block with tacks and then with a glass-ball rubber of about four lbs. in weight pass it to and fro over the leather rubbing hard till you produce the pattern perfectly glazed on the leather' (1830, p.185).

68 An English dressing chest with an unusual use of leather to decorate the fronts of the drawers, c.1950.

69 *A side-chair decorated with* cuir bouilli. *Made for the Great Exhibition by Leake of London, c.1851.*

GILT LEATHER

Originally an Islamic technique and often called 'Spanish leather' on account of this origin, it was made from calves' skins faced with tin foil. They were embossed or punched with patterns which were then painted in colours. The tin foil ground was glazed with a yellowish varnish which gave the 'gold look' to the foil. Gilded and tooled leathers were also produced in a similar manner. Extensively used for wall-hangings, gilt leather was also used for upholstery coverings in the latter part of the 17th century, and was made particularly in Flanders and Holland.

See Spanish leather below, Screen-maker

IMITATION LEATHER

See Coated fabrics

KID LEATHER

A leather prepared from the skins of young goats. King George II had a travelling bed (c.1720) which had a kid skin leather TICKING.

LACQUERED LEATHER

A leather with a finish of coloured lacquer or japan, sometimes known as 'patent leather'. This appears to have been first used in the later 18th century for leather intended for upholstery (see Vernis de Gobelins). In the later 20th century upholstery has been finished with a cellulose lacquer.

MOROCCO LEATHER

A furnishing leather made from sumach-tanned goat skins (sumach is the reddish dried and ground leaves of trees of the *Rhus* genus). This leather was originally from Morocco and the Barbary States and invariably red. It was used in the 18th century for lining desk and table tops as well as for covering chair seats and backs. Chippendale suggested that 'if the seats are covered with red morocco they will have a fine effect' (1762, Plate XV). By the 19th century it had acquired a name for quality and was essentially used for dining, library and club chairs. It was considered 'by far the best leather used for covering purposes, its durability and the fastness of its colour being qualities not common to any other material' (Working upholsterer, 1883, pp.5–6). The Morocco leather suite was the epitome of high-class upholstery in the early 20th century. Although not quite so long-lasting as Moroccos, cowhides became more popular post 1914–18 as they were cheaper, larger and more easily obtained. Aka Maroquin.

PARCHMENT AND VELLUM

Sheep, goat or calf skins treated with lime and not tanned, but dried under tension and finished in a variety of ways. In the 19th century a material called Pelletine was patented by Brown (Pat.no.1839/8193), which was to be made from parchment and printed with designs of wood grains, and so on, and used as a 'veneer'. Vellum was used for decorative purposes in early-20th-century furniture by the Italian designer Carlo Bugatti.

RAWHIDE

An untanned split cattle hide, preserved by a liming process which does not convert the skin to leather. As it dries, it shrinks, making it ideal for drum seats.

ROAN

Cured sheep skins tanned with a sumach preparation. In the 19th century, roans were used in conjunction with Morocco leather to cover outside chair backs when the seats and insides were upholstered in Morocco. 'Some of the best roans, when quite new, so closely resemble morocco that an experienced man often finds it difficult to decide offhand which is which. Roans are not so difficult to work as moroccos, being more elastic and supple' (Working upholsterer, 1883, p.6).

RUSSIA LEATHER

A particular process of leather preparation which produced supple sweet-smelling hides. The process involved steeping the hides in a variety of preliminary baths to remove hair by lime washing. After scraping they were then washed again in mixes which might be of flour and yeast, or dog and pigeon dung, depending on the recipe. They were then put into a mix of oatmeal and water to undergo a slight fermentation, then they were washed in running water. This was followed by a steeping in a mix of birch, or possibly willow, or poplar bark and oil. The visible cross-hatching scores are a result of the hammering process which left a distinctive diaper pattern. This was due to the use of textured wood blocks to agitate the skins while still moist, so as to allow the penetration of the oil and the partial breakdown of fibres. When tanned and dry, the skins were rubbed gently with birch oil and finished. Russia leather was widely used for upholstery in the mid to late 17th and all of the 18th centuries in England and America. In January 1660, John Sapsorard of Writtle, Essex had '4 Russia leather chairs' in his parlour (Steer, 1969, p.90). In 1703, the Capitol in Williamsburg was furnished with 'seven doz: of Russia leather chairs [for] furnishing the rooms above stairs' (Gloag). Embossed Russia leather was still recommended by Loudon for library table tops (1839, p.1055).

SCORCHED LEATHER

A reddish-brown leather with a pattern (often a damask pattern) which was embossed with the use of a hot plate and a mould underneath. Favoured in the 17th century for protective cases for furniture items.
See also Damask leather, above

SKINS

Hair skins are untanned hides which are cleaned and dressed. Often used for rugs, they have also been incorporated in upholstery, especially in the 20th century. Zebra, pony, and cow skins have all been used. Snake skins have also been used as 'veneer' especially in French Art Deco cabinet and chair decoration.

SEALSKIN (AKA SOYLE)

A hair-hide type, cured by drying on frames and having alum worked into the surface. In 1737, Samuel Grant of Boston, Mass., bought '9 red sile skins [for] making 25 seats' (B. Jobe, cited in Cooke, 1987, p.88). They have been used for sling seat covers and for covering trunks and cases. In other situations they have been used as a polishing aid (similar to SHARKSKIN). Moxon (1677) recommended sealskins as an alternative to rushes (see Grasses) for polishing turned work.

SKIVERS

The top grain split of a sheep skin often used to line desk tops or writing slides. Varying from paper thin to c.1 mm ($\frac{1}{32}$ in), it is available in a wide variety of colours, finishes and effects, often copying superior leathers.

SPANISH LEATHER

A decorative leather finished with gilding, used for wall-hangings and chair covers during the 17th century. Chippendale notes how a 'Slider [should be] covered with green cloth or Spanish leather for writing upon' (1762, Plate CXXVI).
See Gilt leather, above

TURKEY LEATHER

A 17th-century term for inlaid gilded leather, originally of Turkish or North African origin. Evelyn recorded seeing 'a cabinet of Maroquin or Turkey leather so curiously inlaid with other leathers, and gilding, that the workman demanded for it 800 livres' (Diary, 25 May 1651). Also refers to leather tawed (softened) with oil before the hair side is removed.
See also Morocco leather, above

Clouzot, Henri (1925), *Cuirs Decorés*, Paris: Librairie des arts décoratifs.
Davis, Charles T. (1885), *Manufacture of Leather*, Philadelphia: H. C. Baird & Co.
Garbett, Geoff and Skelton, Ian (1987), *The Wreck of the Metta Catharina*, Truro, Cornwall: New Pages, pp.23–8 (see Russia leather).
Muhlbacher, Eva (1988), *Europaïsche Lederarbeiten*, Berlin: Staatliche Museen zu Berlin.
O'Flaherty, F. and Roddy, W. T. (eds) (1956–65), *The Chemistry and Technology of Leather*, 4 vols, New York: Reinhold.
Waterer, John (1948), 'The Art of cuir bouilli', in *Country Life*, 5 November, pp.934–5.
— (1968), *Leather Craftsmanship*, London: G. Bell.
— (1971), *Spanish Leather: History of its use from 800 to 1800 for Mural Hangings, Screens, Upholstery, Altar Frontals, Ecclesiastical Vestments, Footwear, Gloves, Pouches and Caskets*, London: Faber and Faber Ltd.

Leather cloth
See Coated fabrics

Lemonwood
See Degame

Leno
An open-work gauze weave fabric sometimes interspersed with areas of plain weave. The warp threads are twisted in pairs before weaving, the pairs cross and recross each other between picks of weft. In 1819, George Bullock had in stock '7 pieces of figured leno, green stripe, figured buff and citron coloured leno' (Levy, 1989, p.185). Occasionally used for window curtains in the 19th century, in the mid 20th century these cloths were made up into curtains and used as 'light filters'.

Leopard wood
See Snakewood

Letter wood
See Snakewood

Light alloys
See Aluminium, Magnesium

Lignum vitae (*Guaiacum spp.*)
A West Indian timber, imported into Europe since the early 16th century. A heavy wood with an average density of 1230 (c.77 lb/cu ft), it has a dark greenish-brown to black heartwood, with a bright yellow sap wood, a fine and uniform texture but an interlocked and irregular grain. The name 'wood of life' owes itself to the idea that it was a cure for venereal diseases. This explains why it was often used for utensil turnery in the 16th and early 17th centuries. In the later Stuart period from c.1660 it appears as veneer but it was most widely used by Dutch makers. With its streaked heart and pale sapwood it made good OYSTER VENEERS in PARQUETRY in the late 17th century and small veneers in the 18th century. By the early 19th century, Sheraton described it as 'a very hard and most ponderous wood and is of a resinous quality of a blackish yellow colour in the middle and of a hot aromatic taste' (1803, p.261). Not much used for furniture since then.
See Cocuswood

Lilac (*Syringa vulgaris*)
A light-yellow to salmon-pink coloured timber with brownish streaks. Lilac is a hard and strong timber with a close smooth texture. It was employed in the making of TUNBRIDGE WARE during the 18th century.

Lima wood
See Brazilwood

Limba
See Afara

Lime wood (*Tilia spp.*)
A European timber with an average density of 560 (35 lb/cu ft). It has a creamy yellow colour, darkening to yellow-brown, with a fine uniform texture and a straight grain. It cuts well across or with the grain, and resists splitting, therefore it has been popular with carvers. Used in Roman times, it came to particular prominence from the 1660s onward, the Grinling Gibbons school of carving particularly favouring

this timber. In the 19th century it was used for chair frames as 'from its inert character it makes an excellent ground for japanned and inlaid work, and is used for the frames of the best japanned chairs, inlaid with mother-of-pearl' (Blackie, 1853, p.45).

American lime
See Basswood

Limed oak
A decorative finishing process which pickles oak with a coating of slaked lime brushed into the surface. It was then either left unpolished, lacquered or wax polished. The resultant grey-white speckled look was a hallmark of the early-20th-century cottage style.

Linen
The yarns spun from the fibres of the flax plant (*linum*) and the fabrics made from them. It has been used extensively, but is often woven in conjunction with other yarns, either as a warp or weft, making a 'union' cloth.
See, for example, Canvas, Crankey, Crash, Dornix, Fustian, Haircloth, Hessian, Holland, Silesia, Southedge, Ticking

Lining
The preparing of the interiors of fancy cabinet work, which included sloping writing surfaces, flaps of cabinets which are used for writing or, most especially, the lining of small boxes. The materials used included coloured papers (often black designs on a coloured ground or marbled papers), and various textiles. In the 19th century women were usually employed in this work, but if jewel boxes needed velvet finishes, the work was often given over to men. In 1850, Mayhew reported that the women who were mostly responsible for this work were paid 15s per dozen. Although in the poorer end of the trade the women were often wives of the fancy cabinet-makers who made the work, in the better end of the trade the work was sent to outworkers. Cabinet-makers were also responsible for the lining of the tops of library and reading tables with cloth or leather.

Mayhew, H. (1850), *Morning Chronicle*, LXIV, 8 August.

Lining up
The method of fixing a framework to the underside of a top to increase its strength and apparent thickness. Also known as thickening or thicknessing up.

Linseed oil
The product of the crushing of seeds from the flax plant. The processing of linseed oil by either cold pressing (lighter) or hot pressing (darker) was followed by bleaching to clear the colour. The raw oil could then be used but the 'boiled' variety was more usual. After heating, to lessen the drying time, drying agents were added to further improve the setting properties. Once prepared, it was applied by simply rubbing over the work. Loudon particularly recommended 'cold-drawn linseed oil alone' as a timber finish that would, once polished, resist boiling water and hot dishes better than any French polish (1839, p.1063).
See also Polish, Varnish

Linsey
Linsey wool or black flock was a woollen rag-based material which was prepared from old woollen cloth. It was popular in the 1950s as a top stuffing for cheap- and medium-quality upholstery.
See Woollen flock

Linsey-Woolsey
A coarse cloth with a linen warp and a woollen weft, hence the name. Known since the 15th century and, although often used as a clothing fabric, hangings have been recorded made from this material. An early American reference is in the 1646 inventory of John Fairfield of Wenham which listed 'Green lincye woolsie curtaynes'. In England, Essex resident Mary Willis (1681) had 'one great hutch with a set of striped linsey woolsey curtains and a vallance' (Steer, 1969, p.165). Daniel Defoe described the division of labour in their manufacture: 'The Hangings, suppose them to be ordinary Linsey-Woolsey are made at Kidderminster d'yd in the country, and painted or water'd at London' (1727, I, p.333). It remained as a dress fabric into the 19th century.

Linter felt
See Cotton flock

Lip(p) work
See Straw, Wicker

Lipping
(a) A solid fillet of timber, plastic or metal extrusion that is let into a board so that the edge is protected against break-away problems. Plastic or wood edge strip is an alternative material that is glued to the exposed edge.

(b) Lipping is also a term for the moulded framework which is made to surround a table designed to be fitted with cloth or needlework, among others.

Lloyd Loom (Woven paper furniture)
Perhaps one of the most successful man-made materials that was ideal for furniture, was Lloyd Loom. The invention of the process that combined the making of furniture from a (usually) bentwood frame and a woven integrated surface material is credited to Marshall B. Lloyd. In 1917 he patented a method of weaving a sheet of partly wire-reinforced twisted paper strips, to produce a flexible sheet material that imitated wicker but had its own characteristics: Lloyd Loom was advertised as 'neither cane nor wicker-superior to either'. The material for woven paper furniture was very fine grain kraft paper produced in thin sliced rolls (also known as FIBRE-RUSH). These were unwound into long strips and passed through a gum bath before being twisted into threads and wound onto spools. This formed the weft of the material, the warp being the same paper yarn but with a core of 18 gauge steel wire. This latter feature was the key difference between Lloyd and his competitors. The final sheet size was up to 102 cm (40 in) wide.

Initially successful in the making of perambulators, it was an even greater success for furniture. In its heyday, between 1920 and 1940, over one thousand designs were produced by the Lloyd company in the United States and by the British licensee, Lusty, in Britain. In the 1930s, the products were also made on metal frames as well as on bentwood ones.

Although used as part of the British Utility range, as well as being produced after the lifting of controls, Lloyd Loom did not retain its pre-war eminence and it has gradually declined as a product range until 1968 when the British makers, Lusty's, closed down. Revivals have subsequently been marketed (see Plate XX).
See also Fibre-rush

Curtis, L. (1991), *Lloyd Loom Woven Fibre Furniture*, London: Salamander.

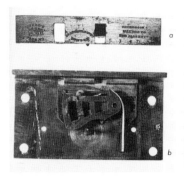

FAR LEFT
70 The Lloyd Loom factory in Menominee, Michigan, showing the manufacture of sheets of shaped and flat material, c.1922.

LEFT
71 Example of a Chubb patent lock, early 19th century.

72 Example of a tumbler lock, c.1770.

Locks

A mechanism intended for fastening lids and drawers, and which has been used since the first furniture. Although usually for security, they were often decorative in their own right. Simple rotary locks were used in small quantities by Ancient Egyptians, and from the Middle Ages (14th century) hand-made iron locks were sometimes sunk into wooden frames of furniture. In the 16th and 17th centuries locks consisted of bolts protected by wards, that is, obstructions between the keyhole and the bolt. From *c.*1660 outside-mounted locks diminished in use and disappeared altogether in favour of locks inserted into frames.

In Europe, irregular-shaped keyholes were first used to limit access but were not particularly satisfactory. Continental long locks with keyholes in the centre of drawers were let into the front of the drawer, whilst English locks were short, with the keyhole at the top of drawer. This meant that the lock was fitted into the back of the drawer and was therefore flush with the back of the drawer front.

English locks were initially made from wrought iron; from the late 18th century they were made in brass and iron, as well as in steel from about the end of the 19th century. Early locks had wards or ridges as obstacles to false entry, but in 1778 Robert Barron developed double-acting tumblers; and by 1784, Joseph Bramah had developed a circular lock in which the key had no contact with the bolt.

Locks can be classified either by their mechanism or the use to which they are put, but these are not mutually exclusive.

MECHANISM-BASED LOCKS

Back spring warded lock
A simple till lock which allowed the bolt to be held open or closed by a flat spring. The ward is a length of thin curved metal fitted inside the case, making a barrier to be matched by the key slots before the bolt can be moved.

Bramah or lever locks
A patented lock mechanism from 1784 (Pat.no.1430) and 1789 (Pat.no. 2232) which employed a complicated mechanism in a small space, replacing fixed wards with a movable lever. The radial arrangement gives the compact shape. The mechanism operates by a key which enters at the centre and pushes against spring resistance to operate the mechanism. The number of slots in the key corresponds to the number of slides, varying between four and twelve, depending on the level of security required, resulting in many millions of combinations. Chubb invented a detector lock in 1818 (Pat.no.4219) using six or more levers (a lever threw out the mechanism if picked).

Spring and tumbler lock
A lock with a spring-loaded tumbler ending in a square pin which drops into a notch in the bolt. To open, the tumbler must be lifted with a key. In 1778 Robert Barron patented (Pat.no.1200) a double-action tumbler lock in which the key had to by-pass wards and lift both tumblers. Mayhew and Ince specified 'extra good warded spring and tumbler locks to shoot twice' in a bill to Croome Court, September 1781–May 1782 (Beard, 1993, p.107). Sheraton noted their use for book case and wardrobe doors.

Habit de Marchand Miroitier Lvnettier

USE-BASED LOCKS

Bird's beak lock
A lock that has the tongue made so that it will spring sideways upon extension by the key action. Used on tambours, piano falls and cylinder top tables.

Box lock
A lock with link plates for tea chest and wine cisterns. The bolt operates horizontally rather than projecting, making contact with the lugs on the strike plate.

Cut cupboard locks
Made to fit flush into the door. Suitable for either right- or left-hand cupboard doors for bookcases and wardrobes.

Drawer or Till lock
Cut flush into the back of the drawer front with a bolt that projects into the fore edge above. Made from iron and, after 1750s, from brass as well.

Espagnolette lock
A locking system which engages both ends of a vertical rod. Used for windows, cupboard doors and so on.

Hasp lock
Wrought-iron lock usually with a staple plate, square or shield-like in shape with chamfered edges.

Mortise lock
A lock usually let into the edge of a door so that it is invisible on the door face when closed. These were recommended by Sheraton for doors and sliders of cylinder tables (Sheraton, 1803, p.262).

Straight cupboard lock
A lock that simply screws to the door.

Dickinson, H. (1941–2), 'Joseph Bramah and his inventions', in *Transactions of the Newcomen Society*, XXII, London.
McNeill, I. (1968), *Joseph Bramah, A Century of Invention 1749–1851*, Newton Abbott: David and Charles.

Locustwood

(a) Black locust (*Robinia pseudoacacia*): See Robinia

(b) Honey locust (*Gleditschia tricanthos*): A timber native to North America, especially in Carolina and Virginia. Although known, it has been little used for any constructional purpose as it splits easily. Aka Mesquite.

(c) Courbaril (*Hymenea courbaril*) or West Indian locust: See Courbaril

Logwood (*Haematoxylon campechianum*)
See Stains

London plane
See Plane wood

Looking-glass maker
A specialist who prepared GLASS plates for MIRRORS, whose trade was usually incorporated with that of a glass grinder. Once the mirror had been prepared it was then framed by a specialist framer. In 1664 The Worshipful Company of Glass-Sellers and Looking-glass Makers was incorporated, and by the first quarter of the 18th century the trade was well established. The glass-grinder 'buys [the glass plates] from the glass house rough, and it is his business to grind them even and then polish them, which is done by sand and water' (Campbell, 1747, p.173). They were then silvered.
See also Frame-maker, Mirror glass

Child, Graham (1990), *World Mirrors, 1650–1900*, London: Sotheby's Publications.
Wills, Geoffrey (1965), *English Looking-glasses, a Study of Glasses Frames and Makers, 1672–1820*, New York: A. S. Barnes & Co.

Loop knots
See Knots and knotting

Looped tufting
See Tufting

Loose covers
See Protective furnishing

Loose pin hinge
See Hinges

Loose seats
See Drop-in seat

Loper

The sliding bars that pull out from a bureau or table top to support the fall flap of a bureau or the leaves of an extending table.

Low relief

See Carving

Lumbayo (*Heritiera spp.*)

A reddish-brown timber which works easily, but is unreliable so is only used as a cheap substitute for mahogany or cedar. First imported into England from Java and the Philippines c.1914. Now known as Mengkulang (*Heritiera javanica*).

Lumbercore

See Blockboard

Lustring or Lutestring

A lustrous silk TAFFETA fabric with a ribbed pattern. It was made from a taffeta which was stretched and covered with a syrupy gum (or beer) dressing, and dried in front of a fire to give a gloss finish. Alternatively, the yarns were so treated before weaving. They could be plain, striped, changeable, patterned or brocaded. Introduced into England from France in the early 17th century, in 1639 a patent was granted to Peter La Dorée for glossing plain and figured satins (see also Grosgrains). By 1698 the Royal Lustring Company was established by charter to concentrate upon the making and selling of this fabric. An advertisement in the *London Gazette* in 1697 stated that 'their warehouse shall be opened every day to sell Allamodes, Renforces and Lustrings'.

Lustring was also imported from France and Italy during the 18th century, so in 1736 it was recorded as 'a glossy sort of French silk' (*Dictionarium Britannicum*). In 1792 'Three French grey lustring window curtains' were recorded at Newby Hall (Low, 1986, p.154). It was still used as a furnishing fabric in the early 19th century. George Smith recommended lustring for fire screens, 'where the stands are wholly mahogany, the mounts may be covered with lustring in flutes with tassels to suit' (Smith, 1808, p.20), and in 1809 fashionable bed curtains were 'of blue satin lined with white lutestring and trimmed with a narrow gold edging' (Ackermann, May 1809, p.331). Lustring was still being recommended in the 1840s for curtains for drawing rooms.

Great Britain, Parliament (1698), *An act for the better encouragement of the Royal Lustring Company and the more effectual preventing the fraudulent importation of lustrings and alamodes*, London.

Macassar ebony (*Diospyros celebica*)

See Ebony

Machine decoration

The decoration of furniture by 'machine' has been a part of the repertoire since the early use of turning lathes, the development of moulding machines, and in the 19th century the development of carving machines and a whole range of other specialist processes. From the mid 19th century many firms specialized in providing embossed or machine-cut carvings, mouldings, marquetry panels, decorative veneered panels, turnings, all of which would be simply applied to carcases. During the 20th century further effects were achieved by the development of machine processes as well as new materials, scoured grain by wire brush or sand-blasting techniques, embossed and impressed reproductive techniques, and applied moulded ornaments. See also Carving machines, Embossing, Marquetry, Router, Turning

74   *In the second half of the 19th century the American woodworking machinery industry was paramount. The J. A. Fay company first patented this carving and moulding machine in 1876.*

Patent Carving and Edge-Molding Machine.
With Patent Friction Reversing Countershaft.

Machines and machinery use

To fully locate the development and use of machines in furniture-making, it will be useful to distinguish three major categories which equate to the main processes. Firstly, machines for preparing and shaping timber, which include circular SAWS, planers, mortisers, borers, dovetail cutters and VENEER cutters. Secondly, machines for processing and shaping parts, which include band saws, scroll or fret-saws and LATHES. Thirdly, machines for decorating independently, which include routers, moulders, embossers and CARVING machines. These machines can also be categorized into other divisions. Some machines were owned and operated by entrepreneurs outside of the industry and they operated either a bulk service for cutting and preparing timber, or they let space in their workshops for individual users. Other processing machines were often of a size or price that enabled a small workshop to employ them and were able to be operated by either human or non-human power.

Initially machines were 'powered' by human, animal or water, using shafting, pulleys and belting. After the water wheel, which was mainly used in sawing, the steam engine developed in the 18th century, was gradually introduced into furniture factories in the 19th century in conjunction with the line shaft which supplied power to a range of machines. The gas-powered engine enjoyed a vogue in the later 19th century as it was smaller, less troublesome and less expensive than steam power. The application of electricity occurred in the early 1900s, when the Oliver company in the USA developed machines with built-in electric DC motors. Developments were rapid from then: AC motors were developed c.1912, improved machine bearings and cutting tools enabled speeds to be increased dramatically. Most importantly, electric motors allowed machines to be positioned where required.

Expansion came in World War I when woodworking machinery was employed in a multitude of tasks, from manufacturing tent-pegs to machining propellers for aeroplanes. Progress was now swift as speed, accuracy and control were continually improved. Examples of change were related to safety and speed. By the 1880s the exposed gear wheels were gradually enclosed. The cylindrical cutting head was developed around 1900 to replace the dangerous square cutter-head, and the introduction of precision ball-bearings, high-speed steel, high-speed motors based on frequency changers all improved safety. Other important developments from the early 20th century included compressed air for clamping and driving motors and the development of portable electric tools (first devised in 1909). The story of the development of machinery since then has been one of continuous improvement in speed, quality and complexity. The use of semi-automatic, automatic, numerically-controlled and computer-programmable machines is now standard in the furniture industry.

DETAILS OF PARTICULAR MACHINES

Block clamper
A machine in use by the 1920s, devised to clamp timber blocks around a piece of small cross-section so as to enlarge the cross section. This was used especially in the case of turned legs, where a portion of the leg is to be materially larger than the remaining sections, such as bulbous or melon-shaped table legs.

Board jointer
A specialized automatic continuous-feed power machine used to join smaller panels of mixed sizes together at the edges by cutting tongues, grooves, dovetails (aka Linderman joint) or variations on these joints which can then make up panels. The simple square-edge joint was most common. Developed in the 1920s, versions are still used today.

Boring machine
A machine intended to drill single or multiple holes into timber components for dowels, mortises or slotting. By the 1920s automatic double-end boring machines were used to bore ends of rails simultaneously. Horizontal or vertical versions were used and a range of specialized models were developed.
See also Mortiser, below

Carver, multiple spindle
See Carving

Clamper
See Block clamper, above

Dovetailer
Although Bentham had attempted to make a comprehensive patent for joint cutting in 1791 and 1793 (Pat.nos 1938 and 1951), it was not until 1851 that a dovetail machine was patented by fancy cabinet-maker H. J. Betjeman (Pat.no.13588). By 1855 the dovetailing machine had been developed in America. The Burley Dovetailing machine was alleged to have been able to produce seventy-five to one hundred dovetail joints per hour. In 1870 Charles Knapp received a patent for a dovetailing machine which cut joints using a dowel in the side of the drawer front, which fitted into a hole in the drawer side. Modern spindle moulders can have attachments for dovetailing.

Four cutter
Another name for a combined machine which completes the planing and moulding of all four sides of a board. Each cutter has an integral motor and the machine may have more than four cutters.
See also Planers, below

Fret-cutter
See Fretwork

General (Universal) woodworker
By the end of the 19th century, machines that combined a number of operations had been developed. These often combined band, circular and fretsaws, mortising, boring and moulding devices.

Mortiser
Mortise-cutting machines were devised by the end of the 18th century. They were operated by hand or power and used cutters such as chisels (hollow), chains or twist bits. In 1834 American George Page developed a foot-powered mortising machine. In 1876 the American Greenlee Bros developed the hollow chisel mortiser. Specialized mortisers included borers with revolving and oscillating drills which made very narrow mortises, and hinge mortisers which cut the required depth out to receive a hinge. Multi-cutters can be programmed to cut many mortises at one time.

Moulder
See Spindle moulder, below

Planers and Planing
Early attempts at mechanizing the planing process were made by London bedstead-maker, Leonard Hatton, who patented a machine for planing boards in 1776 (Pat.no.1125). In the same way as saws, planing machines had been developed by simply trying to replicate the reciprocating human action. In 1791 Bentham again improved upon the original scheme, first with a reciprocating plane, c.1780, and then one based on the rotary principle for which he obtained a patent in 1791 (Pat.no.1838). In 1802 Joseph Bramah devised a more satisfactory process (Pat.no.2652). Like the saws, they were designed to assist large users rather than being supplied to cabinet workshops. However, this meant that timber mills were often in a position to supply prepared timber that was planed ready to work, rather than rough boards. This was clearly an advantage to the small-scale maker who bought nominal amounts of raw material to make up and sell on a cyclical basis. In 1827 Malcolm Muir of Glasgow patented a planing machine (Pat.no.5502), and in 1851 William Furness of Liverpool exhibited a planing machine at the Great Exhibition. All planing machines were then based on the rotary knife principle.

In 1828 American William Woodworth patented a planing machine that was the basis for many later models, as it not only passed timber over the rotary cutter heads, but held it firm against them. By the early 20th century, work was first taken to the buzz planer and one side was planed, it was then sent to the roughing planer to be uniformly planed to size. By the 1920s the Straitoplaner or planer-thicknesser was developed. This machine, also called an 'under and over' planer, flattens boards on one face and then planes the second face to the correct thickness in one operation, removing any 'wind' in the boards, ready for the finishing planer. The planer-moulder or 'four cutter' can cut all four sides of timber simultaneously. The finishing planer then prepares the boards for veneering or finishing.

Router
A machine devised for cutting away surplus wood either as a boring, edging, grooving or moulding operation. By using jigs and a particular cutter, the router can be made to follow any particular design. In the 1950s the router was used to cut away dark surface veneer to reveal lighter veneer beneath.

Rubbing
Automatic rubbing machines that smooth the tops and sides of cabinet work after finishing were commonplace in American furniture factories after World War I. It was said that these machines would 'coarse rub, fine rub, rottenstone, and polish equal to handwork' (*Machine Woodworker*, February 1912, p.10).

Sander

A wood-working machine that is fitted with a continuous sanding roll that has work applied to it for finishing or scouring. Varieties include endless bed, roll feed, stroke, hand block, belt, variety flat belt disk, jig or spindle, air drum and scroll. In 1877 the first true sanding machine was made by the Berlin machine works in USA. In 1892 the English Ransome Company introduced the patent Invincible three-cylinder sandpapering machine. Various shaped sanders devised in conjunction with jigs have meant that complicated sanding operations have been dramatically simplified. The automatic turning sander was also devised in the early 20th century as a simple combination of lathe and sander which used sandpaper strips to abrade a profile onto a component. In the late 20th century a furniture factory would have belt sanders, edge sanders, upright ribbon sanders, pneumatically inflated sanders, flap sanders, turning sanders, lever stroke sanders and through-feed sanders with a variety of abrasive grades, starting coarse and finishing fine.

Saws

See Saws

Shaper

A machine tool with a steel table on which pieces of timber stock can be clamped. Cutting spindles are fitted to guide rollers mounted on a swing beam, which ensures that the roller runs against the contoured former or jig. The timber passes the cutter block, removing wood to the required pattern.

Spindle moulder

A machine tool that operates a high-speed spindle mounted with cutters so that work can be placed against the cutters to create a selected profile. In 1873 Richard Bitmead commented that the rotary moulding cutter or Toupie was quite new to English manufacturers, although it had been used for some time on the Continent. He said it was particularly useful for Gothic or medieval work 'as more chamfering can be done by it in one hour than could be done by handwork in a day' (Bitmead, 1873, p.74). This machine could also take dovetailing attachments. In the 20th century it remained an important machine for cutting mouldings and joints including dovetails which could be profiled to demand.

Tenoner

Developed in the 1830s by famous American machine maker J. A. Fay. Initially rounded cutter blocks made rounded ends to the tenoners. Developments produced the single-end tenoner and finally the double-end tenoner which was designed for the bulk cutting of tenons in boards at both ends at the same time.

Universal joiner

A small machine developed in the 1850s which was arranged to saw and cut mouldings and joints as required. Aka general joiners.

See also Planes, Saws, Veneering

Bale, M. P. (1880), *On Woodworking Machinery, its Rise, Progress and …*, London: C. Lockwood and Co.
Ball, A. M. (1937), *Woodworking Machinery for Small Workshops*, London: Technical Press.
Chambers, W. (1854), *Things as they are in America*, Philadelphia: Lippincott, Grambo.
Dodd, G. (1876), *Dictionary of Manufacturing Mining, Machinery and the Industrial Arts*, London.
Ingerman, E. A. (1963), 'Personal experiences of an old New York cabinetmaker', in *Antiques*, November.
Mansfield, H. (1952), 'Woodworking machinery. History of its development 1852–1951', in *Mechanical Engineering*, no.12, December.

75 *The development of woodworking machinery was continual, but the requirements of wartime often acted as a spur to improvements. This English double-end tenoning machine dates from c.1947.*

Parks, B. A. (1921), 'Engineering in furniture factories', *Mechanical Engineering*, vol.43, no.2, February.
Ransome, J. S. (1896), *Modern Woodworking Machinery*, London: W. Rider.
Ransome & Co (1879), *Illustrated Catalogue of Patent and Improved Woodworking Machinery*, London: The Company.
Richards, J. (1872), *A Treatise on the Construction and Operation of Woodworking Machines Including a History of the Origins and Processes of Woodworking Machinery*, London.
— (1885), *On the Arrangement, Care and Operation of Woodworking Factories and Machinery Forming a Complete Operator's Handbook*, London: E. & F. N. Spon.
Schmidt, R. (1861), *Machinery for Woodworking*, Leipzig.
Sims, W. (1985), *200 years of History and Evolution of Woodworking Machinery*, Burton Lazars: Walders Press.
Tice, P. (1983), 'The Knapp dovetailing machine', in *Antiques*, vol.CXXIII, May.
US Commissioner of Labor (1898), *Report on Production by Hand and Machine*, Washington: Govt Printing Office.
Wallace, J. & M. (1929), 'From the master cabinet-makers to woodworking machinery', in *Transactions of the American Society of Mechanical Engineers*, October.

Madeira

See Mahogany

Maderón

A proprietary composite man-made material developed in Spain during the 1990s by Silio Cardona. It is created from crushed almond shells and other ligno-cellulosic material, combined with polymer resin and then moulded to shape. Its high average density leaves a very smooth surface finish. The shaped parts are then assembled with epoxy resin. The final assembly is varnished and painted as required. (Byers, *50 Chairs*, 1997, pp.128–31.)

Madrona (*Arbutus menziesii*)

A North American timber with an average density of 760 (48 lb/cu ft), light to medium red in colour with an irregular grain. The burrs are valuable as veneers.

Magnesium

The lightest of common metals, when alloyed it is used occasionally for furniture as an alternative to ALUMINIUM. It was developed post World War II as a result of the search for an ultra-light aircraft material (compare: steel 500 lb cubic foot weight, aluminium 168 lb, and magnesium 100 lb). The low specific weight allowed components to be made of strong sections with little increase in mass.

Anon. (1948), 'New trends in furniture', in *Plastics*, June, pp.300–3.
Pannell, E. V. (1943), *Magnesium, Its Production and Use*, London: Pitman.

Magnolia (*Magnolia grandiflora*)

A North American timber with an average density of 560 (35 lb/cu ft). It is creamy-white to tan-yellow with frequent purplish streaking, a fine and uniform texture and a straight grain. The wood of the ever-green variety has been used for furniture in the southern states of America since the 18th century. It was used for cheap furniture in the early 20th century (Boulger, 1908, p.165), and between the wars it was marketed in America as POPLAR for the exterior work of furniture.

In the USA magnolia is also known as strawberry wood, although this is light to medium-red in colour, with irregular grain and burrs. Aka Cucumber wood.

Mahogany

A hard, heavy, durable wood with a close grain, it was ideal for cabinet-making as well as being workable in both solid and veneer, and often being available in large board sizes. One of the reasons for its popularity with cabinet-makers since early in the 18th century was succinctly recorded by Nicholson: 'logs of mahogany may be cut into planks of such amazing breadth as to afford table tops of immense width' (1826, p.9). For consumers, its strength, its ability to take a high polish, its light red colour which deepened on exposure, as well as its exotic connotations satisfied many of their needs.

Although probably known in Europe by the 17th century, there is little surviving evidence that is proven. However, one clear indication of its growing importance was the beginning of the government's collection of mahogany import statistics in 1699. The commercial introduction of mahogany as a viable business proposition rested upon the abolition of import duties in 1721, through the Naval Stores Act. Although not directly intended, the change inevitably assisted the cabinet-maker in his search for novelty, so that by 1743 Mark Catesby could remark that the 'excellency of this wood [mahogany] for all domestic uses is now sufficiently known in England' (Catesby, 1731–43). A contemporary also commented on this taste for exotic timbers:

My Lords contemptuous of his Country's Groves,
As foreign Fashions foreign Trees too loves:
Odious! upon a Walnut-plank to dine!
No-the red-veined Mohoggony be mine!
Each Chest and Chair around my Room that stands
Was Ship'd thro' dangerous Seas from distant Lands
(Thomas Wharton, 1748, *Poems on Several Occasions*, cited in Symonds (1955) p.117)

The mahogany trade had become so important that by 1771 another Act (11 Geo. III cap 41) was passed, which extended the freedom from duty to all American timbers because mahogany 'had become very useful and necessary to cabinet-makers'. The continuing success of mahogany as a furniture timber was acknowledged in the early 19th century:

The exquisite beauty of the finer kinds of mahogany, the incomparable lustre of which it is susceptible, exempt also from the depredation of worms, hard, durable, warping and shrinking little, it is pre-eminently calculated to suit the work of the cabinet-maker. Accordingly, these admirable properties, added to its abundance, and the largeness of its dimensions, have occasioned it to be manufactured into every description of furniture.
(Smith, *c*.1816, p.91)

The continual use of mahogany alongside other woods that moved in and out of popularity is revealing. It is an example of the establishment of particular timber types that were recognized as being appropriate to a particular item, room or use. In the case of mahogany, it was especially destined for the dining room (although examples of most furniture types which use the same timber can of course be found). A French visitor to England noted:

that the English are so much given to the use of mahogany; not only are their tables generally made of it, but also their doors and seats and the handrails of their staircases. Yet it is just as dear in England as in France … At all events, their tables are made of most beautiful wood and always have a brilliant polish like that of the finest glass.
(Marchand, J. (ed.) (1933), The Mélanges sur l'Angleterre of François de la Rochefoucauld: 1784', *A Frenchman in England*, trans. S. C. Roberts, p.30)

However, it was not always the height of fashion. In 1808, George Smith said 'when used in houses of consequence [mahogany] should be confined to the parlour and bedchamber floors' (p.xiv). During the 19th century mahogany was selected for particular usage, so that it would be graded as table wood, chair wood, and veneer logs. In the case of tables the choice of log was determined by the design. For example, if a telescope table was being considered, long and wide boards were required; in the case of a pillar table, smaller boards were used. In either case attention was paid to blemishes, grain and colour. For chair wood, longer lengths were recommended so that multiple cuts could be simply made. The timber itself could be of a less interesting colour and figure than table wood. Veneer logs 'require more skill and greater knowledge of cabinet-making for their selection than those for any other purpose in the trade' (Blackie, 1853, p.34).

The American experience was similar. Henry Fearon noted that 'Mahogany yards [in New York] are generally separate concerns … Mahogany is used for cupboards, doors, banisters, and for all kinds of cabinet work … Veneer is in general demand and is cut by machinery. Chests of drawers are chiefly made of St. Domingo mahogany' (1818, p.23).

The types of mahogany imported changed over time. Initially supplies came from Jamaica and it was known as Jamaica wood (see below). By the late 1740s this source of timber had been substantially worked out, although other sources of supply opened up. These included the West Indies, Cuba, Honduras, Mexico and, in the 19th century, West Africa. (See varieties below.) In recent years conservation issues have meant that the supply of mahogany has become more difficult although Central and South America continue to supply large quantities.

African mahogany (*Khaya ivorensis*)

A West African mahogany variety with an average density of 560 (35 lb/cu ft), which was imported, in considerable amounts around the period 1820–40. Knight recorded that 'A new species of mahogany has been lately introduced in cabinet work which is commonly called Gambia' (1830, p.176). The *Khaya senegalensis* was popular for a while but was discontinued when it was found that it lost its colour and turned a dull dirty purple, that it was poor in glue holding, and was liable to distort. However, by the end of the 19th century a substantial trade had developed in another variety of African mahogany (*Khaya ivorensis*), which gave much better results. During the 20th century the African varieties have been used extensively in furniture in solid, veneer and plywood forms. The SAPELE variety (*entandrophragma cylindricum*), which when radially cut gives striped veneers, induced a fashion for a period, especially during the 1950s–60s.

Baywood (*Swietenia macrophylla*)

A mahogany that was sourced in Central America (Campeachy on North West Yucatan). Popular in the early 19th century as a fine veneer as well as solid timber, baywood lost some of its importance as it was found that its colour deteriorated after exposure. By the mid 1850s it had lost its prestige and was mainly used for frames, interior parts of construction and solid work. Although in 1882 an American journal noted that 'The forest of Yucatan and Central America are full of this beautiful wood and the new railroads which are opening up Mexico to commerce will certainly bring this and other beautiful and now costly woods to our markets at prices within reach of all' ('Furniture', *Inland Architect and Builder*, May 1883, p.54). Central American mahogany was still called baywood into the mid 20th century.

Brazilian mahogany
See Andiroba

Ceylon mahogany
See Jackwood

Cherry mahogany
See Makoré

Cuban (Havana) mahogany (*Swietenia mahogani*)
A timber with an average density of 550 (34 lb/cu ft) that is light red when first cut but darkens upon exposure to a richer, deeper colour. A hard and heavy timber with a close straight grain, it often supplies remarkable figurings. It was first imported into England in the early 1760s. In 1793 it was charged at 17.5 per cent more to work than ordinary mahogany (*Cabinet-maker's London Book of Prices*, 1793). Sheraton described it as being somewhat harder than Honduras but with no figure in the grain: 'Generally used for chair wood for which some of it will do very well' (1803, p.184). It became more important from 1808 after the establishment of direct trade with Cuba. It was generally regarded as inferior to Spanish or Jamaican mahogany. Indeed blemishes often marred later supplies, so it was recommended that Cuban mahogany supplied with faults should be used for rails of telescopic tables and for beds for veneering (Blackie, 1853). In the 1850s, board supplies over 48 cm (19 in) wide were called 'table-wood' and were cut into leaves, shelves and tops.

Gaboon mahogany (*Aucoumea klaineana*)
See Gaboon

Guadeloupe wood
A fine mahogany (?) from Guadeloupe in the West Indies. Used by Chippendale for 'a very neat work table of guadalupe wood with a hexagon top', supplied to Sir Lawrence Dundas in 1764 (Gilbert, 1978, p.159). In the same year Chippendale used this wood for a 'neat box' for Lord Coventry. Its source is interesting, as Guadeloupe was a French possession under brief occupation by the British for a short period during the Seven Years' War (1756–63).

Hispaniola mahogany
See San Domingo

Honduras mahogany (*Swietenia macrophylla*)
First introduced in the 1760s, by the latter part of the 18th century this variety had supplanted the West Indian timbers to a great degree. It was sourced in Central America (south-east Yucatan-Belize) and had a deep reddish-brown colour, a uniform grain and a softer texture than West Indian varieties, although it paled to golden or even greyish shades after exposure. Sheraton said it was 'the principal kind of mahogany in use amongst cabinet-makers' (1803, p.254). It was specially used for carcases, drawer linings and cheaper furniture, and was still recommended for such work in the 1920s. This mahogany was also called Baywood on account of Belize being in the Bay of Honduras.

Horseflesh mahogany
See Sabicu

Jamaica mahogany (*Swietenia*)
A mahogany variety imported through much of the 18th century. Supplies from various West Indian islands were forwarded from Jamaica under the general name of Jamaica wood. However, it remained the benchmark for other grades and sources. Its importance was noted in 1853: 'Of the earlier importations, those from the island of Jamaica furnished a great proportion of the largest and most beautiful wood' (Blackie, p.29). In 1826, Nicholson said of mahogany 'that of Jamaica is much more durable and beautiful and appears as if the pores were filled with chalk' (1826, p.9).

Madeira (mahogany) (*Persea indica or canariensis*)
A West Indian name for mahogany. In 1663 Gerbier noted that 'precious woods are to be had … in the West Indies, some … as hard as marble; beside rare Madeira and other variously figured' (Gerbier, 1663, p.108). American references to Madera or Madeira imply Bahamas mahogany rather than the Jamaican variety. It was also known as CANARYWOOD, being described as an inferior kind of mahogany, light yellow in colour.

Mexican mahogany
By the later 19th century Mexico was supplying mahogany that was 'a good substitute for Honduras in joiners and cabinet work, and is used most extensively in that way' (Laslett, 1894, p.266).
See also Baywood

Philippine mahogany
See Lauan

Pink mahogany
See Agba

Rattan mahogany
A variety from the island of Ruatan, hence the corruption of name. It was imported from c.1745 and was considered inferior to Jamaica mahogany. In fact Sheraton referred to 'Ratan' as 'a kind of bastard

mahogany' (1803, p.294). However, it was an ideal timber for carcase work as it was cheaper but of good size and a relatively light weight.

San Domingo mahogany (*Swietenia mahogani*)

San Domingo or Spanish mahogany was derived from the West Indian island of Hispaniola. It was a very hard, heavy wood, deep red in colour, which darkened upon exposure, sometimes having an attractive figuring. It provided a mahogany with a range of figure, a hard texture and straight grain, which was ideal for construction, as well as for crisp carvings. Sheraton noted that San Domingo 'produces dying [sic] woods and mahogany of a hardish texture, but is not much in use with us' (1803, p.252). This reference probably refers to the interruption of trade caused by the Napoleonic wars (1799–1815). Just over twenty years later, Nicholson specifically recommended Spanish mahogany for dining tables as the wood table surface was exposed at the dessert course (1826, p.6). It continued to find favour during the mid 19th century. In 1853 it was noted that 'wood from the city [St Domingo] is chiefly of a rich generous hue, varying from gold colour to ruby, but its superiority over other importations consists principally in the transparency and beauty of figure by which it is distinguished' (Blackie, p.32). It was still recommended at the end of the 19th century, but 'owing to the very small dimensions … in the supply that comes to us [it] goes solely to meet the demand for cabinet and ornamental purposes' (Laslett, 1894, p.261).

Spanish mahogany
See Mahogany (San Domingo)

Swan river mahogany
See Jarrah

White mahogany
See Prima vera

Bowett, Adam (1994), 'The commercial introduction of mahogany and the Naval Stores Act of 1721', in *Furniture History*, XXX, pp.43–56.
— (1998), 'The Jamaica trade, Gillow and the use of mahogany in the eighteenth century', in *Regional Furniture*, 12, pp.14–57.
Chaloner and Fleming (1850), *The Mahogany Tree …*, Liverpool: Rockliff and Son.
Lamb, George (c.1935), *The Mahogany Book*, Chicago: Mahogany Association Inc.
Payson, William F. (ed.) (1926), *Mahogany Ancient and Modern*, New York: Dutton.

Maidou (*Pterocarpus pedatus*)

An East Indian (especially Burmese) wood with highly decorative veneers which are similar to PADOUK or AMBOYNA.

Makoré (*Tieghemella heckelii*)

A West African hardwood with an average density of 730 (46 lb/cu ft). It has a pinky-red to blood-red heartwood, is often straight grained, and has a range of figures especially roe. Once known as 'hard pear' in the Cape province and used by the Dutch colonists for cabinets. It is a good substitute for Cuban MAHOGANY and was widely used in later-20th-century cabinet work. Selected timbers show a mottled broken stripe or drapery figure. Aka African cherry, Cherry mahogany.

Malachite

A hydrous carbonate of copper resulting in a mineral showing a range of vivid green colours with black veins which are zoned or banded concentrically or parallel in alternating shades. It is mined in Russia and Australia. It has been used for furniture decoration, particularly for items intended as imperial and royal presents, over a long period of time. The Russian Imperial stone-cutting works at Peterhof, and the Ekaterinburg factory were famous for their decorative malachite items from the later 18th century. However, it was in the early to mid 19th century that the manufactory at St Petersburg, established by M. Davidoff, began to produce malachite furniture, some of which was shown at the 1851 Great Exhibition.

Fragments of malachite are sawn by circular saws into thin leaves or plates of c.2–3 mm ($\frac{1}{12}$–$\frac{1}{8}$ in) thick. For curved surfaces, bent saws cut the malachite, which seems to have been very precarious and which resulted in slightly thicker leaves. The process of jointing was achieved by making a recess on the edge of one piece to fit a projection on another, with consideration of the final pattern effect. Davidoff's achievement was to avoid joints that were straight with no reference to the natural veins or lines of the material (the old method). The malachite leaves, once veneered to an iron, copper or stone surface, were cemented and polished. A paste for filling spaces and awkward areas was made from malachite fragments mixed in green cement.

Chenivière, A. (1988), *Russian Furniture*, London: Weidenfeld and Nicolson, pp.259–73.

Mallet

A wooden tool for driving wooden handled chisels and for knocking timbers together. It has a slightly curved-edged rectangular head and is commonly used by carpenters and joiners for knocking wooden components together. The carver's mallet has a particular shape which may be called bell or bun shaped. It is made from beech or boxwood, close-grained for strength, and is so shaped to allow the carver to strike the chisel from any angle without moving his grip on the handle.

Manchester velvet

See Velvet

Manchineel (*Hippomane mancinella*)

A West Indian and Central American timber, known as a cabinet wood since the 18th century, it is tawny-yellow variegated with brown and with an odour of lavender. A 1762 inventory of Powderham lists bookcases as manchineel (but actually PADOUK) (Gilbert and Murdoch, 1993, p.49). In the same year 'manchenille' was recommended to American cabinet-makers as 'a very fine ornamental wood' (Hinckley, 1960, p.60). However, the furniture-makers Gillows of Lancaster were rather circumspect about this timber. They warned their agent in the West Indies to avoid 'mangenill' [sic] being mistaken for mahogany, which they considered far superior to manchineel (Ingram, 1992, p.46).

In the 19th century it was considered desirable. It has been described as having 'the character of mahogany and is similarly used but is less common' (Holtzapffel, 1846, p.93). A later comment states that 'The wood is a most beautiful material for furniture, finely variegated with yellow, brown and white; it is very close and hard, and susceptible of a high polish' (Blackie, 1853, p.43).

Mangrove (*Rhizophora mucronata*)

A timber from tropical swamplands with the colour and character of red mahogany. One type was identified which was 'hard, straight grained and elastic which stands almost better than Spanish mahogany, and it is therefore preferred for straight edges and squares' (Holtzapffel, 1846, p.93).

Manilla wood

An unidentified timber known in the early 19th century. It is probable that this timber was shipped from the Philippine port of Manila. In the 1811 *London Cabinet-maker's Union Book of Prices*, the working of Manilla wood is priced at 12 per cent more than mahogany.

Mansonia (*Mansonia altissima*)

A West African hardwood with an average density of 630 (39 lb/cu ft) which is dark greyish brown with bands of purple. A fine smooth texture and straight grain makes this an excellent cabinet-making wood. Introduced into Europe in the 1930s, it has been used as a substitute for black (American) WALNUT, which it resembles, and is sometimes known as African black walnut.

Maple (*Acer*)

The timber of maple was used in Greek and Roman furniture as an alternative to THUYA. It was especially used for beds and tables as it was highly prized for being extremely white or covered with wavy spots (bird's-eye maple). Maple has also been used in Central European furniture since the medieval period. During the 17th and 18th centuries, maple was also used in marquetry, sometimes stained. In France, maple, or *bois d'érable* was widely used during the early 19th century. Henry Mayhew noted that in England, 'maple (chiefly foreign) is used for furniture, and of late has been extensively wrought into picture frames' (20 June 1850, LVII).

Bird's-eye maple

Young buds unable to break through the bark cause the particular decorative effect known as bird's-eye. These are then grown over and build up into a mass of nodules. When sawn through, they reveal an attractive amalgamation of swirls, dots and wavy figure that often seem to resemble birds' eyes. Evelyn noted that joiners sought it 'for tables, inlayings, and for the delicateness of the grain, when the knurs and the nodosities are rarely diapered which does much to advance its price' (1662, p.65). He particularly recommended Italian and Austrian varieties.

In the late 18th century a British taste developed for bird's-eye maple, especially on fancy furniture. It was specifically recommended for bedroom furniture, as it was apparently 'suggestive to the fancy of purity and happiness' (Blackie, 1853, p.21). This maple was also recommended for interior work in davenports or similar drawing-room furniture, as it was a contrast to the dark exterior wood. The FANCY CABINET-MAKERS simply 'cut it with scissors and pasted it in with thick shoemaker's paste' (Bitmead, 1873, p.27). Imports from Canada were used for this interior work as well as for exterior veneers.

European maple (*Acer platanoides*)

The European field maple is a hard timber that wears and turns well. It is creamy white with tinges of red or yellow, with a straight grain and figures such as bird's eye, tiger, curly or ripples. This maple is similar to SYCAMORE and is also chemically treated to produce HAREWOOD. In the mid 19th century it was noted that 'except in rural districts, European maple has been used to a very small extent in the manufacture of furniture' (Blackie, 1853, p.19).

Hard (Rock) maple (*Acer saccharum*)

This variety is found in the eastern half of North America, and is known as sugar maple or black maple. It has an average density of 720 (45 lb/cu ft) and is creamy white with a reddish tinge, sometimes with a dark brown heart. It has a fine and even texture, a generally straight grain, and a distinctive figure is found on plain sawn surfaces, some-times with figure such as fiddle back, tiger stripe and if rotary cut, the 'bird's-eye-maple' effect. American maple wood was particularly specified for a commode and matching tabourets in Ackermann's *Repository* (November 1818, Plate 99). In the mid 19th century Loudon noted that 'like the curled maple it is used for inlaying mahogany. Bedsteads are made of it and portable writing desks which are elegant and highly prized. To obtain the finest effect, the log should be sawn in parallel to the concentric circles' (1844, p.412). In the 1920s, as 'sugar maple' it was one of the principle American furniture woods used, usually in the solid with figured versions used as featured effects.

Japanese maple

Derived from *A. palmatum*, it closely resembles *A. saccharum* but is slightly darker. In Britain it has been used in the 20th century as a substitute for Hard maple.

Queensland maple (*Flindersia brayleyana*)

A highly decorative Australian hardwood that is not a member of the maple family. It has an average density of 550 (34 lb/cu ft), red to dark red with a medium texture, an interlocked grain and a close stripe figure. It is rather closer to SATINWOOD than true maple. It has often been used for panelling, cabinet work and turning. It also produces very attractive decorative veneers including moiré, ripple, fiddleback, striped and bird's-eye effects.

Red maple (*Acer rubrum*)

A North American (Canada and Eastern USA) timber very similar to soft maple. It is creamy brown to white, heavy and hard and straight grained with less lustre than the hard maple. This maple was the commonest wood in 17th-century America, being especially preferred by turners. In the 20th century it has been used for chair-making upholstery frames in the USA. When curled, it is valued for veneers. Aka Tiger maple.

Soft or Silver maple (*Acer saccharinum*)

A North American timber which is similar to hard maple but with an average density of 530 (33 lb/cu ft). With a delicate creamy white sapwood and a reddish-brown heartwood, it is lighter and softer than hard maple. It works well and was widely used as a side chair timber during the 18th century in America. In the 20th century it has been used for cheap furniture. Aka White maple.

Maracaibo ebony

See Partridge wood

Maracaybo

A province of Venezuela which gives its name to a 'furniture wood of moderate size, as hard as good mahogany and in appearance between it and tulipwood' (Holtzapffel, 1846, p.94). Sometimes called Maracaybo cedar, but is not of this family.
See also Verawood

Marble

Ranges of metamorphic rocks including limestone that have been recrystallized by violent earth movement. Marbles are available in a wide range of colours and patterns and can be worked in the solid, as a veneer, as mosaic or as inlay. A distinction between ancient and modern marble is important. The former being marbles from quarries now unknown or disused; modern marble being from those that were/are operational at the time of production.

Marble has been used in a range of furniture types, as well as a base for PIETRE DURE work, but is most well known for its employment as table and commode tops. Its early use is Italian in origin, and although not usual in England until 18th century, there are many exceptions. The Duke of Wurttemburg's secretary commented upon 'tables of inlaid work marbles of various colours, all of the richest and most magnificent description', when he visited Theobalds in 1592 (Rye, 1865, p.18). The effects of the Grand Tour, as well as an interest in the geology of marble encouraged a desire for exotic types for use on table tops in the 18th century, so much so that it was common to stain white marble to imitate the more costly versions. Robert Dossie in his *Handmaid of the Arts* (1758) discussed methods of staining alabaster, marble, and other stones to achieve these effects. The fashion for marble returned in the early 19th century, and by 1851 the taste was so widespread that artificially coloured SLATE and other marble imitations were developed.

PROCESSING
Marble slabs were sawn into thicknesses by saws in combination with water and grit. The selection of the correct cutting line to reveal the best markings was very important. Once cut into blocks, gritty paste was used to smooth the surface. This was repeated with ground-up earthenware for further smoothing. Polishing was achieved by rubbing the marble with rags, soaked in emery paste and lead. The final rubbing was made with ROTTENSTONE.

TYPES OF MARBLE
Many marbles are named after the quarry location, but there are also general type names:

Black Belgian
A marble with a compact grain and a dense black colour. Used widely as a substitute for PARAGONE, and, in the 19th century, as a ground for Florentine mosaics.

Brescia
Any marble split naturally and reset with fragments of other materials, for example, shells, jaspers and so on, on a dull background.

Brocatelle(o)
A marble comprised of broken fossil shells.

Cipolino
A marble with whitish ground streaked with bands of green like an onion.

Encrinital
Marbles containing fossil encrinites, crinoids or stone lilies. When cut in various directions they impart peculiar star-like patterns to the marble.

Griotte
Marbles of bright or deep red-coloured spots veined with black upon a dark brown background.

Lumachello
Figured marble caused by sections of small shells, so closely united as to form the body of the marble. Shells may be white, black or brown and the uniting material varies. The fossil shells are often near perfect in preservation and less crushed than Brocatello.

Madrepore
Those marbles containing fossils creating an effect of white and grey spots with regular dots or stars within.

Mona marble
A form of serpentine and crystalline limestone found in Anglesey.

Occiato
Lumachello marble with a violet ground colour with round fossil shells, closely placed resembling eyes.

Onyx
A quartz-like rock allied to agate with brown-, black- and white-coloured alternating bands.

Paesina
Marbles veined so that they appear to represent landscapes.

Pavonazella
Antique marble supposedly resembling the plumage of a peacock.

Portor
Marbles with a black ground and yellow veins.

Verde
A brescia marble of bright shot green with streaks of green, black and white.

Marbles are sourced all over the world, and many local quarries have supplied marbles to furniture-makers. For example, English marbles were commented upon by Defoe in 1727. In Dorsetshire he noted that 'there are also several Rocks of very good marble, only that the veins in the stones are not Black and White, as the Italian but grey, red, and other colours' (Defoe, 1727, p.209).
See also Pietre Dure

Blagrove, G. H. (1888), *Marble Decoration and Terminology*, London: Technical Press.
Dubarry de Lasale, J. (2000), *Identifying Marble*, Paris: H. Vial.
Grant, Maurice H. (1955), *The Marbles and Granites of the World*, London: Printed for the author by J. B. Shears.
Manners, J. E. (1979), 'From quarry to table top', in *Country Life*, 24 May.
Tomlinson, J. M. (1996), *Derbyshire Black Marble*, Matlock Bath: Peak District Mines Historical Society.

Marble paper
See Paper

Marblewood
A term for an 18th-century composition of glue and a mass of wood chippings and shavings, which may have been coloured to produce a turned solid, or a lump that could be sliced as a veneer.
See also Ebony (Andaman)

Marbling
A paint effect to reproduce the look of marble that appears to have been known since at least the Middle Ages for architectural applications. It was certainly used in the 17th century for chimney-pieces and wainscoting and has continued into the 20th century.

The technique was described by Salmon (1701, pp.897–8), where he suggested that the piece be painted one colour, and whilst still quite wet, the thinned second colour should be dribbled to make major veins. When it had further dried, the second colour was again dripped on but the vein effect was broken up with a feather or suchlike. After two or three days drying, it was varnished. A more accomplished description was offered in the mid 18th century:

To marble upon wood. Take the white of eggs, beat them up till you can write or drawer therewith; then with a pencil or feather draw what veins you please upon the wood; after it is dry'd and harden'd for about two hours, take quick lime, mix it well together with wine, and with a brush or pencil paint the wood all over; after it is thoroughly dry, rub it off with a scrubbing brush so that both the lime and the whites of eggs may come off together; then rub it

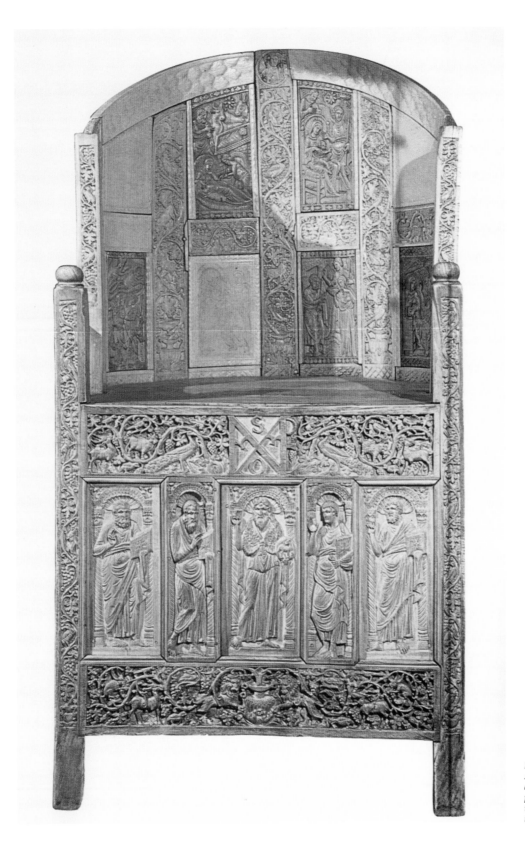

I   *The Throne of Maximian.*
A 6th-century Byzantine chair
decorated with carved ivory
panels. The work is in part made
up on a framed construction
technique.

III A fine example of late-17th-century oyster veneering in walnut with stringing additions.

II An extraordinary chair made from chiselled steel. Produced by Thomas Rucker of Augsburg in 1574, it is a virtuoso piece. Augsburg was a centre of furniture-making in this period.

IV   An early-18th-century green lacquer cabinet.

*V   A fine walnut armchair from
the early 18th century with
original needlework.*

VI   A fine mahogany English
chest of drawers, c.1770. The
drawer fronts are veneered with a
fine matched crotch veneer.

LEFT
VII   The ball and socket joint of the rear leg of a Shaker chair was a hallmark of their work. It cleverly took into account the common practice of leaning a chair on its back legs.

BELOW LEFT
VIII   The sumptuous effects achieved by the combination of rosewood and brass are seen in this inlaid cabinet by George Bullock.

BELOW RIGHT
IX   The use of tole (painted metal) panels in conjunction with japanning is demonstrated effectively in this Regency cabinet decorated with chinoiserie motifs, c.1815.

X   *A salon suite based on a
typical form, decorated with
papier mâché views, c.1850.*

XIV   An Ashburton marble inlaid table top, c.1860.

XV A demonstration piece
showing the versatile flexibility of
bentwood. This chair was used by
Thonet from 1867 as an
exhibition and demonstration
piece. Although it looks
continuous, it is made from two
lengths of bentwood.

XVI A Wakefield Rattan chair built upon a platform rocker base, c.1884–90.

XVII   A cut-glass sideboard made by Osler and Co of Birmingham, England, c.1887.

XVIII   A buffet cabinet
designed by J. V. Cissarz. It was
intended specifically to employ
pre-formed cabinet-making
boards. Hessisches
Landesmuseum, Darmstadt.

XIX The fashion for bamboo
had been widespread in the West
from the 18th century. This
example of a bamboo and lacquer
cabinet dates from c.1900.

XX A rare chair showing the
Lloyd Loom material and the
additional hand-applied 'fitch
work' in its skirt, c.1931.

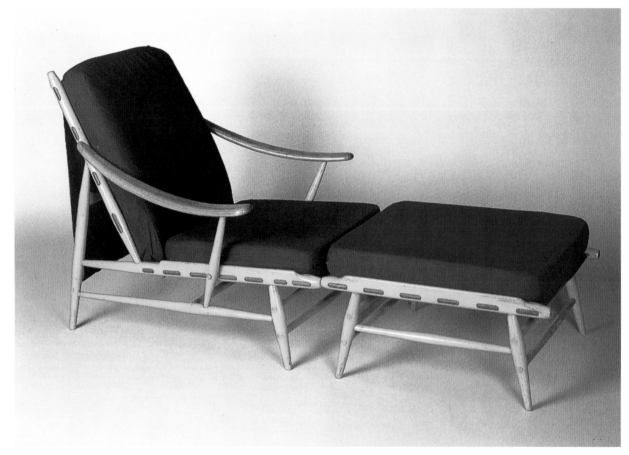

XXIII   An Ercol lounger chair, c.1960. The chair demonstrates the continuation of traditional but mechanized chair-making techniques, combined with modern upholstery practice (latex cushions and rubber webbing).

XXIV   A mock-up of an easy chair, c.1990, showing particle board panels, pre-formed upholstery fillings and polystyrene 'show-wood' decoration.

with a linen rag till it is smooth and fine; after which you may lay over a thin varnish and you will have a fine marbled wood. (Smith, 1756, p.148)

Another rather more bizarre method was also advocated by Smith. In this recipe a mix of plaster of Paris, quicklime, salt, oxblood, coloured stones and glass pieces were beaten into a powder, made into a paste by adding vinegar, beer and sour milk and then brushed over the wood. When it dried it was smoothed with pumice and then oil finished, presumably having the appearance of a marble slice.

Marbled furniture had not always been accepted so readily. In 1827 it was commented that 'in painting chairs it is sometimes the practice to marble them; nothing can be in worse taste, as no imitation should ever be introduced where the reality could not be applied if persons chose to go to the expense – and who would choose a marble chair' (Whittock, 1827). However, the 19th century was to achieve remarkable standards of marbling. One of the most famous exponents was the well-known painter-stainer Thomas Kershaw who in 1860 received a patent (Pat.no.1476) for his marbling process and the associated tools which he designed to create impressive fancy marble and wood-grain effects.

See also Graining

Jervis, S. (1986), 'Prince of grainers and marblers: Thomas Kershaw (1819–98)', in *Country Life*, 10 April, pp.939–41.
Spencer, Stuart (1989), *The Art of Woodgraining*, London: Macdonald Orbis.
Whittock, Nathaniel (1827), *The Decorative Painters' and Glaziers' Guide*, London: Isaac Taylor Hinton.

Marcella

A term for quilted work which stitched two thicknesses of fabric together in such a way as to leave spaces in between so that rovings of cotton were inserted in-between to create a padded effect. It probably originated in Marseilles during the 18th century. The handwork method was eventually superseded by a loom process which produced a double cloth with a heavy weft cord effect. In 1774 Chippendale supplied 'a marcela quilted peticoat and cover' to a 'deal toylet table on castors' to Ninian Home for Paxton House (Gilbert, 1978, p.274). In 1763 a machine had been patented by Robert Elsder and George Glasgow for 'weaving and quilting in the loom' (Pat.no.786). Its success was probably dubious, since in 1783 the London based Society for the Encouragement of Arts, Manufactures and Commerce offered a premium 'to encourage the making in the loom, [of] an imitation of that species of needlework long known by the name of Marseilles quilting' ('Transactions', cited in Montgomery, 1984). By the 19th century it was sold by the yard and used for making toilet covers, dressing table mats and other such items.

Maroquin

A name for Morocco LEATHER.

Marquetry

A process of laying small pieces of veneer material in a pattern or design onto a substrate. Not to be confused with inlay, which is put into a substrate. Marquetry originated in Egypt, with great skill being achieved over a long period. One example from the New Kingdom (1575–1075 BC) has an estimated 33,000 pieces, glued in a herring-bone fashion. The practice continued in Byzantium and was much later developed in Northern Italy by monks for INTARSIA work.

The next important step occurred in the mid 16th century when the fretsaw was developed. This made more intricate cutting out possible, and encouraged the jigsaw cut which allowed the overlaying prin-

77 *An English chest of drawers showing the marquetry-worker's skilled use of veneers, especially in the oyster form, c.1690.*

ciple, rather than inlaying as previously. The development of veneer-cutting mills also ensured a better and more regular supply of veneers (see further, VENEERS). Early use in England is confirmed (?) by the Lumley inventories of 1590 which list 'chaires and stooles of walnuttre and markatre and cubbordes of walnuttre and markatre' (Walpole Society, p.29). The full-scale marquetry process, which had been developed in conjunction with veneering in the later 17th century, was still popular in the early 18th century. The marquetry method involved laying a variety of wood veneers of differing colours and sizes onto a ground to build up a picture. This could be laboriously done using individual cuts, but was soon made easier. The required pattern was drawn upon paper which was pricked through to make the required number of copies. The selected veneers and the chosen pattern were put together in a sandwich form with a waste piece on either side to prevent splintering. The sandwich was then placed into a vice with two jaws or chops, one fixed and one movable. The latter jaw was operated by a cord fixed to a treadle, so that the sandwich could be held tight whilst the pattern was being cut by the saw.

Various methods were used to heighten the three-dimensional effect. Different coloured timbers produced major contrasts, whilst smaller sections were dipped into hot sand to produce a graduated shaded effect (see SAND SHADING). Evelyn described the process: 'the sand is to be heated in some very thin brass pan, like the bottom of a scale of balances: this I mention because the burning with iron or aqua fortis is not comparable to it' (1662, p.240). He even specified the type of glue that was most satisfactory for marquetry: 'the fine and more delicate work is best fastened down with fish glew, to be had of the drougist by the name of Ichtyocolla' (ibid.).

Once the veneers were cut into the required patterns and colourings, they were fitted to one another and, if necessary, into the ground veneer. The finished panel was then papered, glued and allowed to dry. When ready, the panel was laid in position onto the carcase or other part and glued down with a hot caul or sand bags. Pressure of weights or screws held the marquetry panel tight until it was dry.

During the first quarter of the 18th century the pictorial designs, made up from small sections of various-coloured woods, were often of floral or seaweed styles, with the fine detail being achieved by thin saw cuts in the veneers. Evelyn mentioned 'Berbery for yellow, holly for white, our inlayers use fustic, locust or acacia, brazil, prince and

rose wood for yellow and reds, with severall others brought from the Indies' (1662, p.240). In this marquetry form, the pattern was often cut into more easily managed sections which required a greater skill, as each section was fitted separately to make up a full design. Other designs are known as seaweed or arabesque marquetry, which used only two woods, one for the pattern and one for the ground. By the latter part of the 18th century (post 1760s) the detailed effects of the mainly neo-classical and symbolic images were accomplished by finely engraving the surface of the marquetry.

With the development of the French HORSE or English DONKEY, in the second half of the 18th century, further improvements in marquetry preparation were made. This device clamped the package of veneers to be cut in such a way that it allowed an increased capacity, in other words, so that twelve veneers at a time could be sawn. It also meant that the marquetry-worker could sit down to the work rather than standing as he would have done previously, at jaws mounted on a workbench.

Sheraton's comments about marquetry (which he still calls inlay) are revealing: 'in cabinet-making [marquetry] was much in use between twenty and thirty years back; but was soon laid aside, as a very expensive mode of ornamenting furniture, as well as being subject to a speedy decay' (1803, p.357).

However, in the 19th century there was a growing demand for marquetry, and despite specialization (see Marquetry worker), mechan-

ized manufacturing methods were attempted. In 1878, H. R. Paul noted that a wardrobe by Howard and Sons had 'some machine-made marquetrie [sic], which is simply an abomination'. His report goes on to describe how the 'abomination' was created:

It is made by cutting the pattern with a stamp, placing it on the veneer that is to form the ground, and squeezing the one into the other by machine pressure … Anyone may imagine the ragged edges left by such a process. In fact the wood must become pulp before it can do what is intended. (*Society of Arts Artisans Reports on Paris Exhibition*, Paris, 1878, p.419)

The report ends with a sombre announcement that says that 'so long as wood is wood, and until a machine can be invented to deal with it as wood, marquetrie will have to be made by hand' (ibid.). Although it was clear that high-quality marquetry began to be a luxury, it was ideally suited to the magnificent products of some later-19th-century manufacturers including Jackson and Graham, Gillows, Herter Brothers, Emile Gallé, and Louis Majorelle. By 1919, printed marquetry transfers which gave the effect of marquetry work were marketed. This was in addition to ready-made marquetry parts that had been known for a long time.
See also Imitation marquetry, below

Arabesque marquetry
A form of marquetry in which the design is based on the intricate interweaving of flowing vegetation, based on infinite correspondence, following Islamic models. It was used from the later Renaissance onward as surface decoration and was particularly popular in the latter part of the 17th century. It usually employs only two contrasting woods.

Endive marquetry
An all-over marquetry pattern popular in the later 17th century, associated with seaweed-style marquetry but the pattern relying on a formalized endive leaf.

Imitation inlay and marquetry
As demand for furniture grew during the 19th century, it is not surprising to find inventive minds turning to methods of imitating marquetry. One of the most successful was John Dyer, who in 1861 patented a process that produced an imitation of marquetry on the surface of deal or pine furniture. His simple method consisted of coating a cheap wood surface with gum, size or wax and then applying blocks, stencils or transfers to the surface. The dry surface was then French polished. The process was acknowledged as being an exciting development by Lorenzo Booth. He praised the partnership of Dyer and Watts for their 'honest intentions': 'These gentlemen have directed their attention, first to treating a common material with first rate workmanship and superior design; and secondly they have involved and introduced a decorative system, which is simple, effective and expressly suited to their common material' (Booth, 1864, p.16). The *Art Journal* was even more glowing in their account of the firm's products: 'Messrs Dyer and Watts claims from us a most decided expression of our approval and admiration – not only because of its intrinsic elegance, but also because, being so excellent, it is in every respect adapted to both the requirements and the means of the community at large' (1863, p.80). Finally, G. W. Yapp, commenting on the painted furniture of Dyer and Watts, pointed out that painted ornament should not necessarily be made to imitate inlaid work. He said, 'on the contrary, it is capable of effects quite beyond the reach of marquetry' (1885, Plate cxix). This was perhaps the vindication of an imitative process that was a success in its own right.

George Maddox openly declared in his catalogue of bedroom furniture that his suites 'were made of polished deal with the additions of ornamental borders, centres etc. of imitative marquetrie [sic] having all the appearance of being really inlaid and being equal in every respect to satinwood and marquetrie' (c.1865).

Jeux de fond
Mosaic marquetry shapes used to create a decorative background.

Marqueterie en plein
Inlaid solid carved detail to a depth of 9 mm (⅜ in) or completely through the surface.
See also Inlay, Intarsia (Relief intarsia)

Mosaic marquetry
A decorative process, described as mid-way between artistic marquetry and TUNBRIDGE WARE, was invented by a M. Marcelin, a French marquetry-worker who exhibited mosaic marquetry at both the London 1851 and Paris 1855 exhibitions. It was made by gluing together pieces of wood so as to make a mosaic pattern, then this was cut at precise angles. These blocks were then sliced into as many thicknesses as required and laid down as a mosaic veneer (Wyatt, 1856, p.311).

A noteworthy patent that attempted to reproduce very fine marquetry or parquetry effects is the 'mosaic veneer' process. This patent was taken out in 1867 (Pat.no.1598) by the American Mosaic Veneering Company of New York. In this instance it did not use wood parts but rather a 'plastic' material. The process involved forcing the material through a metal plate with the appropriate design upon it, then drawing the resulting rods together and gluing and hardening them. Finally the bundles were sliced into veneers ready for application.

The wood mosaic process remained a fascination. In 1878, Harriett Spofford wrote in glowing terms of the American practice of importing Indian marquetry: 'No marquetry exceeds for curiosity, that which is occasionally brought now from India, known as the mosaic of Bombay and made of microscopic cubes of wood that produce a fine effect' (cited in *19th-Century America*, # 262). Around 1890 Tiffany (New York) introduced wood mosaic which 'was produced by a new method of work. The patterns … are made of thousands of squares of natural wood, 16th of an inch in size, of different colours, and each individual square surrounded by a minute line of metal' (ibid.). This definition seems to refer to a form of TUNBRIDGE WARE with added metal strips in the built-up block.

Oriental marquetry
A patented French process devised by Madame Rosalie Duvinge in 1877 (Pat.no.118,8370). The method was based on the idea of 'a mosaic combined with metal cloisonnes for objets d'art and furniture'. The materials used included ivory, brass, pewter, copper and traditional and exotic woods and mother-of-pearl. The 'marquetry' was usually built up on an ivory ground divided by metal 'cloisonnes' and filled with quality wooden marquetry.

Seaweed marquetry
A particular marquetry design and process that imitated the flowing nature of arabesques, thus being likened to seaweed. It was usually only made from two timbers (often walnut and holly, or box), a base and a contrast. Also called scrolled marquetry.

See also: Boulle, Contre-partie, Donkey, Inlay, Parquetry, Pietre dure, Pounce, Première-partie, Sand shading, Straw marquetry, Tunbridge ware

Amateur (1875), *Amateur's Practical Guide to Fretwork, Woodcarving, Marquetry etc.*, London: Kent & Co; C. H. Savory.

Bellagiue, G. de (1968), 'English marquetry's debt to France', in *Country Life*, CXLIII, 13 June, pp.1594–8.
Bemrose, W. (1872), *Manual of Buhl and Marquetry*, London: Bemrose and Sons.
Champion, C. W. (1889), Mansion House Committee, *Reports of Artisans on the Paris Exhibition*, pp.133–7, Paris, 1889.
Denning, D. (1896), *Fretwork and Marquetry*, London: Upton Gill.
Diderot, Denis et al. (1751–65), 'Ebenisterie', 'Marqueterie', 'Menuiserie' and 'Teinture sur le bois', in *Encyclopédie*, 17 vols, Paris: Briasson.
Fitzgerald, L. V. (1907), *Marqueterie Staining*, London: Upton Gill.
Flade, Helmut (1986), *Intarsia Europaïsche Einlegekunst aus Sechs Jahrhunderts*, Dresden: Verlag der Kunst.
Hawkins, David (1986), *The Techniques of Wood Surface Decoration*, London: Batsford.
Jackson, F. Hamilton (1903), *Intarsia and Marquetry*, London: Sands and Co.
Kisluk-Grosheide, D. (1999), 'Maison Giroux and its "Oriental" Marquetry Technique', in *Furniture History*, XXXV, pp.147–72.
Lincoln, William (1971), *Art and Practice of Marquetry*, London: Thames and Hudson.
Ramond, P. (1981), *La Marqueterie*, Paris: Dourdan.
Streeter, C. (1971), 'Marquetry', in *Bulletin of the Metropolitan Museum of Art*, 29, 418–29.

Marquetry workers
During the height of the fashion for marquetry, in the second half of the 18th century, some cabinet-makers specialized as 'inlayers'. However, there is little evidence of a specialist trade being established to any degree at this time. But by the end of the 18th century there was a trade in ready-made marquetry, centred on small, easily repeatable designs such as paterae and shells, which seems to indicate a specialism. One example from the United States was Thomas Barrett of Baltimore who in November 1800 had in stock '1316 shells for inlaying into furniture'. By the mid 19th century there was a need for specialists in

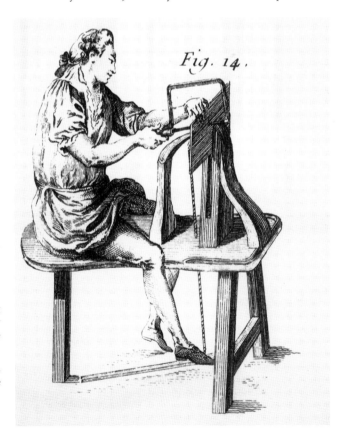

79 *A French marquetry worker shown sitting on his donkey, operating the jaws to hold the pack of veneers, and cutting them using the fret or marquetry saw, c.1770.*

response to the growing demand for full-scale marquetry work. These workers were in turn divided between designers, cutters, dyers and assemblers. Mayhew recorded that in London in 1850 there were just over one hundred such craftsmen, due to the fact that 'the beautiful art of marqueterie, which had fallen into disuse in this country, experienced a revival ten or twelve years ago [1838–40]'. Later on in the century veneer merchants marketed ready-made veneer panels and inlays.
See also Boulle cutter

Kirkham, P. (1980), 'Inlay, marquetry and buhl workers in England
  c.1660–1850', in *Burlington Magazine*, CXXII, pp.415–19.
Mayhew, H. (1850), *Morning Chronicle*, Letter LXIV, 8 August.

Marsh grass
See Grasses

Mask wood
An Australian timber resembling satin wood, which was favoured there in the later 19th century.

Masonite
See Hardboard

Mason's mitre
See Joints

Mastic
See Resins

Masur birch
See Birch wood (Karelian)

Matching
See Veneering (Special effects)

Matching planes
See Planes

Matelassé
A cotton, rayon or silk 'double' fabric, woven with two sets of warp and weft threads so that one set is the back, the other the front. The two faces are interlaced at intervals, where the pattern occurs. The patterns are like quilting, often of one colour, with a rich flowered design which only shows as a relief or embossed effect. Introduced in the late 19th century, it remained a furnishing fabric into the second half of the 20th century.
See also Marcella

Matted seats
Chair seats made from a range of GRASSES, STRAW and RUSHES were said to be matted. As the same materials were used to make floor and bed mats, the connection is clear. An Essex inventory from 1686 listed five 'mated chaires' (Steer, 1969, p.182) and in 1692 a reference is made to 'matted chair-maker' Thomas Smith. In the same year, playwright John Dryden referred disparagingly to theatre-goers who 'to save coach hire, trudge along the street, then print our matted seats with dirty feet' (1692, *Cleomenes*, Prologue, The Works of John Dryden, 18 volumes, Edinburgh: Archibald Constable and Co, 1821, Vol.VIII, p.246).
  Examples of matted seats were found in New England from the

1660s and it is possible that these were particularly made with twisted corn-husk twine. The term was still being used in 1745 when Defoe commented on the supply of chairs: 'The chairs if of cane are made in London; the ordinary matted chairs, perhaps in the place where they live' (*Complete English Tradesman*, p.266). The tradition continued into the 19th century: Loudon noted that corn husks were twisted together to form a twine which is then braided and used for seat bottoming (1839, p.1087).
See also Grasses, Painting, Rush seats, Wicker

Mattress-making
A branch of upholstery work that was undertaken by specialist mattress-makers. The principle of filling a mattress was based on either a 'stuffing' or a 'layering' process. The first method was to fill the mattress 'bag' with the required fillings from one open end, the second method was to lay filling materials into an open case and attach the top cover when the whole case was filled. The manufacturing process originally used special mattress frames to ensure a rectangular shape and for ease of stuffing. Once the mattress-maker had filled the case, he temporarily slip-stitched the top in place so that he could insert the tufts. In better-quality mattresses the sides were also stitched to create a better shape. The side stitches were visible and could be up to three layers. A rolled edge might be created by sewing through the fillings close to the top and bottom sides. Then it was passed to an upholsteress to seam up and bind the edges. The mattress-maker was 'only reckoned [to be] a third-rate hand, and the price paid for making [mattresses] is much lower than for other upholstery work' (Bitmead, 1912, p.23). The craft was gradually taken over by machine-assisted assembly processes of pre-fabricated parts after World War II, although some handmade work is still produced.
See also Mattress, Tufting

Davies, V. and Doyal, S. (1990), 'Upholstered mattress construction and
  conservation', Scottish Society for Conservation and Restoration, in
  Conservation of Furnishing Textiles, Post prints of the Conference held at the
  Burrell Collection, Glasgow, March 1990.
Ludlam, A. J. (1947), *The Craft of Mattress and Bedding Production*, London:
  Furniture Record.

Mattress
In simple terms, a textile case which is stuffed full of soft and flexible material such as COTTON fibres, FEATHERS, FLOCK, HAIR, leaves, MILL PUFF, MOSS, PINE HAIR, SEAWEED, STRAW, TOW or other such suitable filling, which is primarily designed to be slept upon. The intention originally was as a support for the top feather bed (see also Palliasse below). John Evelyn explains his recommendation of beech leaves for filling mattresses as they 'offered the best and easiest mattresses in the world to lay under our quilts instead of straw, because besides their tenderness and loose lying together, they continue sweet for seven or eight years long before which time straw becomes musty and hard' (1662, p.47). Beech leaves were still recommended in 1840 as 'they remain sweet and elastic for years' (*Daily Wants*). The use of a selection of different fillings in various mattresses to make something of a 'system' was considered by Sheraton:

for delicate persons I offer my opinion how they should have their beds made:
first to begin with a straw mattress, then a flock ditto, on which the feather bed
is to be laid and lastly a hair mattress; but if it should feel too firm then a very
thin flock mattress may be placed upon it.
(1803, p.44)

In the 1840s a similar mattress system was recommended. The first mattress onto the bed frame should be

of straw, … very thick and as hard as a board; … the second mattress is made of horse hair or wool for large beds; and for children, of chaff, seaweed, beech leaves, cocoa nut fibre, paper, and many other things of that sort … for the poor, mattresses are often filled with mill-puff or flock, and for children, bran might be a good substitute.
(*Workwoman's Guide*, pp.198–9)

The idea was still current as late as 1949 (Bitmead, 1912, 5th impr. 1949). Bitmead recommended a palliasse or straw mattress for beds with lath bottoms. In addition, a mattress stuffed with cotton (although animal hair was also widely used, as were wool or flock), coconut fibre or weeds and mosses such as ALVA MARINA.

Box spring mattresses
Probably developed soon after the adoption of springs for upholstery. They were certainly being made by upholsterers in the 1860s. The mattress was built up on a wooden frame using bed springs tied in a similar way to spring UPHOLSTERY with cord, canvas covering, stuffing materials and top cover. They were referred to as 'French' when made with a wooden-side frame and therefore a 'firm edge', and 'German' when the springs came to the edge and were held in place by bamboo strips creating a 'sprung edge'. They were usually used in conjunction with a soft mattress or overlay and a BEDSTEAD.

Palliasse
A mattress or bed support made from STRAW. The best were made from wheat straw. Of early origin, they survived as part of the 'bed' well into the 20th century. Their making was described by Bimont who particularly noted the use of straw and said that it should be arranged evenly by hand and then compacted to create an edge and finally stitched (1770, p.49). Indeed this remained the basis of palliasse or straw-mattress making. To achieve a satisfactory product, a complicated process of making required that the straw was all running the same way in the mattress. This required the palliasse ticking to be suspended in a frame so that the maker could ram straw into the case and pack it down. When this was finished, the case could be sewn and tufted in the manner of a mattress (Bitmead, 1912, p.23).

Spring mattresses
These are interior-sprung mattresses which have a built-in support system such as pocketed (nested) springs, coil springs or interlaced (woven) spring systems, usually upholstered with layers of fillings and a final TICKING.
See also Bed springs

MDF (Medium density fibreboard)
A man-made wood-based sheet material that is composed of fine fibres of timber that are mixed with urea-formaldehyde resin and additives to form a felted 'mattress-like' material. This is then subjected to heat and pressure to create rigid boards and panels. This material, which was developed in the 1960s in the USA, is seen as a very acceptable substitute for solid wood, with many features that commend it to the furniture-maker. It is very smooth and can be machined without breakout or material loss, and can be finished with a variety of materials directly to its surface (for example, paint, print or laminate), with little preparation. Contrary to particle board, it needs no extra edging or surface treatment.

FIRA (1985), *Medium Density Fibreboard, its Manufacture, Processing and Applications*, Stevenage: FIRA.

Measuring
See Bevel, Callipers, Dotter, Gauge, Rods, Setting out, Sweep, Templates, Trammell, Vergier, Wood square

Mechanical fittings and mechanisms
See Bed mechanisms, Castors, Chair mechanisms, Table opening and extending mechanisms

Mechanical joints
See Joints (Finger) (Knuckle) (Rule)

Meranti (*Shorea spp.*)
A large family of timbers from Malaya and Indonesia including red, light red, white and yellow versions. A considerable variation in the properties of the species occurs, and it has been imported in mixed lots. They have been particularly used for the construction of the sides and bottoms of drawers in the 20th century. Aka Tanguile.

Red meranti
Two versions are employed: the light red which is similar to African mahogany and has an average density of 530 (33 lb/cu ft), whilst the dark red has an average density of 690 (43 lb/cu ft), and is more uniform than the lighter version. In the second half of the 20th century red meranti has been used for veneers, cabinet work and especially drawer making. Used to some extent in North America from the late 19th century as a mahogany substitute. Aka Tanguile.

White meranti
A timber with an average density of 650 (41 lb/cu ft). Almost white when first sawn, then darkens slightly to a buff shade.

Yellow meranti
A timber from Indonesia with an average density of 560–650 (36–40 lb/cu ft). Yellow to dark-red in colour with a moderately coarse texture and an interlocked grain, it is used for veneers, cabinet work and substituted for more expensive timbers.

Mercury gilding
See Gilding

Merino
A 19th-century merino wool upholstery fabric which had a soft finish similar to cashmere and was used for hangings and as an upholstery cover. It was made up into damask cloth for dining- and drawing-room hangings and upholstery as it 'makes up beautifully, not requiring lining' (Smith, 1826). It was also especially specified for upholstering bedroom furniture supplied to Sir Titus Salt in 1866 (*Furniture History*, III, pp.66–75).

Mesquite
See Locustwood (Honey)

Metal
See Aluminium, Brass, Bronze, Copper, Gold, Iron, Silver, Steel, Zinc

Metal mounts
See Hinges, Locks, Ormolu

Metal thread
See Cloth of gold, Needlework (Embroidery)

Micro-mosaic
See Mosaic work

80   An English occasional table made with glass columns, mirror glass to the base and edge, with an etched glass top surface, c.1938.

Mill puff

A cheap mattress filling, made from the dust, remains and ends of cloth from the mills. Of an even lesser quality than FLOCK. It needed up to 23 kg (50 lb) weight to fill a double mattress.

Mirror glass

The earliest mirrors used obsidian or polished metal as a reflective surface, although glass was apparently used in Ancient Egypt. By the 13th century a form of mirror was made from glass globes that were blown and, whilst still hot, injected with molten lead or tin. When coated and cooled, they were cut into small mirrored pieces. This technique, with the addition of mercury, continued to be used for curved and concave mirrors.

From c.1500 the manufacture of glass plates, combined with the tin-mercury process of 'silvering' became the common method of making mirrors for 400 years. The method of silvering was as follows: A piece of tin-foil was laid on a marble slab. Once the layer of oxide was removed from the tin surface, a layer of mercury 3–5 mm (⅛–¼ in) thick was poured onto the tin. The glass, having been cleansed with washed ash and polished with linen cloth, was then slid over the mercury in one movement. The next process was to weigh down the glass to encourage bonding and amalgamation. After further evaporating processes, the mirror was left to harden for anything up to a month.

A thin blotting paper is spread on a table, and sprinkled with fine chalk; and then a fine lamina or leaf of tin, called foil, is laid over the paper; upon this mercury is poured, which is equally to be distributed over the leaf with a hare's foot or cotton. Over the leaf is laid a clean paper and over that the glass plate. The glass plate is pressed down with the right hand, and the paper is drawn gently out with the left; which being done, the plate is covered with a thicker paper, and loaden with a greater weight, that the superfluous mercury

may be driven out, and the tin adheres more closely to the glass. When it is dried, the weight is removed, and the looking-glass is complete.
(Barrow, 1758, p.339)

The first-known of these mirrors were produced in Venice in 1507, when the Dal Gallo brothers obtained a privilege for making this mirror type. The Venetians had established a lead in the supply of glass mirrors from the early 16th century. This was due to the technical development of the 'broad' or Lorraine process of glass-making which involved blowing a tube of glass until it reached the appropriate size, when it was then sliced lengthways and afterwards flattened within an annealing chamber. Clearly this process was limited to the finished sizes that could be made, and there were associated problems found in the thinness of the glass, which limited the amount of polishing as well as having a tendency to warp; but this did not deter market growth. Indeed, the marketable value of glass and mirrors was not lost on English entrepreneurs. In 1621, Sir Robert Maunsell petitioned the King for the right to develop a looking-glass factory. His business employed 'strangers from foreign parts to instruct natives not only in making Crystalline Morano glasses but also Looking Glass plates and theyre foyling' (cited in Schweig, 1973). After 1660, George Villiers, 2nd Duke of Buckingham, was granted a patent for making mirror plates at premises in Vauxhall, London, which according to Evelyn were 'far larger and better than any that came from Venice' (cited in Wills, 1965, p.56). Indeed, importation of mirror glass was forbidden in 1664, the same year that the Worshipful Company of Glass Sellers and Looking-glass Makers was established. In 1675 there were eighty-five members including twenty grinders of mirror plates.

Although there was an industry in England, such was the quality and prestige of French mirrors that they were imported in quantity. The mirror glass was often imported in an unfinished state and it was necessary to process it further in England. This is the sort of work that might have been carried out by furniture businesses which had glass rooms and employed grinders and polishers. As glass-mirror finishing involved grinding, polishing, silvering and cutting to size, the specialist glass grinder was often employed. The glass-grinder 'fixes [plate glass] horizontally in a weighty frame, and [it] is rubbed backward and forward upon another plain, on which sand and water is constantly running … the glass being thus on both sides ground perfectly true [is] afterward polished with emery and putty' (Collyer, 1761, pp.57, 149).

The process of grinding used a range of sands and water. The process commenced with hard and coarse sands which were gradually overtaken by finer and finer grades until the final application of powdered finishing sand. In some cases a rough plate was fixed on a bed and another smaller plate was lowered on top of this one with a weight added. The grinding of two plates was therefore facilitated. Polishing was the final process and this involved bedding the glass sheet in plaster of Paris on a stone table top so that it would remain firm. A small wooden block with handles and an underside covered in rough woollen cloth was the main tool for rubbing the polishing materials into the glass. The polisher used 'emery to take out the scratches … then tripple (which is rust of old iron) for clearing the grinders ground … Afterwards white putty is used which is the polishers finishing' (*The Plate Glass Book*, 1757, cited in Symonds, 1936, p.10).

A useful gadget to assist the polisher was a hoop of yew wood attached to a wooden frame on the ceiling, to which the polishing block was fixed. This was set up so that the hoop acted as a spring and returned the block to the starting position, thus aiding the workman's arm.

Often the glass grinder was also responsible for silvering the back to make mirror glass. Such is the case of James Welch, who offered for sale a 'great variety of peer [sic], chimney, or sconce glasses, fine dressing glasses, coach, chariot or chair glasses' (Symonds, 1955, p.155). Silvering was also carried out by cabinet-makers. The inventory of the Bastards' business in Blandford, Dorset, taken in 1731, lists '24 lb of quicksilver at 5s 6d per pound; 35 of tinfoile at 18d and two marble and two common stone tables for silvering glasses: wooden frame and other utensils of ye same; 65 lead weights for ye same use at 7lbs each'. In addition there was a large stock of glass (Legg, 1994, p.31).

By the mid 18th century, the techniques of glass-making had improved sufficiently to create extraordinary mirror sizes. According to contracts made by Chippendale, the size of 243 × 117 cm (96 × 46 in) was not unusual, and his company was even able to supply mirrors of 289 × 228 cm (114 × 90 in), but this was undoubtedly exceptional.

A major development occurred in the mid 19th century which helped to meet the continuing demand. From c.1850, following the experiments of Justus von Liebig, a German chemist, mirrors were 'silvered' using a solution of silver nitrate reduced by an aldehyde, to deposit a brilliant mirror surface on the glass. The backs were finished with a red lead or paint. The development of continuous process furnaces improved production rates by the later 19th century. However, it was not until the first years of the 20th century that the old tin-mercury amalgam method finally gave way to 'silvering' by spray methods which deposit silver nitrate in an ammonia-based medium onto the prepared glass.

See also Frame-maker, Glass, Looking-glass maker, Speculum

Child, Graham (1990), *World Mirrors, 1650–1900*, London: Sotheby's Publications.
Hadsund, P. (1993), 'The tin mercury mirror: its manufacturing technique and deterioration process', in *Studies in Conservation*, vol.38, pp.3–16.
Roche, S., Courage, G., Devingey, P. (1957), *Mirrors*, London: Duckworth.
Schweig, B. (1973), *Mirrors: A Guide to the Manufacture of Mirrors and Reflecting Surfaces*, London: Pelham Books.
Symonds, R. W. (1936), 'English looking glass plates and their manufacture', in *Connoisseur*, 97, May, June, July.
Wills, G. (1965), *English Looking-glasses: A Study of Glass, Frames and Makers, 1672–1820*, London: Country Life.

Mitre cramps
See Cramp

Mitre joint
See Joints

Mitre square
A tool used for the accurate marking of 45-degree mitres. Moxon noted that with the mitre square, 'picture frames and look-glass frames are commonly made' (1677, p.85).

Mock cushion
An upholstery technique that creates the effect of a loose cushion by sewing and piping the fixed seat in such a way as to appear separate.

Mockado
One of the new draperies introduced in the later 16th century. It was a velvet type, similar to modern moquette. With a linen warp and a wool weft it was either plain or embossed.
See Moquette

Modernism
A term that refers to the period c.1920 to 1970 which represented a search for a totally new style appropriate to the 20th century. Based to a great extent on FUNCTIONALISM, it was an all-embracing movement that treated architecture as the mother-art but with all other arts and crafts linked to it. The movement developed its own language and vocabulary based on functional theory, modern materials (such as PLYWOOD, STEEL, GLASS) and a disavowal of decoration for its own sake. The powerhouse of the developments was found in Germany and France and, after 1933, in America. The development of a machine aesthetic coincided with the attraction of new materials and manufacturing methods which seemed to have an inevitability about them. The products of the Bauhaus set a benchmark for Modernism, but a host of well-known architects and designers (including Marcel Breuer, Le Corbusier and Gerrit Rietveld) experimented with new forms and produced icons of furniture design which have been developed further ever since.

Mohair or Mocayare
A term that refers both to a finished cloth as well as to the hair of the Angora goat.

(a) It was a highly prized fabric from the very late 16th century, but in Europe it was woven with wool or silk mixes with the mohair yarns. In the 17th century mohair was a ribbed silk fabric like Gros de Tours that had been watered (moiré). In 1675 the Countess of Manchester had a room 'hung with six pieces of haire, called silk watered mohaire' (Fowler and Cornforth, 1974, p.132). The particular watered effect was produced by calendering two cloths together so that the ribs on one marked the face of the other. In 1710 'a strip'd mohair stuff' was used as a covering for a chair and stool in Dyrham Park. Whilst in the New Nursery at Dyrham there was 'a mohair silk bed lined with green sarsenet' and 'four pieces of mohair stuff hangings' (Walton, 1986, p.61). By the mid 18th century it was clearly described as

a kind of stuff, ordinarily of silk, both woof and warp, having its grain wove very close. There are two kinds, the one smooth and plain, the other watered like tabbies: the difference between the two only consists in this, that the latter is calendered, the other not.
(Chambers, 1728, repeated by A. Rees, 1819)

(b) The second definition is possibly derived from the Arabic *mukayyar* (cloth of goat's hair). It was a fine CAMLET type of fabric made from the hair of the angora goat, but can be confused with moiré. The French for mohair is *mouaire*. In the mid 19th century, mohair yarn was made into

many kinds of camblets, which when watered, exhibit a beauty and brilliance of surface unapproached by fabrics made for English wools … Also large quantities of what is termed Utrecht velvet, suitable for hangings and furniture linings for carriages are made from it abroad. Recently this kind of velvet has begun to be made at Coventry, and it is fully anticipated that the English made article will successfully compete with the foreign one in every essential quality.
(James, 1857, p.465, cited in Montgomery, 1984)

By 1884 it was also noted as a mohair cloth woven with mohair yarns. It was considered to be virtually indestructible and was widely used in public transport work. It was still used in mid 20th century for its lustre and hardwearing properties.
See also Moreen

Moiré
Originally a French term for a mohair fabric (see Mohair), later a silk fabric with a ribbed effect. Later still the term referred to any 'watered' fabric.
See Grosgrain, Harratine, Mohair, Moreen, Tabbinet

81 A table top executed in glass mosaic by H. Stevens of Pimlico. The table was exhibited at the 1851 London Great Exhibition.

Moiré antique

A variety of Grosgrain silk very fine and heavy. 'Its ... watered appearance is produced by forcing moisture through the folds by means of a screw, or hydraulic press ... Width 22 to 36 inches' (Brown and Gates, 1872, cited by Adrosko, 1990, p.109).
See also Grosgrain

Moquette

A 16th-century wool pile VELOUR, with linen warp and weft, and an extra wool warp for the pile, plain or figured, and sometimes stamped with patterns after weaving. Known in France as moucade (Anglicized as MOCKADO). Originally seen as a carpet-type fabric, and used as such on upholstery. In the 1590 inventory of Cassiobury there were 'three chairs in mockado' in Lady Morison's chamber (Beard, 1997, p.31). Another early reference is to 'sic pieces of hangings of red mockadowe' recorded in the Hardwick inventory of 1601 (Boynton, 1971, p.24). Tufted mockado was voided to create a pattern of pile and ground. More recent examples of moquette are more like velvet. The best qualities have a wool pile on a cotton ground, but cotton and rayon piles were also introduced in the mid 20th century. It was amongst the most popular textiles for upholstery in post-war Britain.
See also Caffoy, Plush, Velour

Mora (*Mora excelsa*)

A timber from Guiana and Trinidad. It has an average density of *c*.1030 (64 lb/cu ft) and is chestnut brown to red, resembling mahogany in colour. With a coarse texture, an interlocked grain, it is a difficult timber to work but has sometimes been used as a substitute for ROSEWOOD or MAHOGANY, especially when figured.

Moreen (Morine)

A worsted material with a decorative finish often with a horizontal rib and stamped or watered effects in imitation of moiré CAMLETS. It was used in the 18th and early 19th centuries for drapery and upholstery. In 1809 it was noted that 'morone continues still in use, and the more

so, where economy is requisite, which article also has experienced an improvement by being embossed in a variety of patterns' (Ackermann, vol.1, March 1809, p.188). However, by 1839 it was suggested that moreen 'should never be used in cottages'. It 'used to be employed for the hangings of best beds and bed-room windows ... [but] is now considered as apt to harbour moths and other vermin; and therefore in these economical times, it is much less used than formerly' (Loudon, p.1080, fig.1982).

By 1872 it was described as 'A coarse all wool fabric woven plain. It is usually dyed in plain colours, heavily sized and pressed, or tabbied, to imitate watered goods. The colours are generally permanent, and the goods durable. It is used for covering cushions and furniture. Width 24 to 27 inches' (cited in Adrosko, 1990, p.109).

Cummin, H. (1940), 'Moreen – a forgotten fabric', in *Antiques*, 38, pp.286–7.

Moreton Bay chestnut
See Blackbean

Morocco cloth
See Coated fabrics

Morocco leather (French: *Maroquin*)
See Leather

Mortise and tenon
See Joints

Mortise lock
See Locks

Mortising machine
See Machines

Mosaic marquetry
See Marquetry

Mosaic work

Originating in the ancient world, the idea of using small cubes of marble, stone, glass, and such others set into a bonding agent was revived in Renaissance times and was developed upon the back of the excavations of Roman remains in the 18th and 19th centuries. In a number of cases, original excavated classical mosaics were re-used as table tops. However, originals were very scarce and valuable, so copies were soon made. The trade centred upon Rome, initially in the Papal workshops.

Various terms are used to describe particular mosaic techniques. These include *Opus alexandrium* – a mosaic of small, black and white square stones. *Opus romanum* – an Ancient Roman technique for floor decoration using tesserae in patterns. *Opus sectile* – a form of marquetry (not tesserae) in which pieces of stone and others are fitted together to make an image in jig-saw fashion. This was the precursor of PIETRE DURE. *Opus tesselatum* – a mosaic with tightly fitted square tesserae which do not reveal any background. *Opus vermiculatum* – a mosaic made with irregular shapes set in worm-shaped patterns that follow a design naturally.

By the mid 19th century a new technique was introduced. This used glass tesserae which could be formed into many shapes and coloured with a very wide range of shades. The technique, which was developed by Benedetto Boschetti, allowed the mosaicist to trace outlines onto the base of his composition and then, by painstaking assembly, build up a pictorial surface with minute glass pieces which resulted in a 'painted' effect. Two table tops using the improved glass tesserae technique were exhibited in London during the 1851 Great Exhibition.

Micro-Mosaic
Made from minute tesserae, first developed in the Vatican workshops during the second half of the 18th century. Some work may contain as many as 1400 tesserae per 6.5 square cm (square in). The technique is based on *smalti filati*, that is, glass threads drawn and cut into tesserae which are then fitted onto the surface. The invention of this method is attributed to Giacomo Raffaelli from *c*.1775. Improvements occurred in the 19th century with more and more brilliant colours added to the palette.
See also Intarsia, Marble, Pietre dure, Tunbridge ware

Fischer, P. (1971), *Mosaic History and Technique*, New York: McGraw-Hill.
Gonzalez-Palacios, A. et al. (1982), *The Art of Mosaics: Selections from the Gilbert collection*, Los Angeles: Los Angeles County Museum.
Hanisee, J. (1989), 'Mosaic tables in the Gilbert collection', in *Antique Collector*, 60, 11, pp.92–9.
Sherman, A. (1971), *The Gilbert Mosaic Collection*, West Haven, Conn.: Pendulum Press.

Moss

A cryptogamous plant grown in clusters and sometimes used for filling MATTRESSES. In 1792, Thomas Smith of Doncaster, advertised a secret method of cultivating and harvesting moss especially for use in bedding (*Doncaster Journal*, 9 October). In the early 20th century it was noted that 'Other weeds and mosses, the products of Italy and America, are used for the same purpose, [that is, filling mattresses] and are cheaper than horse-hair and wool' (Bitmead, 1912, p.17).
See also Alva Marina, Mattress, Spanish moss

Mother-of-pearl

A layered calcium-carbonate lining of the pearl oyster and other shells. It has a lustrous and iridescent sheen (resulting from refraction of light through the layering) and has been used for furniture inlays and decoration for many centuries. Many varieties and colours are available, including the large saltwater pearl oyster (*Aricula margaritifera* or *Meleagrina margaritifera*), found mainly in warm seas, and the freshwater pearl oyster (*Unio margaritifera*) which is found in rivers and lakes throughout Europe, Asia and North America. Mother-of-pearl is also found in the shells of the cuttlefish (*Nautilus pompilus*), from tropical waters, and the red abalone (*Haliotis iris*) found in the Pacific. Other sources include Ceylon, California, and Japan. Each plate will vary in colour depending on its source, and the range includes black, pink, white, blue-green and green-yellow, while some are stained by the worker. The trade names for pearl were 'snail', the ordinary shell; 'Japanese', which was wavy and variable in colour; 'blue, green, or pink', which were the most expensive. The shell has to have its outer crust removed by abrasion or acids before the mother-of-pearl can be worked. It is then cut up to a millimetre (–$\frac{1}{16}$ in) thick and used as inlay or as part of a marquetry design in a similar fashion to wood veneers. It can also be engraved by covering with wax and incising the design onto the wax surface. An application of nitric acid will burn the shell to the design and, after washing, mastic can fill the engraved spaces of the design.

Mother-of-pearl was used during the Renaissance all across Europe, a splendid example being a bed bought by Francis I with 'marqueté à feuilages de nacre de perle' (Mercer, 1969, p.124). In England, the Earl of Northampton's inventory of 1614 listed: 'An ebony cabinett inlaid with mother-of-pearle' (*Archaeologia*, vol.42), and in the Tart Hall inventory of 1641 there was 'a large trunke of mother-of-pearl with two drawers' (Cust, 1911, p.100).

The taste continued into the 17th and 18th centuries across Europe. In the Netherlands marquetry incorporating the material was particularly made by Dirck van Rijswick, who, in the late 17th century, was famed for his floral mother-of-pearl inlays on black marble. In Germany it was particularly used for table tops, and from the early 17th century, the cabinet-maker Sommer used mother-of-pearl to great effect as a contrast to pewter and other metals. The Berlin cabinet-makers, the Spindler brothers, worked in mother-of-pearl marquetry during the 1760s, whilst the Italian cabinet-maker Piffetti used mother-of-pearl for specialized marquetry effects. Mother-of-pearl was also prominent as chest ornament in conjunction with bone and ivory, as well as sometimes being combined with tortoiseshell in English Boulle work.

In the 19th century, mother-of-pearl was again used to contrast with the fashionable darker woods in French furniture of the 1840s. In English papier mâché furniture of the 19th century, mother-of-pearl is commonly associated with the work of Jennens and Bettridge, who in 1825 patented (Pat.no.5137) a method of fixing slivers of the material to the surface of paper mâché objects before the final varnishing process. The fashionable revivals of the mid 19th century in the USA, especially the Louis XVI revival, all used mother-of-pearl as a component of their designs. The spectacular use of the material was recorded in a bedroom suite made for the Takoor of Moore by Samuel and Co of Houndsditch, London, in 1883. The suite was completely veneered in mother-of-pearl and was appropriately exhibited at the London International Fisheries Exhibition.
See also Burgauté work

Digby, S. (1987), *The Mother-of-pearl Inlay Furniture of Gujarat*, Oxford: Oxford University Press.
Grun, H. (1963), *Perlmuttkunst in Alter and Neue Zeit*, Vienna.
Kisluk-Grosheide, D. (1997), 'Dirck van Rijswick (1596–1679), a master of mother-of-pearl', in *Oud Holland*, 111, 2, pp.77–94.
Ritchie, Carson (1974), *Shell Carving*, Cranbury, New Jersey: Barnes and Co.

Moulding machines
See Machines

Moulding-planes
See Planes

Mouldings

A distinction is made between mouldings in solid work which move into the panel from the frame edge, and applied mouldings which stand proud of the frame. Descriptions of mouldings are based on the following nomenclature: 'st(r)uck' when worked in the solid or 'planted' when added afterwards: 'bolection' when laid to cover the joint between two surfaces at differing levels, for example a joint between a panel and frame: 'bedded' when laid in a groove.

The use of mouldings is generally decorative but they have a very early origin as most designs were based on prototypes established by Classical architecture. Originally they were cut into solid wood, but with the advent of panelled construction they could also be applied. The application of decorative mouldings to carcase furniture, ranging from a simple cock bead to a drawer front through to an elaborate built-up cornice, meant that techniques of producing mouldings changed in relation to prevailing styles. Mouldings were usually applied in two forms: In one case they were built up on a backing of inferior wood; alternatively they were produced as a composite of sev-

82 *The wave moulding machine was developed in the late 17th century. This later-18th-century French model is based on the same principle. A template fits under the workpiece for the cutter to follow the shape required.*

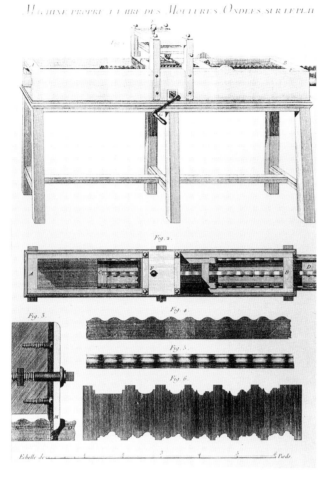

a mill in 1850 and saw four steam-driven moulding machines. He noted that 'whatever the pattern, the machine will cut at an average twelve feet per minute. A simple form thus prepared would occupy a skilled and quick mechanic one quarter of an hour' (Mayhew, 1850, Letter LXII, 25 July). In the mid 20th century, mouldings were generally cut by a spindle moulding machine. Two or more mouldings may be worked on differing faces at the same time with four-cutter and six-cutter machines.

TYPES OF MOULDINGS

Astragal
A semi-circular moulding often found on door fronts, especially in the doors of glazed cabinets and bookcases. It also refers to the tracery mouldings holding glass in cabinet doors.

Bead
A semi-cylindrical moulding either called recessed or cock. When the moulding is cut from the surface of the base material and remains flush with the surface, it is recessed; when it is fitted onto the surface, it is a cock bead.

Bed moulding
The moulding fitted into the space between a vertical surface and an overhanging horizontal surface or cornice.

Bolection moulding
A projecting moulding of ogee shape with an outward face used in the early 17th century to frame around panels, and then in the 18th century, was also used for larger-sized panels.

Channel moulding
A continuous groove or channel cut into or gouged out of a surface, to give a decorative effect. It was often used in conjunction with columns. Compare with FLUTING.

Housed moulding
A moulding that is glued in a rebate with a long and short shoulder to the frame.

Wave moulding
An undulating reeded moulding used in the 18th century, that resembles a wave motion. An early attempt at mechanizing what was initially a hand process was the wave-moulding machine. It mechanically produced an undulating reeded band by a process akin to copying a template model. This particular moulding was often executed in ebony, ivory or stained sycamore. Roubo described this machine and its companion, the channel-moulding machine (1774, Plates 313, 314). Moxon also described its operation:

as the rounds of the rack ride over the round edge of the flat iron, the rack and riglet will mount up the iron, and as the rounds of the waves on the underside of the rack slides off the iron on edge, the rack and riglet will sink and so in progression ... The riglet will on its upper side receive the form of several waves.
(1703, pp.106–7)

Wave, E. J. (1923), *Furniture Mouldings, Full-size Sections of Moulded Details of English Furniture from 1574 to 1820*, London: Benn.

Mountain ash
See Rowan

Mounts (Metal)
See Ormolu, Sheffield plate, Silver

eral simpler moulded shapes, thus offering a large variety of decorative possibilities, relatively simply. Indeed, the range of choice could be further extended by adding carving, contrasting veneer, tracery, inlay or even marquetry to the moulding surface.

The moulding tools were initially made by the cabinet-maker himself, but as the demand grew specialist moulding-plane-makers set up in business. The plane-maker was usually able to make any profile of cut to a customer's requirements, whilst the home-made SCRATCH STOCK or standard irons continued to be used for the more simple mouldings. The standardization of moulding-planes occurred around 1770, but this did not mean a limiting of variety. Examples quoted by Humell indicate that some American woodworking shops had as many as 143 varieties of moulding-plane in their tool collection (Kebabian and Lipke, 1979, p.50). See also Planes

Changes in taste affected moulding-plane use. Martin pointed out that 'cabinet-makers have but few moulding-planes, almost the whole of their mouldings have been formed with about a dozen pair of hollows and rounds. Since beading has been so much in fashion, planes for the purpose have been introduced' (1819, p.115).

Nevertheless moulding mills were established during the 1840s in England particularly to take advantage of Muir's 1827 patent mechanism and the abundant supplies of Canadian YELLOW PINE that was generally soft to work and free of knots. Henry Mayhew visited such

Mulberry (*Morus nigra*)
A timber introduced into Europe around the 10th century. It has an average density of 640 (40 lb/cu ft) and has a white to yellow sapwood with golden to reddish brown colouring with dark streaks in the heartwood, a coarse texture and an often irregular grain. Despite its reputation, it seems to have been little used for furniture. Evelyn wrote about the 'incomparable benefit of it … for its timber, durableness and use for the joiner and carpenter' (1662, p.110). Evelyn suggested its main use was in cask- and vessel-making. Loudon (1839) also confirms this usage. However, by 1913 it was described thus: 'The wood of the black mulberry is but yellow when fresh, but it acquires in the course of time a brownish-red tint. It takes a good polish and is often used for making furniture' (Elwes and Henry, 1913).

Indian mulberry (*Morus laevigata*)
An Indian timber with an average density of 720 (45 lb/cu ft), it is hard, close grained and darkens on exposure. It has been used for carving and turnery. Howard considered that 'it deserves to be better known and more widely used as a cabinet wood' (1920, p.162). It was made up into 'art furniture' for display at the 1924 British Empire Exhibition.

White mulberry (*Morus alba*)
An Asiatic timber considered suitable for furniture by Roubo, but little used being grown principally to supply silkworm food. The French writer Bergeron recommended the white mulberry, which he described as very similar to elm but very close in the grain and suitable for furniture and turning (Holtzapffel, 1846, 1, p.94).

Muninga (*Pterocarpus angolensis*)
An East African timber with an average density of 620 (39 lb/cu ft). It is reddish brown with streaks of golden red or yellow, with a medium texture and an irregular grain. Used for high-class cabinet work and veneers in the 20th century. Aka BLOODWOOD.

Muntins
A term used in relation to panelled framing where the muntin is the vertical division and panel support in the main body of the work. Stiles are a specific type of muntins which form the outside frame of chests, often including the leg.

Muskwood (*Olearia argophylla*)
(a) A brownish yellow timber from the Australasian (especially Tasmania) silver-leaved musk-tree. It has BURRS at the butt end, which produce fine mottled effects highly prized for cabinet work and turnery. It was recommended for veneering fancy furniture and pianofortes in the early 20th century.

(b) (*Trichilia moschata*) A fragrant and resinous Jamaican timber. Aka ALLIGATOR wood.

Muslin
A lightweight open-textured cotton cloth of plain weave, with a very fine spun yarn, originally imported from India in the 17th century, but the later French and Swiss versions were more useful to the upholsterer. Muslin was used for curtains during the 17th century and took over from cambric, lawn and linen. Chambers defined it as 'a fine sort of cloth wholly cotton; so called, as not being base, but having a downy knap on its surface resembling moss … There are various kinds of muslins brought from the East Indies; chiefly Bengal' (Chambers, 1752). It was commonly used for inner curtains during the 19th century and occasionally as main curtaining up to the 20th century: 'When employed in the decoration of bedrooms, boudoirs etc., they [muslin curtains] should always have a transparent [sic] of coloured silk or white satin placed underneath' (Bitmead, 1949, p.35). The heavy, wide unbleached muslin is used for the inner or first covering on high-quality upholstery work.
See also Cambric, Dimity, Gingham

Mutenye (*Guibourtia arnoldiana*)
A Central African timber with an average density of 880 (55 lb/cu ft). It is yellow brown to reddish tinged with black streaks, moderately hard and heavy with an interlocked grain and an attractive figure. Used as a decorative veneer in cabinet-making and as a substitute for WALNUT in the later 20th century.

Myall (*Acacia pendula*)
A rich dark violet-brown Australian timber with an average density of 1200 (75 lb/cu ft). Known since *c*.1845, it has been used for veneers, fancy boxes and other such uses, and by 1920 was noted as 'an ornamental wood much prized by cabinet-makers and turners' (Howard, 1920, p.162).

Myrtle
Pacific or Californian myrtle (*Umbellularia californica*): A North American timber with an average density of 600 (38 lb/cu ft). It is golden brown to yellowish green, with a straight, occasionally irregular grain, a firm texture and distinct rays. It produces mottled and swirling stumpwood clusters and burrs, so is used for fine inlay and veneering. Soaked logs can produce the so-called 'black myrtle'. Aka ACACIA, Mountain laurel or Pepperwood.

Tasmanian myrtle (*Nothofagus cunninghamii*)
A Tasmanian timber with an average density of 720 (45 lb/cu ft). It is a salmon-pink to brown colour, hard, heavy and very tough. Its smooth, close grain made it suitable for all kinds of furniture work. In the early 20th century it was 'much employed by cabinet-makers for various articles of furniture. Occasionally planks of it are obtained of a beautiful grain and figure, and when polished its highly ornamental character is sure to attract attention' (Spon, 1901, p.148). Not a true myrtle.

Nailing
A method of fixing timber, textile, leather or other materials, using nails, to frames either for a practical and/or a decorative effect. Although generally associated with upholstery and decorative finishes, nails were widely used in cabinet-making both in early slab construction and later factory work.
See also Construction, Driving bolt

Close nailing
An upholstery technique widely used in the 18th century, which was both a decorative finish as well as a practical fixing for the top covers of chairs. The gilt or brass nails were fitted close together with no gap between them, and often followed the outline of the frame.

Double nailing
A method of decorative nailing used in the 18th century in conjunction with upholstery, which employed two rows of nails. Chippendale suggested that certain chairs 'are most commonly done with brass nails in one or two rows and sometimes the nails are done to imitate fretwork' (1762, p.3).

83 *A mid-17th-century English side-chair showing the leather seat and nailing pattern which was both practical and decorative.*

Secret nailing

A nailing method which hides the nail under a gouged piece of wood that is not severed but glued back after the nail has been punched in.

Triple nailing

A decorative method of fixing leather or other fabrics using three rows of brass nails, sometimes in a pattern.

Nails

The use of nails in connection with woodwork is an example of very early methods of fixing. Bronze pins or nails were used in Egypt as early as the Old Kingdom to fix copper or gold foils to furniture frames. Roman iron clavus nails were made by hand, using nail rods which remained the basis of nail making until the 18th century. The rods were cut to size, the heads were rounded by hammering and the stems were usually irregularly tapered with a point. The nail-maker partly cut through the rod and put the point in a predetermined hole in a swage block. Then he broke off the rod through the partial cut and hammered the projecting end so that it spread and formed a head. Once cooled, the nail would easily come out of the block. They were sometimes finished for decorative reasons or as a prevention against staining.

In the Middle Ages gilded, silvered or tinned nails were used, and later varnished finishes were applied. In July 1692 John Reynolds charged Knole 'for new fileing 300 and ½ of the old nails at 2s & 6d p. hundred and varnishing them' (Beard, 1997, p.295). Nails were customarily sold by weight or price. In 1764 Samuel Norman had in stock 'sixpenny trunk nails, sixpenny clout nails, fourpenny ditto, threepenny ditto, two penny ditto, half inch brads, inch ditto and inch and half ditto' in quantities measured in thousands (Kirkham, 1969, p.508).

By 1800 cut nails were made by machine. Ezekiel Reed patented the process in America in 1786, and in England Thomas Clifford patented his method in 1790 (Pat.no.1785). Initially these machine-made blanks were hammer-headed, which was a hand operation, but they were soon 'headed' by machine also. In these cases the tapered nail was cut from a sheet, and then the nail was clamped and hit with a hammer to make the head. By 1825 the cut-nail machine combined the operations of cutting and making heads. The distinction between the two is that the handmade nail has a taper on all four sides, whilst the machine-cut nail only has a taper on two sides. By the mid 19th century the machine-made round steel wire nail appeared and the process was fully mechanized.

See also Tacks

Brads

A wedge-shaped nail with a slight projection on one side used in joinery and cabinet-making. Sheraton lists joiners' brads, flooring brads, batten brads, bill brads and quarter brads (1803, p.93).

Brass nail

Upholstery nails with heads 6–20 mm (¼–¾ in) in diameter. Early examples from the 16th century were cast in one piece with a square-shaped tapered shaft, and this remained the method until manufacturing developments in the latter part of the 19th century made them from wire shanks and stamped heads.

Initially used for nailing leather to wooden chests, by the 18th century they were used for decorative finishes often in two or three lines (double or triple nailed). In addition to outlining frames upholstered with fabric alone, they were also used to fix braids, fringes and other trimmings. The inventory of the business of Bastard's of Blandford (1731) lists 'about 20 thousand of brass nails for coffers and coaches and chairs ye means 4s, [total] £4.0s.0d' (Legg, 1994, p.32).

Bullen (Bullion) nail

Large gilded or silvered copper nails used to finish upholstery. In 1637 Ralph Grynder invoiced Queen Henrietta Maria for '350 large bullen nayles for the couche chears & stooles at 9s a hundred' (Beard, 1997, p.289). By the 18th century they were described as 'nails with round heads, and short shanks, lined and lacquered … used in hanging rooms, setting up beds, covering of stools, chairs, couches, desks, coffins, &c.' (*The Builders' Magazine*, 1774, p.92).

Copper pin nail

A small tack-like nail used for fixing cloth and trimming in 18th-century upholstery.

See also Gimp pins, below

Cut clasp nail

A rectangular section nail 2.5–15 cm (1–6 in) long used for a strong grip, especially for panelling work.

Gimp pins

Small thin coloured nails used for PASSEMENTERIE attachment. Known in the 18th century as copper pin nails, they are today made from fine cut steel.

Nickel-headed pins or imitation screws
Short nails with a countersunk or rounded head cut with a slot to look like screw heads. Used in cheap work.

Panel pins
Thin round nails of 1.25–6 cm (½–2½ in) long, made from bright steel or occasionally brass. Small bright steel nails have been used to fix light plywood and hardboard to carcases and frames.

Prince's metal nails
Prince's metal was an alloy of three parts copper to one of zinc giving a gold colour. Chippendale used '5,080' prince's metal nails in his 1760 commission for Sir William Robinson for eight large elbow chairs (Gilbert, 1978, p.142).

Rose-head nails
Hand-made nails have been referred to as rose headed on account of the petal effect of the hammered head.

Round wire nails and lost-head round wire nails
Machine-made nails for case making and cheap assembly.

Stucco nails
Large nails with round brass heads with points 2.5–25 cm (1–10 in) long 'necessary in fixing large looking glasses' (Sheraton, 1793, p.273).

Veneer pins
Similar to panel pins but even thinner in size (like wire) with clumped heads. Used for securing veneer during the process of laying veneers with cauls.

The term Nail is also a traditional needlework measurement of approximately 5.5 cm (2¼ in).
See also Tacks

Bodley, H. (1983), *Nail Making*, Shire Albums: Princes Risborough.
Bradley-Smith, H. R. (n.d.), *Chronological Development of Nails, Blacksmith and Farriers' Tools at Shelburne Museum*, no.7. c.1966.

Narra (*Pterocarpus indicus*) (USA)
See Amboyna, Padouk

Needles
Upholsterers have always used needles as an integral part of their furnishing practice. A range of specialist needles have been developed for particular applications, including 40 cm (16 in) needles for tufting mattresses, 21 cm (8–9 in) regulating needles, 15 cm (6 in) needles ideal for quilting and stitching, whilst a range of common sewing needles are used for joining materials. Curved or bent needles, either single or double pointed, are used for sewing rolls and backs, as well as for sewing gimps, passementeries and so on to covers. In addition, special curved spring needles are used for upholstery work. In 1649, Randle Holme specifically mentioned the specialist 'pack or matting needles made of iron or steel with a long eye bending upwards at the point, the bottom side is flat and the bending side round' (Book iii, v, p.273).
See also Regulator

Needlework (Embroidery)
Embroidery is a term that refers to the processes and methods of applying decorative needlework to a textile ground or animal skin by an EMBROIDERER. The range of threads, stitches and patterns is very wide and the processes have a 4000-year history. Embroidery was initially used in furniture work for portable items such as table covers,

cushion and pillow covers. As embroidery is an embellishing process, which increases the luxuriousness of the work, it is not surprising that it was highly valued, and when showing signs of wear would be re-used in other situations. APPLIQUÉ was one of the early uses which reworked valuable embroidery.

In the 16th century BLACKWORK was popular, but by the beginning of the 17th century CREWEL embroideries were most frequently encountered. An example from Hardwick Hall (1601) gives an indication of quality: 'a tester bedes head and double vallans of black velvet imbrodered with silver gold and pearle with sivines and woodbines fringed with golde silver and black silk' (Boynton, 1971, p.24). The range of stitches used and types of work produced in the 17th century are indicated in the following lines:

For Tente-worke, Raisd-worke, Laid-work, Frost-worke, Net-worke
Most curious Purles, or rare Italian Cut-worke
Fine Ferne-stitch, Finny-stitch, New-stitch and Chain Stitch,
Braue Bred-stitch, Fisher-stitch, Irish-stitch, and Queen Stitch
All these are good and these we must allow
and these are everywhere in practice now.
(John Taylor, *The Needles Excellency*, 1634)

By the 17th century wool needlework on canvas became the fashion, and it was often seen as a woman's duty to supply needlework for chairs either for upholstered seats and backs or for drop-in seats (see Plate V). During the 18th century ready-made kits were available for this purpose. Saint Aubin mentions that 'some merchants in shops selling chairs and sofas, have canvas on hand on which shaded designs are already embroidered. Only the background remains to be filled in to amuse those who do not wish to expend much effort' (1770). In Bath, for example, 'the Matrons of the City, their daughters and their maids [were] flowering the [coarse FUSTIAN] with Worsted, during the intervals between the Seasons to give the Beds a gaudy Look' (Wood, 1742, vol.2, pp.3–4).

During the 18th century embroidery and needlework were variously used for upholstery and bed-hangings, including some imported embroidery from India and the Far East (for example, 1720 State bed, Erthig). Embroidering naturalistic flower motifs on plain satin grounds in the later 18th century was popular for bed furniture or for occasional pieces, such as pole screens. In the early 19th century a taste for embroidery in satin stitch with coloured silks or metal thread for the backs of sofas and loose cushions was evident. The work was carried out on velvet or plain silk, often in classical motifs.

In the 19th century, BERLIN WOOL-WORK was introduced, and from the mid 19th century revivals of traditional methods were encouraged so that embroidery returned to favour with a wide range of designs, methods and techniques being introduced or re-introduced as 'work for ladies', or as examples of Arts and Crafts philosophy.

See also Appliqué, Berlin wool-work, Chenille, Crewel work, Embroiderer, Gros point, Knots, Passementerie (Purl), Petit point, Quilting, Stitches and stitching especially Flame stitch, Stumpwork, Turkeywork

Bridgeman, Harriet and Drury, Elizabeth (1978), *Needlework: An Illustrated History*, London: Paddington Press.
Caulfield, S. and Savard, B. (1882), *The Dictionary of Needlework*, London.
Clabburn, P. (1976), *Needleworkers' Dictionary*, London: Macmillan.
Digby, G. W. (1963), *Elizabethan Embroidery*, London: Faber.
Edwards, Joan (1975), *Crewel Embroidery in England*, London: Batsford.
Morris, Barbara (1962), *Victorian Embroidery*, London: Barrie and Jenkins.
Saint-Aubin, C. G. de. (1770), *Art of the Embroiderer*, Paris, trans. N. Schuer, Los Angeles: Los Angeles Museum, 1983.
Swain, Margaret (1970), *Historical Needlework*, London: Barrie and Jenkins.

Neo-Classicism
A style that was a reaction to the ROCOCO, developing *c.*1750 and which was based on archaeological discoveries in Greece and Rome in association with the interest inspired by the Grand Tour. The simpler geometric forms, and classical ornament supposedly reflected a sober and rational change from the whimsical Rococo. It was particularly associated with France and England. In France neo-Classicism moved from the Louis XVI style and the highly sophisticated ébénistes of that period through the Directoire to the Empire style. In England it was Robert Adam and George Hepplewhite that were particularly associated with the style. By the end of the 18th century, a sophisticated and francophile interpretation of neo-Classicism was promoted by Henry Holland and Thomas Sheraton, which was eventually to become the REGENCY style.
See also Federal, Ormolu, Satinwood

Nettletree
See Hackberry

Nettle wood (*Celtis australis*)
A Mediterranean timber which is yellow, heavy and hard. It resembles SATINWOOD and was used in the 19th century for furniture, carving and musical instruments. Loudon commented that 'when it is cut obliquely across the fibres, it very much resembles satinwood. It is principally used for furniture and by sculptors in wood' (1844, p.1415).

Nickel plating
A metal treatment and an alloying element. Nickel is used as a protective and ornamental coating for metals that are susceptible to corrosion. The nickel plate is deposited by electrolysis in a nickel solution on to metals like iron and steel, to give a highly polished finish. It is particularly associated with German tubular steel furniture of the mid to late 1920s.

Nigerian cedar
See Agba, Guarea

Nigerian pearwood
See Guarea

Nigerian satinwood
See Ayan

Nitro-cellulose
See Lacquer (Synthetic lacquer)

None-so-pretty
See Passementerie

Norwich work
See Turkeywork

No-sag springs
See Springs

Nutmegwood
Another name for PALMYRA WOOD. In 1774, Chippendale supplied Burton Constable with 'a very neat pembroke table of Nutmeg wood cross banded with white' (Gilbert, 1978, p.280).

Nutwood
Alternative name for HAZEL wood.

Nylon
See Plastics (Nylon-polyamide)

Oak (*Quercus spp.*)
One of the most important timbers in the history of furniture-making. Oak has been a specific and a more general description of a number of timbers (see below). Although used for centuries in the solid for all types of furniture-making by carpenters, joiners and cabinet-makers, oak has also been used by cabinet-makers either as a base for veneering or in the veneer form itself. The most important in furniture-making have been the European and American oaks.

European oak (*Quercus petraea*)
A hard, heavy wood with an average density of 600–700 (40–45 lb/cu ft). Its timber varies from creamy-white to dark brown depending on the source. Distinctions between English oak and imported oaks must be made, as differing conditions affect the timber. The British oak being heavier and stronger than continental versions, it was more often used for construction than for furniture-making, so it is not surprising to find that furniture and panelling were often made from imported, frequently Baltic timbers. These timbers would come in a range of colours, often light-tan to biscuit in colour, and they were usually of high-quality, free of knots, with a fine grain and a mild character. Prussian timber was often darker brown in colour with a fine 'silver grain'. The characteristic silver ray effect on quartered surfaces was due to broad medullary rays that were revealed by RIVING, or later quarter-sawn conversion methods.

The trade in imported oak has been long established. References to timber imported into England can be found as early as 1253 (Chinnery) and by 1662, John Evelyn wrote of English oak that it was 'of much esteem in former times till the finer grain'd Norway timber came amongst us which is likewise of a whiter colour. It is observed that oak will not easily glew to other wood, nor not very well to its own kind' (Evelyn, 1662, p.108). In the 16th and first half of the 17th centuries oak was amongst the most common furniture woods. William Harrison said 'Nothing but oak was any whit regarded' (cited in Wolsey and Luff, 1968, p.21). The trade continued to be important, as Sheraton confirmed: 'the oak used by cabinet-makers is imported from Russia, Norway, Sweden, and the United States of Holland, some in logs, and some cut into various thicknesses' (1803, p.276). When riven or quarter-sawn, these imported boards were called wainscots or clapboards.

Early-19th-century taste for English oak was reflected in the *Repository* which noted of a pier table that 'the plinth and margins … of the oak transversely cut and highly polished, … in splendour rivals the foreign woods' (Ackermann, August 1818, Plate 98). Imports continued in the 20th century and large quantities were received for furniture-making from Czechoslovakia (known as Austrian oak) as well as Baltic, Dantzig, Odessa and Adriatic oaks.

American red oak (*Quercus rubra*)
A Canadian and North-eastern USA timber with an average density of 770 (48 lb/cu ft), a whitish sapwood and a pink- to red-brown heartwood, used for both veneer and solid construction. Red oak was much used by American furniture-makers in the 17th century, not least because it was easy to plane and rive: in New England the conversion of oak was nearly always based on RIVING, which was a benefit in both ease of conversion as well as in its resistance to warping. Although it

was soon recognized in the 17th century that red oak would be a valuable export timber, the problems of decay on the long sea-voyage precluded this trade until well into the 19th century, when eventually it was exported in large quantities. By the beginning of the 20th century, the quantity of oaks shipped from Canada and USA exceeded any others. Although not comparable to the figure and colour of British oak, the imported timber has been used extensively in non-show-wood areas of 20th-century cabinet work.

American white oak (*Quercus alba*)
An oak variety sourced in Eastern USA and South-eastern Canada. Similar to the European oak (*quercus robur*), especially in respect to working properties and grain, it has a yellow-tan to reddish tone. This oak has a very obvious ray formation and can be distinguished from red oak by the tylosis that is present. Riven white oak was used in American furniture in the 17th century, although red oak was the more popular. In the 20th century white oak has been used as quarter-sawn and rotary cut veneer.

Australian silky oak (*Cardwellia sublimis*)
A timber with a light pinkish-brown colour, a close grain and wavy figure, it is usually cut on the quarter to reveal prominent rays. 'Silky Oak' is coarse, even textured with a straight grain, but it is not a true oak. It is good for steam bending but is most often encountered as veneer in furniture.

Bog oak
See Bog oak

Botany bay oak
Knight says this 'forms very beautiful furniture. The ground is an uniform brown with large dark blotches' (1830, p.179). He identifies it separately to BEEFWOOD.

Brown oak
A colour change caused by a fungal attack by *Fistfulina hepatica*, sometimes known as 'foxiness', rendering the heartwood a darker shade which is often a rich reddish brown. This can occur in most species of the oak. It was much sought after in the 19th century so that 'even when in a state of decay, or in its worst stage of foxiness, the cabinetmaker prizes it for its deep red colour and works it up in a variety of ways' (Laslett, 1894, p.96).

Green oak
Oaks which are attacked by the fungus *Chlorosplenium aeruginosum* have weakened timber, but provide a bright greenish-blue wood which could be used for veneer and inlay, especially in TUNBRIDGE WARE.

Grey oak
Oak timber that has been treated with sulphate of iron.

Japanese oak (*Quercus mongolica*)
First introduced to the West early in the 20th century, it has an average density of 650 (41 lb/cu ft). The wood is a pale biscuit colour with a straight grain. Large quantities of this timber were used before World War II in cheaper British furniture manufacture. It was also especially suitable for post-World War II tastes for effects such as silver-grey oak, 'Jacobean oak', limed oak, fumed and golden oak.

Turkish oak (*Quercus cerris*)
Variety found in Asia Minor. Numerous rays give a very showy figure.

WAINSCOT
A name for quarter-cut European oak which has a showy surface pattern and is usually straight and true. The origin of the word is probably in the Dutch word *wagenschot* (a wagon shaft) or possibly from the Dutch *waeg schot* (a wall covering or defence). Although wainscot has been used to describe all oaks, it was initially used to refer to high-quality wood, but was soon commonly used for referring to the imported oak timbers from the Baltic countries during six centuries of importation. Inventories often specify furniture as being made from wainscot: for example, Margaret Haward of Writtle, Essex, had 'a pair of wainscot drawers' (Steer, 1969, p.264) and an Essex inventory from 1663 lists 'one wainscott chair' (Steer, 1969, p.95). From the 17th century it also referred to wall panelling itself, probably because oak was the most favoured material for this purpose. It survives today as 'wainscoting' although this has now diminished to a small (usually softwood) timber band around the base of walls.

See also Fumed oak

Chinnery, V. (1979), *Oak Furniture*, Woodbridge: Antique Collectors Club.

Obeche (*Triplochiton scleroxylon*)
A tropical West African hardwood introduced in the 20th century. It has an average density of 380 (24 lb/cu ft) and is creamy-white to pale straw yellow, with a moderately fine to even texture and an interlocked grain which often gives a faint stripe on quartered sections. It is soft and light, fairly durable, easy to work and takes stain and polish well. If exposed to iron compounds under moist conditions, blue stains appear which are valued for marquetry work. In the 20th century it has been extensively used for plywood and interior joinery, especially drawer linings and shelves in furniture.

Offset hinge
See Hinges (Necked or offset)

Ogeche (*Brosium alicastrum*)
A yellowish-brown hardwood from South America with a close even grain. Similar to maple in appearance and used for veneers and cabinet-making during the 20th century.

Oil gilding
See Gilding

Oils
Viscous liquids derived from seeds or nuts have long been used in furniture finishing. The main oils used in furniture work are known as drying or fixed oils (that is, convertible into solids by absorbing oxygen when exposed in thin films) or the essential oils which readily vaporize. The drying properties can be increased by heating or boiling; for example, boiled LINSEED OIL. In some cases they have been applied directly, whilst in others the oils are part of particular recipes. See Polish, Tung, Varnish

Ingle, E. (1915), *A Manual of Oils, Resins, and Paints for Students and Practical Men*, London: C. Griffiths and Co.

Oil stain
See Stains

Olive
A shaped piece of wood the size of an olive. In the 18th century they were covered with fabric and used to fasten upholstery: William France supplied '4 Olives to tye back the curtains [of a bedstead]' to Sir Lawrence Dundas in 1764–5 (Beard, 1997, p.307). More recently the

term refers to a wooden button inserted to hide a screw or bolt in a hole, often in a show-wood chair frame.

Olive ash
See Ash

Olivewood
European olivewood (*Olea europaea*)
A hard, close-grained timber with an average density of 920 (58 lb/cu ft). It has a yellowish-green colour with wavy mottled figure and is hard, heavy and very smooth. It was used for veneers and parquetry in the late Stuart period and into the 18th century. Due to its relatively small size it was ideal for OYSTER veneers. By the early 20th century it was still used for veneers and thin boards for boxes.

East African olivewood (*Olea hochstetteri*)
A timber from Kenya with an average density of 880 (55 lb/cu ft). It is a pale brown timber with grey-brown and black streaks which create a marbled effect. It has a fine texture and an even, lightly-interlocked grain and has been used for furniture and turnery during the 20th century.

Opepe (*Nauclea diderrichii*)
A West African timber with an average density of 740 (46 lb/cu ft). It is a decorative orange to copper-brown colour with an interlocked grain and a coarse texture. The vivid colour and figure make it a useful veneer.

Orangewood (*Citrus aurantium*)
A yellowish white timber, indigenous to southern Europe but widely cultivated, which is hard, heavy and tough. The small size limits its use to fancy work. It has been occasionally used for stringing in the 17th and 18th centuries as well as for main surface and inlay work in German and Scandinavian furniture.

Oregon pine
See Douglas Fir

Orham wood
A Canadian species of ELM often called rock elm, which is coarser than English elm. The name is probably a corruption of the French word for elm: *orme*.
See Elm (American)

Oriental wood
See Walnut (Australian or Queensland)

Ormolu
An English term that is now a generic name for gilded BRASS or BRONZE mounts. The name is derived from the French *bronze doré d'or moulu* meaning bronze gilded by the mercury GILDING process. In the 19th century ormolu also referred to an alloy of copper, zinc and tin, which produces a 'gold-colour' metal used for furniture mounts.
See Gilding

Gentle, Rupert and Feild, Rachel (1975), 'The genesis of English ormolu', in *Connoisseur*, CLXXXIX, June, pp.100–15.
Goodison, Nicholas (1974), *Ormolu: The Work of Matthew Boulton*, London: Phaidon.

Orrice
See Passementerie

Osiers
Flexible twigs of the WILLOW tree which is grown especially for basketry.

Overlays
(a) Prepared materials that are laid on and not in a surface. These would include IVORY, MARQUETRY, MOSAIC and FRETWORK, all of which may be applied to a carcase.

(b) The term also applies to bedding such as quilts and duvets.

Overstuffing
A thick upholstery padding that extends over the frames of chairs and sofas, and blurs the outline of the inner frame. From the mid 19th century, thick overstuffing became a feature of upholstery design, initially reflecting price and status.

Oxidizing
A finish (copper and silver were the most popular) made by producing oxides (metal salts) on metal surfaces for fittings and other metal furnishings. Articles were usually plated with a cyanide solution to give a thin copper deposit. The article was then covered with a solution of ammonium, potassium or sodium sulphate, after which it was rinsed and dried. A variety of brown, grey or black finishes were achieved. The effects can be imitated by applying bronze powder (or other metallic) in varnish, bronzing liquid over black (or other colour) japan, and then baking.

Oystering
A form of VENEERING which uses thin slices (*c.*1.5 mm/$\frac{1}{16}$ in) of branch wood from trees such as OLIVE, LABURNUM, MULBERRY or WALNUT. They are then laid side by side on the surface to be covered in such a way that they create a pattern of circles. First used in Holland, the process was introduced to England in the later 17th century. Variations include the butterfly cut which slices the branches into veneers at a 45-degree angle, so creating elliptical shapes. The benefit of this angled version was not only visual; less exposed end grain made for more successful adhesion (see Plate III).

Padding
See Upholstery fillings

Padouk
African padouk (*Pterocarpus soyauxii*)
A Central and West African timber with an average density of 720 (45 lb/cu ft). It has blood-red heartwood that tones upon exposure to a dark purple-brown with red streaks, a coarse texture and a mixed grain. It is ideal for decorative veneers, high-class joinery and cabinet-making. Imported in the early 20th century, it is also widely known as a superior dye wood. Used in the USA as a furniture wood in the early 20th century.

Andaman padouk (*Pterocarpus dalbergioides*)
Sourced in the Andaman Islands, this hardwood has an average density of *c.*780 (49 lb/cu ft). It is a rich crimson to brick-red colour with occasional dark streaks. Its interlocked grain often produces a roe or striped figure on quartered surfaces, while its texture is medium to coarse. It is hard to work, but finishes cleanly. Used in the 18th century for high-quality chairs and commonly called ROSEWOOD. Used for high-class joinery and billiard tables, while selected logs, especially root boles, are converted into decorative veneers. Aka Narra and VERMILION WOOD.

Burma padouk (*Pterocarpus macrocarpus*)
Sourced in Burma and Thailand since the mid 1850s. The timber has an average density of 880 (55 lb/cu ft). It is orange-red to brick-red, streaked with darker lines but matures to golden reddish-brown. It has a coarse texture and interlocked grain. Used for billiard table frames, high-class joinery and quartered decorative veneers. Some trees offer a narrow broken and mottled striped figure which is very ornamental. Used in the USA for furniture in the early 20th century as vermilion wood or East Indian mahogany. Aka Narra.

See also Amboyna, Maidou, Manchineel and Rosewood

Painted satin
See Satin

Painted silk
Originally an imported fabric used as a wall-hanging, it was later an upholstery fabric, popular in England particularly between 1790 and 1810. A delicate effect was achieved by using water-colour paints on a plain silk fabric. They were usually made into panels for chair seats and backs, or for small furniture items such as fire screens. Hepplewhite suggested that medallions of printed or painted silk might be used for circular-backed chairs (1794, p.3), and Sheraton noted painted silks in his *Drawing Book* (1791–4), particularly describing the 'printed and painted silks executed of late by Mr Eckhardt, at his manufactory in Chelsea'. Around 1793, Eckhardt and Co had established a 'Royal patent manufactory of painted silk, varnished linen cloth, paper, etc' in London. In 1798 Francis and George Eckhardt patented various processes for this technique (Pat.no.2208).
See also Printed silk

Painted taffeta
Decorative designs painted upon TAFFETA cloth. The Duchess's dining room at Woburn had 'the chairs and sofas of painted taffeta' when Arthur Young visited in 1768 (Young, 1771, p.29).

Painted velvet
Painted velvet was a fashionable upholstery cover in the early 19th century. The practice of painting velvet has been called 'theorem painting', where the theorem is a STENCIL and the paint is made from water-colour and gum arabic. Ackermann illustrated a 'Dress Sofa' (January 1821, Plate 9), which was designed to have a printed white velvet covering. A little later Nathaniel Whittock considered 'the downy surface of the velvet and the brilliancy of the liquid colours used to produce fruit and flowers, [gave] it a decided superiority over any other kind of flower painting, for ornamenting bellropes, ottomans &c.' (Whittock, 1827). It was evident that painting on velvet was very much a pastime for women to provide decoration for the home. The *Elegant Arts for Ladies* (c.1856) suggested that stencilled designs on velvet would 'look very handsome [on] music stools, the front of pianos, ottomans, banner screens, pole-screens and borders for table cloths' (cited in Hodges, 1989, p.23).

Whittock, Nathaniel (1827), *The Art of Drawing and Colouring Flowers Fruits and Shells ... Painting on Velvet*, London: Isaac Taylor Hinton.

Painting
Paint is a coloured suspension in a base which is applied to surfaces and creates a film. Many formulae refer to paint products, including those based on water, oil, casein (soured skimmed milk) and tempera. It is one of the oldest techniques of furniture decoration and finishing, and has been used at various times ever since. Painted furniture can be simply divided into three major groups: The first uses furniture features as a surface upon which to represent images; the second decorates a surface with colour or pattern; the third is the use of paint in simulation of other materials. These very general groupings can be further divided between a small amount of fine painted decoration added to a cabinet, an all-over paint finish and combinations thereof.

Painted finishes for furniture have been known since ancient times and are therefore one of the earliest forms of furniture decoration. In Ancient Egypt the painted stool (using a tempera paint material) was a relatively common form of seating. In the Middle Ages, there are sporadic references to painted furniture during the 10th to 12th centuries and by the time of Henry III (1216–72) references to these items were often seen in Royal accounts. In the 15th century many famous Italian artists were employed as specialized painters of chests. The spectacular Florentine cassone represents the high point of Renaissance painted furniture. Apart from the high-style Renaissance work there was already a furniture painting tradition in Europe, a tradition that was to remain central to much vernacular furniture well into the 19th century. In this tradition, painted finishes served to disguise poor-quality timber and provided an opportunity to introduce some much-needed brightness into a room. The variety and styles of these finishes and their importance in enhancing common furniture with attractive patterns, simulations of high-quality materials (for example, tortoiseshell, marble, fine timber and so on), or simply with plain colour, are a necessary reminder that nearly all social groups wanted to enjoy attractive surroundings.

There was a clear taste for painted furniture during the first half of the 17th century both in large and small households. During the later 18th century there was a general revival of painted furniture. However, it was from the 1770s, in the high-style markets, that a taste developed for furniture made in light-toned woods such as HAREWOOD and SATINWOOD which featured delicate natural colourings or GRISAILLE work. Painted motifs (often produced by well-known painters such as Kauffmann, Zucchi and Pergolesi), sometimes in combination with marquetry, supplied the correct degree of delicacy, whilst the chosen designs often reflected the architectural features, wallpaper or printed textiles of a particular room. These were usually painted onto wood veneer, but were sometimes painted onto COPPER panels which were then fitted to furniture. Towards the end of the 18th century painted beechwood chairs in lampblack or grisaille were fashionable. Again there were degrees of painted finish. In some cases, paint would be applied onto veneer to create simple border designs, or in other cases the whole piece might be finished with a paint decoration. Hepplewhite noted that the tops of commodes may be of inlaid or painted satinwood (Hepplewhite, A. and Co, 1794, p.14).

By the early 19th century, Sheraton recorded how furniture painting was a specialism: 'The principle thing which constitutes this as a distinct branch of painting is the general use of size and varnish colours, by which it is performed with much greater dispatch and effort. Yet the prices allowed in the country, at least in many parts of it, are so poor, that the painter can hardly distinguish furniture from common oil painting' (1803, p.422). He also gives information on specific painting of rush-bottom chair-seats which should be built up by three priming coats using white lead ground in linseed oil, followed by coats of colour with Spanish white and a final top coat of colour in turpentine. Sheraton admonishes: 'They who use any kind of water colour for rush bottoms, [who] entirely deceive the purchaser, for it rots the rushes and by the sudden push of the hand upon the seat, the colour will frequently fly off' (op.cit., p.423). Sheraton also gives specific details of painting chairs either with a green or a black background as well as instructions on painting lines of decoration on chair frames.

Despite Sheraton's plea, the application of water-colour painted designs onto plain wooden surfaces became general. One of the problems associated with this type of painted furniture was spelt out in the section devoted to wardrobes in *Hints on Houses and House Furnishings* (1851). It was pointed out that 'in order to meet the great desire for cheapness cabinet-makers give a coat of size to such articles as they wish to paint and upon this a coat of water colour of any required shade'. The purpose of this process was to allow the colour to dry on the surface so that, when varnished, it appeared as good as japan. Only when the varnish wore off and the paint soon deteriorated, did the cheapness of the process reveal itself. According to the writer, this problem was particularly associated with common washstands.

Painted furniture of various types continued to be made, often being applied as a small decoration, but it was not until the commercial development of industrially applied lacquers and coatings in the early 20th century that painted surfaces became fashionable for complete furniture pieces.
See also Combing, Fancy chair-making, Graining, Japanning, Lacquer, Marbling, Stencils

Croney-Hawke, N. (1976), 'William Morris and Victorian painted furniture', in *Connoisseur*, 191, January.
de Dampierre, F. (1987), *The Best of Painted Furniture*, London: Weidenfeld.
Fales, D. (1972), *American Painted Furniture 1660–1880*, New York: Dutton.
Kirk, J. T. (1980–1), 'Tradition of English painted furniture', in *Antiques*, 117, May 1980, pp.1078–98, October 1980, pp.738–47, January 1981, pp.184–97.
Maufe, P. (1928), 'Modern painted and decorated furniture', in *Architectural Review*, 63, pp.32–5.
Painted Wood: History and Conservation (1998), Proceedings of a symposium organized by the Wooden Artefacts group of the American Institute for Conservation of Historic and Artistic works, 11–14 November 1994 at Williamsburg, Los Angeles: Getty Conservation Institute.
Rider Lea, Z. (1960), *The Ornamented Chair*, Rutland, Vermont: Tuttle.
Ritz, G. M. (1971), *The Art of Painted Furniture*, New York: Van Nostrand Reinhold (trans. from German).

Palampore
A single panel of mordant-painted, resist-dyed Indian cotton (chintz), similar to PINTADO. First introduced to England in the early 17th century (*c*.1614), they became increasingly popular during the century and were often made into quilts. They were also used in America during the 18th century.

Paldao (*Dracontomelum dao*)
A Philippines timber with an average density of 740 (46 lb/cu ft). It is grey-brown with a tinge of green, with irregular dark brown to black streaks similar to walnut, a medium texture and a variable grain. It is mainly converted into highly decorative veneers for high-quality furniture. Possibly the 18th-century 'Guiney wood' imported from Papua New Guinea.

Palissander
See Rosewood (Brazilian)

Palliasse
See Mattress

Palm
From the mid 19th century timber from palm trees was known variously as COCONUT, LEOPARD, NUTMEG, PALM, PALMYRA, and

PORCUPINE wood. In the early 20th century the *palmier* timbers were favoured by some French makers working in the Art Deco style, especially Printz and Legrain.

Palmyra wood (*Borassus flabelliformis*)
The wood of the Asian palm tree, especially those grown in Sri Lanka. It was used in TUNBRIDGE WARE since the end of the 18th century. According to Bitmead, the veneers 'when polished have a lapideous gloss and beauty, which rival those of agate' (1873, p.80).
See also Nutmegwood

Panacoco (*Robinia panacoco*)
A timber from French Guiana and Brazil. It has a black lustrous heartwood and is very compact and durable. Introduced in the 1870s, it was then considered a most valuable wood for cabinet work.

Panel
An important element in the CONSTRUCTION of panelled furniture, it was a loose board held in place by a framework of grooved stiles and rails. After the introduction of cabinet-making techniques it was less important, but panels remained a feature of joinery in parts of furniture-making, especially in the construction of backs. In the 20th century panel work was revived in factory-made furniture especially in conjunction with PLYWOOD.
See Construction

Panel saw
See Saws

Panelled construction
See Construction

Panelling
A method of letting in a veneer panel with or without a bordering STRING. Often simulated by inlaying strings in a flush surface. In the late 18th century panels were formed in a range of shapes by strings on frames of tables.

Panes
Widths of fabric of varying colours and weave, joined together or applied over another cloth in such a way as to create a framed effect, often to fit walls but also for upholstery coverings. Early records note the use of panes on curtains and hangings in the 16th century. In 1509, Edmund Dudley had 'vij paynes of course tapstree werk' in the Great Chamber (Beard, 1997, p.282). It became particularly fashionable from the mid 17th century. The inventory of Tart Hall in 1641 had the Great Chamber 'hanged with payned red and yellow damask hangings' (Cust, 1911, p.99). The process was known as paning.

Paper
A variety of papers are used by cabinet-makers and upholsterers for very different purposes, including packing, designing, decoration and assembly work. Large-sized roll paper, called cartoon paper, was used for full-size drawings in factory work. In the production department gummed paper tapes were used to join smaller veneers ready for assembly and application (see Tape joint), and newsprint was pasted to protect veneer work in the press or for gluing up and making up marquetry. For decoration, marbled papers have been used at least since the 18th century to line trays and drawers.

Amongst the most important has been cartridge paper. It was

widely used for packing and wrapping furniture in the 18th century as well as for preparing working drawings. In 1764–5 William France invoiced Sir Lawrence Dundas for 'Taking down the cartridge paper hangings from the Blue damask hangings in the Drawing room, and putting up in the long room, over the blue damask drawing room, to preserve the crimson damask hangings from the dust &c., while the floor is taken up and new laying' (Beard, 1997, p.307). Cartridge paper is sometimes called Whatman paper after a well-known maker, and has been used for working drawings and sketches well into the 20th century.
See also Lining

Paper birch
See Birchwood

Paper furniture
Paper has been used in applications such as CARDBOARD, LLOYD LOOM and PAPIER MACHE.
See also Cardboard, Papier mâché

Paperwork decoration
See Filigree

Papier mâché
A malleable, mouldable substance that has been used for a variety of furnishings and furniture in Europe since the 17th century. Papier mâché is a broad classification of five different, though related, processes. The first is the process that Clay patented. It consisted of pasted sheets of paper that were laid over variously shaped cores. This was found to be the best form for furniture as the moulds could be made from iron or brass, ensuring a consistent shape. The second variety was formed into thick sheets or boards by pressing paper pulp between dies. The resultant panels were generally flat and could be used in interior decoration, for bedstead ends, door panels or other flat cabinets. In addition, the panels were employed by the carriage-making trade. The process was further developed by pressing pulp into matrices to form a variety of shapes, especially suitable for architectural work. The third process consisted of making a fibrous slab from coarse fibres, earthy matter, chemical agents and cementing size. This mass was passed through rollers which produced a uniform board, which could then be finished and decorated like papier mâché. Carton Pierre was the fourth process. This was made from pulp paper mixed with whiting and glue, pressed into moulds, backed with paper, then hardened and dried. It was usually destined for use as architectural ornament. The fifth process was known as Ceramic papier mâché. This was made from paper pulp, resin, glue, drying oil and sugar of lead. The plastic material that resulted could be moulded into any form and was especially used for architectural decoration.

The origins of papier mâché can be traced to India and other parts of the Orient. An early use of the form is in pasteboard used in Germany, France and Italy in the 1580s, but the earliest mention of the material in England appears to be in Robert Boyle's essay *Of Man's Great Ignorance of the Uses of Natural Things*, published in 1672. In this work Boyle referred to the use of papier mâché as being suitable for 'frames of pictures and divers pieces of embossed work and other curious movables'. However, there is no evidence that the material was much used before the mid 18th century.

In 1749, William Duffour of Soho claimed to be the original maker of papier mâché and it has been suggested that his French surname may give some credence to the suggestion of others that the craft of papier mâché manufacture in Europe was first established in France. Eighteenth-century commentators like Robert Dossie refer to French snuff-boxes made from papier mâché, and in 1763 Peter Babel, a papier mâché worker, refers to his raw material as 'an invention of modern date, imported by us from France and now brought to great perfection'. According to Jean-Felix Watin, it was *c.*1745 that Guillaume Martin of the famous 'vernis Martin' lacquer process, improved papier mâché production to make small boxes which were varnished. Henry Clay is credited with producing papier mâché goods, including furniture, on a commercial scale in England. Clay was an apprentice of John Baskerville, a famous paper-maker and japanner from Birmingham who had experimented with paper panels. In 1772 Clay took out a patent (Pat.no.1027) for making 'high varnished [paper] panels for rooms, doors, cabins of ships, cabinets, bookcases, screens, chimney-pieces, tables etc'. The panels were made by layering pasted paper sheets together in a mould, soaking them with linseed oil and then drying the pressed panels to form a rigid shape. In the early 19th century the hand-layered method was superseded by the manufacture of 'blanks', and later still the panels were made with up to 120 sheets of paper, layered to create a strong shape for furniture.

The ornamenting of papier mâché was an integral part of the process. One of the very earliest patented processes was taken out by John Skidmore in 1786, which was for: 'Ornamenting japan wares with foil stones, Bristol stones, paste, and all sorts of pinched glass, sapped glass, and every other stone, glass, and composition used in or applicable to the jewellery trade' (Pat.no.1552). This is a very early indication of the impending mid-19th-century penchant for inlay and glass decoration in papier mâché. Two more patents, one in 1809 by Charles Valentine (Pat.no.3219) for producing landscapes on japanned surfaces, and another in 1812 by Thomas Hubball (Pat.no.3593) which replaced pigments with coloured metallic ores, further developed the ornamenters' repertoire (see Plate X).

However, the name of Jennens and Bettridge, the successors to Clay's business, remains the most successful of the papier mâché manufacturers and ornamenters. The reason for their fame perhaps rests on their use of unusual materials to decorate the blank shapes.

84 *Papier mâché was employed in a wide variety of furniture for panels as well as for moulded objects. This English bedstead has panels decorated with mother-of-pearl and painted decoration, c.1851.*

Their patent of 1825 (Pat.no.5137) for 'preparing and working pearl-shell into various forms, applying it to ornamental uses in the manufacture of japan ware', signalled the most well-known phase of papier mâché furniture decoration. This was the so-called mother-of-pearl 'inlay'. In fact the process was not inlaid but rather applied to the surface and was fixed by layers of varnish. At the height of their success, Jennens and Bettridge were employing sixty-four men, solely as full-time decorators. In 1847 Jennens patented the technique of softening dry panels with steam so they could be mounted in a male/female mould and pressed into shapes and dried (Pat.no.11670). This process ensured large-scale batch production.

The importance of papier mâché as an applied decoration and carving substitute was confirmed in 1773, when John Pickering patented a method of making ornaments with paper to resemble wood carving for furniture applications (Pat.no.1058). In 1840 Charles Bielefeld noted 'that Papier mâché is applied to the enriched cornices of bookcases and cabinets, to the mouldings and corners ands centre ornaments of panelling [sic] on their doors and sides; to the enriched scroll legs of cabinets and pier tables in the old French style' (Bielefeld, 1840, p.6).

The taste for papier mâché had declined by the latter part of the 19th century and it was gradually abandoned. It was, however, revived for use during World War II for pilots' bucket seats, glider wing tips, tail planes and such others. This led to a consideration of the material for shell chairs. Despite the introduction of quick-setting glues and heat sources to enable the shells to be produced rapidly, it was nevertheless unable to compete commercially with plastics.

Aitken, W. C. (1866), 'Papier mâché manufacture', in S. Timmins (ed.), *Birmingham Resources and Industrial History*, London: R. Hardwicke.
Bielefeld, C. F. (1840), 'On the use of the improved papier mâché in furniture', in *Interior Decoration of Buildings and in Works of Art*, London: The author.
DeVoe, S. (1971), *English Papier Mâché of the Georgian and Victorian Periods*, London: Barrie and Jenkins.
Dickinson, G. (1926), *English Papier Mâché, its Origin, Development and Decline*, London: Courier Press.
Lindsey, G. (1876), 'Papier mâché', in G. Philips Bevan (ed.), *British Manufacturing Industries*, London: Edward Stanford.
Reyden, D. van der and Williams, D. C. (1988), 'The technology and conservation treatment of a nineteenth century English papier mâché chair', in *Wooden Artifacts Group speciality session*, 1986, AIC Meeting, Chicago.
Toller, J. (1972), *Papier Mâché in Great Britain and America*, London: Bell.

Paradise wood
See Eaglewood

Paragon
From the French word *barracan*. A coarse worsted fabric, ribbed, printed or watered, used for hangings and upholstery from the 17th century to the mid 18th century. It can also be described as a double CAMLET. Well-known by the early 17th century, in 1684 'his Grace's dressing room' in Dublin Castle had curtains of yellow paragon with squab cushions of yellow damask covered with paragon protective covers (Clabburn, 1988, p.251). Whilst in 1693, William Lash of Suffolk County (USA) had 'Parragon curtains and vallaines and bedstead and curtain rods and testercloth' (cited in Montgomery, 1984, p.317). It was generally out of use by the mid 18th century, being usurped by HARRATEEN, MOREEN and DAMASK.

Paragone
A black flint used as a ground for Florentine mosaics and PIETRE DURE from the early 17th century. It was used in other factories including the Gobelins and Naples. Being a good foil, it was also often used in conjunction with polychrome stone compositions of floral design. Its use was revived in the mid 19th century for the same purpose.

Parana pine
See Pine

Parcel gilt
A medieval term that simply means partly gilded. Often applied to silver ware, it also refers to decorative furniture that has small amounts of gilding applied to detail as highlights.

Parchment
See Leather

Parnella wood
An unidentified timber, the making up of which was charged at 20 per cent over standard mahogany work in 1793 (*Cabinet-makers' London Book of Prices*, 1793, p.263).

Parquetry
A particular form of MARQUETRY in which the design is geometric and the elements of the marquetry are cut to reflect this. The earliest form might be oystering, which was popular in the late 17th century. In 18th-century French furniture, cube parquetry was especially popular as it gave a three-dimensional effect to surfaces. The terms *placage aux compartements* or *tarsia geometrica* and *frisage* refer to this method.

Particle board
A man-made board in which graded ligno-cellulosic particles (often wood, including forest waste, bough wood and thinnings) are bonded together with a synthetic resin. They are then processed by pressing on plates, by a continuous method or by extrusion under pressure to produce a stable board material suitable for veneering. It should be regarded in its own right and not seen as an inferior substitute for solid wood. Grades for various work include: standard, fine surface, superfine, paper-faced, melamine-faced and PVC faced. The major benefit for manufacturers of furniture is that the boards are non-directional, so that the movement problems associated with veneering on solid timber are avoided.

Particle board was developed in the late 1930s (Pfohl patent) and was commercially produced in Germany and Switzerland from 1941. It was introduced onto the British market from 1946–7, although it was not seen as a furniture material until the later 1950s. In 1955 Michael Sheridan noted that particle board, although used in panelling headboards and occasional table tops, was not considered suitable for carcase work at that time, and it was not mentioned in a 1956 English manual of contemporary cabinet design and construction. In comparison, German furniture manufacturers had established early on their own wood-chipping plants, in order to control the quality and supply of the product.

When particle board was introduced into furniture-making, it marked the beginning of a major change in the CONSTRUCTION of furniture as it used prepared panels supplied by outside merchants. Particle board is now a major part of furniture manufacturing. Its features of flatness, smoothness and freedom from warping, as well as dimensional stability, to say nothing of relatively reasonable cost, have ensured that it has been the basis of the mass market in cabinet furniture around the world (especially KD construction). Its applications have been extended beyond cabinet work in recent years. Its use in the making of UPHOLSTERY frames for inexpensive upholstery has been inevitable in terms of price consciousness.

Wood was not the only material used as a base for particle boards. The residue of linen preparation from flax was converted into flaxboard, and sugar-cane residue was made into BAGASSE board.

TYPES OF PARTICLE BOARD

Decorative
A finished board with either a veneer or laminate surface ready prepared.

Flake or wafer
A board with large shavings laid horizontally over each other, which produces a higher tensile strength than standard board.

Graded density
A board with a gradual change from the thicker core to the finer surface.

Oriented strand
A three-layered board with long strands of wood shavings layered in one direction, each outer layer being at 90 degrees to the other as in plywood.

Single layer
Boards with similar-sized particles throughout. Used as a base for veneer work.

Three layer
A board of coarse particles sandwiched between two outer layers of finer density, with a high resin content. Used when a smooth surface finish is required.

Akers, L. E. (1966), *Particle Board and Hardboard*, Oxford: Pergamon.
Anon. (1955), 'New uses for particle board', in *Art and Industry*, January, pp.16–21.
Mitlin, L. (1968), *Particle Board, Manufacture and Application*, Sevenoaks: Pressmedia Ltd.

Partridge wood (*Caesalpina granadillo*)
(a) A timber sourced in Venezuela, Brazil and Central America, with an average density of 1200 (75 lb/cu ft). The exposed heartwood is deep purplish red-brown, with a stripy to marble-like figure with a variable grain and a fine and even texture. The streaks sometimes resemble partridge feathers. It was used in the later 17th century for inlay and marquetry and in the later 18th century as a surface veneer. In the mid 19th century it was still recommended for cabinet work and turning. It was sometimes called CABBAGEWOOD and varieties were also distinguished as red, brown, black or sweet partridge (Holtzapffel, 1846, p.99). Aka Acapu, Granadillo, Maracaibo ebony.
See also Angelim

(b) A name for the speckled appearance of OAK wood attacked by a saprophytic fungus *Stereum frustulosum*.

Passementerie or **Passemaine**
The decorative trimmings associated with soft furnishings and upholstery. Passementerie was originally formed from the tying off of the warp ends on finished woven cloth. The fringes were knotted into patterns and it was soon clear that this decorative finish could be made to stand alone on its own heading. It also had practical applications as it could disguise joins in narrow fabric, creating a panelled effect. Its early use in upholstery work is confirmed by Elizabethan inventories which often list 'passamaine lace of gold' (Beard, 1997). Although passementerie was woven and sold by specialist dealers, it

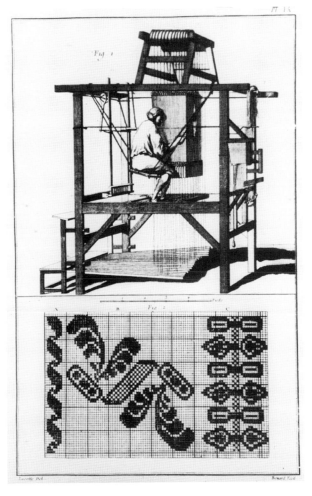

85 *A French passementerie loom and the squared paper pattern that was used by the weaver, c.1780.*

was also made by ladies as a pastime. For example, Gerrit Jensen supplied Queen Mary with '2 engines to make fringe'.

In the 18th century, passementerie was sold by specialist 'lace men'. The *London Tradesman* defined this trader as one who sold 'all sorts of gold and silver lace, gold and silver buttons, shapes for waistcoats, lace and networks for robeings and women's petticoats, fringes, bugles, spangles, plates for embroidery and orrice, and bone-lace weavers, gold and silver wire, purle, slesy, twist etc.' (Campbell, 1747, p.147). Styles of passementerie followed the vagaries of fashion but remained an integral part of the upholsterers' and decorators' repertoire. However, it was commercially acknowledged as a speciality of France. Diderot's *Encyclopédie* (pp.116–19) illustrates the special looms including the various wheels and bobbins.

The manufacture of passementerie is based on three stages: spinning, weaving and decorating. Spinning involves twisting yarns into stiff gimps or plied cords. The core of the trimming is made and then covered with coloured yarns. This process is worked by a large wheel and a tensioned bar which allows the threads to tighten and shorten as the wheel is turned. The weaving process can be simply a two-treadle loom. The warp forms the top of the fringe, while the weft can be pulled out to the required length of fringe. The bullion fringe has an additional twist inserted by the spinner so that it plies up the warp. A cut fringe is made similarly but without the extra twist. It is then cut after removing from the loom. Complicated designs can be made with twenty or more treadles for the warp operation. Gimped braids have a metal rod parallel with the warps, so that the gimp can be twisted round them to make projections at the sides. Any other decoration can then be sewn in.

BRAID

A woven trimming in the form of a band. Now generic, it was originally a narrow woollen tape used for binding or as the base for a more complicated trim. In the 17th and 18th centuries, references to lace often really referred to braid, as early examples were plaited on cushions in the manner of bobbin lace. Braid is usually used to emphasize shape or to cover seams.
See also Galloon, below

CORDS

The simplest of trimmings, often combined with tassels. They were made from a twisted cotton or worsted core, frequently with a silk wrapping. Various diameters of cord were used: the narrowest to cover seams, the thickest as tie-backs or swags for drapery. Cord was produced domestically or in factories using cord wheels which twisted the yarns. Cord is used to emphasize shapes and outlines or as an edging for appliqué.
Piping cord, see below

FRINGES

A decorative border of hanging threads and cords often employed on curtains to improve the drape. Early fringes appear to be simple forms hanging directly from a netted heading: later tasselled or tufted fringes were made from floss silk. An early indication of the wide range available was made by Randle Holme. Referring to bed valances in 1649, he listed bed fringes as 'Inch fringe, caul fringe, tufted fringe, snailing fringe, gimpe fringe with tufts and buttons and vellum fringe' (1905, iii, xiv, p.16). One hundred and fifty years later, Sheraton recorded that 'The French have now begun to use fringe at the bottom of their chair backs' (1803, pp.214–15). See specific types below.

Ball fringe
Made with a variety of sizes and details, but always including bobbles or balls.

Belladine fringe
Made from raw Levant silk. In 1735 Stephen Langley supplied to Chiswick House '170 ounces of the best fine green Baladine silk fringe cut, made wt [with] a broad head to be used to ye 10 chairs, 2 Saffoys and hangings' (cited in Beard, 1997, p.303).

Bullion fringe
Usually recognized by a thick twisted cord- or rope-like fringe of 8–30 cm (3–12 in) thickness. Cotton bullion fringe was chiefly used for bedroom furniture in the later 19th century.

Campaign fringe
Has small bell-like tufts. The name is an Anglicization of the French *campagne*.

German fringe
Made from white cotton of 4–8 cm (1.5–3 in) in width, used for trimming blinds and bed furniture.

Trellis fringe
Knotted in macramé fashion.

GALLOON

A narrow, closely woven decorative braid, tape or ribbon, made from wool, silk or cotton, combined with silk or worsted yarns. Produced in a wide range of widths, weights, textures and so on. Used in the 17th century to create a border for fabrics used on chair backs. Also used to cover edges and seams in gold or silver thread and silk.

GIMP

From the French word *guiper*, to wrap. Originally a cord wrapped with silk or cotton or worsted wool which made an open-work braid. Now an open-work trimming, made from silk, wool or cotton, often twisted with a cord or wire running through it. The strands are looped, plaited or twisted to make a pattern like wickerwork. More complex gimps include 'embassy', which is stiff and symmetrical for use in straight work, and 'shell', which is flexible and looser. It has been widely used as a finish to the edges of upholstery.

LACE

(a) A 16th-century term for ornamental BRAID. The term derives from the early method of plaiting braid on long cushions in the manner of bobbin lace. It was fixed onto upholstery in order to break up large areas of cloth by banding or bordering. It could be of silk, gold or silver thread. In the 19th century, American references to Coach or Broad Lace refer to braids about 5 cm (2 in) wide made from worsted, wool, or cotton and linen, often with a warp patterned design.

(b) An open-work textile often of linen or sometimes metal threads, first made in Italy and Flanders in the late 15th century. Lace is either needlepoint or pillow lace. The former is a type of embroidery developed from knotted nets (filet), open-work based on leno weave or drawnwork. However, needlepoint is made from a single thread and needle, whereas pillow lace is made from many threads wound on bobbins and twisted together in different ways. In the late 17th century the expensive Venetian needlepoint lace was usurped by the *point de France* technique which was used in place of the Venetian lace for interiors and drapery. This in turn was superseded by the lighter Argenton needle lace. Lace styles were often known by the place of origin, for example Alençon, Brussels, Nottingham and Venice.

By the mid 19th century machine-woven lace was being made in very large quantities, especially for curtains but also for a wide range of other furnishing decoration. In the *Workwoman's Guide* lace was recommended for bed decoration in conjunction with fringes as a border feature (1840, p.193). Lace has been in decline as a furnishing fabric since the mid 20th century.

NONE-SO-PRETTY

A small figured braid, tape or ribbon used on upholstery in the 18th century. London cabinet-maker Samuel Norman had in stock '12 pieces of nonsopretty' in 1764 (Kirkham, 1969, p.509). The colour-matching of these tapes to furniture coverings was required in some cases.

ORRICE

A braid woven in a variety of patterns from gold or silver threads used in the late 17th and early 18th centuries. By the 19th century it was a general term for all kinds of GALLOONS used in upholstery.

PIPING

The trimming of edges or seams by means of a fine cord enclosed in a tube-like, bias-cut sewn fold. At the end of the 17th century piping was used to accent cushions and edges and to outline the forms of upholstery work. Later it was used to link seams in leather and cloth. Piping cord is the basis for folded tapes over French seams, as well as cords stitched directly to the seam. The cord is made from cotton or compressed paper fibres which give a firmer edge.

PURL

A decorative trimming made from fine gold or silver or wire tightly bound in silk covering, coiled round a thin rod and pushed off to form a flexible tube for use with embroidery. Used in the 16th and early 17th centuries.

RUCHE

A narrow trimming material with running stitches along its length which, when drawn up, produces a frilled or quilled effect. When the centre threads are pulled up, the ruche edges project in a double frill. This may be cut or uncut.

TASSELS

A form of passementerie which is distinguished by its pendant shape and threaded appearance. Simple tassels are made from double-looped threads wrapped in cord. Larger tassels have a shaped core, which is then built up with threads. This is joined at the junction to a cord, by a process called snailing, using thread worked with a needle. Widely used in window treatments, to hold back bed curtains and to decorate pelmets. Special weighted tassels were made for fire-screen balances. Sheraton described their use: 'The weight of the screen must be ascertained, and then a lead tassel is formed of equal weight, with a hole through the centre to take a line, which is then covered and worked as any other tassel' (1803, p.317).

Boudet, Pierre and Gomond, Bernard (1981), *La Passementerie*, Paris: Dessain and Tosca.
Donzel, C. and Sabine, M. (1992), *L'Art de passementerie, et sa contribution à l'historie de la mode et de la décoration*, Paris: Chêne.
Fowler, John and Cornforth, John (1974), *English Decoration in the Eighteenth Century*, London: Barrie and Jenkins.
Gasc, Nadine (1973), 'Des dorelotiers aux passementiers', exhibition catalogue, Paris, Musée des Arts Décoratifs.
Heutte, R. (1972), *Le Livre de la passementerie*, Paris: Dourdon.
Hogarth, S. D. (1997), 'Goldlace to Girth webs – the evolution of a trade in York', in *Textile History*, 28: 2, pp.185–200.
Jackson, Linda Wesselman (1987), 'Beyond the fringe: ornamental upholstery trimmings in the 17th, 18th and early 19th centuries', Edward S. Cooke (ed.), in *Upholstery in America and Europe from the Seventeenth Century to World War I*, New York: Norton.
Levy, S. (1983), *Lace, a Visual History*, London: Victoria and Albert Museum.

Pastiglia

Originating in Italy during the Renaissance, pastiglia is a gesso-like paste used to decorate surfaces. It was made from the powder which resulted from ground lead being exposed to vinegar vapours in a container and then being mixed with an egg white binder. It was either applied to furniture items whilst still wet, when decorative moulds could be pressed into it before it had dried, or the motifs were moulded and then glued to the surface after setting. The resulting pattern was then painted or gilded. The usual furniture form was a casket or box and the pastiglia was apparently scented before application. It is likely that these were produced in both Ferrara and Venice.

Winter, P. de (1984), 'A little known creation of Renaissance decorative arts; the white lead pastiglia box', in *Saggi e Memorie di Storia dell'Arte*, no.14, pp.9–131.

Pau amarello (*Euxlophora paraensis*)

A Brazilian timber with an average density of 890 (56 lb/cu ft) and a warm golden colour. In the 1920s it was noted that it is 'never imported on a commercial basis, although it is such a handsome wood that it would be much sought after in furniture' (Howard, 1920, pp. 208–9). Aka Brazilian satinwood.

Peach wood

A nineteenth-century variety of BRAZILWOOD used for dyes.

Pearl shell

See Mother-of-pearl

Pearwood (*Pyrus communis*)

A timber native to Europe with an average density of 700–800 (45–50 lb/cu ft). It has a pink-brown to yellowish-white colouring, and a very fine even grain and texture. It has been used for vernacular furniture from about the 15th century, for inlay in Elizabethan and Jacobean furniture, and extensively for picture frames and bracket clocks in the 17th and 18th centuries. In 1613 Gervase Markham wrote: 'If you chuse timber for joint-stooles, chairs, or chests, you shall then chuse the oldest pear-tree to be found, for it is both smooth, sweet, and delicate, and though it be a very soft wood, yet in any of these frames it is an exceedingly long laster' (*The English Husbandman*, 1613, p.68, cited in Bowett, 1993). In addition it was used for carving in the late 17th and early 18th centuries, especially for picture frames and furniture stands. When stained black it could imitate EBONY for use as inlay, split balusters or mouldings. Evelyn recommends its use 'for its excellent colour'd timber … especially for stools, tables, chairs, pistol-stocks, instrument-makers, cabinets and very many works of the joyner (who can make it easily to counterfeit ebony) and Sculptor, either for flat or embossed works' (1662, Appendix, p.72). The wood has been popular in France and America for provincial furniture styles. From the 18th century pearwood was also used as a base for stained stringing and PENWORK.

Pegs

A wooden pin or wedge used to join pieces of timber together within the solid or as a through tenon. They were used before nails, screws or adhesives, and long after in some cases: pegs remain a reliable method of jointing in some applications. Pegs were never quite round and were on occasion tapered. The variable shrinkage rates meant that in some cases pegs would eventually stand proud of the surface.

Penistone

A heavily milled woollen broadcloth woven in the Penistone district of Yorkshire from the mid 16th century. The Hardwick Hall inventory of 1601 lists 'two curtains of grene penistone for the windowes' [of the low great chamber] (Boynton, 1971, p.31).

Penwork

This form of painted decoration for furniture, especially for small items such as boxes, tables and cabinets, was developed in the early 19th century. One of the earliest references located so far is when Rudolph Ackermann referred to decoration 'on a black ground, in imitation of Indian ivory inlaid work' (Ackermann, June 1810, p.396). It consisted of drawn and inked decoration in a multitude of patterns and was carried out by artistic ladies, as a pastime. Light-coloured woods such as pear, sycamore, holly, chestnut or pine were generally used, sometimes with a GESSO foundation, to give a smooth surface for the painting. Most penwork designs were carried out on black backgrounds laid onto wood surface, but there are examples with white or emerald-green backgrounds. Dark-red or imitation-tortoiseshell backgrounds are also known. Occasionally gilding was used and especially in the 1830s and 1840s other colours were usual for parts of the work.

The process usually started with a surface stopped out or 'voided' in black water-colour, then the basic design was traced or painted and

86 A fine example of a small cabinet decorated with penwork on a simulated ebony ground. This form of decoration was popular in the first quarter of the 19th century, England.

the details added in Indian ink with a pen or fine brushes. The final operation was to glaze the surface with coats of transparent varnish.

Penwork was used to decorate the borders of printed TUNBRIDGE WARE and Scottish Mauchline ware in the early 19th century, but other examples of the technique were carried out by amateurs. Indeed, designs were professionally produced for copying by amateurs. In 1822 the *Repository* featured a shop called 'The Temple of Fancy' which held 'an extensive collection of handsome screens, both plain and ornamented, screen-poles, elegant stands for table-tops and chess boards, card-racks, flower ornaments, and white-wood boxes, in a variety of shapes, for painting the inlaid ebony and ivory, with every requisite useful for painting and ornamenting the same' (Ackermann, January 1822).

In 1827 Nathaniel Whittock's *The Decorative Painters' and Glaziers' Guide* included instructions (p.98) for preparing work pieces for ladies:

As the work in imitation of inlaid ebony and ivory is now so fashionable, and the process is in every respect similar to any other kind of japanning, it is mentioned in this place, as great inconvenience is felt by many painters from their not having the knowledge of the proper method of preparing the ground for ladies to paint upon, or of varnishing and polishing it after the painting is finished.

Penwork remained a popular method of decorating furniture into the 1880s.

Hughes, G. (1964), 'The vogue for penwork furniture', in *Country Life*, 23 April.
Hyde Park Antiques (1989), 'Penwork the Triumph of Line', exhibition catalogue, 12 October–20 November, New York.
Riley, Nöel (1983), 'The elegant and useful accomplishment of penwork', in *Antique Collector*, March, pp.52–5.
Tingry, P. F. (1804), *The Painters' and Varnishers' Guide*, London: Keasley.

Pernambuco
See Brazilwood

Peroba rosa (*Aspidosperma peroba*)
A Brazilian and Argentinean timber with an average density of 780 (49 lb/cu ft). It is rose-red to yellow, streaked with purple or brown which darkens on exposure to a dark brown. It has a fine texture often with an interlocked grain, and has been used in the 20th century for fine furniture. Aka Araracanga.

Perpetual
A wool twill fabric made from white SERGE (also called Perpetuana),

introduced in the late 16th century and used widely in the 17th century for bed hangings and upholstery. The cloth was soaked and softened in oils and urine, then dried on tenterhooks. It was then folded, placed on a coal-fired hot press and the upper plate screwed down. In 1638/9 Anne, Viscountess Dorchester, had a 'redd perpetuana bedd' in a nursery, as well as a 'French bed of green perpetuana' (cited in Clabburn, 1988, p.251). A little later, Ham House also had a 'french bed stead hung with blew perpetuana leased with gilt leather, and a counterpoint of blew perpetuana' (Thornton and Tomlin, 1980, p.22). Celia Fiennes (1698) recorded the process of preparing serges in Exeter in great detail (1982, pp.197–8).

Perpetuana
See Perpetual

Persimmon (*Diospyros virginiana*)
A North American timber with an average density of 800 (50 lb/cu ft). It has a pale-coloured sapwood with a small core of blackwood, a straight grain, and a fine and even texture. With markings of light yellow and brown-and-black streaks, it has been used as veneer, especially in the USA.
See also Ebony

Petit point
A type of embroidery that is used for upholstery work such as DROP-IN seats, chair backs and loose CUSHIONS. It produces a fine, closely worked and even surface which allows for detail in the pattern. It is worked on fine canvas, usually in a frame, and tent stitch (single stitches slanting upwards from left to right over one cross of canvas) is usually employed. The Gobelins stitch is sometimes employed for petit point work. In this case the stitches are over two threads in height and one in width. This creates a shaded effect which can be used in conjunction with the tent stitch. Fine woollen and sometimes silk yarns are used to create pictorial images, often against a dark background.

Petticoat
The drapery associated with dressing and toilet tables. Chippendale explains that 'the petticoat goes behind the feet of the table which looks better' (Chippendale, 1762, Plate CXIX). The petticoat for dressing tables remained a decorative soft-furnishing feature into the mid 20th century.

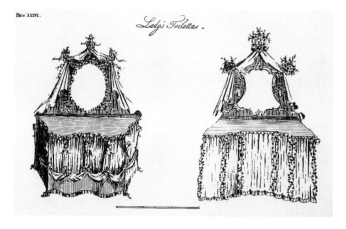

87 The soft furnishing associated with dressing tables included petticoats to fit around the table section. These designs for petticoats were produced by Ince and Mayhew, London, and published in 1759.

Pewter inlay

Pewter is a metal based on an alloy of tin and lead approximately in the proportions of 80/20. It has been used as a furniture decoration on occasion since the 17th century. Used either as cut sheet or sometimes melted and poured into pre-cut cavities, pewter is usually associated with high-style furniture as inlay, or as a component of BOULLE marquetry. It was favoured by English makers such as Gerrit Jensen, and a little later in the early 18th century Coxed and Woster imaginatively used pewter as a stringing, in conjunction with burr veneers. In the later 18th century, French makers such as Weisweiller combined brass and pewter marquetry with ebony. In 1774, Englishman Joseph Jacob patented a method of decorating furniture using tin-foil, lead or pewter, beaten or rolled into sheets for applying to cabinets and other articles (Pat.no.1065). Pewter remained useful for marquetry work and was particularly used by Arts and Crafts designer Baillee Scott towards the end of the 19th century.
See also Boulle work

Pheasant wood

See Angelim, Teak

Philip and cheny

A plush pile fabric on a warp yarn ground, woven in Norwich by 1608. The name is derived from the French *phelpe et chaîne*, *phelpe* being plush and *chaîne* being warp. The name was soon abbreviated to CHENEY.

Philippine mahogany

See Lauan, Meranti

Piano hinge

See Hinges

Pickled finish

An effect on cabinet work (often pine) that has been particularly applied to French 'provincial' styles. Various woods can be pickled by using a combination of bleach (caustic soda), white shellac, fillers and glaze. Similar results come from the stripping of a painted finish, leaving any fillers or remaining paint used to create a white-veined appearance on the surface.
See also Weathered oak

Pierced carving

See Carving

Pietre dure

Pietre dure (*pietra dura* in the singular) are hard or semi-precious stones that are worked with versions of lapidary techniques and are used in creating decorative objects as well as being a decoration for furniture and interiors. Originating in Italy, the full name, *Commesso di pietre dure* indicates that the stones are 'combined', that is, so close that seams do not show. Also called Florentine mosaic, the technique was derived from *opus sectile*, the original MOSAIC marquetry. It is a process in which decorative panels are made up from a mosaic of irregular-shaped semi-precious stones. This 'jigsaw' is glued to a slate base for stability: in this it is similar to marquetry in wood. If coloured stones are inlaid into a marble base they are an intarsia process. The stones used include AGATE, CHALCEDONY, GRANITE, JASPER, LAPIS LAZULI, MALACHITE, PORPHYRY, and various MARBLES.

As in other specialist trades who often supplied furniture-makers,

88   An example of the recycling of furniture parts. A 19th-century English table is set with 17th-century pietre dure panels, c.1867.

there was a sub-division of labour. The designer was the *invenzione*, the artist or sculptor who prepared the *modello*. The design was followed by stone selection carried out by the *sceglilore di pietre*, often a painter, expert in colour selection and choice. He made an ink and pencil tracing, then made an outline of the section shapes for various stones to be used. These were then cut out and glued to prepared stone slices cut from a block by the *segatore col filo* (wire cutter or sawyer). Further specialists included the *commettitor*, a specialized cutter-out, and the *fruttista*, a carver of whole fruits. Following the setting out, the *spiantore* smoothed or levelled off stones and the final polish was undertaken by the *lustratori* or polisher.

The working methods have been known, particularly in Italy, since Classical times, especially for small items and jewellery. As it is not a process that is easily mechanized, manufacturing methods and tools have remained the same for many centuries. Once the paper cut-out designs had been glued to the selected stones, the stone was then cut to a thickness of 2–4 mm (*c*.¹⁄₁₆–⅛ in). If it was particularly fragile, it would be lined with a section of slate. The cutting process used a bow saw with an iron wire 'blade', which was used in combination with a spatula covered with abrasive paste. The cut was made, like marquetry, with a slight angle to its edge so that pieces may fit together with very little space gap. The ground material was either cut in a similar way, using a drill to make a starting hole for the wire saw if necessary, or by chiselling away a few millimetres depth of a solid top, leaving dividing sections to create part of the pattern. In the 19th century the Italian technique was based on the following process: The marble slab about 3 mm (¹⁄₁₆+ in) thick had the design drawn upon it and was cut out using a fine saw and files; the hard stones were worked into the pattern by lapidary techniques, the whole was then prepared, polished and finished; finally it would be mounted as a veneer to a thicker slab.

In the Renaissance the processes were revived for use in the decoration of furniture and later for other *objets d'art* and even interiors. The earliest recorded maker was Benedetto Peruzzi from Padua in 1379, but the major revival seems to have occurred in Milan and it was from here that Cosimo I de Medici poached craftsmen to help him establish a workshop in Florence. A workshop was duly founded in 1588 under his auspices, which later became known as the Opificio delle Pietre Dure. Evelyn recorded his visit:

The Court of Justice, under which is a stately arcade for men to walke in, and over that the shops of divers rare artists who continually worke for the greate Duke. Above this is the renowned Ceimeliarcha, or Repository, wherein are hundreds of admirable antiquities, statues of marble and metal, vases of porphyrie etc. ... here were divers incomparable tables of Pietro Comessa, which is a marble ground inlay'd with severall sorts of marbles and stones of divers colours, in the shapes of flowers, trees, beasts, birds and landskips like the natural. In one is represented the town of Ligorne by the same hand who inly'd the altar of St. Lawrence, Domenico Benotti, of whom I purchased 19 pieces of the same work for a cabinet.
(*Diary*, 24 October 1644, p.107)

Other centres developed: Rome was one and Venice another, whilst in Naples in 1737, the Royal Pietre Dure factory was founded by the King of Naples. Using Florentine artisans it quickly established itself and it is now difficult to distinguish its early work from the Florentine versions. This factory eventually closed in 1860. Although the most prestigious work was carried out in Italy, the taste for pietre dure spread across Europe. For example, the Miseroni family from Milan worked for Rudolf II in Prague, as did the Florentine Cosimo Castrucci, who devised a pictorial landscape approach to the work. In late-17th-century Paris the Gobelins workshops employed Florentine workmen. Later, under Louis XVI, French ébénistes including Carlin and Weisweiler favoured the re-use of pietre dure taken from cabinets of that period for use in their 'modern' cabinets. In 1759, the Buen Retiro workshop was established in Madrid, Spain, by Charles III using Italian craftsmen and management. Active from 1763 to 1808, it was well known especially for the production of table tops, some of which are still in the Prado Museum.

English examples of this taste for pietre dure must include the outstanding Badminton cabinet which was made in Florence for the third Duke of Beaufort in 1726. In this case the cabinet was made up and shipped to England complete with assembly instructions. Another famous piece, the Kimbolton cabinet designed by Robert Adam for the Duchess of Manchester, was used to provide a setting for pietre dure panels that had been brought back to England from the Grand Tour. The panels are recorded as being made in 1709, but the cabinet was not constructed until the 1770s.

During the 19th century large quantities of ready-prepared stones exported from Italy were often mounted onto furniture. French makers were particularly fond of using them, but there are many English examples to be found also. They were generally mounted on side cabinets and were either glued onto the surface or let into a veneer which was usually ebony or ebonized. They were sometimes also mounted in frames and used to decorate walls as pictures. Although the Italians remained pre-eminent in the craft, the taste for hard-stone decorated furniture was such that many local materials in other countries were pressed into service (for example, Ashburton marbles in England) along with the development of a range of inventions to imitate the effects. For example, early-19th-century table tops were made in England from irregular-shaped marble mosaics bedded in cement, rubbed down and polished. These 'scrap' or patchwork tables were superseded by designs that used the marbles deliberately. In the late 1830s, John Adam of Matlock first started the pietre dure process. Derbyshire work followed the Italian pietre dure processes, but as they used softer marbles and were able to stain some stone, they undercut the market of the imported work. The Duke of Devonshire, at close-by Chatsworth, encouraged local workers to imitate the superb Florentine work in his collection and in the 1840s and 1850s the Derbyshire industry boomed. William Adams, owner of Old Mawe's Museum at Matlock, Derbyshire, noted that

the beautiful style so long adopted at Florence was introduced into Matlock ten years ago by the author, the first specimen being a butterfly ... This work advanced from butterflies to sprigs, birds, flowers, and foliage of every description, and some of the most beautiful and perfect workmanship are now done in this country, and introduced as ornamental tables, inlaid vases etc. into many of the first noblemen's houses.
(*The Gem of the Peak*, 1845, 4th edn, p.408. Cited in Wills, 1971)

The process involved cutting panels of black or rosewood colour marble, into 3 mm (1/16+ in) thicknesses. These were fret-cut so that open spaces were prepared to receive the other coloured marbles and fluorspars to make the pattern. The whole panel was then fixed to a thicker marble bed and polished. Even this process was easier, as the stones were all of approximately the same hardness. The regeneration of the Derbyshire industry in the 1840s and 1850s led to a good supply of marble tops, but they were usually expensive. By the 1850s there were more than fifty masters working in this trade. Indeed it was so successful that steam-powered marble saws were developed to cut slabs of marble into suitable panels. The saws used toothless blades in conjunction with a continual stream of sharp sand and water. However, by the mid 1890s only one firm remained as tastes changed irrevocably (see Plate XIV).
See also Malachite, Marble, Mosaic work

Cornforth, John (1988), 'Princely pietre dure', in *Country Life*, December 1, pp.160–5.
Giusti, Annamaria (1992), *Pietre Dure: Hardstones in Furniture*, London: Philip Wilson.
Gonzalez-Palacios, Alvar (1977), 'The Laboratorio della pietre dure in Naples: 1738–1805', in *Connoisseur*, CXCVI, pp.119–29.
— (1981), *Mosaici e Pietre Dure*, 2 vols, Milan.
Honor, Hugh (1958), 'Pietre dure and the grand tourist', in *Connoisseur*, CXLI, May, pp.213–15.
Hughes, G. B. (1955), 'Derbyshire marble mosaic and inlay', in *Country Life*, 22 December, pp.1486–7.
Koch, E. (1987), 'Pietre Dure and other artistic contacts between the courts of the Mughals and that of the Medici', in *A Mirror of Princes: The Mughals and the Medici*, Bombay: Marg, pp.29–56.
Thornton, Peter (1978), 'John Evelyn's cabinet', in *Connoisseur*, April, p.254.
Tomlinson, J. M. (1996), *Derbyshire Black Marble*, Matlock Bath: Peak District Mines Historical Society.

Pietra paesina

An Italian stone of calcareous rock found in the bed and edges of the Arno river. It is employed in inlay pictures (usually a landscape), which uses the natural veining and colouring caused by faults, in combination with painting to produce a pictorial image.

Pigeon wood

An 18th-century term referring to the deep red-brown wood from a Jamaican tree. The name possibly derives from the attractiveness of the tree's fruits to birds, especially pigeons, rather than its markings and colourings. There are occasional records of its importation and use for furniture. In 1756, P. Browne noted that 'this shrubby tree is greatly esteemed on account of its wood' (Browne, *Jamaica*, p.368). In 1768 the Earl of Shelburne purchased 'a neat mahogany hexagon table with a Pidgeon wood border' from Chippendale (Gilbert, 1978, p.255). Aka Sea-side grape.

Pin cushion work

A specific form of upholstery technique, originating in the 18th century, for making seats and back pads of delicate, often moulded chair frames, so that the upholstery work appears as applied pads or 'pin cushions'. This work is usually carried out without a first stuffing, so the filling must be accurately laid to ensure evenness of line and appearance.

Pin hinge
See Hinges

Pincers
A tool for gripping and levering metals, cloth and so on. Carpenters' pincers are hinged jaws with a range of variants usually used for pulling nails. Upholsterer's pincers have an extended jaw to act as a fulcrum and the jaw plates are serrated to grip material. They have a specialist use for stretching covers over padding before nailing, or for web-stretching if the material is too short to be used with a WEB STRAINER.

Pincore foam
See Latex

Pine (*Pinus spp.*)
A general term applied to trees and wood of the coniferous genus *Pinus* or various other allied coniferous genera.

Bunya pine (*Araucaria bidwillii*)
An Australian timber with an average density of 440 (28 lb/cu ft). It is light coloured, straight grained and attractively veined. In the 20th century it has been used as a plywood species and for cheap furniture. It was considered 'strong and good and full of beautiful veins, works with facility and takes a high polish' (Spon, 1901, p.130).

Hazel pine
See American red gum

Hoop pine (*Arauacaria cunninghamii*)
A creamy ivory softwood with a close and even texture and an average density of 560 (35 lb/cu ft). Used on occasion for inexpensive cabinet work in the 20th century. Aka Moreton Bay or Queensland pine.

Huon pine (*Dacrydium franklinii*)
A Tasmanian pine with an average density of 350 (22 lb/cu ft). Pale brown to yellowish-brown, it has been likened to bird's-eye maple: 'many little knots stud its whole surface with dark spots, shaded off with the natural satin colour; and this peculiarity will well reward the enterprise of a manufacturer, as furniture made of this would be an absolute novelty' (Bitmead, 1873, p.83). Although scarce by the early 20th century, it was one of the 'most suitable woods for bedroom furniture, bearing a strong resemblance to satinwood' (Spon, 1901, p.143). Aka Heron pine.

Kauri pine (*Agithis australis*)
A softwood which is sourced in the East Indies, New Zealand and Australia. It has an average density of 480 (30 lb/cu ft), is pale creamy brown to pinkish-brown in colour and has a fine, even texture and a straight grain. It also produced on occasion rich mottled, shaded effects in certain growths which were valuable as furniture timber. In the 19th century the New Zealand variety was the chief timber export of that country. In 1873 it was believed that, 'when it becomes more known, [it] will no doubt be much used in furniture' (Bitmead, 1873, p.83). In the 1920s 'mottled Kauri' was sought after for cabinet work.

Oregon pine
See Douglas fir

Parana pine (*Araucaria angustifolia*)
A softwood from South America with an average density of 540

(34 lb/cu ft). The sapwood is often whitish which differentiates it from the heartwood which is brown to dark brown and flecked with red streaks. It produces large knot-free boards of even texture which make it suitable as a furniture and plywood timber.

Pitch pine (*Pinus palustris*)
Exported from southern USA since the mid 19th century. It has an average density of 580 (36 lb/cu ft), and is orange-yellow in colour. It is very resinous (a source of turpentine) but durable and was therefore used for church and school furniture, especially in the early 20th century.

Ponderosa pine (*Pinus ponderosa*)
This knotty pine from North America has an average density of 480 (30 lb/cu ft). It has a deep-yellow to reddish-brown heartwood. Aka Knotty, Californian white, Western yellow.

Red pine
See Rimu or Scots pine

Scots (red) pine (*Pinus sylvestris*)
The red pine or 'fir' of commerce. Its colour actually varies from yellow to reddish brown. The annual rings are clearly marked by contrasting light and dark zones of the early and late woods. It is subject to confusion as in England, if it originates from northern Europe it is known as 'red' or red DEAL (provincial term), and as yellow DEAL (London term) if it originates from southern Europe. Its geographic origins are also indicated by commercial names such as Baltic, Siberian, Polish etc. Evelyn refers to 'fir' from Norway as being

long, straight, clear and of yellowish colour. It is exceeding smooth to polish on, and therefore does well under gilding work, and takes black equal with the pear tree. Both fir and especially pine, succeed well in carving, as for capitals, festoons, nay statues, especially being gilded because of the easiness of the grain to work, and take the tools every way.
(1662, p.128)

Nearly 150 years later it was still valued. 'The wood of this tree [Scots pine] is the red or yellow deal esteemed the most durable of any' (Sheraton, 1803, p.285). Aka Redwood.

Western white pine (*Pinus monticola*)
Similar to Yellow pine, it has an average density of 410 (26 lb/cu ft) with a yellowish-white sapwood and pinkish-yellow to pinkish-brown heartwood. It is straight grained, compact and easily worked. It has been widely used in furniture-making.

Yellow pine (*Pinus strobus*)
English trade name for North American WHITE PINE. It has an average density of 380 (24 lb/cu ft) and is a pale straw colour with thin dark parallel lines running through the grain. It has a straight grain and a fine even texture. Used in America for secondary construction, especially for corner blocks and slip seats. In 1853 one authority said it was introduced into England c.1818 as a commercial timber and has 'almost superseded the red and white pines or Baltic timber which up to that period were the only kinds available for the purposes of the cabinet-maker' (Blackie, 1853, p.4). Fifty years later it was considered 'best suited to cabinet-making purposes, and forms the ground for nearly all veneered and hidden work' (Spon, 1901, p.351). By 1922 it was noted that 'it is the softest but most reliable of the pine woods, but getting scarce' (Wells and Hooper, 1909, p.345). Aka New England pine, Weymouth or Quebec pine.
See also Spruce

Forest Products Research Laboratory (1960), *A Handbook of Softwoods*, London: HMSO.

Pine hair or **Wool**
The needles of pine trees that were used for inexpensive MATTRESS fillings in the 19th century. In 1884 Beck recorded their use in Silesia, and they were available from wholesale suppliers in America in the late 1880s.

Pine state hair
Another name for EXCELSIOR.

Pink mahogany
See Agba

Pinking irons
A specialist upholstery tool made in a variety of shapes with serrated or scalloped edges. They were used for cutting ornamental designs in leather or cloth, to create decorative effects for trimming, buttons and so on.
See also Punches

Pintado
In the 16th century pintado (Portuguese for spotted) was cheap block-printed cotton cloth. In the 17th century pintadoes were resist-dyed, mordant-painted cloths similar to CHINTZ. It was widely used for quilts, curtains, cupboard cloths and so on. In 1609 the East India Company had 'pintadoes of all sorts, especially the finest … I mean such as are for quilts and fine hangings' (Irwin and Brett, 1970, p.4). A little later, Evelyn recorded how he 'supp'd at my Lady Mordaunt's at Ashley: here was a roome hung with Pintado, full of figures greate and small, prettily representing sundry trades and occupation of the Indians, with their habits &c: very extraordinarie' (*Diary*, 30 December 1665). Its popularity was curtailed in 1720 when it was illegal to 'use [pintado] or wear in or about any bed, chair, cushion or other household furniture' (Irwin and Brett, p.5).
See also Chintz, Palampore

Piping
See Passementerie

Piqué
See Tortoiseshell

Pit saw
See Saws

Pit sawing
See Conversion

Pitch pine
See Pine

Plaid or **Plod**
A striped and checked twilled woollen fabric like the modern tartan. In 1641, the Countess of Arundel had 'a couch bed, covered with scotch plad, thereon 4 little cushions of the same' (cited in Cust, 1911, p.98). It was still fashionable in 1710 when Dyrham Park had a 'Plod room' furnished with '5 pieces of Scots plod hangings, 2 window curtains and vallans of the same' and 'four chairs, 2 stools couch and three cushions' all covered in the same (Walton, 1986, p.58). Plaid, as an essentially Scottish fabric, was revived in the 1850s by Queen Victoria and Prince Albert at their residence in Balmoral Castle where they maintained the habit of furnishing rooms in plaid.

Plane wood (*Platanus spp.*)
A European timber with an average density of 620 (39 lb/cu ft). It is a light reddish-brown hardwood timber with conspicuous and numerous rays on quartered material showing as a decorative fleck. The wood is straight-grained and fine to medium textured. Sheraton recorded it as 'a very white wood, close in grain and rather tough; and in many places in the country used by cabinet-makers instead of beech for painted chairs, or for the fly joint rails of card and pembroke tables' (1803, p.288). It was still used as a substitute for BEECH or BIRCH chair frames in the 1920s. Plane wood can be treated chemically to produce HAREWOOD with a silver-grey background with brown flecks. Lacewood refers to quarter-cut timber which reveals a lace-like figure, with a light spotted, brown colour.

WESTERN PLANE (*Platanus occidentalis*)
A North American timber exported to England for furniture by the early 20th century and especially used for bedroom suites. Boulger noted that 'the cabinet-makers of Philadelphia object to the wood when plank from its tendency to warp; but when well seasoned it stands well', and is 'imported into England for furniture' (Loudon, 1844, cited in Boulger, 1908, p.255).
See also Buttonwood, Sycamore

Planes
The plane is a wood-working tool with a sharp blade protruding from a base that has the major benefit of removing a continuous shaving of wood rather than a chip. It is more controllable, and therefore finer work can be achieved more accurately. In fact the built-in control means that the worker only has to apply strength as driving force. It was apparently first used in Roman times. The variety of planes are myriad, but Salaman (1975), although discussing well over one hundred variations, has divided them into three main categories; preliminary shaping (bench), fitting and close adjustment, and finishing and smoothing (moulding). In all cases the essential requirement is the fitting of cutting irons into a body or stock.

Astragal
A moulding-plane which works a semi-circular profile which is used to create the tracery moulding on glazed doors, to finish a wooden door edge or to separate more complex mouldings.

Block
A small metal (iron) plane designed for use with one hand. The low pitch of the iron means that cross-grain work is easier and is therefore ideal for end-grain work in the mitre block or shooting board.

Bull-nose
An iron plane for finishing rebates and angles. It is of small size with the mouth close to the fore-end.

Compass
A bench plane with concave and convex sole plates designed to adjust to any curve for smoothing curved surfaces.

Dovetail
A plane with acute-angled chamfers for cutting sides and bottom corners of sliding dovetails.

Drawer
A special grooving plane designed to cut grooves in drawer sides ready to take the bottom board.

Fillister
A general name for rebating planes fitted with fences. These may

be fixed-standing fillisters for simple cutting, or regular rebates, or moving fillisters which have an adjustable fence.

Hollows and rounds
Matched pairs of moulding-planes with one sole hollow or concave, the other round or convex. A full set of cabinet-makers' hollows and rounds included 18 pairs from 3–38 mm (⅛–1½ in) rising in sixteenths.

Jack
A common form of bench plane up to 43 cm (17 in) long, which was used for the first smoothing of rough surfaces before the trying plane was applied. This was sometimes called 'jacking up' work. Aka Fore plane or Strike block. Known to Moxon (1703).

Jointer
The longest of the bench planes, between 66 and 76 cm (26 and 30 in) long with a 8 cm (3 in) sole. See Trying plane. Known to Moxon (1703).

Matching
A pair of planes that were specially designed to be used to cut tongues and grooves in timber. One shaped for the tongue, the other matching one for the groove.

Moulding
A wide range of specialist planes designed to cut the full range of ornamental mouldings including cavetto, bolection, ogee, round hollow, cove, fillet, flute and others. Known to Moxon (1703).

Plough
A fully adjustable plane used for grooving panels and cutting joints. The use of these planes by turners was specifically excluded in an agreement between the joiners and turners made in 1632. Known to Moxon (1703).

Rabbet
A plane with the iron the same width as the stock, used for cutting rebates or rabbets, that is the upper edges of boards, so that a similarly cut piece can fit into it. Known to Moxon (1703).

Scraper
A handle to hold a SCRAPER tool. It is not a plane but allows the cabinet-maker to scrape veneers or surfaces or to remove paint etc. See Toothing plane, below.

Smoothing
Originally a bench plane made with a wooden stock, it has gradually been replaced by metal versions. Intended to perform smoothing operations in woodworking shops, it often becomes an all-round planer. Known to Moxon (1703).

Table
Matched pairs of moulding-planes, used to cut the rule joints on the flaps of folding table tops, and so on.

Tongue
Complements the plough plane.

Toothing
A scraper plane with a near-vertical toothed iron. This scrapes the surface prior to veneering or gluing. The cutter has a serrated edge which will scratch away timber without lifting the grain. Useful for working difficult grained timbers before scraping.

Trying
Also called a jointer, the trying plane is used for truing the surfaces and edges of long boards. The trying planes were 51–6 cm (20–2 in)

long, whilst the jointer was 71–6 cm (28–30 in) long. It was used to shoot long joints, table tops and others.

Goodman, W. (1993), *British Planemakers From 1700*, Needham Market: Roy Arnold.
Greber, J. (1991), *The History of the Woodworking Plane*, trans. Seth Burchard, Albany, New York: Early American Industries Association.
Jones, C. (1985), *Planers, Matchers and Molders in America*, Seattle: C. Jones.
Mayhew, Henry (1850), *Morning Chronicle*, Letter LXII, 25 July.
Tompkins, Charles (1889), *A History of the Planing Mill*, New York: Wiley.

Plaques
See Ceramic

Plastics
A wide variety of plastics have been adapted and used for an increasing range of processes in the furniture industry. These have included: ADHESIVES; structural bonding – either with or without reinforcement (PARTICLE BOARD); moulded or cast as components of finished articles; surface materials – LAMINATES; powder coatings; LACQUERS and resins; upholstery FOAM and overlays; LEATHER CLOTH; synthetic fibres for textile coverings; WEBBING; small parts such as DRAWERS, handles, HINGES, knobs, as well as decorative accessories which can be moulded, extruded or otherwise shaped and fabricated. Plastics can be simply classified as natural plastics, semi-synthetics and synthetics. Natural plastics include the following materials: AMBER, GUTTA PERCHA, HORN, SHELLAC and TORTOISESHELL.

SEMI-SYNTHETICS

Casein formaldehyde (Erinoid, Casco)
Developed in the 1880s, casein was a well-known ADHESIVE, but was mainly known as the basis of artificial ivory or horn products. It was occasionally used as a veneer for cabinets in the early part of 20th century.

Cellulose acetate (Celanese)
A non-flammable cellulose which replaced the nitro-cellulose with acetic acid. It was commercially available from 1911 and was developed over the following years into a wide range of household goods. Further developments in the latter part of the 20th century have led to the basic material being modified to an extent that it is suitable for upholstery, woven 'wicker-style' chairs, and fabricated forms such as the (1969) Plia chair.

Cellulose nitrate (Parkesine, Xylonite, Ivoride, Celluloid)
In 1856, Alexander Parkes patented a chemically produced plastic substance which he called Parkesine. It was made by the action of nitro-cellulose on cellulose (e.g. cotton waste) but was inflammable. Being based on cellulose nitrate, it was too brittle to be really successful. By 1870 Wesley Hyatt in the USA had developed Parkes's recipe and produced Celluloid (nitro-cellulose and camphor). In the first part of the 20th century it was used as imitation HORN, TORTOISESHELL and IVORY. It was popular for small decorative and useful objects as well as for billiard balls, which were the main idea behind the experiments at the time. In furniture, celluloid was sometimes used in thin sheets for marquetry and in lines for inlay, as well as being the base of cellulose nitrate lacquers that were standard for much of the 20th century.

Viscose (Rayon)
Fibres made from cellulose treated with sodium hydroxide and carbon disulphide. In 1892 viscose rayon was patented, but its impact on furnishing fabrics was not felt until after 1920 when the industry was fully established.

89 *The Blow plastic inflatable chair caught the spirit of the 1960s. Designed in 1967 and using electrically welded transparent PVC, it was fun, portable, relatively cheap and not intended to last.*

Vulcanite (Ebonite)
A man-made substitute for EBONY developed in the mid 19th century. It was made from natural rubber which was heated with the addition of up to 30 per cent of sulphur. The resulting material was very hard, black and strong but with a close resemblance to ebony. It was used for piano keys and fine detail in furniture decoration.

SYNTHETICS

ABS (Acrylonitrile-butadiene-styrene)
A synthetic terpolymer plastic available since c.1948 which is particularly impact resistant. Mostly vacuum-formed, it was used for chairs in the mid 1960s. ABS was also used for injection-moulding chairs (Kartell), as well as for storage systems, tables and other items. In the 1990s recyclable ABS has been used as a material for making chairs again.

Acrylic (*Polymethyl methylacrylate*): Perspex, Lucite, Plexiglas
A transparent and rigid thermo-plastic which could be moulded to shape. Like many other plastics, acrylic was either used to imitate other materials or was used for its own properties. By 1937 the acrylic plastic Lucite was introduced into the USA as a furniture material but often imitated other styles. By the 1970s acrylic was being widely used for tables, racks, and so on (see Plate XXII).

Bakelite
A form of thermo-setting plastic derived from the reaction of phenol-formaldehyde which sets solid when heated and was the first completely synthetic resin. Patented in 1909 by Leo Baekland, it was initially intended to be a synthetic substitute for SHELLAC. Baekland realized that the material could be used for strong heat-resistant moulded products. Although it had to be filled to reduce brittleness, it was used a great deal for plastic household goods and radio sets and some furniture in the early part of the 20th century.

The first furniture use of phenolic mouldings appears to be in 1926, when the Simmons Company of Racine, Wisconsin, produced a reproduction-style chair-frame made from eight separate phenolic mouldings with an upholstered timber-framed seat and back (Katz, 1978, p.60). In 1932, in a very different design mould, a French manufacturer used phenolic plastic for one-piece outdoor table tops, chair seats and backs, and achieved some commercial success. An interesting use was from 1928 when a process called *bois glacé* was introduced: wooden surfaces were coated with a transparent phenolic liquid called Catalin as a replacement for glass tops.

Carbon fibre
A treatment of acrylonitrile fibres by heat (pyrolysis) which gives the fibres (aligned in parallel with the axis of the filament) great strength whilst maintaining their silk-like quality and light weight. The fibres are used in the late 20th century in conjunction with resins in a similar manner to GLASS FIBRE. The material has been used to make items such as chairs and table tops.

Melamine formaldehyde
The plastic most associated with decorative laminates such as 'Formica'.
See Plastic laminates

Nylon-polyamide
A generic term used to describe a group of man-made products by synthetic means all of which are super-polyamides. Nylon has characteristics of strength, resistance to water and mildew, and is a malleable plastic. In furniture it is used for many applications including drawers, runners, catches, hinges. As a furnishing fabric nylon jersey has been used in particular to make covers for shell chairs.

Polyester
Thermosetting plastics used in the manufacture of synthetic fibres. Devised during World War II polyester is most important as the resin used for glass fibre bonding and wood finishing.
See Glass fibre reinforced plastic

Polyethylene (Polythene)
A lightweight thermo-plastic material devised in the 1930s which in a low density version is widely used in many domestic situations. As high-density rigid polythene it is used in injection or blow moulding of a wide range of objects including furniture. In 1964 the Italian manufacturers Kartell, produced a child's stacking chair, using injection-moulded polythene.

Polypropylene
Although the use of this plastic was discovered as early as 1954, it was not until 1963 that it made its mark as a furniture material. The world-famous injection-moulded Hille stacking chair seat was the first self-supporting chair to be single injection-moulded in mass production. This advance was a major breakthrough as it used a new material to produce a self-supporting shell that could be fitted to a variety of bases. Although these were promoted and sold to the domestic market, large-scale contract use was the most important outlet. By using an inexpensive plastic material, combined with the injection-moulding process, the product could be sold at very competitive prices. Although, from an ergonomic point of view, there was some criticism of the initial design, a second revised design was introduced and this has remained hugely successful. In the 1990s polypropylene has been used as a recycled material for dining chairs.

Polystyrene
A rigid transparent plastic especially used in moulded products. Although first developed in the 1930s, polystyrene was only widely used in furniture when the high-impact version was developed. In 1967 the use of high-impact polystyrene (HIPS) for components was still relatively new, but it was stated that 'It is now possible to reproduce a plastic part that is almost impossible to distinguish from wood' (cited in Skinner and Rogers, 1968, p.156). The desirability of this, from the manufacturers' point of view, was that plastic parts were necessary to meet price points, sustain regularity of supply and standardization, and still maintain an element of style. The customer demand for more ornate surfaces was often prohibitive in traditional materials, so even for small runs plastics were economical. Apart from the cost factors, the plastic suppliers sold other advantages of plastic over wood. There was no movement or shrinkage, plastic was more impact-resistant than wood, and it was easier to colour match to other

parts of a group. American manufacturers were particularly happy using plastic for reproductions of Colonial and Early American and other decorative styles: 'You can put in extra design without extra cost … merely put the detail into the mold, including the wood graining' (ibid., p.157). The versatility of plastics meant that the material was able to be fabricated into both progressive or traditional designs. For example, in 1965, high-impact polystyrene was used by Arkana to produce their innovative Mushroom range of dining and occasional furniture designed by Maurice Burke. This was the first furniture to be rotationally moulded using polyurethane-filled bases and a double skin. Whilst the Arkana Mushroom range was an example of contemporary design, many manufacturers continued to use plastics as a replacement for wooden components in traditional designs. These could range from fascia mouldings to complete frames.

Polyurethane

One of the most important synthetic plastics used in furniture. It may be flexible, rigid, structural, or supplied as a textile coating. Most well known as an upholstery FOAM when flexible, and as CHAIR-FRAME shells when rigid. Less well known is the structural use of injection-moulded rigid polyurethane foam which can mould right-angles into designs. The polyurethane coating resin, which created a fashionable 'wet-look' upholstery cover in the 1970s, was found to be unsuitable due to peeling of the surface coating after a little wear.
See also Chair frames, Plastic foams

Polyvinyl chloride (PVC)

A rigid or plasticized thermo-plastic material first commercially developed in 1928–30. Furniture developments using PVC material occurred in the 1940s with the development of inflatable PVC cushions. The first use of such an arrangement was in the Numax chair made by Elliot Equipment. This had PVC bag-cushions fitted onto a metal or timber frame to make a chair. In 1944 the American Gallowhur Chemical Company produced a chair with a PVC 'tyre' in the shape of a doughnut, fixed to a timber frame with netting. PVC has also been used as a surface coating for extruded tubing to cover metal legs, and as a cover coat for steel panels. As an upholstery fabric it was vacuum-formed over a frame in minutes.
See Coated fabrics

Urea formaldehyde

A thermo-setting plastic used for decorative laminates for tables, and so on. Its most important use was as a plywood bonding resin which worked well in three-dimensional shapes.
See Adhesives

PROCESSES

The methods of processing plastics are as many and varied as the raw material. However, they can be organized into basic groups which will indicate the method which is dependent on the nature of the supply of the plastic material. Furniture components may be cast, moulded (compression, transfer, injection, extrusion, pultrusion, vacuum, blow, rotational), fabricated, press laminated, coated (curtain, dip, roller), bonded, thermo-formed (drape, vacuum, bubble) or extruded.

Buttrey, D. N. (1964/1976), *Plastics in Furniture*, London: Applied Science Publishers.
Guncheon, J. (1941), 'Furnishing in plastics', in *Studio*, February, pp.34–9.
Katz, S. (1978), *Plastics, Design and Material*, London: Studio Vista.
Kovaly, K. (1970), *Handbook of Plastic Furniture Manufacturing*, Stamford, Conn.: Technomic Publishing Co.
Plastics in Furniture (1965), A Symposium held at Brunel University.
Schwarz, S., Seymour, S. and Goodman, Sidney H. (1982), *Plastics, Materials and Processes*, New York: Van Nostrand.

90   *Some furniture shapes lend themselves to plastic materials and the processes associated with them. The Panton stacking chair is an example of successful moulding. Designed in 1960, it was manufactured from 1967.*

Society of Plastics Engineers (1970), *Plastics in Furniture*, National Technical Conference, 10–12 November 1970, St Louis, Mo., New York: The society.

Plastic foams

The development of plastic foams has been of major significance in the furniture industry of the second half of the 20th century. Although urethane foam was discovered in 1848, and Otto Rayner discovered polymerization in 1937, it was not until 1952 that Bayer developed the principle and in 1953 that du Pont followed. Polyurethane-ether (polyether) foam is a purely synthetic material based on the interaction of a polyol and an isocyanate with water. The process of foam-making is based on polymer formation and gas generation which create a mix that rises like a loaf. When cured, it can be cut to size also like a loaf. The cured foam can then be converted into a range of shapes including upholstering pads, cushions and wraps. The plastic foam can also be bonded in chip form, and different densities may be glued together. Although widely used as a component, it was not until 1967 that one of the first applications of polyurethane to make frameless furniture appears with the Throwaway sofa by Willie Landels. In 1969 Gaetano Pesce used the flexible character of plastic foam to create the Up chair which could be vacuum-packed to one tenth of its 'normal' size.

Sayed, I. M. (1984), *Foams Used in Upholstery*, Vienna: United Nations Industrial Development Organization.

91 An example of a sophisticated fully upholstered American platform rocker-chair with walnut frame and silk brocade cover, c.1880. The mechanism is almost entirely hidden.

Plastic laminates

A sandwich of printed paper pattern, clear formaldehyde laminate and substrate melded together to create a surfacing material that is impervious to water, scratch resistant, and hard-wearing. Laminates have a thickness range of 0.5–1.5 mm (⅟₃₂–⅟₁₆ in) and are made by pressing underlay sheets of phenolic resin-impregnated paper and overlay sheets of melamine-impregnated paper at high pressure and temperatures with a decorative sheet in-between. Post-forming grades are used for moulded edges, and solid colour 'laminates' (Colorcore) were developed by 1982.

The earliest laminate was patented in 1918 (applied for in 1913). Initially designed as a replacement for mica in insulation work, it was not until 1927 that US patents for 'lithographed wood-grains of light colour, employing an opaque barrier sheet to block out the dark interior of the laminate sheet' signalled the beginning of laminates as they have become known in furniture applications. In the 1930s technical developments including the lamination of real wood veneers into the laminate and the use of melamine-resins rather than the thio-resins, encouraged a real interest from furniture-makers. This was expressed in a demand for melamine-topped dining sets as a replacement for enamelled table tops, which when combined with steel frames became the ubiquitous Dinette sets.

Discussing plastic laminates in the English furniture trade, Denise Bonnett argued that: 'Nothing quite so significant has made such an impact on the furniture trade for many years' (Bonnett, 1956, p.99). It was likely that its success owed something to the fact that it was fundamentally a veneering process, already so familiar to the trade.

Lewin, Susan G. (1991), *Formica and Design*, New York: Rizzoli.

Plastic webbing
See Webbing

Plate glass
See Glass

Plates

A metal mount, often brass, which is applied to the corners and edges of cabinets for protection or decoration. For example, in the later 17th century japanned cabinets, copied from Chinese originals, had double lock plates, corner and angle plates fitted. Metal plates are also associated with early-19th-century military and travelling furniture. In these cases, the plates were usually brass strips fitted to the edges and corners of articles such as chests, bookcases, writing boxes.

Phillip, J. (1984), Catalogue of *Exhibition of Travelling and Campaign Furniture*, Hitchin: Phillips of Hitchin Ltd.

Platform

(a) An upholstery suspension system which uses a one-piece elasticated, diaphragm, flexolator or fab-web support. Early experiments with GUTTA PERCHA using its elastic properties were applied to a form of platform springing. At the 1851 Great Exhibition, H. Pratt displayed a brass chaise-longue fitted with 'elastic' gutta-percha sacking (Class 26, Item 403). The real success came one hundred years later when platform seating support was made from a resilient rubber diaphragm designed for use in show-wood framed chairs and sofas. Introduced in the 1960s by the Pirelli company, it was a useful way of supporting loose cushions on a tensioned supporting system that was simply held to the show-wood frame by four hooked bolts. Later, various textiles were used to create a flat suspension for cushions.
See Springs, Webbing

(b) The term also applies to the finished seat of an upholstered easy chair before laying on a seat cushion.

Platform rocker

Rocking chairs that are fixed to a stationary base but with a built-in rocking spring mechanism are called platform rockers. The arc-shaped rocking frame was attached to a fixed base with a linking spring to enable the pivot-rock action. It was initially an American invention. An early development was the patent taken out by D. Harrington on 23 April 1831 for a rocking chair which used combined steel carriage springs. Other patentees developed improvements that removed the extended rocker sections. In 1870, an American designer, Theodore Palmer, patented an 'oscillating rocking chair' which relied on the tension of spring steel arms built into the chair to provide a rocking motion as the user pivoted the seat on the underframe (US Pat.no. 102,701). From this date the platform rockers gained popularity. One of the simplest and most effective types of platform spring was patented in 1879 by Beiersdorf and Bunker of Chicago. This simple spring unit had two coil springs located in a small frame, which was the link between the fixed base and the rocking seat unit. In 1882 the American maker, George Hunzinger, patented an 'improved' mechanism based on two tension springs simply attached to the rocker and base frame (US Pat.no.264,880). The platform rocker principle is still used today.

Pleating

A method of shaping fabrics into decorative effects by sewing or pressing. Widely used on curtains, loose covers and bed hangings. They vary in style and include box, goblet, organ, pencil, French: most of them defining the resulting shape.
See also Tufting

Plough plane
See Planes

Plum (*Prunus domestica*)

A fruitwood with a deep brownish-red heartwood and a contrasting yellow sapwood. As with other fruit woods it was used by country cabinet-makers as well as inlayers and turners from the 16th century onward. Evelyn noted that 'pear and plum tree give the deepest red, and approached nearest in beauty to Brazil [wood]' (*Silva*, 1662, III, iv, p.236). It was used on occasion in the 18th century for fine furniture, both in the solid and as veneer.

Wild plum (*Prunus spinosa*) is especially associated with Tunbridge ware, and as *bois de prunier* it was used in 18th-century France, as well as in Germany and Scandinavia.

Plumes
See Feathers

Plush

A pile velour cloth woven from woollen, goat-hair (mohair) or silk yarns with a longer and softer nap than VELVET, used for upholstery. It was less expensive than velvet but produced a similar rich effect with a longer and less dense pile. Plush was a French speciality from the later 17th century (French: *pluche*) and remained an important upholstery fabric into the 20th century. It was defined by Chambers in 1741 as being 'composed of a weft of a single woollen thread, and a double warp, the one wool of two threads twisted, the other goats-hair. Some plushes are made entirely of worsted and other composed wholly of hair'. It may also be plain or embossed. In 1639 Anne, Viscountess of Dorchester, had '1 bed to lye on it of purple plush … with a canapie, the outward vallance of purple plush laced with silver lace and silver fringe' (cited in Clabburn, 1988, p.253). In 1710, Dyrham Park had various furniture items upholstered in 'striped plush' (Walton, 1986, p.59). In 1881 it was said of mohair that its 'luster and elasticity peculiarly fit mohair for its chief use, the manufacture of Utrecht velvets, commonly called furniture plush' (cited in Grier, 1988, p.303). Mohair plush has a short, stiff pile and an even, close finish, whereas silk plush had a longer and less uniform pile. A mohair pile woven into a linen foundation was widely used for contract furnishings, especially in the later 19th century.
See also Mohair, Velvet

Plywood (Sperrholz or contreplaqué)

A term devised (first recorded in OED in 1907) to describe the building up of layers of wood veneer (usually at 90 degrees to each other) to make a material that is stronger and more flexible than the original parts.

Some form of plywood was used by the Ancient Egyptians in their woodworking, but this had little direct effect on furniture development. Wherever the origins of plywood were, the concept was well established by the mid 18th century, when cabinet-makers were commonly using three-ply veneers to create fretwork galleries on tables and candlestands. The reason was that this laminated or ply process was stronger than solid wood of equivalent dimensions, especially when the designs that were to be fretted into it were very finely drawn. The ply process was not limited to frets and galleries. Chairs had back splats composed of layers of mahogany in three plies. In the early 19th century, Sheraton described the practical benefits of built-up plywood work. In a design for a Universal Table, Sheraton describes its making as follows: 'the framing is three inches broad, and mitred

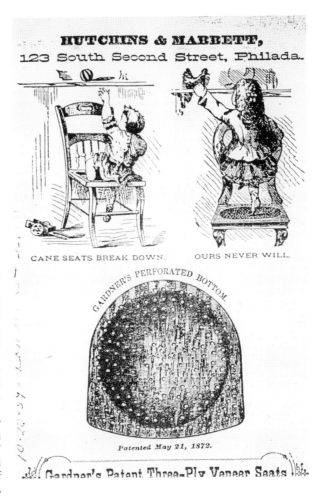

92 *The problems that plywood could solve were graphically shown in this advertisement for Gardner's replacement seats, c.1880.*

at the corners; and the panels are sometimes glued up in three thicknesses, the middle piece being laid with the grain across and the other two length ways of the panel, to prevent it warping' (1793, pp.293–4).

Sheraton also suggested that bookcase pediments should be made up in a similar way: 'the facia or ground board, glued up in three thicknesses, having the middle piece with the grain right up and down'. Sheraton clearly gave considerable thought to the problem. He noted 'that if any faulty or shaken veneers were cut into 3 feet lengths, and as many of them glued together as to be a proper thickness for the ground of a card table top, they may afterwards be cut down to 3 and ½ widths, and jointed again as solid wood' (Sheraton, 1803, pp. 129–30). In this case the plies were used to restrain the movement of the timber, in addition to giving strength and rigidity.

Again in the 19th century, the process of building up plies was generally to achieve a stable surface rather than a technique that could be used to create new shapes in furniture. Plies, whilst giving strength to cut-out surfaces, were also useful in creating a flat surface that did not warp. This was particularly important for marquetry and Boulle workers. One manual required: 'the ground whereon the pieces are to be ranged and glued is ordinarily of oak or fir, well dried, and to prevent warping, is composed of several thicknesses glued together, with the grain of one layer intersecting the direction of the other' (Martin, 1819, p.112). The value of this method was again noted later. The finest

Parisian ébénistes prepared their *placage* or base for marquetry or Boulle work by using plies of poplar and oak wood glued together with crossed grains. They were then veneered with the appropriate ground wood for the final surface finish (Jackson, F. H., 1903, p.113). The previous examples all used ply as a solution and not as a particular material.

The development of design and manufacturing processes that deliberately exploited plies of wood either in plywood or LAMINATE form may have started in Germany in the early part of the 19th century. It might be argued that the Biedermeier style encouraged this search for a flat, stable base so that the plain and flush surfaces of carcases as well as the veneered frames of sofas would not warp. During the 1830s the Thonet company were producing head and side boards for bed frames and sofas in a built-up veneer form, which were shaped in presses. Alongside these specific developments was a more general method of ply construction called press work. Press work describes the process of building up furniture components by layering a number of veneers in a criss-cross fashion in a mould or CAUL. The process allowed shaped frames to be produced from thin sections of 'plywood'. In 1866 it was new enough to receive the comment: 'Among the recent applications of this art [that is, veneering] may be noticed press-work' (Tomlinson, 1866, vol.iii, p.712). He further describes 'a machine recently constituted for moulding the thin veneers into curves of single or double curvature so as to enable them to be employed for making dished and spheroidal articles'. As late as 1877 press work was still regarded as new enough to be reported in the British trade press. It appeared that it was often made with 'some strong plain wood such as black walnut and rosewood or other fancy wood for the exterior' (*Furniture Gazette*, 18 August 1877, p.120).

This method, also called 'built-up veneer work', was especially used to manufacture sewing-machine cases. The standardization of material made it ideally suited to the production of large numbers of similar objects, and it was for this reason that it was most successful in the sewing-machine industry. The process, which was developed by the French Manufacturing Co of Cincinnati, started in 1865. In 1867, Mr E. F. French obtained a patent, and in the following five years another four patents were granted, all relating to the plywood construction of sewing-machine cases:

The process consists in the making of the cases and the tables each from one board; in the former instances the corners being rounded without joints, the two ends of the boards being securely glued together on one side, each board being composed of seven layers of veneers, each one-eighth of an inch thick, five of whitewood and two of walnut, also glued and pressed together, the grains of the veneers running alternately transversely, by which a firm board is made that cannot, as with solid wood, warp or crack. (*Furniture Gazette*, 31 January 1874, p.109)

Other inventors employed plywood's own special qualities in furniture design. The patent taken out by John Mayo of New York in 1865 appeared to be prophetic:

By adopting the well-known process of wet and dry heating in course of manufacture, the several scales of wood may be brought to such a state of pliability as to assume any desired form by compression in a matrix or upon formers and by using different degrees of thickness, in connection with cements of different kinds, the character of the article made can be either rigid or flexible.
(Cited in Perry, 1948, p.35)

Further experiments on the lines patented by John Mayo continued. The patent of Isaac Cole (US Pat.no.148,350), taken out in March 1874 in the United States, has been seen as a landmark in the history of design. Cole designed a 'new and improved veneer chair' which used plies of veneer to create a continuous seating surface, a back and a support. Although this chair does not appear to have been made commercially, the history of plywood and its use in furniture took a significant leap in 1872. In that year George Gardner was granted a patent for a three-ply veneer or plywood seat (US Pat.no.127,045). The aim of this patent was to protect the production of a replacement for the traditional cane seat. The principle was very simple: a piece of shaped three-ply was prepared to whatever form was required for the creation of the seat and then it was simply nailed onto the chair frame. It was soon obvious that the labour-intensive process of CANING was to decline as a general practice, as a direct result of this new seat.

The concept of the ply-seat was developed in a slightly different way by the Thonet company. Their experiments led them to apply the technology of plywood, together with machine-impressed designs, to produce a 'thermo-plastic' seat, sometimes with a raised design, sometimes with a plaited design, and at other times with pierced holes. The use of perforations in both Thonet and Gardner seats was not only for ventilating purposes, but also to increase the decorative appeal of an otherwise plain seat. In addition to these, the choice was widened further by the use of seats produced in 'imitation intarsia'. This was realized by a process of branding a seat with a design resulting in a two-tone effect. See also Embossing

The value of plywood as a substitute for solid wood in the construction of furniture was fully recognized once the rotary cutting of logs into continuous veneers became a commercial proposition. Although there were many patents and inventions during the century pertaining to rotary cutting, it only became cost-effective in the 1880s. The corollary to this invention was the realization that a suitable glue would be essential. Experiments in Russia produced a blood albumen and casein cement (see Adhesives) that was water-resistant and strong enough to make a complete bond between veneers. These experiments and developments were part of the European reaction to the success of the Gardner company in the USA. Early plywoods were bonded with vegetable glues, hence they had virtually no moisture resistance and the material became derided to a degree.

Christian Luther set up a firm in Tallin (Reval), Estonia, to exploit the European demand for plywood. Around 1884, Luther's experiments with three-ply led him firstly to develop chair seats, and then, by 1892, fully-assembled bentwood and ply furniture. It has been suggested that the first production of steam-pressed plywood sheets occurred around 1895, when pieces suitable for tea-chests were imported into London by E. H. Archer, the founder of the Venesta plywood company (Wood and Linn, 1942, p.188).

According to Nikolaus Pevsner, an independent investigation into the use of plywood for furniture-making was made by Karl Schmidt, known for the establishment of the Deutsche Werkstatten. He was asked to produce a cabinet designed by J. V. Cissarz, which had flush doors. Taking the three-ply chair seat principle, he developed it into five-ply and attempted to make a flush-faced cabinet (see Plate XVIII). The successes eventually came and in 1902 Schmidt was able to establish a plywood factory in Rehfelde near Berlin (Pevsner, 1937, pp. 75–6).

Plywood was soon accepted in commercial cabinet furniture manufacturing. The American Come-packt furniture Co described the making of their furniture in 1901; 'wherever possible we make use of a laminated five ply top for the tables … These tops cost considerably more than solid tops but we know they will never warp or get out of shape' (Come-packt Catalogue, 1901, Winterthur Library).

One of the major uses was to substitute solid wood drawer-bottoms

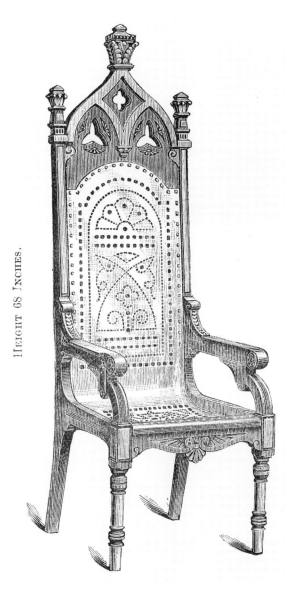

HEIGHT 68 INCHES.

FAR LEFT
93 *Plywood was soon accepted
as a suitable furniture
component. This 'Officer's chair'
in perforated veneer (plywood) is
a good example. Gardner and Co,
New York, c.1884.*

LEFT
94 *The development of plywood
for applications other than
furniture created opportunites for
designers who were able to
transfer the technology. This
plywood chair has its seat panel
bent in two planes, an idea
developed from wartime plywood
leg splints.*

with plywood, and by 1927 this method had become almost universal. In many instances plywood was also introduced for the backs, tops and dustboards of furniture. Apart from the savings these innovations introduced, it is clear that another major benefit of using ply components could be found in the weight reduction of the furniture. The development of true plywood, from its substitute for solid wood in panel situations, to its use in the manufacture of curved and bent surfaces, progressed through the early to mid part of the 20th century. Various architects and designers experimented with the material during the 1920s, and although Alvar Aalto is commonly credited with the first successful use of bent plywood, there were many experiments before his seminal products. For example, in 1927–8 Geritt Rietveld designed a steel-framed plywood-seated chair, which combined the two 'modern' materials: steel and plywood. Gerald Summers used aeroplane ply as an experimental material for furniture-making which resulted in the curved surfaces that were the hallmark of his company,

Makers of Simple Furniture. In his designs, the economy of production, requiring only four basic steps and a cold moulding process made his single-sheet bent-plywood armchair an exciting proposition. Thirdly, in 1936, Marcel Breuer designed the famous plywood Isokon long chair and associated furniture, all using bent plywood. Although these designs were not popular, the ideas that came from these avant-garde pioneers were assimilated by the commercial manufacturers quite easily. Bent plywood was used in the construction of many 'moderne' or 'art deco' influenced trade designs for anything from coffee tables to cocktail cabinets.

One major development in the use of plywood for furniture was the three-dimensional forms introduced by Charles Eames and Eero Saarinen in 1940. The jury of the Museum of Modern Art's (New York) competition of organic design in home furnishings, awarded these chairs first prize. The exhibition catalogue (1941) recorded the importance of these chairs: 'A significant innovation was that, in the case of chairs by Saarinen and Eames, a manufacturing method never previously applied to furniture was employed to make a light structural shell consisting of layers of plastic glue and wood veneer molded in three-dimensional forms'. The Eames's attempts to develop the organic armchair show something of the spirit of invention that involved making plaster moulds, layering veneer and glue foil alternately, sealing the load and then pressing a heated vacuum membrane against the whole so that the glue melted and the veneers took the mould's shape after 4–6 hours pressure.

During World War II, Charles and Ray Eames worked with the Moulded Plywood Division of Evans Products to further develop

95 An experimental British
sideboard with veneered stressed-
skin panels and metal extrusions,
produced for the Board of Trade,
c.1946–8.

95 An experimental British sideboard with veneered stressed-skin panels and metal extrusions, produced for the Board of Trade, c.1946–8.

awareness of this fact should go a long way to dispelling the prejudice towards plywood in furniture.

In a comment immediately after the war it was recognized that, 'the use of this "new" material was largely the means whereby it was found possible to offer attractive and serviceable furniture within the reach of the lower income classes' (*Working Party Report*, 1946, p.54). Despite this, the practical application of suitable designs for manufacture incorporating plywood, did not appear to have been exploited to the full at this time. The *Working Party Report* (Board of Trade, 1946) considered that although constructional and design changes had begun to be made, there was great potential to develop them further with plywood. In addition, the same report showed some foresight when they questioned the time-consuming processes of building up flat or curved panels by edge jointing (coopering) and cramping boards. They asked how long would it be before a reconstituted material was used which would avoid the problem of built-up boards. This acknowledgement of plywood, and by implication other board material, seems to have foreseen the developing panel process for furniture-making.

The situation in the USA was slightly different to Europe. A British 'Productivity Team' (1952) made comment about the relatively small part played by plywood in the American furniture industry at that time. They noted that the trade would rather use solid timber or 'core-stock' similar to blockboard. This was in some measure due to the easier availability of hardwoods in the USA.

The developing use of plywood necessitated changes in furniture CONSTRUCTION. Plywood panels encouraged flush surfaces in cabinet design, and the supply of pre-formed moulded shapes could be used for chair and seat parts. Not surprisingly, it was the architect-led contract market that encouraged these developments. A good example would be the Hillestak chair of 1949–50, designed by Robin Day for Hille, which used pre-formed plywood for the backs and seats, combined with a laminated wood spine.

The possibilities of plywood being used in a batch production system where standardized parts were readily available for straightforward assembly, was clearly advantageous. For example, the production of 'tubes' of bent ply and LAMINATES pre-formed to shape would allow parts to be sliced off to make complete arm sides or frames, whilst the development of moulds enabled many complex shapes to be built up, which could easily be fitted to frames.

Plywood continued to be an innovative material for 20th-century designers. One example is the development of the one-piece plywood NXT chair by Peter Karpf in 1991. This uses the strength of plies in diagonal as well as vertical and horizontal make-ups, and has resulted in a chair weighing only 3.5 kg (8 lb) but capable of normal use.
See also Veneers

Boulton, B. (1921), *The Manufacture of Plywood and Glue*, London: Pitman.
Deese, M. (1992), 'Gerald Summers: Makers of Simple Furniture', in *Journal of Design History*, 5, no.3.
Knight, E. V. and Wulpi, M. (1927), *Veneers and Plywood*, New York: Ronald Press Co.
Logie, Gordon (1947), *Furniture from Machines*, London: Allen and Unwin.
Perry, T. D. (1948), *Modern Plywood*, New York: Pitman.
Shand, P. Morton (1936), 'Timber as a reconstructed material', in *Architectural Review*, February, pp.75–89.
Venesta Ltd (1948), *Our First Fifty Years 1898–1948*, London: Venesta Ltd.
Wainwright, S. (1927), *Modern Plywood*, London: Benn.
Westwood, B. (1939), 'Plywood – a review', in *Architectural Review*, 86, pp.123–42.
Wood, Andrew (1963), *Plywoods of the World: Their Development, Manufacture and Application*, revised edn, Edinburgh: W. & A. K. Johnston.
Wood, Andrew and Linn, T. G. (1942), *Plywoods, Development, Manufacture and Application*, Edinburgh: W. & A. K. Johnston.

their work. The use of plywood components in items as varied as leg splints and gliders was developed and again provided the breakthroughs that would eventually feed into commercial furniture products. Their 1945 children's chair made of two pieces of moulded ply was the first post-war use of their innovative production methods.

The difficulties of combining different types of material was highlighted by Eames's work. Originally the technique of cycle welding (developed by Chrysler to bond rubber to wood or metal) was first considered by Eames and Saarinen for the fixings in their chairs designed for the Organic Design in Home Furnishing Competition in 1940. As this method was reserved for the war effort, the chairs had to be fixed in another way. In 1945–6 a satisfactory mass-production technique for connecting the parts of the chair was finally achieved on the assembly line, by gluing the shock mounts to the wood pieces with a resorcinol-phenolic adhesive, applied with heat and pressure. The legs were then screwed to the shock-mounted spine, and the seat was attached to the legs and spine by four additional shock mounts.

Quite clearly the development of plywood during the war was to have far-reaching effects on the furniture industry. In World War II, major developments such as the work of the Eames's, as well as sandwich or stressed skin plywoods made the material respected in its own right. In Britain, plywood had been used very successfully in building gliders, landing craft and most especially in the Mosquito plane. Commentators who noted that the fuselage of Mosquito planes and Vampires were constructed of plywood, considered that public

Pocket screwing

A method of fixing table tops and the like by boring an oblique hole through a rail and screwing it up. The hole is then hidden by a BUTTON or OLIVE.

Pocket springs

See Springs

Point d'Hongrie

See Stitches (Flame)

Poker work

A method of decorating wood surfaces by burning the wood with heated tools. It is one of the most elementary methods of decorating and was often practised as a hobby in the 19th-century home. It has affinities with XULOPYROGRAPHY, the art of charred wood engraving, which enjoyed a brief period of success in the mid 19th century.

Probably first used for producing designs on North Italian cedar and cypress chests in the 15th century, it was also used in 17th-century Italian work. Writing in England in 1819, T. Martin thought that this form of decoration, which resembles painting on wood, 'had lately been discovered'. After a full description of the process, he had high hopes for it: 'We may fairly expect from the specimens we have seen of this ingenious mode of painting that the panels of our cabinets may be made to exhibit performances in this way that shall rival the most successful attempts at imitative art' (1819, p.118).

See also Burned wood-carving process, Xulopyrography

Thompson, W. D. (1901), *Poker Work; Including Coloured Poker Work and Relief Burning*, London: L. U. Gill.

Pole lathe

See Bodger, Lathe

Polish

The process of burnishing a surface or a surface coating, or the application of a finish such as wax (see below), oil (see below) or French polish (see below). The desire to polish furniture surfaces to protect, enhance the colour and to provide a shine, have long been part of the furniture-maker's business. The Romans used oil of cedar and juniper as well as wax to polish their wooden furniture (Richter, 1966, p.124). In the Middle Ages, polishing with waxes and oils was deemed not so important since medieval furniture was often painted. After painted surfaces declined in favour of decorative wooden surfaces, from the 16th century, oils such as nut, poppy and linseed, and later waxing became popular finishing materials. Both oil and wax continue to be used in furniture finishing, alongside a wide range of more sophisticated products and recipes.

Of all the processes of furniture-making that could be mechanized, polishing seemed to be the least likely. Nevertheless, in the USA alone, thirteen processes were patented between 1790 and 1873 for machines to polish cabinets. By the 1920s they were apparently common in American furniture factories, either as automatic machines or portable hand-held machines.

BUTTON POLISH

See Resins (Lac)

FRENCH POLISHING

Friction varnishing or French polishing was the most important furniture finishing innovation of the 19th century. Nicholson explained that this 'new and durable mode of polishing or varnishing … consists in

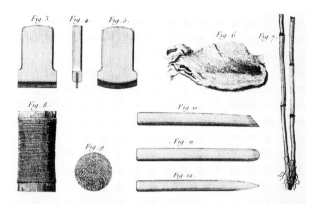

96 *Eighteenth-century polishing equipment is illustrated in this plate from Roubo. The sticks, fish skins and bundles of rushes are clearly shown.*

applying a considerable quantity of transparent gum-lac over the surface, so that the surface of the gum appears as if it were the surface of the wood' (1826, p.7).

It was significant that it became a completely separate part of the trade with its own specialist workers, price lists and trade secrets. French practitioners of the art are said to have been established in London as early as 1808, but writers in the second decade of the century were still claiming its novelty. In 1818 Thomas Gill found French polishing to be 'nearly new' in furniture-making (pp.371–2), although he pointed out that hitherto it had been used for lathe turned work, especially musical instruments. There were soon numerous recipes including the following example published in 1820:

Take of mastic one ounce, sandarac one ounce, seed lac one ounce, shell lac one ounce, gum lac one ounce, gum arabic one ounce and virgin wax quarter of an ounce; these reduce to powder, and put into a bottle with a quart of rectified spirits of wine; after standing some hours, it will be fit for use. Application: Make a ball of cloth and on it put a little of the polish: afterwards wrap over the ball a piece of calico, which touch on the outside with a little linseed oil; then rub the furniture hard, with a circular motion until a gloss is produced, finish with one third of the polish to two thirds of the spirit of wine. (Brown, *Rudiments of Drawing …*, 1820)

In 1823 the 'new' process was praised again:

The Parisians have now introduced an entirely new mode of polishing which is called plaque, and is to wood precisely what plating is to metal. The wood by some process is made to resemble marble, and has all the beauty of that article with much of its solidity. It is even asserted by persons who have made trial of the new mode that water may be spilled upon it without staining it. (*Mechanics Magazine*, 22 November 1823)

In 1829 it was still seen as a comparatively modern process which was beneficial to the furniture:

The method of varnishing furniture by means of rubbing it on the surface of the wood, is of comparatively modern date. To put on a hard face, which shall not be so liable to scratch as varnish, and yet appear equally fine, the French polish was introduced. (Stokes, 1829, pp.100–1)

By the 1830s it was fully accepted that

in large towns such as London and Edinburgh, where the art of polishing furniture forms a distinct operation, what is called French polish is by far the best for bringing out the beauties of wood, and giving it a brightness and richness of colour which nothing else hitherto invented can produce. (Loudon, 1839, p.1063)

The reason for his encouragement was that 'it is not liable to crack or show scratches like varnish'. However, although it was a highly popu-

97 With the advent of furniture-making factories, large quantities of varnish were required. In the case of Harris Lebus, London, they established their own polish-manufactory to keep a regular supply, c.1910.

lar finish with the public, design critics hastened to condemn the process. Charles Eastlake, comparing it to hand (wax) polishing, incorrectly said 'The present system of French-polishing, or literally varnishing, furniture is destructive of all artistic effect in its appearance, because the surface of wood thus lacquered can never change colour, or acquire that rich hue which is one of the chief charms of old cabinet work' (1868, p.83). Arthur Hayden, an early-20th-century antiquarian, denigrated the practice in the following terms: 'High polished surfaces and veneers and that abomination French polish which is a cheap and nasty method of disguising poor wood, brings furniture within the early 19th century days when a wave of Philistine banalities swept over Europe' (Hayden, 1905, p.236).

By the 20th century the process of application still remained specialized and time-consuming. The French polishers had established themselves as a separate part of the trade, and therefore in many instances they worked in their own workshops, although in larger factories they were employed as hands. In early-20th-century factories, both men and women were employed as polishers, the women usually working on small items and the cheaper work. Two circumstances hastened its general demise: changes in polishing technology and new consumer demands. The improvement brought about by the new spraying techniques can be seen in that it took up to nine and a half hours to polish a sideboard by hand (plus an allowance for the hardening-off time), whereas by nitro-cellulose spray it took only twenty-five minutes. The new synthetic lacquers were more resistant to wear and tear and the taste for a high-shine finish also declined.

GARNET POLISH
See Resins (Lac)

GLAZING (aka Slake, Finish or Telegraph)
A cheap, later-19th-century polishing finish comprising mastic (1 oz), benzoin (5 oz) and methylated spirit (5 gills). This was applied in one or two steady sweeps over a previously prepared surface.

OIL POLISHING
This original process, which rubbed oil (sometimes mixed with a mild abrasive like tripoli or brick dust) into the timber, was time-consuming. The surface was rubbed, allowed to dry to touch, then re-oiled and burnished. Although there were many recipes, in the later 19th century the process could involve using a surface filler, followed by a coat of shellac which, in cheap work, was rubbed down with raw oil and then cleaned off. For better quality work the process was similar but used three coats of varnish, each of which was allowed to harden. This was then followed by a rubbing of ground pumice stone and oil which polished the varnish coat. French cabinet-makers used tripoli as an abrasive, and oil instead of brick dust. Evelyn mentions that

there is a way so to tinge oak after long burying and soaking in water which gives it a wonderful politure [polish] as that it has been frequently taken for a coarse ebony. The process of putting walnut into a hot oven so that the oils in the timber are heated and rise to the surface so that they can be used to polish the surface.
(1662)

Evelyn also recorded the idea of oil polishing for particular timbers: 'Ebony, Box, Larch, Lotus, Terebinth, Cornus, etc, which are best to receive politure, and for this linseed oil or the sweetest nut oil does the effect best' (ibid.).

Although considerably overstated, Neve indicated the apparently beneficial preservative effects of linseed oil as a finish: 'It was experimented with in a walnut-tree table, where it destroyed millions of worms immediately, and is to be practis'd for tables, mathematical instruments, boxes, bedsteads, chairs &c. Oyl of walnut will doubtless do the same, is sweeter and better varnish' (Neve, 1726, p.261). In the papers of John and William Myers of Wheldrake, Yorks (1778) the following method of oil-polishing is recorded:

To polish mahogany doors oyle it over with linseed oyle over night then in the morning take sum brick dust put it into a silk stocking or anything that is fine then dash it over the door and take a piece of new carpitt or any woolon cloth and rub it. Oyle coats after another with brick dust and oyle until you make a glow till you can see your self in it.
(Cited in Gilbert, 1991, p.18)

This practice was clearly quite common; indeed Sheraton noted that 'the general mode of polishing plain cabinet work is ... with oil and brick dust'. Sheraton listed the methods of his day: '1. soft wax and a little red oil; 2. unsoftened wax; 3. the general mode being linseed oil (plain or stained with alkanet) rubbed with brick dust which creates a putty which results in a fine polish; 4. chairs are usually polished with a wax mixture rubbed in with a polishing brush' (1803, pp.289–90). A little later, Loudon noted that cold drawn linseed oil alone, rubbed for several hours until a bright polish was obtained, was ideal for table tops and was more effective than French polish for tables (1839, p.1063). In the 1880s oil polishing was still described as 'the best and most perfect finish that can be given to hardwoods ... for it can be varied to suit all conditions. It is the cheapest and best for common chamber or parlour suites, and at the same time can be made the most beautiful for the highest-priced furniture' (Yapp, c.1885, p.22). Oil finishes were revived for unpolished matt wood surfaces such as teak in the 1950s and 1960s.

WAX POLISHING
Known in the ancient world for giving a lustrous shine to timber, the use of wax was revived from the early 16th century. Wax finishes were noted by Evelyn. After describing a black staining method, he gave the recipe: 'melt some beeswax, mixing it with your lamp black and size, and when tis cold, make it up into a ball and rub it over your former black, lastly, with a polishing brush (made of short stiff boars bristles) labour it till the lustre be to your liking' (Evelyn, 1664, ii, pp. 3, 4). A little later, Moxon gave a description of 'in the lathe' wax polishing in which

they hold either a piece of seal-skin or Dutch reeds (whose outer skin or film somewhat finely cuts) pretty hard against their work, and so make it smooth enough to polish. Hard wood they polish with bees-wax, viz. by holding bees-wax against, till it hath sufficiently touched it all over; and press it hard into it by holding hard the edge of a flat piece of hard wood made sizeable and suitable to the work they work upon, as the work is going about. They then set a gloss on it with a very dry woollen rag, lightly smeared with salad oil. (1677, p.213)

Wax finishes were also illustrated by Roubo (1772) who discussed hard and soft wax methods. The hard wax was a process for veneered furniture, of rubbing liquid beeswax onto a surface with a small bundle of grasses tied in a 56 × 10 cm (22 × 4 in) cylinder, which then forced the wax into the pores of the wood. The use of cork was to be avoided as it might generate too much heat. The surface was then buffed to remove excess wax. This method produced a high-gloss finish. For solid wood furniture Roubo recommended a soft wax and tallow mix. The surface to be finished was warmed and the wax mix was applied by brush and then buffed.

The waxing process (in this case mixed with turpentine) was also used in England. This would seem to have produced a less glossy finish than the above, and it was still recommended for interior wood-work in Sheraton's *Dictionary*. In 1793 the *Cabinet-makers' London Book of Prices* noted that 'Polishing the outside of any work with hard wax to be double the price of oil polishing' and 'Ditto with turpentine and wax to be half the price extra for oil polishing'.

The application of wax using corks, brushes and linen rubbers was still common in the early 19th century. Indeed, Tingry noted that 'Many cabinet-makers are contented with waxing common furniture such as tables, chests of drawers etc', and went on to say that wax seemed preferable to varnish: 'This seems to be the case with tables of walnut-tree wood exposed to daily use, chairs mouldings and for all small articles subject to constant employment' (1832, pp.57–8). This 'kind of polish is used in various stained articles, as also for chairs and bedsteads' (Nicholson, 1826, p.12). Other recipes included wax composition (aka Furniture paste) which was made from beeswax dissolved in turpentine, with the addition of one-sixteenth part powdered rosin or copal varnish (Loudon, 1839, p.1064). For black stained furniture a heel-ball of black wax was used, or a method called CHAR-COAL POLISHING, which gave a black finish like ebony, was also employed.

Wax polishing was more common in America and could be used on its own or as a finish over varnished surfaces. Beeswax was recommended partly because it acted as a filler and top coat in one; for example, beeswax was used 'to fill up all the chinks and crevices of the top of a gaming table' (Cotton, 1725, p.13). In America, during the 18th century, beeswax was exported and Bayberry wax was used on occasion as a finishing wax. Carnauba wax from Brazil was not available until the mid 19th century.

See also Finish, Lacquer, Varnish

Anon. (1921), *The French Polisher's Handbook, with a Section on Gilding and Bronzing*, London: P. Marshall & Co.
Anon. (n.d.), *A Practical Guide to French Polishing, Including Furniture Polishing, Graining, Staining, Varnishing, Japanning, Wax and Dull Polishing and Stencilling*, Wyman, SPL.
Bairstow, P. and Waterhouse, A. (1993), *French Polishing*, London: Batsford.
Bitmead, R. (1876), *Practical French Polisher and Enameller*, London.
Denning, D. (1895), *Polishes and Stains for Woods: How to Use and Prepare Them*, London: Upcott Gill.
Field, J. (1919), *The French Polisher's Handbook, How to Polish from the White*, Bolton: Field, J.
Gill, T. (1818), 'On French varnish for cabinet work', in *Annals of Philosophy*, XI, pp.119, 371, London.

Godla, J. (1991), 'The use of wax finishes on pre-industrial American furniture', in *Papers Presented to the Wooden Artifacts Group*, AIC annual meeting, Albuquerque, New Mexico.
Mussey, R. D. (1982), 'Old finishes and early varnishes', Techniques 6, in *Fine Wood-working*, March/April, pp.71–5.
Standage, H. C. (1892), *Practical Polish and Varnish Maker*, London: E. F. and N. Spon.

See also bibliography for Finish

Polishers

Prior to the development of French polish, wood finishing was undertaken by the cabinet-maker. With the introduction of FRENCH POLISH-ING in England, *c*.1815, a separate trade was developed by immigrant French and native craftsmen who worked at all levels of the trade. In 1851 the English census listed 4294 French polishers. Polishing was sometimes undertaken by women workers, but de-skilling occurred in all parts of the trade, due to polishing's demise in the face of spray finishing in mechanized plants, in the early to mid 20th century.

Anon. (1885), *French Polishers' Trade Price List*, London: Wyman.
Hervé, F. (1897), *French Polishers and Their Industry*, London.

Pollarded wood

The crown of a tree is a poll, therefore the removal of the crown or top branches is known as pollarding. The top of a young tree and its branches are removed, and each season they are trimmed back so that the growth is concentrated into a large bulbous shape on the top of the trunk. When mature, these can be cut and sliced as burrs. OAK, POPLAR, WILLOW and ELM are all suitable trees for this process which creates knurls and BURRS. Pollarded oak was widely used in the early part of the 19th century for burr-oak furniture. Rudolph Ackermann noted 'The manufacture of British woods such as pollarded oak and elm cut transversely near the roots is so well understood and so beautiful when thus applied, that they need no other recommendation to the admirers of superior furniture' (Ackermann, January 1824, Plate 135). In France the pollarding of WALNUT trees was fashionable.

Polyanthus wood

A timber which appears to have been given an exotic label for promotional purposes. Its botanical identity is not yet known. In 1821 Robert James, a cabinet-maker from Bristol, was described as a 'manufacturer of the beautiful polyanthus wood'. His advertisement explains that this wood 'will be found to excel any other yet offered, for beauty of colours, and variety to the imagination, exhibiting on its highly polished surface, Woods, Landscapes, and in some instances Animals, fish &c. are represented which has a grand and pleasing effect' (cited in Walton, 1976).

Walton, K. M. (1976), 'Eighteenth century cabinet-making in Bristol', in *Furniture History*, XII, pp.59–64.

Polychromatic turning

See Turning

Polychrome

A term that refers to the use of more than one colour, usually paint; it is often used to describe medieval and 19th-century Gothic revival furniture decorated in such a fashion.
See Painting

Polyester lacquer

See Lacquer

Polyether
An abbreviation of Polyurethane-ether.
See Plastic foam

Polyethylene
See Plastics

Polymethyl methylacrylate
See Plastics (Synthetic, Acrylic)

Polypropylene
See Plastics

Polystyrene
See Plastics

Polyurethane lacquer
See Lacquer

Polyvinyl chloride
See Coated fabrics (PVC), Plastics

Pommelle
See Sapele

Ponderosa pine
See Pine

Poplar (*Populus spp.*)
A European hardwood with an average density of 400–560 (25–35 lb/cu ft), it is creamy whitish-yellow to grey in colour, with an even texture and a close straight grain. Poplar was occasionally used by Romans for veneering, and is sometimes found in medieval chests where part of the trunk is cut to form a lid (example in Hereford Cathedral *c.*1440). In the 16th and early 17th centuries it was used, sometimes stained, for inlay and marquetry, whilst in America in the 17th century it was used by turners for chair legs and such like. In the 18th century it was used in Germany in both solid, veneer and inlay, whilst burrs (resembling amboyna) were especially favoured in the Biedermeier period. In Italy the *populus serotina* has been used for secondary parts in cabinet work, and this use for interior cabinet work was revived in the 20th century. Poplar has also been a plywood timber and certain cuts sometimes provide an effect known as 'peanut shell graining'.
See also Aspen, Cottonwood, Tulipwood, Whitewood

Porcelain, inlays and plaques
See Ceramic

Porcupine wood (*Cocus nucifera*)
A timber from the coco PALM with variegated markings resembling porcupine quills. The brown variety is known as PHEASANT wood.
See Coconut, Palmyra

Porphyry
A hard igneous rock composed of feldspar crystals embedded in rock, the name coming from *pupura* or purple colour. Often the white/red feldspar crystals are embedded in a red ground. Known in Roman times, it was usually limited to imperial use. A porphyry throne was used in the installation of Popes (Cloisters of St John Lateran, Rome,

Sedes Stercoraria). It was especially favoured in 16th- and 17th-century Florentine and Roman MOSAIC work, and was used on occasion in the 18th century for table slabs, in place of marble. In the 1850s the London Polytechnic Exhibition showed a table, 1.78 m (5 ft 10 in) in diameter, made from porphyry inlaid with pieces of various colours and supported on a porphyry fluted pedestal.

Castro, Morcati Di (1987), 'The revival of the working of Porphry in sixteenth century Florence', in *Apollo*, CXXVI, 308, pp.242–8.

Post-Modernism
A style that reacted against the MODERNISM and FUNCTIONALISM of mid- to late-twentieth-century design. Inspired by Pop art and an interest in popular culture, it developed into a multifaceted style equally at home in any of the arts. Building on the pop culture of the 1960s, post-Modern design developed a style which was witty, ironic and eclectic in its sources and was intended to bridge the gap between high and low culture. Part of this was the upsetting of traditional design conventions, which were replaced by a wide range of eclectic imagery and design approaches. Furniture produced in this idiom has been associated with the use of colour, pattern and unashamed borrowing of historical models often juxtaposed in incongruous ways. The revival of ART DECO motifs and imagery was one particular aspect of the style.

Pounce
A powdery coloured substance such as SANDARAC, pipeclay or charcoal, which was dusted over a perforated patterned sheet to transfer a design to the surface below. When lightly heated, the substance adhered to the wood to give a clear outline for accurate pattern cutting. Known since at least the 16th century, pounce was particularly used for replicating designs in MARQUETRY work. The process was facilitated by a pounce box. The pom-pom was a variation on the process, using asphaltum, in the late 19th century and onward.
See also Marquetry

Power tools
Any wood or metal-working tool that is portable but has an electric (mains or battery) or compressed air power supply. The first hand-held power tools were operated from light sockets. One of the first was a router produced in 1909, a portable jointer was developed in 1914, and in 1918 the first direct motor drive bench saw was available.

Prairie grass
See Grasses

Preen
Man-made or synthetic rubber foams produced under a variety of trade names: Aeropreen, Sorbopreen, Vitapreen.
See also Foam, Latex

Première-partie
When laying VENEERS where there are only two materials, the background in one panel can often be the infill in the other. With particular reference to BOULLE work, première-partie refers to the panel with the most valuable material, while 'contre-partie' refers to the process of compensation of material in these sorts of designs or to the panel with the less valuable material predominating.
See also Boulle work

Press
See Veneers

Press work
See Plywood

Prickall
An upholsterer's tool that was described in 1649 as 'a kind of awl …
[which] with the blow of a hammer on the head is made a hole to put
and drive the shank of a brass nail into wood which would not drive
otherwise' (Holme, 1649, III, V, p.273).
See also Awl

Prima vera (*Rosodendron Donellsmithii*)
A Central American and Mexican timber with an average density of
460 (28 lb/cu ft). Creamy yellow to yellow-gold in colour, it has a
straight grain, a streaky figure and a coarse texture. Used in the USA
during the later 19th century for cabinet-making. In the 20th century
it has been used as a fine furniture wood for bedroom and dining
suites in the USA. Aka White mahogany.

Primitive construction
See Construction (Dug out)

Prince's metal
A BRASS alloy of c.75 per cent copper and 25 per cent zinc, pickled in
dilute spirit of vitriol (sulphuric acid), then immersed in nitric acid
before the final burnishing.
See also Nails

Prince(s)wood (*Cordia gerascanthus*)
A West Indian timber, brown with irregular markings, hard and heavy
with a smooth, close grain. In 1756, Jamaican 'Spanish Elm or Princes-
wood … is generally esteemed as one of the best timber woods in the
island' (P. Browne, p.170). Now known as Canalete. In 1679 Ham
House had a scriptoire of 'Prince wood garnished with silver'
(Thornton and Tomlin, 1980, p.83).

Printed cotton
Printed cottons imported from India were used in European furnishing schemes from the late 16th century. These were hand-printed
cloths finished with mordants (metallic oxides) which reacted with the
dye to fix the colours in the fibres. English manufacturers began to
copy the designs and the process by using carved wooden blocks. In
1676 William Sherwin was granted a patent for 'a new way for printing broad calicoe' in 'the only true way of East India printing and
stayning such kind of goods'. From the mid 18th century the printing
in intaglio by flat engraved copperplates was developed. This method
was first established in Ireland in 1752 and later in England. The
printers used 91 cm (36 in) square plates in combination with a press,
but though limited to single colour prints, they had a long repeat
pattern potential, ideal for bed curtains and drapery. By 1756 copperplate printing was soon a speciality of London until the technique
was taken to France by 1770 when *toiles de Jouy* were printed by C.P.
Oberkampf at his works in Jouy-en-Josas. In the 1790s Oberkampf
used engraved copper rollers to replace the flat plates.

The important copper rotary-cylinder printing invention was
patented by Thomas Bell in 1783, but it was not until thirty years later
that commercial production was really significant in England. This resulted in faster printing, multi-colour results which, after 1830, took
advantage of the new dyestuffs which were becoming available. The

'furniture print' intended for curtains, the filling and the chair seat
was especially popular in the early 19th century.

Although screen printing was known as early as the second half of
the 17th century, it was not until the 1920s that commercial production
was possible. This still remained a hand operation until the 1950s
when the process was mechanized, and it is now the most economical
method of printing cloth.
See also Chintz

Clark, Hazel (1985), *Textile Printing*, Aylesbury: Shire.
Clayton, M. and Oakes, A. (1954), 'Early calico printers around London', in
    Burlington Magazine, XCVI, pp.135–9.
Montgomery, F. (1970), *Printed Textiles: English and American Cottons and Linens
    1700–1850*, London: Thames and Hudson.

Printed silk
Plain silk fabrics that are overprinted with designs. Sheraton recommended 'French printed silk or satin, sewed on to the stuffing with
borders round them' or even pasting the silk onto a rebated top rail
panel with a gold bead edging for drawing room chairs (1793, p.387).

Printing
The application of decorative finishes to furniture by printing processes (including silk screen and lithography) has a long history. As
early as 1638, William Billingsley patented a method of printing furniture and so on with liquid gold and silver (Pat.no.121). In 1739,
Stephen Bedford of Birmingham devised a method of printing single-
colour transfer prints, imitating engraving, on small wooden objects
(Pat.no.737). However, the process of transfer printing was in fact a
19th-century invention and was used to especially ornament iron or
brass bed posts and frames. Thermography was a particular printing
process, devised by a Felix Abate of Naples in 1854, which exposed
veneer-wood to the evaporation of hydrochloric acid or sulphuric
acid, either in vapours or dilution. A paper or cloth design was pressed
on to the treated veneer and, as soon as the wood was heated, a 'most
perfect and beautiful representation of the printing instantly appears'
(*Furniture Gazette*, 13 December 1873, p.590). In 1859 a process of imitating sepia drawings by charring the surface of the wood with heated
engraved cylinders was invented by Mr Brigg. In this case a cylinder
was heated by gas to allow some control over the temperature of the
charring process. Once the shadow effect had been obtained, the surface was rubbed down and polished. Following the developments of
photography, the copying process was used by the photographic
transfer of designs to wood. This was the Pixis method of transferring
photographs to wood (Haldane (1883), *Workshop Receipts*, pp.193–5).
The idea was revived in the mid 20th century for use on areas such as
cabinet doors and chests, but was usually associated with screen
printing or plastic laminates.
See also Stencils, Xylography

Pritch awl
See Awl

Protective furnishing
Loose or fitted covers for chairs and sofas, bookcases, table and
commode tops, and beds, which were intended to protect the finer
materials underneath, were often supplied by upholsterers. The
covers might be made from LEATHER, BAIZE, DRUGGETT and others,
and linen HOLLAND was popular in the 19th century for the making
of protective and storage covers. PAPER covers were also used in a
variety of situations, mainly as dust and light protection. The commonplace nature of protective covers can be seen in the household of

Sir Richard Worsley: in c.1779 the housekeeper's store room had '8 crimson serge cases for gilt chairs … 2 damask leather covers for pier tables … green baize covers for pictures and glasses … [and] 2 green and white stripe cases for sofas' (Boynton, 1965, p.51). The three main areas requiring protection were upholstery, beds and fine cabinet work.

BED PROTECTION

In the 17th century prestige beds, especially, were supplied with a set of 'case curtains' and extra rods to keep the main fabrics clean and dust free. By the later 17th century, the importance of keeping expensive beds clean was noted by Daniel Marot who annotated one design for a bed with outer case curtains as necessary 'pour conserver le lit contre la poussière' (Thornton, 1978, p.177). They were still needed for prestigious beds much later. In 1786 Sir John Griffin-Griffin was supplied with 'an outside polished curtain rod, made to fold on the Doom, with a set of Irish cloth curtains to draw round the bed' (Beard, 1997, p.310). These curtains, costing £1. 15s. 0d., protected the state bed which had cost him £398 in total.

CABINETS AND TABLE PROTECTION

The supply of fitted covers for globes and of cases for cabinets, table tops and triads began during the 17th century. Sometimes they made a dual contribution, being decorative in their own right. In 1649, Randle Holme recorded 'A Turky table cover or carpett of cloth or leather printed' (XIV, p.15). By the 18th century they were in common use and were included in many invoices and inventories. Chippendale supplied '2 Damask leather covers lin'd and bond with gilt leather' to the half-round sections of dining tables for Paxton (Berwick). In 1803 Sheraton explained how 'covers for pier tables [were] made of stamped leather and glazed, lined with flannel to save the varnish'. He goes on to say: 'Lately they have introduced a new kind of painted canvas, varnished and very elastic in its nature and will probably answer better than leather' (1803, p.336). Bookcase covers (in this case for the protection of books) made from silk were designed so that they were

suspended within side and at the top of the case by a spring roller, in the manner of a blind, and is made to draw to the bottom of the case where spring locks are placed to receive the means for confining it; they are confined to the sides by grooves, and thus become as protecting as doors would be, without their weight or inconvenience.
(Ackermann, vol.X, July 1813, p.42)

The desire to protect expensive furnishings continues with the use of 'table felt', loose covers and dust sheets.

UPHOLSTERY PROTECTION

Fitted but removable top covers for upholstery were also known as slip covers. The idea of a set of covers that gave a fitted look but were simply removable at will, either for purposes of protection or pattern change, has been popular for many centuries. Occasionally this practice was reversed and the finer covers were fitted only when required. The range of protective furnishings was necessarily wide. In 1588 Robert Dudley had a carved and embroidered walnut chair that was sufficiently important to have 'a case of buckerom to the same' (Beard, 1997, p.284). In 1663 Samuel Pepys explained how he was 'alytering my chairs in my chamber, and set them above in the red room, they being turkeywork; and so put their green covers upon those that were above, not so handsome' (Diary, 11 October 1663).

In 1773, Chippendale advised Lady Knatchbull that 'serge is the most commonly used [for covers] but … you might chose some sort of calico' (Gilbert, 1978, p.57). Hepplewhite illustrates a wing easy chair and noted that they may 'have a linen case to fit over the canvas stuffing as it is most usual and convenient' (The Cabinet-maker and Upholsterer's Guide, 1794, p.3). Loudon describes how

A very cheap yet tasteful loose sofa cover may be made of glazed self-coloured calico, with a narrow piece of different coloured calico or shawl bordering, laid on about a couple of inches from the edge. This kind of cover lasts clean much longer than one of common printed cotton.
(1839, p.325)

The particular use of linen holland is shown in a representative example of a 19th-century housekeeping manual:

When chairs are fitted up with damask, merino, stuff, horse hair, or other material that does not wash, they are generally covered with Holland, chintz, or glazed calico, which protects them from dust and dirt, and are easily removed, when required for company. Holland covers are the most durable, but too cold; chintz, unless very strong, should be lined with thin glazed calico. The cover should be made exactly to fit the chair or sofa, with or without piping at the edge, and with the loops sewed on three of the sides underneath, and a pair of strings on the fourth side; the cover is firmly fastened down by passing one of the strings through the three loops and making it tie.
(Workwoman's Guide, 1840, p.206)

Baumgarten, Linda (1993), 'Protective covers for furniture and its contents', in American Furniture, pp.3–14.
Clabburn, P. (1989), 'Case covers', in The National Trust Book of Furnishing Textiles, Harmondsworth: Penguin, pp.166–76.
Montgomery, Florence (1984), 'Case covers', in Textiles in America 1650–1870, New York: Norton, pp.123–7.

Pterygota (Pterygota bequaertii)

A tropical West African timber with an average density of 570–640 (35–40 lb/cu ft). It is pale yellow to white, with a fairly coarse texture and an interlocked grain. Used in the 20th century for plywood and utilitarian furniture, sometimes as a substitute for beech or ramin.

Pull over edge

An upholstery term referring to the method of fitting a top cover by pulling the cloth over the leading edge and sides to create a convex shape in which the seat and borders are one continuous piece of fabric.

Pumice stone

A porous lava stone used in POLISHING a variety of surfaces. In the 19th century it was particularly used for polishing the surfaces of woods which were open grained. The process involved wetting the surface and rubbing with a flat piece of pumice and allowing to dry. The process was repeated until the desired degree of smoothness was achieved. Fine-ground pumice on a damp cloth was also used for polishing japanned, varnished and painted goods. Cabinet-makers were particularly advised to smooth the expansions in AMBOYNA veneers by the action of pumice and oil (Blackie, 1853, p.42).

Punches

A range of steel tools designed for particular piercing, driving or decorative marking of wood or metal. Various trades employed differing models to perform specialized tasks:

Buhl punch or Carver's or Steel punch
Made with a shaped point in a variety of designs for low-relief carving and infill designs within high-relief work. Frosting punches make small indentations, in particular shapes such as circles, stars and other groups of small designs for infill work.

Upholsterer's punch
Has a serrated edge and is used for cutting out tufts for mattresses and ornamental finishes.

Veneer punch
Has an irregular outline and is used to cut out blemishes in veneer, such as holes or cracks. A replacement piece is then cut with the same tool and can be fitted in the space.

Punch work
A decorative process which uses PUNCHES with various-shaped ends to cut a pattern into a wooden surface. Although a feature of 17th-century cabinet work, it can be found in 19th-century work as well.

Purl
See Passementerie

Purpleheart (*Peltogyne spp.*)
A Central American and tropical South American timber, especially from British Guinea, with an average density of 980 (62 lb/cu ft). The name is derived from the deep purple colour when freshly cut which, upon exposure, matures to a rich browny black. With a fine texture and a variable grain, it is a superb furniture timber. Sometimes interlocked grain may produce a striped figure on quartered surfaces. The best coloured veneers are obtained from saw-cut veneers since steaming (for rotary cutting) adversely affects the colouration.

Known as *bois d'amarante* in France, it was extensively used in the 18th century for marquetry, parquetry and full surface decoration. Roubo confusingly recorded that Amaranth (purpleheart) was *'appellé par les Anglois Mahageni ou Magohini : espèce de bois violet que les hollandois nous vendent'* (known by the English as Mahogany: a kind of purple wood sold to us by the Dutch) (1772, p.770). It has been used for stringing and banding since the 18th century. In America it has been used to a limited extent for marquetry, billiard tables and fancy cabinet work. Widely used in England during the 19th century, it was imported in the round, in logs 2.40–3 m (8–10 ft) long and 15–23 cm (6–9 in) in diameter. According to Knight, '[Purplewood] has lately been introduced into this country' (1830, p.179). A mid-19th-century description noted that,

Purple wood, called also Amaranthus, is a product of Brazil, and like most other woods of small growth and irregular shape, is imported in the round state … Purple wood is sometimes confounded with kingwood and violet wood, but these are frequently figured whereas purple wood is usually plain. It is used for buhl-work, for marquetry, and turning, and is sold by weight. (Blackie, 1853, p.40)

It is still used for fancy turning, inlay and marquetry in the 20th century. Aka Amaranth, Violetwood.

PVC
See Coated fabrics, Plastics

Pyrography
See Burned wood-carving process, Poker work, Xulopyrography

Quadrant hinge
See Hinge

Quadrant stay
See Stays

Quarter sawing
See Conversion

Quartering
See Veneering

Quaruba (*Vochysia spp.*)
A Brazilian and Central American timber similar to mahogany but with an average density of 520 (32 lb/cu ft). It is reddish-brown in colour, varying considerably in texture and workability. It has a coarse open grain and flecked surface. Its tendency to distort and its brittleness have not prevented its importation during the latter part of the 20th century.

Queensland maple (*Flindersia brayleyana*)
See Maple

Queensland walnut
See Walnut (Australian)

Quilling
See Filigree

Quilting
A technique of sandwiching material and filling to create a padded effect. Initially used in saddlery and armoury for padded overlays, it was adapted to upholstery techniques during the 17th century. The connection with the origins of upholstery and the role of the saddler and carriage-maker is clear (see Upholstery). Quilting was also a well-known technique in the preparation of 18th- and 19th-century bed 'furnitures'.
See also Marcella

Rabbet or **Rebate**
A continuous rectangular channel cut along a piece of wood, usually to receive a panel or other component. It may be cut manually or by a rebate plane, or if multiple copies are required a side FILLISTER plane is used.

Rail
A general term used to denote many horizontal parts of furniture or woodwork.

Raised work
See Stumpwork

Ramin (*Gonystylus bancanus*)
A hardwood from South East Asia with an average density of 650 (41 lb/cu ft). It is a straw colour, with a moderately fine texture and an even grain but with little decorative value. Used in cheap furniture construction in the latter part of the 20th century.

Rattan (*Calamus*)
Rattan is derived from a climbing palm found in the East Indies and had been known to furniture-makers for a long time as the source of CANE used for chair seats and backs. Cane is simply the pared 'inner bark' of the rattan palm (*Calamus rotang*), whilst REED is the core of that palm. Whereas cane has been used in furniture since at least the 1650s for the infill of seats and backs, the reed or the inner part of the plant was discarded until the mid 19th century.

By around 1840 American businessman Cyrus Wakefield started to sell rattan to basket-makers, who used the inside reed, and sold the outer skin to chair-makers for seating. His business grew and developed a wide range of rattan products as well as specialized machinery to process it. The popularity of rattan furniture grew in these years, as well as the demand for cane seating and so on. In the USA rattan was particularly recommended because 'the principle excellence of cane [rattan] as a material for chairs, sofas, baskets etc., are its durability, elasticity and great facility of being turned and twisted into an almost endless variety of shapes' (Wheeler, 1851, p.199). In 1897 the merging of the Wakefield business with the Heywood company, who were making similar products, became the Heywood-Wakefield Co.

The taste for rattan furniture continued and was adopted by progressive designers as well as traditionalists. Rattan was available in an enormous range of styles, colours and finishes (including bronzed, gilded and coppered) to suit all parts of the market. In many cases it was further embellished with trimmings and paint work by the owners.

Even a straightforward natural material such as rattan has been the subject of imitation. In America, during the 1950s, the idea of fabricating a rattan substitute was introduced. The 'rattan look' was created from round-section steam-bent wood which was coloured to the tone of cane and charred at intervals to give a natural look (see Plate XVI). See also Cane, Lloyd Loom, Wicker

Adamson, Jeremy (1993), *American Wicker*, New York: Rizzoli.
United Nations Industrial Development Organization (1996), *Design and Manufacture of Bamboo and Rattan Furniture*, Vienna: UNIDO.

Rattan wood
See Mahogany

Ratteen or **Rateen**
A thick twilled KERSEY type woollen cloth with a friezed or curled nap. Postlethwayt defined it as 'a thick woollen stuff, quilled, woven on a loom with four treadles like serges and other stuffs that have the whale or quilling – there are some prepared like cloths, others left simply in the hair, and others where the hair or nap is frized' (1751). Sheraton (citing Chambers) says that they are mostly made in France, Holland and Italy and are generally used in linings (1803, p.294). During the 18th century rateen was used for upholstery, bed hangings and curtains.

Rattinet
A thin woollen material of a thinner substance than RATTEEN used, among other uses, to line curtains. Similar to SHALLOON. Chippendale supplied Edward Knatchbull with '67 yards fine buff Rattinet to line curtains' in the late 1770s (Gilbert, 1978, I, p.233).

Rawhide
See Leather

Rebate
See Rabbet

Recliner chair mechanisms
See Chair mechanisms

Recycled materials
Although a number of furniture-making materials have been recycled at various times, including timber wood, carvings, upholstery fillings and covers, these have been for reasons such as economy or scarcity of the material. In the late 20th century materials that have been used for other purposes have been recycled to make furniture. These have included plastic shampoo bottles, car seats, broken glass and manhole covers. For the more commercial market materials such as MADERON, recycled plastics (see POLYPROPYLENE, POLYETHELYENE) and CARD-BOARD have been incorporated into 'green design'.

Red alder
See Alder

Red gum
See American red gum

Red maple
See Maple

Red pine
See Pine (Scots)

Red river gum
See Eucalyptus wood

Red sanders
See Sanderswood

Redwood
See Sequoia

Reed
(a) The inner core of the RATTAN plant after the removal of the outer cane. Used in the USA from *c*.1880 by the Wakefield Rattan Co for chair-making as an alternative to cane furniture. Since the reed furniture had had its glossy outer coating removed, it could easily be stained or painted, rather than left natural as cane or rattan.
See also Rattan

(b) Reeds are also the name for the strip components of TAMBOUR doors. In 1793 it was suggested that they were glued up in two thicknesses or were made up in two differing colour woods (*Cabinet-maker's London Book of Prices*, 1793).
See also Grasses

Reeding
A simple but elegant form of carving which is based on a series of parallel convex mouldings. It is the reverse of FLUTING. A popular decorative technique in the later 18th century.

Regency
The period 1790 to 1840, although not just the period of the Regency, describes the general changes in taste influenced by the Greek revival, the Egyptian and French Empire tastes and the continuation of a version of the NEO-CLASSICAL taste. Furniture was characterized by the use of strongly figured woods such as EBONY, MAHOGANY or ROSE-WOOD. Decoration included JAPANNING, PENWORK, BRASS inlays and mounts. The revival of BOULLE work was associated with this style and George Bullock was one of its major exponents.
See also Satinwood, Verre églomisé

Regulator

An important tool of the upholsterer. A regulator is a steel spike, 15–30 cm (6–12 in) long with a flattened base and a tapering point. It is used to position (regulate) filling material through the hessian or calico (or similar) covering so that the correct profile is constructed.
See also Stuffing stick

Relief intarsia

See Intarsia

Renaissance

An artistic movement that was established by the early 15th century, which was to have a profound effect on all the arts. Initially the artist and the craftsman were equal and the two worked together on projects such as painted cassone, but a gulf developed between them in the 15th century which has remained to this day. Renaissance style was based on Roman orders and original features in conjunction with an interest in Man and Nature. The basis of much of the design was a system rather than simply ornamental forms, although details such as the acanthus, mouldings, shells, swags and putti were all part of the repertoire. Ranging from Italian INTARSIA and painted cassone to English OAK tables, chairs and cabinets, from massive architecturally proportioned mid-European presses and cupboards to the finest and most skilfully made cabinets that were themselves works of art, the Renaissance saw the flowering of the furniture-makers' craft. Towards the end of the period, furniture was designed to complement the interior, although these schemes are often classified as Mannerist, Baroque or neo-Classical. In the second half of the 19th century, a Renaissance revival took place which combined the motifs of the original style with carving, porcelain insets and marquetry work. MAHOGANY, ROSEWOOD and WALNUT are featured woods, and upholstery is important in this revival.
See Intarsia, Inlay, Joiner

Rep(p)

A furnishing textile, usually of cotton, wool or silk, with a fine warp and a thick weft which gave it a distinctive transverse, corded or ribbed effect. As an upholstery fabric it was popular in the 19th century. Gobelins or Printed rep was produced to look like tapestry and was introduced in France in the 1870s. Tycoon rep, although usually described as a dress fabric, was used by do-it-yourselfers for upholstery as it was cheaper and gave a warm and soft effect in imitation of printed Eastern designs. In the late 19th century, 'furniture rep' was a flowered cotton fabric whilst a 'worsted rep' was plain coloured and used for curtains and upholstery. By the early 20th century cotton rep was also widely used.

Resins

A natural or synthetic material which is insoluble in water, though usually soluble in drying oils, turpentine or alcohol. Resins are widely used in making PLASTICS, LACQUER and VARNISHES. Natural resins are all derived from vegetable matter (particularly conifer trees, and in other cases tropical trees) apart from shellac, and have been used since early times in various applications.

Acrylic
See Plastics

Anime
A fossilized resin found in East Africa. Very hard and nearly as insoluble as AMBER, it is not soluble in alcohol, but only dissolves in high temperature oils. However, it dries quickly so that it was substituted for COPAL in fixed oil varnishes and used to impart a high gloss.

Balsam
Resinous exudations of the trees (especially coniferous).
See further, below

Benzoin
A resin taken from the tree *Styrax benzoin* from Sumatra, or the *Laurus benzoin* grown in America. It was used in the manufacture of varnishes from the 16th to the 19th centuries on account of its lustre and relative hardness, but most especially for its scent. Not used in the later 20th century.

Camphor
A resin distilled from *Cinnamomum camphora*. Used as an ingredient in varnish-making, often as a softener and in making celluloid.

Colophony
See Rosin (below)

Copal
A tree resin sourced in the West Indies, South America and Africa from a number of tropical trees including *Copaifera langsdorfii*, and located in various shapes and sizes in the ground. It is a constituent of a hard, shiny and transparent varnish. Like other 'hard' resins it can only be made into a solution by liquefying with heat and then mixing with a hot drying oil. The name is possibly derived from the Aztec word *copalli* (resin) and the resin was introduced to the West *c*.1577. Sheraton gives a recipe for a high-quality varnish: By dissolving copal in linseed oil, then diluting it with spirit of turpentine, a 'beautiful and transparent varnish, which when properly applied and slowly dried, is very hard and durable. This varnish is applied to snuff boxes, tea-boards and other utensils' (1803, p.173). A few years later it was still praised as it will 'neither dissolve in spirits of wine nor essential oils, except by a certain process. It may however be dissolved by digestion in linseed oil. Copal varnish is superior to any other' (Nicholson, 1826, p.6). Its particular benefit was in its lack of colour and relative hardness. It remained popular as an ingredient of varnish until the 1940s.
See Vernis Martin

Dammar
The resin of South-East Asian trees of genus *Agathis*. When dissolved in turpentine, it could produce a clear varnish.

Elemi
Resin obtained from Central and South America from a variety of trees (for example, *Burseraceae*) which is used in varnish-making for toughness and flexibility.

Fossil resin
See Amber

Kauri
A resin from coniferous trees of the species *Agathis* found in New Zealand. The East Indian variety of kauri pine (*Agathis alba*) produces a resin (Manila COPAL) which can also be found fossilized. Introduced *c*.1823, it is of lesser quality than copal but was widely used in early-20th-century VARNISHES. This variety has also been used for furniture in the second half of the 20th century.

Lac (shellac)
A resinous substance secreted by the lac insect (indigenous to South East Asia) upon the twigs and young branches of certain trees, in particular, species of fig. The female lac insects, *Laccifer lacca*, exude

a secretion that accrues and coalesces, forming hard, resinous layers that eventually completely cover the twigs of the trees. Stick lac was the crude lac after scraping from the twigs. When this was ground and washed, it granulated into seed-lac which is the partially purified state. When melted, strained and formed into sheets, it is known as shellac. Shellac varies in colour from yellow to deep orange. When bleached, it is known as white shellac. The term shellac is often applied to a solution of the resin in alcohol, which is used as a varnish (French polish). Lac was imported into Europe by the second half of the 17th century and used as a spirit varnish resin. It was the basis of lacquers for cabinet work through the 19th century.
See Varnish (Shellac)

Button polish: A grade of shellac, used in French polishing recipes. The name derives from the button-shaped discs into which the SHELLAC formed after processing. The 'buttons' were translucent orange, so the shellac quality could be seen when held to the light.

Garnet polish: A grade of shellac, used in French-polishing recipes, that is red-brown in colour. It is used mainly for mahogany, walnut and similar darker-coloured timbers.

See also Japanning, Polish, Varnish

Mastic
A resin from the *Pistacia lentiscus*, a small Mediterranean sumach tree. Mastic is almost colourless and is soluble in alcohol and turpentine; it was used in the making of spirit and essential oil varnishes. Although it dries rapidly, it darkens and becomes brittle with age. Often used to finish painting in the 18th century, it was also used neat as an infill, in conjunction with brass, probably to create a tortoiseshell inlay effect (see examples of infill in Gilbert and Murdoch, 1993, pp.51–2).

Rosin (Colophony)
The distilled balsam from pine trees, in effect the remains after turpentine has been distilled off. When warmed, it liquefies and becomes sticky. Mixed with beeswax, it was used as a glue for stone mosaic work. In the 19th century it was mixed with SHELLAC to cheapen French polish.

Sandarac
A North African resin in small yellow scales, from the THUYA (*Tetraclinus articulata*), which is either dissolved in alcohol to make spirit-VARNISH or in oils to make an oil-varnish. A mix of linseed oil and sandarac was a varnish recipe in use in the 17th century. It was a main ingredient in French varnish during the later 18th century. Softer than shellac and less brilliant, it was therefore used for a pale varnish for lighter-coloured woods. It was not much used in the later 20th century. Aka Gum juniper.

Shellac
See above, Lac

Synthetic resins
See Plastics, especially cellulose nitrate, cellulose acetate, phenol formaldehyde

Turpentine
Trees from the genus *Pinaceae* (pines) yield common turpentine which distils into oil of turpentine and leaves a residual rosin or colophony. Larch give Venice turpentine and firs produce Strasbourg turpentine and Canadian balsam. Oil of turpentine is a common ingredient in spirit varnishes.

Barry, T. H. (1932), *Natural Varnish Resins*, London: Ernest Benn.

Mantell, C. L. et al. (1942), *The Technology of Natural Resins*, New York and London: J. Wiley & Sons.

Reversible seat
A cushion which has a face cloth on both sides. See also Seasonal furnishings (Eckhardt's patent reversible seat)

Rhus vernicifera
See Lacquer (Urushi)

Riffler
A double-ended file or rasp with two curved heads tapered and shaped, which are especially used by carvers. The styles vary but include squared, oval or sharp edges, with rasp or file finishes. They are used for smoothing concave parts of carved work.

Rimu (*Dacrydium cupressinum*)
A coniferous New Zealand timber with an average density of 560 (35 lb/cu ft). It has a pale yellow sapwood and a light brown to red heartwood. With a fine, even texture and a straight grain, it is often cut into veneers for cabinet work. In the early 20th century it was an important timber. 'It is largely employed in the manufacture of furniture, the old wood being handsomely marked like rosewood, but of a lighter brown hue' (Spon, 1901, p.144). It was noticed how 'working as readily as Birch, and comparable in strength to Oak, it is likely to replace satin walnut, which it somewhat resembles, as a cabinet wood, being far more reliable than that timber' (Boulger, 1908, p.262). It can produce fine burr veneers. Aka Red pine.

Rip saw
See Saws

Riving
A method of timber CONVERSION used in the 16th and 17th centuries, which was done single-handedly as opposed to pit sawing. As a simple one-man method a large reinforced mallet called a Beetle was used to drive in large iron wedges to split timber baulks. As the timber sections became smaller, a maul or MALLET and a FROE were used. By positioning the froe onto the end grain of the baulk of timber and knocking it with the maul, the wood could be 'worked' to split along the rift. Riving allowed the radial surfaces of the baulks to become the working face, which meant easier working and less distortion or movement.

Roan
See Leather

Robinia or **Acacia** (*Robina pseudoacacia*)
A widely distributed tree with an average density of 710 (45 lb/cu ft), it has a dull, yellow colour with brown veins, a coarse texture and a straight grain. Known to the Ancient Egyptians, the variety *acacia nilotica* was an indigenous species widely used as a furniture timber until the Third Dynasty. It was introduced from America (where it was known as LOCUSTWOOD) to Europe in the 17th century where it was used for inlays and bandings. In the 19th century it was said that 'in North America it is more highly valued by the cabinet-maker and turner, than any other native timber' (Blackie, 1853, p.47). Some authorities have seen it used as a substitute for SATINWOOD. Today it is used for cabinet work and decorative veneering.
See Locustwood (Black locust in USA)

Rock crystal

A very hard clear quartz mineral found in a wide variety of deposits throughout the world. The yellow variety is known as citrine, whilst the purple variety is amethystine quartz. This natural quartz material was used in the surface decoration of exotic pieces of furniture over many centuries. Excavations in the Assyrian Sennacharib's Palace found several portions of a throne in rock crystal. In the mid 14th century crystal was used in the form of thin pieces combined with silver for the decoration of a *faudesteuil* for King John of France. In the 16th century it was used in Italy for pietre dure work and its difficulty of working meant it often became part of the jeweller's repertoire. In the 17th century, following a German tradition, rock crystal along with other semi-precious stones were introduced into cabinets. King Charles I owned 'a rich cabinet of cristal with silver gilt and copper gilt, in a red chest lined with crimson satin' (Jervis, 1989, p.285). As with other highly exotic materials, cabinets worked with rock crystal were often made as gifts for dignitaries. French examples from the late 17th century include the gifts to the King of Siam: for example, a large cabinet of rock-crystal with decoration of silver-gilt flowers. Naturally the material was also used for chandeliers, but its use declined with the improvement in blown crystal glass at the end of the 17th century.
See also Glass

Rococo

Originally sprouting from the BAROQUE, Rococo was developed in the late 1690s by Jean Berain and Pierre Le Pautre in France. By the early 18th century the Régence (1715–23) developed it further, but it was only later, in the 1730s, that the rest of Europe was affected. The style is particularly characterized by a vitality of movement that is expressed in asymmetrical motifs, C and S scrolls, the incorporation of CHINOISERIE, and a taste for exuberant designs such as *bombé* commodes. Lacquer, paint and applied ormolu were often part of the decorative schemes which were frequently designed as a complete interior. Upholstery reached new heights of luxury in the search for comfort and style, and a wide range of 'new' furniture types were developed. The Rococo revival occurred in the early 19th century in England and then in Germany from where it soon spread to America. The extravagant work of J. H. Belter, Charles Baudouine and Alexandre Roux testify to this *nouveau riche* taste.
See Carving, Chinoiserie, Gilding, Lacquer, Mahogany

Rods

A method of marking out patterns onto timber prior to cutting was to use 'templates' called rods. These consisted of 1 cm (½ in) pine boards which had drawn upon them a full-scale plan of the component to be made. This was shown complete with joints and rails, so that accurate measurements could be taken for timber stock. The use of rods as 'working drawings' was clearly beneficial in the factory processing of furniture that had been made from a high number of components.
See also Setting out

Rolled edge

A description of an upholstery technique favoured in the latter part of the 19th century. It consisted of a thick padded roll of filling material fixed to the leading edges of chairs and sofas. It was often covered in a contrasting material to the main body of the upholstery, and in some cases was bound with cord.

Rosewood

A name for a variety of different species which are identified as heavy, dense, dark-streaked timbers of the *Leguminose* order. Generally it varies from light hazel to nearly black and is renowned for its streaky purple-black figure. The name 'rosewood' was originally given to PADOUK on account of its rose colour. When Indian rosewood was introduced in the late 1750s it was called 'black rosewood' to distinguish it from padouk.

Brazilian rosewood (*Dalbergia nigra*)

A Brazilian hardwood, heavy, dense and durable with a dark purplish-brown colour and a variegated figure. It is mostly straight-grained with a coarse texture. Referred to by Evelyn as an inlay, in the 18th century it was occasionally used as veneer. After the opening of direct trade with Brazil in 1808 it became much more common. Its size was important in the 19th century. Knight noted that imports were commonly of 56 cm (22 in) wide logs which were then cut into veneers, with solid sections being used for legs and the like (1830, p.176). Its popularity continued so that it could be said that 'next to mahogany, it is the most abundant of furniture woods, a large quantity is cut into veneers for upholstery and cabinet work, and solid pieces are used for the same purposes' (Holtzapffel, 1846, p.104). It remained a cabinet wood, becoming popular in the Art Deco style and again in the 1960s for high-class 'modernist' furniture in Europe. Aka Rio, Bahia, Jacaranda or Palissander.

Honduras rosewood (*Dalbergia stevensonii*)

A timber exclusive to Belize, with an average density of 1000 (63 lb/cu ft). Pink to purplish-brown with black markings, it has a variable grain and a medium to fine texture. Not much used in the 18th century but occasionally called West Indian rosewood. During the 19th century it was considered to be 'an inferior kind … so soft, porous, and ill coloured, as to be fit only for the manufacture of ordinary furniture' (Blackie, 1853, p.24). In the 20th century it has been widely used for decorative veneers and turnery.

Indian rosewood (*Dalbergia latifolia*)

A distinctive hardwood with an average density of 830 (52 lb/cu ft). It is coloured rose to purple dark-brown with purple-black streaks. It has a uniform texture and is moderately coarse with a ribbon grain figure due to narrow interlocked grain. Widely used for decorative veneers and turnery. Introduced in the late 1750s and then called black rosewood to distinguish it from PADOUK (which had originally been called rosewood on account of its colour). Popular in the 19th century for furniture-making, it was referred to as East Indian Blackwood or Sissoo.
See also Cocobolo, Granadilla

Rosin

See Resins

Rottenstone

A decomposed siliceous limestone that in powdered or 'brick' form, and in combination with oils, has been used to polish surfaces such as BOULLE work, pearl and metal work since the 17th century at least. It was in use up to the middle of the 20th century to create highly polished surfaces by friction rather than abrasion.
See also Polish

Router

A hand or machine tool that gouges out patterns into a wooden surface. Various types include beading, circular, lining, ovolo and stringing. Also used *c.*1950 to cut through surface veneers to reveal substrata of differing coloured laminated woods as a decorative feature. Simple hand-made versions for routing curved lines were easily assembled from a block, an arm and a piece of cutting steel. The SCRATCH STOCK did the same job, but for straight lines near edges.

Routing

The process of cutting out lines, grooves or patterns in a surface ready to receive inlays or other features. It also refers to cutting out shapes in solid wood. Routing may be done by hand using a ROUTER tool, or by machine. The stringing router is an example of a specialist tool used by cabinet-makers to prepare for inlaying STRINGING.

Rowan (*Sorbus aucparia*)

A European timber with an average density of 640 (40 lb/cu ft). It is a light reddish-brown colour with a fine uniform texture, and is easy to work. It has been used to a small extent in Europe for cabinet work, carving and turnery. Aka Mountain ash.

Rubbed joint

See Joints

Rubber cloth

See Coated fabrics

Rubber foam

See Latex

Rubber suspensions

See Four point platform, Webbing (Rubber)

Rubberized hair

New latex technology encouraged the use of rubberized HAIR, and the first use of this composite material appears to have been in cockpit seats during 1929. It is fabricated from curled hair that has been formed into a pad using a natural or synthetic rubber binder. It may be moulded to particular shapes.

Ruche

See Passementerie

Rugging

An inexpensive upholstery filling made from jute rags and other materials such as carpet and HESSIAN. It has a tendency to pack down in time but has been used in cheap mattresses.

Rule joint

See Joints

Runners

See Drawers

Running stitch

See Stitches

Rush seats

Early references indicate a medieval usage, but it was for much of the 17th century that rush-seated chairs were popular and acceptable throughout Europe. 'Rush', as a defining word for materials used for BOTTOMING, is all embracing and could refer to a range of materials including bulrush, Dutch rushes, flags, marsh grass, reed, seagrass, sedge (for these, see Grasses), twine and basswood. Regional techniques and styles varied, but a trade seems to have been established in England in the mid 17th century. At this time American methods followed those of England in this respect.

On occasion, rush seats would be painted. In the French royal court, rush-seated chairs were sometimes japanned and were often supplied with a squab cushion. The idea of painting the rush seat for decoration and preservation appears again in the early 19th century. Sheraton gives details:

Rush bottom seats ought always to have their seats primed with common white lead, ground up in linseed oil, and diluted with spirits of turpentine. The first priming preserves the rushes, and hardens them; and, to make it come cheaper the second coat of priming may have half Spanish white in it, if the price require it. The third coat should be ground up in spirits of turpentine only and diluted with hard varnish, which will dry quick … They who use any kind of water colour for rush bottoms, entirely deceive the purchaser for it rots the rushes, and by the sudden push of the hand upon the seat, the colour will frequently fly off.
(1803, pp.422–3)

In the later 19th century, rush seating was adopted by the craftsmen and designers of the Arts and Crafts movement, as the material represented many of the qualities they stood for. The well-known ebonized framed Sussex chair made by Morris and Co is such an example, of which many others occur in regional furniture as well as in reproductions.

Plaited rushes were also woven into 'mats' to lay on bed webs or ropes, to provide support for the mattress.
See also Grasses, Matted seats

Holdstock, Ricky (1989), *Seat Weaving in Rush, Cane and Corol*, Lewes: Guild of Master Craftsman.

Russia leather

See Leather

Russell

A wool satin-weave damask-like textile, woven in Norwich from at least 1547. The name derives from *Rijssel* the Dutch name for Lille, from where the technology was taken. They were hot pressed in order to create a 'satin-look' and were also called Norwich satins and Norwich fustians. In Isaac Smith's 1787 inventory of his Boston, Mass., home there was an 'easy chair in green russell, 6 mahogany chairs russell bottoms, 1 set green russell curtains' (Montgomery, 1984, p.337).

Rustic furniture

Furniture frames that have been either made from unfinished or natural parts of a tree or are carved to resemble branches, roots or trunks of trees, are often defined as being in the rustic style. Popular in the mid 18th century, they continue to be used for garden furniture designs.

In 1765 Robert Manwaring produced a design book in which over a quarter of all the plates represented 'Rural Chairs for Summer Houses' or 'Rural Garden Seats'. The details are instructive in the understanding of the making process:

[The chairs] may be made with the limbs of Yew or Apple trees, as Nature produces them, but the stuff should be very dry and well seasoned; after the bark is peeled clean off, shute for your pitches the nearest pieces you can match for the shape of the back, fore feet and elbows; if you choose to have strait seat rails, you may extend the small boughs over them, fastening them with screws where it is necessary, the bottoms let down with a rabbet, some of them are

usually blocked, provided the seats are made in wood; they are generally painted in various colours.
(Manwaring, 1765, p.22)

A taste for rustic furnishings remained into the mid 19th century. Shirley Hibberd warned about poorly made rustic furniture which used infected wood:

[The wood] soon began to decay within by dry rot, which seldom gave any outward sign, so that a rustic structure in which the process had long been active, would preserve its respectable appearance until the final collapse came, when it would subside into a wreck, and to the owner's surprise, be found to have long consisted only of an outer shell of varnish or paint and a mass of mere dust within.
(*Rustic Adornments for Homes of Taste*, 1870, pp.395–6)

Rustic furniture-making apparently required some sensitivity in its making. Charles McIntosh suggested in 1853 that 'It is next to useless to employ a carpenter [since] they work too much by square and rule, and from habit give their work too much the appearance of art'. He considered that 'all rustic work should be made by an intelligent labourer who has a natural [talent] for these things'. The sort of person McIntosh had in mind, as well as the materials to be used, is made clear. He suggested wintertime because this was when workmen 'can put together the material picked up from time to time during their usual occupations in the woods and forest' which included 'curious excrescences found on old trees, and the natural bent branches' (McIntosh, *The Book of the Garden*, Edinburgh, 1853, vol.1, pp.687–8, cited in Gilborn, 1987).

In the USA during the latter half of the 19th century the camps in the Adirondacks region of New York State developed a distinctive form of rustic furniture. This consisted of three forms: mosaic twig work, the use of BIRCH and birch-bark, and the use of CEDAR. In mosaic twig work split twigs were applied in geometric patterns to the surface of cabinets and cupboards. By using a range of differing coloured woods, naive patterns could be simply created. The birch and birch bark and the cedar woods were also combined with twig mosaic on occasion. The demand soon meant that 'imported' rustic furniture was used in the area and beyond, with factories in Indiana shipping large quantities of rustic furniture made from HICKORY. Firms such as O'Brien Bros of Yonkers, Laurelton Rustic Manufacturing Co and The Old Hickory Furniture Co of Martinsville supplied large numbers of rustic tables, chair and accessories, in some cases up to the 1940s (see Plate XII).

See also Iron (Cast), Terracotta

Gilborn, C. (1987), *Adirondack Furniture and the Rustic Tradition*, New York: Abrams.
Heckscher, M. (1975), 'Eighteenth century rustic furniture designs', in *Furniture History*, XI, pp.59–65.
Mack, D. (1996), *Rustic Furniture Companion*, Asheville N.C., Lark Books.
Stephenson, S. (1979), *Rustic Furniture*, New York: Van Nostrand.

Sabicu (*Lysiloma sabiqu*)

A Central American (Honduras), Cuban and West Indian timber similar to rosewood and mahogany with an average density of 770 (48 lb/cu ft). It is chestnut brown with darker stripes, with an even texture and a close grain. Used in England from 1750 for veneer banding, as well as occasionally in the solid and for veneering. When exported from the West Indies to America in the later 18th century it was sometimes referred to as HORSEFLESH MAHOGANY. In 1793 working it was charged at 17.5 per cent more than standard mahogany (*Cabinet-makers' London Book of Prices*, 1793). It was specified for the staircases in the 1851 Great Exhibition. By 1894 it was sometimes mistaken for

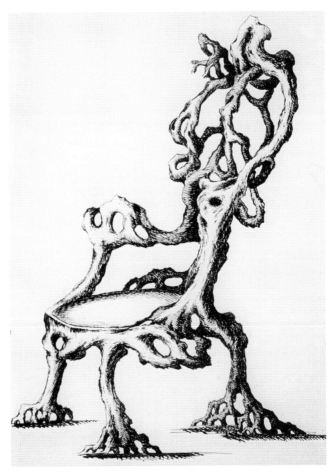

98 The 18th-century rustic style was reproduced in pattern books along with other styles. This pattern for a 'root chair' of rustic design is from Edwards and Darly, A New Book of Chinese Designs, 1754.

rosewood and 'on this account of considerable value … is much prized by cabinet-makers and others who employ it for furniture' (Laslett, 1894, p.279).

Sackcloth

'Sacking' was a bottoming cloth for beds and chaise-longues and was widely used before caning was popular in the 17th century. In 1637 Ralph Grynder supplied Queen Henrietta Maria with 'double sack-cloth and girth for three chairs and three foulding stooles' (Beard, 1997, p.290). In 1764, the London cabinet-maker, Samuel Norman had in stock '15 sacken bottoms of several sizes' (Kirkham, 1969, p.508). For beds, it was tacked to the rebate of the frame or fitted with a canvas edge and held in position by ropes. In 1793 cabinet-makers charged specifically for 'nailing in the sacking' of press beds (*Cabinet-makers' London Book of Prices*, p.40). Sacking as a bed support was still in use in the 19th century (see BED cords), but was gradually replaced by laths, springs and bed-bases.

Saddle bags

A later-19th-century term for the fine 'carpet upholstery' covering, with designs drawn from and imitating the Middle Eastern saddle bags of camels. It has also been used to refer to cheap classes of dining-room furniture.
See also Carpet

99 *The delicate process of sand-shading veneers is shown in this plate from Roubo. The tongs for holding a piece of veneer in the hot sand are also shown.*

Saddling
See Bottoming

San Domingo mahogany
See Mahogany

Sand bag
A sand-filled bag used as a weight to apply pressure to hand-laid veneers during the glue-setting process. They were sometimes held in place by a GO BAR, and have been especially useful for components, such as curved legs.
See also Veneering

Sand box
A box or a bag filled with warm sand. Veneer pieces are laid on top of the sand and the shaped component is laid on the veneer. Finally a weight is placed on top to press the veneer and base together. It is only suitable for hollow or serpentine work, such as drawer fronts.

Sand shading
A process in the preparation of MARQUETRY veneers which involves dipping the prepared pieces into hot sand so as to shade and change the colour. The longer the insertion, the darker the shading will become.

Its early association with INTARSIA is not surprising as colour manipulation was essential to the process. Vasari (1550, p.262) particularly mentions a kind of intarsia accomplished with woods that are tinted and shaded. Evelyn described the process: 'When they [cabinet-makers] would imitate the natural turning of the leaves in their curious compartments and bordures of flower work, they effect it by dipping the pieces so far into hot sand as they would have

shadow.' He also points out that the correct process is undertaken by placing the sand in a brass pan: 'This I mention because the burning with irons, or aqua-fortis is not comparable to it' (1662, p.240). It remains one of the best methods of colouring wood pieces.

Sandalwood (*Santalum album*)
An Indian and East Indian wood with an average density of 940 (59 lb/cu ft). It is yellowish-brown with a firm texture, a straight and very close wavy grain, and a characteristic fragrance. Used in the mid 19th century for the manufacture of small cabinets and for the interior work of items such as escritoires, musical instruments, fans, it has also been used for inlays.

Burmese sandalwood
See Kalamet

West Indian sandalwood
See Amyris

Sandarac
See Resins

Sandblasting
A decorative technique applied to glass and timber to give a roughened surface texture. Used to create 'decorative' effects in the USA in the 1930s by applying the blast against a stencil.

Sanderswood (*Adenanthera pavonina*)
An Indian and East Indian timber with an average density of 800 (50 lb/cu ft). Yellowish-grey to brown, it is occasionally like rosewood in colouring. Howard noted that 'it would be useful in this country, as it already is in India for cabinet work' (1920, p.4).

SANDERSWOOD, YELLOW (*Ximneia americana*)
A substitute for SANDALWOOD. Aka Wild olive or Hog plum.

Sanding machine
See Machinery (Sander)

Sandpaper
See Abrasives

Santa Maria (*Calophyllum brasiliense*)
A timber from the West Indies and Central America (Honduras), with an average density of 640 (40 lb/cu ft). It is a pale pink to reddish-brown timber with interlocked grain, often giving a stripy effect when quarter-sawn. It was sometimes used as a substitute for Mexican MAHOGANY in cabinet work. By the end of the 19th century it was not very abundant and has now become scarce.

Sapele (*Entandrophragma cylindricum*)
A West African hardwood with an average density of 640 (40 lb/cu ft). It is medium darkish-red brown, with a fairly fine texture and an interlocked grain, and a noticeable and characteristic regular stripe on quarter-sawn surfaces. It is fairly easy to work and takes an excellent polish, so has been a widely used furniture wood in the 20th century. Particularly used for high-quality chair-making, it is also prized for finely decorated veneers and has an easily recognizable figure. When blister figure appears, it is also known as plum pudding MAHOGANY, or snail quilt mahogany.
Aka Pommelle

Sapodilla (*Achras zapota*)
A genera of tropical American and West Indian timbers which are generally reddish-brown, heavy and hard. They are the commercial source of GUTTA PERCHA, balata and chicle gum, though sometimes the timber is used for turnery.

Sappan
See Brazilwood

Sapwood
The outer part of a tree trunk beneath the bark, which contains the living cells of the tree. There is often a distinction between heartwood and sapwood in colour. The difference varies between species, from very little in quantity or distinction to as much as 60 per cent, as in red gumwood.

Sarc(s)enet
A thin silk fabric introduced in the Middle Ages and possibly derived from the word Saracen. Used in the 15th century for curtains, for example, 'Curteyns of white Sarsenette' were supplied to a bed made for Louis de Bruges in 1472 (*Archaeologia*, XXVI, 279–80). Another example is dated 1537, when it was used for bed curtains for Katharine of Aragon (Beard, 1997, p.282), and its use continued into the 17th century. The 1679 Ham House inventories list varieties of sarcenet including changeable, clouded, florence, persian and striped (Thornton and Tomlin, 1980, p.166). These were used for blinds and PROTECTIVE FURNISHINGS. In the early 20th century it was still employed for chair backs, draperies, and so on.

Sassafras (*Sassafras officinale*)
A timber from the laurel family, with an average density of 480–530 (30–33 lb/cu ft). It is a dark to light silver-brown colour more commonly known for the use of its root in medicine. In the 19th century it was sometimes used for cabinet-making on account of its scent (Holtzapffel, 1846, p.105), and has been used for decorative veneers in the late 20th century.

Sateen
A soft cotton fabric made in a sateen weave (weft satin weave) with a lustrous surface. Although generally used as a lining material for curtains and drapery, in the later 19th century it was used in American upholstery. In the 20th century 'Glosheen', a heavy sateen with multicoloured flower prints or in plain colours, was used in the 1960s for small chairs and loungers.

Satin
A glossy fabric which is woven so that the fine warp threads float over the weft to give a closely woven, sheen-like effect. Originally a luxurious silk fabric, but when made from coarser yarns, it was called satin of Bruges, or Bridges (see below). It was probably imported into England during the 13th century. In 1392, the Earl of Arundel's will included 'the bed of red and blue satin with half celour' (Eames, 1977, p.80). Satin continued to be used for bed furniture and hangings, and by the end of the 17th century it was also painted. In 1710 a closet in Dyrham Park had 'a window curtaine of painted sattin', and in the Best Bed Chamber there was a 'sattin counterpane flower'd with gold' (Walton, 1986, p.59). Hepplewhite recommended the use of satin bedhangings: 'where a high degree of elegance and grandeur are wanted' (1794, p.18). In the 19th century it was widely used as an upholstery fabric. George Smith suggested that 'in elegant drawing rooms plain coloured satin … assumes the first rank as well for use as richness' (Smith, 1808, p.xii). It is now made from a variety of fibres.
See also Caffar, Caffoy, Damask

SATIN DE BRUGES
A smooth-faced cloth woven from a combination of silk warp and linen weft, imported widely in the 17th century. The 1601 Hardwick Hall inventory recorded 'a table carpet of tissue and purple wrought velvet, lined with crimson sattin bridges' (Boynton, 1971, p.24). It was still identified as a furnishing fabric in the late 19th century.

SATIN DE LAINE
A plain or printed all-wool satin, sometimes imitating woven patterns if printed. Used for curtains and upholstery in the 19th century.

Satin walnut
See American red gum

Satiné (*Brosimum lanciferum*)
A timber from Guiana and Guadeloupe with an average density of 1000 (63 lb/cu ft). It is grey-red to deep rich red and is tough and hard, but works and polishes well. In 1920 it was noted that 'this valuable, highly decorative wood is insufficiently known or appreciated in England … In France however, it has been extensively used and is highly valued for its unusual qualities' (Howard, 1920, p.247). Varieties include satiné *rouge* (red-brown) and satiné *rubanné* (lighter). Aka Bois de féroles.

Satinwood
A fine timber with varieties from India, the Far East, Australia and the West Indies (see below). These timbers generally have a golden-yellow colour with a fine texture and narrowly interlocked grain producing a variety of figures. They are usually used as veneer or inlay. An early example from 1765 was when Mayhew and Ince supplied Earl Coventry with '2 very fine sattin wood and holly commodes'. When Sophie von la Roche made her famous visit to Seddon and Co in 1786, she saw a 'thousand articles of straw-coloured satinwood charmingly finished with all the cabinet-maker's skill' (cited in Gilbert and Wood, 1997, p.33). In 1793 it was charged at 12 per cent more to work than ordinary mahogany.

Satinwood was especially effective as a background for later-18th-century cabinets with painted decoration, as well as for Federal and Regency designs in general. It remains a classic timber for these styles in reproduction.

Australian satinwood (*Zanthoxylum brachyacanthum*)
A bright yellow timber, it is silky, soft, close grained and easily worked. Used in cabinet work in the early 20th century.

East Indian satinwood (*Chloroxylon swietenia*)
A variety with an average density of 990 (62 lb/cu ft) which was mainly used for cross bandings due to the narrowness of available pieces. Sheraton considered that 'East India satinwood is of the hardest texture, and of a small rich figure in the grain, and I think no instance in nature yet discovered does exceed the beauty of the richest sort of it … The wood runs narrow and is used in general only for cross banding' (1803, p.314).

West Indian satinwood (*Zanthoxylum flavum*)
A variety with an average density of 890 (56 lb/cu ft) which has been preferred because of size and workability. It is darker than the East Indian variety with a closer grain. This satinwood has been used since

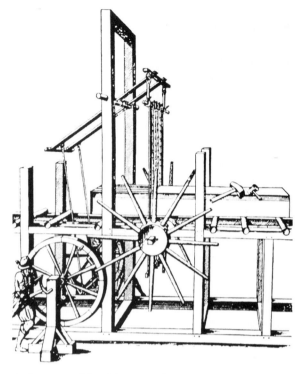

100 A large mechanical frame sawmill used in the 15th and 16th centuries. Probably these sorts of machines were mostly employed in preparing joiners' work.

the later part of the 18th century for panelling, turning, veneering and inlay. Sheraton recorded its popularity:

[West Indian wood is] often more valuable than the East Indian because of its breadth and general utility … This is amongst cabinet-makers a highly valuable wood the best of which is of a fine straw cast, and has therefore a cool, light, and pleasing effect in furniture, on which account it has been much in requisition among people of fashion for about 20 years past.
(1803, p.314)

It began to lose its pre-eminence in the 1820s. Knight considered that 'it is now not much used in cabinet work' (1830, p.178), and by 1853 it was reported that

[satinwood] presented an agreeable variety to the more sombre coloured woods, of which drawing room furniture had been commonly manufactured and for a number of years it was extensively used in preference. That it did not retain this eminence is to be accounted for partly from the caprice of fashionable taste, and partly from the fact that when polished with bee's wax, the mode then in use, it speedily gave off its colour and presented a pale blanched appearance. This defect has been remedied by the introduction of French polish, which preserves the colour; but the wood had fallen into disfavour before the remedy had been discovered, or rather before it had found its way to Britain.
(Blackie, 1853, p.22)

This variety was revived in the early 20th century for the highest class of bedroom suites. Sometimes called prickly yellow wood (on account of its knobbly bark) or simply yellow wood.
See also Saunderswood

Stevens, C. (1984), 'Satinwood furniture', in *Collectors Guide*, November, pp.44–7.

Saunderswood (*Pterocarpus santalinus*)

An Indian and East Indian timber with an average density of 1100–1200 (65–75 lb/cu ft). It is dark red to almost black with striped colour-ing and an interlocked grain. Apart from providing a bright red dye used by French polishers, the timber has been employed for inlay work and small turnings. Sheraton noted it as 'A kind of wood brought from the East Indies of which there are three kinds, white, yellow and red' (1803, p.302). Aka Ruby wood, Santal.

Savanna wood

A timber mentioned specifically in the Federal Society of Philadelphia cabinet-makers' price lists *c*.1800 as being charged extra for working with (Hinckley, 1960, p.37). It is possibly a variety of southern pine, or a corruption of Havana (mahogany) wood.

Saw horse

See Trestles

Sawmills

The early history of sawmills is inevitably difficult to unravel. Beckmann (1817, p.222) suggests that as early as the 4th century AD, sawmills for timber-cutting were in use in Germany. Around 1250 Villard de Honnecourt published designs for sawmills, and it is recorded that water-driven sawmills were in use in Augsburg by 1322, and by 1420 a sawmill was established in Madeira. In the 1550s Norwegian timber was commonly cut into deals by sawmills, and mills were also established in Holland, France, Silesia and Sweden during the 16th century. Although initially intended for the cutting of softwood boards, thin veneers were also cut by the mill method from *c*.1587.

The growth of the trade in the export of timber from Europe and (later) North America meant that the value of sawmills, operated by running water and built near stands of timber, was well-established. Indeed, it was the only practicable way of supplying the increasing demand for pre-cut boards, for a wide range of applications.

The slow acceptance of sawmills in Britain stems from the fact that it was unprofitable to run one, when sawn timber could be imported more cheaply than it could be cut in England. Even though England was therefore not in the forefront of sawmill developments, there were some attempts to develop the mechanized process and the earliest recorded patent that tried this in England was in 1629, when Hugh Bullock received a patent (Pat.no.45) 'for an engine for cutting timber into plank or board'. In 1683, John Booth received a patent (Pat.no.230) for an 'engine for sawing timber and boards without the aid of wind or water', with yet another following in 1703 for George Sorocold (Pat.no.369). It seems safe to assume that these were aimed at the requirements of primary converters and bulk users such as ship and joinery trades, rather than the furniture trade specifically.

Further serious consideration of the problem did not come again in England until 1761 when the Society of Arts awarded a premium to James Stansfield for a plan of a sawmill. This was subsequently built in 1767–8 by Charles Dingley at Limehouse, London, using wind vanes to power it. The vested interests of the pit-sawyers prevailed over innovation; they envisaged the mill putting their livelihoods at risk, and so burned it.

Most sawmills built in the 17th century were based on attempts to replicate the reciprocal motion of the human arm and hand saw. Barely twenty years after the pit sawyers' action at Limehouse, the Society of Arts could report that in 1782 sawmills were well established in England. However, the attitude of the sawyers did not change and Mayhew recorded the sawyers destroying a horse-drawn mill in the early years of the 19th century. Development was rapid from there on, although yet again the spur did not come from the cabinet-making trade but rather was a result of naval requirements. Samuel Bentham was commissioned by the government to tour the Baltic countries to investigate their power-sawing processes, and upon his return he patented his own ideas and began to produce various wood-working machines. In 1791 Bentham developed the principle of saw segments mounted on a circular disc, which enabled sawing to be carried out more speedily and efficiently. In 1805 another engineer, Marc Isambard Brunel, took out a patent for very large circular saws, particularly associated with VENEER cutting, and in 1807 further developed the mechanical saw in association with naval block-making machinery.

These developments did not directly affect the furniture trade, although the possibility of regular control over timber purchase and conversion was clearly useful to makers. The 1731 inventory of John Bastard of Blandford, Dorset, a business whose interests covered building, joinery and furniture-making, specifically lists 'The Engine and wheel for sawing'. Although it is likely that this was a vertical frame saw, as it was housed in a shop which listed large quantities of deals and 'square stuff', there is no evidence to suggest that it was based on designs by any of the patentees mentioned above, or was even a 'mill' operation (Legg, 1994, p.35). In fact, at least one major 18th-century company had its own facilities. In 1786, Sophie von la Roche commented on Seddons of London, who '[had] their own saw-house, in front of which lie blocks of the finest exotic woods, in quantities equal to the piles of firs and oaks seen at our sawmills' (Gilbert & Wood, 1997, p.33). Other quality makers, Linnell for example, are recorded as having saw-pits in their yard, whilst others only had drying rooms and store rooms, the assumption being that timber had been already cut elsewhere.

By 1825 it was said that sawmills were common all over Britain. With changes in import regulations, which favoured American square-hewn timber rather than Baltic sawn timber, there was a greater demand on the sawmillers. The interest in developing powered sawmills had its heyday between 1842 and 1852, when 34 English patents were taken out relating to the cutting and sawing of wood. However, even as late as 1862 half of the Royal Navy's timber requirements were still hand converted.

In America from the 17th century, the sawmill was important to the economy and became one of the mainstays of the expansion westward from the coastal regions. By the beginning of the 19th century, the sophistication and importance of these mills (now steam-powered) for plank, board and rotary cut veneer is clear:

Steam saw mill and mahogany yard Richardson and Co. Having recently put into operation their improved patent rotatory veneer cutters, propelled by steam power, are prepared to cut veneers of any given dimension … they also saw boards, plank, &c. in the best manner, with an improved vertical saw … Fine veneers cut to convenient sizes, can be supplied for shipping on the shortest notice … [to] any part of the United States.
(*Poulson's Daily Advertiser*, Philadelphia, 10 August 1825)

During the 19th century sawmills were often part of larger timber undertakings which imported, exported and seasoned woods for all the woodworking trades. Henry Mayhew described the 'application of machinery to the carpentry and joinery trade'. He noted three mill arrangements, all with steam power; one for making mouldings, another for planing timber and a third for veneer-cutting. According to Mayhew the steam moulding mill had been established within the last ten years, the planing mills within the last twelve years and the veneering mill for forty years (Letter LIX, 4 July 1850).

Timber conversion still remains a specialized trade which may be carried out in the country of origin, or after importation.

Bale, M. P. (1883), *On Saw Mills. Their Arrangement and Management and the Economical Conversion of Timber*, London: C. Lockwood and Son.
— (1899), *Handbook of Sawmills and Wood Converting Machinery*, London.
Beckman, J. (1817), *History of Inventions*, London: Longman, Hurst, Rees, Orme and Brown (Sawmills, pp.222–30).
Cooney, E. (1987), 'Eighteenth century Britain's missing sawmills; A blessing in disguise', in *Construction History*, vol.3, pp.31–55.
Forman, B. (1970), 'Mill sawing in seventeenth century Massachusetts', in *Old Time New England*, 60, 220, Spring, pp.110–30.
Louw, H. (1992), 'The mechanisation of architectural woodwork, in Britain from the late eighteenth to the early twentieth century', in *Construction History*, vol.8, pp.21–54.
Mayhew, H. (1850), *Morning Chronicle*, Letter LIX, 4 July.
Medlam, Sarah (1991), 'Parts ands materials, sawmills in 1820s', in *Regional Furniture*, V, pp.31–41.

Saws

Although the splitting or RIVING of timber was perhaps the first method of converting a log or trunk, and one that lasted for many centuries, a more reliable and accurate method was to be required for more particular and delicate work. The origins of saws can be found in the Neolithic period when men cut a variety of materials with flint flakes. These were very crude and difficult to manage so other materials were introduced that included copper, iron, bronze, a form of steel and obsidian.

The copper saw was introduced during the first Dynasty (*c.*3000 BC) in Egypt. This was followed by saws of cast bronze which were developed in the New Kingdom (*c.*1500–1000 BC). With the cutting edge raked towards the handle, the saw strokes were all made on the pull motion. The difficulties these features caused were rectified by the development of alternate settings of the saw teeth. It was not until Roman times and the introduction of iron on a larger scale that the modern setting of the teeth was introduced. It was realized that a set made it easier to saw, thereby avoiding clogging.

From early times, large timbers were lashed to posts to hold them steady whilst shorter ones were hand-held and cut with a smaller saw (see tomb wall paintings at Saqqara *c.*2500 BC, in Baker, 1966, p.298). The Romans used large and small frame saws, hand saws and double-handled cross-cut saws. This selection was clearly necessary as fine quality veneering and woodworking required these special tools. The Minoans introduced large saws up to 1.70 m (5 ft 7 in) long and 20 cm (8 in) wide, often designed to fell timbers with a two-man operation.

Roman-style saws continued well into the Middle Ages, and remained satisfactory until the early 17th century when improvements were made. Developments in steel manufacture meant that wider strips of steel could make wider blades and therefore do away with the wooden stabilizing frame, as well as give a more reliable blade. The necessary balance between hardness, smoothness, stiffness and flexibility within the saw blade was surely a test of the blade-maker's skills.

With the development of the cabinet-maker, and a growing demand for finer work, the range of saws and tools in general grew. Moxon lists pit saws, bow saws, whip saws and tennant saws (1677, p.98), whilst the well-known inventory of Philadelphia cabinet-maker Charles Plumley lists 5 hand saws, 4 tennant saws, 3 beam saws and 3 small saws in his workshop in 1708 (Forman, 1988, Appendix 1). By the mid 18th century English saws were approaching their contemporary form, so by 1803 Sheraton listed the types used, including hand, ripping, pannel, tenon, sash, dovetail, bow, baluster and bench saws (1803, p.302). The growth of specialist converters, machines to process timber and the development of specialized machines for preparing parts ready-cut, meant the need for a full kit of saws gradually grew less important for commercial furniture-makers.

101 A large horizontal band saw, used to convert logs into planks. This example is from Plumbridge's sawmill in High Wycombe, c.1904.

Armchair-maker's (*scie à araser de menuisier*)
A special saw designed to cut the shoulders of tenons on carved, curved parts of chair frames. It is made with a stock (similar to a plane) fitted with a saw blade on one side. Using a box-shaped cramp and a template, accurate cutting of the joints was ensured, even on complex, shaped members of a frame.

Back
A general term for saws which have a stiffening strip of iron or brass fitted along the top edge of the blade. Used for cutting joints and fine work. Specific back saws include bead, carcase, dovetail, kerfing and tenon. The strip is tapered and split in order to provide a spring tension feature.

Band
A band saw is, in principle, a tensioned steel belt with serrated edges that runs over two powered wheels. These may be set vertically or horizontally. Invented and patented by William Newbery in 1808 (Pat. no.3105), it was never used commercially at that time due to a problem with the quality of the saw-toothed metal band which was unable to withstand the high friction rates. Nevertheless developmental work continued, and in Germany in 1831 a Berlin pattern-maker named Stutzer exhibited a band saw. In 1836 Ferdinand Selle, a Potsdam cabinet-maker, was awarded a patent for a band saw. However, neither of these designs seems to have had great commercial success. It was in 1855 that the breakthrough came: Msr Perin, a veneer specialist from Paris, used spring steel and a simple repair technique to overcome the tensioning difficulties of the saw. This turned out to be successful, but took some years to become fully established. Its potential then realized, it was developed in many ways. Horizontal models were soon introduced, and as the quality of the blades improved, the scale of saws increased so that by the end of the 19th century very large logs were being sliced with giant band saws, as well as small models being used in delicate work. Band saws are now conveniently arranged for use by a wide range of makers.

Bead
A small back saw with a blade 8–15 cm (3–6 in) in length and with no set, for cutting out fine work.

Betty(e)
A frame saw with the tension of blade held directly between the two ends. Used by chair-makers for sawing out chair arms and other curved parts.

Bow
A frame saw in which the blade is strained between two side pieces by a twisted cord and toggle stick. The blade is usually very narrow (in British models) and can be turned to any angle. This gives the saw a useful curved-cutting ability.

Buck
Similar to the bow saw but with a fixed blade limiting it to cross-cutting.

Buhl
See Fretsaw below

Carcase
Early 19th-century trade name for a back saw, possibly used for cutting joints in the frame or carcase of cabinets.

Circular
The circular saw was a major step forward in the preparation of wood, in that it cut on a continuous rather than on a reciprocal basis. Its origins are unknown but English developments appear to have started with the patent of Southampton-based Samuel Miller (Pat.no. 1152, 5 August 1777). In 1791 Samuel Bentham developed the principle of saw segments mounted on a disc (see also Veneer). In 1805 Brunel took out a patent for large circular saws (Pat.no.2844) particularly associated with veneer cutting and in 1807 developed the saw further in association with block-making machinery. By 1821 the Shakers, at their village in Waterlivet near Albany, NY, had developed a water-powered circular saw, and in Germany at least two attempts were made to develop the circular saw. In 1817 Alois and Martin Munding received a patent for a circular saw, and in 1818 Stober, a Munich entrepreneur, introduced an English pattern circular saw into Germany.

The importance of large powered saws for converting timber has been recognized in the development of the timber, joinery and furniture trades (see Sawmills). However, one of the most important developments was not on this scale at all. The small circular saw of up to seven inches in diameter, often operated by a treadle, was one of the keys to the success of small-scale furniture-makers. This saw allowed makers of cheap furniture to square up, mitre and rabbet cleanly and accurately: 'The cheap furniture-makers could not work at the price they do if they did not use this saw' (Bitmead, 1873, p.67). According to Bitmead, in cheap carcase work the frame is not dovetailed together, rather the ends are simply rebated and nailed. This method of rebating using a circular saw was particularly useful for drawer making, which traditionally used dovetail joints. The advantage of this cheap method was that a dozen drawers could be made in the time it took to dovetail-join just one. This obviously had great advantages when such objects as Davenports and chests were being made. In the late 19th century, the value of the foot-operated circular saw to 'slop' workers was such that with this one machine they could produce parallel, mitred and tapered cuts with ease.

Compass
A keyhole, or lock saw, designed to cut holes and small shapes in wood. They are tapered with pistol handles and are without set.

Coping
Similar to a Boulle saw, the coping saw is a small bow saw with a very narrow blade held in tension by a metal bow. Introduced in the early 20th century, it is used for cutting small work such as dovetails and tenoning. It is also employed for scribing.

Cross-cut
A large one- or two-man saw used for cutting timber across the grain.

Dovetail
A small saw with a 15–25 cm (6–10 in) blade with 6–8 teeth per cm (15–22/in) to cut dovetails, small mitres and delicate work.

Frame
A saw of great antiquity which was initially made like a bow so that the blade could be held in tension by green wood. There were two types, a rectangular frame and an H frame. Both types eliminated the old problem of buckling blades. Later the frame saw was used with a very thin blade to cut veneers. This later use continued until the 19th century with blades of 120–50 cm (4–5 ft) long and 10–12 cm (4–5 in) wide. The following are all frame saws: bow saw, bucksaw, buhl saw, coping saw, fretsaw, pit saw, scroll saw.

Fretsaw or Scroll (aka boulle or buhl saw)
The fretsaw or scroll saw, developed from the simple marquetry cutters saw, was one of the simplest and most useful tools for the cabinet-maker. This special saw has a deep 50 cm (20 in) U-shaped frame which holds a blade of 12–15 cm (5–6 in) long. The blades are sometimes so fine that they are little more than serrated wire. Based on the design of a bow saw, the fretsaw is used to cut out curved shapes in thin wood, plywood and veneer.

Since the 16th century, when they were used by intarsia workers, fretsaws have been associated with fine and delicate cutting out. They were commonly used by Boulle-workers and marquetry-workers, as well as intarsia masters. The distinctive U frame, and the thin wire-like blade demonstrate the possibility of cutting a shape at some distance from the edge of the material.

Hand
A generic name for wide-bladed saws ranging in length from 25–76 cm (10–30 in). They include the rip saw, panel saw and the compass saw.

Jigsaw
A narrow-bladed saw held in a frame with a supporting table for the work to be cut upon. It operates with a reciprocating motion using a treadle, flywheel or spring. Developed in the late 18th century, jigsaws were used for cutting all sorts of FRETWORK. The foot-operated saws introduced in the 1860s thus meant that in the USA at least, they 'place[d] household decoration, indeed the complete furnishing, within the means of everyone' (William and Jones, *Beautiful Homes*, 1878).

The first treadle-operated fretsaw machine was patented in 1865. This operated with a single blade, so it could cut out intricate shapes and satisfy the demand for the most elaborate decoration. It was also beneficial in that it kept the blade vertical and was estimated to be three times as fast as hand tools. In 1878 Paterson said that 'excellent fret cutting machines have in great measure superseded hand-cutting in this branch and provide a very cheap and effective means of decoration' (Paris, 1878, p.96). The development of the fretsaw to a state of reliability and the fact that the power source could be human, steam or later electric stimulated its speedy adoption. The demand for fretted designs grew to a point where there developed a separate trade of FRET-CUTTER. He produced fretted parts for supply to furniture and piano makers. They also made small items which they themselves sold. Although fret cutters tried to maintain a 'mystery' around their trade, the importation of cheap and simple fret machines from America in the 1880s encouraged manufacturers large and small to use them.
See also Fretsaw above and Fretwork

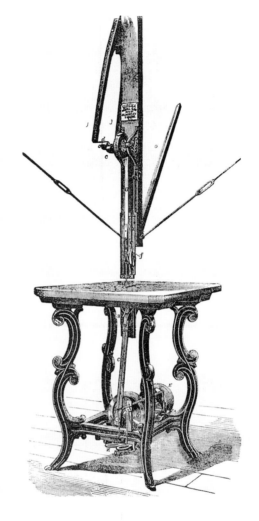

102   *The American-made Eureka jigsaw, c.1880. The rococo scrolled frame confirms a reluctance to take on a particular machine aesthetic at this date.*

Open
A general term that includes the cabinet saw, compass saw, crosscut saw, panel saw and ripsaw.

Panel
A lightweight hand saw used for cross-cutting softwoods, plywoods and so on, to give a cleaner finish through finer teeth.

Pit or Whip
A range of long-bladed open or framed saws usually 150–210 cm (5–7 ft) but known up to 3 m (10 ft) in length, used for slash-converting timber in a saw-pit. Moxon noted that these saws were set so that the kerf or cut was almost 6 mm (¼ in) wide 'but for fine and costly stuff they set it finer to save stuff' (1677, p.97).
See Conversion

Rip
The longest version of the hand saw, with coarse teeth and a long blade (up to 75 cm/30 in). It was widely used for 'ripping' down the grain length of timber.

Tenon (Tennant)
A back saw known since at least the 17th century and used to cut out tenons and other cross-cut work.

Veneer
See Veneers

Disston, Henry & Sons Inc. (1926), *The Saw in History, a Comprehensive Description of the Development of this Most Useful of Tools*, 9th edn, Philadelphia: H. Disston & Sons Inc.
Grimshaw, Robert (1880), *Saws, the History, Development, Action, Classification and Comparison of Saws of all Kinds. With Appendices Concerning the Details of Manufacture, Setting, Swaging, Gumming, Filing, etc.*, Philadelphia: Claxton, Remsen and Haffelfinger.
Jones, Chandler (1992), *Bandsaws*, Seattle: C. Jones.
Jones, P. and Simons, E. N. (1961), *Story of the Saw*, Spear and Jackson.
Linnard, W. (1981–2), 'Sweat and sawdust: pit-sawing in Wales', in *Folk Life*, 20, pp.41–55.
Reichmann, C. (1988), 'The tools that fuelled the fretwork frenzy', *Chronicle of the Early American Industries Association*, vol.41, 1, pp.1–2.
Worssam, S. W. (1892), *History of the Bandsaw*, Manchester: Emmott and Co.

Say(e)

A lightweight woollen or silk material of twill weave described as 'a sort of thin woollen-stuff or serge' (Bailey, 1736). Often used for linings, says were also woven into 'beds'. These were specially woven says of coarser yarns up to 360 cm (4 yd) wide, intended for bed hangings. In 1551 Henry Parker of Norwich had a 'trussing bed with a tester and valance of red and greene saye, panyd, three curtains of the same' (Hall, H., 1901, pp.150–1). Says could also be printed. In 1601 Hardwick Hall had a 'canopy of yellow saye stayned with birds and Antikes' (Boynton, 1971, p.25). It was later mainly used for clothing.

Scagliola

An imitation marble. It was made from a variety of recipes, but was essentially a mix of finely ground and calcined gypsum or plaster of Paris, selenite, isinglass, colouring matter and sometimes marble chips. Once the mixture was prepared, one or two coats of rough plaster were applied to a surface and keyed. Several batches of superfine plaster were then tinted, sliced and beaten together, and the scagliola chips were added. A veined effect was simulated by drawing coloured threads through the mix. Once the surface was set and smoothed, it was polished with linseed oil. If required, a high gloss finish could be achieved. An alternative method was the painting of a marble design on the wet plaster mix, then fixing the colours by heat. Sir William Chambers described a recipe in 1769 to Mr W. Hall:

> The composition for the foundation is bitts of tile or well-baked brick and bitts of marble mixed with lime for river flints – a sufficient quantity to bring the whole to a consistency of a paste. Then a finer paste of the same composition but with less marble is laid on … and having beat it for some time then strew in bits of marble of different kinds and beat them in the paste, then when dry put on a paste composed of powder of tiles, lime and soapwater, for otherwise it never takes a polish … smooth and polish it with a clean polished trowel before it drys, then rub it with linseed oil and a woollen cloth. N.B. The Italians give what colour they please by mixing with the paste Brown, red Vermilion, Yellow Occar, or any colour that agrees with Lime.
> (Cited in R. Edwards, 1964, p.425)

Of Roman origin, scagliola's manufacture was revived during the 16th century in Italy, and by the 17th century it had reached a high state in works by Guido del Conte (Sassi). Evelyn wrote 'I have frequently wondered that we never practised this in England for cabinets' (*Diary*, 17 October 1664). By the 18th century Italian masters such as Enrico Hugford and his pupil Lamberto Gori produced many pictures and table tops in this material. Hugford's particular technique used scagliola pastes as semi-fluids to create tonal control, giving an effect of painting first, then secondly a pietre dure illusion of fine in-

lay. Scagliola was commonly used in 18th-century interiors, and slabs were made for table tops and commode tops for furniture.

Scagliola was produced in England from the mid 18th century. According to Sir William Chambers, the best scagliola products in England were made by Richter and Bartoli of Newport Street. They do seem to have had a serious interest in the business, as John Richter took out a patent in 1770 (Pat.no.978) for inlaying scagliola into marble or metals, to imitate birds and flowers. They supplied Nostell Priory with 'two statuary tables inlaid of scagliola according Messrs Adam's desaing for the Salon at Nostell at 75 guineas each' (Gilbert, 1978, p.173), as well as '2 Tables of Scagliola at £65.00 each' to Croome Court, in 1768 (Beard, 1993, p.101). With the establishment of reliable suppliers in London, its popularity apparently continued apace. Vincent Bellman started a manufactory in London in 1790, and in 1808 George Smith recommended its use. The COADE STONE Company also manufactured it from *c*.1816.
See also Marble, Marbling

Massinelli, A. M. (1997), *Scagliola, L'arte della pietro di luna*, Editalia, Rome.
Pulman, J. (1845), 'On the manufacture of scagliola', in *Builder*, 11 January, pp.50–1.
Wragg, R. B. (1957), 'The History of scagliola', in *Country Life*, 10 October, pp.718–21.

Scarf joint
See Joints

Scorched leather
See Leather

Scots pine
See Pine

Scouring
An abrasive technique, using rushes as part of a finishing process.
See Grasses (Dutch Rushes)

Scraper
A finishing tool, often home-made from steel plates, which have had an edge turned on them. They were ideal for cleaning up hardwood after 'smoothing up' and prior to final sand papering. Cabinet-makers and chair-makers employed scrapers, but the chair-makers' version differed in that it was honed to a bevel of 60 degrees as opposed to the square cut of the cabinet-making version. The chair-makers also fitted their scrapers into a split wooden stock some 30 cm (12 in) in length. Machines for scraping were developed in the USA by Whitney and Co, of Massachusetts, in the 1850s. They became widely popular in Europe after a display at Paris in 1876.

Scratch carving
See Carving

Scratch stock
A scraping tool designed to produce simple mouldings up to an inch wide, on edges of panels or to form grooves for inlays. Usually made by the craftsman for his own use. Two pieces of wood held together make the fence and the handles, and the cutters were made from old saw blades or steel plates shaped to the required profiles. Although superseded by routers, they have been used on occasion for small work, such as repairs.

Screen-maker

A specialist tradesman described in the 18th century as one who 'deals in leather, of which their gilt-leather screens are made, and are of kin to the joiner, as they make their own frames to mount their screens on … some of them are little inferior to Upholders as they frequently sell other goods besides screens' (Campbell, 1747, pp.175–6).

Screwdrivers

A tool designed to fit the slots of SCREWS to facilitate turning. Designed to work in conjunction with screws, they naturally followed the same development. As with many tools, a wide range of specialist screwdrivers of varying sizes and complexity have been made, including ratchet versions and the Philip's screwdriver designed to screw cross-cut headed Philip's pattern screws.

The London pattern screwdriver has broad flat blades and a flat handle. Cabinet screwdrivers have a round blade and an oval handle. By the early 20th century power driven screwdrivers were recommended for cabinet works. McKnight's automatic screwdriver was fitted to a flexible tube which rotated once pressure was applied to screws. It was available by 1912. The Moline automatic screwdriver, which worked on the drilling principle with a stand and treadle operation, was developed at the same time.

Screws

Screws were made and used for furniture work from the late 17th century but were scarce until the mid 18th century. They were initially hand-cut from iron, and were hand-filed, inevitably resulting in an irregular thread and slots. These screws have a tapered thread and core, while the hand-cut top slots were shallow and irregular. In 1731 three gross of wood screws were valued at £4. 1s. 0d. (Legg, 1994, p.31). From c.1760, partly lathe-made screws were used for fixing hinges and securing tops. These had a clearer diminishing spiral. Job and William Wyatt patented a screw-making machine in 1760 (Pat. no.751) 'for cutting screws of iron called wood screws'. These had no points but less taper than hand-made screws, though with a similar section groove and a flat head. From early in the 19th century, machine-made screws came into general use. In 1817 the thread-cutting machine was devised which used iron wire to produce a screw with a turned head distinguished by concentric ring marks. This development was to produce a regular screw with an even head, a regular thread and a blunt end.

The modern gimlet-point screw dates from an American invention (US Pat.no.11,791) which was produced in England by Nettlefold from 1854. The process produced pointed screws with regular and standardized sizes. In 1858 the design was amended to allow a taper along the length, so the thread core tapers into the shank.

Screws are also cramps: 'one of the mechanical powers, much used by cabinet-makers in gluing pieces of wood together. For this purpose, they have various hand screws and caul screws, which they use in veneering, and is one of the most effectual methods in that art' (Sheraton, 1803, p.302).

Dickinson, H. (1941), 'Origin and manufacture of woodscrews', in *Transactions of the Newcomen Society*, XXII.
Kebabian, P. B. (1994), 'Thomas Harvey and the manufacture of woodscrews', in *The Chronicle of the Early American Industries Association*, 47, 3, September, pp.84–7.

Scrim

A thin canvas used to line or bottom a chair. Occasionally it has been glued to wooden panels to give stability.

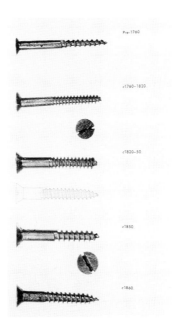

103 A series of examples of screws showing the development from pre-1760 to 1860.

Sea wrack grass
See Grasses

Sealskin
See Leather

Seasonal furnishings

The intention of having differing upholstery covers for the particular season of the year, for example the French practice of silk damask hangings for the winter and printed cotton for the summer. This need was met by various sets of drapes and covers that could be changed at will, or less commonly the use of slip seats (drop in) and reversible or loose back cushions and removable arm pads. These were known as *à chassis*. An ingenious chair design was patented in 1798 by Anthony Eckhardt (Pat.no.2208), which was based on a seat pad fixed on swivel pegs to the frame, so that it could be turned through 180 degrees to even out wear or change the top cover instantly. This design included a model that allowed the back and seat to exchange places.
See also Protective furnishing

Seasoning and Preservation

The seasoning process makes timber lighter, more stable, easier to work and more durable. This is achieved by drying out green wood to its equilibrium moisture content, in other words a balance between the moisture content of the environment in which the wood will be used and that of the timber. All timber has a moisture content (typically, about half its weight is in moisture when a tree is cut), which usually makes it unsuitable for most furniture-making until it has been reduced to its equilibrium moisture content, although unseasoned wood is sometimes used in construction (see Green construction).

Some understanding of timber technology and the necessity for seasoning to prevent warping and cracking was clearly achieved early on in wood-working, although not necessarily brought to any high degree of refinement. Initially, methods of seasoning included the placing of the timber in running water, burying it in the earth, drying it by burning the outside of a pile of timber, or covering a timber pile

104   The mechanization of the seasoning process was common by the early 20th century. This American kiln is being loaded with mahogany boards, c.1926.

with dung. As early methods of seasoning were only adequate, and in no real sense controlled, the making process itself often called for additional 'seasoning' processes. For example, when table tops were jointed up, Sheraton recommended more than once that made-up tops for tables and cabinets should stand to shrink as much as possible before they were finally glued and assembled (1793).

Although open-air seasoning was recommended in the 19th century, the need for speedy processing in response to a greatly increasing demand, meant that drying rooms in workshops were more important (see below, Kiln drying). Inventions in wood processing were often eccentric. For example, in c.1825 James Atlee devised a process of squeezing wood through rollers that were progressively closer to each other, in order to extract sap. By the early 20th century, other developments in mechanized seasoning were in use and the science of timber seasoning was developing rapidly. However, some early-20th-century manufacturers in England were not very exact about timber drying. In one factory, seasoning was done 'in the cellar with sticks between the timber and it was left down there for three or four weeks … we judged when it was dry by its weight' (Radford, 1981, p.37). In fact, in cheap furniture the creaking and cracking of poorly seasoned timber was a particular feature. Changes in weather could still affect finished goods, even those made with seasoned timber. In one factory in the early 20th century, the repairing of split tops and sides caused by weather changes was a common practice at certain times of the year.

AIR DRYING
A method of natural drying (seasoning) of timber in the open air, which is characterized by the sawn planks being stored with sticks between them to allow the drying process to be facilitated by circulating air (hence the term 'in stick'). As all wood shrinks across the grain, it is necessary to maintain a regular stack with a weighted top to avoid any distortion to the boards. A rough rule of one year's seasoning to a couple of centimetres (one inch) of timber equates to a moisture content of 15–20 per cent. Regulation of the process has often been difficult. In Ancient Egypt the high temperature was conducive to speedy drying-out, so damp mats were laid over timbers to slow down the rate. In Ancient Rome it was the practice that some woods were covered with manure so that they would not dry out too quickly. Nevertheless the open air was the favoured method of seasoning for centuries.
See also Kiln drying, below

BURYING
Burying timber in a desiccating material was another attempt to try to control the rate of seasoning. Romans buried wood (especially the

prized thuya) in corn for periods of seven days at a time, then the corn was renewed and the process repeated. Much later, in 1720, a method was patented (Pat.no.427) known as the Cumberland method, which was 'a process of heating, drying, seasoning and bending timber wood plank or board'. It consisted of burying the timber in wet sand and heating it until the required desiccation had been achieved.

CARBONIZING AND SMOKING
A seasoning method which smokes or chars the outer layer of timber, rendering it dry and sealed against rot or infection. The earliest references to seasoning by smoking are found in Virgil and Hesiod. Roman timber smoke-rooms were established near baths as a heat source, so that warm smoke would dry and harden the timber. This process was used in France until the mid 19th century. Indeed some commercial methods, which were developed in the 1890s in the USA and England, operated baking or smoke-curing methods. The charring of timber to preserve it was usually applied to shipbuilding and would appear to be inappropriate for furniture.

GIRDLING
This process was to cut the tree bark all round, near the base, to inhibit growth and start the drying process before felling. Not only did it allow for the moisture content to reduce, but it also lightened the weight of the trunk once felled. This method was practised in Ancient Rome. Pliny noted that 'some with good results leave the timber after cutting it around into the pith, in order that all moisture may flow out while it is standing' (xvi, 222). The method was used in the 19th century for Far Eastern timbers, especially for teak, prior to export.

IMPREGNATION METHODS
A number of seasoning processes were based on the idea of replacing the sap by a substance that was a preservative and/or an antiseptic. One of the earliest was Kyanizing, patented by John Kyan in 1832, in which mercuric chloride (corrosive sublimate) was impregnated into timbers (Pat.no.7001). Loudon suggested this process was particularly useful for spare draw-leaf tables which were stored in enclosed spaces to be 'steeped in deuto-chloride of mercury (corrosive sublimate) as suggested long ago by Sir Humphrey Davy, and as recently employed by Mr. Kyan for the prevention of dry rot by neutralising the causes of vegetable fermentation' (1839, p.1047). In 1838 Sir William Burnett patented a seasoning method which impregnated timber with zinc chloride (Pat.no.7747). This was known as Burnettizing, and the process was still being used in the 1920s in England and the USA.

In c.1913 William Powell devised a system of seasoning timber by boiling the wood in a saccharine solution without pressure, which apparently encouraged the timber to absorb the carbohydrates into its cell walls whilst simultaneously expelling the natural sap and moisture. It was then dried at a high temperature. This process, known as 'Powellizing', only took a few days from the felling of the timber to factory use. Its speed and lack of odour made it useful for furniture and it was used commercially in High Wycombe.

Recent developments in the application of polyethylene glycol (PEG) have resulted in up to 90 per cent reductions in the shrinkage of green wood. This has been used in large turnings and carved work which can be made to shape and then treated without traditional seasoning.

KILN DRYING
This mechanized, accelerated seasoning is based on placing timber in chambers of hot air or steam. A low temperature and high relative humidity to start with, moving towards a higher temperature and a

lower relative humidity, meant that seasoning only took 5 to 30 days per couple of centimetres (inch) of board, with moisture contents as low as 6–8 per cent.

In the 18th century some cabinet-makers 'seasoned' timber on their own premises. Thomas Chippendale had a room for the 'drying of wood on the Roof which is covered with boards and pitched over a German stove' (Gilbert, 1978, pp.40–1). By the early 19th century the commercial interest in seasoning encouraged invention. In 1844 David and Symington patented a process of seasoning which used blasts of air at increasingly higher temperature rising from 150°F (50°C) for green wood to 400–500°F (200–50°C) (Pat.no.10126). By the mid 19th century it was still common practice to place wood in drying rooms which were heated to several degrees above the likely temperature they would normally be subjected to. The use of specially heated rooms with ingress for hot, dry air, and space for the exit of moist warm air was developed especially for building timbers.

In the early part of the 20th century the Nodon-Bretonneau process was devised. This was a seasoning method based on electrolysis: The planks were stacked with wet mats between them. The mats acted as electrodes and an alternating current was passed through the stack for a period of hours. The method apparently produced harder and stronger timbers with less warping. Around the same time another method of kilning, using warm air, was introduced. The Erith method used warm, very moist air which avoided 'case hardening'. The benefits of these new, rapid seasoning methods meant that more timbers could be used satisfactorily. Ash, birch, aspen and sycamore, traditionally seen as difficult to work, avoided warping by the use of the new and speedy steam-heated kilning processes.

SMOKING
See Carbonizing, above

WATERING
A seasoning method using the action of running salt water to 'wash' the timber of sap. Medieval processes involved the immersion of timbers in running water, then they were dried in an upright position, which allegedly reduced the risk of worm infestation. The process was still used in the 1900s by chaining timber baulks down in water for a period, then carefully air drying them. Rare and fine timbers such as EBONY were immersed in water for long periods, and then covered for slow drying. HOLLY is sometimes boiled in water and then wrapped to dry slowly.

Blake, E. G. (1924), *The Seasoning and Preservation of Timber*, London: Chapman and Hall.

Seaweed
An aquatic algae found on the shores. Processed seaweed was used as an upholstery and bedding filling during the 19th century.
See Alva marina, Grasses (Sea wrack)

Seaweed marquetry
See Marquetry

Secondary wood
The timber used in the construction of cabinet carcases, as opposed to the surface or exposed timbers. The secondary woods are often of a lesser quality decoratively but should be structurally appropriate.
See also Construction

Sedge
See Grasses

Seersucker
A textile of mixed silk and cotton, often striped, and with a crêpe appearance, originally from India. Since the end of the 17th century it has been used for curtains and hangings. A 'pair of searsucker curtains and vallens' were listed for Thomas Hunt of Boston, Mass., in 1734 (Cummin, 1960, p.36). Modern seersuckers are striped cottons with puckered surfaces.

Cummin, H. (1940), 'Early Seersucker', in *Antiques*, 38, pp.231–2.

Sequoia (*Sequoia sempervirens*)
An American softwood with an average density of 410 (26 lb/cu ft). It has a dull reddish-brown heartwood and a distinctive growth-ring pattern with a fine even texture and a straight grain. Used for plywood manufacture as well as for decorative veneers. During the early 20th century it was used for interiors (drawers and robe backs) of cabinet work by large-scale makers in England. The bark is often used as a component of PARTICLE BOARDS.

Serayah
See Meranti

Serge
A twill (diagonal ribbed) weave, worsted-warp and woollen-weft cloth. It was used as a chair-covering material as well as for curtains, valances and protective furnishings from the 15th century. Like SAYE, serges were sometimes called 'beds' on account of their use and width. In 1691, William Bird of Essex had a 'gray serge quilt, the like curtains and valans, curtain rodds, bedstead and six serge chairs' (Steer, 1969, p.207). In 1778 Thomas Chippendale supplied Sir Edward Knatchbull with '48 yards Buff Serge in bags to the window curtains' (Boynton, 1968, p.103), probably to protect the curtains.
See also Perpetual, Say(e), Shalloon

Serpentine
A mineral formed from hydrous magnesium silicate, which is dark green or dull green with coloured markings which are sometimes mottled, resembling serpents' skin. The antique serpentine was found in Egypt, whilst since Roman times a Tuscan type has been used in Florentine architectural intarsia. The red-spotted, dark green serpentine from the Lizard area of Cornwall was also sought after. Used on occasion for table tops and inlays.

Serpentine springs
See Springs

Service wood (*Sorbus torminalis*)
A very hard, fawn coloured, fine grained timber from Europe which is similar to pear, often with a dark heartwood. Figured logs have been used for furniture since the 17th century. Evelyn noted that it 'being of a very delicate grain for the turner, and divers curiosities and looks beautifully and is almost everlasting; being rubbed over with oil of linseed well boiled, it may be made to counterfeit ebony, or almost any Indian wood coloured according to Art' (1662, p.63). By the early 19th century it was scarce.
See also Rowan, Whitebeam

Set work
See Turkeywork

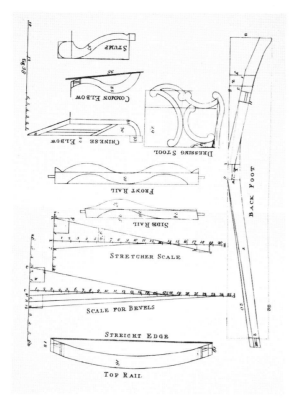

Setting out

The need to mark out work directly onto timber or metal has been a basic requirement in all furniture-making. The emphasis on the necessity of a knowledge of geometry, which was often described in pattern books and manuals, is evidence of this. Examples of setting out work to obtain the best use of raw materials are also shown in manuals. For example, Robert Manwaring's *The Cabinet and Chair-maker's Real Friend and Companion* of 1765 shows various methods of setting out work.

In early-20th-century cabinet-making, the setting out sheets and a material cutting list were handed to a 'marker-out' who selected and cut 'stuff' for the cabinet-maker. The 'setter-out' marked the prepared stuff to length and indicated joints for machining. They were then set-out with pencil marks or RODS where the joints, rails and so on were to be cut. The development of jigs and stops has done away with this process.
See Rods

Sewing machines

The introduction and development of industrial sewing machines had an impact on the upholstery trade inasmuch as the sewing of covers and cushions was facilitated to keep up with the demand for upholstered furniture from the end of the 19th century onwards. The multiple pre-cutting and sewing of covers and cases meant that less-skilled labour could be used to fit them and trim the upholstered work.

Shading

See Marquetry, Sand shading

Shadow wood

A form of decorative plywood used in England in the 1950s. It was produced by impressing diamond patterns into the top layer of the plywood by heated rollers.
See also Plywood

Shagg

A heavy worsted material with a long nap. Used in the 18th century for clothing and upholstery work. In 1710, Dyrham Park had 'two Dutch chairs with shagg cushions' (Walton, 1986, p.62).

Shagreen

There are a variety of interpretations of this material, the most usual referring to dried fish skins that are coloured and used as veneers for cabinet work. The derivation of the word may be from the Turkish word *saghri* meaning the croup of an animal. Originally shagreen was the untanned skins of asses, horses and camels likened to parchment. The characteristic grain effect was artificially obtained by pressing small seeds into new skins, which were then shaved and dyed. Drying the skins made them hard and rigid. They were probably first introduced from China and Japan into Europe in the 17th century and were used in the Jacobean period for covering items such as small desks, and in the 18th century for boxes, tea caddies and so on. In the second half of the 18th century, specialist makers like John Folgham of London established businesses as shagreen case-makers, selling items such as writing desks, knife cases and travelling requisites finished in shagreen.

The alternative name of Galuchat is derived from the 18th-century Msr Galuchat, who used the material for covering sheaths, using the skin of a small spotted dog-fish which was either chlorine-bleached and left plain, or tinted blue or green to emphasize the granular structure.

Shagreen is also made from highly polished skins of sharks and rays, which are occasionally dyed black, but more usually green. More recently sharks (*Caniculus*) or dogfish and rays' skins, having a naturally granular surface (which can be stained) have been used. Most special is the ray-fish skin (*Sephen*) which is covered with round calcified papillae like small pearls. This skin takes stains well and is often associated with Art Deco furniture, especially that of Ruhlmann and Iribe.

Shagreen cloth was woven with a pebble effect to imitate the leather in the early 18th century and used to cover chests and cases.

Caunes, Lison de (1994), *Galuchat*, Paris: Editions de l'Amateur.

Shalloon
An inexpensive twill worsted fine-yarn SAYE type cloth used for lining and, occasionally, upholstery. They were sometimes glazed and hot pressed. *Serge de Châlons* was in use by the mid 17th century in England and was still in use in the late 18th century. In 1793 cabinet-makers charged specifically for 'putting on the tammy or shalloon with braid on each side of each pannel' of a folding fire screen (*Cabinet-makers' London Book of Prices*, p.211).
See also Rattinet

Sharkskin
See Shagreen

Shave
A general term for a cutting iron that is mounted into a wooden stock which is shaped for convenience, so as to be two-handed. Chair-makers' shaves were widely used by Windsor and other chair-makers.
See also Drawing knife, Scratch stock

Sheet glass
See Glass

Sheet steel
See Steel

Sheffield plate
A metal made from copper sheets that are fused between thin layers of silver to form a material that can be worked like silver. Discovered *c.*1740, it was used commercially from the 1760s for 'silverware'. In some instances Sheffield plate has been used in furniture-making. A table exists, made *c.*1825, that had a mahogany frame to which was bolted a Sheffield Plate top and four legs. Other examples include its use in stamped hardware, especially handles and backplates.

'An old Sheffield Plate table' (1961), in *Antique Collector*, 32, p.128.

Shellac
See Resins (Lac), Varnish

Shells (Chair)
See Chair frames

Shellwork
A popular amateur pastime for decorating mirror frames and cabinets, sometimes in conjunction with FILIGREE paper. Introduced in the 17th century, the process was mainly taught to and used by amateurs. An advertisement in the December 1703 *Edinburgh Gazette* told of a London gentlewoman who taught 'shell-work in sconces, rocks or flowers' (cited in Edwards, 1964, p.467). During the 18th century and well into the 19th century the practice continued to be seen as being particularly appropriate for young ladies. In *c.*1856 shellworking was recommended as 'an elegant drawing room occupation, as well as one calculated to call forth the artistic taste and inventive powers of the worker' (*Elegant Arts for Ladies*, cited in Hodges, 1989, p.16).
See also Ivory, Mother-of-pearl

Shoe piece
A piece of timber that supports the back splat of a chair onto the back seat rail. Variations include two separate pieces supporting the splat or shoes that are built in from the seat rail complete. The former was more widely used in the 18th century.

Shruff
See Excelsior

Side irons
A component of 19th- and 20th-century bedsteads. The L-shaped cast-iron bars held the bed together by fixing to the head and foot boards as well as supporting the bed springs. Aka Angle-irons.
See also Bed springs, Bedstead, Chills

Silesia
A fine linen and/or cotton furnishing fabric originally made in Hamburg and sometimes called 'sleazy'. It was thin and coarse but was used from the mid 18th century for lining and blinds. Cabinet-makers William Vile and John Cobb invoiced the Earl of Coventry for work at Croome Court in 1757 for '52.5 yards of Silesia to line your cotton for a furniture to the 2 bedsteads' (Beard, 1997, p.305). In the early 19th century it was specially woven in a range of widths to suit various-sized window blinds.

Silicon carbide paper
See Abrasives

Silk
A generic name given to the fibres and the cloth woven from the product of the cocoon of the mulberry silk moth. It produces a very versatile yarn that is both attractive and practical. It has a natural lustre, is easily dyed and is very strong. Filament bundles direct from the cocoon produce the best silk, while spun silk from the remainder is made into a more heavy duty fabric. Raw silk still has a gummy ex-udence upon it. Of Chinese origin, silk weaving has been known for four to five thousand years. Introduced into Europe as early as 200 BC as a cloth, sericulture was developed by the 10th century in Spain and a little later in Venice and Genoa. Genoa remained supreme in the manufacture of furnishing silks until the late 18th century, although by the 17th century other centres had been established in France and England. The main fabrics produced from silk were ARMOZEEN, BAUDEKIN, BROCADE, DAMASK, DUCAPE, DURANCE, GROSGRAIN, LAMPAS, LUSTRING, MATELASSE, MOHAIR, PASSEMENTERIE, REP, SARCENET, SATIN, TABARY, TABBINET, TABBY, TAFFETA, VELVET.

CLOUDED SILK
The use of dyed warp yarns before weaving created a decorative, shaded cloud-like pattern in the cloth. Ham House had 'clouded lute-string' lining the leather table covers in 1677 (Thornton and Tomlin, 1980, p.45), and in 1710 there was a 'Clouded Room' in Dyrham Park with six pieces of clouded silk hangings, a clouded silk bed lined with 'yellow strip'd' persian and a counterpane of the same (Walton, 1986, p.62).

Anquetil, J. (1996), *Silk*, Paris: Flammarion.
Rothstein, Natalie (1990), *Silk Designs of the Eighteenth Century in the Collection of the Victoria and Albert Museum*, London: Victoria and Albert Museum.
Thornton, Peter (1965), *Baroque and Rococo Silks*, London: Faber and Faber.

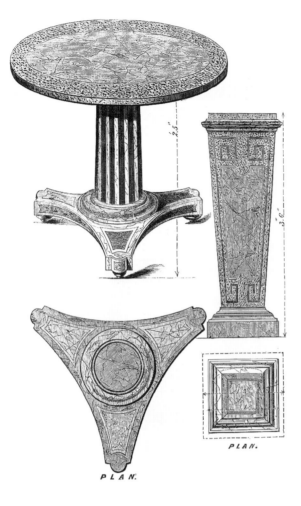

107   The London-based Pimlico slate works developed a range of items using slate as the base material. This design for a circular slate table and pedestal, c.1850–5, is typical.

PLAN.

PLAN.

PLAN.

Silver

The use of silver either in the solid or as a form of veneer can be found in Roman furniture where it was used for plating or veneering as well as for solid parts of furniture, such as fulcra (Pliny, XXXIII, 144). Silver continued to be used as an inlay in Byzantine times. It returned to fashion in the 16th century and became a German speciality for inlays and marquetry. For example, in 1577 Zacharias of Hradec had a silver-gilt armchair and table decorated with ornament and jewels. During the 17th century the English Council of State sold off a silver table and frame all laid over with silver and silver painted furniture, and Evelyn was impressed by the Duchess of Portsmouth's dressing room as containing amongst others 'tables, stands, chimney furniture, sconces, branches, braseras, etc. they were all of massy silver and without number' (*Diary*, 4 October 1683). It continued to be used as an inlay and as a component of marquetry, especially in some German furniture of the 17th and 18th centuries.

By the 19th century silver furniture was becoming a rarity but remained viable for exhibition work and one-off pieces; for example, the American Gorham Co built a dressing table and stool in solid silver for the 1900 Paris Exhibition.
See also Silvering, Silver plate

Bencard, M. (1992), *Silver Furniture*, Copenhagen: Rosenborg.
Hayward, J. H. (1958), 'Silver furniture', in *Apollo*, LXVII, pp.71, 124, 153, 220.

Silvering

The use of thin silver leaf applied as a decorative finish similar to GILDING was introduced onto pre-Restoration furniture. In the later 17th century silvering was particularly applied to underframes for chests. It has occasionally been used since. In 1775 Chippendale supplied silvered girandoles, looking-glass frames and the ornaments on a table for Edwin Lascelles (Gilbert, 1978, p.209). In the 20th century Edward Maufe designed a dressing table which was covered in silver leaf (V&A Museum, London).

Silver maple

See Maple

Silver plate

A metal plating specialism which was occasionally applied to cabinet fittings. Early use is recorded in 1399: 'a table … of wood plated (thickly?) with silver-gilt' (Eames, 1977, p.221). Trade catalogues show cabinet hardware made from the material which appears to have been popular in America. A Philadelphia silver-plater announced in 1809 that he had 'silver plated knobs for cabinet ware of the newest fashion and warranted superior to any imported' (*Aurora General Advertiser*, cited in Fennimore, 1991, p.88). It is distinct from SHEFFIELD PLATE.

Silverwood

Another name for Harewood

Single lapped dovetail

See Joints (Dovetail)

Sinuous springs

See Springs

Sisal

A fibre obtained from the Agave plant, it was used prior to the 1930s as a filling for mattresses and cushions. Used in the USA as an inexpensive stuffing, sometimes in a rubberized version. It has also been made into pads for use over arm and spring units.

Sissoo (*Dalbergia*)

See Rosewood (Indian)

Skewers

Important upholsterers' tools, also called Pins, which are from 8–13 cm (3–5 in) in length with a spike end, and the tops bent over to form a loop. Used particularly in iron-backed work (see Frames) and also to hold covers in place while setting out before nailing or sewing.

Skins

See Abrasives, Leather, Shagreen

Skivers

See Leather

Slate

A clay-like sedimentary rock that splits into thin plates. Its use in furniture has been widely known in connection with the beds of billiard tables and as a backing for *commesso* work in Florence particularly. Apart from these special applications, slate furniture enjoyed a vogue in the mid 19th century. The furniture made for Penrhyn Castle in North Wales is a famous example, where 'in order to show what can be done with slate, various articles of furniture are placed in the rooms occupying the places usually filled by carved wood and marble' (Louisa Costello, *The Falls, Lakes and Mountains of North Wales*, 1845, p.86, cited in Marsden, 1993).

The process of imitating marble by decorating slate slabs was, however, a successful 19th-century innovation. Originally invented and patented by George Magnus in 1840 (Pat.no.8383), the process involved floating mineral colours in prepared water onto a slate bed and then firing the decorated slate so as to create a glaze. This fired surface not only looked like marble but bore a tactile resemblance to it as well. The benefits of slate were also that it was stronger than ordinary stone. With slabs up to 2.4 m (8 ft) long and with a thickness of a couple of centimetres (half an inch), large table and sideboard tops could be safely made and used. Glazed slate was particularly used for loo-table tops, consoles and chiffoniers and billiard tables. The critic Digby Wyatt commended Magnus for taking an ordinary material and 'giving to it form and ornamentation' and for 'raising a school of artists and for applying to it hundreds of new purposes which it could be better and more cheaply adapted than those which it displaces' (1856, p.318).

Magnus was not the only person experimenting with imitations of marble. In 1848 Elizabeth Wallace patented a process that used coloured glass to replicate marble (Pat.no.12075). This was exhibited at the 1851 Great Exhibition, and could apparently be used to decorate wall linings, picture frames, tombs and articles of furniture. At the same exhibition, a Thomas Gushlow also showed a specimen of slate made in imitation of china which was also adapted for table tops (Class 26, Item 37a). The use of slate for billiard table tops was common by the mid 19th century, but its application to making the legs, in place of timber, was an important change in maintaining the table's stability.

In the 20th century designers have occasionally employed slate as a curiosity.

Marsden, Jonathan (1993), 'Far from elegant yet exceedingly curious', in *Apollo*, April, pp.263–70.

108 *An English painted slate-topped, tip-up table made with slate panels on the column to give support, c.1845.*

Slip covers
See Protective furnishing

Slip seats
See Drop-in seat

Slot dovetail
See Joints (Dovetail)

Slot screwing
A method of fixing components by screws, whereby the screw is located in a slot in the receiving board, designed to allow for expansion and contraction. Also a secret fixing method.

Smoothing plane
See Planes (Smoothing)

Snakewood (*Brosimum guianensis*)
A Central and South American timber (especially Surinam) with an average density of *c*.1300 (81 lb/cu ft). It is light red with a deep vivid red heartwood, with black shades interspersed. It is hard, but with a fine and even texture, durable and difficult to work, and is always of small dimensions. Used as a facing, veneer or inlay in the later 17th century, and occasionally for veneers in the 18th century. In the 19th century, it was 'principally used for bordering and small work' (Knight, 1830, p.179), and by 1853 'Its adaptation to cabinet-work being much restricted by the smallness of its size, it is principally used in veneering picture-frames and in turnery, and in the more expensive kinds of walking sticks' (Blackie, 1853, p.40). Aka Letter wood (UK), Leopard wood or Speckled wood in USA.

Bowett, A. (1998), 'The age of snakewood', in *Furniture History*, XXXIV, pp.212–25.

Soft maple
See Maple

Soft pine
See Pine (Western white, Yellow)

Softwood
Timber obtained from coniferous trees which are a lesser form than the hardwoods, in botanical terms. However, they may well be physically harder than botanically classified hardwoods.

Sorrento wood
An ash-grey timber 'much used by French cabinet-makers and by fancy cabinet-makers in London' (Bitmead, 1873, p.79). It is SYCAMORE or LIME that has been coloured by particular streams near Sorrento (Italy) by being laid in the water for several months. It was fashionable for work boxes and Tunbridge ware. In some cases MAPLE was coloured to imitate Sorrento wood, especially for bedroom furniture.

Soss hinge
See Hinges (Cylinder soss)

Southedge
A linen textile used for linings and blinds in the 17th century. The Hengrave inventory of 1603 listed 'two great southedge curtyones for ye great window' (Thornton, 1978, p.358). Aka Soultwitch.

Sowetage
A coarse fabric used for lining upholstery from the 16th century onward.

Spanish cedar
See Cedar

Spanish chestnut
See Chestnut (European or Sweet)

Spanish mahogany
See Mahogany

Spanish moss (*Tillandsia usneoides*)
A type of vegetable matter (epiphyte) growing on other plants (especially trees) in the swampy areas and on the coast of the Gulf states of America, especially Louisiana and Florida, as well as in South Carolina. It grows in trees and hangs down like a beard. When 'ripe' it is harvested and prepared for upholstery use. The removal of the tough outer skin leaves black fibres that are similar in appearance to curled hair. When dried it is very resilient and has been widely used as an upholstery stuffing, being equivalent to medium quality hair. In 1810 a visitor commented on the preparation which included burying 'it underground until the niterbark of the fibre which is soft and damp rots away, and when it is taken up and washed it has exactly the resemblance of horse hair and makes a very comfortable mattress' (cited in Michie, 1985, p.47). Certainly used commercially by the early 1800s, it was considered by some as second only to hair in the 1930s. Aka Spanish beard, Barba Hispanica.
See also Moss

Speckles
See Aventurine

Speckled wood
See Snakewood

Speculum
An alloy of two parts copper and one part tin, producing a metal capable of being brought to a bright, highly polished finish. It is not STEEL although the material is sometimes misleadingly referred to as such. Widely used for reflecting telescopes and adapted for some looking-glasses before the general introduction of MIRROR glass. The recipe for mirror-quality speculum was: 'for flat looking-glasses melt refined copper then add fine tin, as soon as they melted add red tartar, white arsnick, and nitre, keep in a melted state for three to four hours then cast into moulds' (Salmon, 1701, p.853). In 1641 'a steele glasse with a frame done about with brass' was recorded in an inventory of Tart Hall (Cust, 1911, p.99).
See also Mirror

Spelter
See Zinc

Spike grass
See Grass (Marsh)

Spindle moulder or **Toupie**
See Machines

Spindle wood (*Euonymus europaeus*)
An almost white timber with a fine uniform texture. It is hard and heavy with a straight grain, but is usually only available in short lengths. Used in 18th-century marquetry when a white colour was required, as well as a base wood for staining. However, its main use was for gunpowder, skewers and spindles (hence the name). Aka DOGWOOD.

Spirit stain
Stains such as ALKANET which dissolve in alcohol.

Splints
Strips of wood split from green saplings including white OAK, HICKORY and ASH. Used in North American vernacular furniture for woven seats and backs of chairs.

Split baluster
A baluster turning that is cut in half and applied to surfaces. These could be made by gluing two blocks of wood on either side of a board. This composite was then turned in the lathe. When the design was completed, the two turned halves were soaked away from the centre board.

Split leather
See Leather, Rawhide, Skivers

Sponge (natural)
One of the most unlikely materials for upholstery work was natural sea-sponge. Around 1868 the American Patent Sponge Co offered for sale patent sponge as a substitute for curled horse hair. By a process of mixing natural sea-sponge with water and glycerine, which was then evaporated to leave a stable product, they apparently produced an upholstery stuffing that was inexpensive, easy to use and germ free. The products of latex extract are sometimes referred to as sponge rubber or sorbo. Whether this forerunner of FOAM was successful is not known.
See also Latex, Preen

Pacific Elastic Sponge Company of California (1868), Catalogue, San Francisco: the Company.

Spray
See Finishing equipment

Spring and tumbler lock
See Locks

Spring bars
An American upholstery spring system which was in use by the turn of the 20th century. It comprised three or four conical springs attached at their small ends to a flat metal bar, which was then fitted to the frame. It was found in cheaper furniture as it eliminated the skilled spring-tying process.

Spring edge
The creation of a resilient front edge to upholstery and bedding work is known as a spring edge. By fitting springs right up to the front rail of a frame and fixing them with a wire or BAMBOO rod to give controlled flexibility, a resilient and comfortable effect is achieved which is superior to a firm edge where the cover cloth is simply pulled over the fixed frame and filling.

Spring units
Pre-fabricated spring units which can be simply nailed into a chair frame, thus saving on time and skilled labour.

Springs
A resilient device used as support for upholstery and bedding work. Although the coil spring is the most well known (see below), many versions and varieties have been employed in upholstery work.

CENTRIPETAL
A spring mechanism for a chair that has four hoops of spring steel radiating from a centre. The arrangement, patented by Thomas Warren in 1849 (US Pat.no.6740), was initially adapted from railway coach seating by the American Chair Co, and was used on mid-19th-century American rocker chairs. The principle was based on the leaf spring, but in this case the leaves were not straight but inverted back on themselves to form an ellipse or semi-circle. Chairs with this springing were exhibited at the 1851 London Great Exhibition and were very well received. 'The springs are connected to another centre

piece, which sustains the seat of the chair on a vertical pin; on this the chair seat revolves, while at the same time the springs sustaining the seat from the underframe give it an agreeable elasticity in every direction' (The *Illustrated Exhibitor*).

COIL
These springs, originating in the requirements for carriage suspension, probably found their first upholstery use in the 18th century for chamber or exercising horses. The 1793 *Cabinet-makers' London Book of Prices* charged for making chamber-horses, including 'springs each … and for fixing the springs and girth webbing each', and included charges for 'turning of the springs' (1793, p.208). Mattresses were also made with interior springs, but it is difficult to show whether they preceded upholstered chairs or vice-versa. It has been suggested that true sprung upholstery was a Biedermeier invention and it was Georg Junigl, a Viennese upholsterer, who was first granted a patent in 1822 for upholstery springs. This patent was: 'for his improvement on contemporary methods of furniture upholstery, which, by means of a special preparation of hemp, and with the assistance of iron springs, he renders so elastic that it is not inferior to horsehair upholstery' (Himmelheber, 1974, pp.89–90). However, this probably was a codification of previous practice and not a major advance. The phrase 'improvement on contemporary methods' would suggest that this is so.

In England the acceptance of upholstery springs seems to have grown rapidly. In 1826 Samuel Pratt took out a patent (Pat.no.5418) for 'improvements in the application of springs to beds, couches and seats to be used on ship-board for the prevention of sea sickness'. This consisted of wire springs, twisted into circular or angular coils in the shape of an hourglass, which were attached to webbing inside the upholstered seat. In 1828 Pratt had developed the spring further, and his new patent (Pat.no.5668) was for 'elastic beds, cushions seats, and other articles of that kind'. This latter development was applied to sprung cushions and simple spring units for upholstery rather than as sea-sickness prevention. Pratt's patent defined the 'spring unit' in such a way as to indicate that it had the advantages that would be its selling points for many years. These included the sprung edge, the advantages of reversibility and the fact that they could be either built into furniture or be fitted to a removable cushion.

Although the use of springs in upholstery has been traced to at least the mid 18th century (see above), it can be assumed that spring upholstery for general domestic use was not widely introduced into the furniture trade until the 1830s. However, in 1834, it seemed that there were few workmen who had a sound knowledge of spring upholstery: 'They [the upholsterers] will be found pretending to know, rather than [being] really and truly acquainted with the art; the necessary result of which has been that the public have been dissatisfied with the spring-stuffed sofas, and they have, consequently, grown

109   The use of exposed centripetal springs in this chair design was unusual in 1851. Nevertheless the American Chair Co were praised for this exhibit in the 1851 London Great Exhibition.

110   The use of bi-conical springs in the 1790s in this Sheraton design for a chamber horse confirms that these were known before the 1820s.

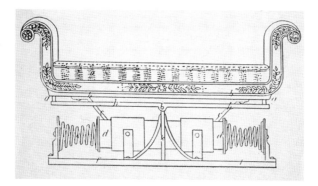

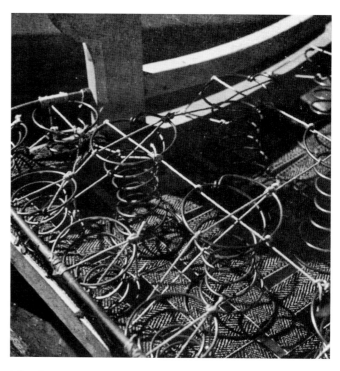

into disuse' (Crofton, 1834, p.47). This implies that spring seats were available generally before 1834, but upholsterers had little idea as to their correct application. Crofton hoped his publication would enable young upholsterers to learn so that: 'the art of spring-stuffing may then be reinstated in its original perfection' (op.cit., p.60).

In 1839 Loudon confirmed that the use of 'spiral springs as stuffing has long been known to men of science; but so little to upholsterers, that a patent for using them was taken out, some years ago, as a new invention. Beds and seats of this description are now, however, made by upholsterers generally'. Loudon went on to say that 'springs may be had from Birmingham by the hundred weight' (1839, p.336). His statement indicates the very few years' delay before the trade whole-heartedly embraced the idea of springs.

Although springs were available commercially, furniture-makers continued to produce their own springs. Sheraton recorded the making process and the reason for cone-shaped springs: 'strong wire [is] twisted round a block in regular gradation, so that when the wire is compressed by the weight of those who exercise each turn of it may clear itself and fall within the other' (Sheraton, 1791, Plate 22, Appendix). In 1835, upholsterer John Hancock of Philadelphia had '2 blocks for making springs' and 43 kg (6 st) of iron wire in his stock-in-trade sale (Conradsen, 1993, p.53).

The earliest attempts at securing springs were to the solid boards, as used in chamber-horses, with the result that they did not have the same degree of resilience that came with the later use of webbing. Some early-19th-century American sofas exist with iron coil-springs stapled directly to board or slatted bottoms in the manner of the chamber-horses of the 18th century. This method of fixing bed bases was in fact patented in 1831 by Josiah French of Ware, Mass. (Grier, 1988, p.227). The resulting upholstery was inevitably heavier and less resilient than the conventional methods of using webbing, but it enabled spring upholstery to become available to another level of the market.

Various techniques were invented to assist in the making of upholstered chairs. The first was simplifying the setting of springs in the interior seat. In 1853 Finnemore patented a method of fixing springs in upholstery and mattresses (Pat.no.1652). His method used springs with loops formed at the top and bottom. The springs were held in place by straps that passed through the loops on the spring. A simple solution to the seat-springing problem was to make a spring unit which simply had to be inserted into the frame. An important process was patented by Louis Durrieu in 1864 (Pat.no.1054). This patent consisted of a set of springs connected at top and bottom, using the continued wire of the springs which allowed them to make their own frame. The obvious advantages of this process over individual hand-knot tying resulted in not only a consistent product but also the possi-

bility that the unit could be developed so as to fit onto chair backs and sides as well as in loose cushions.

The manufacture of springs remained a manually controlled operation for most of the century. In 1871 the *House Furnisher* could say that this was not for want of machines but rather for the 'want of uniformity in the wire' (May, p.42). The problem was that soft spots in the spring wire needed to be removed before it could be made up into springs. This could be done manually because the maker could see the flaws, but machine processes could not develop until reliable supplies of wire were available. These problems were reflected in consumer complaints. In 1877 the Garret sisters complained that iron springs were 'always out of order and cannot have their anatomy readjusted without the intervention of the manufacturer, by whom alone the complexity of their internal structure is understood' (cited in Grier, 1988, p.117). Even later, in 1889, complaints were still being voiced about the poor quality of English springs, especially in comparison with French ones. A report on upholstery from the Mansion House Committee visiting the Paris Universal Exhibition in 1889, complained that all this was even more annoying as the cost of springs was a nominal part of the cost of an upholstered job.

Attempts to speed up the springing process also included the continuing development of the fitting of springs without webbing support. These methods used in England and America included wooden battens to which springs were nailed, a platform of intertwined coiled wires called a lace web to which springs were clipped, and metal laths with springs pre-fitted by the manufacturer. In 1878 it was reported that a Paul Roth of New York was exhibiting machinery that would produce a stitched edge, pack the hair into a seat and tie the springs (*Furniture Gazette*, 23 February, p.106).

By the mid 20th century, traditional methods of springing were being challenged. In the same way that foams revolutionized the filling of cushions and the padding process of upholstery, changes in spring technology allowed a move away from the coil-sprung plat-

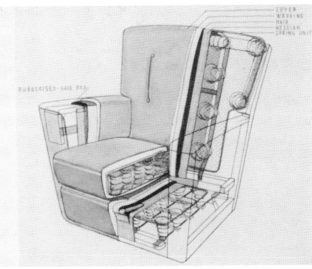

113   The use of pre-fabricated springs units continued to de-skill the upholstery process. This English example shows the units mounted on steel laths, as well as a pre-fabricated spring cushion, c.1950.

form that was the mainstay of upholstery prior to World War II (see Suspension systems). The hour-glass shaped coil spring had remained the same since its invention, with a range of sizes for particular applications: 13 cm (5 in) for couch scrolls, 15 cm (6 in) for seats for small chairs, 18–25 cm (7–10 in) for seats of easy chairs, couches and backs.

FISH-MOUTH

A serpentine spring with the addition of a small section of spring metal to the leading edge, designed to create a 'sprung edge'. When fixed in situ, the resultant effect resembles a fish mouth.

NO-SAG

A patented form of serpentine springing for upholstery that is based on a zigzag-shaped length of spring steel that is fixed under convex tension from one side of a frame to the opposite side.
See Serpentine, below

POCKET

A straight-sided coil spring enclosed in a calico pocket or sleeve. Each pocket was sewn or clipped together in such a way as to create a mattress with a degree of independent operation for each spring. Patented in 1901 by Vi-spring and mainly used in mattresses.

SERPENTINE

A type of upholstery support based on zigzag-shaped lengths of spring wire which are fitted in convex tension between rails. These springs enable upholsterers to fit a support system into a deep-profile chair or sofa, without the skills involved in traditional upholstering.

SINUOUS

See Fish mouth, Serpentine, above

SPRING UNITS

In the very late 19th century the newly invented assembled spring unit was made up from a number of coil springs fastened together with clips and surrounded by a bent-wire frame. The developments were encouraged by the burgeoning motor-car industry. These factory-made spring units had steel spring bars as a substitute for webbing; the conical springs were clipped on, and steel wire was used to clamp and secure the springs in a grid instead of the lashing process. The whole spring unit was then covered with canvas and upholstered as required. The types included single, double and triple layers of springs (all riveted to steel base laths). The cheapest was made from two diagonal laths with five springs fitted in a cross; a better quality was made with three laths each way with nine springs. All were fitted with a wire mesh top. These were a useful innovation for speeding up the process of laying springs into a frame for a fully upholstered chair. Further developments included interior-sprung seat cushions that were often used in conjunction with the spring units.

TENSION

In 1841 John Wilkie, an upholsterer, and Charles Schiewso, a musical instrument maker, patented an early form of tension spring which used the principle of expansion and contraction of small springs mounted on straps (Pat.no.8861). This was an important development as it avoided the need to have a deep seat to accommodate the original hourglass-shaped coil springs. This concept was developed further when in 1856 George and William Hooper patented 'improvements in springs for carriages, and for the cushions of carriages, chairs, mattresses, beds and similar articles' (Pat.no.282). This patent relied on the idea of compensating springs made from rings or strips of vulcanized India rubber. Yet another example and a precursor of the modern tension spring was invented by William Searby in 1857 (Pat.no.2939). This consisted of a piece of elastic metal, wood or bone compressed into a curved form. Each end was attached to a buckle and strap which were fixed to the frame of the furniture, and used lateral tension to create a spring. Arched metal laths fixed under tension were also used in France for outdoor chairs and later for railway-carriage seating. In the 20th century the introduction of the tube-shaped tension spring, sometimes encased in cloth, allowed chairs to have the spring benefits without the deep frame profiles that were needed to accommodate full coil-springing. This was particularly useful for fireside and wing chairs of all types. The development of this type of tension spring is credited to Willy Knoll, who patented his method in 1928 (Pat.no. 322,638). It was a success and formed the basis of the famous Parker-Knoll range of tension-sprung chairs from the 1930s onward.
See also Four point platform, Upholstery

WOOD

Thin laminated strips of timber occasionally fitted to beds in a convex shape, to act as a firm suspension for mattresses. The idea appears to have originated in Switzerland.

Grier, K. (1988), *Culture and Comfort, People, Parlours and Upholstery, 1850–1930*, New York: Strong Museum.
Holley, D. (1981), 'Upholstery springs', in *Furniture History*, XVII, pp.64–7.
Thomas, D. G. (1976), *A. Howard and Sons, Upholsterer's Spring Makers, A Short Record of the Firm's History*, Greater London Industrial Archaeological Society.

Spruce (*Picea spp.*)

A term referring generally to the genus *Picea*, commercially known in the 19th century as white pine, deal or fir. It has a density of 440 (28 lb cu ft), and the whole wood is light yellow-brown and is recognized by the knotty character of the boards. It has an even, parallel grain and a hard texture. It is mainly found in Northern Europe.

In 1853 stock sizes of spruce for furniture use were recommended as follows: 12.7 mm (½ in) boards for use as plain deal backs, 19 mm (¾ in) boards for use as bed bottoms, and 31.8 mm (1¼ in) wide used for tenter frames (Blackie, 1853, p.6). Spon noted that 'it is fine grained and does well for gilding on, also for internal joinery, lining furniture and packing cases … It is a nice wood for dresser-tops, shelves and common tables' (1901, p.131). Aka Whitewood.

Stained glass
See Glass

Stains and staining

Dyes and stains were important in the cabinet-maker's repertoire, the distinction between them being that stains colour the surface, whilst dyes penetrate the material and effect a colour change due to chemical reaction. In either case the choice of substances for achieving colour change was immense. For many centuries the more commonly used dyes were natural such as ALKANET, LOGWOOD, verdigris, copperas, and barberry root, whilst ARCHIL, DRAGON'S BLOOD, and BRAZIL-WOOD were regularly used as stains. As with some other processes, the resourcefulness of the cabinet-maker was sometimes the only limitation on developments in the field and many and various recipes can be found in instruction manuals. The use of stain was usually to disguise poor-quality timber, and to imitate that of better quality, so many stain recipes attempted to imitate mahogany, walnut or ebony. In fact a stain can be made to almost any shade by mixing dry colour with boiled linseed to make a paste and then thinning it with turpentine. Evelyn noted a concoction of plum tree wood with quick-lime and urine for a red stain (1662, p.240). He also recorded a black stain:

> there is a black which joyners use to tinge their pear tree with, and make it resemble ebony, and likewise fir and other woods for cabinets, picture frames etc. which is this – Take logwood, boyle it in ordinary oyle, and with this paint them over, when tis dry, work it over a second time with lampblack and strong size. That also dry, rub off the dusty sootiness adhering to it with a soft brush or cloth.
> (Evelyn, 1662, p.241)

Interestingly the same recipe was offered by Sheraton some 150 years later. During the 17th century staining was an important part of the MARQUETRY process, but by the end of the 18th century 'The art of staining wood was more in use at the time when inlaying was in fashion which required most of the primitive colours; at present red and black stains are those in general use' (Sheraton, 1803, p.308).

In the early 19th century, the woods used as a base for staining were holly, pear and beech and most often used for chairs, sofas and bed-steads. The recipes for rosewood and ebony were straightforward, but mahogany could be produced by a process which involved rubbing the surfaces with dilute nitric acid and then covering the article with hot sand and placing it in an oven (Nicholson, 1826, p.11). Loudon, discussing the finish of Windsor chairs, noted that they 'were frequently stained with diluted sulphuric acid and logwood; or by repeatedly washing them over with alum water, which has some tartar in it, they should afterwards be washed over several times with an extract of Brazil wood' (1839, pp.318–20). This apparently gave a mahogany-like finish.

The 19th century saw staining develop into a batch process for some articles. Whittock described how chairs were dipped in vats of boiling dye to give a rosewood colour: 'at the principle manufactories they are dipped in a large copper containing the boiling stain and then taken out and allowed to dry before they are dipped again' (1827, p.72).

By the early 20th century, stains available to the furniture-maker included aniline dye stains, stains of plant origin and chemical origin.

PLANT STAINS INCLUDE THE FOLLOWING:

Alkanet-root

A dye from the root of the plant *Anchusa tinctoria*, found in Europe, which was used to make red oil for colouring furniture. It is easily soluble in either oils or alcohol. According to Sheraton, if it was mixed with LINSEED OIL, rose pink and DRAGON'S BLOOD, all ground together and then boiled for twelve hours and strained, it would revive timber, especially MAHOGANY. Sheraton goes on to say:

All hard mahogany of a bad colour should be oiled with it, and should stand unpolished a time, proportioned to its quality and texture of grain; if it be laid on hard wood to be polished off immediately, it is of little use; but if it stands a few days after, the oil penetrates the grain and hardens on the surface, and consequently will bear a better polish, and look brighter in colour. (1803, p.6)

It was also used in the 19th century for imitation work: 'Oil coloured by alkanet is used for staining wood in imitation of rosewood' (Ure, 1839, I, p.89).

Brazilwood
An important dyewood. Sheraton noted that brazilwood (or brasil-etto) was 'an American wood, of red colour and very heavy', adding that 'the wood is imported for dyers, who use it much' (1803, p.95).

Dragon's blood
A red gum resin exuding from the palm *Daemonorops*. The name was also applied to the juice of the 'dragon tree' *dracaena draco*. Stalker and Parker state that 'the best is the brightest red and freest from dross. You may buy it in drops (as the Drugsters call it)' (1688, p.4). In the mid 18th century Salmon mentions two sorts: 'lumps wrapped in long narrow leaves called drops or tears of dragon's blood and common dragons blood in lumps or cakes which is inferior' (1758, p.221). The extracted resin was evaporated, powdered and added to spirit varnish to darken and redden timbers.

Fustic
A West Indian tree that was important for inlay work, which yields a yellow dye imported in long sticks, often used in the 19th century for dyeing linens.

Indigo
A tropical shrub (*Indigofera*), the stem and leaves of which give a dye, once largely used in calico printing.

Logwood (*Haematoxylon campechianum*)
A bright red dye-wood timber from Central America, especially the west coast of Yucatan. Known in England since at least 1581. Although providing red dyes, it was also used as a way of staining wood black. If an alkali such as soda of potash was added, the colour changed to a dark blue or purple, hence the black effect obtained through multiple washes. Stalker and Parker's recipe for staining woods black explains the process: 'boil it [logwood] in a water and vinegar, then take galls and Copperas well beaten and boil them well in water with which stain your work so often till it be the black to your mind' (1688, p.83). Aka Campeachy.

Madder-root (*Rubia tinctorium*)
A plant indigenous to the Levant but widely cultivated in the Mediterranean area and India. It imparts a red colour when soaked in water or spirits.

Nut-galls
A growth found on twigs of oaks (especially Turkish oak), produced by the puncture of the twig by insects. Nut-galls contain a large quantity of tannic and gallic acid and were used extensively as dye stuffs.

Persian berries
Berries from a species of blackthorn common in Persia and Turkey. Gathered in an unripe state, they furnished a yellow dye during the 19th century.

Red-sanders
A tree that yields a dye of a bright garnet-red colour. Used by French polishers for dyeing polishes, varnishes, revivers and so on, especially in the 19th century.
See also Saunderswood

Turmeric (*Curcuma longa*)
The root of the plant imported from China and the East Indies. It supplies a yellow dye used in making Dutch pink- and gold-coloured varnishes.

CHEMICAL STAINS WERE DERIVED FROM:

Acetic acid
A stain can be made from iron filings soaked in vinegar (acetic acid). Especially useful for butternut, which will turn almost black whereas chestnut will turn a soft yellowish-brown.

Ammonia
Aka Hartshorn, an ammonia solution (originally sourced from harts' antlers) used to fumigate mahogany and oak. It has also been used prior to staining to give a base colouring to a timber.

Bichromate of potash
A brick-brown finish can be obtained for oak or chestnut by staining with bichromate of potash, and then rubbing the surface with linseed oil.

Iron sulphate
By boiling oak in a mixture of sulphate of iron and water, a grey stain will be imparted.

Nitric acid
Aqua fortis is the traditional name for nitric acid. Used as a colourant which, when diluted with water, provides a range of yellow-red colours, depending upon its strength. Bitmead noted that in the USA the practice of imitating old mahogany by brushing walnut over with a weak nitric acid solution was common (1873, p.82).

Permanganate of potash
A purple dye which can create a range of stains including near black to light brown, widely used to reproduce 'antique' effects (see Ash).

Picric acid
A bitter yellow acid compound sometimes used to create an 'antique' effect of oak.

Silver nitrate stain
A caustic chemical compound. It has been used as a weak solution on chestnut which is afterwards fumed with ammonia to give a dark brown.

Sulphuric acid
A heavy corrosive acid sometimes used in recipes for ebonizing. When diluted with water it can make a yellow stain. Aka vitriol.

Tannic acid
See Nut-galls, above

See also Dyeing of wood, Lampblack

Mussey, R. (1982), 'Old finishes and early varnishes', Fine Woodworking Techniques 6, in *Fine Woodworking*, March/April, pp.71–5.
New, S. (1981), 'The use of stains by furniture-makers, 1660–1850', in *Furniture History*, XVII, pp.51–60.
Whittock, Nathaniel (1827), *Decorative Painters and Glaziers' Guide*, London: I. T. Hinton.

116 A stay quadrant mounted in the side of a drawer of an English painted secretaire commode, c.1785. When the drawer is shut, the drop-flap mechanism is completely hidden.

Stamped velvet
See Velvet

Staple hinges
See Hinges

Staple(s)
A fixing method widely used in later-20th-century upholstery and cabinet-making. Especially used in conjunction with cheap furniture for fixing hardboard panels satisfactorily both in structural and non-structural applications. In upholstery the staple gun, usually powered by compressed air, has become the mainstay of the non-traditional trade.
See also Stay

Stay or **Staple**
Curved, usually quadrant-shaped metal arms designed to support fall flaps of bureaux, reclining chair backs and so on. In later-17th-century reclining chair use, they worked in conjunction with a ratchet and were sometimes covered in cloth or were gilded or silvered. In 1637, Ralph Grynder supplied Queen Henrietta Maria with '3 new stays foe the chair backs' (Beard, 1997, p.290). For cabinet work the rule-joint stays open and locks like a folding ruler.

Steam chest
An iron cabinet or zinc tray and box designed to heat glue or cauls, as well as to bend wood. It was assembled and filled with water, then placed on a stove so that steam filled it up and the steam-heating of the piece could begin.

Steel
An alloy of iron and up to 1.7 per cent carbon, sometimes with other elements added, e.g. manganese, phosphorus, sulphur silicon. There are three major types of steel: carbon, mild and alloy steel. Carbon steel is made by heating wrought iron with charcoal to absorb carbon. In 1742 crucible steel developed by Benjamin Huntsman was superior in hardness, due to consistency of production directly from iron. How-

ever, the difficulties of manufacture prior to the Bessemer process of the 1850s meant that limited quantities were made. The Bessemer process used a method which forced air through the molten pig-iron in a converter, thus reducing its carbon content as well as allowing impurities to form a 'slag'. In the 1860s the Siemens Martin 'open hearth' method allowed the use of both pig-iron and scrap and by the 1950s an improved oxygen method had been developed. Alloy steels have other metallic substances fused into the base metal. Stainless steel, for example, has a percentage of chromium added.

The use of steel prior to the late 18th century was limited in furniture partly because of its cost. When it was used it would be for plaques, mirrors and very occasionally chests and chairs. One of the most extraordinary chairs made from forged steel with chiselled reliefs and figures was made in c.1574 by Thomas Rucker of Augsburg for Emperor Rudolph II. Chiselled steel cabinets were made at Nuremburg and Augsburg in the late 16th and early 17th centuries for export, and in the 17th century the Galleria workshops at the Uffizi produced steel furniture (see Plate II).

The most well-known 18th-century steel furniture was made in the Russian manufactory of Tula. Originally set up in 1712 as an ordnance factory, Tula began to make a range of decorative objects by the 1730s. These included X-shape chair supports with open-work scrolls decorated with inlays of softer metals such as brass or bronze. Decoration later included blued steel, chiselled relief work, gilding and multiple metal decoration. The famous facet cutting of blued steel became a feature by the mid 18th century.

The excavations of classical remains in the later 18th century encouraged a taste for steel furniture. The material lent itself well to the severe lines of furniture designed after the classical manner. The political associations made during the French Revolution with gilded and upholstered furniture encouraged a revised taste, often for very simple polished iron and steel furniture, including chairs, benches, hammocks, ladders and folding furniture. Specialist craftsmen, the *'fournisseurs en acier poli'* developed the special skills of using tempering ovens to control the colouring of the metal.

Once steel became more accessible in the 19th century, it was developed in separate forms, including strap, wire, sheet, rod and later tube (see below). In the 20th century, metal has taken a major place in the furniture-maker's repertoire, be it for domestic or contract use. For the avant-garde in the 1920s and 1930s, tubular steel furniture particularly represented modernity, whilst manufacturers saw the potential of a developing market. In 1923 the American Simmons Company made bedroom furniture from steel. With a range of nine suites, each with eleven pieces, they were making 300 units a day, which was expected to rise ten-fold when a new factory was on-line. The manufacturing used electrically welded seamless tubing, and product differentiation was achieved by a variety of finishes. For example, at the top of the range, furniture was painted with a wood grain effect. On the other hand, parts of the trade, especially in England, did not immediately welcome the material. In 1931 it was found that:

a striking technical change in the post-war years has been the steady invasion of metal work. Already metal furniture has invaded the office, the kitchen and the nursery and perhaps in a few more years metal tables, chairs, sideboards and bookshelves will be common. This change of course attacks the whole 'furniture' trade as hitherto understood by operatives and employers. Metal furniture requires neither sawyers, machine wood-workers, carvers nor French polishers. Already the furnishing trades are alive to this menace and retailers are praising the superior look of wood to their customers with a view to maintaining a preference in its favour.
(*New Survey of the Life and Labour of London*, 1931, p.217)

However by the 1940s another generation of designers were claiming metal as an ideal material for mass producing furniture. Charles Eames gave his rationale behind this material use:

Metal stamping is the technique synonymous with mass production in this country, yet 'acceptable' furniture in this material is noticeably absent. By using forms that reflect the positive nature of the stamping technique in combination with a surface treatment that cuts down heat transfer, dampens sound, and is pleasant to the touch, we feel that it is possible to free metal furniture from the negative bias from which it has suffered. (Cited in Neuhart and Eames, 1989, p.97)

Ironically, most of Eames's designs were executed in wood or plastics, sometimes with metal underframes or legs. Mass-produced stamped metal chairs did not develop quite in the manner that Eames had envisaged.

Pressed sheet and strip steel

The use of strip steel was introduced into furniture with the production of garden chairs by Francois Carré, who patented his design in 1866. He used curved steel strips to give durability and elasticity to his chairs. In the 1860s bent steel strips were used to manufacture a range of chairs, generally for public space or garden use. The use of strip steel for the seat and back and a rod structure for the frame ensured a comfortable design with durability and strength. The chairs were made in France by the Société Anonyme des Hauts-Fourneaux & Fonderies du Val d'Osne and in New York by the firm Lalance and Grosjean. Perhaps some of the earliest applications of sheet metal to furniture in this century can be found in the burgeoning office-furniture market. By 1920 there was a large manufacturing sector producing metal furniture such as filing cabinets, desks and work benches. A successful off-shoot of sheet steel used presses to form a pressed-steel chair. A lightweight stacking chair using this method was produced by Evertaut in England, as well as by the French manufacturer Société des Meubles Multiples in Lyons. Not surprisingly, the nature of the material tended to disqualify it as suitable for domestic furniture, except for its application as internal chair frames.

Other uses for metal in furniture included the wartime development of internal metal upholstery frames. Yet again, this was an idea that had been known and widely used in the 19th century. In that time the frames had been designed to give a flexible curved shape to chairs. In the mid 20th century the metal frames were designed to imitate the shape of an existing wood frame chair. They used rolled steel sections

118   One of the most well-known examples of steel-tube furniture. The Cesca chair by Marcel Breuer also demonstrates the elegant cantilever principle. Designed in 1928 and reproduced from 1965.

with wooden tacking strips and were unimaginatively box-like in shape. Alternatively, metal frames could be much more innovative and some were used to produce more organic shapes with welded steel rod and sewn-in rubberized hair (see below). In recent years, some designers have returned to sheet metals, but these have generally been limited editions and not 'commercial' designs.

Tubular steel

Developments in tubular steel technology began with the German firm of Mannesmann, who, in January 1885, perfected the technique of heating a billet, which was pierced and then rolled into the required tube. It was ideal for the new developments in bicycle design but was too heavy for furniture. A later development by Machinefabrik Sack, in 1921, produced tubes with thinner walls which were therefore lighter and less rigid, in other words more suitable for bending into furniture shapes.

Marcel Breuer was the first to be credited with the initial use of precision steel tubing for furniture, his 'Wassily' club chair of 1925 being the first of a range of tubular products that would be developed world-wide. Once the principle of tubular steel frames had been established, the next important development was the design of the CANTILEVER chair, which was developed independently by Mart Stam, Mies van der Rohe and Breuer. Their work established tubular metal furniture as a type form.

In America, the Ypsilanti Reed Company developed the tubular steel furniture with designs by Donald Deskey for a range called Flekrom. By 1930 the Howell Company of Chicago were making chrome-plated, tubular-framed chairs for indoor use. The Chromsteel Range was also used in several of the model houses in the Chicago

117   The use of sheet steel in contract office furniture has been standard for much of the 20th century. This example of a Roneo typist's desk dates from c.1947.

OPPOSITE PAGE
119   The use of steel rod or wire was developed in the mid 19th century. This chair by Warren Platner, designed in 1966, uses nickel-plated steel rods to create a chair of sculptural form.

World's Fair of 1933, further promoting it as a fashion. The Lloyd Manufacturing Co (see Lloyd Loom) also developed tubular steel furniture, which was again promoted by being used in many displays on the World's Fair 1933 site. (Marshall Lloyd had developed a process for producing thin-gauge steel tubing as early as 1913, called the Lloyd oxyacetylene process.)

Although Breuer- and Miesian-inspired tubular chairs were manufactured in large quantities in the USA, the truly popular ranges of tubular steel furniture came after the war with the 'dinette' sets. These comprised a table with a plastic laminate top, on tubular steel legs, and four tubular dining chairs. In the early 1980s one company was turning out 2000 such sets per day from two factories.

Wire and rod
Iron and steel wire and rod was employed by furniture-makers in the second half of the 19th century. Early examples of twisted wire furniture from France, designed to be used in the garden, were recommended as being 'exceedingly light and unique in appearance, admirably suited for lawns, summer houses, cottages and piazzas' (Wickersham, 1855, p.31). A unique use of wire was developed and patented in 1876 by George Hunzinger. He devised a seat in which steel wires were covered with fabric and fitted to the frame (US Pat.no. 176314). The meshing of wire (covered with thread or braid) formed a seat of great strength and durability which was also surprisingly elegant. Conversely, the well-known ice-cream parlour chair found in the USA was made from twisted steel rods and fitted with a plywood seat. The particular design was patented in 1909 by the Chicago based Royal Metal Manufacturing Co.

The example of steel's flexibility through wire and rod was exploited in furniture manufacturing throughout the 20th century. However, the use of wire and rod, usually in combination with other materials, has became synonymous with the 1950s, both in the 'Contemporary' style in Britain and in the work of designers such as the Eames and Bertoia in the USA. A chair designed and made by Ernest Race and Co, which used a welded rod and a plywood seat to make a semi-traditional style chair for the Festival of Britain in 1951, helped to change British attitudes to metal furniture since the designs were not considered outlandish. As well as complete frames, manufacturers utilized the wire rod as a skeleton for upholstering easy chairs and sofas, but most important for the general market was the adoption of wire rod legs with ball feet. This underframe or leg was found on every furniture object that it could be applied to, from coffee tables to easy chairs.

In the USA, Harry Bertoia designed his famous sculptural wire frame chairs which were recognized as a form of interior sculpture. The shaped wire rods used for the seat-back were bent and formed by hand, whilst the rectangular base rods act simply as support. This was similar to the Eames's where steel rod was used for chair bases in combination with contrasting seat-back materials. This then enabled chairs to be seen as two separate but related parts, the seat and the support.

Steel in its many forms has risen and fallen in popularity as fashion has dictated. For a number of years around the 1970s the 'chrome and glass dining set' which used large-section square or round chromed tube was often seen with a matching upholstered suite made from the same material. These sorts of sets are still available, but are often relegated to the role of a kitchen dinette.

Benton, Tim and Campbell-Cole, B. (eds) (1979), *Tubular Steel Furniture*, London: Art Book Company.
Geest, J. and Macel, O. (1988), *Stühle aus Stahl, Metallmöbel 1925–1940*, Cologne: Walter Konig.
Groneman, C. H. (1949), *Bent Tubular Furniture*, Milwaukee: Bruce.
Leben, U. (1995), 'D'Acier, l'art du mobilier et des objets en fer et acier polis', in *Connaissance Arts*, 520, September, pp.108–22.
Malchenko, M. D. et al., (1974), *Art Objects in Steel by Tula Craftsmen*, Leningrad: Aurora Art
Montclos, B. (1993), 'Mobilier en acier de Toula', in *Estampille, l'objet d'art*, April, pp.52–61.
Ostergard, Derek (1987), *Bentwood and Metal Furniture 1850–1946*, New York: American Federation of Arts.
Pfannschmidt, Ernest (1962), *Metallmöbel*, Stuttgart: Hoffman.
Wilk, C. (1981), *Marcel Breuer: Furniture and Interiors*, New York: Museum of Modern Art, and London: Architectural Press.

Steel carving
See Carving steel

Steel webbing
See Webbing steel

Steel wool
See Abrasives

Stencils and Stencilling
An attractive and simply produced decorative effect that has been successfully applied to a range of furniture. Essentially it is a process of applying designs through a specially prepared template, either by paints or powders, applied to a tacky varnish base. The materials used by stencillers included powdered metals such as brass, zinc, copper, aluminium, silver and gold, or a range of alloys. The stencils, cut from rag paper or card on a sheet of tin or glass with a stencil knife, were toughened in linseed oil. Etching tools, pounces and punches were also part of the kit. Stencilling was widely used in conjunction with paint techniques for vernacular furniture decoration. Introduced from Asia during the 5th and 6th centuries, the process was widely used during the Middle Ages for decorating patterns on walls, furniture and cloth. It remained a popular method of decorating vernacular furniture (especially in the USA) and by the end of the 19th century was industrialized to a degree.

In the 1820s the famous American fancy chair-maker Lambert Hitchcock introduced this form of decoration to his chair production. His stencils typically included stylized flowers and fruit, often in a basket and framed with leaves. Complex tonal effects could be achieved by skilled operators who used the multicoloured bronze powders and stencil frames, directly onto tacky varnish.

In England stencilling was also recommended for imitation inlay work, especially on oak. Bitmead described how to cut a stencil and apply gas-black mixed with thin polish over the stencil. When dry, the work was 'bodied-in' and rubbed down with hair cloth (smooth side down). After this a final coat of polish was laid down. When finished the work appeared inlaid (Bitmead, 1876, p.40).

Fales, Dean (1972), *American Painted Furniture 1660–1880*, New York: Dutton.
Waring, Janet (1937), *Early American Stencils on Walls and Furniture*, New York: Dover, reprint 1968.

Stick furniture
Unlike most chair construction forms, stick furniture used the seat panel as the basis of its construction. Spindles are fitted into the back of the seat to create a backrest, and legs are socketed into the base of the seat for support. The stick method of construction is generally in the province of the turner.

The origins of this type are found in Ancient Egyptian stool construction. The method has remained much the same since then and

was a standard process for centuries. In primitive designs three legs and no back was the basic form. For example, in 1649 Randle Holme described 'a country stool or plank or block stool being only a thick piece of wood with either 3 or 4 pieces of wood fastened in it for feet. Note if these be made long, they are termed either a bench, forme or tressell' (vol.2, bk 3, 14, p.15). More sophisticated effects resulted in the 'Windsor' chair form.

Stinkwood (*Ocotea bullata*)
A South African timber with an average density of 800 (50 lb/cu ft). It has a variable colour between light grey to black, straw to yellow-brown, with a moderately fine texture and a variable grain. Hard and heavy, it is difficult to work. It was used for high-class cabinet-making in Dutch colonial work, but by the early 20th century it was very scarce.

Stitches and Stitching
NEEDLEWORK techniques are based on passing a needle and thread through a cloth in a particular way to create the desired effect. Stitches fall into four basic categories: flat (including satin, cross and herring bone), linked or chain stitches which provide loops on the surface, buttonhole stitches, and knot stitches.

Baste tacks
A flat stitch that holds materials together temporarily with long loose stitches.

Blanket
A link stitch used as an edging stitch to cover a turned-over raw edge of cloth.

Blind
An upholstery technique with the intention of stitching in a manner that pulls fillings towards edges to firm and solidify them. The vertical edges are indented as a result.
See Mattress

Cross
See GROS POINT

Double-stuff
In 17th-century upholstery, the technique of double-stuff stitching, usually in the centre of the seat, was intended to hold the sandwich of stuffing, sackcloth and webbing as a firm and integral whole. The stitching may be in an oval or rectangular form, the former being favoured in American examples and the latter in European chairs.

Feather
An upholstery stitch that has been used to give sharp definition to the edges of upholstered work. It was made in conjunction with the first stuffing of show-wood or gilt-framed upholstery. A row of stitching is placed crosswise around the edge of the seat and is in a herringbone shape. The feather stitch is applied to the top row to compress the edge into a sharp line of stuffing.

Flame
The name for both a stitch and a pattern. As a stitch it refers to the long and short stitch work on canvas, which is also called Florentine, Bargello, Irish or Hungary (*point d'Hongrie*) work. As a pattern, it refers to the graded, shaded design that resembles flames. A fine open canvas is worked with stranded not twisted threads and uses six shades of the same colour. These are sewn in short and long stitches in strict order. The outline of each row is then made in gold or black or other contrast to define it.

Running
A flat stitch which runs the thread in and out of the material in even spaces, e.g. for gathering.

Tent
A flat stitch slanting diagonally and parallel over one thread of the canvas to form a solid background of even lines.
See PETIT POINT

Stone
Amongst the earliest of materials used for 'furniture'. The Neolithic site of Skara Brae in the Orkney Isles used assembled slabs of stone to make surfaces. Stone was used in Greek and Roman times for thrones, and later for fixed seats in cathedrals such as Charlemagne's throne in Aix-la-Chapelle and the Bishop's chair in Hexham. Other examples of medieval stone work are known (for example, Westminster Hall table), as is the use of local stone by peasantry for 'furniture'. The massy nature and difficulty of working, as well as the practical considerations, meant that solid stone furniture was unlikely to be popular. However, particular types of decorative stone have been widely used for centuries, often as a decorative part of an object.
See especially Blue John, Lapis lazuli, Malachite, Marble, Porphyry, Rock crystal, Serpentine, Slate

Stone work
See Marble, Mosaic work, Pietre dure, Pietre paesina, Scagliola

Stopping
A term referring to a variety of materials that are used to fill or stop up defects in timber surfaces prior to finishing. The materials used vary widely but include mixes of waxes and resins, colouring matter, driers and sawdust. The term stopping also refers to cements and putty. Evelyn recorded the use of 'black putty' for ebony:

> wherewith they stop and fill up cracks and fissures in ebony and other fine wood, [which] is composed of a part of the purest resin, beeswax and lamp-black: this they heat and drop into the crannies then with a hot iron glaze it over, and being cold, scrape it even with a sharp chisel, and after all, polish it with a brush of bents; a woollen cloth, felt and a hog'd hair rubber.
> (1662, p.238)

Sheraton gives a similar recipe, which was 'a composition of bees wax, black rosin, red lead, Venetian red, a little yellow ochre, and Spanish brown to imitate the colour of mahogany, and by which to fill up any small hole' (1803, p.142). A different approach was taken by Nicholson who defined cement stopping as 'clear glue and fine sawdust [which] is used for stopping up the holes or defects of hardwood. When the surface is to be painted whiting may be used' (1826, p.4). An alternative recipe was to mix resin, beeswax and colouring. In fine work requiring accurate colouring, the colour was ground in spirits of turpentine to make a thick paste. This was then softened with turpentine varnish. The stopping was effected on the piece, and then the work was allowed to dry and evaporate the turpentine, leaving the stopping very hard and heat resistant. In common furniture work the stopping used was simply glaziers' putty mixed with colour, and in painted work mixtures of whiting and glue were used (op.cit., p.12).
See also Beaumontage, Finish

Straight cupboard lock
See Locks

Strap carving

See Carving (Low relief)

Strap hinge

See Hinges

Straw or Chaff

The dried stalks of corn, wheat and other cereals after harvesting. It has been used as a furniture-making material for centuries in a variety of forms, including upholstery stuffing, for decoration, as a constructional material or for flooring. Straw was used for centuries for stuffing MATTRESSES and bedding. In 1577 William Harrison felt for servants who did not have an undersheet on their bed 'to keepe them from the pricking straws that ran oft through the canvas [of the palliasse] and raised their hardened hides' (Harrison, 1877, *Description of England*, II, p.240). In the 19th century it was still used as an inexpensive upholstery and bedding filler. Loudon noted the use of oat chaff in mattresses in Scotland and maize chaff in Italy (1839, p.336).

For interior upholstery filling work the use of straw was recommended by Bimont in 1770, particularly for the backs of chairs as 'it did not collapse upon the seat' (p.48). A little later the prestigious Gillows firm was ordering quality straw in lieu of hair which was in short supply (Gillows Memo Books, 37, 1784–90).

Straw was also used to make some chairs and to bottom others. In 17th-century turned chairs straw twisted together to make a twine, then plaited and finally woven into chair-seat bottoms. In construction, lipp work was an ancient vernacular process of making chairs, cradles, baskets and so on, which were either built upon an ASH framework to which a straw shell was threaded up, or were made from coiled straw rope (the lip) which was lashed together with strips of bark or other vegetation. The constructional tradition continued into the 19th century when Loudon noted that

Matting is manufactured in many different manners, out of the straw of corn, rushes or other long, narrow, grassy or sedgy leaves. In Monmouthshire easy chairs with hoods like porter's chairs in gentleman's halls are constructed of straw matting on a frame of wooden rods, or stout wire, and chairs are made entirely of straw in different parts of England in the same way as common beehives.
(1839, pp.346–7)

The 'beehive' chair was fashionable in the 1840s in America, according to Webster (1845, p.276).

In the 1990s a PARTICLE BOARD made from wheat straw, glue and binders has been produced as an environmentally friendly product, using a renewable resource which is equally as strong as wooden particle boards.

See also Basketwork, Grass, Matted seats, Mattresses, Rush seats, Wicker

Twiston-Davies, L. (1950), *Welsh Furniture*, Cardiff: University of Wales Press, pp.17–18.

Straw marquetry

A technique of furniture decoration that used split straws, tinted and dyed to produce illustrations of pictorial, biblical or genre type. They were cut to size and glued to paper surfaces. The designs also imitated Hungarian stitch, landscapes, figures or geometric marquetry. These were then used to decorate small furniture items and looking-glasses. This craft was originally developed in Italy and France in the 17th century. John Evelyn noted the 'curious straw work among the nuns even to admiration' that he saw in Milan (May 1646, p.252). In the early 18th century Dr Robert Plot recorded this form of work in England:

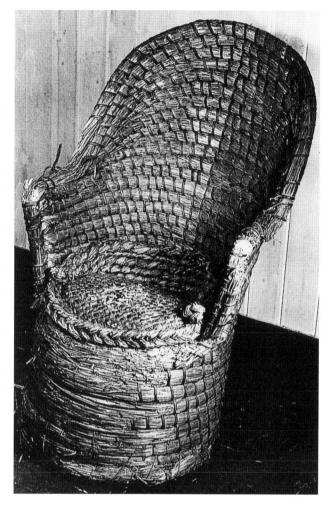

120 *The continuing use of straw as a furniture-making material is shown in this chair of c.1880. The chair also demonstrates the lipp-work or rope technique which builds up the chair in coils.*

by a certain method of first scraping the straw, and cutting it into square pieces, none larger than the 20th or 30th part of an inch, he can lay them on wood, copper, or silver in such order and manner, and that with great expedition, that thereby he represents the ruins of buildings, prospects of cities, churches etc., upon dressing or writing boxes or boxes for any other use. (1705, 263–4)

Plot refers to the artist Robert Wiseman who 'modestly owns that he saw work in Italy that gave him a hint for his invention', thus confirming Evelyn's observations.

From c.1700 Luton and Dunstable were the English centres of the craft, but it was also frequently associated with France. In the 18th century French straw-marquetry furniture included tables, chests, screens, desks and cupboards. During the Napoleonic Wars prisoners-of-war produced fine examples of straw marquetry at Norman Cross, Peterborough, which became a centre for this particular kind of the work.

In the 19th century the taste for straw work grew. In 1815, Grace Service patented a method of manufacturing 'straw with gauze net web and other similar articles for making workboxes' (Pat.no.3930). At the height of its popularity, c.1860, ingenuity in meeting demand meant that 'The tedious process of splitting, opening, flattening, and polishing straws by hand, was superseded by an ingenious little machine, which performs the work more quickly, equally and effectively' (cited in Bagshawe, 1936, p.332). This work was also divided into flat or raised surfaces, the latter being formed by pressing straw in moulds.

The craft had a small renaissance in the 20th century with French designers, Jean-Michel Frank and A. Groult being particularly associated with it on a large scale.

Bagshawe, T. W. (1936), 'Straw marquetry', in *Apollo*, XXII, pp.283–6, and XXIII, pp.332–5.
Caunes, Lison de (1993), *La Marqueterie en paille*, Paris: Editions de l'amateur.
Copper-Royer, J. (1954), *Un joli métier d'art. La Marqueterie de paille*, Paris: Librairie Grund.
Plot, Robert (1677), *The Natural History of Oxfordshire*, Oxford: Mr S. Millers.
Renton, A. (1999), 'Straw Marquetry made in Lübeck, Leiden and London by the Hering Family', in *Furniture History*, XXXV, pp.51–81.

Straw mosaic
Straw mosaic work was a version of straw marquetry, which closely resembled very superior TUNBRIDGE WARE. Developed in the mid to late 19th century, it was seen as a novel decorative technique (*Furniture Gazette*, 13 September 1873, p.36).

Strawberry wood
See Magnolia

Stretcher
A method of strengthening a seat, chair or cabinet frame by supplying a bracing function, usually stretching between the back and front legs. Introduced in the 16th century, its fashionable use was discontinued in the late 18th century. Various types have evolved. These include: the arched stretcher used on the front legs of late-17th-century upholstered chairs; rising stretchers which cross under a chair or table and rise to a central point; the serpentine stretcher which is based upon an X shape but uses two convex curves instead of straight sections; the spur or cowhorn stretcher, and the straight X-shaped stretcher.

Stringing
A narrow strip of wood or metal inlay, typically up to *c*.3 mm (⅛ in) square. It was mainly used in linear form as a contrast to the main timber in a cabinet surface or as a frame for marquetry designs. From the 1550s light-coloured timbers were mainly used to provide this in contrast to darker surfaces. Stringing might take a variety of forms including the porcupine quill stringing which was favoured in late-17th-century England. This was made up from interlaced ivory and ebony strips. SILVER strings were inlaid as was SHEFFIELD PLATE on occasion, especially at the end of the 18th century. During the early 19th century, there was a fashion for BRASS stringing. In the early 20th century plastic imitations were employed. Stringing can be cut to size with a string gauge and then inlaid to a groove made with a scratch stock.

St(r)uck moulding
See Mouldings

Stuffing
One of the procedures in full-upholstery work. The 'first stuffing' refers to the process of laying and fixing padding materials over the prepared base of webs, springs and hessian. The 'second stuffing' refers to a range of methods for fixing fillings laid over the first stuffing. Usually it consists of another layer of padding over which a calico cover finished with a top cover is fitted. Various types of stuffing are identified: pillow stuffing in which the first and second stuffings are tufted to control the fillings; round stuffing which is loose; French stuffing which is the same as 'pillow' but with added quilting rows, close to the edges, to produce a defined edge; and PIN CUSHION stuffing.
See also Upholstery

Stuffing pads
A pre-fabricated upholstery material made from, for example, hair, coir or sisal woven on to hessian backing by a needle process. Used as a speedy way of fixing padding to upholstery frames.
See also Wadding

Stuffing stick
An early and necessary upholsterer's implement which performs the same role as the REGULATOR. Described by Randle Holme as 'tough wood or iron being a little bent at the end with a nick in it by the help whereof all parts of the seat of a cushion, chair or stool are equally filled' (1649, III, V, p.273).
See also Regulator

Stuffover
A term that refers to the form of upholstery that has filling and cover over most of its frame, as opposed to show-wood work. The stuffover process is one of the most complicated and demanding of upholstery work.

Stuffs
A term for woollen and worsted cloths including CALAMANCO, CAMLETS, LASTING, MOREENS, PLAIDS, SHALLOON and TAMMY.

Stumpwork or **Raised work**
A NEEDLEWORK effect that results in raised and decorated reliefs standing proud of the surface. Stumpwork was popular in the mid 17th century when it was ingenious in its use of materials, including wood or parchment moulds covered in silk, wire, lace, sequins, pearls and so on. As it was subject to wear and tear, it was mostly applied to areas such as mirror frames or box tops.

Best, Muriel (1990), *Stumpwork: Historical and Contemporary Raised Embroidery*, London: B. T. Batsford.

Sulphur inlay
White 'putty' inlay which may have been made from white lead, calcium carbonate or sulphur and has been used occasionally for decorative inlay purposes since the 16th century.

Sumach
Staghorn sumach (*Rhus typhina*)
A North American timber with a golden greeny-orange colouring. It is light, soft and close grained and has been used as a dyewood and for inlaying.

Venetian sumach (*Rhus cotinus*)
A southern European, especially Greek, timber used as a yellow dyewood. Aka Zante, FUSTIC.
See Fustet

Sunk carving
See Carving (Gouge)

Superfine
A furnishing textile, recommended by George Smith as the best for the curtains of 'eating rooms and libraries' (1808, p.xii).

Suspension systems
See Platform, Springs, Webbing

Swan neck hinge
See Hinges

Swan river mahogany
See Mahogany

Swash turning
See Turning

Sweep
A tool used by chair-makers to mark the places (for joints) where cross-pieces intersect, to ensure parallel lines in a chair frame. The French term *compas à verge* also refers to it. Later, RODS with nails appear to have been used.
See also Dotter, Vergier

Sweet chestnut (*Castanea sativa*)
See Chestnut (European)

Sweet gum
See American red gum

Sweetwood
See Canella

Sycamore wood (*Acer pseudoplatanus*)
A European timber with an average density of 620 (39 lb/cu ft). It is white to creamy white with a lustre. Straight-grained but often with a curly and wavy figure, it has a fiddleback figure on quartered surfaces. It is good for steam-bending and when chemically treated is sold as HAREWOOD. A pink or mid-brown shading, achieved by steaming to change the colour, is called weathered sycamore. Sycamore stains and polishes well, so when dyed black, it is used as a substitute for EBONY. It also turns well, and has been available in large boards of table-top size.

It has been used as a furniture wood since at least Roman times. Chaucer refers to a 'table of sicmour' (*House of Fame*, Book III), and it was used for floral marquetry in conjunction with walnut in the 17th century. It was popular as veneer and in the solid when satinwood was fashionable in the late 18th century. It was also valued in France for its whiteness, when it was used in marquetry for the sides of perspective cube designs. Many Dublin-made pieces in the 18th century used sycamore. Very specific uses were for painted chairs or the fly-joint rails of card or pembroke tables. In the early 19th century it was noted that when 'sycamore is obtained of a considerable degree of whiteness and figured, it is much esteemed for cabinet work' (Nicholson, 1826, p.61). It was particularly used for the inside fittings of cabinets. In the early 20th century it was still 'highly esteemed on the Continent by turners, cabinet-makers, and carvers' (Boulger, 1908, p.282). During the 1920s it was internationally used for cabinet work.

In America sycamore refers to the PLANE (*Platanus occidentalis*) and is sometimes called BUTTONWOOD. The American plane wood was used by furniture-makers in eastern USA in the 17th century. It sawed easily with the water-powered mill saws, and was occasionally used for chair slats as it bent relatively easily. In 1800 Nathan Coombes, timber merchant of New Jersey, was offering sycamore scantling for bedsteads as well as stocks of buttonwood (Kebabian and Lipke, 1979, p.44). In the 20th century the lumber has been widely used for drawer sides as well as for plywood veneers, which are then used in drawer bottoms.

Synthetic glues
See Adhesives

Synthetic finishes
See Lacquer

Tabaret (Tabouret/Tabourette/Tabaray)
A shaded and striped cloth, defined as a 'medium heavy silk fabric used for upholstery, distinguished by alternate stripes of watered and satin surface, generally in different colours'. In *c*.1779 Sir Richard Worsley had '3 pea-green festoon tabaray window curtains fringed at bottom' (Boynton, 1965, p.42). A little later, Hepplewhite suggested that for window stools, 'the covering should be of taberray or morine, of a pea-green, or other light colour' (1794, p.4), and Ackermann showed a 'beautiful French scroll sofa adapted for the drawing room, which may be made of rosewood, with gold ornaments, and covered with rich chintz or silk tabouret, corresponding with other parts of the furniture' (Ackermann, August 1812, 113). Tabouret was popular in the mid 19th century in the USA for drapery and upholstery, as well as for lining walls: '[it] is never used for any other purpose than for bed and window curtains, and for covering sofas, chairs, ottomans, and coach linings. It is very much used for drawing room and sitting room walls' (Howe and Stevens, 1864, cited in Montgomery, 1984, p.356).

Tabbinet
An upholstery fabric made of silk warp and wool or linen weft, like a poplin, with a watered or tabbied surface, sometimes with figures woven on the watered ground. In 1864 its use was described by an American company: 'It is very much used for drawing room and sitting room walls. Instead of paper, paint or tapestry, and when used for this purpose it is not put on tight and flat like paper or tapestry but fluted and has a magnificent appearance' (Howe and Stevens, 1864, cited in Montgomery, 1984, p.356).

Tabby
(a) The simplest and most common weave type with an alternate warp and weft. When equal, they are called linen weave; when more warps, it is called warp faced; and when more wefts, it is called tapestry weave.

(b) A rich ribbed silk cloth with either a plain or watered surface. Probably of Middle Eastern origin, it was manufactured in England by Huguenots after the Restoration (1660). It occasionally came with a small pattern, when it was known as *tabis à fleurs*. Sheraton describes tabbying as a process 'performed by an engraved roller, which presses it into uneven surfaces, and these reflecting the rays of light differently, makes it appear wavey' (1803, p.315).

Table opening and extending mechanisms
Tables that can be adjusted in size have a long history, as well as a wide range of operations. In 1304 'a table that raises and lowers' was

121 *Table-extending mechanisms have exercised the minds of furniture-makers for centuries. In the early 19th century there was a spate of designs and patented methods of extending tables. This example, based on a concertina movement, develops an existing idea, c.1810–15.*

extend tables include the use of pulleys, endless chains and further developments of the lazy-tong and screw motions. Further developments had to wait until the patent of Robert Jupe in 1835 (Pat.no.6788). Jupe's patented table was based on enlarging a dining table by the addition of segmental pieces. Jupe's patent specification included designs for circular, oval, square and rectangular table shapes. He also showed two differing methods of enlarging the table frame. One was a straightforward pull-out mechanism based on sliding sections, the other a more sophisticated arrangement, which included a mechanical contrivance to swivel the sections out from the centre. This was one of the most successful patented tables, still being available some thirty years later. A variation on the circular extending table was Filmer's design which was opened with a screw-turning mechanism but had extra leaves inserted around the circumference of the table.

The application of a continuous screw which opened the table by the turn of a crank was an important and popular extending method, especially for 'telescope tables'. Among the many types devised, Hawkins's iron tube with a fixed female screw and a revolving male screw, operated by a crank, was popular. Other types included 'tray frame' tables devised by Fairclough, which had a solid screw so that the screw would pull one frame from another, thus extending the table, and a rack and pinion device was developed by Betjeman as well as versions of the original 'diminished slider', based on 16th-century examples.

Many of the mechanisms described continued to be used in a variety of ways into the 20th century. In the later part of the century, the 'flip-up' folding centre leaf (or leaves) system was devised, which was a simple and inconspicuous method of extending tables.

Tacking
The process of affixing fabrics, leather and others to a chair frame. Blind tacking is a method which can disguise the tack line on outside panels by layering the fabric(s) face down, so that they are tacked and pulled over a 'tacking strip' (card or metal) that allows a straight edge to be seen. The other edge is, of course, normally tacked inside the frame.

recorded and in 1420 'a table which can be let down and lifted up at pleasure' was listed in an inventory (Eames, 1977, p.222). In the 16th century the drawleaf (diminished slider) mechanism was introduced and has remained popular ever since. The gateleg method was widely used in the 17th century and again has remained a standard type. Many versions of folding tops or drop-flap tables were devised and patented in the 18th century. The first English patent with a specific space-saving intention was Eckhardt's portable table and portable chair of 1771 (Pat.no.995), which was 'so contrived as to answer all the purposes of the common tables and chairs, and at the same time to lay in the compass of a small box'. This was evidently designed for ease of transport as much as movement within the home. The first patent for an extending table was in 1794 with Sweetnam and Higgs 'improvements in the construction of tables' (Pat.no.2007). The principle of this patent was that a double-flap top would be able to flip over, swivel round and extend the size of the table to twice its original size. The table also had a hollow-framed top which was apparently designed to hold shaving, dressing or writing requisites.

Adjustable dining tables continued to gain the attention of patentees and in 1800 Richard Gillow designed an extending dining table which used wood or metal sliders to pull apart the two tops, ready for insertion of extra flaps (Pat.no.2396). Between 1802 and 1807 four more patents were taken out which related to altering the size of tables. Brown's patent extension table was based on the concertina or 'lazy-tongs' principle with a cross rail and legs between each pair of tongs. This was successfully marketed by Wilkinson & Co of Ludgate Hill. Another improvement on the extension of dining tables was invented by George Remington in 1807 (Pat.no.3090). This consisted of a lazy-tongs motion which expanded tables in a concertina motion similar to Brown's patent of two years previously. However, this patent relied on a pair of legs being attached to each set of tongs.

One of the less well-known table extending devices was patented by William Doncaster in 1814 (Pat.no.3827). Doncaster was not a cabinet-maker and this may be the reason for the eccentric nature of his patent. It was based on the principle of hydrostatic bellows that operated the rising and lowering of a rotary centre in a table. Other attempts to

122 *The ability to extend circular tables was successfully achieved by English patentee Robert Jupe in 1835. From that date until well past 1850 his mechanism was applied to a varied range of circular tables.*

Tacks

A range of varieties of small, sharp-pointed nails with comparatively large heads, used for fixing fabric to frames usually for practical rather than decorative reasons. Like nails, they were classified and graded. In 1637 Ralph Grynder distinguished 'black tacks' in his 1637 bill to Queen Henrietta Maria (Beard, 1997, p.289), but this appears to be a rare, specific reference. Tacks were identified as 1, 2½, 3, 6 and 8 oz types in the inventory of Hancock and Co of Philadelphia in 1835.

Fine
Smaller, more slender tacks used for fixing stronger weave fabrics.

Improved
Tacks with a thick shank and a broad head, used for fixing coarse, open-weave material.

Iron Tacks
The standard tack for upholstery since the 18th century. Originally made from hand-forged shanks and hammered heads. The cut shank was introduced in the late 18th century, and by the early 19th century machine-stamped heads were used in conjunction with cut shanks.

Webbing (blued)
Special large-headed cut-steel tacks, used by upholsterers for fixing webbing to frames.
See also Nails

Taffeta

A plain woven silk fabric stiffened with extra weft threads, often used for cushion covers, bed furniture and drapes from the 16th century onward. In 1537 'two curtaines of taffata paned white and red' refers to the decoration of beds in the household of Katharine of Aragon (Beard, 1997, p.282). The 1601 Hardwick Hall inventory had a 'bed with three curtains of changuable taffety' (Boynton, 1971, p.24), and one hundred years later Dyrham Park's 'Little Red Room' had 'a scarlet taffeta silk bed' (Walton, 1986, p.63). A wide range of effects were applied to the cloth to ensure differentiation. In 1723 Savary des Bruslons recorded that:

Taffetas are made in all colours. Some are glossy, some striped with silk, others are flamed, checked, flowered, or with patterns called *point de la Chine* and *de Hongrie* … Most taffetas are used for women's summer dresses, for linings, scarves, head-dresses, canopies for beds or easy chairs, window curtains, bedspreads and other furnishings.

(See also Painted taffeta.) Sheraton followed these remarks closely when he said 'taffety was remarkably glossy', and was 'made in all colours, some plain, and other striped with gold, silver etc – some are chequered, others flowered' (1803, pp.315–16). This description is taken directly from Chambers's *Cyclopedia* of 1741. In the mid 20th century thin taffetas were used as light-filter cloths for window drapes. See also Lustring, Sarcenet

Tambour

A series of narrow strips or REEDS of timber, mounted onto a canvas backing or steel strips to make sliding doors or shutters for cabinets. They are usually held in grooves on the frame, and can be fixed vertically or horizontally. They were fashionable in France in the mid 18th century and later in England. Sheraton and Hepplewhite both commented on their use, Sheraton pointing out that they were ideal for work where no great strength or security is requisite such as in night tables and pot cupboards (1803, p.316). They were later particularly successful when used on roll top desks, especially in the USA where in the early 20th century the 'curtains' (as they were known) were made up by gluing slats onto a duck cloth cut to size and then fitted into the side grooves of the desk frame.

Tammy

A lightweight worsted cloth which was often glazed. The name appears to originate from the French *étamine* worsted yarn. Woven in Norwich since 1605 and in use during the 17th and 18th centuries for drapery, bed hangings and curtains and for lining fire screens. Chippendale supplied Edward Knatchbull with '3 spring curtains of green tammy complete' and '166 yds. fine tammy lining' (Boynton, 1968, pp.99–100). A specific use was noted in the 19th century when *The Cabinet-makers' Book of Prices* charged for 'putting on the tammy with braid each side' for fire screens (1793). By the end of the 19th century, tammies were described as being composed of 'a union of cotton and worsted … they are plain, highly glazed and chiefly used for upholstery' (Caulfeild and Seward, 1882, p.471).

Cummin, H. (1941), 'Tammies and Durance', in *Antiques*, 40, September, pp.153–4.

Tamo
See Ash, Japanese

Tanguile
See Meranti

Tape joint

The need to join veneers for easier application to panels was addressed by the Comte de Fontainmoreau in 1847, when he patented (Pat.no.11716) a machine for veneer-joining which used the principle of rotary cutting combined with a method of gluing the veneers to a very thin canvas backing. In the 20th century the method was developed to use paper tape or cloth, perforated or not, which joined the veneers together temporarily until they had adhered to their base. The tape was then sanded off. Taping machines are specially designed for the purpose of preparing these veneers.

Tapestry

(a) Although commonly associated with wall-hangings, tapestry has also played an important role in upholstery. Woven on a loom using silk or wool yarns, there is no limit to the number of discontinuous threads that can be used as weft colours since they are inserted by

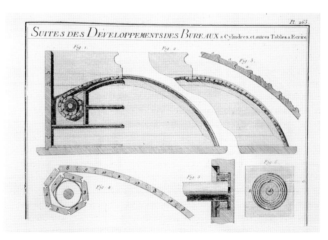

123 *The design and operation of the tambour and cylinder roll are clearly shown in this plate from Roubo, c.1771.*

hand, as needed. By this method the yarn face eventually covered the whole of the cotton warps.

Tapestry is woven on either a high or low loom. In the low warp, the loom is horizontal and the weaver works with the cartoon of the design (drawn in reverse) laid under the loom, whilst working the rear of the tapestry. In the high warp system the loom is vertical and the weaver again works from the rear of the tapestry. The worker can inspect the work as it progresses via mirrors reflecting the front side.

The European tapestry industry was developed around the 11th century, and initially tapestries were used for wall-hangings and door curtains. By the 15th century there were attempts to co-ordinate wall-hangings with loose furnishings and cushions which were woven to match. By the second half of the 18th century there was a fashion for covering chairs with tapestry made to fit exactly the frames of chairs and to match wall-hangings (for example, Osterley Park Tapestry Room). The styles and types of tapestry are usually associated with a particular town or factory. Arras, France, was among the first to be a centre of weaving and gave its name to the tapestry panel. By the mid 15th century Arras declined in importance and Tournai, Brussels and Lille became more important. By the mid 16th century tapestry works had been established in England (Sheldon, and Mortlake, Soho by the 17th century) and in France (Gobelins, Aubusson and Beauvais by the 17th century). The royal tapestry factory at Beauvais was founded in 1664. Throughout the 18th century furniture covers were woven there, often in sets to match wall-hangings. In the 19th century they continued with the manufacture of furniture covers and it was in 1940 that the factory was merged with the Gobelins works. The Gobelins workshop executed tapestry on a high-warp loom with thick warp yarns and soft wool wefts which were beaten up to completely hide the warp and create a horizontal ribbed effect. These were used for chair backs, especially in the late 17th and early 18th centuries. By the early 20th century tapestries were still considered valuable. According to Richard Bitmead,

Tapestry is, in fact, generally speaking, only employed by the upholsterer to give variety to the furniture when the house to be furnished consists of more than the usual number of rooms. Among the varieties of this furnishing material, the tapestries of the Gobelins and the Savonnerie hold the first rank but not being articles of commerce, are rarely to be met with except in royal residences. There are however, some excellent imitations of these materials, the tapestries of Beauvais and Aubusson among the number, but they are expensive and are only employed in the manufacture of first-class upholstery. (1912, p.33)

Occasional examples of modern interpretation of the technique occur. In the 1920s the French furniture designer Pierre Chareau worked with Jean Lurcat to design and produce tapestries in a modern idiom for upholstery covers.

(b) Tapestry is also a term for a machine-woven cloth in which all or nearly all the colours are found in the warp yarns. These imitation tapestries were woven on the Jacquard loom from the 1830s. The Neuilly or Jacquard tapestry was a later-19th-century imitation of Gobelins tapestry, where the weft creates the design with up to twenty-four weft colours. All cotton versions were woven in France, Belgium and Philadelphia from around 1890 and were considered expensive. Hand block-printed coarse rep could also produce a tapestry-like effect which was preferred by some as more like the real thing, as opposed to the Jacquard tapestry which resembled needlework. The so-called Cluny tapestry was a strong, thick cloth made of wool and silk especially for hangings and curtains, which was introduced into England around 1875 (Cole, 1892).

Tapisseries de Bergame
Coarse woollen tapestry with hemp warps, used for wall-hangings and upholstery, especially in the 17th century. They often had large patterns woven into them, but were generally a second-rate product imitating high-style tapestries.
See also Appliqué, Berlin wool-work

Dossie, R. (1758), *Handmaid to the Arts*, London: printed for J. Nourse, pp.479–502.
Thomson, W. G. (1973), *A History of Tapestry*, London: Wakefield, E. P. Publishing reprint of 1906 edition.
Thornton, P. (1960), 'Tapisseries de Bergame', in *Pantheon*, VI, XVIII, March.
Weigert, R. A. (1962), *French Tapestry*, London: Faber and Faber.

Tasmanian myrtle
See Myrtle

Tasmanian oak (*Eucalyptus sp.*)
An Australian timber with a density which varies depending on species between 640–800 (40–50 lb/cu ft). It is pale to light brown with a pinky cast, a straight to variable grain and an open texture. Used for furniture, plywood and decorative veneers. It is not a true oak.

Tassels
See Passementerie

Teak (*Tectona grandis*)
A hardwood from the region of India and Burma with an average density of 640 (40 lb/cu ft). It is light golden-brown in colour with an uneven coarse texture and a straight grain. Although used occasionally in 17th century Goan furniture often inlaid with ebony, it first came into European prominence in the 19th century as a furniture wood. Bitmead noted that teak was 'much used by cabinet-makers at the beginning of the present century [19th] for carcase work, for ends, drawers stuff etc. … The cheap table makers purchase old ship timber for loo-table pillars etc. [and] after it is turned, it is veined with a feather and black stain and passed off for walnut' (Bitmead, 1873, p.178). In the mid to late 20th century, teak veneers were extensively used in a wide range of popular furniture in Europe and North America.

Bastard teak
A finely figured wood sold in the early 20th century as 'Pheasant wood' and used for bandings and centres.

Telescopic actions
See Table opening and extending mechanisms

Templates
Gauges or patterns made especially for particular works, designed to act as a guide or gauge in production processes. Especially used for angles, joints, curved work and chairs.
See also Jig, Rods

Tenon saw
See Saws

Tension springs
See Springs

Tension top

A tight cover fixed over upholstery fillings and mattresses, which is without buttoning or tufting to hold the fillings in place.

Tent stitch

See Stitches

Terracotta

A composition material made from clay and sand which is fired without glaze. During the 19th century it was used to make rustic furniture, especially for garden use. The Wilnecote works near Tamworth produced a range of 'Rustic ware' which was glazed, and from 1862, William Baddeley produced rustic terracotta objects including garden seats, in which 'his imitations of bark etc. and of various woods and plants were remarkably good' (Jewitt, *The Ceramic Art of Great Britain*, 1878, vol.I, p.425).
See also Rustic furniture

Terry

In the 19th century terry was a horizontally ribbed warp-faced fabric often with a wool face and a cotton weft. Silk was also used for terry weaves with a worsted weft and silk warp which was sometimes woven to create a damask effect. It is similar in appearance to REP.

Therming or Thurming

A turning process in which a square section moulding is achieved. Sheraton described therming as the same as tapering, that is producing a table or chair leg with its thickness diminishing towards the ground. He particularly noted that it seemed unnatural to him to take all the tapering from the inside of the leg, a practice he decried (1803, p.316). By the 20th century machine lathes thurmed components by fixing the timber to a drum so that each side is offered to the knife in succession.

Thermography

See Printing

Through tenon

See Joints (Mortise and tenon)

Thrown work

A term used to describe turned work.

Thuya (*Tetraclinus articulata*)

A softwood from North Africa, especially Morocco and Algeria, known as *citron* in the ancient world and the source of SANDARAC. It has a rich golden brown to orange-red colour, while the timber is fine-textured and aromatic, glues easily and polishes exceptionally well. The stems of the tree swell at the base, which is partially buried in the soil. The burrs grow underground as a root burr, so the stump grows each time the tops are coppiced. The timber was dug out rather than felled and was most often converted into highly prized veneers. There are often problems in veneer laying due to the potential disintegration of the veneer, due in part to the lack of integrity in the sheets.

It is possible that the name is derived from the Greek word *thyon* meaning an African tree. Thuya was used in later Egypt for table tops especially, where the fine effect of the cut timber could best be shown off. It was also amongst the most prized timbers for furniture in Roman times. According to Pliny the reason was the same as for the Egyptians before him: Thuya has a resplendent grain described as 'wine mixed with honey, the veins being particularly refulgent' (Pliny, XIII, 91–6). The value of the timber must also have been an attraction. Cicero's famous thuya table, allegedly costing half a million sesterces, could, incidentally, still be seen in Pliny's time, one hundred years later. The taste for thuya table tops, in combination with ivory legs, encouraged a special guild to be established in Rome which looked after the interests of the thuya and ivory workers.

Thuya was re-discovered in the 18th century and was again desired for its warm brown colouring, wavy-lined graining and small birds' eyes resembling AMBOYNA (but with fewer spots grouped in sixes). From the 1860s it was exported from Algiers to Europe and during the early 20th century was used by Art Moderne craftsmen as a flamboyant timber. Not to be confused with the genus Thuja (cedar).

Ticking

A linen, and later cotton, twill weave material, specially suited to MATTRESS covering. Known at least by the early 18th century for enclosing FEATHERS and other fillings, they are usually woven to produce a striped effect, traditionally of blue and white or pink and white. To ensure featherproofing, it was the custom to rub the underside of the cloth with beeswax or a gum made from a mix of turpentine and rosin before filling. Later-20th-century bed-tickings have been made from decorative damasks. Types include flock tick at 5.5 oz, feather tick at 7.5 oz and hair tick at 8+ oz per square yard.
See also Crankey, Damask

Tigerwood (*Macherium spp.*)

A South American, especially Guianan timber with a bright chestnut-red colouring and black spots. It is hard and heavy with a close grain, making it a valuable cabinet-making wood.
See also African walnut (USA), Goncalo alves (USA), Zebrawood

Tiles, ceramic

See Ceramic plaques, inlays and tiles

Tin

A metallic element that can be worked on its own or as an alloy with copper to produce bronze. The early use of tin as a component of furniture decoration is recorded by Theophilus who showed how to use it to decorate furniture (c.1120, Book 111, p.72). His examples included painted stools, chairs and beds that were mounted with copper plates and then inlaid with tin. In 1770 a Msr Clement in Paris used tin as the base for panels decorated with painted fruit and flowers. This was a development of the application of TOLE. Tin was also intended to line dining-room pedestals used as plate warmers (Hepplewhite, 1794, p.7). A little later it returned to its decorative use. Stokes gives the recipe for imitating silver stringing by preparing a mix of tin and quicksilver that can be laid into the grooves and then dry polished to a silver effect (1829, p.48).

In 19th-century America, tin (either as a sheet or recycled from containers) was sometimes punched with decorative designs and used for 'windows' in food safes and cupboards.
See also Tole, Whitesmith

Tissue

A class of textiles woven on a draw loom. They had a second warp to act as a twill binder. The satin ground had a second weft of loosely twisted yarns to create a figure in the weft, which were often made from gold or, principally, silver threads. A bed in the Ingatestone in-

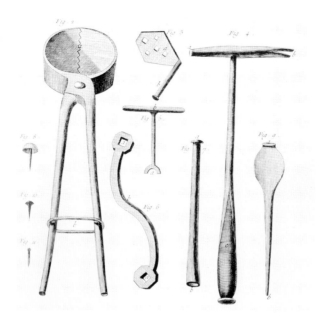

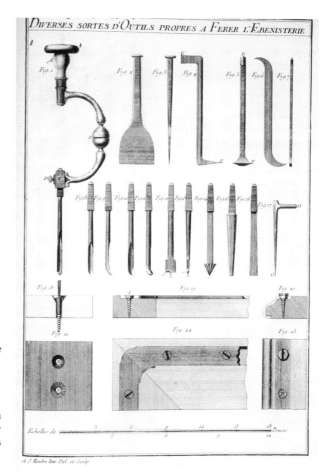

ventory of 1600 had furnishings of 'tysshew layde with crimson silke and goulde lace' (cited in Thornton, 1978, p.357).
See also Brocatelle

Toilet
Fabrics used for bed quilts, counterpanes and such furnishings, with a fine face in plain weave, stitched down according to a design by means of a tightly woven binding warp. Sometimes the figure stands out in relief.

Tola
See Agba

Tole (*Tôle peinte*)
Tole is lacquered and decorated TIN plate or sheet IRON that is fabricated into a number of objects or inserted into others. One of the earliest establishments to make tole was in Usk, Pontypool, when *c.*1680 Thomas Allgood developed a coal by-product that adhered to metal by heat, which was a black asphaltum varnish. Trays, tea caddies, and other small items were the basis of the trade which was carried on in Usk and Birmingham. The trade was also developed in France so that by the 1790s beds, tables, vases, boxes and desks were being decorated in this manner. Aka Pennsylvania ware (see Plate IX).
See also Japanning

John, W. D. (1953), *Pontypool and Usk Japanned Wares*, Newport, Mon.: Ceramic Book Co.
Samoyault, Jean Pierre (1977), 'Chefs-d'œuvre en tôle vernie de l'époque consulaire et impériale (1801–1806)', in *Revue du Louvre et des musées de France*, XXVII, pp.322–34.

Tongue and groove
See Joints

Tongued mitre
See Joints

Tool chests
A craftsman's tools were a valuable asset, so it was common practice to insure tools and look after them well. Tools might be carried in a basket, bag or box, but for cabinet-makers the tool-chest was the normal storage for his own tools. The best examples were made in the 18th century with a simple but sturdy frame and outside finish. The insides were lined with mahogany, fitted with tools racks, nest of drawers and storage compartments, and were sometimes decorated very elaborately, often with marquetry designs.

Rees, J. and Rees, M. (eds) (1994), *The Tool Chest of Benjamin Seaton*, Tools and Trades Society.

Tools
Many of the 'standard' range of woodworking tools were available by the beginning of the Bronze Age. From this period there began a continuing refinement of them with the exception of the plane, which was developed by the Greeks. The early Egyptians used copper then bronze for their tools, but iron was favoured in the classical world. Iron gave the Greeks and Romans great improvements in tool-making and use. These included socketed heads, sharper edges and raked teeth saws which all allowed greater precision.

An early discussion about woodworking tools and their uses is found in Johann Amos Comenius's book of Latin grammar, *Orbis Sensualium Pictus*, which gives descriptions of carpentry, cabinet-making and turning (1659, reprint 1966). For example, the box-maker (cabinet-maker) 'smootheth hewen boards with a plain upon a work board, he maketh them very smooth with a little plain, he boarth them thorow with an augre, carveth them with a knife, fasteneth them together with glew, and cramp-irons and maketh tables, boards, chests &c' (trans. Charles Hoole, 1685). In this account, the kit of tools, which includes PLANES, AUGERS, GLUE and CRAMPS, clearly indicates a joiner rather than a carpenter working in solid wood. A little later in 1717, an inventory of William Howell, a cabinet-maker working in Boston, Mass., gives a list of tools and materials that were in his shop at the time. The list includes: a variety of planes designed for particular parts of the cabinet-making process including block, smoothing, rebating and toothing versions; CHISELS and files, as well as DRILLS and bits, along with a variety of SAWS, AUGERS and gimlets. These tools have much in common with the trade of the joiner, it is only when the 'finering hammer and pincers', the 'fine saw', 'walnut fenere', 'eighty pounds of lead', 'nus skin', glue and beeswax are also accounted for, that the inventory clearly indicates a CABINET-MAKER rather than a JOINER (cited in Forman, 1988, p.49).

The growing range of tools and the increasing reliability of the metal components used during the 18th century enabled cabinet-makers to have a degree of flexibility and application to individual circumstances, as well as an increasing certainty as to the quality of the end product. Sophie von la Roche, writing in 1786, suggested that it was the calibre of tools that helped to make the superior products of the London business of Seddon and Company. She was so impressed that she recorded how she would like to have seen 'the hand-tools used in this work [Seddon's cabinets] being manufactured in Birmingham; for I held some of them in my hand, and looked upon them as the most valuable and beneficent inventions' (cited in Gilbert and Wood, 1997, p.34). It was in fact in Sheffield that a new, harder, cast STEEL was produced by Benjamin Huntsman which had brought improvements to cutting tools amongst other articles, but this would have soon been known in Birmingham and elsewhere where tools were manufactured.

For particular tools see Adze, Auger, Awl, Bench screw, Bevel, Bit, Brace, Bradawl, Breast bib, Callipers, Carver's clip, Chisel, Clamp, Cramp, Dotter, Drawing knife, Drills, Driver, Driving bolt, Folding wedges, Froe, Gauge, Hammer, Handscrew, Holdfast, Lathe, Mallet, Mitre square, Needles, Pincers, Pinking irons, Planes, Power tools, Prickall, Punches, Regulator, Riffler, Router, Saws, Scraper, Scratch stock, Screwdrivers, Shave, Skewers, Stuffing stick, Sweep, Tool chests, Trammel, Travisher, Trestles, Tufting board, Web strainer, Wood square

Arnold, R. and Walker, P. (1974–6), *The Traditional Tools of the Carpenter and Other Craftsmen*, 4 vols, London: Arnold and Walker.
Gaynor, J. and Hagedorn, N. (1993), *Working Wood in Eighteenth Century America*, Williamsburg, Virginia: Colonial Williamsburg.
Goodman, W. L. (1964), *The History of Woodworking Tools*, London: Bell.
— (1971), 'Some Elizabethan woodworkers and their tools', in *Furniture History*, VII, pp.87–93.
— (1972), 'Woodworking apprentices and their tools in Bristol, Norwich, Gt. Yarmouth and Southampton', in *Industrial Archaeology*, 9, 4, November.
— (1976), 'Tools and equipment of the early settlers in the New World', in *Chronicle of the Early American Industries Assoc.*, 29, 3, September, pp.40–51.
— (1981), 'Christopher Gabriel, his book', in *Furniture History*, XVII, pp.23–41.
Hummell, C. F. (1968), *With Hammer in Hand: The Dominy Craftsmen of East Hampton New York*, Charlottesville: University Press of Virginia.
Kebabian, P. and Lipke, W. (1979), *Tools and Technologies: America's Wooden Age*, Vermont: University Press, pp.43–65.
Mercer, H. (1929), *Ancient Carpenters' Tools with Lumbermen's, Joiners' and Cabinet-makers' Tools in use in the Eighteenth century*, Doylestown: Bucks County Historical Society.
Moxon, J. (1677), *Mechaniks' Exercises or the Doctrine of Handy Works*, reprint 1970, Praeger.
Proudfoot, C. and Walker, P. (1984), *Woodworking Tools*, Oxford: Phaidon Christies.
Roberts, K. D. (1989), *Some 19th Century English Woodworking Tools*, Fitzwilliam, NH; the Author.
Salaman, R. (1975), *Dictionary of Tools Used in the Woodworking and Allied trades 1000–1900*, London: Unwin Hyman.
Walker, P. (1982), 'The Tools available to the mediaeval woodworker', in *Woodworking Techniques before AD 1500*, S. McGrail (ed.), Brit. Archaeol. Rep., Int. Ser., cxxix, Oxford, pp.349–56.
Welsh, P. (1966), *Woodworking Tools 1600–1900*, Contributions from the Museum of History and Technology, United States National Museum Bulletin 241, Smithsonian Institution.

Toon wood (*Cedrela toona*)
See Australian red cedar

Toothing planes
See Planes

Tortoiseshell
A translucent material that is rarely derived from tortoises, rather being prepared from the upper shell or carapace of turtles, especially of the hawk's bill turtle (*Chelone imbricata*). The carapace covers the back, and is dark brown, amber and red. The thinner plastron covers the abdomen, and is often clear or yellow blonde. Many types are semi-transparent and they all have thermo-plastic properties. The preparatory processes included boiling and clamping the shells into moulds and allowing them to settle to produce a flat area. As many shell-plates were quite small, it was common practice to fuse them together to create larger surfaces, whilst in lesser-quality work the plates often were simply abutted together. Almost all shell was painted on the reverse side to provide a coloured background, which was then covered with thick paper to disguise any joins. Enhancing the tortoiseshell colouring can be achieved by colouring the adhesive which joins a paper backing to the tortoiseshell plate: red lead or vermilion for red; lapis lazuli for blue effects; zinc-white for pale effects. In addition, gold powder was also added.

The use of tortoiseshell is ancient. Pliny tells of 'Carvilius Polio a man of prodigal habits and ingenious in inventing the refinements of luxury, was the first to cut the shell of the tortoise into laminae and to veneer beds and cabinets with it' (Pliny, 9, 39). It came back in fashion in Italy and the Low countries during the 17th century as a veneer for cabinets, tables and frames. The South German *Wunderkammers* and the Antwerp cabinets on stands, which were veneered with tortoiseshell in contrast to black ebony or completely over the whole piece, are fine examples of the genre. Tortoiseshell cabinets are known to have been in England from *c.*1600. An English inventory of Tart Hall (1641) notes 'a little ebony square table inlayde with Toreaux shels' (Cust, 1911, p.99). Tortoiseshell, in conjunction with other materials, has also been an essential component of BOULLE marquetry since the 16th century. Its use was revived in Art Deco furniture, especially by the French makers Ruhlmann, Groult and Leleu.

IMITATION TORTOISESHELL
The imitating of tortoiseshell could be done by painting, by staining similar materials like horn, or later, by plastic materials. Stalker and Parker noted that 'before japan was made in England, the imitation of tortoiseshell was much in request for cabinets, tables and the like' (1688, p.79). They published recipes for the counterfeiting of tortoiseshell and noted its use for glass-frames and small boxes. One such required

whiting laid on close grained wood, smoothed and finished with lacquer and silver leafs on top. Collins earth and size mixed and applied to the leafs to imitate larger sections of shell. Sanguis droconis [dragon's blood] mixed with gum water to imitate streaks. Finally build up coats of shellac to finish. (ibid., pp.79–81)

Tortoiseshell could also be imitated in a more solid form. The French authority Plumier describes the process of producing imitation shell in detail. By softening horns to a pulp in a lye wash, one was then able to mould them into flat plates. They were then covered in a mix of quicklime, litharge and lye so that they would develop the distinctive, partly opaque, partly transparent effect of real tortoiseshell. Apparently this was available exported from England with ready-coloured tints (1749, p.258).
See also Boulle

PIQUÉ
A decorative process which inlays small strips of gold or silver into tortoiseshell for effect.

Dent, H. (1923), 'Piqué a beautiful minor art', in *Connoisseur*, London, p.2.
O'Connor, S. (1987), 'The identification of osseous and keratinaceous materials', York: United Kingdom Institute for Conservation (UKIC), occasional papers, v.
Thurston, K. (1985), 'Use of tortoiseshell as a decorative medium', in *Antique Collecting*, June, pp.6–9.

Totara (*Podocarpus totara*)
A New Zealand softwood with an average density of 640 (40 lb/cu ft). It has a reddish colour and a straight and even grain which was easily worked. Used locally for joinery and construction work, it was first used in England during the 19th century for cabinet work. In 1845 it was noted that the timber was 'found to work up into very handsome sideboards, tables and bookshelves' (E. J. Wakefield, 1845, *Adventures in New Zealand*). The London cabinet-maker Levien had a collection of fine New Zealand timbers and exhibited a cabinet in totara and lime at the 1851 Great Exhibition. In 1920 it was still considered to be one of the most valuable timbers of New Zealand, both as a substitute for mahogany and for its fine burrs (Howard, 1920, p.295).

Levien, M. (1976), 'The furniture of J. M. Levien', in *Connoisseur*, 191, pp.50–7.

Tow
A by-product of the processing of bast fibres, especially flax. After heckling, the line and tow are separated. The line is spun into linen yarn and the tow is used as a foundation in upholstery work, chiefly on seats and arms. It was certainly in use after 1679, and has been used to make spring edges for seats in US upholstery. In the later 20th century it was still used for upholstery foundations in the USA.

Trades
The interdependence of specialized trades both in the wholesale and retail sectors is noticeable from early on in furniture history. Guilds, as well as manufacturers and retailers who specialize in a particular class of work have been a feature of the industry for centuries. This process of growth was gradual, but an example of the growth can be seen in 1886 when Britain had over 250 trades associated with the business of making and supplying furniture and furnishings.

For particular trades see Arkwright, Bed-joiner, Blacksmith, Bodger, Boulle cutter, Box maker, Brazier, Buckram-maker, Cabinet-maker, Cane chair-maker, Carpenter, Carver, Chair-maker, Cofferer, Embroiderer, Fancy cabinet-maker, Fancy chair-maker, Frame maker, Fret-cutter, Gilder, Joiner, Looking-glass makers, Marquetry worker, Polishers, Screen-maker, Turner, Upholsterers, Whitesmith

Trammel
For carpenters a trammel was a simple rod (up to 1.5 m/5 ft long) with two adjustable points which can scribe circles. For cabinet-makers it was an instrument for marking out ovals or ellipses. It was composed of a diagonal cross, each arm of which had two grooves at right angles in which pins or pencils are set so they can slide. They were usually made by the cabinet-maker himself. Aka Beam compass.

Transfer prints
See Printing

Travisher
A chair-maker's SHAVE with a long radius and a shallow curve. Used to finish and clean up Windsor seats after the adze and the draw knife (scorp) have taken off the bulk.

Trestles
A part of the equipment of an upholstery workshop. A pair of trestles enables the upholsterer to work on couches and large chairs with easy access. In 1760 the furnishing business of Samuel Norman listed ten 'board and trestle' sets in his inventory (Kirkham, 1969, p.509). Also called saw horses which have been used singly or in pairs, to assist in cutting timber.

Trimmings
See Passementerie

Triple nailing
See Nailing

Tripoli
A soft grey to yellow fine earth of decomposed siliceous matter, sourced in North Africa and elsewhere. Yellow tripoli or French tripoli was used for polishing light-coloured woods that would otherwise be stained. Red tripoli came from brick earth found in Sussex and was also used for polishing purposes. In 1688 it was noted that 'you must have Tripoly to polish your work after it is varnished which must be scraped or finely pounded and sifted' (Stalker and Parker, 1688, p.2). It was still used in the 19th century as a polishing compound.
See also Rottenstone

Trying plane
See Planes

Tubular steel
See Steel

Tufting
A method used by upholsterers to ensure that the fillings of CUSHIONS and MATTRESSES remain level. Cords were inserted through the thickness of the pad and held by a bunch of threads that stopped the cord being pulled through the pad. This technique was introduced in England and America in the mid 18th century and suited the flatter, squarer design of their chairs, rather than the more fashionable domed seats favoured in France. Sometimes the process was worked under the top cover, although this might be marked by BUTTONING. In the later 19th century, the diamond tufting method was developed. See below for types of tufting:

Diamond

A tufting technique that creates a regular, decorative diamond shape usually on the backs and seats of upholstery. The 'extra' cloth used was often sewn into pleats.

Jiffy

A ready-made tuft and cord which can be speedily and simply inserted through mattress or cushions with a specially adapted needle. Widely used on mattresses and cushions in the 20th century.

Looped

A form of fixing for upholstery fillings. Introduced in the 17th century, it was simply a loop of thread that held a tuft of fabric or linen, to even the strain on the surface fabric. It was later superseded by buttoning in upholstery, but remained a feature of mattresses.

Machine

The demand for buttoned furniture ensured that templates (TUFTING BOARDS) would be developed further into tufting machines. For furniture use these machines or presses were generally designed to clamp together the top material and filling, and then button it through with pins and washers. This built-up 'blanket' of backing, stuffing and material top-cover could then be applied to a sprung frame with much more speed and ease than the traditional hand-layering process. Naturally this encouraged the division of labour and a consequent reduction in the skill required for upholstering chairs and sofas. Machine processes developed in the USA in the 1890s. The Novelty Tufting Machine by the Freschl Company, which mechanically tufted backs and seats of upholstery jobs, was apparently operated by boys and was alleged to have taken the place of twenty-five skilled workmen. In the USA these machines were nicknamed 'hay-balers'.

Mattress

A method of holding firm fillings in mattresses. It is simply done by passing a needle and strong thread through the thickness of the mattress and catching little tufts of worsted yarns or circles of red leather, and then returning the needle and tying off the end firmly. The spacing is maintained by letting the stitches fall opposite the middle of the previous row of stitches. Once fitted, the tufts hide the stitch and ornament the surface.

Tufting boards

A TEMPLATE the size of the finished upholstery/bedding section with holes drilled appropriately to the design, enabling simple and easy tuft insertion.

Tula cut steel

See Steel

Tulip-tree (*Liriodendron tulipifera*)

A whitewood, from eastern North America, the tulip-tree is commonly known as tulip poplar or yellow poplar although it is part of the magnolia family. It has an average density of 490 (31 lb/cu ft), is light yellow to brown, without features, with a straight grain and is easy to work. When first cut, it is bright canary yellow but tones to a light yellow-brown with a satiny lustre. It has a fine even texture and its stain-taking qualities make it ideal for factory-made furniture. Some trees yield a curly grain called blister figure which has been used as veneers for decorative panelling and cabinet work.

Whitewood was a timber that was popular with furniture-makers in 17th-century America. It was mill-sawn and used as boards and if it was the primary timber, was often painted. Commonly used in coastal Connecticut, New York and Pennsylvania, it was also made into the seats of American Windsor chairs and used as a secondary construction wood, especially for corner blocks and seat rails. It was later a plywood species. In the 20th century as American WHITEWOOD it has been used in concealed cabinet work and was imported into the UK in large quantities for general furniture trade use before 1939. Aka CANARYWOOD (GB), CUCUMBER WOOD, POPLAR or Yellow poplar or WHITEWOOD (USA).

Tulipwood (*Dalbergia spp.*)

An attractive cabinet-making timber that is usually creamy-tan to pink in colouring with parallel streaks of pinky rose, thus reproducing something of the effect found in varieties of tulip. In the mid 19th century tulipwood was described as flesh-red with streaks of a deeper tint. This timber, either imported from Brazil or the East Indies was used especially as veneer and for cross-banding in the 18th and early 19th centuries. It was supplied in small sticks 5–18 cm (2–7 in) in diameter, often with blemishes, and was therefore only used for small items of cabinet work. The colours fade easily and Sheraton recommended varnishing to protect the beautiful effects against the sun. He also noted that it was ideal for cross banding (1803, p.323–4). By 1830 its principle use was still banding, but 'it is [also] employed in smaller articles, such as caddies and ladies work tables' (Knight, 1830, p.178). It was used for veneers and banding in the early 20th century.

The East Indian version was considered superior and was apparently held in great esteem by French cabinet-makers. It had a straighter grain, was less hard and showed a greater contrast of figure, making it a superior cabinet-making wood. Aka Pinkwood in the USA, *Bois de rose* in France.

Tunbridge ware

A generic name for a variety of decorative surface finishes applied to small cabinet work, especially boxes and caskets, but also including table tops and small furniture items. The original version of Tunbridge ware was recorded by Celia Fiennes in 1697, when she noted 'shopps full of all sorts of toys, sliver, china, milliners, and all sorts of curious wooden ware, which this place is noted for the delicate neate and thin ware both white and Lignum vitae wood' (1982, pp.126–7). Prior to *c.*1830 the decoration was made by standard marquetry and inlay methods, but it was, by all accounts, very skilfully produced:

The wood principally used for this purpose is holly, [which] furnishes a prodigious variety of the prettiest ornamental inlays that can be imagined, some of which are so excellent in their kind, that it is hard to believe that they are not assisted by the pencil. But besides holly, they use no small quantity of cherry-tree, plum-tree, yew, and sycamore: the yew especially is of late become very fashionable, and the goods vineered with it are certainly excessively pretty.
(Benge Burr, *History of Tunbridge Wells*, 1766, cited in Pinto, 1970)

By around 1830 a new range of woodwork was developed, which included miniature parquetry and tessellated mosaic work. These processes meant that designs could be replicated in batches. The process was based on building up a block of shaped hardwood rods (usually squares, triangles and rhombuses) to reflect the desired pattern. In the tessellated mosaic technique, the designs were prepared by artists and then transferred to squared paper so that each square was indicative of a colour graduation. The band-maker then chose timber veneers approximately 15 × 2.5 cm (6 × 1 in) and less than 2 mm (⅟₁₆ in) thick that were close to the required colours. These were then glued together to form a solid block. One block was prepared for each column of the charted design. The sliced blocks were assembled in accordance

126 *An example of fine-quality Tunbridge ware work-table made by Edmund Nye of Tunbridge Wells, c.1850.*

with the pattern and then glued and pressed together so that they eventually had the whole design running through the full depth of the block. By careful slicing at 90 degrees to the block, it was cut into mosaic veneers which were then laid onto a whitewood base. Although the centre of this work was Tunbridge Wells in Kent, specialist makers worked in other locations, sometimes in conjunction with a turnery business.

See also Penwork

Austen, Brian (1989), *Tunbridge Ware and Related European Decorative Woodware*, London: Foulsham and Co.

Gill, M. (1985), *Tunbridge Ware*, Princes Risborough: Shire.

Holtzapffel, C. (1847), *Turning and Mechanical Manipulation*, vol.2, London, pp.763–9.

Pinto, Edward (1970), *Tunbridge and Scottish Souvenir Woodware*, London: Bell.

Tung oil

A drying oil obtained from trees of the genus *Aleurites* or *Vernicia*, used in varnishes.

Tupelo (*Nyssa aquatica*)

A timber variety from the South-eastern USA with an average density of 550 (34 lb/cu ft). With a grey to light brown or ivory colouring, it has a fine uniform texture and an interlocked grain, giving a striped appearance on quarter-sawn surfaces. In the USA and England during the first half of the 20th century, it was used for the cores of panels, as well as on occasion for exposed parts in cheaper grades of furniture or painted furniture, such as breakfast sets. It was also imported in the early 20th century for the inside linings of cheap cabinet work.

Aka Black gum, Gumwood

Turkey leather

See Leather

Turkeywork

An upholstery cloth which is made either as carpet with a turkey knot pile on a single linen warp and double linen weft, or with wool yarns drawn through canvas and knotted to form a pile. In either case the work proceeded on a loom and was not needlework. Once the weaving process was completed, the cloth was removed from the loom, the edges were finished, the pile clipped tidy, and the whole was washed to soften the cloth.

Early references to turkeywork (as carpet) occur. In the 1509 inventory of Edmund Dudley there are '23 cussins of carpett work' and '3 coverings for cussins of carpet worke' (*Archaeologia*, LXXI, 1921). In the 1588 Kenilworth inventory there is a 'turquoy carpette of Norwiche work' (Halliwell, 1854, p.147). The height of fashion for turkeywork appears to have been the latter 17th century. Randle Holme wrote regarding the furnishing of a dining room: 'A turkey table cover, or carpett of cloth or leather printed. Chaires and stooles of turkeywork, Russia or calves leather, cloth or stuffe or of needlework. Or els made all of Joynt work or cane chaires' (1649, bk III, ch.XIV, p.15). A little later in 1667, Pepys fell out with Mrs Martin over 'her expensefulness, having bought turkeywork chairs' (*Diary*, 14 April 1667). However, she was clearly fashionable.

In 1683 it was claimed that 'five thousand dozen of Sett-work chairs (commonly called turkeywork chairs, though made in England) were yearly made and vended in the Kingdom, and great quantities of these chairs were also vended and sent yearly beyond the seas' (cited in Symonds, 1934, p.180). This referred to a petition against CANE seat chair-makers who were seen to be stealing the trade enjoyed by English wool workers. The cane chair-makers retorted by pointing out

the problems of cloth upholstery including 'the dust, worms and moths which inseparably attend turkeywork, Serge and other stuff-chairs and Couches' (Symonds, 1951, pp.13–14).

Turkeywork continued to be used into the early 18th century. For example, chairs purchased between 1704 and 1733 for the House of Commons included over 150 chairs with turkeywork covers. By the 1730s, however, it had begun to lose popularity. Aka Carpet, Norwich work, Set work.

Hughes, G. B. (1965), 'The Englishness of Turkeywork', in *Country Life*, 11 February, p.309.

Swain, M. (1987), 'The Turkeywork chairs of Holyrood House', in E. S. Cooke (ed.), *Upholstery in America and Europe from the 17th Century to WWI*, New York: Norton.

Symonds, R. W. (1934), 'Turkeywork, beech and japanned chairs', in *Connoisseur*, 392, March.

— (1951), 'English cane chairs', in *Connoisseur*, April.

Turkish chair

A 19th-century term that referred to the deeply-buttoned iron wire back chairs that were fashionable in the period 1880–1900. The name related to ideas of comfort and luxury and appears to have no direct connection with Turkey. However, the ottomans, divans and the SADDLE BAG chairs of the same period relate directly to the taste for an assumed 'Turkish style'.

See Chair frames

Turkish oak

See Oak

Turners

The craft of turning was practised continuously in northern Europe from Roman times. Manuscript depictions of the workers and the results of their work confirm this. The craft was organized early on. A Fellowship of Turners was established in London in 1310, and the London Turners' Company was granted its charter in 1604. The Turners' Company was often in dispute with other woodworkers. They particularly complained about those who 'work and turn in the shops and houses of joiners … and do teach and instruct joiners in the art of turning'. In 1632 the Court of Aldermen laid down that

turning and joyning are two several and distinct trades and we conceive it very inconvenient that either of these trades should encroach upon the other, and we find that the turners have constantly for the most part turned bedposts and the feet of joyned stools for the joyners and of late some joyners who never used to turn their own bedposts and stool feet have set on work in their own houses some poor decayed turners, and of them have learned the feate and art of turning which they could not do before. And it appeareth unto us by custom that the turning of Bedposts, Feet of tables, joyned tools do properly belong to the trade of a turner, and not to the art of a joyner and whatsoever is done with the foot as have treddle or wheel for turning of any wood we are of the opinion and do find that it properly belongs to the turners.
(Phillips, 1915, pp.27–8)

Although the high point of the turners' craft was in the late 17th century, they remained important as suppliers to cabinet-makers and upholsterers. In 1747 it was noted that 'common turners chairs were sold at the turners' shop' (Anon., *General Description of all Trades*, 1747, p.57). They also supplied parts as well as whole furniture, with some turners developing into wholesalers. By the early to mid 19th century, turning had become mechanized but divisions in the craft continued. Mayhew discusses the general turner, the tassel and fringe turner, hardwood turners, bobbin turners and 'slop' turners. The general turner would produce bed posts, table legs and pillars, drawer knobs and beading, all principally in mahogany. They would also turn legs for chair-makers. The tassel and fringe turner made components for upholstery work mainly in alder, lime or chestnut. The hardwood turner made small items and speciality work, and the slop workers were working as sweated labour for low piece-work rates (Mayhew, 1850, Letter LXVII, 29 August).

Champness, R. (1966), *The Worshipful Company of Turners of London*, London: Lindley-Jones and Brother.

Stanley-Stone, A. (1925), *A History of the Worshipful Company of Turners of London*, London: Lindley-Jones and Brother.

Symonds, R. W. (1939), 'Craft of the English turner,' in *Apollo*, May, pp.223–6.

Turning

Turning is a decorative process where the method creates the design and decoration in one operation. The technique is based on fixing a work-piece between two pointed centres and then spinning it. Once rotating, by bow string, wheel or other system, an edged tool is applied to cut away the surface as required. It can be compared with another old technique, the potter's wheel, where in both cases the item has been referred to as being 'thrown' or actually spun round. For example, in 1604 'xijd [was] paid to the dish thrower, [for] ij days making of a chere' at Shuttleworth House (Symonds, 1939, p.225).

Prime force was commonly supplied by a flexible pole or sapling for a pole lathe, or by a suspended 'bow' or a large fly-wheel turned by hand. The pole lathe and the bow only allowed cutting on the down stroke, whilst the fly-wheel enabled the possibility of continual turn-ing. The efficiency of the simple traditional methods are illustrated by the continued use of the pole lathe by chair bodgers well into the 20th century.

Turning was best accomplished by the use of non-porous hard-woods with straight grain and few knots, a close texture and a strength along the grain. Such timbers as ash, walnut, beech and fruit woods have always been considered the best. Alternatively the turning of green timber which shrinks across the grain meant that when turned components were fitted into seasoned wood, they would shrink one way and tighten up naturally.

The origins of the process can be traced to ancient times, when lathes were well known. There is evidence of the Egyptian use of a 'proto-lathe' but archaeological evidence suggests that turning was invented around 1000 BC, probably in a number of regions simultaneously, but was only fully developed in Hellenistic times, with an early image of the lathe dating from the 4th century BC. Plato matter-of-factly refers to turning and lathes and said that carpenters were responsible for sawing, boring, planing and turning wood (Richter, 1966, p.124).

By the Middle Ages the technique was quite sophisticated (Theophilus, 1120, ch.61) and evidence of turned work is widely found in wood, metal and other materials. The development of the pole lathe was instrumental in the success of turning, but further developments also occurred (see LATHES). Moxon wrote an essay on the 'Art of Turning', which was an important benchmark in technical description (tool use and so on).

Having thus fitted it into the lathe they begin to work with the sharp-pointed grooving tool, or else with the triangular grooving tool, and with the point of either of these tools break the grain of the wood, by laying small groves upon its surface, til they have pretty well wrought away extruberances, and brought the work tolerably near an intended shape … Afterward they cut down and smooth … and bring the work into a perfect shape … Lastly they polish with Bees-wax … and set a gloss on it with a very dry woollen rag lightly smeared with salad oil.
(1703, pp.167–236)

One of the most common forms of the turned designs for the frames of tables and chairs was based on a multiple repeat of small ball shapes. As one of the oldest forms of turning, known in Ancient Greece, it found renewed popular success in the late 17th century. Its use is confirmed by Randle Holme who described this form as 'wrought with knops and rings all over feet. These and the chairs are generally made with three feet' (1649, iii, ch.14, ill.73). It was widely used for table and chair legs as well as cabinet stands in North Europe and America in the mid 17th to early 18th centuries, and resurrected in the late 19th century for a range of items, especially easy-chair frames.

Technical developments improved the possible designs that could be turned. The swash or two-axis method was a form of ornamental turning that cuts the pattern obliquely to the axis; in other words, two axis turning that allows a shaped spindle to be turned with the use of a buckle, off centre. This turning method was an important development as it allowed complete rear chair stiles to be turned in two simple operations on the lathe (Forman, 1988, pp.204–5).

Another development was a spiral turning design which produced two, three or four twist sections to make the interlocked design patterns. Used on legs of tables, cabinets, stands and chairs, it attracted the attention of a 17th-century inventor, John Ensor of Tamworth, Staffordshire. He was responsible for a mechanical technique that was 'able to make such not only of two, but of three or four twists, or more if he pleaseth; and that in so little time, that he can turn twenty of

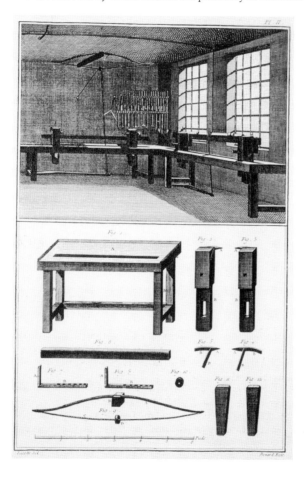

127   An illustration of the simple equipment required to set up a turning lathe. The table, the stocks and their wedges, and the sprung bow are sufficient to start turning, c.1770, French.

these, whilst one is cut and rasped, the only ways they could make such at London and Oxford' (Plot, 1686, ch.IX, p.384).

By the early 19th century steam-power was used to operate turning lathes in mills; however, the hand-operated trade, especially in 'slop' work, continued. The basic lathe with a wheel collar and mandrel operated by foot pressure remained, although Mayhew noted that the big-wheeled lathes, turned by hand, were very rarely used (1850, Letter LXVII, 29 August).

The factory use of automatic copying, twist, back knife and multiple lathes has been common through most of the 20th century.

POLYCHROMATIC TURNING

A 19th-century process of combining inlay with turning. The term relates to a process of inlay that is combined with turning. In its simplest format it comprised a turned part that then had similarly turned studs inlaid into it in the manner of a band. A more complex process was the lamination of blocks of varying coloured woods that were glued together, then turned and possibly studded, revealing their colours. Thirdly, the lathe was used for creating geometric inlay. The basis of this was a circular disc of an appropriate size which was in turn inlaid with other coloured circular discs of varying sizes: these were then finally fitted into pieces of furniture.

See also Lathes, Therming, Turners

Abell, S. G. et al. (1987), *A Bibliography of the Art of Turning and Lathe and Machine Tool History*, North Andover, Mass.: The Museum of Ornamental Turning Ltd.
Audsley, G. A. (1911), *The Art of Polychromatic and Decorative Turning*, London: G. Allen and Co.
Bergeron, H. (1816), *L'Art du tourneur*, Paris: Hamelin-Bergeron.
Gascoigne, M. (1859), *Handbook of Turning*, London: Saunders and Otley.
Maurice, K. (1985), *Sovereigns as Turners*, Zurich: Verlag Ineichen.
Salivet, L. G. (1792), *Manuel du tourneur*, Paris.

Turpentine
See Resins

Twiggen

A reference particularly used in the 17th century which refers to WICKER work and especially chairs. In 1588 'A twiggen cheare xijd' was listed in an inventory (Lancashire wills, Cheatham Society III, p.136) and in 1662 Evelyn referred to OSIERS as a recommended material 'for all wicker and twiggie works' (*Silva*, p.86). In 1649 Randle Holme explained of a particular type of hooded chair that 'These chairs [are] called twiggen chaires because they are made of osiers and withen twigs: having round covers over the heads of them like to a canopy' (1905, vol.ii, 2: 14).

See also Osiers, Wicker

Twill

A weave system in which two or more warp threads are passed over by wefts with a staggered arrangement, creating a herringbone or diamond design.

Twine

A form of cord made from flax or hemp used for upholstery work. Twines are characterized by being composed of two or more yarns. The various types of twine used include fine twine for buttoning, stitching twine and LAID CORD for lashing.

Underglass painting

See Verre églomisé

Universal machines

See Machines

Upholsterer

See also Upholstery

The craft of the upholders, a medieval form of the word upholsterer, was initially carried out by the COFFERER, who had been responsible for using leather as a covering for trunks and later chair seats, or by the saddler. In 1390 'A Saddler makes a chair for the Comte de Nevers inner chamber in wood garnished with cloth padded with down' (Eames, 1977, p.200). The fitting up of domestic textiles in large households was originally carried out by the *tapissier* and the *fourrier*. Their work included the supply of canopies, wall tapestries, table carpets and other soft furnishings for interior decoration. It was all these trades that were to be subsumed by the upholsterer during the 17th century.

Although references to upholders can be found as far back as 1258 and they were recognized as a separate 'mistery' in 1360, the nature of their trade at that time bore little relationship to what is now known as upholstery work. However, they gradually achieved a degree of respectability when in 1465 the Upholders were granted a coat of arms. In 1474 a petition was presented by the Mistery of Upholders which indicated that their wares already included feather beds, pillows, mattresses cushions and quilts. This petition demanded more control over scurrilous makers who filled mattresses with 'cats tails and thistle down' and thereby brought the Upholders into disrepute. This appears to have been a recurring problem since in 1495, and again in 1552, Acts were passed forbidding the use of stuffings, other than feathers or down. These measures began to control some of the apparent excesses, as in 1626 the Upholders' Company was granted a Royal Charter indicating a recognition of their changed circumstances.

Originally they were dealers in old clothes, old beds, old armour and other diverse sorts of materials. The upholsterers' shabby and unsavoury image took some time to shake off. In Stow's *Survey of London* (1598), he observed that Birchin Lane in the City of London 'had for the most part dwelling Fripperers or Upholders that sold olde apparel and householde stuffe' (cited in Houston, 1993, p.4). Their reputation remained suspect well into the 17th century. At times they were accused of handling stolen property and of selling contrary to the established customs of the City of London. An early example of the use of the name 'upholsterer' from 1613 is recorded in Sir Richard Boyle's diary payments made to 'the uphoulster for sylck ffringe and making up the chaires and stools and window cusshen of damask' (Edwards, 1964, p.626).

By the 17th century, the upholsterer was providing his services for the supply of textiles and the making up of them for elaborate bedsteads, draperies and so on. In addition, he was involved in funeral directing as well as beginning to become involved in the actual upholstering of chair frames supplied by the chair-maker. This involvement with various aspects of society, and the growing importance of the interior and its decoration, meant that many upholsterers were becoming advisers and even arbiters of taste. In addition they were increasingly employing and over-seeing the work of other tradesmen and, eventually, the upholsterer was often given charge of whole schemes of decoration. As wealthy clients were beginning to require interiors that were consciously co-ordinated, it was the upholsterer who began to play a pivotal role in the supply of house furnishing. This role was to eventually develop into the profession of interior decorator. Several 17th-century upholsterers became wealthy and had a certain prominence in society.

However, it was the important influence of France that is most noticeable at this time. In the Lord Chamberlain's accounts, John Casbert is recorded as an upholsterer supplying furniture, canopies and royal yacht decorations, while other listed names, such as John Poitevin, Francis La Pierre, and Philip Guibert testify to the French connections. Indeed there were even examples of imported Parisian upholstery work to be found in England.

These instances begin to demonstrate that the role of the upholsterer was more that of an orchestrator and co-ordinator than simply of a tradesman. Although the upholsterer could only operate successfully with the assistance of the silk mercer, the passementier, the embroiderer, the cabinet-makers and a whole range of other subcontractors including feather dressers, linen drapers, glass merchants, blacksmiths, carvers, gilders and the whole spectrum of building crafts people, it was the upholsterer who was responsible for the works and who often took a profit on their contribution. Indeed it was noted at the time that the upholstery business was potentially able to provide a very profitable living.

By the mid 18th century the upholsterer's speciality as an arbiter of taste was fully recognized by contemporary commentators, and this established a particular relationship between retailer and customers that has remained to this day. Campbell was happy to say about the upholsterer that 'He is that man on whose judgement I rely on the choice of goods; and I suppose he has not only judgement in the materials but taste in the fashions, and skill in the workmanship' (1747, p.170). Campbell continues by describing the upholsterer, whose

genius must be universal in every branch of furniture: though his proper craft is to fit up beds, window curtains, hangings and to cover chairs that have stuffed bottoms. He was originally a species of the Taylor, but by degrees has crept over his head, and set up as a connoisseur in every article that belongs to a house.
(ibid., p.170)

An example of the actual duties of an employee of an upholstery firm is indicative of the work that was carried out. The upholsterer stayed at the client's house, often for months at a time. One example from the bills of Thomas Chippendale shows that in 1773 an upholsterer named Reid stayed at Harewood House for 24 weeks and 3 days. The client was later charged for Reid's time for

fixing the Damask hangings of the state bedchamber and dressing room, fixing the gild borders of both rooms – unpacking and fixing the state bed, window Curtis [sic] with cornices, glasses and sundry other furniture. Laying down carpetts, listing doors, making a cushion to an easy chair, taking down all the Venetian blinds, cutting out new tapes to do – washing the laths and fixing again, making canvas and paper hangings to the state bed chamber and

Habit de Tapifsier.

was to these that Campbell was referring when he described 'the young man who has a mind only to be a mere upholder and has no prospect of setting up in the undertaking way. He must handle the needle so alertly as to sew a plain seam, and sew on the lace without puckers, and he must use his sheers so dextrously as to cut a valance or counterpaine with a gentle sweep according to a pattern he has before him' (1747, p.120).

In addition to the wide-ranging upholstery tasks, the upholsterer also became involved in funeral and mourning furnishings. The supply and fitting of black cloths throughout the house, as well as the supply of coffins and other paraphernalia that were associated with the funeral rituals, kept upholsterers busy. The connection between death and appraisal is evident in the preparation of inventories, but descriptions of this aspect of their trade seems to indicate that upholsterers were also adjudicators in conflicts between parties. Campbell suggested that they always valued things at a low price as 'they are obliged to take the goods if it is insisted on, at their own appraisement'. Upholsterers sometimes also added the title 'Brokers of old goods' to their trade cards, an aphorism for second-hand dealers, no doubt resulting from their work as appraisers.

The importance of the upholsterer in the early 19th century is testified to by the growth in numbers of practising tradesmen listed in trade directories, as well as an increasing number of pattern and design books specially aimed at this particular business. These works included George Smith's *A Collection of Designs for Household Furniture and Interior Decoration* (1808), Ackermann's *Repository of the Arts* (1809–28), John Taylor's *The Upholsterer's and Cabinet-maker's Pocket Assistant* (1825), and Thomas King's *The Upholsterer's Sketch Book of Modern Designs* (1839). Equally important was the publication in 1834 of Crofton's *The London Upholsterer's Companion* which was a comprehensive account of the processes of upholstery, including the newly revived interior springing. The publication of this trade manual which consolidated contemporary knowledge of upholstery techniques demonstrates the growth of the business of upholstery. Not long afterwards, *The Workwoman's Guide* (1840) was published, perhaps giving an indication of the role played by women in the practical sewing and making-up of upholsterers' requirements.

In the 19th century the role of the upholsterer began to change. One path was for successful entrepreneurs who had developed upholstery businesses into comprehensive furnishing firms to continue to dominate the better class of trade. The other path was for the working upholsterers to remain as skilled craftsmen who were employed in the workshops of the larger enterprises. For the high-quality trade, craftsmen remained 'all rounders' for much of the century. Indeed it would be unjust to claim that the upholsterers' skills deteriorated during this time, for some of the products of the 19th century were amazing in their proficiency and imagination in the cause of comfort and taste. At other levels, attempts were introduced to further divide the labour of upholstery workers. The descriptions of the trade in the mid 19th century confirm the continuing role of the upholsterer. Mayhew, writing in 1850, commented:

The upholsterers who confine themselves to their own proper branch, are the fitters up of curtains and their hangings, either for beds or windows; they are also the stuffers of chair and sofa cushions and the makers of carpets and of beds; that is to say they are the tradesmen who in the language of the craft do the soft work or in other words, all connected with the cabinet-makers art in which woven fabrics are the staple.
(Letter LXIII, 1 August)

As well as this soft work, many upholsterers were still involved with funeral directing and the appraising business.

130 The extensive nature of the upholsterer's craft is demonstrated in this French caricature of c.1670–90. The craft included seating, drapes, bedding, interior decoration, and even fancy furniture items.

dressing rooms and fixing, making serge covers for the state bed, glasses &c and covering up do [ditto] taking down cleaning & covering up sundry furniture about the house.
(Cited in Gilbert, 1978, p.208)

The co-ordinating role of the upholsterer as a full house furnisher was always important, but the specialist emphasis on material and draperies never went away. These were usually associated with the conversion of textiles into finished 'upholstered goods'. This role in the decorating process involved them in making and fitting beds, curtains, hangings, and making stuffed chairs with tight and loose covers. Indeed the 'proper craft' of upholstery itself demonstrated some sub-division. For example, the actual cutting out of expensive materials was seemingly left to male workers, whilst cheaper female labour was often employed for all the sewing as they 'never served an apprenticeship to the Mystery'. Other examples of division are in the evidence of chair-stuffing being a separate skill, whilst the chair-frame maker had been a distinct trade for a long time. There were of course upholsterers who did not rise to the full decorator status and it

131 Until the 19th century many trades had their workshops and retail premises located in the same building. This engraving shows a French upholstery shop with customers, workers and deliveryman, c.1770.

131 Until the 19th century many trades had their workshops and retail premises located in the same building. This engraving shows a French upholstery shop with customers, workers and deliveryman, c.1770.

The publication of practical manuals on upholstery techniques from the 1870s onward, indicate the decline of the apprenticeship system and the rise of a new breed of upholsterer. In addition to this change, the growth of department stores that divided up the various components of the upholsterer's work into departments dealing separately with cabinet-making and furniture, soft furnishings, upholstery and the supply and fitting of carpets, meant further division of labour and loss of prestige.

In the USA during the 19th century, the upholsterer's craft was much diminished by a series of developments which reduced the skill levels required to make upholstered work. The introduction of pre-fabricated spring units, buttoning machines and electric sewing machines meant that the bulk of the craft skills disappeared.

Indeed in the 20th century the role of the factory upholsterer has diminished further with continual developments in pre-fabrication of seats, cushions and other elements of upholstery, which, combined with the staple gun, have meant that upholstered furniture can be produced by semi-skilled labour. However, there remains a place for skilled craftsmen who are able to work with traditional methods and materials. The demand for traditional-quality new work, such as from heritage organizations, and for other sorts of re-upholstery will ensure the future of the craft.

See bibliography following Upholstery

Upholstery

All upholstery consists of four basic elements: the frame, the supporting system, the padding or cushioning, the outer cover. Although textiles and various fillings had been used to make cushions and squabs since the Middle Ages, it was not until the 16th century that anything like true upholstered furniture was made, as the peripatetic nature of life among the upper classes was not conducive to fixed furnishings. After a more sedentary way of life had been established, the demand for comfort grew rapidly and a range of upholstered articles began to meet their needs. Chair backs and seats were covered with fabric and some examples had the whole frame covered with cloth. Sir John Harington noted:

would it not become the state of the chamber to have easye quilted and lyned forms and stooles for the lords and ladies to sit on which fashion is now taken up in every merchant's hall as great plank forms that two yeomen can scant remove out of their places, and waynscot stools so hard that since great breeches were layd aside, men can skant endewr to sitt upon.
(*Nugae Antiquae*, 1804, vol.I, p.202, cited in Jourdain, 1924, p.194)

Upholstery was a combination of the long established wooden-framed chairs, the girth webbing derived from animal harnessing, the quilted padding used by armourers for protection within suits of armour, and applied decorative textiles. The techniques of upholstery, and the four basic elements were well known by 1588. The reference to the making up of stools with '2 dussen of gyrthwebe for 3s., 700 garnishing nails for 1s 9d, four pounds of deer hair at 1s 4d., nine skins, and fringe at 11s.' indicated this clearly (Nathaniel Bacon, Stewards Account 1587–9, cited in Clabburn, 1988). Less than one hundred years later, Randle Holme fully explained the process of making a chair:

Girth it, is to bottom it with girth webb, stret drawn and crossed.
Canvice it, is to nail the canvice on the top of the stool or chair frame, over the girth webb.
Rowle it, is to put rowls on the top edges.
Stuffing, is to stuff it with hay, wool, flocks or feathers.
Fringing, is to nail the fringe about the stool seat at the sides.
The seat is that place sitten on.
Backing is to nail the back on a chair suitable to the seat.
Garnishing is the finishing with brass nails.
(1649, 1, bk 3, ch.3, p.97)

By the beginning of the 17th century, variants of a simple upholstered back stool (or farthingale chair) were known in many European countries. By the end of the century all the upholstery techniques (with the exception of springing and certain stitching methods) were known and used. Whilst the techniques of upholstery at this time were elementary, the effects were often sumptuous due to the rich textiles employed. The simple chairs developed longer and taller upholstered backs, and set a standard that remained well into the 18th century. The more comfortable easy chair, that developed in the 18th century, seems to have derived from invalid or sleeping chair models. These especially comfortable chairs had large down-filled cushions and padded backs filled with horsehair. Most forms of upholstered chair were finished with decorative trimming, piping or nailing.

The early techniques of upholstering were simple but workmanlike. Webbing, canvas and a variety of stuffing materials were employed to make up the seat or back. By the Restoration, most fashionable families were employing upholsterers to supply comfortable seating and other furnishings often decorated with elaborate trimmings. During the mid 18th century the upholstery procedures followed a similar pattern. Webbing was stretched to form an interlaced support over which was fixed hessian. Curled hair was laid onto this, and stitched through to the webbing to prevent excessive movement. A roll edge was made by fixing a tube of stuffing material to the front rail to maintain the shape at this wear point. A layer of linen was fixed over the hair, and then the final top covering was close fitted. In these systems the filling quality was all important. Hay, wool, and hair were common, but there were also various attempts to develop alternative fillings. The ideas ranged from feather cushions to pigs' bladders filled with air.

TUFTING, a technical development, which was originally meant to stabilize the fillings, soon turned into a design feature. This technique, introduced in England and America in the mid 18th century, suited the flatter, squarer design of their chairs rather than the more fashion-

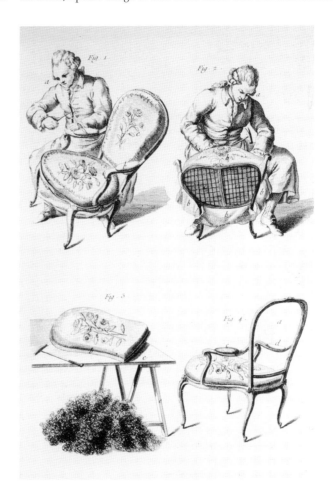

FAR LEFT
132   The skills of the upholsterer and his assistants is demonstrated in the State Bed at Osterley. Designed by Robert Adam and made between 1776 and 1778, it includes examples of most of the upholsterer's skills.

LEFT
133   The work of the 18th-century upholsterer is seen in this plate from the Encyclopédie. It shows the technique of sewing and tacking as well as the use of horsehair, and the technique of 'pin-cushion' (loose-back) work.

134   *High-quality upholstery is still built up by hand, using techniques that have been developed over the last three centuries. This English example shows the sewing of a roll edge, c.1950.*

able domed squab seats favoured in France. Loose seats and backs were also introduced because the often elaborate mouldings made it impossible to fix covers tightly. In addition, it meant that seats could be re-upholstered or removable covers could be used for the various seasons.

SPRINGS, originating in the requirements for carriage suspension, found their first use in chamber or exercising horses. Some 19th-century American sofas exist with iron coil-springs stapled directly to board or slatted bottoms. The resultant upholstery work was inevitably heavier and less resilient than the conventional methods of using webbing, but it enabled spring upholstery to become available at a lower level of the market.

Whatever processes were devised to simplify the methods of spring stuffing, the problem for chair manufacturers still remained: that the full upholstering of an easy chair or sofa was a skilled trade that successfully resisted mechanization for a long time. The most difficult parts consisted of the tying of the spring bed and the processes of even stuffing and tufting. However, techniques were invented to assist in the making of upholstered chairs. The first was simplifying the setting of springs in the interior seat. A simple solution to the seat springing problem was to make a SPRING UNIT which just had to be inserted into the frame. The sewing of covers was aided by the use of the industrial SEWING MACHINE, but otherwise it seemed that the mechanical assistance that became available in other parts of furniture-making was not possible for upholstery. However, as buttoned or tufted upholstery was a major feature of the period, it is not surprising that attempts were made to try to simplify the process by mechanized means. It was not until the end of the century that a satisfactory method was marketed (see Tufting). There was also an attempt to mechanize other parts of the upholstery process: In 1878 it was reported that a Paul Roth of New York was exhibiting machinery that would produce a stitched edge, pack the hair into a seat and tie the springs.

Whatever the merits of these machines, they were not exploited commercially, and it is fair to say that the British upholstery trade at least remained generally unaffected by changes in technology until the introduction of man-made fillings, latex and plastic foams and staple guns in the 20th century. The production of a fully upholstered chair was based on the craftsman constructing the shape onto a pre-formed wood, or sometimes, iron frame. This called for considerable skill in technique as each chair had to be built up in carefully balanced

135   *The upholstery trade in England had not changed dramatically by the early 20th century. The London workshop shown here has a wide range of work going on at the same time, and there appears to be little division of labour except between seamstresses and upholsterers, c.1901.*

layers. The main change in the process was the gradual division of labour into the three stages of stuffing, cutting out of covers and covering. However, as chairs were usually made to order in a wide variety of fabrics, the integration of the upholstery business into the factory situation was a slow process that still remained based on workshop practice well into the 20th century.

It is clear that the internal spring revolutionized upholstery practice and design in the 19th century. During the 20th century, the nature of all of these elements changed in varying degrees. Perhaps the most significant change has been the gradual use of ready-made parts such as spring units, needled and layered fillings on paper backings, foam and polyether cushioning all cut to size, as well as ready-made frame sections, and the pneumatic staple gun, all of which has meant that the skills of an upholsterer have changed. Twentieth-century developments in upholstery were to change the internal structure, and new materials began to be used in substitution for traditional ones. The traditional method of upholstery frame-making often relied on the separate craft of FRAME-MAKERS. The latter built wooden frames to a specification and then delivered them to upholstery workshops. These frames were usually frameworks for the suspension and covering, and in many cases were completely hidden after upholstering. At various times fashion has favoured 'show-wood' upholstery, which called for exposure of the frame. This varied from a hint of frame, such as an arm knuckle, to a fully polished show-wood frame with loose seat and back cushions, which demanded considerable frame-making skills. In addition to wooden frames, the revival of the 19th-century idea of metal frames was used both for internal and external frames.

The technical changes in upholstery have related to both the internal structure and the external coverings. At the beginning of the century the spiral spring was supreme, but in the 1930s tension springs were introduced into Germany and England. This released the designer from having to create a deep section in a chair to accommodate the spiral springs: he could produce a more elegant easy chair whilst retaining the benefits of metal springing. In 1929 the development of latex-rubber cushioning was patented by Dunlop. When made up into cushions, this became an ideal partner to the tension-sprung chair. Post-war developments included the four-point suspension (one-piece rubber platform) and the introduction of rubber webbing by Pirelli. Both these processes hastened the demise of the traditional

spring until the introduction of serpentine metal springs, which enabled manufacturers to produce a traditional-looking upholstery range without the cost of a fully sprung interior. Metals were also utilized by designers like Ernest Race, who created new lightweight organic-shaped chair and sofa frames from metal rods.

In the late 1940s, the hammock principle used in upholstery, based on aircraft seating, with rubberized hair filling, was patented by Christie Tyler. This was again taken up in the 1960s and early 1970s, when there was a fashion for chairs made from chromed tubular steel fitted with hammock cushions. With the 1960s' advances in technology and design strategies, chairs were produced which included frame, structure and padding in one item. The PLASTICS revolution that allowed this was responsible for an incredible range of very varied objects, including: the Sacco chair filled with high resistance foamed polystyrene balls; the Blow chair in inflatable PVC; the Pratone of integral foamed polyurethane foam; or even the Up chair, made from polyurethane foam, vacuum packed in a box which 'came to life' in your living room as it was unpacked. In the contract market, plastics became a valuable material for seating work.

Plastics also earned a place in post-war upholstery with the introduction of polyether and polyester FOAMS for cushions and padding. Developments continued with substitutes for most traditional materials, for example, man-made fibrefill in place of cotton-fibre wrap. External coverings have been revolutionized by the use of PVC-coated fabrics, which were themselves a substitute for the earlier leathercloths. Although upholstery design for the high street market has remained stubbornly traditional, a variety of innovations have been introduced into the manufacturing processes. These include frames made from particle board or plywood, pre-formed plastic arm, wing and leg sections, and even complete plastic frames for 'Queen Anne' chairs (see Plate XXIV).

Contemporary upholstery work has ranged from the practical to the highly experimental. The exploitation of materials such as stretch fabrics to create sculptural shapes, the imaginative use of foams to create fantasy furniture and the re-introduction of traditional products such as wicker, cane and grass point to interesting developments in the future. Advances in the construction of 'traditional' upholstery have not been great in the latter part of the 20th century. Techniques of fabric cutting and parts' supply on a multiple basis have speeded up these aspects of the work. The 'cell system' of production has also resulted in economies of time and material, whilst the fixing of outer fabrics by the pneumatic staple gun, which began in the 1950s, must be the greatest advance in speedy assembly. Subtle developments have derived from this process itself. For example, in order to avoid an unsightly line of tacks on the top of the back of furniture, a hidden tacking strip was devised to fix material to backs.
See also Air cushions, Banding, Bonegrace, Bottom linen, Chair frames, Cord seats, Cushions, Drop-in seat, Fat Bag, Lead moulding, Loose covers, Mattress, Nailing, Needles, Palliasse, Passementerie, Petticoat, Platform, Pleating, Quilting, Reversible seat, Seasonal furnishings, Slip covers, Springs, Turkish chair

Anderson, M. and Trent, R. (1993), 'A catalogue of American easy chairs', in *American Furniture*, pp.213–34.
Anon. (1885), *Practical Upholstery*, By a working upholsterer, Wyman and Sons.
Bast, H. (1947), *New Essentials of Upholstery*, Milwaukee: Bruce Publishing.
Beard, G. (1997), *Upholsterers and Interior Furnishing in England 1530–1840*, London and New Haven: Yale.
Bland, S. (1995), *Take a Seat, the Story of Parker-Knoll 1834–1994*, Baron Birch.
Cooke, E. S. (1987), *Upholstery in America and Europe from the Seventeenth century to World War I*, New York: Norton.
Crofton, J. S. (1834), *London Upholsterer's Companion*, London: The author.
Garnier-Audiger, A. (1830), *Manuel du tapissier, décorateur, etc*, Paris: Roret.
Grier, Katherine (1988), *Culture and Comfort*, Rochester, NY: Strong Museum.
Houston, J. F. (1993), *Feather Beds and Flock Beds, Notes on the History of the Worshipful Company of Upholders*, Sandy: Three Tents Press.
Michie, A. H. (1985), 'Upholstery in all its branches: Charleston, 1725–1820', in *Journal of Early Southern Decorative Arts*, XI, (2).
Nothelfer, K. (1942), *Das Sitzmöbel. Ein Fachbuch für Polsterer, Shulbauer*, Ravensburg.
Ossut, C. (1994), *Le Siège et sa garniture*, Paris: Vial.
Passeri, A., Trent, R., Jobe, B. (1987), 'The Wheelwright and Maerklin inventories and the history of the upholsterer's trade in America 1750–1900', in *Old Time New England*, 72, pp.312–54.
Symonds, R. W. (1956), 'Crafts of the upholsterer', in *Antique Collector*, June, pp.103–8.
Tierney, W. F. (1965), *Modern Upholstering Methods*, Bloomington: McKnight.
Upholstery Conservation, Pre-prints of a Symposium held at Colonial Williamsburg, February 1990, East Kingston: American Conservation Consortium.
Walton, K. M. (1973), *English Furniture Upholstery 1660–84*, Temple Newsam, Leeds.
— 'The Worshipful Company of Upholders of the City of London', in *Furniture History*, IX, pp.41–51.

Upholstery fillings

For upholstery fillings, anything from pigs' hair to seaweed has been considered as a possible contender. Whilst curled hair has been recognized as one of the most successful natural fillings, many others have been more or less satisfactory (see Algerian fibre, Alva marina, Cat's-tail, Chaff, Chipfoam, Coir, Cotton flock, Down, Excelsior, Feathers, Fibrefill, Flags, Foam, French hair, Hair, Hair substitutes, Hemp, Kapok, Latex, Linsey, Mill puff, Moss, Pine hair, Pine state hair, Plastic foam, Rubberized hair, Rugging, Seaweed, Sisal, Spanish moss, Sponge, Straw, Tow, Wadding, Washed flock, Wool, Woollen flock).

Apart from those mentioned elsewhere, there were a number of other attempts to employ materials as upholstery fillings. In 1843 Richard Brooman patented the use of convolvuli (Pat.no.9863) as a mattress and upholstery filling. In 1863 Thomas Ghislin patented 'Improvements in the treatment of certain foreign plants and the application of fibres derived therefrom' (Pat.no.1953), which was partly intended for upholstery use. These plants were to be broken down and their fibres used as stuffing or they might be woven into cloth as a substitute for horsehair.

Upholstery fixings

See Back tacking, Bible front, Buttons and loops, Cane edge, Case rods, Flies, Hooks and eyes, Knots (Lashing), Laid cord, Quilting, Rolled edge, Staples, Stitches, Tacks, Tension top, Tufting, Twine, Webbing, Zips

Upholstery technique

See Buttoning, Couching, Double-loop stitches, Edge treatment, Hammock, Knotting, Mattress making, Mock cushion, Nailing, Overstuffing, Panes, Pin cushion work, Pleating, Pull over edge, Quilting, Rolled edge, Stitching, Stuffing, Stuffover, Tacking, Tufting, Van Dyking

Urea formaldehyde

See Adhesives

Utile (*Entandrophragma utile*)

A West African sapele timber with an average density of 670 (42 lb/cu ft). It has a pinky brown to deep red-brown colour with a uniform and moderate texture, and an interlocked grain which produces an irregular stripe figure. It has been widely used for furniture and cabinet-making during the latter half of the 20th century.

Utrecht velvet
See Plush

Vacuum moulding
The process of making materials shape themselves to a pre-determined form by laying them over a former and removing air, so that the ensuing vacuum ensures that the material bends to take the shape of the mould. Used in plastic and plywood production as well as for veneering work. It is especially useful when working with complex shaped surfaces. In 1941 Charles and Ray Eames developed their 'Kazam' vacuum machine for bending plywood in two planes and this idea was commercially adopted soon after. By the 1950s vacuum moulding machines were standard furniture factory equipment.
See also Plastics, Veneers

Van Dykes
According to Holtzapffel, a 'technical term for brass metal borders' (1847, vol.II, p.736). The term also refers to elongated triangle-shaped inlays laid alternately in light and dark timbers. These are often found on backgammon boards and in Tunbridge ware. It has been suggested that the name may be derived from the artist Van Dyke, who often painted his subjects with pointed 'triangular' beards.

Van Dyking
A method of cutting out fabric for buttoned back upholstery work, especially in leather. The term refers to the serrated edge of the pattern when cut. The zigzag edge has diamond-shaped pieces fitted to it in such a way that the joins follow the creases of the buttoning pattern and ensure a good match of hides or pattern.

Varnish
A surface finishing material and process that used RESINS dissolved in liquids to create a thin, solid but relatively transparent film which was ideal for wood finishing. The name varnish is derived from *vernix*, Latin for amber. Varnish finishing for wood was known in Ancient Egypt and has remained part of the repertoire ever since. Inevitably, the range of recipes is wide and varied, although some seem to be more useful than others. For example, in the 15th century the following recipe was recorded: 'To make wernysch: Take a galon of good ale, and put thereto iij. ounces of gumme of Arabyke ['gum acacia'], and boyle a galon into a quarte and kepe yt welle' (T. Wright and J. O. Halliwell, *Reliquiae Antiquae*), which demonstrates the continuing use of gum acacia, a varnish ingredient known as far back as Ancient Egypt.

The 17th century saw the beginning of the use of true varnishing on furniture. As the finer-grained timber veneers were introduced, a liquid which when dry produces a hard clear finish to furniture was clearly desirable. In 1664 Evelyn referred to oil varnish as 'Joyner's varnish' and also refers to tree and nut oils that 'made an excellent varnish for pictures, for woodwork and to preserve polished iron from rust' (*Silva*, 2, 1, p.22). Evelyn also mentions the introduction of the 'incomparable secret of the Japan and China varnishes which has hitherto been reserved so choicely amongst the virtuosi … they varnish their work with china varnish which infinitely excels linseed oyl' (ch.31, 3). Evelyn describes high lustre China varnish (spirit) made from four parts gum lac to one part gum sandarac dissolved in alcohol. He explains the method:

The wood which you would Vernish, should be very clean smooth and without the least freckle or flaw; and in case there be any, stop them with a paste made of Gum Tragacanth, incorporated with what colour you design: Then cover it with a layer of varnish purely, till it be sufficiently drench'd with it: Then take seven times the quantity of varnish, as you do of colour … apply this with a very fine and full Pencil; a quarter of an hour after, do it over again, even to three times successively; and if every time it be permitted to dry, before you put on the next, 'twill prove better: Within two hours after these four layers (or sooner if you please) polish it with Preslc [French *prêle*] (which our cabinet-makers call as I think Dutch Reeds) wet, or dry; not much imports it, though in doing this, you should chance to discover any of the wood; since you are to pass it over four or five times as above; and if it be not yet smooth enough, Preslc it again with reeds, but now very tenderly: Then rub it sufficiently with Tripoly and a little Oyl-olive, or water: Lastly cover it once or twice again with your vernish, and two days after, polish it as before with tripoly and a piece of Hatters Felt.
(*Silva*, 1662, pp.238–9)

The range of varnishes can be simply categorized as oil varnishes, shellac, spirit varnishes and synthetic varnishes.

OIL-BASED VARNISH
The earliest varnishes, from around 250 BC, were based on natural resins dissolved in hot linseed oil and these varnishes (from many differing recipes) remained standard well into the 20th century. The oil-based varnishes mainly used resins such as sandarac, amber, rosin or colophony, copal, amber, mastic and kauri. The fixed-oil varnishes, mainly made with amber or copal, were the most durable but took a while to dry. They were occasionally accelerated with a drier such as litharge. These varnishes were also sometimes thinned with turpentine to ease application. On occasion known as rubbing varnishes, since once dried hard they could be abraded with soft stone such as pumice or rottenstone to produce a brilliant shine.

Sheraton gives detailed instructions for preparing and applying these varnishes (1803, p.327). The full process for cabinet finishing involved 'rushing' the surface (that is, rubbing down with rushes), applying a coat of copal varnish, three layers of white spirit varnish, which was 'rushed' off, then four more coats were added at daily intervals. Polishing could then begin. Using pounded pumice stone and water, the surface was rubbed level and cleaned off and then allowed to dry. The final part involved rottenstone and water, then cleaning up with oil and flour as a final finish. Although Nicholson considered copal varnish difficult to make, he noted that it 'may be procured [ready-made] of japan-manufactures or coach makers' (1826, p.31). It was described in detail by American author Ernest Hazen in 1843:

To give the work a complete finish four coats of [copal] varnish are successively applied … after the application of the first coat, the surface is rubbed with a piece of wood of convenient form; after the second, with sand-paper and pulverised pumice stone; after the third with pumice-stone again; and after the fourth with very finely powdered pumice-stone and rotten-stone. A little linseed oil is next applied and the whole process is finished by rubbing the surface with the hand charged with flour.
(vol.II, p.144)

SHELLAC VARNISH
The secretion of the lac insect that accrues and coalesces forming hard, resinous layers is dissolved in alcohol which evaporates and leaves a film (see Resins, Lac). Stalker and Parker quote both seed-lac and shellac, preferring the former as the latter 'though it may be polished, and look well for the present, yet like a handsome Ladies beautiful face, it has no security against the injuries of time' (1688, p.18). They described the process of applying a clear varnish to olive wood and walnut: 'After applying ten to twelve coats of seed-lac varnish (with the top removed for later use), dried between each coat and polished with rushes, apply the top part of the varnish in six coats. After three days standing, apply powdered tripolee and rub till it acquires a gloss' (loc.cit.). For lower-quality goods, oil varnish was applied in fewer

coats and not surface polished. Stalker and Parker also discussed 'shell-lac' varnish, which they considered

> a fit varnish for ordinary work that required not a polish; ... Your common Varnish-dawbers frequently use it, for 'tis doubly advantageous to them; having a greater body than the seed-lac, less labour and varnish goes to the perfecting of their work; which they carelessly slubber over, and if it looked tolerably bright til tis sold, they matter not how dull it looks afterward. (1688, p.10)

By the mid 18th century the spirit varnishes included 'shellac varnish', 'a clear varnish made with sandarac gum', 'a very beautiful Chinese (copal and sandarac) varnish', 'the excellent (sandarac, mastic, camphor and turpentine) varnish of Mr. Ward of England', 'Chinese (shellac, mastic and sandarac) varnish of all colours', 'a perfectly beautiful Chinese (sandarac, mastic and shellac) varnish', 'another Chinese (copal) varnish for all kinds of colours', 'a varnish as beautiful as that of the Chinese (shellac and alcohol)', 'a French (shellac and sandarac) varnish' (Plumier, 1749, 12: 4). By the 19th century, a wipe-on solution of shellac in alcohol was developed in France and is commonly called FRENCH POLISH.
See also Japanning

SPIRIT VARNISH
The spirit varnishes are solutions of natural RESINS (for example, benzoin, mastic, dammar, sandarac) in volatile solvents, usually oil of turpentine or alcohol, which evaporate off thus leaving the surface slightly more pliable and less likely to crack. Probably not known before the 16th century, they were common in cabinet-making during the 17th and 18th centuries and have remained so. In America colophony resin in turpentine was a common and inexpensive varnish popular during the 18th and 19th centuries. However, spirit-based varnishes deteriorate as the resins oxidize, discolour over time and become brittle.
See also shellac, above

SYNTHETIC RESIN VARNISH
See Plastics

See also Amber, Finish, Gums, Japanning, Lacquer, Resins, Vernis Martin

Anon. (1818), *Cabinet-makers' Guide: or Rules and Instructions in the Art of Varnishing, etc.*, London: Arliss.
Dossie, R. (1758), *Handmaid to the Arts*, London.
Hasluck, P. N. (1903), *Wood Finishing*, London: Cassell.
Matteillo, J. J. (ed.) (1941), *Decorative and Protective Finishes*, New York, Wiley.
Mussey, R. D. (1982), 'Old finishes, early varnishes', in *Fine Woodworking Techniques*, 6, Mar/April, pp.71–5.
— (1987), 'Transparent furniture finishes in New England, 1700–1825', in *Old-Time New England*, lxxii, pp.287–311.
Seymour, R. B. and Mark, H. F. (1989), *Organic Coatings; Their Origin and Development*, London: Elsevier.
Stalker, J. and Parker, G. (1688), *A Treatise of Japanning and Varnishing*, London: Tiranti, 1960
Tingry, P. (1832), *The Varnishers' Guide*, London: Sherwood, Gilbert and Piper.
Watin, J. F. (1755), *L'Art du peintre, doreur, vernisseur*, Paris.

Varnished gilding
See Gilding

Vegetable dyes
See Dyes

Vegetable glues
See Adhesives

Vellum
See Leather (PARCHMENT AND VELLUM)

Velour
A plain or figured cut-pile all-cotton fabric, in which the pile is usually made from additional warp yarns which are raised over rods set in place of wefts, to create loops which can either be cut or left uncut.

Velvet
A luxurious warp pile fabric woven over wires or 'face to face', originally made from silk, but now made with a variety of pile yarns such as silk, acrylic, mohair, cotton or wool. It is woven in a selection of finishes and a range of weights from dress to heavy upholstery. The velvet weave technique can also make corduroy, which is woven with a weft yarn long-floated between each ground weft in such a way that ridged effects are made. When the pile is uncut to make looped pile effects, these create cloths such as terry, Brussels or moquette.

Velvet was introduced into Europe (especially Italy) in the early 13th century. It was used early on for furnishings. The 1509 inventory of Edmund Dudley describes both clothing and furnishings made from velvet, including sparvers (curtain or canopy) and cushions (Beard, 1997, p.282). Amongst the best early velvets were those from Lucca, Florence and Genoa. These were figured furnishing velvets with a satin ground and a multi-coloured pile which could be cut or uncut or even a mixture of both. The cut and uncut pile was sometimes called Cisele. The large patterns and bold colours made them popular in the late 17th century and through much of the 18th century. Little velvet appears to have been manufactured in England until the immigration of the Huguenots from 1685.

Although originally silk, velvet fabrics with a cotton pile were introduced in the mid 18th century. These were known as Manchester velvets. They were popular after around 1760 and are now known as VELOUR. George Smith suggested that for a field bed 'the borders [might be] cut out in black Manchester velvet and sewed on' (1808, p.5).

Various special effects may be applied to velvet as to other fabrics. Stamping the silk face with irons applied under pressure to create a raised pattern and a ground effect pattern was not uncommon. Other special effects either applied or woven in created 'antique' velvet, broderie (cut pile same height or lower than uncut pile), ciselé (cut pile is higher than uncut), pile on pile (pile of two or more heights), terry, voided (areas left completely free of pile) and velveteen.
See also Caffoy, Mockado, Plush (Utrecht velvet)

Marinas, F. De (1993), *Velvet: History, Techniques, Fashions*, London: Thames and Hudson.

Veneers
A thin slice of (usually) decorative material that is intended to be fixed to a solid substrate. Veneers may be of many different materials (see HORN, IVORY, MOTHER-OF-PEARL, MARBLE, TORTOISESHELL, and so on), but usually refer to wood products.

First used by the Ancient Egyptians, probably due to timber shortages, the process seems to have been ignored by the Greeks but revived by the Romans. The Roman use was regretted by Pliny, when he complained of 'the luxury that displays itself in covering one tree with another, and in bestowing upon the more common woods a bark of higher price' (XVI, 232). It was not until the relative peace and prosperity of the Renaissance that the ancient art could be revived properly (see VENEERING).

Veneers are prepared and selected according to the end use. The

136 *An example of masur birch veneer. The distinctive pattern is revealed by rotary-cutting.*

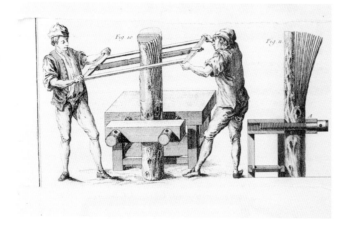

137 *The cutting of veneer by hand was a skilled occupation requiring a straight eye and a steady hand, c.1770. The limitations of this process were exposed once mechanical methods were developed in the early 19th century.*

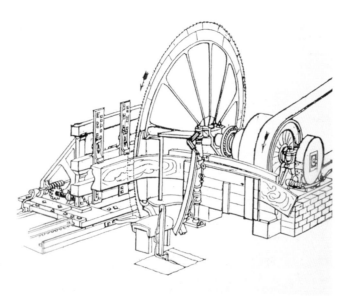

138 *Improvements in veneer cutting occurred in the early 19th century, when Marc Brunel devised his circular veneer saw, c.1810.*

finest and most decorative are designated as 'face quality', which is defined as a fine veneer with the particular characteristics associated with the timber that it is cut from. The other extreme is the 'backing grade' veneer. This is a featureless veneer used for utilitarian purposes. Within these basic classifications are numerous differences based on the nature of the actual veneer when it is opened up from the log. Apart from the natural veneers, a variety of 'man-made' veneers have been produced. These are often laminated veneers in which a selection of veneers are glued together under pressure and then cut vertically (see FINELINE). These may also be angle-cut laminated veneers to create various effects. Alternately, veneer may be dyed by having colour injected into the living tree or having the cut veneers dyed to shade.

VENEER MANUFACTURING PROCESSES

The production of veneer was originally a hand-cutting process whereby the timber baulk was held upright in a vice and the sawyers cut slices down the length of the timber. The hand veneer-cutter was able to cut *c*.2 veneers to the centimetre (5 to 6 to the inch), whilst for finer work, from smaller baulks of timber, a cabinet-maker could cut *c*.3 veneers to the centimetre (7 or 8 to the inch). Chambers noted of veneers that 'in order to saw 'em the blocks or planks are placed upright in a kind of sawing press' (1728).

There were attempts to mechanize the process quite early on. The first patent that relates to the production of veneers was taken out in 1635 by Sara Jerom and William Webb for an 'engine for cutting timber into thin scales, for making band boxes, scabbards for swords and the like' (Pat.no.87). Three years later, in 1638, Sara Jerom took out another patent for the same description (Pat.no.120). These early patents were isolated, and the period between 1700 and 1830 was the heyday of the hand sawyer and hand veneer-cutter. An attempt to replicate the hand process was devised in France. The rising wood veneer-cutting machine was patented by a Msr Cochot of Auxerre in 1799 and is still found occasionally in use today. The log was lowered into a pit, then fitted onto a rack and pinion mechanism, geared to the cutting speed of the saw. As the log rose up against the blade, so the sheet of veneer fell away.

In 1806, Marc Isambard Brunel obtained a patent for machine-cutting veneers and thin boards (Pat.no.2968). This was the beginning of successful mechanization. Soon after this, Brunel, with partners, set up a veneer and saw mill in Battersea. The principle that Brunel first used was based on a horizontal knife to slice veneers from a log. The basis of the process was that the knives would be held in line and they would extend beyond the block to be cut. The knife would then reciprocate as the log was brought forward to the blades. The machine, according to Holtzapffel, 'answered moderately well with straight grained and pliant woods, such as Honduras mahogany, but there were serious objections to its use for woods of irregular, harsh and brittle grain such as rosewood' (1847, p.806). He goes on to point out that this was a shame 'as the splitting machine converted the whole of the wood into veneer without waste, whereas the veneer saw on average cuts one third of the wood into saw dust' (loc.cit.).

Brunel's next attempt after abandoning the knife-cutting process was the application of the circular saw. His initial experiments were again unsatisfactory due to the friction of the saw that made it buckle and twist. To overcome this, Brunel nicked the saw-blades to avoid buckling and eventually developed this idea so that his final saws were made up of segments of saw blade that were attached to a circular casting which could be of very variable size. The mill was described by a visitor in the *British Register*:

in a small building on the left, I was attracted by the action of a steam engine of 16 horse power and was ushered into a room where it turned, by means of banding, four wheels fringed with fine saws. I beheld planks of mahogany and rosewood sawed into veneers 16th of an inch thick, with a precision and grandeur of action that was really sublime ... A large sheet of veneer 10 feet long by 2 feet broad was separated in ten minutes, so even and so uniform that it appeared more like a perfect work of nature than one of human art! (Local History Collection, Battersea Library)

This was not a unique example, as in 1827, a provincial sawmill in Barnard Castle, County Durham, employed 'one veneer saw plate and segments' (Medlam, 1991, p.34). The incredibly long-running success of Brunel's saw system was noted by the trade press: 'the soundness of this conclusion [Brunel's segment blade device] has been proved for half-a-century, as nothing in the way of substantial improvement has been added to the machine ... [In the full development of this mill] eleven machines were at work on the ground, the diameter of the saws being from 7' to 17', the largest of the saw teeth being of the gauge of five to the inch' (*House Decorator*, 15 April 1881). The report noted that veneer was cut at the rate of about 30 cm (1 ft) in four seconds, a great improvement in speed:

Saws for veneers are built of a circular cast-iron wheel upon which are fixed segments of soft steel. Upon the soft steel are fixed hardened steel serrated blades which are the cutting edge of the saw. This saw is capable of handling up to 24 feet long and 5.5 feet wide timber. The number of veneers usually cut varies between 15 with a six inch wide plank and eight with a sixty inch wide plank. (loc.cit.)

By the 1830s four methods of preparing veneers were operative: hand saw, circular saw, rotary knife and plane. Although sawn veneers have been considered superior to sliced or rotary cut (in this process the logs are usually moistened by steam to facilitate the knife cuts), the growing demand for veneers encouraged developments that led to speedier conversion.

The application of steam to the veneer-cutting process and the centralization of the process was a natural development, as was the combination of sawmill, timber and veneer supplier into one company. Henry Mayhew, writing about the application of machinery to the carpentry and joinery trade in 1850, confirmed that veneers were 'now exclusively made by means of steam machinery'. Discussing veneer mills further, he noted that the mill he visited in London was the largest in the world with 2.5 ha (6 acres) of ground next to a canal. He described the saw room as 37 m (120 ft) long and 27 m (90 ft) wide, containing eight circular saws, varying between 2 m (7 ft) and 5 m (17 ft) in diameter.

Apart from the application of steam engines, the veneer sawing process was further developed in the mid 19th century. The horizontal saw frame was introduced to do finer cutting work than the circular saw was capable of. This was achieved by the use of fine-ground saws and resulted in an increased production of veneers. The disadvantages of saw cutting, such as limited veneer sheet size, slow speeds, and waste through saw dust, were overcome by the development of the knife-cutting process, essentially either a slicing or a peeling operation.

The rotary knife-cutting or peeling process was important not only for veneers but also for the development of PLYWOOD. In a report published in 1817 it was said that a Russian piano-maker in St Petersburg was producing 'sheets of veneer of about a hundred feet in length, and four, five or even more in width'. This claim was countered by the allegation that cabinet-makers in Furth [Germany] had been producing peeled veneer for a long time prior to 1817. In England in 1818 Henry Faveryear developed (Pat.no.4324) a machine for rotary cutting logs, but this does not seem to have been adopted. However, in 1822 a prototype of a 'peeling machine' was made by the Vienna Polytechnic Institute. A short time later the process was developed in the USA and, as the 'Improved Patent Rotary Veneer cutter propelled by steam power', it was used by Richardson and Co of Philadelphia in 1825. The first rotary veneer-cutting machine that was patented in the United States was designed by John Dresser of Stockbridge, Mass., in 1840. It was also in Russia that the cutting of veneers by a rotary method was seriously developed. It is noteworthy that it could be

139 *The success of the Brunel saw is shown in this photograph of a saw built on his principles and used continuously from 1860 to 1934.*

140 *The importance of the rotary cutting of veneer is found in plywood production, but also in the increased variety of figure that can be revealed by the 'peeling' process.*

141 *Developments in veneer cutting took a leap forward with the introduction of the Arbey knife-cutting veneer machine. This enabled a much more economic use of the log (no waste in sawdust) and allowed far more veneers to the centimetre or inch than was previously possible.*

either hand- or power-operated, and the machine design was simply based on the common turning lathe. A British patent for continuous rotary veneer-cutting machinery was registered by Comte Fontain-moreau in May 1847 (Pat.no.11716). His main claim was that the timber log could be cut, whatever its width. It did not need to be cross-cut to fit the jaws of the machine and therefore it yielded larger slices of veneer.

A major benefit of rotary cutting was noted by the *Mechanics Magazine*. In a notice published in 1848 they referred to a veneering machine that was able to cut a roll of maple veneer 91 m (300 ft) long and 90 cm (3 ft) wide from a log 90 cm (3 ft) long and 51 cm (20 in) in diameter which easily reveals the bird's-eye figure (12 February 1848, p.155). George Dodd pointed out the different methods used in Britain and the Continent: 'the English usually adopt the method described [Brunel's vertical cutting saw], but on the Continent a singular mode is practised of cutting a continuous veneer in a spiral form. The English plan wastes a little more wood, but yields stronger veneers than the foreign' (1858). The British trade press continued to report on the rotary system as if it were new and, as late as 1881, the *House Decorator* reported that:

a new and highly successful machine is the rotary, on the principle of the knife – a system highly favourable to wood in the round and to figure, as in the case of bird's-eye-maple, found only on the face of logs. The number of veneers in this case is greatly increased as there is nothing lost by the saw or with the rib or set of the same marking the face of the veneer.
(15 April, p.285)

According to this article the veneers were so thin that it was not practicable to use inlay or banding for further decoration.

Whatever the problems or merits of the rotary system, it had shown that the application of knives in veneer-cutting was successful.

It was the French who then revived Brunel's original but unsuccessful idea of knife-slicing a log. The benefits of the process were extolled in 1875. It was reported that Arbey's knife-cutting process could not only cut 39–59 veneers per cm (100–50 veneers per in) but also leave the surface so even that it was ready for use straight from the cutters. It is also interesting to see that Arbey offered a choice of steam-powered or hand-operated machines (*Practical Magazine*, 1875, pp. 207–8). It was only two years later that the well-known London saw millers and timber suppliers, Esdaile's, were advertising the new process. They said that 'veneers can now be cut by the new knife-cutting process whereby all waste is avoided and a product is given of from twenty-eight to one hundred veneers to the inch' (1877).

By 1878 it was claimed that 'knife cut veneers will soon be universally used [as opposed to saw cut], even though the saw cut takes polish better and is more solid' (*Furniture Gazette*, 19 October, p.265). These changing techniques of veneer cutting follow the demands of the trade. With a need for more and cheaper veneers, the benefits of the knife-slicing machine, which produced up to twelve times the number of veneers obtainable from the same log were obvious.

With the development of rotary cutting, the PLYWOOD industry became established. The process allowed a regular-sized sheet of veneer to be available for making up into panels, usually using cheaper non-decorative timbers for the inner plys. The improvements contributed to a cost reduction through central processing and a better use of raw materials, which resulted in the availability of fashionable furniture for a broader market range.

Callahan, J. C. (1990), *The Fine Hardwood Veneer Industry in the United States, 1839–1990*, Lake Ann, Michigan: National Woodlands Publishing Co.
Knight, W. and Wulpi, M. (1927), *Veneers and Plywood*, New York: Ronald Press.

VENEER SUBSTITUTES
Between 1855 and 1865 there were nine patents taken out for veneer substitutes. One of the most promising was Vulcanized rubber or Vulcanite, used to produce veneer. The rubber solution was rolled into thin sheets which could be plain or embossed. These were then dipped into boiling water until they were very flexible and were then applied as veneer. The obvious advantage was that they would cover the sharpest curves and angles (*Furniture Gazette*, 18 August 1877). A year later James Budd devised a method of using a 'varnish' of glass, in place of wood, as a veneer – the object here being to reduce the cost and at the same time produce a high finish that could imitate any other surface type whilst remaining impervious to atmospheres, and so on (*Furniture Gazette*, 16 November 1878). It attracted considerable interest and included the Duke of Norfolk amongst its patrons.
See also Laminates, Plastic, Wood substitutes

Veneering

The basic process of applying veneers to surfaces involves a few simple tools and the requisite materials. There are two traditional methods of hand-laying veneers: by the hammer or by the caul. The hammer method was used for simple flat work with pliable and mild veneers. The process involved the warming of both the veneer and the base, followed by the spreading of glue to both surfaces. The veneer was then rubbed down onto the base and the hammer was applied to the surface, thus removing all the air to obtain a good adhesion. The caul method is based on applying heat and pressure to the veneer in relation to the shape, dimension and form of the base. Sometimes the cauls would be made of sandbags which were especially suitable for round or hollow work, otherwise they would be purpose-built, often out of pinewood, to fit those pieces to be veneered. The pressure required to bond the two parts might be obtained by GO BARS. If the veneered parts were shaped, sand-bags or lead weights were used to hold down the veneer to the base or, if it was a large piece, the use of specially shaped cauls might be required.

These practices which had endured since the 17th century were beginning to be inadequate for the larger volume of furniture being made during the 19th century. As with machine tools, large manufactories used steam power to heat the CAULS which were largely made up from iron boxes with screws and clamps. Shops without steam power used a thick iron plate heated with gas jets in the same way. In contrast, the manual method which involved the prepared panels being put in a press and then held down by planks and poles which abutted against the beams of the workshop, continued to be used.

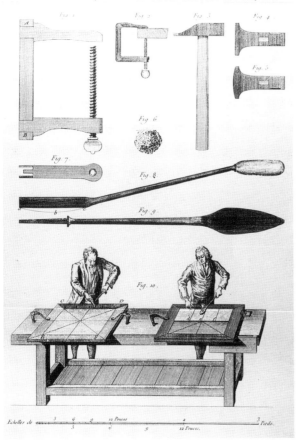

George Bullock had 'a large cast iron plate with iron screws and 2 stoves for drying and laying veneers, faced with lead' (Levy, 1989, p.182).

By the 1860s there were attempts to mechanize the veneering process, either to speed it up or to make it more reliable. Again, the basic processes of the 20th-century industry were devised in the 19th century. The tower press and the vacuum press were two of the most important methods. In 1861 the cabinet-maker Charles Board patented the tower press. His invention used the idea of a stack of presses that were heated and cooled alternately so as to melt the glue and then set it rapidly. In addition to the benefits of speed, the multiple processing of panels was a major advance.

The invention and patenting of a caul, operated by electro-magnets was devised by A. McIvor, a chemist from Edinburgh University. This, in essence, was using the force of the electromagnet to force down the caul onto the surface of the veneer, thus pressing it against its baseboard. McIvor also devised a version of the vacuum-bag method of veneering which used a flexible diaphragm and a steam exhauster to create a vacuum over the work to be veneered, thus creating adhesion. Both these methods obviated the need for the craftsman to apply his own energy.

In addition to the improvements in basic veneering methods, there were other attempts at developing greater decorative possibilities within the veneering process. Many of these were aimed at achieving effects that could not be made with the traditional methods. For ex-

ample, Amies invented the method of veneering in relief, which was intended to represent carved surfaces. It was a process that involved using two moulds, male and female. These moulds were heated and a sheet of veneer was placed between them. The hollow part was filled with a plastic substance and the veneer pasted with paper and then glue. Next, the sandwich was heated again and pressurized, allowing the veneer to take the shape of the mould and thus producing an imitation of a carved surface. When dry, these veneered shapes could be used in any decorative design.

In 1849 John Meadows patented a process which allowed veneer to be continuously carried, without a break or joint, over all forms of curved surfaces or angles. The method was based on a series of cauls hinged together, with screw pressure applied to each part of the gadget. In *The Cabinet-maker's Assistant* it was noted that 'several excellent examples of its efficiency were displayed in the Great Exhibition of 1851'. However, it was also pointed out that: 'This invention seems best adapted for veneering surfaces (of mouldings or other) of such frequent use, and determined form and dimension, as would warrant the preparation of a fixed series of cauls adapted to them' (Blackie, 1853, p.4).

Nonetheless examples continued to be suggested. In 1871 a Birmingham cabinet-maker, J. E. Tysall, patented a method of inlaying by cutting inlay into a carcase, then veneering over the top, and finally carving out the pattern again to reveal the underneath inlay. A similar process, patented in 1875 by two cabinet-makers from Camden Town, J. Thornton and J. Thallon, was used for inlaid marquetry. This rather contradictory name involved the use of relief-cut rollers that impressed the pattern onto the surface, which was then planed level to reveal a marquetry-like design. All these variants on the basic process of veneering illustrate attempts to either copy more expensive methods or to achieve effects that would otherwise be unobtainable. The available evidence does not indicate a great deal of interest from the bulk of the trade, most of these processes remaining specialized and limited.

SPECIAL EFFECTS IN VENEERING

The matching of sliced veneers was recognized early on for its decorative possibilities. As the sliced veneers only slowly change their figuration, they can be used to create patterns themselves by turning them like a book: running them next to each other or at random; cutting them into quarters, diamond quarters or reverse diamonds, herringbones, or diapers, closed squares, butterfly wings, rosettes or diagonal crosses (see Plate VI).
See also: Banding, Book matching, Caul, Composite veneers, Diamond

142 The veneering technique was well known by the 17th century and the basic practice has remained substantially the same as it was then. This plate from Roubo shows the laying of veneer and the tools used.

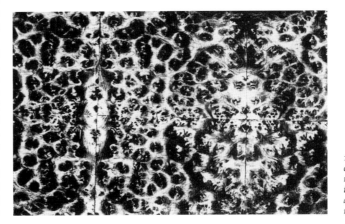

143 The astonishing effects that can be achieved by veneer matching are demonstrated in this example of thuya veneer. It also shows the effect of quarter matching.

matching, Diaper work, Feather banding, Oystering, Sand bag, Sand box, Sand shading, Stringing, Tape joint, Veneers

Hobbs, E. W. (1928), *Modern Furniture Veneering*, London: Lockwood.
— (1934), *Veneering and its Possibilities*, London: Cassell.

Venturine
See Aventurine

Verawood (*Bulnesia arborea*)
A tropical American timber with an olive green to brown colour, imported from Maracaibo in the late 19th century and used as a substitute for LIGNUM VITAE.

Verdigris
Green 'deposit' forming on copper, bronze or brass. The effect can be recreated by applying dilute acetic acid on copper.

Vergier
A measuring stick based on the 'verger' or rod which helped chairmakers to mark out intersections on frames. The French *compas à verge* was a more specialized version.

Vermilion
A textile referred to in the 1654 Ham House inventory (in a chamber, now Mrs Henderson's) as 'a window curtiane of white wrought vermilion'. In addition there was a 'French bedstead with curtaines, valance, counterpoint and all furniture belonging to it of the same', as well as 'two chairs, eight stooles two carpets all of white vermilion' (Thornton and Tomlin, 1980, p.28). It is generally considered to have been made from cotton. Writing about Manchester's trades in 1641, Lewis Roberts noted that 'they buy cotton wool in London that comes from Cyprus and Smyrna, and work that same in to fustians, vermillions and demities which they return to London where they are sold' (cited in Montgomery, 1984, p.372).

Vermilion wood
See Padouk

Vernis des Gobelins
This particular varnishing method which produced a transparent lacquer, was developed at the Gobelins royal workshops around 1713. This varnish was particularly used to lacquer leather and cloth for hangings and upholstery.

Wolvesperges, T. (1995), 'The Royal Lacquer Workshop at the Gobelins, 1713–1757', in *Studies in Decorative Arts*, II, 2, pp.55–76.

Vernis Martin
The lacquering products of the French family Martin were called vernis Martin. This became a generic name for all lacquers produced in France in the 18th century. In 1730 the Martin brothers were granted a patent to manufacture varnish, and this was renewed in 1744 and again in 1753. The *Manufacture Royale des Vernis Martin* was the name of the workshops which were run as a family business, with two younger brothers Robert and Martin Le Jeune joining the business after 1748. Two sons of the elder brothers also joined. All the family members, except one of the younger brothers (Martin Le Jeune) had the title of *Vernisseur du roi* conferred upon them.

The lacquer was based on a COPAL lacquer recipe which was mixed together by melting turpentine, amber, copal, colophony and linseed oil. The time-consuming application method was to give the decor-

ated surface six coats of varnish. These dried and after two or three days were rubbed down with a pumice powder and water mix. Another ten to twelve coats were applied and allowed to dry for up to a week. They were then again rubbed with a water and pumice mix. Another polishing, using emery and water, was then washed off and a final polish was given using rottenstone. An oil rubbing to clean it up was itself cleaned off with wheat flour and cloth.

The technique, similar in appearance to oriental lacquering was produced in a wide range of fashionable colours, from deep red and black, to paler shades, through to whites. From the mid 18th century surfaces were pre-prepared with a sized ground and were then painted with contemporary scenes in the manner of Watteau or Boucher. An antique finish was created by *craquelure*, which simulated the effect of an ageing painting where the paint has dried and cracked in a web form. The final task was to lacquer the whole surface of a piece of furniture. A contemporary description (1753) describes the various options:

> when the pieces [to be decorated] have reached the first state, they are then polished with a file or rasp to prepare them to receive paint: then they may be varnished, colours may be applied either by combining and blending them with varnish … or by applying them in sections in the manner of a checkerboard, or by applying them beneath the polished varnish, or by mixing powders and metal filings with varnish into a paste, which the painter then spreads onto the particular piece.
> (Cited in Dampierre, 1987, p.26)

The reputation of the vernis Martin was so great that in 1759 the English Society for the Encouragement of Arts offered a reward for 'the making one quart at least of the best, most transparent and colourless varnish equal in all respects to Martin's at Paris'.

Crowder, S. (1753), *Genuine Receipt for Making of Famous Vernis Martin*, Paris.
Czarnocka, Anna (1994), 'Vernis Martin, the lacquerwork of the Martin family in eighteenth century France', in *Studies in the Decorative Arts*, Fall, pp.56–73.

Verre églomisé and Under-glass painting
This technique, often used to decorate mirrors, was based on engraving gold leaf, which was applied to glass. The name is derived from Jean-Baptiste Glomy, an 18th-century designer and framer who apparently made frames for prints with this type of decoration. He died in 1786, and it was only in 1825 that his name was given to the process by French archaeologist, Carrand. Although it has this later appellation, the method of decoration was known to the ancient Romans, and was written up in 14th-century Italy by Cennino Cenninni. His working method was to take the glass, and lay a coat of glair (white of egg and water) as a base for the design. This was then covered by gold (or silver) leaf. When it was dry, it was finely engraved, the background removed and the surface then painted in colour. An alternative recipe called for the design, cut into paper, to be placed on a previously varnished glass surface. When the varnish was dry, the paper was moistened and removed. The design was then filled with colour and backed by silver leaf (Barrow, *Dictionarium Polygraphicum*, 1735, (1st edn) vol.1, p.114).

The method was widely employed over Europe and later in America. It was used in German furniture of the 15th and 16th centuries for plaques inserted into furniture cabinets. It was also used for English mirror borders in the early 17th century, often on a blue background. In mid-18th-century France, panels of verre églomisé were sometimes incorporated into cabinets, whilst in Baltimore, Federal furniture and clocks sometimes included oval-shaped glass panels with gold and black allegorical paintings represented in verre églomisé. In the English 'Regency' period the process was sometimes

used to decorate the friezes of mirrors, and in France it was revived in the 1840s as a contrast to the taste for heavy, dark woods. The technique was also used in Russia, particularly for desks, in the late 18th century and early 19th century. It was adopted for large sheets of glass and was incorporated into working furniture (that is, table tops, friezes, pediments and so on), even if it was to withstand heavy use. Simple underglass painting was often used in conjunction with true verre-églomisé work.
See also Glass

Vert antique

A painted or chemically realized effect that imitates the appearance of patinated or corroded bronze castings. The process has also been called bronzing, and *patina antiqua*. The technique was apparently developed in the early 19th century. An 1837 French guide to the techniques of *Bronzage* says that

Bronzing, which forms today one of the bronze manufacturing branches … has only existed as a speciality for forty years, and was not as widespread then as it is today … Up until 1825 only one tint of bronzing was known, which was vert antique which … sought to imitate as closely as possible, bronze exposed to corrosion of the weather … or again like Florentine bronzes, in which the colour was altered by time or interior vapours.
(Cited in Mussey, 1994, p.244)

Apart from patination techniques using powdered metals and lacquers, there were also methods based on gilding practice and varnishing to colour. There was also a wide range of paint and glaze techniques that reproduced the effect of vert antique and bronze or other metals.

Mussey, R. (1994), 'Vert Antique decoration on American furniture', Symposium of Wooden Artifacts group, American Institute for Conservation, Williamsburg, November 1994: Getty Conservation Institute.

Vinhatico (*Plathymenia reticulata*)

A tropical American timber also called Brazilian or yellow mahogany with an average density of 590 (37 lb/cu ft). An orange-yellow colour with variegated streaks, it tones to a deep reddish-brown. Fairly light and soft but durable with a straight or roey grain, and a medium to coarse texture. It was used in a Gillow commission of 1811 when mahogany bookcases with 'Venetico' additions were supplied to Tatton Park (*Furniture History*, 1970, p.25). In the mid 19th century it was said that Vinhatico resembled CANARYWOOD and several yellow woods were called Vinhatico (Blackie, 1853, p.44). Called yellow wood in USA.

Violetwood
See Kingwood, Purpleheart

Virginia walnut
See Walnut (American)

Vulcanite
See Plastics, Veneers

Wadding
Sheets of carded fibres which are needled, bonded or felted onto a textile backing for stuffing and wrapping purposes in upholstery work. Wadding can be made from cotton, wool or man-made fibres. An early English reference to a 'felting machine', devised to prepare ready-made stuffings covered with hessian, was patented by Christopher Nickels in 1841 (Pat.no.9012).

Wainscot
See Oak

Walnut (*Juglans spp.*)
A timber with a greyish-brown background with dark, smoky streaks, but variable in colour, depending upon growing conditions. The most desirable cuts were made to expose dark striated figure sometimes from stumps, burrs and crotches, as well as the roots of the tree. The various names such as English, French (also known as Grenoble), Italian or Circassian, all refer to the one species *Juglans regia*, the trade name being allegedly dependant on origin. Walnut is an ideal furniture timber in many ways as it is easily worked, even grained, strong but relatively light in weight. A very varied grain pattern makes it even more desirable in veneer form.

Its early use in the Elizabethan period can be seen in the Paget inventories of 1552, where six walnut stools were listed. By 1584 the family had a desk, a table and a sealed bed, all in walnut (Wolsey and Luff, 1968, appendix A), and later in the Lumley inventory of 22 May 1590 there were 'chairs and stooles of walnuttre and markatre, fourmes of walnuttre' (Walpole Society, vi, 1918, p.29).

By the early 17th century walnut was clearly a sought-after furniture wood. Francis Bacon in his *Natural History* (1626) declared walnut the best timber for tables, cupboards and desks. Whilst in 1635 Gervase Markham encouraged Englishmen to 'make choyse of the finest walnut-tree you can find … for joyned tables, Cubbords, or Bedsteads' (Markham, *English Husbandmen*, p.57, cited in Forman, 1988, p.3). With the revival of fashionable taste from 1660 onwards, it is not surprising to find Evelyn praising walnut:

In truth were this timber in great plenty amongst us we should have far better utensils of all sorts for our houses, as chairs, stools, bedsteads tables wainscot cabinets etc. instead of the more vulgar beech subject to worm, weak and unsightly; but which to counterfeit and deceive the unwary, they wash over with a decoction made of the green husk of Walnuts. I say had we a store of this material especially of the Virginia, we should find an incredible improvement in the more stable furniture of our houses.
(1662, p.59)

Evelyn also praised the French use of walnut, particularly in inlaying work, which used 'the fine and close timber about the roots which is admirable for fleck'd and chambletted works'. However, European walnut was a victim of fashion. An 1776 edition of Evelyn's *Silva* noted that 'formerly the walnut tree was much propagated for its wood, but since the importation of mahogany and the Virginia walnut it has considerably decreased its reputation'.

In the early 19th century it was noted that 'mahogany has now nearly superseded its [walnut's] use in furniture' (Nicholson, P. and M., 1826, p.61), but twenty-five years later in France Nosban (1843) noted that it rivalled mahogany (Viaux-Loquin, 1997, p.142). During the 1870s to 1880s walnut-veneered bedroom furniture found favour again in England, and it has fluctuated in popularity as a tasteful furniture timber ever since.

African walnut (*Lovoa trichilioides*)
A hardwood from tropical West Africa with an average density of 560 (35 lb/cu ft), it is bronze to orange-brown with gum lines, causing black streaks, with the grain producing a ribboned, striped effect in many examples when quarter-sawn. It is not a true walnut but a member of the mahogany family. It is difficult to work due to spiral grain, but is more resistant to fungi than European versions. Widely used for cabinet work and veneers. Aka Tigerwood (US name).

American walnut (*Juglans Nigra*)
A timber derived from the Eastern USA with an average density of 620 (39 lb/cu ft). It has a fine figure and rich purple-brown colour which has made this timber a useful cabinet wood. It has excellent working properties and takes polish well. Moderately hard and more difficult to work than the European variety, it also supplies highly valued veneers coming from crooks, burrs, forks and stumps. Also known as black or Virginia walnut, it is a little darker than the European version and was imported into England during the 17th century. In 1630 William Strachey, First Secretary of Jamestown, wrote to London explaining American walnut's qualities:

of walnutts there be three kindes, the black walnutt, which is returned home yearly by all shipping from thence and yields good profit, for it is well bought up to make waynscott, tables, cubbordes, chairs and stools of a delicate grayne and cullour like ebonie, and not subject to the worms.
(Cited in Forman, 1988, p.31)

In the first half of the 17th century Virginia walnut was clearly fashionable. King Charles I owned 'one oval folding table of spotted virginia wood' (possibly burr?) (Jervis, 1989, p.287). English importations of black walnut exceeded those of European walnut for much of the 18th century as a consequence of the Naval Stores Act 1721. However, by the early 19th century Sheraton recorded that 'the black Virginia was much in use for cabinet work forty to fifty years since in England but is now quite laid aside since the introduction of mahogany' (1803, p.331). However, in the mid 19th century there was a revived demand for American walnut for the interior parts of cabinet work which was to be veneered on the outside with the more expensive European walnut. In the mid 19th century it was also imported as a substitute for the rarer European timbers. Importations of black walnut had been considerable, even though one commentator considered that 'in quality it is decidedly inferior to that of European growth … It is, however, serviceable when wrought in the solid, for the inferior parts of articles of which the principle parts are to be veneers with finer wood and for chairs, couches, pillars, brackets, balls and the like' (Blackie, 1853, p.23). However, large root boles, stored in dung heaps for a considerable time, apparently produced beautiful specimen veneers which were highly valued.

Throughout the 18th century black walnut was favoured for American side-chair frames, and around the 1860s to 1870s it was a popular timber for medium- to high-grade Chicago furniture, as it was easily obtained from Indiana and Ohio. This demand had the effect of clearing supplies, and costs went up as sourcing went further afield.

By the 20th century Boulger noted that 'Before the middle of the 19th century it was only used in England for carcase ends, frames for veneering, and other inferior purposes; it has now increased four-fold in price, and is more used than European wood, its uniform colour recommending it to shop-fitters and as a basis for painted or other ornamentation in the cabinet trade' (1908, p.295). In the 20th century it has been used extensively for library, office and dining room furniture, as well as for fittings in buildings.

Australian or Queensland walnut (*Endiandra palmerstonii*)
It has an average density of 740 (46 lb/cu ft) and is a variable brown colour with pinky overtones and striped figure, sometimes with a grey cast. The grain is often interlocked, giving a chequered or striped effect when cut on the quarter. It is difficult to work, although more lustrous and slightly heavier than true walnut, and is recognized as a high-quality timber for cabinet work, veneers and marquetry. It was introduced into England around the period 1924–5, and has been used in the USA for bedroom and dining suites. Queensland walnut is not a true walnut, although it posseses many of the characteristics. Aka Orientalwood (USA).

Black Sea or Circassian walnut
A finely figured species with an open grain.

Burr walnut
These are the excrescences found on the trunks of walnut trees that provide highly decorative veneers.

Butternut (*Juglans cinera*)
See Butternut

East Indian walnut
See Kokko

Italian walnut
Southern European timber of good quality, light brown with darker stripes. In the 1920s it was expensive due to the amount of sapwood waste.

Satin walnut
See American red gum

South American walnut (*Juglans neotropica*)
A South American timber with an average density of 640 (40 lb/cu ft). It has a coarse texture, a variable grain, and its striped veneers are highly prized.

Jakway, B. G. (1939), *The Story of American Walnut*, American Walnut Manufacturers Assoc.: Chicago.

Washed flock
A woollen filling material used by upholsterers and mattress makers. Washed flock contains not less than 50 per cent wool, either old or new.

Water beds
See Coated fabrics

Water colour finish
A finishing treatment known in the 19th century to give an ornamental effect to furniture at an inexpensive price. The method was simply a process of painting-in a design that, when dry, was polished over to make it permanent. One of the problems associated with buying this type of painted furniture was spelt out: 'In order to meet the great desire for cheapness, cabinet-makers give a coat of size to such articles as they wish to paint and upon this a coat of water-colour of any required shade' (*Hints on Houses and House Furnishings*, 1851, p.5). The purpose of this process was to allow the colour to dry on the surface, which was then varnished and appeared as good as japan. Only when the varnish wore off and the paint soon followed, did the cheapness of the process reveal itself.

Water gilding
See Gilding

Water seasoning
See Seasoning

Water stain
See Stains

Wave moulding
See Mouldings

Wax
See Polish

Wax inlaying
The inlaying of MASTIC in brass has been recorded in furniture of the second quarter of the 18th century. This appears to have demonstrated an attempt to create an imitation of tortoiseshell or exotic timbers set with brass.

Wax polish
See Polish

Weathered oak
A decorative finishing process which used a weak caustic soda and lime mix brushed onto the surface. This was allowed to dry and then cleaned off and finished with a wax or lacquer. Oak is acidic, so the effect of the alkali was to darken it.

Web strainer
A bat-shaped implement used by upholsterers to strain webbing on a seat frame. It may have an aperture and a dowel to hold a loop of webbing, or it may be made with a rebated end and a metal strap which holds the webbing tight.

Webbing
A closely woven narrow fabric used in the foundation of upholstery. The webbing may be used to give shape and support to a chair or sofa frame, seat or back, support a spring platform, or it may be tensioned to support loose cushions or to build up a drop-in seat. The principle of webbing is that it should be resilient and not stretched as tightly as possible.

The earliest webbing was known as girth web, the word coming from the girth straps that were used to attach saddles and so on onto an animal. The webbing was woven by girth weavers, which was a branch of narrow weaving (see Randle Holme quote in UPHOLSTERY). First recorded in 1381–2, its use in chair-work was recorded in 1582

when Thomas Grene, a COFFERER, was paid for 'bottoming double girth webb and work' (Beard, 1997, p.284). Its use for bed supports was later recorded in 1634 when Sir Thomas Herbert noted that 'The better sort sleep upon cots or beds two foot high, matted, or done with girth web' (*Travels*, p.149). Since the 16th century the supporting system for upholstery has been based on varieties of webbing laid across the seat cavity of a chair or sofa frame. The Upholders' Company Byelaws of 1679 refer to the fact that 'all chaires, stoles, cowches and squabb whatsoever they be made of shall be cross girt in the bottome with new sailcloth being made to be put on sale by any person using the trade of an Upholder' (cited in Houston, 1993, p.58). Its application may be either by the so-called French webbing method, using *c*.10 cm (4 in) wide web which is close fitted and completely covers the base, or English web *c*.5 cm (2 in) wide which is used to create a more open criss-cross mesh. Both these methods are used worldwide.

Webbing can be made from natural materials including linen, jute or cotton, or in the 20th century from synthetics such as reinforced rubber or polypropylene. The nature of the yarns used in making the web is often a useful indicator of age and history of some upholstered furniture. For example, fibre analysis would indicate that if the yarn was cotton the web was made in the 20th century, if made of jute, it would be post 1830, and if of either flax or hemp it is likely to have been made prior to that date. The method of weaving is also an indicator. Initially, before 1700, webbing was made in a plain weave, which was fairly open and irregular. By 1800 the texture was more dense. From the beginning of the 19th century a twill weave was introduced, as plain weave was being derided as cheap. A distinction also existed in the 20th century between English and Scottish webbing (superior) and Belgian or Continental (for use in less strained areas, such as backs and arms of work).

Best black and white
A reference to the black and white herringbone pattern that is a feature of high-grade webbing.

Jute webbing
A less expensive, but more resilient form of webbing for upholstery introduced in the 19th century.

Plastic webbing
The use of 'webbing' made from polypropylene or similar (Fabweb) has been adopted for hammock-shaped chairs and chairs designed for outdoor use.

Rubber webbing
The use of rubber for upholstery suspensions was patented in England by Auguste Fournier (Pat.no.2080) in July 1862 for 'webs of vulcanised rubber interlaced and fixed to framework'. In 1877 vulcanized 'Indiarubber springs' were used by George Sims in his Sybarite patented folding chairs. Apart from these isolated examples of use, elastic webs had to wait until the reinforced rubber webbing that was developed in 1948 by the Pirelli company. In 1950 they set up a company called Arflex to develop foam-rubber furniture. Marco Zanuso was commissioned to develop the potential of the conjunction of foam and rubber webbing in upholstery. The rubber webbing was designed to be fixed to wood or metal frames, so it was versatile enough to be hidden within traditional seating, or it could be used as a revealed support in a minimal design. According to Zanuso the exciting possibilities of the new materials were such that 'one could revolutionise not only the system of upholstery but also structural, manufacturing, and formal potential' (Bangert, 1988, p.33).

The combined advances of latex cushions and rubber webbing were

144   An example of an English chair frame, webbed ready for springing, c.1950.

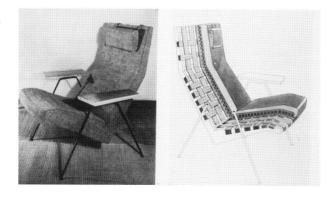

related to the design developments of popular chairs and sofas in the 1950s onward. The show-wood frame, which echoed a Scandinavian ideal of open-plan living in which cabinets and upholstery were related in timber type, was extremely popular. Even if traditional-style suites were required, the new materials meant that they could be produced at a lower cost and faster pace than the original built-up support system (see Plate XXIII).

Steel webbing
Steel bars measuring 2 cm (¾ in), plain, perforated or corrugated and punched so springs may be easily fitted. Cheaper upholstered furniture used this webbing method.

Milne, E. C. (1983), *History of the Development of Furniture Webbing*, private print, Leeds.
— (1984), 'Development of English webbing', in *Antique Collecting*, May, pp.8–12.

Webbing (blued) tacks
See Tacks

Wedge
A wedge is a small cut of timber used to hold legs firmly into chair seats. When working with selected green wood, which shrinks but does not warp, this form of fixing is enough to give stability. The wedges used in the High Wycombe area of England were split out with a hatchet and then finished with a draw SHAVE. This gave stability as the splitting followed the grain of the tree. Later saw-cut versions were prone to breakage as there was no account taken of the grain structure.

Wedging
A form of construction that uses WEDGES of wood to hold legs into holes or similar.
See Construction (wedged)

Weights
A useful component of various furniture objects, especially patent, adjustable or metamorphic furniture. They were provided by the plumber as they were chiefly made from lead. The main use of weights was as a counterbalance. For example, Chippendale made a metamorphic desk for Edwin Lascelles in 1772, in which 'the front of the secretary [was made] to rise with ballance weights' (Gilbert, 1978, p.206). Sheraton, discussing a dressing glass, noted that 'the weights are suspended sometimes to tambour glued on to webbing' (1793, Appendix, Plate XVII). As a component of 'metamorphic' furniture, they were also useful to facilitate rise and fall mechanisms. The 1798

patent of Day Gunby for 'entire new weights, bolts, and springs' was intended to operate 'all kinds of desks, tables, chairs, stools, tambour frames, bedstead and various articles' (Pat.no.2248).

Welding
A method of joining two or more metal pieces together. Welding is a major part of the assembly process of metal furniture. There are three main systems: fusion welding, forge welding and gas welding. In fusion welding, the edges of the two pieces to be joined are heated to melting point and then brought together. In forge welding, the parts to be joined are heated to molten temperature and then they are hammered together to fuse. This is the oldest form and was in use up to the latter part of the 19th century. The electrical processes were gradually introduced from about 1877. In gas welding (oxyacetylene) an intensely hot flame heats the welding rods, which are placed at the joins to be made, so that the rods melt and fuse the pieces together. Arc welding uses the arcing of electricity between the metals to be welded and an electrode generating heat. In spot welding, the metals are fixed between two electrodes so that, when a current is passed, they heat and fuse. Electronic and laser beam welding are now common in industry.

Wenge (*Millettia laurentii*)
A Central African (Zaire) timber with an average density of 880 (55 lb/cu ft), introduced in the 20th century. It has a dark brown heartwood and very close black veins. It is straight-grained, with a coarse texture, and is used for decorative veneers and turnery. During the 1960s to 1970s it was particularly popular in Europe for cabinet-making.

West Indian satinwood
See Satinwood

Western hemlock (*Tsuga heterophylla*)
A timber from the western seaboard of North America, but also grown in the United Kingdom. It has an average density of 500 (31 lb/cu ft), with a lightish yellow colour which deepens to warm brown. It has a straight grain. Used for hidden carcase parts such as drawers and backs of cabinets, or for furniture which is to be painted or stained.

Western red cedar (*Thuja plicata*)
From British Colombia and northern west USA. It has an average density of 370 (23 lb/cu ft), a red-brown heartwood with a yellow sapwood, and is straight-grained with a rather coarse texture. This is not a true cedar and is not widely used in furniture.

Wheel mechanisms
The fitting of wheels to furniture in order to provide mobility, usually for furniture that is intended to be moved beyond the confines of a room, has been used for special-purpose furniture for centuries. In particular, wheels have been fitted to chairs and beds intended for invalid use, and more recently to dinner wagons and trolleys.
See also Castors

White mahogany
See Prima vera

White pine
See Yellow pine

Whitebeam (*Sorbus aria*)
A European timber with an average density of 720 (45 lb/cu ft). It is pinkish-grey to brown with dark streaks, with a uniform texture and a straight grain. Reasonably hard and heavy, it is used for turnery and carving. Known as *bois d'alisier* in French 18th-century marquetry. Aka Alisia wood.

Whitesmith
A worker in white metal, usually TIN. The whitesmith finishes and polishes work and is not involved in heavy founding.

Whitewood
A name applied to Norway SPRUCE.
See also Basswood, Canarywood, Tulip-tree

Wicker
Strictly speaking, wicker is a particular form of basketry work in which the general shape of the object is produced by a warp of stiff rods, called stake frames. The word appears to derive from the old Swedish word *vika* meaning to bend. It is now a generic term that embraces a number of natural materials that have, at various times been made into furniture by weaving processes. It is usually made from whole or split rods of WILLOW (withy), called osiers, using techniques based on basketry, but other materials used include CANE, FIBRE-RUSH, RATTAN, REED and STRAW.

Wicker is one of the oldest materials that have been in constant use. Wicker furniture was known in Ancient Egypt from *c.*3000 BC, and existing examples, such as the Thebes chests in Cairo, show techniques that have not altered in over five thousand years. In the Roman Empire, wicker was clearly a popular medium for furniture, as basket-like, tub-shaped wickerwork chairs appear on a number of stone reliefs. An interesting item noted from 1374 was a wicker chest covered with leather (Eames, 1977, p.115). Without doubt, it remained a useful material for vernacular furniture and was certainly widespread by the 16th century. The establishment of the Company of Basket-makers in the City of London in 1569 is an indication of the growing importance of the trade.

During the 17th century, wicker chairs were common all over Europe, sometimes with arms and often with a hooded back to improve stability. Dutch genre paintings of interiors sometimes show the 'bakermat', a special wicker seat designed for nursing, which was made with a long trough in front to allow the swaddling process to be completed easily. Wicker was also widely used for cradles, bird-cages, screens and other items, depending on the region. The terms 'twiggen', 'basket' and 'wicker' became interchangeable in the 16th and 17th centuries. John Evelyn mentions the use of willow osiers for all 'wicker and twiggie work' (1664, p.42) and Randle Holme's talks of 'Twiggen chaires because they are made of Owsiers and Withen twigs' (1649, II, xiv, p.14). These forms of chairs remained popular at local levels well into the 19th century. Wicker was also widely used for hooded chairs, for children's commode chairs, as well as for other applications such as venting sides for cabinets and, later, for invalid carriages.

In America, during the 17th century, settlers often brought wicker furniture as well as the techniques with them. Although by the 18th century wicker was considered an inferior medium for furniture, in the 19th century it experienced a massive revival when wicker furniture was designed both for indoor and outdoor use. Wicker furniture met a very wide range of criteria, thus making it acceptable to various consumer groups. For designer reformers for example, its simple material, which was generally left natural or at worst stained, together with its obvious, revealed construction, were important markers of honesty. Rather than being applied to the surface, ornamental designs could be woven into the material and become an integral part of the furniture. From a stylistic point of view, the material lent itself to a wide range of designs, and it could be decorated as extravagantly as required. This included loose cushions, ribbons and bows, drapes and lace, and by the end of the century they were also being painted and upholstered. More importantly, the general public's growing awareness of sanitation and health issues saw wicker as a natural, clean material, synonymous with country living and good health, which may be confirmed by wicker's associations with baby carriages and invalid chairs. Lastly, the growth of a market for furniture designed to be used in a summer setting, either in the garden or in a conservatory, encouraged lightweight, easy-to-handle suites for which rattan was an ideal material. Various new models were designed, the croquet chair for example had a wicker frame, a button back, a long seat, a wrap-around back and an integral arm. WILLOW was also used in combination with rattan to create a range of decorative and comfortable chairs in the 1870s and 1880s. By the turn of the century, wicker furniture was being enjoyed all over Europe.

The material was also adopted by Modernist designers. Mies van der Rohe's bent metal chair and the British Pel chairs often used wicker in conjunction with tubular steel. Other manufacturers met the following demand for less expensive models. Inevitably, attempts at cost reductions in the weaving process led to a change in design from the tightly-woven (closed) to the looser, open styles, which in turn may have opened up a gap in the market for inexpensive, closely woven models – a gap that was easily filled by LLOYD LOOM.

The wider popularity of these materials coincided with the post-World War II interest in open-plan interiors and the lighter-weight furniture required for them. Examples can be found all over Europe and the USA. In this period three techniques were employed to provide a variety of styles and cost brackets. The first of these was the fully woven, where the warp is the frame; the second where thicker canes making a frame were tied together at intervals, and the third where multiple loops of cane were fitted into the frame and tied or pinned to the framework and bound at intervals. It remains popular.

146   Wicker is one of the earliest furniture-making materials. This relief sculpture from c. AD 235 demonstrates the sophisticated type of wicker chair that was in use in Roman times.

147 *The development of wood-substitutes was related to the expansion of the market for furniture. By the later 19th century there were many types of substitute available. The Ligline carved decoration, c.1910, made by the Ornamental Products company of Detroit, was one of the more successful types.*

See also Art fibre, Cane, Lloyd Loom, Matted seats, Osiers, Reed, Straw, Twiggen, Willow

Adamson, Jeremy (1993), *American Wicker: Woven Furniture from 1850 to 1930*, New York: Rizzoli.
Bobart, H. H. (1911), *Records of the Basket-makers' Company*, Dunn Colling: London.
Corbin, P. (1978), *All About Wicker*, New York: E. P. Dutton.
Curtis, Lee (1991), *Lloyd Loom: Woven Fibre Furniture*, London: Salamander.
Di Noto, A. (1984), 'Presence of wicker', in *Connoisseur*, 214, June, 78–85.
Edlin, H. (1949), *Woodland Crafts in Britain*, London: Batsford, pp.100–14.
Freese, E. (1867), *Zeichnungen für Korbmacher und Korbmöbel Fabrikanten*, Kiel.
Heywood Bros (1982), *Heywood Bros and Wakefield Company. Classic Wicker Furniture. The Complete 1898–99 Catalogue*, New York: Dover.
Heywood Co (1926), *Heywood-Wakefield and Co. A Completed Century 1826–1926*, Boston: The Company.
Kirkham, Pat (1985), 'Willow and cane furniture in Austria, Germany and England c.1900–1914', in *Furniture History*, XXI, pp.121–31.
— (1985), 'Dryad cane furniture', in *Antique Collecting*, February, pp.11–13.
— (1986), *Harry Peach: Dryad and DIA*, London: Design Council.
Ottilinger, Eva (1990), *Korbmöbel*, Salzburg: Residenz Verlag.
Saunders, Richard (1976), *Collecting and Restoring Wicker Furniture*, New York: Crown Publishers.
Scott, Tim (1990), *Fine Wicker Furniture 1870–1930*, West Chester PA: Schiffer Publishing.
Thompson, F. (1978), *The Complete Wicker Book, the History of Wicker Furniture and Accessories From Antique to Modern*, Des Moines: W H Books.

Wild service
See Service wood

Willow (*Salix alba*)
A European timber with an average density of *c*.400–80 (25–30 lb/cu ft). It has white to pinkish colourings, a fine even texture and a straight grain which takes a polish well. When cut into veneers, it often produces a moiré effect. It was used for bed frames in Ancient Rome (Ovid Metam, viii, 656) and was also apparently well-adapted for luxurious reclining chairs. Pliny writes:

other willows throw out osiers of remarkable thinness, adapted by their suppleness and graceful slenderness for the manufacture of wicker-work. While from a whiter willow the bark is peeled off, and being remarkably tractable … is also found particularly useful in the construction of those articles of luxury, reclining chairs.
(Pliny, xvi, 37/668 174)

It is the raw material of WICKER, for which purpose it is grown on OSIER beds. The thinner pieces are used as rods for weaving, the thicker ones as stakes for the framework, and when split they are known as skeins which are used for binding. Boiling the rods allows the bark colour to stain the twigs. Loudon recorded how FANCY CHAIRS 'are first caned and then covered in patterns with willow (split willow rods) of different colours, produced by staining, so as to very successfully imitate various kinds of woods' (1839, p.1061). In the 19th century, skeined willow was made by splitting it into regular strands, which was then used for seating by High Wycombe chair companies.
See also Wicker

Windsor chair-maker
See Chair-makers

Windsor chair-making
See Chair-making

Wiremesh
A decorative component of furniture, often made from BRASS which is used most commonly for facing doors. 'In any commode or cabinets which have a part of their ornaments gilded, wire suits well with it' (Sheraton, 1803, pp.332–3).

Wirework
See Brass, Iron, Steel

Wood square
An important 'tool' for the cutting out of upholstery and drapery materials. When material is placed on the CUTTING-OUT BOARD, the front edge is brought level and the tool can then square the material across with great accuracy. Bitmead suggested that it should 'be made of old, seasoned mahogany, and be about 4ft. in the blade and 20 in. in the stem. These squares can be made by any cabinet-maker, or indeed joiner, for they are not generally stocked at tool-shops' (1912, p.7).

Wood substitutes
Although there had been attempts to produce some wood substitutes prior to the 19th century, it was during this period that developments grew rapidly. The search for a reliable and consistent material that could be easily worked was a clear response to the rising demand for decorative furniture. In particular this related to CARVING work. In the early 19th century there was difficulty in obtaining good carvers, so it is not surprising that when a demand occurred substitutes were developed. Nicholson mentions casting ornaments or mouldings using fine glue, and fine sawdust or wood raspings which can then form a paste (1826, p.3). This was then inserted into an oiled mould, packed tight and weighted. When dry it could be fixed to the appropriate surface. The same formula is given for cement-stopping, used to stop up defects in hardwoods.

The nature of these materials and the intentions of the makers are obvious in a rider to the trade catalogue of O. A. Nathusius of New York, a producer of patented artificial wood ornaments. They said that 'No provision is made for screws, as they [the ornaments] are designed more especially for a cheaper class of work and are intended to be attached in the simplest manner by glue and brads' (1877, Henry Francis du Pont, Winterthur Library Collection).

During the 19th century, as can be seen by the large number of patents that were taken out for this category, interest in the possibilities of wood substitutes was strong. Between 1855 and 1876 there were 68 English patents relating to wood substitutes. Most of the wood substitutes attempted to use wood waste combined with chemicals to produce a paste that could be moulded and then set. The processes varied from chipped wood, boiled in caustic soda and then pressed and rolled (Pat.no.112), to wood pieces ground down on a grindstone, then mixed with water and moulded under pressure (Pat.no.217). Others were more exotic: In 1852 a Mr Pidding patented an amalgam of coal, peat, shrubs, shells, bark and other materials, which was mixed with glue and carbonized (Pat.no.13911). In the same year Moses Poole patented 'Improvements in the manufacture of tables, sofas, bedsteads etc.' His improvement was based on producing a hard substance from India rubber and sulphur with or without other materials. The resulting product was then intended to be either made into veneer for wooden frames or wrapped around iron-framed furniture (Pat.no.14299). As can be seen from this last patent, not all these materials were meant to be used as a substitute for solid wood.

Developments of the basic method of producing artificial wood were devised by Harrass of Thuringen. In 1883 a report on his process mentioned the recipe as including sawdust, animal blood, ground wood and glutinous flour. The process involved placing this mixture into metal moulds to produce the requisite shapes. It was different from BOIS DURCI in that it had pasteboard applied to its underside to give a regular base for fixing, and the possibility of veneering the face of the object was included. With the advent of PLASTICS in the early 20th century, these sorts of substitutes were gradually replaced.
See also Bois durci, Composition, Particle board, Veneer substitutes

Wood wool
See Excelsior, Pine state hair

Wool
(a) The scoured and washed virgin sheep's wool which has been used as an upholstery and bedding filling. It may be used pure or as an ingredient in WOOLLEN FLOCK and its varieties.

(b) Animal wool that has been spun into yarn. The two main distinctions being between wool and worsted. The latter is tightly spun from long staple fibres, ensuring a more parallel arrangement in the yarn creating a finer cloth.

Woollen flock
A filling material used by upholsterers and mattress-makers and once considered superior. In 1474 the Mistery of Upholders (sic) petitioned the Lord Mayor of London against the use of 'imitation flock' by complaining about 'mattresses stuffed with hair and flocks and sold for flocks … cushions stuffed with hair and sold for flocks which have been deceivably made to the hurt of the King's liege people' (Houston, 1993, p.5). Sheraton recorded it as 'a kind of wool used by upholsterers for mattrasses' (1803, p.210). Used in the 20th century, it should be not less than 70 per cent wool obtained from the finishing processes of newly woven, felted or knitted woollen textiles. 'Washed flock' contains not less than 50 per cent wool, either old or new. 'Washed woollen mixture' contains 70 per cent animal fibre, whether old or new. Flock can use recycled, shredded wool cloth which is often matted into a felt. The difference between 'carded' flock and 'ground or pulled' flock is self-evident. In 1949 it was noted that there are 'various graduations, ending in the veriest rubbish, composed of old woollen cloths, rugging, and rags of different kinds which are torn to pieces

and cleaned by powerful machinery, and rendered fit for the purpose of stuffing' (Bitmead, 1949, p.16).

Wormy chestnut
See Chestnut

Worsted damask
See Damask

Woven paper
See Lloyd Loom

Wrought iron
See Iron

Wych elm
See Elm

Xulopyrography
A more involved process than pyrography or POKER WORK. It was a process of carving or engraving into a charred wood surface so that the shading of colours resulting from variations in the depth of cutting could be graduated to suit the design.
See also Burned wood-carving, Poker work

Xylography
In the 19th century a craze for pseudo-scientific names for wood treatments and finishes abounded. The prefix xylo- (Greek for wood) was adopted by a number of inventors for their particular processes. Xylography, which was a grain printing operation, was one of the most widely reported of these processes. It was first noted in January 1869 (*Society of Arts Journal*, pp.155–9). The technique was based on the simple idea of taking a decorative wood board and applying a coat of oil paint to it. A paper sheet was then rolled over this and the print was transferred to the paper. It was then a matter of rolling the print onto the inferior surface. Further developments occurred in October 1873, with the granting of a patent to Thomas Whitburn of Guildford for his process of printing decorative designs on wood (Pat.no.48). The process used the idea of engravings or electrotypes which were printed onto a wood surface using a printing press.

In 1877 there appeared a series of advertisements for the process, developed by Whitburn and Young. These, along with the fact that the process was exhibited at the Paris Exhibition of 1878, could indicate some commercial success. Thomas Paterson noted in 1878:

> that among the specimens [of xylography] are some panels of pine with representations of flowers and leaves, in which the natural brilliancy of the wood is not deadened by any process of dyeing. This greatly heightens the effect produced, and if the process is a cheap one, as one would suppose it should be, it might become a very valuable addition to the means at the disposal of the decorator or cabinet-maker.
> (Paris, p.390)

Xylonite
An early plastic used widely for inlays and marquetry. As an ivory substitute, it was called ivorine.

Xylotechnography
Developed by the 19th-century British firm Trollope and Sons, this decorative process involved staining wooden surfaces with transparent colours to achieve an effect similar to inlaying. It was sometimes used in order to achieve an effect of inlaid ebony and ivory.

148 *The technique of xylotechnography, which imitated the inlay of ebony and ivory, enjoyed a fashion in the 1870s. This cabinet was displayed at the London 1871 exhibition by the inventors, Trollope and Sons of London.*

Yacca wood (*Podocarpus coriacea*)
A timber from an evergreen tree of Jamaica, sold in short crooked pieces 10–30 cm (4–12 in) thick. In the mid 19th century it was used in England for cabinet, marquetry work and turning (Holtzapffel, 1846, p.109). It was still recommended as a cabinet wood in 1894. Aka Yacher.

Yellow birch
See Birch (Canadian)

Yellow meranti
See Meranti

Yellow pine
See Pine

Yellow wood
See Fustic, Poplar, Vinhatico (USA)

Yew (*Taxus baccata*)
A European softwood timber, with an average density of 670 (42 lb/cu ft). It produces figured golden orange to reddish-brown heart wood with a contrasting light-coloured sapwood with occasional streaks. It is a tough, close-grained but relatively easily worked timber. Sometimes the trunk is composed of vertical shoots that have fused together with air spaces, hence clean planks above 20 cm (8 in) or so are difficult to obtain. This feature and the contrasting heart and sapwood often create a decorative effect. In some cases furniture, especially table tops, has been made to take advantage of this natural phenomenon. Yew may also produce attractive BURRS which were used in veneer for knife boxes and caddies. It bends very well and is always associated historically with generations of English bowmen. It is superb for CHAIR-MAKING and is also ideal for TURNING and takes a good polish.

It was used in ancient furniture for 'the ornamental work attached to chests, footstools and the like' (cited in Richter, 1966, p.124). In the 17th century it was used by turners for knobs and spindles, and by cabinet-makers for veneers and parquetry. After the Restoration it was employed in solid and veneer, and it continued to be used for various items throughout the 18th century. Evelyn recorded how 'by the seasoning and divers manners of cutting, vigorous infolation, politure and grinding, the roots of this tree (or of even our common and neglected thorn) do furnish the inlayer and cabinet-maker with pieces rarely undulated and full of variety' (1662, p.156). It was especially suited to chairs, including Windsor chairs. In 1775 it was noted that 'the [yew] wood is in less estimation than formerly, but it still give a high price to the cabinet-maker' (William Boutcher, 1775, *Treatise on Forest Trees*, Edinburgh, cited in Symonds, 'Furniture of yew wood', *Old Furniture*, July 1929, pp.5–16).

During the early 19th century in France and England it was revived as a decorative veneer, in place of restricted imported timbers. Loudon noted that yew was

universally allowed to be the finest wood for cabinet-making purposes. Tables made of yew, when the grain is fine, according to Gilpin, are more beautiful than tables of mahogany, and the colour of its root is said to vie with the ancient citron [thuya]. It is generally employed in the form of veneers and for inlaid work.
(Loudon, 1844, p.946)

By 1908 it was noted that 'Yew is employed to some extent at High Wycombe and Worksop in chair-making and on the Continent in turnery' (Boulger, 1908, p.301). In recent years it has been used for reproduction furniture in 18th-century styles.

Zante
See Fustic

Zebrano (*Microberlinia biscilata*)
A West African timber with an average density of 740 (46 lb/cu ft). It has a golden yellow to pale brown hardwood with streaks of brown, deepening to a black hue. Its coarse texture and interlocked grain, when cut into quartered surfaces, create zebra-like stripes which have been used for cabinet work occasionally. Aka zebra wood.

Zebrawood (*Astronium fraxinifolium*)
A timber with an average density of 940 (59 lb/cu ft). It is reddish-brown with dark stripes, with a close texture which planes and polishes well. Derived mainly from Honduras and Brazil (occasionally from Asia), it was used in the late 18th century for cross-banded bor-

ders or occasionally as an all-surface veneer (for example, Gillows). Its figure is very obtrusive and was often used in combination with 'quieter' timbers. Sheraton noted its extreme scarcity in 1803, but large-scale importations began in 1808 with the opening of direct trade with Brazil. In 1830, zebrawood was proclaimed as 'the produce of a large tree, and we receive it in logs of two feet wide. It is a cheap wood and is employed in large work [such] as tables' (Knight, 1830). In 1846 'the zebrawood is considered by upholsterers to be intermediate in general appearance between mahogany and rosewood so as to form a pleasing contrast with either of them' (Holtzapffel, 1846, p.110). In the 1850s, it was noted that zebrawood 'has long been extensively used in the manufacture of drawing room furniture, for which, in apartments that are imperfectly lighted, its smart and garish colouring renders it peculiarly suitable' (Blackie, 1853, p.27). By the early 20th century it was only used for veneers and bandings. The name zebrawood is no longer accepted: it is now known as GONCALO ALVES. Sometimes known also as TIGERWOOD (USA) or Andaman MARBLEWOOD (*Diospyros marmorata*).

Zettawood

A timber from British Guiana which is a fine close-grained, hard and heavy wood which is described by Bitmead as 'a beautiful wood of a bright-red chestnut colour, with small peculiar black particles, mostly isolated though occasionally concurrent. This is used for various ornamental purposes, and for small fancy cabinet-work nothing excels it' (1901, p.133).

Zinc

A hard, bluish-white brittle metal, also known as spelter, which is a component of BRASS alloy. Used in the 18th century for lining cupboards of sideboards and pedestals as a warming compartment. During the 19th century, zinc was used in a number of furniture applications, both as decoration for INLAY work and as a construction material.

Another use was to take advantage of the hollow-casting process discovered in 1833. For example, the Austrian firm of Kitschelt exhibited a table cast in zinc at the 1851 Great Exhibition, in London. In PAPIER MACHE work, thin lines of sheet-zinc were used for stringing, in conjunction with mother-of-pearl. A particular inlay process was devised in 1883 that forced a pre-determined pattern of zinc sheet into a wooden surface by means of heavy pressure:

Here the thin slices of wood are glued fast to board, and on it is placed a piece of zinc, in which has been punched a scroll or other design. This metal plate is somewhat thicker than the sheet of wood. The whole board is then submitted to a roller which forces the metal into the surface of the veneer, which is then planed until the zinc itself is reached. This is of course forming a pattern which has been fairly squeezed into the surface of the solid wood.
(Mateaux, 1883, p.153)

Zinc-plated components have occasionally been used for fittings in 20th-century furniture. When a surface is coated with zinc dust by a heating process, it may be described as sheradized.

Zips

Although first developed and patented in 1851, it was only in 1893 that a commercial application of the slide fastener was produced, and it was not until 1913 that Gideon Sundback patented the familiar zip that has been the basis of all modern developments. They are now a key component in 20th-century upholstery, especially for the fixing of cushion covers onto feather, foam or latex interiors, as well as for loose covers.

Bibliography

PRIMARY SOURCES

Ackermann, R. (1809–28), *The Repository of Arts*, London:
R. Ackermann.

Amman, J. and Sachs, H. (1568), *The Book of Trades (Standebuch)*, (New
Introduction by B. A. Rifkin), New York: Dover, reprint 1973.

Anon. (1747), *A General Description of all Trades*, London: T. Waller.

Anon. (1778), *Valuable Secrets Concerning Arts and Trades*, Dublin:
J. Williams.

Anon. (1818), *Cabinet-makers' Guide: or Rules and Instructions in the Art
of Varnishing, etc.*, London: Arliss.

Anon. (1881), *Young Ladies' Treasure Book*, London: Ward Lock.

Arkell, G. E. and Duckworth, G. H. (1903), in C. Booth, ed., *Life and
Labour of the People of London*, London: Macmillan.

Aves, E. (1893), 'The Furniture Trade', in C. Booth (ed.), 'The Trades
of East London', *Life and Labour of the People of London*, London:
T. Cox.

Bailey, W. (1736), *Dictionarium Britannicum*, London: T. Cox.

Barlow, P. (1836), *A Treatise on the Manufacture and Machinery of Great
Britain*, London: Baldwin and Cradock.

— (1861), *Encyclopedia of Arts, Manufactures and Machinery*, London:
J. J. Griffin and Co.

Barrow, J. (1735, 1758), *Dictionarium Polygraphicum*, 2 vols, London:
C. Hitch and L. Hawes.

Beck, W. (1882), *The Draper's Dictionary*, London: The Warehouseman
and Drapers' Journal Office.

Beckmann, J. (1817), *History of Inventions*, London: J. Walker and Co.

Bigelow, J. (1840), *The Useful Arts*, Boston: T. Webb.

Bimont, M. (1770), *Principes de l'art du tapissier*, Paris: Lottin l'aîné.

Bitmead, R. (1873, 1901), *The London Cabinet-maker's Guide to the
Entire Construction of Cabinet Work*, London: Lockwood and Son.

— (1876), *The Practical Upholsterer and Cutter-out*, London: Lockwood.

— (1873, 1900), *French Polishing and Enamelling*, London: Lockwood
and Son.

— (1912/1949), *The Practical Upholsterer and Cutter-Out*, London:
Technical Press.

Blackie, W. and Sons (1853), *The Cabinet-maker's Assistant*, Glasgow:
Blackie.

Book of Trades or the Circle of Useful Arts (1837), Glasgow: Richard
Griffiths & Co.

Book of Trades or Library of Useful Arts (1804), London: Tabart and Co.

Booth, L. (1864), *The Exhibition Book of Ornamental Designs for
Furniture*, London: Houlston and Wright.

Boulger, G. S. (1908), *Wood, A Manual of the Natural History and
Industrial Applications of the Timbers of Commerce*, London: Edward
Arnold.

Boyle, R. (1672), *Of Man's Great Ignorance of the Uses of Natural Things*,
London, cited in Wills, G. (1965), *English Looking Glasses – a Study
of Glass, Frames and Makers, 1672–1872*, London: Country Life,
p.138.

Brown, Richard (1820), *Rudiments of Drawing Cabinet and Upholstery
Furniture*, London: The author.

Browne, P. (1756), *The civil and natural history of Jamaica*, London:
printed for the author.

Cabinet-makers' London Book of Prices and Designs of cabinet-work …
(1788), printed for the London Society of Cabinet-Makers.

Cabinet-makers' London Book of Prices and Designs of cabinet-work …
(1793), printed for the London Society of Cabinet-Makers (2nd edn
enlarged and revised).

Campbell, R. (1747), *The London Tradesman*, Newton Abbot: David
and Charles, reprint 1969.

Catesby, M. (1731–43), *The Natural History of Carolina, Florida, and the
Bahama Islands*, London: printed at the author's expense.

Caulfeild, S. F. A. and Seward, B. C. (1882), *The Dictionary of
Needlework*, London: Upton Gill.

Cennini Cennino (1437), *Il Libro dell'Arte, The Craftsman's Handbook*,
ed. and trans. D. V. Thompson, 1960, Dover: New York.

Chambers, E. (1728, 1741, 1752), *Cyclopedia or Universal Dictionary of
Arts and Sciences*, 2 vols, London: James and John Knapton.

Chippendale, T. (1762), *The Gentleman and Cabinet-makers' Director*,
3rd edn, London: printed for the author, reprint Dover NY 1966.

Codman, O. and Wharton, E. (1897), *The Decoration of Houses*, New
York: C. Scribner's Sons.

Cole, G. (1892), *A Complete Dictionary of Dry Goods*, Chicago:
J. B. Herring.

Collyer, J. (1761), *The Parent's and Guardians' Directory*, London:
R. Griffiths.

Comenius, J. A. (1659), *Orbis Sensualium Pictus*, Menston: Scolar
Press, reprint 1966, trans. Charles Hoole, 1685.

Commissioners of Patents (1869), *Patents for Inventions, Abridgements
of Specifications Relating to Furniture and Upholstery 1620–1866*,
London.

Cotton, C. (1725), *The Compleat Gamester*, reprint 1970, Barrie. Mass.:
Imprint Society.

Crofton, J. (1834), *The London Upholsterer's Companion*, London: The
author.

Defoe, D. (1727), *Tour Through Great Britain*, reprint 1927, London:
Peter Davies.

— (1727/1969), *The Complete English Tradesman*, New York: Kelley.

Degerdon, W. (1893), *The Grammar of Woodwork*, London: Macmillan.

Dempsey, G. D. (1852), *The Machinery of the Nineteenth Century*, parts
1–4, London: Atchley and Co.

Denning, D. (1891), *The Art and Craft of Cabinet-making*, London:
Whittaker.

Denning, D. (1895), *Fretwork and Marquetry*, London: Upton Gill.
— (1931), *Art and Craft of Cabinetmaking. A Practical Handbook*, London: Pitman.
Deville, J. (1878–80), *Dictionnaire du tapissier de l'Ameublement français*, Paris: C. Claesen.
Diderot, D. (1751–72), *Encyclopédie ou dictionnaire raisonné des sciences, des arts et des métiers*, 1793, Paris: Briasson.
— (1771), *Recueil planches sur les sciences, les arts libéraux et les arts méchaniques*, Paris: A. Livourne.
Dodd, G. (1843), *Days at the Factories, Manufacturing Industry in Great Britain*, London: C. Knight, W. Clowes.
— (1844), *Textile Manufactures of Great Britain*, London: Charles Knight & Co.
— (1852), *Curiosities of Industry and the Applied Sciences*, London: Routledge.
— (1858), *Novelties, Inventions and Curiosities in Arts and Manufactures*, London: Routledge.
— (1876), *Dictionary of Manufacturing Mining, Machinery and the Industrial Arts*, London: Virtue.
Dossie, R. (1758), *Handmaid to the Arts*, 2 vols, London: J. Nourse.
Dresser, C. (1873), *Principles of Decorative Design*, London: Cassell, Peter & Galpin.

Eastlake, C. (1868, 1878), *Hints on Household Taste*, London: Longman.
Edwards, G. and Darby, M. (1754), *A New Book of Chinese Designs*, London: the authors.
Ellis, G. (1915), *Modern Practical Carpentry*, 2nd edn, London: Batsford.
Ellis, W. (1742), *The Timber Tree*, London: T. Osborne.
Elwes, J. and Henry, R. (1906–13), *The Trees of Great Britain and Ireland*, Edinburgh: private print.
Evelyn, J. (1620–1706), *The Diary of John Evelyn*, E. S. de Beer (ed.), Oxford: Oxford University Press.
— (1662), *Silva, A Discourse of Forest Trees*, 5th edn 1729, printed for J. Walhoe et al.

Fearon, H. (1818), *Sketches of America, A Narrative of a Journey*, 2nd edn, London: Longman.
Fiennes, C. (1982), *The Illustrated Journeys of Celia Fiennes*, London: Macdonald.
Forrest, T. (1779), *A Voyage to New Guinea …*, London: J. Robson.
Du Fouilloux, J. (1611), *The Noble Art of Venerie or Hunting*, London: Thomas Purfoot.

Gay, G. (1895), 'The Furniture Trade', in *One Hundred Years of American Commerce*, Chauncey Depew (ed.), vol.2, New York: D. O. Haynes and Co.
Gerbier, Sir F. (1663), *Counsel and Advice to all Builders … as also in respect of their works, materials …*, London: T. Mabb.
Gill, T. (1827–30), 'On French varnish for cabinet work', cited in *Annals of Philosophy*, XI, pp.119, 371, London: Richard Taylor.
Guilmard, D. (1860), *Le Menuisier moderne*, Paris: D. Guilmard.

Hakluyt, R. (1589), *Virginia Voyages*, Oxford: Oxford University Press, reprint 1973.
Haldane, W. (1883), *Workshop Receipts*, London: Spon.
Hale, Sarah (1840), *Workwoman's Guide*, London: Simpkin Marshall and Co.
Hall, C. (1912), *Wood and What we Make of it*, London: Blackie.
Hall, J. (1840), *The Cabinet-makers' Assistant*, Baltimore: J. Murphy.

Halphen, G. (1845), *Rapport sur l'exposition publique des produits de l'Industrie française de 1844*, Paris.
Harrison, W. (1887), *Description of England in Shakespeare's youth*, London: Trübner.
Hasluck, P. N. (1890), *The Cabinet Workers' Handybook*, London: Crosby Lockwood and Son.
— (1907), *Cabinetwork and Joinery with Working Drawings*, London: Cassell.
Havard, H. (1887–90), *Dictionnaire de l'ameublement et de la décoration*, Paris: Quantain.
Hazen, E. (1843), *Popular technology, or professions and trades*, New York: Harper Bros.
Hepplewhite, A. and Co (1788/1794), *The Cabinet-maker and Upholsterer's Guide*, London: Taylor.
Herbert, Sir T. (1634), *Travels*, London: printed by W. Standsby and J. Bloome.
Hibberd, S. (1870), *Rustic Adornments for Homes of Taste*, London: Groombridge and Sons.
Hints on Housing and House Furnishing or economics for young beginners, London: Groombridge and Sons.
Hodgson, F. T. (1891), *The Practical Upholsterer*, New York: Industrial Publications.
— (1910), *The Practical Cabinet-maker and Furniture Designer's Assistant*, Chicago: F. J. Drake & Co.
Holme, R. (c.1649), *The Academy of Armory or a Storehouse of Armory and Blazon*, printed for the author, Chester, vol.ii, I. H. Jeayes (ed.), Roxburghe Club, London, 1905.
Holtzapffel, C. (vol.I 1846, vol.II 1847, vol.III 1850), *Turning and Mechanical Manipulation*, London: The author.
Hope, T. (1807), *Household Furniture and Interior Decoration*, reprint 1970, London: Tiranti.
Howard, A. L. (1920), *A Manual of Timbers of the World*, London: Macmillan.
Howard, G. S. (1788), *The New Royal Encyclopedia*, London: Alex Hogg.

Ince, W. and Mayhew, J. (1759), *The Universal System of Household Furniture*, London: Robert Sayer.

Jackson, F. H. (1903), *Intarsia and Marquetry*, London: Sands and Co.
Jewitt, L. (1878), *The Ceramic Art of Great Britain*, 2 vols, London: Virtue and Co.
Joiner (1839), *The Joiner and Cabinet-maker*, Knights Guides to Trade, London: C. Knight.
— (1883), *Joiner and Cabinet-maker; His Work and its Principles*, London: Houlston Industrial Library.
Jupp, E. B. (1887), *An historical account of the Worshipful Company of Carpenters of the City of London*, London: Pickering and Chatto.

Kauffman, C. H. (1805), *Dictionary of Merchandise*, Philadelphia: James Humphreys.
King, T. (1839), *The Upholsterer's Sketch Book of Modern Designs*, London: J. Weale.
Knight, C. (1830), *A Description and History of Vegetable Substances used in the Arts and Domestic Economy; Timber Trees*, London: Charles Knight and Co.
— (1831), *The Working Man's Companion*, 3rd edn, London: Charles Knight and Co.
— (1851), *Knight's Encyclopedia of the Industries of all Nations*, London: Charles Knight and Co.

Langley, B. (1740), *The City and Country Builders and Workman's Treasury of Designs*, London.

Laslett, T. (1894), *Timber and Timber Trees*, London: Macmillan.

Lawford, H. (c.1855), *The Cabinet of Marquetry, Buhl and Inlaid Wood*, London.

Levien, J. (1861), *The Woods of New Zealand and their Adaptability to Art Furniture*.

London (1851), *Exhibition of the works of all nations, 1851: reports by the juries on the subjects in the thirty classes in which the exhibition was divided*, London: Clowes.

The London Cabinet-maker's Union Book of Prices (1811), by a committee of masters and journeymen: printed for the Committee.

The London Cabinet-maker's Book of Prices for work not provided in the Union book (supplementary).

London International Exhibition (1851), *Reports of the Juries*, London: HMSO.

London School of Economics (1931), *New Survey of the Life and Labour of London*, London: LSE.

Long, E. (1774), *History of Jamaica*, reprint 1970, London: Cass.

Loudon, J. C. (1835, 1839), *An Encyclopedia of Cottage Farm and Villa Architecture and Furniture*, revised edn, London: Longmans, Orme, Brown, Green and Longmans.

— (1844), *Arboretum and Fruticetum Britannicum*, vols 1–4, London: Longmans.

Macquer, Phillipe de (1773), *Dictionnaire raisonné universel des arts et métiers*, 5 vols, Paris: Didot.

Manwaring, R. (1765), *The Cabinet and Chair-maker's Real Friend and Companion*, London: Henry Webley.

Marshall, W. (1796), *On Planting and Rural Ornament*, London: G. Nicol.

Martin, T. (1819), *The New Circle of the Mechanical Arts containing Practical Treatises on the Various Manual Arts, Industries and Manufactures*, London: R. Rees.

Mateaux, C. (1883), *The Wonderland of Work*, London: Cassell.

Mayhew. H. (1850), *The Morning Chronicle Survey of Labour and the Poor*, vol.5, Caliban Books, 1982.

Montagu, M. (1861), *The Selected Letters of Lady Mary Wortley Montagu*, reprint 1970, London: Longman.

Moreland, F. A. (1889), *Practical Decorative Upholstery*, Boston: Lee and Shepard.

Mortimer, T. (1763), *The Universal Director*, London: printed for the author.

— (1766), *A New and Complete Dictionary of Trade and Commerce*, London: S. Crowder.

Moxon, J. (1677, 1703), *Mechaniks Exercises or the Doctrine of Handy Works etc.*, New York: Praeger, reprint 1970.

Neve, R. (1726), *The City and Country Purchasers' and Builders' Dictionary*, Newton Abbott: David and Charles, reprint 1969.

Nicholson, M. (1824), *New Practical Builder and Workman's Companion*, London: T. Kelly.

Nicholson, P. and M. (1826), *The Practical Cabinet-maker, Upholsterer*, London: H. Fisher, Son & Co.

Nosban, M. (1843), *Nouveau Manuel complet du menuisier, de l'ébéniste et du layetier*, Paris: Roret.

Paris (1855), *Reports on the Paris Universal Exhibition of 1855*, London: HMSO.

Paris (1867), *Modern Industries; A Series of Reports on Industry and Manufacturers as Represented in the Paris Exhibition in 1867*, by twelve British workmen of the Paris excursion committee, London: Macmillan.

Paris (1867), *Reports of Artisans Selected by a Committee Appointed by the Council of the Society of Arts to Visit the Paris Universal Exhibition of 1867*, London: Bell and Daldy.

Paris (1867), *Reports on the Paris Universal Exhibition of 1867*, London, 1868: HMSO

Paris (1878), *The Society of Arts. Artisans Reports on the Paris Universal Exhibition of 1878*, London: Sampson Low.

Paris (1889), *Reports of Artisans selected by the Mansion House Committee to visit the Paris Universal Exhibition of 1889*, London: C. F. Roworth.

Parker, J. H. (1859), *Domestic Architecture in England from Richard II to Henry VIII*, Oxford and London: J. H. and J. Parker.

Pepys, S. (1970–71), *The Diary of Samuel Pepys*, Latham, R. and Matthew, W. (eds), London: Bell.

Plot, R. (1686), *The Natural History of Staffordshire*, Oxford: printed at the theatre.

Plumier, C. (1749), *The Art of Turning*, 2nd edn, trans. P. Ferraglio, New York, 1975.

Pollen, J. H. (1877), 'Furniture and Woodwork', in G. P. Bevan (ed.), *British Manufacturing Industries*, London: Edward Stanford.

Postlethwayt, M. (1751), *The Universal Dictionary of Trade and Commerce*, 2 vols, London: J. and P. Knapton.

Practical Carpentry Joinery and Cabinetmaking (1826), London: Kelly.

Practical Upholstery (1885), by a working upholsterer, Wyman.

Purefoy Letters 1735–53 (1931), G. Eland (ed.), London: Sidgwick & Jackson.

Rees, A. (1778), *The Cyclopedia*, London: W. Strahan.

Richards, J. (1872), *A Treatise on the Construction and Operation of Wood-working Machinery Including a History of the Origins and Processes of Wood-working Machines*, London: E. F. and N. Spon.

Rolt, R. (1761), *A New Dictionary of Trade and Commerce*, London: G. Keith.

Roubo, A. J. (1769–75), *L'art du menuisier en meubles*, Paris: Saillant et Noyon.

Salmon, W. (1672 and later edns), *Polygraphice; or The Art of Drawing, Engraving … Varnishing, Colouring and Dying …*, London, printed E. T. and R. H. for Richard Jones.

Savary des Bruslons, J. (1723), *Dictionnaire Universal de Commerce*, Paris: J. Estienne.

Sharp, S. (1767), *Letters from Italy*, London: printed by R. Cave.

Sheraton, T. (1793), *The Cabinet Maker and Upholsterer's Drawing Book*, New York: Dover, reprint 1972.

— (1803), *The Cabinet Dictionary*, New York: Prager, reprint 1970.

Siddons, G. (1827), *The Cabinet-makers' Guide*, 5th edn, 1830, London: printed for Sherwood, Gilbert and Piper.

Sloane, Sir H. (1707–25), *A Voyage to the Islands of Madera, Barbados …*, 2 vols, London: printed by B.M. for the author.

Smith, A. (1776), *An enquiry into the nature and causes of the Wealth of Nations*, reprint 1961, London: Methuen.

Smith, George (1808), *A Collection of Designs for Household Furniture and Interior Decoration*, London: J. Taylor.

— (1826), *Cabinet Maker's and Upholsterer's Guide*, London: Jones and Co.

Smith, Godfrey (1756), *The Laboratory or School of Arts*, London, printed for James Hodges.

Smith, J. (1816), *The Mechanic or Compendium of Practical Inventions*, 2 vols, Liverpool: Henry Fisher.

— (1816), *The Panorama of Science and Art*, 2 vols, Liverpool: Nuttall, Fisher & Dixon.

Sparrow, W. S. (1909), *Hints on House Furnishing*, London: Eveleigh Nash.

Spofford, H. F. (1878), *Art Decoration Applied to Furniture*, New York: Harper & Brothers.

Spon, E. (1882), *Workshop Receipts*, London: Spon, reprint 1932.

— (1901), *Spon's Mechanic's Own Book: A Manual for Handicraftsmen and Amateurs*, London: Spon.

Stalker, J. and Parker, G. (1688), *A Treatise of Japanning and Varnishing*, London: Tiranti, reprint 1960.

Stedman, J. (1796), *Narrative of a Five Year Expedition Against the Revolted Negroes of Surinam …*, London: J. Johnson.

Stokes, J. (1829), *The Complete Cabinet-maker and Upholsterer's Guide*, London: Dean and Munday.

Strauss, G. L. M. et al. (1864), *England's Workshops*, London: Groombridge and Son.

Talbert, B. J. (1873), *Gothic Forms Applied to Furniture and Decoration for Domestic Purposes*, Boston: Osgod and Co.

Taylor, J. (1634), *The Needle's Excellency*, London, reprint 1995, Austin, Texas: Curious Works Press.

Taylor, J. (1825), *The Upholsterer's and Cabinet-maker's Pocket Assistant*, London: sold by J. Taylor Architectural Library, High Holborn.

Technical Repository (1822–7), vols 1–16, London: T. Cadell.

Theophilus (Ms *c.*1120), *On Divers Arts*, trans. John Hawthorne and Cyril Stanley Smith, New York: Dover, 1979.

Thunberg, C. P. (1793), *Travels in Europe, Africa and Asia*, London, printed for F. and C. Rivington.

Tingry, P. F. (1832), *The Varnishers Guide*, London: Sherwood, Gilbert and Piper.

Tomlinson, C. (*c.*1854), *Cyclopedia of Useful Arts*, 2 vols, London: Virtue.

— (1866), *Illustrations of Trades*, London: SPCK.

Ure, A. (1839), *Dictionary of Arts, Manufactures and Mines; Containing a Clear Exposition of Their Principles and Practice*, London: Longman Green.

Vasari, G. (1550), *Vasari on Technique*, trans. Louisa Maclehouse, New York: Dover, 1960.

Wakefield, E. J. (1845), *Adventures in New Zealand*, London: J. Murray.

Wallis, G. (1854), Special Report, New York Industrial Exhibition, *General Report of the British Commissioners*, House of Commons Proceedings, 6 February.

Watin, J.-F. (1772), *L'Art du peintre, doreur, vernisseur*, Paris: Quillau.

Webster, T. (1845), *An Encyclopedia of Domestic Economy*, New York: Harper Bros.

Wells, P. and Hooper, J. (1909 and later editions), *Modern Cabinet Work, Furniture and Fitments*, London: Batsford.

Wheeler, G. (1851), *Rural Homes*, New York: Chas Scribner.

Whitaker, H. (1847), *The Practical Cabinet-maker and Upholsterer's Treasury of Designs*, London: P. Jackson.

White, J. (1761), *Art's Treasury of Rarities …*, Glasgow: John Tait.

Whittock, N. (1827), *The Decorative Painters' and Glaziers' Guide*, London: T. Hinton.

— (1837), *The Complete Book of Trades*, London: J. Bennett.

Wickersham, J. B. (1855), *Victorian Ironwork: A Catalogue*, reprint 1977, Philadelphia: The Atheneum Library.

William, H. and Jones, C. (1878), *Beautiful Homes or Hints in House Furnishing*, New York: H. Williams.

Williams, H. (1882), *The Workers Industrial Index*, London: 'Labour News' office.

Wood, H. (*c.*1830), *A Useful and Modern Work on Settees, Sofas, Ottomans and Easy Chairs*, London: Ackermann and Co.

Wood, J. (1742), *Description of Bath*, Bath: printed by W. Frederick.

Woodcroft, B. (1854), *Patent and Inventions 1617–1853. Subject Matter Index*, London: HMSO.

Working Man, A (1878), *The Practical Cabinet-Maker*, London.

Working upholsterer (1883), *Practical Upholstery*, London: Wyman and Sons.

Workwoman's Guide (1840), reprint 1975, Doncaster: Bloomfield.

Wright, T. and Halliwell, J. O. (1841–3), *Reliquiae Antiquae*, London: William Pickering.

Yapp, G. W. (1885), *Art Furniture, Upholstery and House Decoration*, London: Virtue.

Young, A. (1771), *A Tour of the North of England*, reprint 1967, New York: Kelley.

SECONDARY SOURCES

19th-Century America Furniture and Other Decorative Arts (1970), New York: Metropolitan Museum of Art, catalogue of an exhibition held at the Metropolitan Museum of Art, 16 April to 7 September 1970, New York.

Adrosko, R. (1990), 'Identifying late 19th-century upholstery fabrics', in *Upholstery Conservation*, Colonial Williamsburg, American Conservation Consortium, East Kingston, NH.

Aitchison, L. (1960), *A History of Metals*, London: Macdonald and Evans.

Aldred, C. (1954), 'Fine Woodwork', in Singer, C. et al. (eds), *History of Technology*, Oxford: Clarendon Press, vol.1, pp.684–703.

Allsop, H. B. (1952–3), *Decoration and Furniture*, 2 vols, London: Pitman.

Ames, K. (1971), 'Gardner & Co of New York', in *Antiques*, XCIX, August.

Ames, K. and Ward, G. (1989), *Decorative Arts and Household Furnishings in America 1650–1920*, annotated bibliography, Winterthur: Henry Francis Du Pont Museum.

Auslander, L. (1996), *Taste and Power Furnishing Modern France*, Berkeley: California University Press.

Aves, E. (1893), 'The Furniture Trade', in C. Booth (ed.), *Life and Labour of the People of London*, London: Macmillan.

Ayres, J. (1981), *The Shell Book of the Home in Britain*, London: Faber and Faber.

Bairstow, J. (1984), *Practical and Decorative Woodworking Joints*, London: Batsford.

Baker, H. (1966), *Furniture in the Ancient World*, London: Connoisseur.

Bangert, A. (1988), *Italian Furniture Design*, Munich: Bangert Verlag.

Barker, G. H. (1937), *Modern Woodwork and Furniture-making*, London: Technical Press.

Beard, G. (1993), 'Decorators and furniture-makers at Croome Court', in *Furniture History*, XXIX, pp.88–113.

— (1997), *Upholsterers and Interior Furnishing in England 1530–1840*, London and New Haven: Yale.

Beard, G. and Gilbert, C. (1986), *Dictionary of English Furniture-makers*, Leeds: Furniture History Society.

Beckerdite, L. (1997), 'Religion, Artisanry, and Cultural Identity: The Huguenot experience in South Carolina', in *American Furniture*, pp.196–228.

Benhamou, R. (1991), 'Imitation in the Decorative Arts of the Eighteenth Century', in *Journal of Design History*, vol.4, I.

Bjerkoe, E. (1978), *The Cabinet-makers of America*, Exton, Pa.: Schiffer.

Board of Trade (1946), *Working Party Report: Furniture*, London: HMSO.

Bonnett, D. (1956), *Contemporary Cabinet Design and Construction*, London: Batsford.

Bowett, A. (1993), Fruitwoods in British furniture-making', in *Furniture Journal*, December, pp.41–5.

Boynton, L. (1965), 'Sir Richard Worsley's furniture at Appuldurcombe Park', in *Furniture History*, vol.I, pp.39–58.

— (1968), 'Thomas Chippendale at Mersham le Hatch', in *Furniture History*, IV, pp.81–104.

— (1971), 'Hardwick Hall Inventory', in *Furniture History*, vol.VII, pp.81–104.

Brown, W. H. (1978), *Timbers of the World*, High Wycombe, UK: TRADA.

Bucksch, H. (1966) *Dictionary of Wood and Woodworking Practice*, London: Pitman.

Byers, M. (1997), *50 Tables*, Crans-Pres-Celigny, Switzerland: Rotovision.

— (1997), *50 Chairs*, Crans-Pres-Celigny, Switzerland: Rotovision.

Cabinet-maker (1892), *A Practical Guide to the Principles of Design and the Economical and Sound Construction of Household Furniture*, London: Ward Lock.

Cescinsky, H. (1931), *The Gentle Art of Faking Furniture*, London: Chapman and Hall.

Cescinsky, H. and Dribble, E. (1922), *Early English Furniture and Woodwork*, London: Routledge.

Chanson, L. (1983), *Traité d'ébénisterie*, 12th edn, Dourdan: Viall.

Chaucer, G. (1994), *House of Fame*, Durham: Durham Medieval Texts.

Chinnery, V. (1970), *Oak Furniture the British Tradition*, Woodbridge: Antique Collectors Club.

Clabburn, P. (1988), *The National Trust Book of Furnishing Textiles*, London: Viking.

Conradsen, D. (1993), 'The Stock-in Trade of John Hancock and Company', in *American Furniture*, pp.39–54.

Cooke, E. S. (ed.) (1987), *Upholstery in America and Europe from 17th Century to WWI*, New York: Norton.

Corkhill, T. (1979), *Glossary of Wood*, London: Stobart.

Cosgrove, J. R. (1932), 'Empire Timbers with Special Reference to Their Uses for Furniture and Decoration', in *Journal of the Royal Society of Arts*, 26 February.

Cotton, W. (1990), *English Regional Chair*, Woodbridge: Antique Collectors Club.

Cummings, A. L. (1961), *Bed Hangings, A treatise on Fabrics and Styles in the Curtaining of Beds 1650–1850*, Boston: SPNEA.

Cust, L. (1911), 'Notes on the collection formed by Thomas Howard Earl of Arundel', in *Burlington Magazine*, XX, November.

Dampierre, F. (1987), *The Best of Painted Furniture*, London: Weidenfeld and Nicolson.

Darling, S. (1984), *Chicago Furniture. Art and industry, 1833–1933*, Chicago: Chicago Historical Society.

Dunbar, M. (1976), *Windsor Chairmaking*, London: Stobart.

Eames, P. (1977), 'Furniture in England, France and Netherlands 12th–15th centuries', in *Furniture History*, XIII, pp.1–276.

Earl, P. (1973), 'Craftsmen and machines. Nineteenth century furniture industry', in *19th Annual Winterthur Conference Report*, Winterthur, Delaware.

Edwards, C. D. (1993), *Victorian Furniture*, Manchester: Manchester University Press.

— (1994), *Twentieth Century Furniture*, Manchester: Manchester University Press.

— (1996), *Eighteenth Century Furniture*, Manchester: Manchester University Press.

Edwards, R. (1964), *The Shorter Dictionary of English Furniture from the Middle Ages to the Late Georgian Period*, London: Country Life.

Edwards, R. and Jourdain, M. (1955), *Georgian Cabinet-makers c.1700–1800*, London: Country Life.

Ettema, M. (1981), 'Technological innovation and design economics in furniture manufacture', *Winterthur Portfolio*, 16.

Fairbanks, J. C. and Bates, E. B. (1981), *American Furniture 1620 to the Present*, London: Orbis.

Farr, M. (1955), *Design in British Industry*, Cambridge: Cambridge University Press.

Fennimore, E. (1991), 'Brass Hardware on American furniture, Parts 1 and 2', in *Antiques*, May, pp.948–55, July, pp.80–91.

Forest Products Research Laboratory (1966), *Timber and Board Materials used in the Furniture Industry*, HMSO: Princes Risborough.

Forman, B. (1988), *American Seating furniture 1630–1730*, New York: Norton.

Fowler, J. and Cornforth, J. (1974), *English Decoration in the Eighteenth Century*, London: Barrie and Jenkins.

Gentle, R. and Feild, R. (1975), *English Domestic Brass 1680–1810 and the History of its Origins*, London: Elek.

Giedion, S. (1948), *Mechanisation takes Command*, New York: Oxford University Press.

Gilbert, C. (1978), *The Life and Work of Thomas Chippendale*, London: Studio Vista.

— (1991), *English Vernacular Furniture 1750–1900*, New Haven and London: Yale University Press.

Gilbert, C. and Murdoch, T. (1993), *John Channon and English Brass-inlaid Furniture 1730–1760*, London: Yale University Press.

Gilbert, C. and Wood, L. (1997), 'Sophie von La Roche at Seddon's', in *Furniture History*, XXXIII, pp.30–4.

Giusti, A. M. (1992), *Pietre Dure – Hardstones in Furniture*, London: Philip Wilson.

Gloag, J. (1990), *Dictionary of Furniture*, London: Unwin Hyman.

Goodison, N. (1974), *Ormolu, The works of Matthew Boulton*, London: Phaidon.

Goodman, W. L. (1964), *The History of Woodworking Tools*, XVII, pp.23–41, London: Bell.

— (1981), 'Christopher Gabriel, His Book', in *Furniture History*, XVII, pp.23–41.

Gregory, A. (1935), *The Art of Woodworking and Furniture-making*, Leicester: Dryad.

Grier, K. (1988), *Culture and Comfort, People, Parlours and Upholstery, 1850–1930*, New York: Strong Museum.

Hall, H. (1901), *Society in the Elizabethan Age*, London: Swan Sonnenschein and Co.

Halliwell, J. O. (1854), *Ancient Inventories of Furniture, Pictures etc.*, London: printed for private circulation.

Hanks, D. A. (1981), *Innovative Furniture in America from 1800 to the Present*, New York: Horizon Press.

Hardouin-Fugier, E. et al. (1994), *Les Etoffes: Dictionnaire historique*, Paris: Editions de l'Amateur.

Hawkins, D. (1986), *The Techniques of Wood Surface Decoration*, London: Batsford.

Hayden, E. (1905), *Chats on Old Furniture*, London: Fisher Unwin.

Hayward, H. and Kirkham, P. (1980), *William and John Linnell Eighteenth Century London Furniture-makers*, London: Studio Vista.

Heal, A. (1953), *The London Furniture-makers, from the Restoration to the Victorian Era 1660–1840*, London: Batsford.

Herrmann, G. (ed.) (1996), *The Furniture of Western Asia Ancient and Traditional. Papers of the Conference held at the Institute of Archaeology, University College London, 28–30 June 1993*, Mainz: Philipp von Zarben.

Hewitt, B., Kane, P. and Ward, G. (1982), *The Work of Many Hands, Card Tables in Federal America 1790–1820*, New Haven and London: Yale University Press.

Himmelheber, G. (1974), *Biedermeier Furniture*, trans. S. Jervis, London: Faber.

Hinckley, F. L. (1960), *Directory of Historic Cabinet Woods*, New York: Crown.

Hoadley, R. B. (1980), *Understanding Wood: A Craftsman's Guide to Wood Technology*, Newton, Conn.: Taunton Press.

— (1990), *Identifying Wood*, Newton, Conn.: Taunton Press.

Hodges, F. (1989), *Period Pastimes*, London: Weidenfeld and Nicolson.

Holley, D. (n.d.), *Origins of Upholstery* (TS), Victoria and Albert Museum, Furniture and Woodwork Collection.

Hooper, J. and R. (1948), *Modern Furniture and Fittings*, London: Batsford.

Hooper, J. (1952), *Modern Cabinet Work, Furniture and Fitments*, London: Batsford, 6th edn.

Hooper, R. (1937), *Woodcraft in Design and Practice*, London: Batsford.

Hordern, R. H. (1937), *Woodworking by Machinery*, London: Pitman.

Hounshell, D. (1984), *From the American System to Mass Production 1800–1932*, Baltimore: Johns Hopkins University Press.

Houston, J. F. (1993), *Featherbeds and Flock Beds, Notes on the History of the Worshipful Company of Upholders*, Sandy, Beds.: Three Tents Press.

Howarth, D. (1984), 'Merchants and Diplomats, New patterns in decorative arts in seventeenth century England', in *Furniture History*, XX, pp.10–17.

Humell, C. F. (1968), *With Hammer in Hand. Dominy craftsmen of East Hampton New York*, University Press, Virginia.

Huth, H. (1971), *Lacquer of the West, The History of a Craft and Industry 1550–1950*, Chicago: University of Chicago Press.

Ingram, K. E. (1992), 'Furniture and the Plantation: Further Light on the West Indian Trade of an English Furniture Firm in the Eighteenth Century', in *Furniture History*, XXVIII, pp.42–97.

Irwin, J. and Brett, K. (1970), *Origins of Chintz*, London: HMSO.

Jervis, S. (1989), 'Furniture in the Commonwealth Inventories', in Arthur Macgregor (ed.), *The Late King's Goods*, Oxford: Oxford University Press.

Johnson, A. P. and Sironen, M. (1928), *Manual of the Furniture Arts and Crafts*, Grand Rapids: A. P. Johnson and Co.

Johnson, W. (1851–6), *The Imperial Cyclopaedia of Machinery*, Glasgow: William Mackenzie.

Jourdain, M. (1924), *English Decoration and Furniture of the Early Renaissance, 1500–1650*, London: T. Batsford.

Joy, E. (1955), *Some Aspects of the London Industry in the Eighteenth Century*, unpublished MA thesis, London.

— (1968), *The Connoisseur's Complete Period Guides*, London: Connoisseur.

— (1974), *English Furniture 1800–1851*, London: Sotheby.

Joyce, E. (1970), *The Techniques of Furniture-making*, London: Batsford.

Kane, P. (1976), *300 years of American seating furniture. Chairs and Beds from the Mabel Brady Garvan and Other Collections*, Yale University: New York Graphic Soc.

Kebabian, P. and Lipke, W. (1979), *Tools and Technologies: America's Wooden Age*, Vermont University Press.

Keeble, A. L. (1930), *Cabinet-making Theory and Practice*, London: Longmans.

Kerridge, E. (1985), *Textile Manufactures in Early Modern England*, Manchester: Manchester University Press.

Killen, G. (1980), *Ancient Egyptian Furniture*, Warminster: Aris and Philips.

Kirk, J. T. (1980–1), 'The tradition of English painted furniture', in *Antiques*, May 1980, October 1980, January 1981.

Kirkham, P. (1969), 'Samuel Norman, A study of an eighteenth century craftsman', in *Burlington Magazine*, III, August, pp.500–11.

— (1982), *Furniture-making in London c.1700–1870 Craft Design, Business, and Labour*, PhD Thesis, University of London.

— (1988), 'The London furniture trade 1700–1870', in *Furniture History*, XXIV.

Knight, E. H. (1878), *New Mechanical Dictionary*, New York: Hard and Houghton.

Kreisel, H. (1970), *Die Kunst des Deutschen Möbels*, Munich: Beck.

Latham, B. (1957), *Timber A Historical Survey of its Development and Distribution*, London: Harrap.

Legg, P. (1994), 'The Bastards of Blandford: an Inventory of their losses in the fire of 1731', in *Furniture History*, XXX, pp.15–42.

Levy, M. (1989), 'George Bullock's partnership with Charles Fraser 1813–1818 and the stock-in-trade sale 1819', in *Furniture History*, XXV, pp.145–213.

Logie, G. (1947), *Furniture from Machines*, London: Allen and Unwin.

Lovell, M. (1991), 'Such Furniture as will be Profitable, The Business of Cabinet-Making in Eighteenth Century Newport', *Winterthur Portfolio*, 26: 1, pp.27–62.

Low, J. (1986), 'Newby Hall: Two late eighteenth century inventories', in *Furniture History*, XXII, pp.135–75.

Lower, A. R. M. (1973), *Great Britain's Woodyard: British America and the Timber Trade, 1763–1867*, Montreal and London: McGill-Queen's University Press.

Lucas, A. and Harris, J. R. (1989), *Ancient Egyptian Materials and Industries*, London: Histories and Mysteries of Man Ltd.

Mabille, Gérard (1995), *Arts et techniques: Menuiserie ébénisterie*, Paris: Massin.

Madigan, M. (1972), *Nineteenth Century Furniture, Innovation, Revival and Reform*, New York: Billboard.

Manzini, E. (1986), *Material of Invention*, London: Design Council.

Marchand, J. (ed.) (1933), 'The Mélanges sur l'Angleterre of François de la Rochefoucauld: 1784', *A Frenchman in England*, trans. S. C. Roberts, Cambridge: Cambridge University Press.

Margon, L. (1975), *Construction of American Furniture Treasures*, London: Constable.

Marshal, G. (1930), 'Furniture', in *Encyclopedia of the Social Sciences*, New York: Macmillan.

Matthew, W. P. (1954), *Practical Cabinet-making*, London: Caxton.

Mayes, L. J. (1960), *The History of Chairmaking in High Wycombe*, London: Routledge.

McIntyre, W. (1984), 'From workshop to factory; the furniture-maker', in *Material History Bulletin*, no.19.

McQuoid, P. M. and Edwards, R. (1954), *Dictionary of English Furniture*, Woodbridge: Antique Collectors Club, revised edn.

Medlam, S. (1991), 'Parts and Materials: A Sawmill in the 1820s', in *Regional Furniture*, V, pp.31–41.

Meiggs, R. (1982), *Trees and Timber in the Ancient World*, Oxford: Clarendon Press.

Mercer, E. (1969), *Furniture 700–1700*, London: Weidenfeld and Nicolson.

'Mercury' Dictionary of Textile terms (1950), Manchester: Textile Mercury.

Michie, A. (1985), 'Charleston upholstery in all its branches 1725–1820', in *Journal of Early Southern Decorative Arts*, MESDA.

Montgomery, C. (1966), *American Furniture, The Federal Period*, London: Thames and Hudson.

Montgomery, F. (1984), *Textiles in America, 1650–1870*, New York: Norton.

Myer, H. (1976), *Myer's First Century 1876–1976*, London: Horatio Myer and Co Ltd.

Nelson, G. (1947), 'The Furniture Industry', in *Fortune*, January.

Neuhart, J. and Eames, R. (1989), *Eames Design: The work of the office of Charles and Ray Eames*, London: Thames and Hudson.

Nisbet, H. (1927), *Grammar of Textile Design*, New York: Van Nostrand.

Nothelfer, K. (1942), *Das Sitzmöbel. Ein Fachbuch für Polsterer, Stuhlbauer*, Ravensburg: O. Maier.

Noyes, E. (1941), *Organic Design in Home Furnishing*, New York: MoMA.

Oliver, J. (1966), *Development and Structure of the Furniture Industry*, Oxford: Pergamon.

Ostergard, D. (ed.) (1987), *Bentwood and Metal Furniture, 1859–1946*, Washington: University of Washington Press.

Palmer, F. (1921), *Practical Upholstering*, London: Benn.

Pattou, A. B. and Vaughn, C. L. (1939), *Furniture Finishing Decoration and Patching*, London: Technical Press.

Pelton, B. W. (1949), *Furniture-making and Cabinet Work*, New York: Van Nostrand.

Penn, T. Z. (1984), 'Decorative and protective finishes 1750–1850', *Bulletin of Association of Preservation Technology*, XIV, 1, pp.3–46.

Pevsner, N. (1937), *An Enquiry into Industrial Art in England*, Cambridge: Cambridge University Press.

Pfannschmidt, E. E. (1962), *Metallmöbel*, Stuttgart: Hoffmann.

Phillips, H. L. (1915), *Annals of the Worshipful Company of Joiners of the City of London*, London: privately printed.

Pinto, E. (1962), *The Craftsman in Wood*, London: Bell.

Pliny. *Natural History* (10 vols), trans. H. Rackham (1938–62), London: Heinemann.

Quimby, I. (ed.) (1984), *The Craftsman in Early America*, New York: Norton.

Quimby, I. and Earl, P.A. (1974), *Technical Innovation and Decorative Arts*, Charlottesville: University Press of Virginia.

Radford, V. (1981), *The Stag and I*, published by The Stag Cabinet Company, Nottingham: private printing.

Rendle, B. J. (1969), *Timbers of the World*, 3 vols, London: Benn.

Richter, G. (1966), *The Furniture of the Greeks, Etruscans and Romans*, London: Phaidon.

Ritz, G. M. (1971), *The Art of Painted Furniture*, trans. from German, New York: Van Nostrand Reinhold.

Rogers, N. R. (1935), *The Technology of Woodwork and Metalwork*, London: Pitman.

Rosoman, T. (1986), 'The Chiswick House inventory of 1770', in *Furniture History*, XXII, pp.81–106.

Rye, W. B. (1865), *England As Seen by Foreigners*, London: J. R. Smith.

Salaman, R. (1975), *Dictionary of Tools used in the Woodworking and Allied Trades 1000–1900*, London: Unwin Hyman.

Saumarez-Smith, C. (1993), *Eighteenth Century Decoration*, London: Weidenfeld and Nicolson.

Schniewind, A. (1989), *Concise Encyclopedia of Wood and Wood Based Products*, Oxford: Pergamon.

Schweig, B. (1973), *Mirrors*, London: Pelham.

Scottish SCR (1990), *Conservation of Furnishing Textiles*, post-prints of a conference held at the Burrell Collection, Glasgow: Scottish Society for Conservation and Restoration.

Shapland, H. P. (1926–7), *The Practical Decoration of Furniture*, 3 vols, London: Benn.

Sheraton, T. (1791–4), *Cabinet Maker's and Upholsterer's Drawing Book*, London: T. Bensley.

Sheridan, M. (ed.) (1953), *The Furnisher's Encyclopedia*, London: National Trade Press.

Singer, C. et al. (1955), *Technology and History*, Oxford: Oxford University Press.

Skinner, W. and Rogers, D. (1968), *Manufacturing Policy in the Furniture Industry*, Homewood, Illinois.

Smith, N. A. (1991), *Old Furniture; Understanding the Craftsman's Art*, New York: Dover.

Steer, F. (1969), *Farm and Cottage Inventories of Mid-Essex 1635–1749*, Essex C.C.

Symonds, R. W. (1955), *Furniture-making in 17th and 18th Century England*, London: Connoisseur.

Thamer, H.-U. (1985), *L'Art du menuisier. Work Practices of French Joiners and Cabinet-makers in the Eighteenth Century*, Florence: EUI Working Papers, 85/171.

Thornton, P. (1978), *Seventeenth Century Interior Decoration in England, France and Holland*, London and New Haven: Yale.

— (1984), *Authentic Decor. The Domestic Interior, 1620–1920*, London: Weidenfeld and Nicolson.

— (1991), *Renaissance Interiors*, London: Weidenfeld and Nicolson.

Thornton, P. and Tomlin, M. (1980), *The Furnishing and Decoration of Ham House*, London: Furniture History Society.

Tomrley, C. G. (1940), *Furnishing Your Home*, London: Allen and Unwin.

Tortora, P. (ed.) (1996), *Fairchild's Dictionary of Textiles*, 7th edn, New York: Fairchild.

United States Dept of Commerce (1931), *Furniture, its Selection and Use*, Washington.

Vegesack, A. (1996), *Thonet*, London: Hazar.

Viaux-Loquin, J. (1997), *Les Bois d'Ebénisterie dans les mobiliers français*, Paris: Léonce Laget.

Voss Elder, W. and Stokes, J. E. (1987), *American Furniture, 1680–1880*, Baltimore: Baltimore Museum of Art.

Walton, K.-M. (1986), 'An inventory of 1710 from Dyrham Park', in *Furniture History*, XXII, pp.25–80.

Ward, J. (1851), *The World in its Workshops, A Practical Examination of English and Foreign Processes of Manufacture*, London: Williams, S. Orr and Co.

Watson, F. J. B. (1969), 'The craftsmanship of the Ancien Régime', in *Apollo*, XC, 91, September, pp.180–9.

Welsh, P. C. (1966), *Woodworking Tools 1600–1900*, contributions from the Museum of History and Technology, Paper 51, United States National Museum Bulletin, Smithsonian Institution, Washington, D.C.

West, J. (1962), *Village Records*, London: Macmillan.

Wilk, C. (1980), *Thonet, 150 years of Furniture*, New York: Barrons.

— (1981), *Marcel Breuer, Furniture and Interiors*, London: Architectural Press.

Willan, T. S. (1962), *A Tudor Book of Rates (1582)*, Manchester: Manchester University Press.

Williams, M. (ed.) (1990), *Upholstery Conservation, Pre-prints of a Symposium Held at Colonial Williamsburg*, 2–4 February, East Kingston, NH: American Conservation Consortium.

Wills, G. (1971), *English furniture 1500–1750*, London: Guinness Superlatives.

Wolsey, S. W. and Luff, R. (1968), *Furniture in England, the Age of the Joiner*, London: Arthur Barker.

Wood, L. (1994), *The Lady Lever Art Gallery Catalogue of Commodes*, London, HMSO.

Woodforde, Parson (1924–31), *Diary of a Country Parson 1758–1781*, 5 vols, Milford: London.

Wright, E. and Broadbent, J. (1995), *Soft furnishings 1830–1930*, Glebe NSW: Historic Houses Trust.

PERIODICALS

American Furniture
Archaeologia
Art Journal
Art Union
Builders Magazine
Cabinet Maker
Civil Engineer and Architects Journal
Doncaster Journal
Furniture and Decoration
Furniture Gazette
Furniture History
House Decorator
House Furnisher
Illustrated Exhibitor
Inland Architect and Builder
Iron Age
Journal of Design
Journal of the Society of Arts
London Gazette
Machine Woodworker
Mechanics Magazine
Metal Industry
Philosophical Transactions of the Royal Society
Poulson's Daily Advertiser
Practical Magazine
Regional Furniture
Scientific American
Society of Arts Journal
Sussex Archaeological Collection
Walpole Society [Journal]
Weekly Review
Winterthur Portfolio